The Venture Capital Cycle

The Venture Capital Cycle

second edition

Paul Gompers and Josh Lerner

The MIT Press
Cambridge, Massachusetts
London, England

First MIT Press paperback edition, 2006
© 2004 Massachusetts Institute of Technology

MIT Press books may be purchased at special quantity discounts for business or sales promotional use. For information, please email special_sales@mitpress.mit.edu or write to Special Sales Department, The MIT Press, 55 Hayward Street, Cambridge, MA 02142.

This book was set in Palatino on 3B2 by Asco Typesetters, Hong Kong and was printed and bound in the United States of America.

Library of Congress Cataloging-in-Publication Data

Gompers, Paul A. (Paul Alan)
The venture capital cycle / Paul Gompers and Josh Lerner.—-2nd ed.
   p.   cm.
Includes bibiographical references and index.
ISBN-13: 978-0-262-07255-7 (hc. : alk. paper) — 978-0-262-57238-5 (pb. : alk. paper)
ISBN-10: 0-262-07255-6 (hc. : alk. paper) — 0-262-57238-9 (pb. : alk. paper)
1. Venture capital—United States. I. Lerner, Joshua. II. Title.
HG4963.G66   2004
332′.04154′0973—dc22
                                                                      2004040286

10 9 8 7 6 5 4 3

Contents

Acknowledgments

The research that forms the basis for this book is drawn from many sources. First, we have relied on a number of investors in and consultants to venture capital funds and organizations. Without their cooperation we would not have been able to access the information that forms the basis of these analyses. We thank, in particular, Tim Bliamptis, Mark Dibner, Frank Featherston, Mark Edwards, Michael Eisenson, T. Bondurant French, Steven Gallante, David Gleba, Jim Hirabayashi, Adam Jaffe, Kelly McGough, Lowell Mininger, Robert Moreland, Mark Nadel, Tom Philips, Jesse Reyes, F. M. Scherer, Rolf Selvig, Scott Sperling, David Witherow, and several organizations—the Harvard Management Company, Asset Alternatives, Brinson Partners and its various affiliate limited partnerships, Kemper Financial Services, North Carolina Biotechnology Center, Recombinant Capital, RogersCasey Alternative Investments, the US West Investment Trust, the U.S. General Accounting Office, VentureOne, Venture Economics, and a major corporate pension fund—for generous access to their files. The role of several of our current and former colleagues—in particular, Jay Light, William Sahlman, Jeffry Timmons, and Robert Vishny—as well as Horace Crouch and Robert Wrenn from the U.S. Department of Defense in providing introductions should also be acknowledged.

Second, we relied on the many hours of patient work by our research assistants. The careful and painstaking work of Rob Bhargava, Gabe Biller, Alon Brav, Amy Burroughs, Ben Conway, Jon Daniels, Tim Dodson, Cedric Escalle, Meredith Fitzgerald, Kay Hashimoto, Victor Hollender, Leo Huang, Brian Hunt, Justin Kow, Taras Klymchuk, Mannie Liu, Laura Miller, Krishnamoorthy Narasimhan, Bac Nguyen, Morgen Peck, Patty Pitzele, Kathleen Ryan, Qian Sun, Sanjeev Verma, and Jay Yang was essential to the completion of the analyses in this volume. The revision of the manuscript for the second edition was managed by Nitin Nayar and Dorella Rangel, to whom we are very grateful. Chris Allen and Phil Hamilton of Harvard Business

School and Neil Bania and Michael Fogarty of Case Western Reserve University provided computational support. Dan Feenberg provided us with state-level tax data. The financial support provided by the Center for Research in Security Prices, University of Chicago, the Fuqua School of Business, Duke University, the Center for Science and International Affairs, John F. Kennedy School of Government, Harvard University, the Advanced Technology Program, the Consortium on Competitiveness and Cooperation, the Division of Research, Harvard Business School, the U.S. National Science Foundation, and the National Bureau of Economic Research was also critical in this process. Our two administrative assistants, Marianne D'Amico and Peggy Moreland, provided patient and indispensable support throughout all phases of this project.

Third, we would like to acknowledge the support of our fellow academic professionals. Rick Carter, Charles Lee, Harold Mulherin, Jay Ritter, and Michael Vetsuypens generously shared data from earlier research projects. Alon Brav, who was the co-author of chapters 18 and 20, and Samuel Kortum, co-author of chapter 12, generously gave permission for their work to be included here. Our analyses were greatly improved by the helpful comments of our peers. We would also like to thank Zoltan Acs, George Baker, Michael Barclay, Chris Barry, Eli Berman, Eli Berkovitch, Bruno Bias, Margaret Blair, Lewis Branscomb, Dennis Carlton, Gary Chamberlain, Susan Chaplinsky, Judy Chevalier, Jeff Coles, Francesca Cornelli, Robert Dammon, Douglas Diamond, Joanne Dushay, Jonathan Eaton, Ben Esty, Kenneth Flamm, Martin Feldstein, Joetta Forsyth, Jennifer Francis, Ken Froot, Chris Geczy, Simon Gilchrist, Michael Gibbs, Stuart Gilson, John Graham, Brian Hall, Kathleen Hanley, Robert Hansen, Oliver Hart, J. B. Heaton, Thomas Hellman, Michael Jensen, Shmuel Kandel, Steven Kaplan, Tarun Khanna, Stacey Kole, Randy Kroszner, Kevin Lang, Reuven Lehavy, Ralph Lerner, Marc Lipson, Andrew Metrick, Lisa Meulbroek, Roni Michaely, Wayne Mikkelson, Mark Mitchell, Kaivan Munshi, Kevin J. Murphy, Maureen O'Hara, Steve Orpurt, Peter Pashigian, Sam Peltzman, Alessandro Penati, Mitchell Petersen, Robert Porter, Canice Prendergast, James Poterba, Manju Puri, Raghuram Rajan, Peter Reiss, Edward Rice, Jay Ritter, Nathalie Rossiensky, F. M. Scherer, Bill Schwert, Stephen Schurman, Erik Sirri, Howard Stevenson, Scott Stern, René Stulz, Eli Talmor, Richard Thaler, Manuel Trajtenberg, Peter Tufano, Michael Vetsuypens, Rob Vishny, Joel Waldfogel, Scott Wallsten, Jerry Warner, Michael Weisbach, Ivo Welch, Bob Whaley, Richard Willis, Karen Wruck, Luigi Zingales, a number of anonymous referees, and seminar participants at many universities and conferences for their helpful comments and suggestions. A number of practitioners—

especially Jonathan Axelrad, Tom Judge, Robin Painter, David Swensen, and Katherine Todd—also provided helpful comments. Particular thanks go to the members of our dissertation committees, who read and commented on early versions of a number of these essays: Carliss Baldwin, Richard Caves, Zvi Griliches, Richard Ruback, William Sahlman, Andrei Shleifer, and Jeremy Stein. All errors and omissions, of course, are our own.

Finally, we would like to dedicate this work to Wendy and Jody, without whom this book would not have been possible.

Several chapters in this book are based on previously published material:

Chapter 3: Paul A. Gompers and Josh Lerner, What drives venture capital fundraising? *Brookings Papers on Economic Activity—Microeconomics* (August 1998): 149–92.

Chapter 4: Paul A. Gompers and Josh Lerner, The use of covenants: An analysis of venture partnership agreements, *Journal of Law and Economics* 39 (October 1996): 463–98.

Chapter 5: Paul A. Gompers and Josh Lerner, An analysis of compensation in the U.S. venture capital partnership, *Journal of Financial Economics* 51 (January 1999): 3–44.

Chapter 6: Paul A. Gompers and Josh Lerner, The determinants of corporate venture capital success: Organizational structure, incentives, and complementarities, in Randall Morck (ed.), *Concentrated Ownership* (Chicago: University of Chicago Press/National Bureau of Economic Research, 2000): 17–50.

Chapter 8: Paul A. Gompers, Optimal investment, monitoring, and the staging of venture capital, *Journal of Finance* 50 (December 1995): 1461–90.

Chapter 9: Paul A. Gompers and Josh Lerner, Money chasing deals? The impact of fund inflows on the valuation of private equity investments, *Journal of Financial Economics* 55 (February 2000): 281–325.

Chapter 10: Josh Lerner, Venture capitalists and the oversight of private firms, *Journal of Finance* 50 (March 1995): 301–18.

Chapter 11: Josh Lerner, The syndication of venture capital investments, *Financial Management* 23 (Autumn 1994): 16–27.

Chapter 12: Samuel Kortum and Josh Lerner, Assessing the contribution of venture capital to innovation, *Rand Journal of Economics* 31 (Winter 2000): 674–92.

Chapter 13: Josh Lerner, The government as venture capitalist: The long-run effects of the SBIR program, *Journal of Business* 72 (July 1999): 285–318.

Chapter 15: Josh Lerner, Venture capitalists and the decision to go public, *Journal of Financial Economics* 35 (June 1994): 293–316.

Chapter 16: Paul A. Gompers, Grandstanding in the venture capital industry, *Journal of Financial Economics* 43 (September 1996): 133–56.

Chapter 17: Paul A. Gompers and Josh Lerner, Conflict of interest and reputation in the issuance of public securities: Evidence from venture capital, *Journal of Law and Economics* 42 (April 1999): 53–80.

Chapter 18: Alon Brav and Paul A. Gompers, The role of lock-ups in initial public offerings, *Review of Financial Studies* 16 (Spring 2003): 1–29.

Chapter 19: Paul A. Gompers and Josh Lerner, Venture capital distributions: Short-run and long-run reactions, *Journal of Finance* 53 (December 1998): 2161–83.

Chapter 20: Alon Brav and Paul A. Gompers, Myth or reality? The long-run underperformance of initial public offerings: Evidence from venture capital and nonventure capital-backed companies, *Journal of Finance* 52 (December 1997): 1791–1822.

The Venture Capital Cycle

1   Introduction

Why This Volume?

Over the past two decades the venture capital industry in the United States has experienced dramatic growth. Annual inflows into venture funds have expanded from virtually zero in the mid-1970s to a high of $105 billion in 2000. Disbursements by these funds into portfolio companies have displayed almost as great a growth. Many of the most visible new firms over the past decades—including Apple Computer, Genentech, Intel, Lotus, and Microsoft—have been backed by venture capital funds. This growth has led to increasing attention to the venture capital industry from the popular press, executives of major corporations, and policy-makers worldwide.

Yet despite this recent attention, misconceptions persist about the nature and role of venture capitalists. One claim, frequently encountered in guides for entrepreneurs, is that venture capitalists are purely passive financiers of entrepreneurial firms who are unlikely to add much value. An extreme, though not unrepresentative, example is Manweller's (1997) *Funding High-Tech Ventures*. In a chapter entitled "Venture Capitalists: The Company-nappers," the author observes:

The term Venture Capitalists (V/C) is an oxymoron. It should be U/Bs (Unadventurous Brokers), especially in hard times. V/Cs today prefer to invest in products which are being developed by sedate, well entrenched companies. If that's your company, V/Cs are a good source to approach for additional equity funding.... [The V/Cs] have developed personality traits more akin to professional wrestlers than professional investors. If you've got the time, try it. You'll get a real education in how to string along future vendors.

Another common misperception relates to how venture capitalists unwind their holdings in young firms. As discussed later in the volume, the exiting of venture capital investments is a controversial area, and venture funds have been known to behave in opportunistic ways. But the discussion of this process is often extremely one-sided and not representative of the broader historical record, as this discussion from the Washington Post (Sloan 1997) shows:

Venture capitalists ... take a company public while the ink is still drying on its incorporation papers. Venture capitalists would rather have you risk your money than risk their own. Besides, going public lets them profit now, rather than waiting.

Distorted perceptions about the venture capital industry are commonplace among policy-makers. One of many examples is Dr. Mary Good, Undersecretary of Commerce for Technology, commenting before the U.S. Senate Governmental Affairs Committee (1997):

As the competitive pressures of the global marketplace have forced American firms to move more of their R&D into shorter term product and process improvements, an "innovation gap" has developed.... Sit down with a group of venture capitalists. The funding for higher-risk ventures ... is extraordinarily difficult to come by.

(Similarly extreme and misleading claims, sad to say, have appeared even in the *Harvard Business Review*; Zider 1998.)

More disturbing than these accounts, however, have been the actions taken by entrepreneurs, corporations, and academic institutions based on misconceptions about the venture capital industry. Particularly misguided is the belief that venture capitalists can add little value to young firms aside from money or can be easily duplicated by an institution whose core strengths are very different. These misconceptions have often led to a failure to capitalize on attractive opportunities and to the substantial destruction of value.

One example that illustrates this point is an instance where a university sought to duplicate the role of venture capitalists, with few of the venture funds' checks and balances and little understanding of the potential pitfalls. In 1987, Boston University invested in a privately held biotechnology company founded in 1979 by a number of scientists affiliated with the institution. As part of its initial investment, the school bought out the stakes of a number of independent venture capital investors, who had apparently concluded after a number of financing rounds that the firm's prospects were unattractive. Between 1987 and 1992, the school, investing alongside university officials and trustees, provided at least $90 million to the private firm. (By way of comparison, the school's entire endowment in the fiscal year in which it initiated this investment was $142 million.) Although the company succeeded in completing an initial public offering, it encountered a series of disappointments with its products. At the end of 1997, the university's equity stake was worth only $4 million.[1]

These misconceptions have motivated us to undertake this volume, which draws together our recent research into the form and function of venture capital funds.[2] We have two goals. First, we seek to gather our research efforts into a more accessible volume than the various finance and economics journals in which they originally appeared. Second, we want to draw out some of the common themes in these studies with a series of interpretative essays about venture capital fund-raising, investing, and exiting.

Three key themes run throughout this volume. The first is the tremendous incentive and information problems that venture capitalists must overcome. Venture investors typically concentrate in industries with a great deal of uncertainty, where the information gaps among entrepreneurs and investors are commonplace. These firms typically have substantial intangible assets that are difficult to value and may be impossible to resell if the firm fails. Similarly market conditions in many of these industries are highly variable. The nature and magnitude of the information gaps and uncertainty at each stage of the cycle leave many opportunities for self-interested behavior by the various parties. At each stage of the cycle, the venture capital industry has developed novel checks and balances, ensuring that incentives are properly aligned and increasing the probability of success.

The second theme is the interrelatedness of each aspect of the venture capital process. Venture capital can be viewed as a cycle that starts with the raising of a venture fund; proceeds through the investing in, monitoring of, and adding value to firms; continues as the venture capitalist exits successful deals and returns capital to their investors; and renews itself with the venture capitalist raising additional funds. To understand the venture capital industry, one must understand the whole "venture cycle." The organization

---

1. This account is based on Seragen's filings with the U.S. Securities and Exchange Commission. In a 1992 agreement with the State of Massachusetts' Attorney General's Office, the university agreed not to make any further equity investments. The school, however, made a $12 million loan guarantee in 1995 (subsequently converted into equity) and a $5 million payment as part of an asset purchase in 1997. The firm was merged in 1998 into a subsidiary of another biotechnology company. Even if all the contingent payments associated with the transaction are made, the university will have received far less than the amount it invested.

2. The distinction between venture capital and private equity funds is not precise. Private equity funds include funds devoted to venture capital, leveraged buyouts, consolidations, mezzanine and distressed debt investments, and a variety of hybrids such as venture leasing and venture factoring. Venture capital funds are those primarily devoted to equity or equity-linked investments in young growth-oriented firms. Many venture capital funds, however, occasionally make other types of private equity investments.

of this volume mirrors this cycle. Each part will highlight the interrelated nature of the various aspects of the cycle.

A final theme is how slowly the venture capital industry adjusts to shifts in the supply of capital or the demand for financing. Academics are used to thinking that financial markets instantaneously adjust to the arrival of new information. This does not appear to be true in the venture capital market, where regulatory and policy shifts generate disruptions that take years to resolve. Put another way, long-run adjustments in supply and demand curves can be very slow to respond to short-run shocks.

The nature of venture-backed companies contributes to this slow adjustment. Because venture funds must make long-run illiquid investments in firms, they need to secure funds from their investors for periods of a decade or more. The supply of venture capital consequently can not adjust quickly to changes in investment opportunities, as is the case in mutual or hedge funds. More generally, even identifying which sectors or groups are likely to be receiving too much or too little investment is often difficult. The supply of venture capitalists is also difficult to adjust in the short run. Not only is it difficult to raise a new venture capital fund without a track record, but the skills needed for successful venture capital investing are difficult and time-consuming to acquire.[3] During periods when the supply of or demand for venture capital has shifted, adjustments in the number of venture capitalists and venture capital organizations appear to take place very slowly.

Why a New Edition?

A natural second question is why we have chosen to produce a second edition of *The Venture Capital Cycle*. The answer is twofold.

First, our own scholarship has progressed. This volume contains six new chapters that reflect the research that we have completed over the past five years. These projects explore issues that in the previous volume we indicated as important but did not explore in depth there. These new chapters enhance our understanding of each aspect of the venture capital cycle, from the determinants of the volume of fund-raising by venture funds to the way in which lockup requirements affect the way that venture capitalists liqui-

---

3. Practitioner accounts emphasize that venture capitalists have highly specialized skills, which are difficult to develop or even identify. For instance, Robert Kunze (1990, p. 49) of Hambrecht and Quist notes: "The life of the associate [in a venture capital organization] is akin to playing house. Since associates never make the actual investment decision … it's impossible to tell whether or not they'll be successful venture capitalists if and when they get the chance."

date their holdings in recently public companies. Other new chapters illustrate the consequences of venture capital, such as the impact that these investments have on the pace of innovation in the United States. We have also updated the discussions throughout the volume, for instance, adding discussions of recent academic works by others in the overview chapters that begin each section of the volume.

Second, the venture capital industry has changed dramatically in the past five years. While cycles have always been part of venture capital, the magnitude of the boom of the late 1990s and the bust of the early 2000s is far greater than any earlier events. Reflecting these dramatic shifts, many of the chapters seek to understand the origins and consequences of the cyclicality in the venture business.

This second point can be illustrated by considering the new chapters we have added to the volume in a little detail. Chapter 3 is devoted to what is arguably the most essential question of the industry: What is behind the kind of ebbs and flows we have seen in the venture capital cycle. In this chapter we look systematically at the determinants of the level of fund-raising in the industry, and highlight the importance of tax policy as driver of venture capital fund-raising. We suggest that capital gains taxes do not affect directly the level of venture capital fund-raising, as most investors are tax exempt, but rather indirectly. This is because more individuals decide to become entrepreneurs, and thus the demand for venture capital increases.

One of the big questions suggested by the "bubble years" of 1999 to 2000 is what kind of distortions are introduced when the venture capital market grows dramatically. In chapter 9 we seek to understand one type of distortion: whether the amount paid by venture capitalists for new investments increases noticeably. We relate the level of fund-raising to the amount paid by venture capitalists, and find that money does appear to chase deals. Even after controlling for the changing investment environment, we find that a period of intensive fund-raising was followed by higher valuations paid by venture capitalists.

Venture capital is a modestly sized financial intermediary, far smaller than, for instance, mutual funds. Why, then, should we care especially about venture capitalists and the way they work? The "bottom line" is that we believe that the venture capital process is especially successful at encouraging innovative activities. In chapter 12 we seek to test this claim. We carefully try to sort out causality issues: that is, whether "venture capital causes innovation" or whether "venture capitalists show up where innovation is taking place anyway." We conclude that the answer to the title question is indeed yes.

Numerous governments—in many state and federal agencies in the United States, as well as in Asia, Europe, and Latin America—have launched initiatives to encourage the formation of venture capital pools. Despite the many billions of dollars spent on these programs over the years, there have been few efforts to systematically understand what makes the programs successful. In chapter 13 we examine this issue by looking in depth at a single U.S. program, the SBIR initiative. We conclude that the programs did stimulate new firm growth but only in regions such as Silicon Valley and Massachusetts, where there were already established venture capital communities.

The scandals of the past two years have led us to be especially sensitive to the distortions that conflicts of interests can introduce to the financing process. In chapter 17 we seek to test whether conflicts of interests led to distortions in one part of the venture capital cycle: when investment banks took public firms that they had invested in through their venture capital subsidiaries. It might be thought that these offerings would be overpriced and subsequently perform poorly in the market. Surprisingly, we find little evidence that any such problems occurred.

Finally, one of the ways in which investment banks seek to limit conflicts is by "locking up" investors such as venture capitalists. Essentially, the investors are prohibited from selling their shares for a number of months after the firm goes public. In chapter 18 we look at how lockups are used, and how the behavior of venture capitalists and other investors changes as the lockups expire and they are free to sell or transfer their shares.

Thus we see this new edition as an opportunity both to incorporate the research that we have completed in the past half-decade and to highlight work that addresses some of the most contentious and challenging issues facing the venture capital industry today.

The Nature and History of Venture Capital

Before turning to a discussion of venture capital fund-raising, it is helpful to review the nature and history of the venture capital industry. The venture capitalists' role is an old one. Entrepreneurs have long had ideas that require substantial capital to implement but lacked the funds to finance these projects themselves. While many entrepreneurs have used bank loans or other sources of debt financing, start-up companies that lacked substantial tangible assets, expected several years of negative earnings, and had uncertain prospects have often been forced to struggle to find alternatives. Solutions to this problem date back at least as far as Babylonian partnerships at the time of Hammurabi (Lutz 1932). Venture capitalists represent one solution to financing these high-risk, potentially high-reward projects.

The venture capital industry today is a well established, if modestly sized, industry. The industry consists of several thousand professionals, working at about 500 funds concentrated in California, Massachusetts, and a handful of other states. These individuals undertake a variety of roles. The first is maintaining relationships with investors—primarily institutions such as pension funds and university endowments, but also wealthy individuals—who provide them with capital. Venture capitalists typically raise their capital not on a continual basis, but rather through periodic funds. These funds, which are often in the form of limited partnerships, typically have a ten-year life, though extensions of several years are often possible. Eventually, however, the funds must be returned to the investors, and a new fund raised. A venture organization usually will raise a fund every two to five years. Taken collectively, the venture industry today is managing funds with a total capital, including capital that the investors have promised to provide, even if it is not all drawn down, of about $150 billion.

Venture capitalists play a second role in the review of proposed investments, and the oversight of those that are selected for investment. The typical venture organization receives many dozens of business plans for each one it funds. Although most proposals are swiftly discarded, serious candidates are extensively scrutinized through both formal studies of the technology and market strategy and informal assessment of the management team. (It is not unusual for a venture team to complete 100 or more reference checks before deciding to invest in a firm.) The decision to invest is frequently made conditional on the identification of a syndication partner who agrees that this is an attractive investment.

Once the decision to invest is made, venture capitalists frequently disburse funds in stages. Managers of these venture-backed firms are forced to return repeatedly to their financiers for additional capital to ensure that the money is not squandered on unprofitable projects. In addition venture capitalists intensively monitor managers. These investors demand preferred stock with numerous restrictive covenants and representation on the board of directors.

The final role of venture investors is managing the exiting of these investments. Typically venture capitalists seek to take public the most successful firms in their portfolios. While a relatively modest fraction—historically between 20 and 35 percent—of portfolio firms are taken public, they account for the bulk of the venture returns. Even among these offerings, often a small number of firms account for the bulk of the returns; the distribution is highly skewed. Other, less successful firms are liquidated, sold to corporate acquirers, or else remain operational at a modest level of activity.

Given the intensity of interest in replicating the U.S. venture model, it is easy to forget how young the formal venture industry is in this country. The first modern venture capital firm, American Research and Development (ARD), did not appear until after World War II. It was formed in 1946 by MIT President Karl Compton, Harvard Business School Professor Georges F. Doriot, and local business leaders who sought to commercialize the technologies developed for World War II, particularly innovations undertaken at MIT. The success of the investments ranged widely. Almost half of ARD's profits during its twenty-six years as an independent entity came from its $70,000 investment in Digital Equipment Company in 1957, which grew in value to $355 million. Because institutional investors were reluctant to invest, ARD was structured as a publicly traded closed-end fund and marketed mostly to individuals (Liles 1977).

A handful of other venture funds were established in the decade after ARD's formation. Most, like ARD, were structured as publicly traded closed-end funds (mutual funds whose shares must be sold to other investors, rather than redeemed from the issuing firm). The first venture capital limited partnership, Draper, Gaither, and Anderson, was formed in 1958. Imitators soon followed, but limited partnerships accounted for a minority of the venture pool during the 1960s and 1970s. The remainder of venture capital industry was either closed-end funds or small business investment companies (SBICs), federally guaranteed risk-capital pools that proliferated during the 1960s. The annual flow of money into new venture funds during these years never exceeded a few hundred million dollars and usually was much less.

As figure 1.1 shows, funds flowing into the venture capital industry increased dramatically during the late 1970s and early 1980s. The increase in new capital contributions outpaced growth in the number of active organizations, due to the rigidities that limit adjustments in the short-run supply of venture organizations and venture capitalists discussed above.

An important contributing factor to the increase in money flowing into the venture capital sector was the 1979 amendment to the "prudent man" rule governing pension fund investments. Prior to that date the Employee Retirement Income Security Act (ERISA) prohibited pension funds from investing substantial amounts of money in venture capital or other high-risk

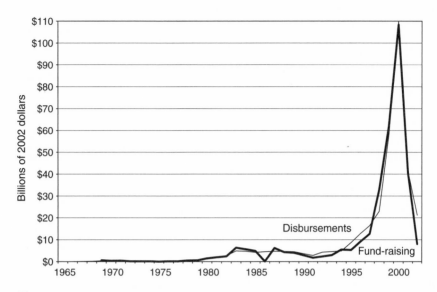

Figure 1.1
Dollar volume of venture capital disbursements and fund-raising, based on tabulations of
unpublished Venture Economics databases. (Data on venture capital fund-raising not available
before 1969.)

asset classes. The Department of Labor's clarification of the rule explicitly
allowed pension managers to invest in high-risk assets, including venture
capital. This rule change opened the door to pension funds' tremendous
capital resources. Table 1.1 shows that in 1978, when $481 million was
invested in new venture capital funds,[4] individuals accounted for the largest
share (32 percent). Pension funds supplied just 15 percent. Eight years later,
when more than $4.8 billion was invested, pension funds accounted for
more than half of all contributions.

An associated change during the 1980s was the increasing role of investment advisors. During the late 1970s and early 1980s, almost all pension
funds invested directly in venture funds. Because venture capital was a small
portion of their portfolios, few resources were devoted to monitoring and
evaluating these investments. During the mid-1980s, investment advisors
(often referred to as "gatekeepers") entered the market to advise institutional investors about venture investments. The gatekeepers pooled resources from their clients, monitored the progress of existing investments,

---

4. The annual commitments represent pledges of capital to venture funds raised in a given
year. This money is typically invested over three to five years starting in the year the fund is
formed.

Table 1.1
Summary statistics for venture capital fund-raising by independent venture partnerships

	1978	1979	1980	1981	1982	1983	1984	1985	1986	1987	1988
First closing of funds											
Number of funds	23	27	57	81	98	147	150	99	86	112	78
Size (2002$ mil)	495	560	1,444	1,984	2,420	6,319	5,608	4,856	51	6,232	4,309
Sources of funds											
Private pension funds	15%	31%	30%	23%	33%	26%	25%	23%	39%	27%	27%
Public pension funds	a	a	a	a	a	5%	9%	10%	12%	12%	20%
Corporations	10%	17%	19%	17%	12%	12%	14%	12%	11%	10%	12%
Individuals	32%	23%	16%	23%	21%	21%	15%	13%	12%	12%	8%
Endowments	9%	10%	14%	12%	7%	8%	6%	8%	6%	10%	11%
Insurance companies and banks	16%	4%	13%	15%	14%	12%	13%	11%	10%	15%	9%
Foreign investors and other	18%	15% .	8%	10%	13%	16%	18%	23%	11%	14%	13%
Independent venture partnerships as a share of the total venture pool[b]		40%	44%	58%	68%	72%	73%	75%	78%	80%	

Source: Compiled from the unpublished Venture Economics funds database and various issues of the *Venture Capital Journal*, except where noted.
a. Public pension funds are included with private pension funds in these years.
b. To calculate the value of independent venture partnerships, we utilize the *Venture Capital Journal* from 1978 to 1994, the *National Venture Capital Association Yearbook* from 1995 to 2001, and Thomson VentureXpert for 2002. This series is defined differently in different years. In some years, the *Venture Capital Journal* states that nonbank SBICs and publicly traded venture funds are included with independent venture partnerships. In other years, these funds are counted in other categories.
c. Foreign investors are not compiled separately in these years.

and evaluated potential new venture funds. By the 1990s, one-third of all pension fund commitments was made through an investment advisor, and one-fifth of all money raised by new funds came through an investment advisor.

A final change in the venture capital industry during this period was the rise of the limited partnership as the dominant organizational form, depicted schematically in figure 1.2. In a venture capital limited partnership, the venture capitalists are general partners and control the fund's activities. The investors serve as limited partners. Investors monitor the fund's progress and attend annual meetings, but they cannot become involved in the fund's day-to-day management if they are to retain limited liability. Venture partnerships have predetermined, finite life spans. The limited partnership agreement explicitly specifies the terms that govern the venture capitalists'

1989	1990	1991	1992	1993	1994	1995	1996	1997	1998	1999	2000	2001	2002
88	50	34	31	54	105	72	97	136	281	421	614	299	125
4,007	2,905	1,771	2,331	2,949	5,524	5,283	9,185	12,676	32,904	62,053	108,382	40,648	8,005
22%	31%	25%	22%	59%	47%	38%	43%	40%	60%	43%	40%	42%	32%
14%	22%	17%	20%	a	a	a	a	a	a	a	a	a	13%
20%	7%	4%	3%	8%	9%	2%	13%	30%	12%	14%	4%	3%	10%
6%	11%	12%	11%	7%	12%	17%	9%	13%	11%	10%	12%	9%	12%
12%	13%	24%	18%	11%	21%	22%	21%	9%	6%	17%	21%	22%	11%
13%	9%	6%	14%	11%	9%	18%	5%	1%	10%	16%	23%	25%	16%
13%	7%	12%	11%	4%	2%	3%	8%	7%	c	c	c	c	6%
79%	80%	80%	81%	78%	78%	84%	84%	82%	79%	80%	82%	73%	82%

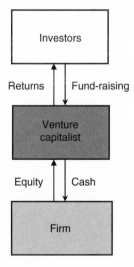

Figure 1.2
Overview of the venture capital process.

Table 1.2
Number and dollar amount of venture capital disbursements for U.S. manufacturing industries, by industry and five-year period

Industry	1965–69	1970–74	1975–79	1980–84	1985–89	1990–94	1995–99	2000–02
Panel A: Venture capital investments								
Food and kindred	1	9	6	23	80	65	136	57
Textile and apparel	4	12	9	19	27	47	106	44
Lumber and furniture	2	8	6	24	62	40	77	41
Paper	2	2	2	2	12	14	32	21
Industrial chemicals	1	1	1	6	18	18	37	13
Drugs	1	12	34	245	554	370	551	469
Other chemicals	1	7	8	10	52	31	58	25
Petroleum refining and extraction	3	3	26	92	27	20	45	31
Rubber products	1	5	6	19	11	12	23	8
Stone, clay, and glass products	0	1	3	14	48	18	21	12
Primary metals	0	3	5	20	44	33	46	81
Fabricated metal products	0	0	0	2	1	3	8	2
Office and computing machines	39	84	108	744	641	224	393	271
Other nonelectrical machinery	12	12	32	254	280	131	213	143
Communication and electronic	23	65	60	497	736	331	968	1,027
Other electrical equipment	0	6	16	36	52	25	63	44
Transportation equipment	1	7	5	6	24	18	58	29
Aircraft and missiles	0	0	0	12	20	9	14	4
Professional and scientific instruments	13	37	70	383	549	237	433	299
Other machinery	7	14	16	62	89	83	140	67
Total	111	288	413	2,470	3,327	1,729	3,422	2,688

Panel B: Venture capital disbursements (2002$ mil)

Food and kindred	5	24	9	30	261	489	1,806	507
Textile and apparel	8	18	17	34	55	377	629	228
Lumber and furniture	5	21	11	33	246	322	850	464
Paper	1	10	3	3	27	96	661	156
Industrial chemicals	0	1	1	51	42	107	431	167
Drugs	0	18	167	766	2,298	3,304	6,764	7,882
Other chemicals	1	49	5	11	191	171	363	289
Petroleum refining and extraction	15	8	113	441	135	97	991	529
Rubber products	1	3	18	35	10	26	86	61
Stone, clay and glass products	0	1	7	42	121	57	105	130
Primary metals	0	10	13	30	82	197	662	2,608
Fabricated metal products	0	0	0	1	0	10	60	4
Office and computing machines	82	496	354	3,999	3,063	1,412	4,746	4,645
Other nonelectrical machinery	79	21	46	832	822	445	1,383	1,998
Communication and electronic	54	232	101	2,146	3,253	2,407	18,823	26,670
Other electrical equipment	0	10	65	96	131	100	330	443
Transportation equipment	0	12	5	11	57	375	520	387
Aircraft and missiles	0	0	0	24	24	26	88	42
Professional and scientific instruments	16	106	140	997	1,781	1,441	4,339	4,837
Other machinery	9	35	27	139	217	865	1,463	552
Total	$277	$1,074	$1,102	$9,721	$12,817	$12,325	$45,101	$52,601

Source: Based on tabulations of unpublished Venture Economics databases.
Note: The count of venture capital investments in each specified period is the sum of the number of unique firms receiving investments in that time period.

compensation over the entire ten- to thirteen-year life of the fund. It is extremely rare that these terms are renegotiated. The specified compensation has a simple form. The venture capitalist typically receives an annual fixed fee, plus variable compensation that is a specified fraction of the fund's profits. The fixed portion of the specified compensation is usually between 1.5 and 3 percent of the committed capital or net asset value, and the variable portion is usually about 20 percent of fund profits. Table 1.1 shows that partnerships have grown from 40 percent of the venture pool in 1980 to 81 percent in 1992.

As a result of this growth, venture capitalists have increased their rate of investment, as figure 1.1 demonstrates. As the rate of investment has increased, venture capitalists continued to focus their investments on information technology and health care, as well as on California and Massachusetts firms. Table 1.2 presents an aggregated summary of investments by industry (in manufacturing firms only) over the past three decades, and table 1.3 provides a summary of investments in the ten states with the most venture capital activity over the past three decades. The result of this growth was intense competition for transactions among venture groups.

The steady growth of commitments to the venture capital industry was reversed in the late 1980s. Returns on venture capital funds declined because of overinvestment in various industries and the entry of inexperienced venture capitalists. As investors became disappointed with returns, they committed less capital to the industry.

The departure of many inexperienced venture capitalists from the industry—along with the robust market for initial public offerings (IPOs)—led to an increase in returns in the 1990s. (Table 1.4 summarizes the exiting of venture capital investments through IPOs as well as comparable data on nonventure capital offerings.) New capital commitments rose accordingly. The surge in fund-raising put upward pressure on prices and led to massive increases in stock distributions to venture capital investors. Additionally venture capitalists responded to greater capital in a variety of ways. First, the amount of money invested in the typical venture-backed company increased. Venture capitalists also increased their compensation and reduced the restrictiveness of the limited partnership agreements that govern their investment behavior.

Once the valuations of small-capitalization stocks began dramatically declining in 2000, these dynamics changed sharply once again. The IPO market shut down, and venture capitalists were left with extensive holdings of unprofitable companies, many of which were built on shaky foundations. These groups dramatically scaled back the pace of new investment and

Table 1.3
Number and dollar amount of venture capital disbursements for all industries in ten states with the most venture capital activity by five-year period

State	1965 –69	1970 –74	1975 –79	1980 –84	1985 –89	1990 –94	1995 –99	2000 –02
Panel A: Venture capital investments								
California	65	179	310	1,863	2,645	1,138	3,192	3,209
Massachusetts	45	93	155	708	1,014	352	894	908
Texas	18	71	84	373	584	215	525	575
New York	28	90	73	311	324	108	531	658
New Jersey	15	35	47	171	291	102	257	261
Colorado	5	22	31	194	258	112	269	245
Pennsylvania	8	21	32	120	290	125	343	298
Illinois	16	29	31	133	214	99	242	244
Minnesota	12	34	42	170	186	79	164	159
Connecticut	3	20	37	136	217	74	200	177
Total, all states	302	847	1,253	5,365	8,154	3,376	9,202	9,257
Panel B: Venture capital disbursements (2002$ mil)								
California	268	672	849	8,251	11,889	9,517	54,603	76,169
Massachusetts	75	191	243	2,389	3,478	2,846	13,089	19,252
Texas	46	172	182	1,427	2,669	2,907	7,922	12,223
New York	39	190	199	846	1,726	1,072	8,223	11,294
New Jersey	40	101	94	455	1,493	1,305	3,511	7,444
Colorado	15	62	56	606	989	858	4,567	6,651
Pennsylvania	22	51	143	455	1,881	1,215	4,078	4,991
Illinois	73	165	144	353	1,485	917	3,463	4,429
Minnesota	8	111	54	332	499	379	2,034	2,542
Connecticut	1	39	104	392	1,799	755	2,473	2,976
Total, all states	$845	$2,379	$2,777	$18,762	$37,796	$28,281	$143,561	$191,974

Source: Based on tabulations of VentureXpert and unpublished Venture Economics databases.
Note: The count of venture capital investments in each specified period is the sum of the number of unique firms receiving investments in that time period.

Table 1.4
Distribution of venture-backed and nonventure IPOs for 1978 to 2002

Year	Number of venture-backed IPOs	Amount raised in venture-backed IPOs	Total number of IPOs	Total amount raised in all IPOs	Venture-backed IPOs as percent of all IPOs (number)	Venture-backed IPOs as percent of all IPOs (amount)
1978	6	$165	50	$566	12.00%	29.11%
1979	4	$76	81	$907	4.94%	8.36%
1980	24	$823	238	$2,719	10.08%	30.29%
1981	50	$962	438	$5,667	11.42%	16.98%
1982	21	$907	198	$2,224	10.61%	40.77%
1983	101	$4,243	848	$21,117	11.91%	20.09%
1984	44	$898	516	$6,080	8.53%	14.77%
1985	35	$1,007	507	$15,664	6.90%	6.43%
1986	79	$2,463	953	$25,772	8.29%	9.56%
1987	69	$1,970·	630	$19,707	10.95%	10.00%
1988	36	$1,125	223	$6,216	16.14%	18.09%
1989	39	$1,365	210	$7,589	18.57%	17.99%
1990	43	$1,560	172	$6,064	25.00%	25.73%
1991	119	$4,715	365	$19,961	32.60%	23.62%
1992	157	$5,308	513	$27,650	30.60%	19.20%
1993	193	$6,031	665	$35,924	29.02%	16.79%
1994	159	$4,190	567	$21,904	28.04%	19.13%
1995	205	$7,685	571	$33,129	35.90%	23.20%
1996	284	$13,495	831	$47,663	34.18%	28.31%
1997	134	$5,249	603	$36,849	22.22%	14.25%
1998	77	$4,063	357	$37,518	21.57%	10.83%
1999	257	$20,841	543	$69,271	47.33%	30.09%
2000	226	$21,652	449	$68,700	50.33%	31.52%
2001	37	$3,118	107	$39,364	34.58%	7.92%
2002	24	$2,474	97	$26,512	24.74%	9.33%

Sources: Barry et al. (1992), Ritter (2003), and various issues of the *Going Public: The IPO Reporter* and the *Venture Capital Journal*.
Note: All dollar figures are in millions of 2002 dollars.

fund-raising as they focused on salvaging their investments. The behaviors associated with the late 1990s, such as the demands for greater compensation, became the focal point for resentment on the part of institutional investors, who believed their interests had been poorly served during this period.

The recent growth and subsequent difficulties of the U.S. venture industry have raised concerns among many venture capitalists and institutional investors about the future prospects of the industry domestically. In response to these changes, investors—and venture capital organizations themselves—are increasingly looking abroad for investment opportunities. Table 1.5 provides an international comparison of venture capital activity. In chapter 21 we discuss some of the future developments that we believe are likely in the venture capital industry.

Limitations of This Volume

Before ending this introduction, three limitations of this book should be acknowledged. First, there are many fascinating topics relating to venture capital that are not considered in this volume. These include the relative performance of venture capital and other financial assets, the degree to which public policies affect the formation of venture capital funds, and the extent to which the U.S. model of venture capital investment can be transferred to foreign markets. Throughout this book we will highlight some of these research opportunities.

Second, we do not attempt to duplicate the guides that explain the intricacies of the venture financing process to practitioners. Numerous excellent volumes exist (especially Bartlett 1995; Halloran et al. 1995; Levin 1995) that document the legal and institutional considerations associated with raising venture financing at much greater depth than could be done in this volume.

Finally, we do not consider many interesting and related forms of financing that also deserve scrutiny. In particular, we define venture capital as independently managed, dedicated pools of capital that focus on equity or equity-linked investments in privately held, high-growth companies. A more ambitious volume might examine the entrepreneurial finance function more generally,[5] while our focus is exclusively on venture capital. This is

---

5. Merton (1995) has argued that the actual institution is not the important element of the financial system, it is the function. The same economic function can be performed by different institutions in different markets.

Table 1.5
Total venture capital invested in 39 nations in 2001

Country	Venture capital invested	Country	Venture capital invested
Australia	1,273	Malaysia	80
Austria	47	Netherlands	208
Belgium	112	New Zealand	46
Canada	3,172	Norway	74
China	1,590	Pakistan	0
Czech Republic	8	Philippines	24
Denmark	172	Poland	28
Finland	159	Portugal	18
France	635	Singapore	1,052
Germany	1,306	Slovakia	3
Greece	36	Spain	125
Hong Kong	1,864	Sri Lanka	0
Hungary	18	Sweden	270
Iceland	7	Switzerland	85
India	1,133	Taiwan	393
Indonesia	9	Thailand	22
Ireland	43	United Kingdom	1,051
Italy	330	United States	41,005
Japan	2,148	Vietnam	3
Korea	1,695		

Note: We utilize the Asian Venture Capital Journal's *2003 Guide to Venture Capital in Asia, 14th edition* (2003) for statistics on the Asian region, Venture Economics' *National Venture Capital Association Yearbook* (2002) for U.S. information, and the European Private Equity and Venture Capital Association's *Annual Survey of Pan-European Private Equity and Venture Capital Activity* (2002) for European data. These figures include first and follow-on investments. European statistics include seed and start-up investments and exclude expansion, replacement capital, and buyout investments. All dollar figures are in millions of 2002 dollars.

partially because of the size of the venture capital market. Although evidence on the financing of these firms is imprecise, Freear and Wetzel's (1990) survey suggests that venture capital accounts for about two-thirds of the external equity financing raised by privately held technology-intensive businesses from private-sector sources.[6]

6. Many more firms receive funding from individual investors than venture capitalists. Freear and Wetzel (1990) report the median financing round raised by private high-technology firms from individual investors to be about $200,000, with 82 percent of the rounds from individuals being under $500,000. A more recent study of high-technology initial public offerings by Fenn, Liang, and Prowse (1998) largely corroborates this survey evidence.

More generally, the venture capital market represents a particularly re-fined, if still evolving, solution to the difficult problems associated with financing young firms. Understanding the approaches developed by these investors—as well as the common problems that the investments face—should be more generally applicable, whether to corporations seeking to en-courage internal entrepreneurship or to policy-makers seeking to promote greater innovation and economic development through start-up companies.

I   Venture Capital Fund-Raising

2   An Overview of Venture Capital Fund-Raising

The process of raising capital and structuring funds is complex and little understood outside the industry. Private equity partnership agreements are daunting documents, often extending for hundreds of pages and addressing almost any possible eventuality. Practitioner discussions of the structure of these firms are rife with obscure terms such as "reverse clawbacks."

But understanding the process of raising a fund and structuring a partnership is central to an understanding of the venture capital cycle. The features of private equity funds—whether management fees, profit-sharing rules, or contractual terms—have long-lasting effects on the behavior of venture capitalists. The choices made in structuring these funds have profound implications for the entrepreneur financing a company through these investors, the investment banker underwriting a firm backed by private equity funds, the corporate development officer investing alongside venture capitalists in a young company, and the pension fund manager placing an institution's capital into a fund.

An example—discussed at length in chapter 16—may help to illustrate how form influences behavior. Almost all venture and buyout funds are designed to be "self-liquidating," that is, to dissolve after ten or twelve years. The need to terminate each fund imposes a healthy discipline, forcing private equity investors to take the necessary, but painful, step of terminating underperforming firms in their portfolios. (These firms are sometimes referred to as the "living dead" or "zombies.") But the pressure to raise an additional fund can sometimes have less pleasant consequences. Young private equity organizations frequently rush young firms to the public marketplace to demonstrate a successful track record, even if the companies are not ready to go public. This behavior, known as "grandstanding," can have a harmful effect on the long-run prospects of firms dragged prematurely into the public markets.

Many features of private equity funds can be understood as responses to an uncertain environment, rife with many information gaps. Investing in a private equity fund is, in some respects, a leap of faith for institutional investors. Most pension funds and endowments typically have very small staffs. At the largest organizations, a dozen professionals may be responsible for investing several billion dollars each year. Meanwhile private equity funds frequently undertake investments in risky new firms pursuing complex new technologies or in troubled mature companies with numerous organizational pathologies and potential legal liabilities.

Limited and general partners have gradually developed a variety of mechanisms to ensure that value is maximized despite these uncertainties. For instance, the "carried interest"—the substantial share of profits that is allocated to the private equity investors—helps address these information asymmetries by ensuring that all parties gain if the investment does well. Pension fund investors frequently hire gatekeepers, who play a consultative role in recommending sophisticated private equity funds with well-defined objectives to their clients. In other cases these intermediaries organize "funds of funds." In addition venture organizations are increasingly hiring placement agents to facilitate the fund-raising process. Specialized investors concentrate on particular niches of the private equity industry, such as buying and selling interests in limited partnerships from institutional investors.

At the same time, other features of private equity funds can be seen as attempts to transfer wealth between parties rather than efforts to increase the size of the overall amount of profits generated by private equity investments. An example was the drive by many venture capital funds in the mid-1980s—a period when the demand for their services was very strong—to change the timing of their compensation. Prior to this point, venture capital funds had typically disbursed all the proceeds from their first few successful investments to their investors, until the investors had received their original invested capital back. The venture capitalists would then begin receiving a share of the subsequent investments that they exited. Consider a fund that had raised capital of $50 million, whose first three successful investments yielded $25 million each. Under the traditional arrangement, the proceeds from the first two offerings would have gone entirely to the limited partners in their fund. The venture capitalists would have begun receiving a share of the proceeds only at the time that they exited the third investment.

In the mid-1980s venture capitalists began demanding and receiving the right to start sharing in even the first successfully exited investments. The primary effect of this change was that the venture capitalists began receiving more compensation early in their funds' lives. Put another way, the net present value of their compensation package increased considerably. It is not surprising, then, that as the inflow into venture capital weakened in the late 1980s, limited partners began demanding that venture capitalists return to the previous approach of deferring compensation.

This tension between behavior that increases the size of the "pie" and actions that simply change the relative sizes of the slices runs throughout part I of this book. By this framework we attempt to understand both the reasons for and the workings of the key features of these funds.

Related Research

While theoretically and empirically oriented economists have extensively scrutinized the interactions between venture capitalists and portfolio firms, the formation of venture funds has received relatively little attention. The rationales for the limited partnership structure and the drivers of variability of capital inflows were little explored. What the limited earlier work focused on was the highly variable commitments to the venture capital industry. Understanding the determinants of this variability has been a topic of some interest. Much of this work has been policy oriented, with attempts to derive implications for programs to promote venture capital.

Various factors may affect the level of commitments to venture capital organizations. Poterba (1987, 1989) argues for the correspondence of venture capital fund-raising to changes in either the supply of or the demand for venture capital. What is meant by supply of venture capital is the relative desire of institutional investors to commit capital to start-ups. The number of entrepreneurs with good ideas who want venture capital determines the demand for venture capital. It is very likely, Poterba argues, that decreases in capital gains tax rates increase commitments to venture capital funds, although the bulk of the funds come from tax-exempt investors. Through a formal model, he showed that a drop in the tax rate can have a substantial effect on the willingness of corporate employees to become entrepreneurs, thereby increasing the need for venture capital. This increase in demand, due to greater entrepreneurial activity, could lead to more venture capital fund-raising.

Other work has approached these issues on a more qualitative basis. Black and Gilson (1998) argue that there should be a strong tie between the health of the public equity markets and venture capital fund-raising, both in the United States and abroad. They consider the health of the venture capital market to depend on the existence of a vibrant public market that allows new firms to issue shares. Only with such a public market can venture capitalists make a credible commitment to entrepreneurs that they will ultimately relinquish control of the firms in which they invest.

Jensen (1991) and Sahlman and Stevenson (1986) discuss the apparent cyclicality in the amount of venture funds raised. They argue that institutional investors are prone to either over- or underinvest in speculative markets such as venture capital. They claim that this apparently irrational pattern of investing can explain the extreme swings in fund-raising. Both works argue that such dramatic swings hinder entrepreneurship and innovation in the American economy.

Jeng and Wells (2000) examine the factors that influence venture capital fund-raising in twenty-one countries. They find the strength of the IPO market to be an important factor in determining venture capital commitments, echoing the conclusions of Black and Gilson. Jeng and Wells observe, however, that the IPO market does not influence commitments to early stage funds as much as to later stage ones. While this work represents an important initial step, much more remains to be done.[2]

A provocative point in the Jeng and Wells analysis is evidence that government policy can have a dramatic impact on the current and long-term viability of the venture capital sector. In many countries, especially in continental Europe, policy-makers face a dilemma. The relatively few entrepreneurs active in these markets face numerous daunting regulatory restrictions, a paucity of venture funds focusing on investing in high-growth firms, and illiquid markets where investors do not welcome IPOs by young firms without long histories of positive earnings. It is often unclear where to begin the process of duplicating the success of the United States. Only very recently have researchers begun to examine the ways in which policy-makers can catalyze the growth of venture capital and the companies in which they invest. (Three recent exceptions are Irwin and Klenow 1996, Lerner 1999, and Wallsten 2000.) Clearly, much more work needs to be done in this arena.

A topic that has attracted far less attention than determining fund-raising patterns is the rationale for the structure of venture capital organizations. The independent private equity firm is an organizational form that has often been hailed as a dramatic improvement over the typical American corporation with dispersed shareholders (Jensen 1993; Shleifer and Vishny 1997b). As we noted in chapter 1, the organizational form that dominates the

---

2. One potential source of confusion is that the term venture capital is used differently in Europe and Asia. Abroad, venture capital often refers to all private equity, including buyout, late stage, and mezzanine financing (which represent the vast majority of the private-equity pool in most overseas markets). In the United States these are all separate classes.

venture industry is the limited partnership. The contracts spell out the compensation and conditions that govern the relationship between investors (limited partners) and the venture capitalist (general partner) during the fund's life. These claims, however, have attracted little prior scrutiny. This absence of attention is surprising given the longevity of the limited partnership as an organizational structure and the unvarying nature of its central features since the Italian commenda of the tenth century (De Roover 1963; Lopez and Raymond 1955).

A recent related work offers possible explanations for the presence of certain conditions in private equity partnership agreements. Lerner and Schoar (2003) examine rationales for constraints on liquidity in private equity limited partnerships. It is commonplace for private equity groups to impose severe restrictions on the transferability of partnership interests, far beyond what is required by securities law. This is particularly puzzling since partnership interests are very illiquid to begin with due to the large stakes held by each investor. They argue that these curbs might allow general partners to screen for long-term investors. A limited partner who expects many liquidity shocks would find these restrictions especially expensive and, therefore, would avoid investing. Thus the limited partners selected will be highly liquid facilitating fund-raising in follow-on funds. Their model shows that restrictions on liquidity are less common in later funds organized by the same venture group, where information problems are presumably less severe. They also find evidence that transferability restrictions are less strict in private equity groups with limited partners that are known to have few liquidity shocks.

An Overview of Part I

In the four chapters that follow, we present four analyses of these issues. In chapter 3, we examine the determinants of fund-raising in the United States. In chapters 4 and 5, we examine the structure of venture partnerships. We show that the need to provide adequate incentives and shifts in relative negotiating power have important impacts on the terms of venture capital limited partnerships. In chapter 4, we consider the more general question of the importance of the limited partnership structure employed by most venture capital funds. Our findings, though tentative, raise provocative questions about the assumptions on this organizational form.

The next chapter explores the suggestions of Poterba and Black and Gilson empirically. We examine the drivers of venture capital fund-raising in independent venture partnerships from 1972 through 1994. We study industry aggregate, state-level, and firm-specific fund-raising to determine if macro-economic, regulatory, or performance factors affect venture capital activity. We find support for the claims about capital gains tax rates: lower capital gains taxes appear to have a particularly strong effect on the amount of venture capital supplied by tax-exempt investors. This suggests that the primary mechanism by which capital gains tax cuts affect venture fund-raising is by increasing the demand of entrepreneurs for capital. If the effect were on the supply of funds, changes in tax rates should have affected the contribution by taxable entities more dramatically.

A number of other factors also influence venture fund-raising. Not surprisingly, regulatory changes such as the Department of Labor's shift in ERISA policies have had an important impact on commitments to venture capital funds. We also show that performance influences fundraising. Higher returns lead to greater capital commitments to new funds. The returns to venture capital have been quite variable.[1] In the early 1980s, returns on venture investments were quite high. From the mid-1980s through early 1990s, however, returns were extremely low. Average returns on venture investments were largely in the single digits. Starting in 1993, returns increased substantially.

These returns were largely driven by the strength of the IPO market. A venture capitalist must liquidate a return in private firms to make money. By far the most profitable exit is an IPO.

A comparison of annual fund-raising by venture capitalists in figure 1.1 with the annual volume of venture-backed IPOs in table 1.4 makes this link explicit. Few firms went public in the 1970s and very little venture capital was raised. The growth of the venture capital industry in the early 1980s was mirrored by a similar growth in venture-backed firms going public. The decline in fund-raising in the late 1980s was preceded by a decline in the IPO market. Finally the growth in venture capital fund-raising in the 1990s was also preceded by increases in IPO market activity.

We offer alternative explanations for the results of our study. We explore the effect of the supply of substitute financing on the supply and demand for venture capital. We find that the availability of bank financing is not a key determinant of venture capital commitments. Additionally we explore the relationship between expected GDP and capital gains tax rates. Finally shifts in technology might be responsible for changes in the level of commitments to venture capital. The results of our state-level analysis show that

---

1. As discussed in chapter 5, the actual calculation of returns for venture investments and their correlation with other asset returns is problematic. New research is needed to improve these measures. See also the discussion in Gompers and Lerner (1997a).

regulatory policies are strongly related to the increase in venture capital commitments during the period of the sample.

Covenants and compensation are critical for aligning the incentives of venture capitalists with those of investors. The limited partnership places restrictions on the ability of investors to intervene in the day to day activities of the venture fund. Few of the common corporate control mechanisms—for example, active boards of directors or a market for corporate control—are utilized in venture limited partnerships. Consequently the terms of the partnership agreement are extremely important for controlling activities of the venture capitalists that might ultimately be harmful to investors.

Covenants and restrictions often play an important role in limiting conflicts among investors and venture capitalists. In chapter 4, we explore two complementary hypotheses that may help explain the use of covenants and restrictions in venture capital limited partnerships. The hypotheses have implications for both cross-sectional and time-series variation in contractual form.

First, because negotiating and monitoring specific covenants are costly, contracting parties should weigh the potential costs and benefits of covenant inclusion. The ease of monitoring and the potential to engage in opportunistic behavior may vary among funds, leading to different sets of optimal covenants in different contracts. Costly contracting implies that more restrictive contracts will be employed when monitoring is easier and the potential for opportunistic behavior is greater.

A second hypothesis relates covenant composition to supply and demand conditions. In the short run, the supply of venture capital services may be fixed, with a modest number of venture partnerships raising funds of carefully limited size each year. Demand for venture investing services has shifted sharply over the past decades. Increases in demand may lead to higher prices when contracts are written. Higher prices may include not only increases in monetary compensation but also greater consumption of private benefits through fewer covenants and restrictions.

In chapter 4, we next examine a sample of 140 executed partnership agreements from a major endowment and two investment managers that select venture capital investments for pension funds and other institutional investors. Because investors in a limited partnership avoid direct involvement in the activities of the fund, the covenants and restrictions in the partnership contract are critical in determining the general partners' behavior. Considerable time and expense are devoted to negotiating the final form of the document. A single limited partnership agreement governs the relationship between the limited and general partners over the fund's life of a decade or more. Unlike other agreements (e.g., employment contracts or strategic alliances), these contracts are rarely renegotiated. The heterogeneity of venture organizations helps us analyze the importance of demand shifts and costly contracting in determining the extent of covenant inclusion in partnership agreements.

The evidence indicates that both supply and demand conditions and costly contracting are important in determining contractual provisions. In univariate comparisons and regression analyses, fewer restrictions are found in funds established during years with greater inflows of new capital, funds in which limited partners do not employ investment managers, and funds where general partners enjoy higher levels of compensation. The evidence illustrates the importance of general market conditions on the restrictiveness of venture capital limited partnerships. In periods when venture capitalists have relatively more bargaining power they are able to raise money with fewer strings attached.

In chapter 5, we examine compensation terms in 419 venture partnership agreements and offering memoranda for funds formed between 1978 and 1992. We explore the cross-sectional differences in compensation (comparing one venture capital organization to another), as well as the time-series variation (how contracts change as organizations become more seasoned). We find that compensation for older and larger venture capital organizations is more sensitive to performance than the compensation of other venture groups. For example, the oldest and largest venture groups command about a 1 percent greater share of the capital gains than their less established counterparts. This greater profit share matters little if the fund is not successful, but can represent a 4 percent or greater increase in the net present value of total compensation if the fund is successful. These differences are statistically significant whether we examine the percentage of profits accruing to the venture capitalists (though these analyses are very noisy) or the elasticity of compensation with respect to performance. The cross-sectional variation in compensation terms for younger, smaller venture organizations is considerably less than for older, larger organizations. The fixed component of compensation is higher for smaller, younger funds and funds focusing on high-technology or early stage investments. Finally, we do not find any relationship between the incentive compensation and performance.

In chapter 5, we also discuss two models that might explain the cross-sectional and time-series variation in compensation, a learning and a signaling model. The empirical results are consistent with the primary predictions of the learning model. In this model neither the venture capitalists nor the investor knows the venture capitalist's ability. In early funds, venture capitalists will work hard even without explicit pay-for-performance incentives because, if they can establish a good reputation for either selecting attractive investments or adding value to firms in their portfolios, they will gain additional compensation in later funds. These reputation concerns lead to lower pay-for-performance for smaller and younger venture organizations. Once a reputation has been established, explicit incentive compensation is needed to induce the proper effort levels. The signaling model, in which venture capitalists know their ability but investors do not, predicts that new funds should have higher pay-for-performance sensitivities and lower base compensation because high-ability venture capitalists try to reveal their type by accepting riskier pay.

Finally, in chapter 6, we contrast the structure and success of investments by venture capital limited partnerships with those of corporate venture programs. The corporate funds have very different organizational forms, typically structured as subsidiaries of the parent firm with little incentive compensation. Nonetheless, they undertake similar investments with similar personnel, suggesting that a comparison with traditional venture funds may help us understand the extent to which the structure of venture capital funds affects their performance. We seek to determine whether the corporate funds are less successful than their independent counterparts. We also examine whether the corporate programs enjoy some benefits that may offset some of these costs. In particular, a substantial body of work on complementarities in the strategy literature suggests that corporate funds select better investments related to their existing business areas or add greater value to the firms in which they invest.

To test these concepts, we examine over 30,000 investments by corporate and independent venture funds into entrepreneurial firms. We examine the ultimate outcome of the firms receiving the capital, the valuations assigned to the firms at the time of the investments, and the duration of the venture organizations or subsidiaries themselves. The evidence supports the importance of complementarities. Portfolio companies receiving funds from corporate investors with a well-defined strategic focus enjoy greater success. Investments are made at a premium, but this may reflect the indirect benefits that the corporation receives. Corporate programs with a well-defined strategic focus are as stable as traditional independent venture organizations. Among the corporate funds without a strong strategic focus, we see significantly less success in the investments and less stability than among the focused funds. Thus it may be that earlier work suggesting the critical nature of the venture capital limited partnership was somewhat misguided. Instead, the evidence argues that strategy and incentives are critical to successful venture capital investing.

Final Thoughts

In short, part I focuses on the two components of venture fund formation. First, it attempts to determine the underlying causes of the venture capital industry's highly variable commitments. Second, it presents analyses that underscore the complexity and multifaceted nature of venture capital organizations. Certainly this is an organizational form that defies facile generalizations. It is clear that this is an organizational structure that has evolved—and continues to adjust—to address the challenging problems posed by investments in entrepreneurial firms. Yet many recent shifts in the structure of these funds, such as the relaxation of covenants during periods of substantial growth, appear to reflect the changing supply and demand conditions for venture capital itself rather than any concerns about the optimal structure for investing. Nor is it clear that the venture capital limited partnership is the only structure in which successful investments into entrepreneurial firms can take place.

Part I ends with more questions than it answers. Will the structures of funds converge over time to a few templates that have been shown to be most effective in generating high returns? Or will the tension among adding features that maximize overall value and those that merely transfer wealth continue to characterize the industry? To what extent will the venture capital limited partnership emerge as the dominant organizational form outside the United States, or will alternative structures predominate?

These questions have become particularly urgent in light of the events in recent years. The run-up in venture capital fund-raising in the late 1990s and subsequent decline in the first years of the twenty-first century, while reflecting earlier patterns, was of a magnitude that far exceeded earlier cycles. This instability and its aftermath are likely to trigger a profound rethinking of the relationship between general and limited partners. Thus, the structure of venture capital organizations is likely to be a topic of continuing interest to academic professionals and practitioners alike.

3   What Drives Venture Capital Fund-Raising?

Introduction

In this chapter we examine the determinants of venture capital fund-raising in the United States over the past twenty-two years. We analyze both industry fund-raising patterns and the fund-raising success of individual venture organizations. Our study focuses on the forces that affected fund-raising by independent venture capital organizations from 1972 through 1994. It provides evidence that regulatory changes relating to pension funds, capital gains tax rates, overall economic growth, and research and development expenditures—as well as firm-specific performance and reputation—affected fund-raising by venture capital organizations. The results were important in promoting venture capital investment.

Our attempts distinguish between supply and demand factors that affect the quantity of venture capital. We find that demand-side factors led the commitment to venture capital funds while capital gains tax rates had an important effect at the industry, state-, and firm-specific levels. Decreases in the capital gains tax rates are associated with greater venture capital commitments. The effect, however, appears to occur through the demand for venture capital as rate changes affect both taxable and tax-exempt investors. Similarly R&D expenditures, especially expenditures by industrial firms, were positively related to venture investments in particular states.

Additionally we present evidence that the Department of Labor's clarification of its "prudent man" rule, which enabled pension funds to freely invest in venture capital, and individual venture firm performance and reputation, influenced fund-raising. Higher returns (as measured by the value of equity held in firms taken public) led to greater capital commitments to new funds. Older and larger organizations also attracted more capital. Our study includes a look at factors that affected venture organizations' decisions to raise funds targeted at early-stage, start-up firms. These funds helped generate new firms and innovation. The results indicate that smaller West Coast venture organizations were more likely to have raised an early-stage venture fund.

Determinants of Venture Capital Fund-Raising

Supply and Demand in Venture Capital

To understand the mechanism through which the venture capital market works, it is important to discuss the factors of supply and demand. Figure 3.1 presents a simple illustration of equilibrium in the venture capital market. Supply of venture capital is determined by the willingness of investors to provide funds to venture firms. The willingness of investors to commit money to venture capital is dependent on the expected rate of return on venture investments. Therefore in the venture capital market, price is

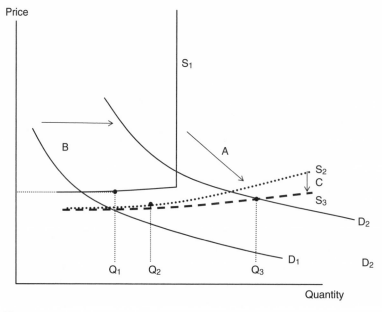

Figure 3.1
Changes in supply and demand in the venture capital market. Equilibrium prior to ERISA is represented by Q_1. After ERISA, the supply curve shifts down to S_2 (A), and the new equilibrium quantity of venture capital is Q_2. Capital gains tax reductions move both demand to D_2 (B) and supply to S_3 (C), and the equilibrium quantity of venture capital moves to Q_3.

the expected rate of return on new venture capital investments. Higher expected returns lead to a greater desire of investors to supply venture capital. As in most supply schedules, the amount of capital slopes upward.

The demand schedule is simply the quantity of entrepreneurial firms seeking venture capital that can supply a particular expected rate of return. As the price increases—the expected return increases—fewer entrepreneurial firms demand capital because the quantity of projects meeting that threshold declines. The demand schedule therefore slopes downward.

We will discuss the equilibria in the supply and demand framework by examining the quantity of venture capital. While any supply and demand equilibrium also implies a particular price (i.e., an expected rate of return), we cannot measure the anticipated rate of return in the venture capital market. Nor does the actual rate of return provide a useful proxy. Returns from venture capital investments can only be observed many years after the original investments because private firms are valued at cost until they are sold or taken public many years later. Because of these accounting policies, the stated returns for venture funds are exceedingly variable and somewhat misleading. (See the discussion in Gompers and Lerner 1997a.[1]) We feel fairly comfortable that the expected rate of return (i.e., price) will not vary substantially across the sample period. As discussed below, however, supply curves for venture capital are likely to be very elastic. Hence changes in equilibrium will have a significantly larger effect on quantities than on prices.

The supply schedule for venture capital is likely to be nearly flat. Investors choose to place money in financial assets because of the expected monetary returns. Because close substitutes for these cash flows exist, either through a single security or combination of securities, investors will have a particular expected return on venture capital that just compensates for the systematic riskiness of the investments (Scholes 1972). If perfect substitutes for venture capital did exist, then the supply curve would be completely flat. We drew the supply curves as slightly upward sloping in figure 3.1. One source of an upward slope would be differential taxes. Because the return on venture capital investments is taxable, investors with higher tax rates will require progressively higher expected rates of return to induce them to invest in venture funds versus some tax-free investment.

---

1. Practices of reporting valuations of companies across various venture organizations are often quite different. Information on fund returns is closely guarded, and even the intermediaries who specialize in compiling this data do not have very comprehensive coverage.

Capital Gains Taxes and Venture Capital Fund-Raising

The effect of capital gains tax rates on commitments to the venture capital industry has been debated in the academic literature as well as in political circles. The effect of reductions in the capital gains tax rate on commitments to venture capital was one of the intended benefits of the 1993 tax reduction from 28 to 14 percent on investments in small companies held for five years.

Poterba (1989) had argued that it is unlikely that capital gains taxes affect venture capital by shifting the supply curve. The supply effect of capital gains tax reductions is illustrated by C in figure 3.1. A reduction in the capital gains tax rate would lower the required expected (before-tax) rate of return on venture investments for taxable investors. This would cause the right-hand side of supply curve S_2 to shift down to S_3. Most investors in venture capital after 1980 have been tax-exempt institutions and the supply effect may therefore have been small.

Poterba then developed a model of the decision to become an entrepreneur. He argued that the capital gains tax rate could have a dramatic effect on this choice. Lower capital gains tax rates make it relatively more attractive for a manager or worker to start his or her own company. Most of a manager's compensation comes in the form of salary and cash bonuses which are taxed at the ordinary income tax rate. Most of the compensation from being an entrepreneur is in the form of capital appreciation on the equity of the company. Poterba argued that reductions in the capital gains tax rates could have a first-order effect on the demand for venture capital as more people are induced to become entrepreneurs and better projects are brought to market. This would increase the quantity of venture capital demanded to D_2 and increase the equilibrium quantity of venture capital to Q_3.[2]

If the capital gains tax rate weighs on commitments to venture capital funds, then we can expect a significant relation at the industry level and at the fund-specific level. In general, lower capital gains taxes lead to increases in commitments to venture capital as a whole as well as to individual funds.

---

2. Anand (1996) examines the effects of capital gains tax rates on investment in the communications industry. For investments by venture capital firms into private communication companies, he finds the level and composition of investment to be affected negatively by increases in the capital gains tax rate. Anand's ability to draw conclusions, however, is limited by the fact that he looks only at one industry. Investments in one industry may be affected by myriad other factors, including technology shifts, tastes, or other investment opportunities. Examining the impact of capital gains tax rates on the quantity of venture capital raised appears to be a much more satisfactory way to address the issue.

We can also shed light on whether Poterba's argument about supply and demand effects is valid. If capital gains taxes affect commitments to venture capital primarily through the demand for venture capital, then we can expect the reductions in the capital gains tax rate to have a positive impact on the commitments of both tax-exempt and tax-sensitive investors. If the effect is primarily due to supply changes, then contributions by tax-exempt investors should be unrelated to the capital gains tax rate. Because we can separate contributions to venture funds by investor type, we should be able to determine whether the demand effects (B in figure 3.1) or supply effects (C in figure 3.1) of decreases in the capital gains tax rate are more important.

The Employment Retirement Income Security Act and Venture Commitments

One policy decision that potentially had an effect on commitments to venture funds via supply changes is the clarification by the U.S. Department of Labor of the Employment Retirement Income Security Act's (ERISA) prudent man rule in 1979. Through 1978, the rule stated that pension managers had to invest with the care of a "prudent man." Consequently many pension funds avoided investing in venture capital entirely: it was felt that a fund's investment in a start-up could be seen as imprudent. In early 1979, the Department of Labor ruled that portfolio diversification was a consideration in determining the prudence of an individual investment. Thus the ruling implied that an allocation of a small fraction of a portfolio to venture capital funds is not imprudent. That clarification specifically opened the door for pension funds to invest in venture capital.

We conjecture that the supply curve for venture capital before the clarification of ERISA might have looked like S_1. The upward inelastic segment of S_1 results because pension funds, a segment of the U.S. financial market that controls substantial amounts of capital, were unable to invest in venture funds. The supply of venture capital may have been limited at any expected rate of return. If the initial demand for venture capital were given by D_1, then the equilibrium quantity of venture capital would be given by Q_1.

After ERISA, the supply curve moved to S_2. The supply curve moved down and flattened out. The supply curve moved down because pension funds, which are tax exempt, required a lower expected rate of return on venture investments than other taxable investors. The curve would not have an inelastic segment because the resources of pensions could now be invested in venture capital funds. When we look at the data, we expect that the quantity of venture capital supplied will increase after ERISA was clarified to Q_2. This effect should only be significant for contributions by pension funds because ERISA regulations have no bearing on other types of investors.

Other Macroeconomic Factors and Venture Fund-Raising

Venture capital fund-raising is potentially affected by other macroeconomic factors as well. Commitments could be affected by both the expected return on alternative investments and the general health of the economy. If the economy is growing quickly, then there may be more attractive opportunities for entrepreneurs to start new firms and, hence, increases in the demand for venture capitalists. Formally, the demand curve would shift to the right. The greater investment opportunity set might be associated with greater commitments to the venture capital industry. GDP growth, returns in the stock market, and R&D expenditures would all be potential proxies for demand conditions.

The level of interest rates in the economy also could affect the supply of venture capital. An alternative investment to venture capital is bonds. If interest rates rise, then the attractiveness of investing in venture capital funds may decline. This would decrease the willingness of investors to supply venture capital at all prices (i.e., at all expected return levels).

Firm Performance and Fund-Raising

In addition to the marketwide factors discussed above, we look for venture capital firm-specific characteristics that may influence fund-raising. First, a substantial body of research examines the relation between past performance and investment. Allocations by investors across asset classes seem to be driven by, in part, the relative performance of various sectors over the recent past. If there is short-run momentum in returns (as shown by Grinblatt, Titman, and Wermers 1995), this response may be rational.

The flow of money into and out of various types of financial institutions in response to performance has been documented extensively of mutual funds. While the early research on mutual funds (Jensen 1968; Ippolito 1989) indicated that mutual fund managers as a group do not significantly outperform the market, recent work has shown cash flows appear to respond to past performance. Sirri and Tufano (1998) found that performance relative to peers in the same investment category is an important determinant of new capital commitments to mutual funds. They examine 690 equity mutual funds and rank the funds by their performance relative to funds that have the same investment focus. They find that the top performing funds in any particular investment style have substantial new commitments to their funds in the subsequent year. The relation between performance and commitments, however, is not linear. Funds that perform poorly do not appear to be penalized in the following year. Money does not leave poorly performing funds. Sirri and Tufano (1998) find that one exception to these findings is new funds. Money does seem to leave a new fund if it is a poor performer.

Chevalier and Ellison (1997) examined how these patterns affect investment incentive functions. They found that funds that have underperformed their peers in the first part of the year have an incentive to increase the riskiness of their portfolios in order to increase the chances that they will end up near the top of the performance charts. If they bet wrong and fail, they will lose few of their current investors.

If the evidence from mutual funds has implications for venture capital, then we can expect recent performance to be positively related to commitments to new funds. It is clear from Sirri and Tufano's (1998) mutual fund results that reputation of the venture organization influences the flow of new commitments when it raises a new fund. Several measures of reputation are important. These include the venture's organizational age and capital under management. Older and larger venture organizations are likely to have more established reputations. They will therefore receive larger capital commitments than similar younger funds.

Industry-Level Analysis

We examine the implications of capital gains tax rates and performance for commitments to venture capital funds by performing two layers of analysis: aggregate flows and commitments to individual funds. The first level of analysis examines the flow of venture capital commitments into the industry. We examine the commitments to new venture capital funds from 1969 through 1994, first by aggregating all commitments in the United States. We then take up an analysis of the level of venture activity on a state by state basis.

Aggregate Fund-Raising Results

Data on annual commitments to U.S. venture capital funds come from the consulting firm Venture Economics. We have checked the entries in this database against the historical information reported in over 400 venture offering memorandums and partnership agreements, as well as against the fund profiles in the *Venture Capital Journal* and *Private Equity Analyst*. The construction of the sample is described in chapter 22. This database is also used in the analysis of individual organizations' fund-raising data in the next section.

In examining fund-raising behavior, we only look at venture capital limited partnerships. First, these partnerships are the dominant organizational form in the industry, accounting for roughly 80 percent of commitments to the venture capital industry in recent years. Furthermore the actual size of SBICs and corporate venture affiliates is often very difficult the estimate. SBICs have access to matching government funds, often several times greater than the amount contributed by private investors. Corporate programs usually do not have a pool of capital specified in advance and are frequently disbanded before investing too much capital. Limited partnerships—with their well-defined size and life span—offer the cleanest estimate of venture capital inflows.

We total the commitments to venture funds each year. Commitments are defined as the pledges that venture capitalists receive for investment over the lifetime of the fund. They are not the amount of money that is actually invested in a given year. Typically venture funds draw on and invest the committed capital over a two- to three-year time period. For example, in 1995 Sierra Ventures raised their fifth fund with aggregate commitments of $100 million. This $100 million would be invested between 1995 and about 1999, but we would classify the entire $100 million as having been committed in 1995.

We also need some measure of returns in the venture capital industry. Ideally we would have year-by-year performance data for individual funds. These data present several problems. As discussed above, calculation of returns is hampered by policies of many venture organizations that potentially delay the write-up or write-down of assets. As a proxy for performance of the venture organizations, we use a measure of the market value of equity held by venture capitalists in firms that went public in a particular year. This measure will be highly correlated with returns on venture funds. Most money in venture capital is earned on firms that eventually go public. Ignoring the companies that do not go public is reasonable because their impact on returns is usually quite small. A Venture Economics study (1988a) found that a $1 investment in a firm that goes public provides an average cash return of $1.95 in excess of the initial investment with an average holding period of 4.2 years. The next best alternative, an investment in an acquired firm, yields a cash return of only 40 cents over a 3.7-year mean holding period. Using the IPO measure also makes sense because marketing documents for venture capital funds often highlight the successful public companies that are backed by the venture organization. We therefore expect the amount of venture capital raised to be a positive function of the value of firms taken public by venture capitalists in the previous year.

In each year we calculate the market value of the equity stakes in firms going public held by each venture capital organization. This value is the number of shares held by the venture organization multiplied by the IPO offering price. We then sum the market values for each IPO in a given year to obtain an annual performance number for each venture capital organization. We then sum across all venture organizations in a given year to get a measure of venture industry performance.

In figure 3.2 we graph the time series of venture capital commitments and the market value of all firms brought public by venture capitalists in each year from 1969 through 1994. We see that from 1969 through 1979, commitments to venture capital and venture-backed IPOs were quite low. Starting in 1980, both commitments to the venture capital industry and the value of firms brought public by venture capitalists rise. The rise of both reversed in 1983. After 1983, it appears that the shift in the venture-backed

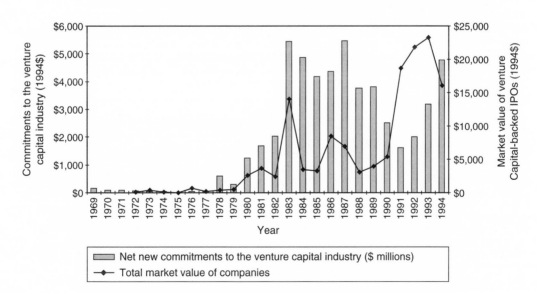

Figure 3.2
Annual commitments to the venture capital industry in millions of constant 1994 dollars. The line graph shows the annual market value of all venture capital-backed firms issuing equity in an initial public offering.

IPO market leads to changes in commitments to new venture funds. For example, increases in the market value of venture-backed IPOs in both 1986 and 1991 to 1992 preceded resurgences in the venture capital market.

The relation between capital gains taxes and venture capital commitments is documented in figure 3.3. The relation is clearly negative. In the 1970s high capital gains tax rates were associated with low levels of venture capital fund-raising. Increases in the capital gains tax rates in 1988 were followed by reductions in venture capital commitments, while the reduction of capital gains for long-held investments in 1993 was followed by a rise in venture fund-raising. This negative relation between venture capital funding levels and capital gains tax rates is clearly only suggestive, because the influence of multiple factors needs to be examined.

Detailed information on the nature of commitments is shown in chapter 1, table 1.1. Several patterns are prominent. First, the volatility of commitments is readily apparent. The level of fund-raising (expressed in 1994 dollars) can vary dramatically from one year to the next. The volatility in venture fund-raising is mirrored by a similar volatility in the IPO market, both for venture-backed companies and for the entire IPO market. We see the dramatic shift from individuals to pension funds over the past fifteen years as the primary capital source for new venture funds.[3]

In order to assess the impact of each of these variables controlling for the others, we present multivariate regressions in table 3.1. Our approach here and in the individual firm regressions is to estimate reduced-form specifications and identify which factors potentially work through demand shifts and which factors work through supply shifts. The time series of data runs from 1972 through 1994. The dependent variable is the natural logarithm of real commitments to the venture capital industry (in millions of 1994 dollars). We present regressions for commitments to the entire venture capital industry, as well as four subgroups: taxable investors, tax-exempt investors, individuals, and pension funds. The independent variables include the natural logarithm of the market value of firms brought public by venture organizations in the previous year (in millions of 1994 dollars), the real return on Treasury bills in the previous year, the real CRSP value-weighted stock market return in the prior year, the previous year's real GDP growth, a dummy variable that equals one for years after 1978 when ERISA's prudent man rule was clarified, and the top marginal capital gains tax rate.

---

3. The measures of the sources of funds are taken from various issues of Venture Economics' *Venture Capital Journal*.

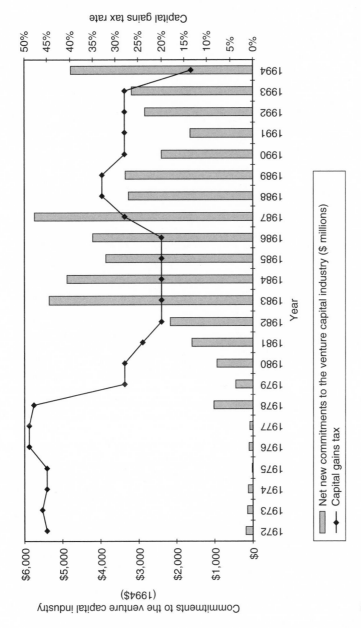

Figure 3.3
Annual commitments to the venture capital industry in millions of constant 1994 dollars. The line graph shows the highest marginal capital gains tax rate effective in that year.

Table 3.1
Regressions for industrywide fund-raising

Independent variable[c]	Dependent variable: Natural logarithm of commitments to the venture capital industry				
	Total	Taxable[b] (1994$ mil)[a]	Tax-exempt	Individuals	Pensions
Natural logarithm of value of all venture capital-backed IPOs in previous year (millions of 1994$)	-0.0124 [-0.06]	-0.0300 [-0.11]	-0.2453 [-1.71]	0.0046 [0.17]	-0.3037 [-1.92]
Previous year's real GDP growth	13.28 [2.01]	16.08 [2.34]	14.48 [3.92]	14.92 [2.10]	12.38 [3.05]
Previous year's T-bill return	0.0022 [0.04]	0.0436 [0.64]	-0.1212 [-3.28]	0.0417 [0.59]	-0.1556 [-3.83]
Previous year's equity market return	0.3836 [0.48]	-0.2240 [-0.22]	0.1648 [0.30]	-0.3920 [-0.36]	-0.1092 [-0.18]
Was ERISA's prudent man rule clarified?	2.172 [3.05]	0.8598 [1.25]	2.183 [5.92]	0.6299 [0.89]	2.454 [6.05]
Capital gains tax rate	-3.835 [-1.66]	-2.068 [-0.96]	-1.803 [-1.65]	-2.498 [-1.52]	-2.726 [-2.14]
Constant	6.551 [3.01]	5.3195 [1.95]	8.579 [5.85]	5.307 [1.88]	8.918 [5.53]
Adjusted R^2	0.824	0.303	0.874	0.250	0.884
p-Value of F-statistic	0.000	0.000	0.000	0.000	0.000
Number of observations	22	17	17	17	17

Note: All regressions are ordinary least squares estimates. [t-statistics are in brackets.]
a. The dependent variable is the natural logarithm of the amount of venture capital commitments (in millions of 1994 dollars) for either all independent private venture capital funds or only those commitments by various groups of investors from 1972 through 1994.
b. Taxable commitments are defined as all commitments from individuals, corporations, or insurance companies. Nontaxable contributions are defined as those from pension funds and endowments.
c. Independent variables include the natural logarithm of the market value of all venture capital-backed firms issuing equity in the previous year (in millions of 1994 dollars), the previous year's real growth in gross domestic product (GDP), the return on T-bills in the previous year, the previous year's CRSP value weighted stock market return, a dummy variable that equals one if the Department of Labor clarified the prudent man rule and allowed pension investment in venture capital (equals one for all years after 1978), and the highest marginal capital gains tax rate effective in that year.

Changes in ERISA's prudent man rule are associated with greater commitments to the venture capital industry, but the effect is not significant for commitments by taxable investors and individuals. As expected, the strongest effect of ERISA's clarification is on contributions by pension funds. An *F*-test of the null hypothesis that the coefficient for pension funds is significantly different from the coefficient for individuals and taxable investors shows that ERISA's effect on contributions by pension funds is different at the 5 percent level. This is consistent with a supply side effect: the easing of pension fund restrictions increased the number of investors wishing to invest in venture capital funds.

Increases in capital gains tax rates have a consistently negative effect on contributions to the venture industry, although the effect is only significant for contributions to the entire industry and contributions by pension funds.[4] While we do find an effect of capital gains taxes on venture capital commitments, it does not appear to be working through the supply side. If changes in the capital gains tax rates have a first-order effect on investors' willingness to invest in venture capital, then the effect will be strongest for individuals and taxable parties. The opposite is true. As Poterba (1989) suggested, the effect of changes in the capital gains tax rate is likely to come through changes in the demand for venture capital. More and better quality managers are incented to become entrepreneurs when the capital gains tax rate declines, and thus the demand for venture capital increases. This increase in demand leads to a greater quantity of venture capital being supplied in equilibrium.

Once other factors are included, the value of firms taken public by venture organizations in the previous year does not appear to have a dramatic effect on contributions. While we cannot rule out a role for IPOs creating liquidity in the venture sector and potentially affecting contributions, we cannot find an effect in the multivariate regressions. This finding is contrary to the arguments of Black and Gilson (1998), who emphasized the importance of a vibrant public market in the development of a venture capital industry. It is consistent, however, with the experience of Israel and Singapore, whose venture industries experienced dramatic growth without having strong domestic public equity markets.

Of the macroeconomic variables, only real GDP growth is important. Increases in the real rate of growth lead to greater commitments to venture

---

4. The coefficients on capital gains tax rates are not significantly different from one another across different investor classes. The purpose of the comparison is simply to show whether capital gains tax rates affect taxable investors only (as the supply effect would predict) or whether they affect all investors equally (as the demand effect would predict).

funds. Once again, this suggests that increasing demand for venture capital is an important determinant of the quantity. Robust economic growth creates new opportunities for entrepreneurs and increases demand for such capital.

One concern may be that because we are using time-series observations on venture fund-raising and the independent variables, the results may be affected by serial correlation in the error terms. The Durbin-Watson statistics for each of the regressions were between 1.88 and 2.00, indicating that such serial correlation does not affect the results. As a diagnostic we also ran Cochrane-Orcutt regressions using a lag term, which did not materially change the results.

State-Level Venture Activity

One difficulty with the analysis in the previous section was the relatively small number of observations. In order to gain additional power for our tests of marketwide venture activity, we examined venture capital activity in each of the fifty states and the District of Columbia from 1976 through 1994. We then examined how state-level demand and supply factors affect venture investing in those states.

Therefore we employ a slightly different approach here than in the preceding sections: rather than examining the formation of venture funds in each state, we measure the actual venture capital investments. This way we account for the difficulty of assigning venture organizations to particular states. Many venture organizations have multiple offices, and correspondingly differing shares of the investments. Venture organizations' headquarters may reflect the need to be proximate to their sources of capital and not their portfolio firms. For instance, many venture organizations are based in New York City, although this has historically been the site of few start-up firms. This pattern is particularly true for groups specializing in the later-stage investments, which typically occur after other groups (who may be geographically more proximate to the portfolio firm) have already joined the board (Lerner 1995).

Again, we use the data of Venture Economics to determine venture capital activity by state. In this case we undertake a special tabulation of the number of companies financed and dollar volume of financing in each state and year between 1976 and 1994. We include all investments by private equity groups into young entrepreneurial firms but exclude investments into leveraged buyouts and restructurings by groups that primarily make venture capital investments.

We also collect a variety of additional data on a state by state basis. Gross state product is compiled on an annual basis by the Department of Commerce's Bureau of Economic Analysis (1997) (also used was Friedenberg and Beemiller 1997). For each state we compiled the total amount of research performed in industry and in academe, regardless of funding source. The state industrial R&D data is compiled by the National Science Foundation (NSF) as part of the Survey of Research and Development in Industry (1980, 1998b). The data pose two problems. First, since 1978 this information has only been collected on a biannual basis. Thus it is necessary to impute the missing years. Second, certain states are persistently missing. In these instances the unassigned R&D in each region is assigned to each suppressed state on the basis of its gross state product (GSP).[5] The allocation of academic R&D expenditures by state is determined using the NSF's annual Survey of Research and Development Expenditures at Universities and Colleges (1998a). We obtain the marginal state tax rate on capital gains through the use of the TAXSIM tax simulation program. We compute the impact of $1,000 of capital gains on a wealthy individual in each state and year, controlling for the possible deductibility of state taxes in federal taxes. (The program is described in Feenberg and Coutts 1993; the simulation and the resulting data are reproduced at *http://www.nber.org/~taxsim/state-rates.*)

Table 3.2 lists venture capital activity in each state by tabulating total number of companies that received venture capital and total amount of venture capital invested from 1976 through 1994. The tremendous concentration of investment in four states is clearly evident. California has by far the most venture investing activity with nearly $20 billion invested (in 1994 dollars). Massachusetts, New York, and Texas are the next most active states and account for the bulk of the remaining capital. It is also clear that many states have almost no venture capital activity. We seek to explore these patterns in a regression framework.

In table 3.3 we present state fixed-effects regressions for the level of venture capital investment per capita (in millions of 1994 dollars) and the number of companies receiving venture capital per capita. We employ an observation for each year in each state, namely a balanced panel. Independent variables include marketwide measures used in the regressions in table

---

5. For instance, in 1977, as in earlier and later years, data for New Hampshire and Vermont are suppressed. Of the $2.4 billion of R&D spending in New England in that year, $2.3 billion is accounted for by Connecticut, Maine, Massachusetts, and Rhode Island. We divide the remaining 65 to 35 percent amount between New Hampshire and Vermont, proportional to their gross state products in that year.

Table 3.2
Summaries of venture capital activity by state

State	Companies financed	Total venture capital invested	State	Companies financed	Total venture capital invested
Alaska	3	$52.11	Montana	17	$49.19
Alabama	75	199.12	Nebraska	15	8.05
Arizona	189	693.91	Nevada	22	25.77
Arkansas	12	14.69	New Hampshire	136	344.32
California	6,154	19,967.67	New Jersey	643	2,019.21
Colorado	609	1,557.01	New Mexico	38	56.47
Connecticut	486	2,094.18	New York	811	2,369.43
District of Columbia	70	210.95	North Carolina	239	612.23
Delaware	26	42.62	North Dakota	4	28.23
Florida	338	779.66	Ohio	342	1,351.21
Georgia	395	872.04	Oklahoma	60	134.78
Hawaii	4	1.23	Oregon	297	789.34
Idaho	12	58.46	Pennsylvania	575	2,292.38
Illinois	514	1,879.06	Rhode Island	85	226.61
Indiana	137	260.33	South Carolina	37	165.86
Iowa	60	143.39	South Dakota	15	7.57
Kansas	46	90.33	Tennessee	235	844.14
Kentucky	59	173.54	Texas	1,254	3,861.13
Louisiana	45	137.59	Utah	117	246.69
Maine	50	126.77	Vermont	313	969.05
Maryland	321	989.15	Virginia	17	61.55
Massachusetts	2,276	5,886.44	Washington	327	835.79
Michigan	267	808.56	West Virginia	16	33.68
Minnesota	483	837.11	Wisconsin	144	269.40
Mississippi	26	32.01	Wyoming	5	4.22
Missouri	107	611.60			

Note: The sample is all venture capital investments by independent venture organizations by state from 1976 through 1994 and denoted in millions of 1994 dollars.

3.1 (logarithm of IPO activity, the previous year's real Treasury bill return, and the previous year's equity market return). In addition we include several variables that might proxy for state-level demand conditions. These include the previous year's growth in gross state product per capita as well as measures of last year's academic and industrial expenditure on R&D (in millions of 1994 dollars) per capita. The R&D expenditure potentially captures demand effects of high-technology firms. If R&D is higher in a state, it may mean that the number of potential entrepreneurs with promising ideas may be greater.

To capture the effect of changes in ERISA's prudent man rule, we include a dummy variable that is equal to one after 1978. To measure the capital gains tax rate burden, we first control for state and federal capital gains taxes separately by including the maximum marginal state and federal capital gains tax rate separately. We then add the federal and state rates to create a variable that captures the total capital gains tax burden in that state.[6]

Table 3.3 shows that both industrial and academic R&D spending are significantly related to state-level venture capital activity. Increases in state R&D levels increase both the amount of venture capital invested as well as the number of firms receiving venture capital. This result suggests that both academic and industrial R&D spending are potentially important for the creation of entrepreneurial firms that demand venture capital.

Similarly growth in GSP per capita is positively related to venture capital activity. This result, consistent with the aggregate results, may indicate the importance of the demand effects; that is, it is important to have a strong growing economy to create new firms that need venture capital financing.

The dummy variable measuring the shift in ERISA policy continues to have a positive effect in the state-level regressions. After the clarification of ERISA, the amount of venture capital invested per capita as well as the number of firms receiving venture capital per capita increases. Finally, capital gains tax rates continue to matter. In the regressions including both state and federal rates, it is only the federal rate that is significantly related to venture capital activity. The state capital gains tax rate is, however, always negatively related to venture capital activity and is of the same order of magnitude as the effect of federal rates. The combined federal and state capital gains rate is also significantly related to venture capital activity. The

---

6. The state tax measure only includes the marginal impact: any savings in federal taxes due to the deductibility of state taxes are factored in. All regressions include state fixed-effects.

Table 3.3
Regressions for state-level venture capital activity

Independent variable[b]	Dependent variable[a]			
	Logarithm of real venture capital investment in the state per million residents		Number of companies receiving venture financing in state per 1,000 residents	
Logarithm of value of all venture capital-backed IPOs in previous year (millions of 1994$)	−0.2008 [−3.35]	−0.1973 [−3.37]	−0.2414 [−1.46]	−0.2372 [1.46]
Logarithm of previous year's real GSP per capita	0.5343 [1.73]	0.5438 [1.77]	4.5621 [4.59]	4.5854 [4.68]
Previous year's real GSP growth in the state	0.0480 [3.11]	0.0478 [3.11]	0.1609 [3.45]	0.1605 [3.45]
Logarithm of previous year's real expenditure on academic R&D per capita in the state	0.7939 [4.88]	0.8032 [5.15]	0.1898 [0.36]	0.2044 [0.39]
Logarithm of previous year's real expenditure on industrial R&D per capita in the state	0.1359 [3.23]	0.1362 [3.24]	0.3208 [2.67]	0.3211 [2.67]
Previous year's T-bill return	−0.1332 [−5.44] ·	−0.1337 [−5.48]	−0.1294 [−1.83]	−0.1295 [−1.83]
Previous year's equity market return	0.0386 [0.15]	0.0235 [0.09]	1.4166 [1.98]	1.3983 [1.99]
Was ERISA's prudent man rule clarified?	1.1713 [6.45]	1.1830 [6.70]	1.6815 [3.32]	1.6948 [3.41]
State capital gains tax rate	−2.5838 [−0.91]		−5.0675 [−0.61]	
Federal capital gains tax rate	−3.4408 [−5.14]		−6.2439 [−3.37]	
Sum of the state and federal capital gains tax rate		−3.3684 [−5.45]		−6.1480 [−3.61]
Overall R^2	0.425	0.425	0.188	0.425
p-Value of χ^2-statistic	0.000	0.000	0.000	0.000
Number of observations	765	765	765	765

Note: All regressions include state fixed effects (not reported). [t-statistics are in brackets.]
a. The dependent variable is the venture capital activity at the state level (either amount invested in millions of 1994 dollars per million residents or the number of companies receiving financing per 1,000 residents) for each year from 1976 through 1994.
b. Independent variables include the natural logarithm of the market value of all venture capital-backed firms issuing equity in the previous year (in millions of 1994 dollars), the previous year's real growth in gross state product (GSP) for that state per capita, the natural logarithm of the previous year's expenditure on academic and industrial R&D per capita in the state (in 1994 dollars), the return on T-bills in the previous year, the previous year's CRSP value weighted stock market return, a dummy variable that equals one if the Department of Labor clarified the prudent man rule and allowed pension investment in venture capital (equals one for all years after 1978), and the highest marginal capital gains tax rate effective in that year at the state and national level.

result confirms the earlier results. Capital gains tax rates do appear to be negatively related to venture capital activity.

Firm-Level Analysis

Sample and Summary Statistics

This section examines fund-raising patterns by individual venture organizations. We perform three levels of analysis. First, we present summary statistics for the database, both in its entirety and segmented by year. We then analyze factors affecting the fund-raising ability of individual venture organizations. Finally, we examine the decision of venture organizations to raise funds with a focus on early- and seed-stage firms. The importance of early- and seed-stage funds in creating new firms is widely recognized. Many of the efforts to stimulate venture activity focus on stimulating seed capital funds. Understanding the unique factors affecting the decision to target these firms is important for potential policy decisions. We examine fund information collected by Venture Economics from 1961 through 1992.

Table 3.4 presents information on the completeness of the venture fund-raising database. In all, we have information on 1,294 venture capital funds. Of those, we have information on the fund size and closing date for 846 (20 of these are missing month of closing). The average venture organization in the sample raised 2.23 funds while the median raised only 1. The maximum number of venture funds raised by an organization is 25. The average venture organization raised $126 million in 1994 dollars while the largest organization had raised over $2 billion.

The time-series distribution of our sample is presented in table 3.5. We see growth in both the number of funds raised and dollar volume of commitments in the early and mid-1980s. The sample also appears to exhibit a slight growth in the size of funds raised (in constant 1994 dollars). If we look at the sum of all the funds in our sample, we have data on $45.0 billion in venture funding which represents nearly all the capital raised by organized venture capital partnerships during the sample period.[7] The lack of size data for 448 of the funds does not impart bias to our results. Our data cover almost all the capital raised over the sample period, and hence the results are clearly applicable to the most important firms.

---

7. The federal government does not collect numbers on venture capital inflows. The Venture Economics database, however, corresponds closely to those of another consulting firm, Asset Alternatives, as well as estimates by practitioners.

Table 3.4
Summary statistics for funds in database

Items in record	Observations			
Panel A: Completeness of records in corrected database				
Month and year of closing and fund size	826			
Year of closing and fund size	20			
Month and year of closing: No size	428			
Year of closing: No month or size	20			
Neither closing date nor fund size	112			

Items in record	Mean	Median	Minimum	Maximum
Panel B: Summary information for each venture organization				
Number of funds raised	2.23	1	1	25
Total funds raised (1994$ mil)[a]	$126.46	$57.11	$0.46	$2,267.02
Closing date of first fund in sample[b]	3/82	7/83	1/63	12/92
Closing date of last fund in sample[b]	5/85	12/86	1/63	12/92

Note: The sample is all funds raised by independent venture organizations included in the Venture Economics Venture Intelligence database. The first panel indicates the completeness of the records of independent venture partnerships in the corrected database. The second panel presents summary information for each venture organization.
a. This tabulation does not include venture organizations where the size of all funds cannot be determined. It does include, however, those venture organizations where the size of some funds cannot be determined.
b. This tabulation does not include venture organizations where the closing date of all funds cannot be determined. It does include, however, those venture organizations where the closing date of some funds cannot be determined. Funds whose month of closing cannot be determined are regarded as closing in July.

Fund-Raising Regression Results

We analyze firm-level fund-raising by using one yearly observation for each venture organization starting with the year that they raise their first venture capital fund. The dependent variable is either a dummy variable indicating whether the venture organization raised a fund or the amount of money (in millions of 1994 dollars) raised in that year. Independent variables include the age of the venture organization, the amount of money it raised during the previous ten years[8] (in millions of 1994 dollars), the value of equity held by this venture organization in firms brought public in that year and the previous year, the value of all venture-backed firms brought public in the previous year, real GDP growth in the previous year, the previous year's

---

8. We look at money raised over the previous ten years because that is the specified life-span of a typical venture capital limited partnership agreement. The ten-year sum provides the best available estimate of capital under management.

Table 3.5
Venture capital funds by year

Year	Funds closed	Funds with size data	Size of funds (1994$ mil)	
			Average	Sum
1961	2	0		
1962	2	0		
1963	1	0		
1964	0	0		
1965	1	1	$41.53	$41.53
1966	1	0		
1967	2	0		
1968	12	0		
1969	16	6	72.95	437.72
1970	14	5	50.25	251.25
1971	13	5	61.32	306.62
1972	11	5	24.22	121.10
1973	13	3	36.47	109.39
1974	11	6	14.41	86.46
1975	11	0		
1976	14	3	38.18	113.51
1977	9	3	28.39	85.18
1978	23	14	30.51	427.09
1979	27	11	43.95	483.46
1980	57	26	47.92	1,245.93
1981	81	47	36.43	1,712.10
1982	98	51	40.96	2,088.79
1983	147	99	55.08	5,452.48
1984	150	106	45.65	4,839.34
1985	99	74	56.63	4,190.56
1986	86	61	72.58	4,427.82
1987	112	95	56.61	5,378.32
1988	78	66	56.33	3,717.95
1989	88	70	49.40	3,457.52
1990	50	36	69.64	2,507.02
1991	34	23	66.47	1,528.73
1992	31	30	67.03	2,010.82
Total	1294	846	$53.22	$45,021.73

Note: The sample is all funds raised by independent venture organizations included in the Venture Economics Venture Intelligence database. The table indicates the number of independent venture partnerships that closed each year, as well as the number which have information on the size of the fund. For those with size data, the distribution of total funds committed each year (in millions of 1994 dollars) is also tabulated.

Table 3.6
Regressions for individual venture organization fund-raising

Independent variable[b]	Dependent variable[a]			
	Model 1		Model 2	
	Was fund raised?	If so, logarithm of fund size (1994$)	Was fund raised?	If so, logarithm of fund size (1994$)
Years since raising last fund	−0.4560 [−15.84]	−21.17 [−7.55]	−0.4692 [−21.58]	−14.15 [−7.02]
Square of number of years since raising last fund	0.0272 [11.94]	0.8710 [3.94]	0.0291 [16.27]	0.5293 [3.28]
Age of venture organization (years)	0.0136 [2.79]	0.9820 [2.32]		
Total venture capital raised during previous ten years for venture organization (1994$ mil)			0.0004 [2.14]	0.1670 [9.56]
Value of equity held in firms brought public this year (1994$ mil)	0.0037 [3.30]	0.3326 [3.50]	0.0029 [2.46]	0.1124 [1.15]
Value of equity held in firms brought public in the previous year (1994$ mil)	0.0091 [4.39]	1.0310 [6.11]	0.0058 [2.58]	0.3742 [2.07]
Total value of firms brought public in previous year by all venture capitalists (1994$ mil)	$1.3 \times E\text{-}06$ [0.23]	−0.0006 [−1.60]	$1.7 \times E\text{-}06$ [0.34]	−0.0006 [−1.72]
Real GDP growth in previous year	−0.0048 [−0.72]		0.0006 [0.08]	
T-bill return in previous year	0.0724 [3.84]		0.0759 [5.45]	
Return on CRSP value-weighted index in previous year	0.0027 [2.37]		0.0036 [2.86]	
Capital gains tax rate	0.0018 [0.31]	−1.1650 [−3.50]	0.0021 [0.41]	−1.8156 [−5.50]
Was ERISA's prudent man rule clarified?	−0.0382 [−0.37]	8.3666 [0.96]	−0.0472 [−0.44]	−5.4530 [−0.66]
Constant	−0.6230 [−2.15]	−0.5752 [−0.04]	−0.6357 [−2.27]	28.99 [1.98]
Log-likelihood	−8159.3		−8197.4	
p-value of χ^2-statistic	0.000		0.000	
Number of observations	5573		5573	

Table 3.6

(continued)

Note: The sample is all funds raised by independent venture organizations included in the Venture Economics Venture Intelligence database. All regressions are Heckman two-stage models. [*t*-statistics are in brackets.]

a. The dependent variables are a dummy variable that equals one if the venture organization raised a fund in that year and the size of funds raised in millions of 1994 dollars.

b. Independent variables include number of years since the venture organization raised a previous venture fund, the age of the venture organization, the total amount of venture capital raised by the organization in the past ten years, the dollar value of equity held by the venture organization in firms taken public this year and in the previous year, the market value of all venture capital-backed firms issuing equity in the previous year (all in millions of 1994 dollars), the previous year's real growth in gross domestic product (GDP), the return on T-bills in the previous year, the previous year's CRSP value weighted stock market return, a dummy variable that equals one if the Department of Labor clarified the prudent man rule and allowed pension investment in venture capital (equals one for all years after 1978), and the highest marginal capital gains tax rate effective in that year.

Treasury bill return, the previous year's stock market return as measured by the annual return on the CRSP value weighted market index, a dummy variable that equals one after 1978 (indicating years after the clarification of the ERISA prudent man rule), and the top marginal capital gains tax rate on individuals.

We estimate a Heckman two-stage model. The Heckman model estimates two equations. The first is the probability that a fund was raised in a given year. The second equation then estimates the amount raised given that a fund was raised in a particular year. This two-stage model is appropriate if the correct decision is that venture capitalists first decide whether or not to raise a new fund. Once they decide to raise a new fund, the venture capitalists then decide the size of fund they wish to raise. The two equations give us insights about factors that affect the probability of raising a new fund and ones that primarily affect the optimal fund size.

Table 3.6 gives the results from the Heckman models. The first regression in each model gives the probability of raising a new fund, while the second regression gives the size of a fund conditional on it being raised. We find that neither the capital gains tax rate nor ERISA's clarification have a significant effect on the probability of a venture organization raising a new fund. The ERISA dummy has no effect on the size of the fund either. The capital gains tax rate does, however, have a significant effect on the size of the fund raised. Lower capital gains tax rates are associated with larger funds. This would be expected if venture organizations raised new funds on a normal cycle that was typically unaffected by external factors. Changes in the capital gains tax rate may affect the quantity of good start-ups to finance as managers are induced to start firms. The greater quantity of good projects would lead venture capitalists to raise larger funds.

We also find that firm performance has a dramatic effect on fund-raising. Both the value of equity held in firms taken public by the venture capital firm in the current year and in the previous year have a positive effect on the probability of raising a new fund and the size of the fund. The effect of the previous year's IPO volume is nearly four times as large as the current year's. This might be due to the long process of raising a new fund (which may take many months). Venture organizations go on "road shows" and gauge investor interest, sign up prospective investors, and generate the necessary documents prior to closing. The more relevant performance is probably the previous year's returns, which are foremost in investors' minds during fund-raising.

Reputation also appears to have a positive effect on the size of the fund raised. Older and larger venture organizations have higher probabilities of raising funds and raise larger funds. The reputation variable potentially captures beliefs about future returns not captured in recent performance variables. The effect of venture organization size is particularly strong on the size of the fund raised. This could indicate that venture organization size is a good proxy for reputation. Venture organization size might also measure the need to raise larger funds. Large venture organizations may have more employees and general partners. In order to keep all of them working at capacity, the minimum fund size needed is substantially higher.

We find that the Treasury bill return in the previous year is positively related to the probability of raising a new fund. This effect may stem from the rapid increase in funds being raised in the early 1980s at a time when real interest rates were high. Both the probability of raising a fund and the size of a new fund raised first decline and then increase with time from the previous fund.[9]

We present the fixed-effects regression models in table 3.7. The fixed-effects models include dummy variables for each venture organization that are intended to pick up unmeasured firm-specific factors. If we find a result even after controlling for firm fixed effects, we can be confident that the effects are robust. We could not estimate the fixed-effects Heckman model. Therefore we run two separate regressions. The first is a fixed-effects logit that estimates the probability of raising a fund in a given year. The second regression is a fixed-effects least squares regression that estimates the size of funds raised conditional on a fund being raised. The approximation to the two-stage maximum likelihood Heckman model is consistent in the estima-

---

9. The regression results are robust to various segmentations of the data, for example, firms located on the West Coast and East Coast.

tions without the fixed effects, so we are confident that the results in table 3.7 are reasonable (Maddala 1987).

In both specifications the capital gains tax rate continues to be a significant factor in venture fund-raising. A decrease in the capital gains tax rate increases the size of funds raised in all the specifications. In the first model the ERISA dummy variable has an important impact. Controlling for firm factors, the ERISA clarification leads to a greater probability of raising a new fund.

Venture organization performance (as measured by the value of equity stakes in initial public offerings) continues to have a positive effect on fund-raising. In the two-stage model with firm fixed effects, the probability of raising a fund increases with greater performance, but the size of the fund does not appear to be affected. We find, however, that the reputation variables have mixed signs in the fixed-effects regression, which are different from the regressions without the firm fixed effects. In the two-stage model the probability of raising a fund is lower for older and larger organizations, but the fund size is larger. As a firm ages, the probability of raising a new fund declines, although the size of funds being raised increases. This lower probability of raising a fund may reflect the retirement of partners within older venture organizations. Unconditionally, older firms are more likely to raise a fund because of their better track record. Controlling for firm effects, however, as a firm ages, it becomes less likely to raise a fund.

Stage Focus Results

We also undertake an analysis of the ability of venture capital organizations to raise a fund that focuses on early-stage investments. The early-stage venture market is often seen as being critical to the success of later-stage investments. Early-stage funds provide new firms with critical financing in their infancy (e.g., see OECD 1996). Many of the policy initiatives undertaken across the country and around the world are aimed at increasing the availability of early-stage capital. Similarly firms in their very early stages are the most prone to capital rationing and liquidity constraints because the uncertainty and asymmetric information are the greatest. If we can understand the incentives to raise a focused fund, we might be able to understand industry dynamics better and may make better recommendations about promoting new entrepreneurial firms.

We divide firms into two categories in this analysis. We indicate whether the funds analyzed above have a stated investment focus on early-stage firms only. (Venture Economics characterizes each fund's focus in their

Table 3.7
Fixed-effects regressions for individual venture organization fund-raising

| | Dependent variable[a] | | | |
| | Model 1 | | Model 2 | |
Independent variable[b]	Logit Was fund raised?	OLS If so, logarithm of fund size (1994$)	Logit Was fund raised?	OLS If so, logarithm of fund size (1994$)
Years since raising last fund	−1.1056 [−18.80]	−2.903 [−1.02]	−1.3034 [−22.83]	2.343 [0.89]
Square of the number of years since raising last fund	0.1069 [16.91]	0.1526 [0.54]	0.1141 [18.74]	−0.2100 [−0.79]
Age of the venture organization (years)	−0.2772 [−11.23]	4.8364 [3.18]		
Total venture capital raised during previous ten years for venture organization (1994$ mil)			−0.0049 [−7.10]	0.1660 [6.41]
Value of equity held in firms brought public this year (1994$ mil)	0.0049 [2.03]	0.0128 [0.10]	0.0056 [2.22]	−0.0764 [−0.59]
Value of equity held in firms brought public in the previous year (1994$ mil)	0.0138 [3.06]	0.2905 [1.38]	0.213 [4.09]	−0.1417 [−0.65]
Total value of firms brought public in previous year (1994$ mil)	$4.1 \times$ E-06 [0.38]	−0.0001 [−0.21]	$-5.0 \times$ E-06 [−0.48]	0.0004 [0.55]
Real GDP growth in the previous year	−0.0315 [−1.42]	−1.875 [−1.42]	−0.0037 [−0.16]	−2.012 [−1.57]
T-bill return in previous year	−0.0160 [−0.43]	−1.727 [−0.77]	0.1154 [3.33]	−1.782 [−0.93]
Return on CRSP value weighted index in previous year	0.0009 [0.28]	−0.1847 [−0.80]	0.0061 [1.94]	−0.1959 [−0.89]
Capital gains tax rate	0.0007 [0.06]	−1.153 [−1.92]	0.0039 [0.36]	−1.506 [−2.45]
Was ERISA's prudent man rule clarified?	2.047 [5.75]	0.7768 [0.04]	0.0967 [0.35]	10.22 [0.67]
Constant	1.434 [1.62]	127.15 [2.77]	1.155 [1.26]	127.60 [2.89]
Log-likelihood/adjusted R^2	−1903.6	0.212	−1939.5	0.252
p-value of χ^2/F-statistic	0.000	0.000	0.000	0.000
Number of observations	5323	1117	5323	1117

Table 3.7
(continued)
Note: The sample is all funds raised by independent venture organizations included in the Venture Economics Venture Intelligence database. Coefficients on the firm dummies are omitted. The regressions for whether the venture organization raised a fund or not are logit. The conditional regressions for size of the venture fund are ordinary least squares estimates. [t-statistics are in brackets.]
a. The dependent variables are a dummy variable that equals one if the venture organization raised a fund in that year and the logarithm of the size of funds raised in millions of 1994 dollars.
b. Independent variables include number of years since the venture organization raised a previous venture fund, the age of the venture organization, the total amount of venture capital raised by the organization in the past ten years, the dollar value of equity held by the venture organization in firms taken public this year and in the previous year, the market value of all venture capital-backed firms issuing equity in the previous year (all in millions of 1994 dollars), the previous year's real growth in gross domestic product (GDP), the return on T-bills in the previous year, the previous year's CRSP value weighted stock market return, a dummy variable that equals one if the Department of Labor clarified the prudent man rule and allowed pension investment in venture capital (equals one for all years after 1978), and the highest marginal capital gains tax rate effective in that year. Dummy variables for each firm are also included to control for firm fixed effects.

database.) Table 3.8 presents summary statistics for venture funds that have a stated early-stage focus and those that do not. We find that funds focusing on early-stage investments are significantly smaller, with a mean [median] size of $42 [$25] million, than are funds that do not focus on early-stage investments (mean of $57 [$36] million). This makes sense because early-stage investments are typically smaller than later-stage investments. The findings in chapter 8 show that the average early-stage investment is only half as large as the mean later-stage investment. Because the amount of time spent during the investment and monitoring process (due diligence, negotiations, etc.) and the need for oversight after the investment is similar, early-stage funds are usually smaller.

We also find that early-stage funds tend to be raised by venture organizations that are slightly older and larger. One possibility is that older, more experienced venture organizations have the necessary knowledge to raise a focused fund. The early-stage funds are, on average, more recent and are more likely to be raised on the West Coast. Clearly, the mix of investments on the West Coast, primarily California, is heavily concentrated on early-stage, technology-based companies. East Coast firms are more balanced and tend to invest in greater fractions of later-stage companies.

In table 3.9 we present multivariate regressions analyzing the determinants of fund focus. We use each new venture capital fund as an observation and examine whether it had an early-stage focus. As the summary statistics hint, smaller funds are more likely to have an early-stage focus. Similarly we find that firms on the West Coast are more likely to raise an early-stage fund. We find that a venture organization was likely to raise a fund with an

Table 3.8
Summaries of venture capital commitments by stage focus

	Funds with stated focus on early-stage firms	Funds without stated focus on early-stage firms	Significance of the difference between early and not early
Size of fund (1994$ mil)	$41.98 [$24.66]	$56.95 [$35.88]	0.000 [0.000]
Amount of venture capital raised by organization in previous funds	$92.20 [$39.54]	$87.58 [$26.64]	0.714 [0.000]
Organization age (years)	4.38 [3.08]	3.77 [0.58]	0.140 [0.002]
Date of fund closing	August 1985 [June 1985]	August 1983 [May 1984]	0.000 [0.000]
Fraction of funds raised on West Coast	38.3%	30.3%	0.017
Fraction of funds raised on East Coast	32.2%	43.6%	0.001

Note: The sample is all funds raised by independent venture organizations included in the Venture Economics Venture Intelligence database.

early-stage focus after the Department of Labor's clarification of ERISA's prudent man rule. This greater probability following the ERISA change appears to be due to the clarification stating that investments will be judged prudent not by their individual risk but by their contribution to portfolio risk. Prior to this amendment early-stage funds might have been viewed as too speculative and might have been more difficult to raise than a later-stage or general purpose venture capital fund. After the amendment, venture organizations could raise focused funds without concern over the perceived riskiness for pension funds.

Alternative Explanations

Supply of Substitute Financing

One alternative explanation for our results might be that the supply and demand for venture capital may be affected by the supply of substitute financing. We have attempted to control for the cost of credit by including the real interest rate. In periods of high real interest rates, venture capital may be more attractive from the entrepreneur's perspective. Similarly, if the availability of bank financing were a major factor in the determination of venture capital commitments, then we should have seen an increase in ven-

Table 3.9
Regressions for stage focus of the fund

Independent variable	Dependent variable (funds with focus on early-stage investments)			
Size of fund (1994$ mil)	−0.0057	−0.0035		
	[−2.82]	[−1.40]		
Age of the venture organization	0.0118		0.0018	
	[0.75]		[0.13]	
Total venture capital raised during previous ten years for this venture organization		0.0247		−3.24 × E-07
		[1.62]		[−0.71]
Was the fund located on the West Coast?	0.4026	0.4619	0.2280	0.2786
	[2.35]	[2.70]	[1.44]	[1.79]
Was ERISA's prudent man rule clarified?	0.7659	0.9025	1.829	1.871
	[1.78]	[2.11]	[4.39]	[4.52]
Capital gains tax rate	0.0208	0.0247	0.0395	0.0404
	[1.36]	[1.62]	[2.70]	[2.80]
Constant	−2.244	−2.502	−4.333	−4.401
	[−3.14]	[−3.49]	[−6.25]	[−6.39]
Log-likelihood	−455.3	−461.9	−557.4	−571.8
p-value of χ^2-statistic	0.002	0.001	0.000	0.000
Number of observations	818	843	1236	1283

Note: The sample is all funds raised by independent venture organizations included in the Venture Economics Venture Intelligence database. All regressions are logit estimates. [t-statistics are in brackets.]
a. The dependent variable is a dummy variable that equals one if the fund raised explicitly stated a focus on early-stage investments.
b. Independent variables include the age of the venture organization, the total amount of venture capital raised by the organization in the past ten years in constant 1994 dollars, a dummy variable that equals one if the firm was located on the West Coast, a dummy variable that equals one if the Department of Labor clarified the prudent man rule and allowed pension investment in venture capital (equals one for all years after 1978), and the highest marginal capital gains tax rate effective in that year.

ture capital commitments in the late 1980s and early 1990s, when bank credit to young, small firms substantially declined. Instead, we see a decline in venture capital commitments over this time period, indicating that bank credit and venture fund-raising moved together.

Challenges in Measuring Expected GDP

A second alternative explanation for our results on capital gains taxes and venture commitments may be the inability to accurately measure expected GDP growth. If expected GDP growth is somehow correlated with capital gains tax rates, then we might be incorrectly interpreting the significance to capital gains tax rates. In unreported regressions, we modeled expected

GDP growth using the previous four years of real GDP growth. Instead of lagged GDP growth, we reestimated the regressions using the expected GDP growth rate. Results were qualitatively the same as in the preceding two sections. This is not surprising since the expected GDP growth rate is primarily affected by last year's growth.

Changes in Technological Opportunities

Finally, the growth in venture capital commitments may have less to do with policy changes and more to do with changes in the number of technological opportunities. In fact the rise in state-level R&D expenditures indicates this to be the case. With changes in technological opportunity causing increases in venture capital investments, we can expect several measures of technological innovation to lead increases in venture fund-raising. In particular, Kortum and Lerner (1998) show that a surge of patents occurred in the late 1980s and 1990s. This suggests that some of the recent growth in venture capital fund-raising in the mid-1990s was due to increases in technological opportunities. The increase in venture fund-raising in the late 1970s and 1980s (the period of our sample), however, was not caused by such technology shifts. The state-level analysis shows that even if we control for R&D spending, it is the regulatory policies that have the most effect.

Conclusions

In this chapter we examined the determinants of fund-raising for the venture industry and individual venture organizations. Our analysis examined supply and demand effects as well as the impact of individual firm performance and reputation. Our results suggest that demand for venture capital plays the most critical role in the fund-raising process. Capital gains tax rates matter, with lower rates leading to a greater quantity of venture capital raised. However, their effect in stimulating demand for venture capital is through commitments by tax-exempt pension funds, which are the least affected by changes in the capital gains tax. Additionally our industry level analysis presented evidence that ERISA clarification in rules governing pension fund investment generally increased commitments to industry. Other macroeconomic factors such as higher GDP growth and increases in R&D spending can lead to greater venture capital activity.

Fund performance is an important determinant of the ability of venture organizations to raise new capital. Firms that hold larger equity stakes in firms that have recently gone public raise funds with greater probability and raise larger funds. Reputation, in the form of firm age and size, also is a positive factor in the ability to raise new capital.

In this chapter we further provided evidence that the decision to raise an early-stage venture fund is affected by pension regulations. The probability of raising a focused fund increased after ERISA's clarification. There was also greater early-stage activity in smaller funds and venture organizations on the West Coast where technology-based start-ups were more prevalent.

The findings we presented have a variety of implications for policy-makers who wish to stimulate venture capital activity. Our results indicate that regulatory reform and policy decisions have an effect on commitments to the venture industry. While the capital gains tax rate is an important driver of venture capital fund-raising, blanket reduction in capital gains tax rates may be a blunt instrument for promoting venture capital. Our analysis suggests that an important factor for the increase in venture capital is increases in the number of high-quality start-ups. The greater the number of firms that meet with success, the greater will be the demand for venture capital. Policies that increase the attractiveness of entrepreneurship and promote technological innovation will have more effect on venture capital investments than across-the-board cuts in the capital gains tax rate. Furthermore the results highlight the highly localized nature of venture capital activity. Countries that wish to promote venture capital activity may consider concentrating efforts rather than spreading resources uniformly around the country. This is in contrast to many of the efforts that various countries have instituted.

Venture capital is increasingly regarded as an important component of the U.S. economic landscape. While policy-makers have often tried to affect the flow of funds into the sector, little has been known about the real impact of such policy measures. This chapter begins to answer those questions and points toward areas for future research.

4   How Are Venture Partnerships Structured?

Here we explore the use of covenants and restrictions in long-term contracts governing venture funds. As discussed in chapter 2, the initial partnership agreement governs the partnership over its life. This agreement is important because it is the crucial mechanism for limiting the behavior of venture capitalists. Many of the oversight mechanisms found in corporations—for example, powerful boards of directors and the market for corporate control—are not available here. While limited partners can serve on advisory boards that review certain policy issues, if they become involved in the day-to-day management of a venture fund, they risk losing their limited liability (Levin 1995). No liquid market for partnership interests exists, and limited partners are frequently restricted from selling their partnership interests. Consequently the primary remedy for the limited partners is legal action triggered by a violation of the covenants.[1]

We analyze 140 U.S.-based independent private partnerships primarily engaged in venture capital investments in equity or equity-linked securities of private firms with active participation by the fund managers in the management or oversight of the firms. We characterize each venture partnership using a series of proxies that measure the probability of opportunistic behavior and supply and demand conditions for venture capital services. We examine whether fourteen major classes of covenants are included in each agreement, and how the inclusion of covenants varies with these proxies.

The results indicate that both sets of proxies are important in explaining the number of covenants. In univariate comparisons, the most significant

---

1. For accounts of recent litigation, see Asset Alternatives (1994a) and Ely (1987). For a more detailed discussion of the latter case, see *Lincoln Nt'l Life Ins. Co. v. Silver*, 1987 U.S. Dist. LEXIS 240 (N.D. Ill., Jan. 13, 1987), count dismissed, 1990 U.S. Dist. LEXIS 13667 (N.D. Ill., Oct. 4, 1990), 1991 U.S. Dist. LEXIS 13584 (N.D. Ill., Sep. 24, 1991), 1991 U.S. Dist. LEXIS 13857 (N.D. Ill., Sep. 30, 1991), adopted, summary judgment granted, 1991 U.S. Dist. LEXIS 15758 (N.D. Ill., Oct. 30, 1991), 1991 U.S. Dist. LEXIS 15804 (N.D. Ill., Oct. 30, 1991), summary judgment granted, 1992 U.S. Dist. LEXIS 8968 (N.D. Ill., Jun. 23, 1992), motion granted, motion denied, 1993 U.S. Dist. LEXIS 11325 (N.D. Ill., Aug. 12, 1993).

differences are associated with measures of relative supply and demand conditions, especially the inflow of venture capital in that year. In regressions—whether cross-sectional analyses of the entire sample or first-difference analyses of those organizations that raised multiple funds—both sets of proxies have significant explanatory power.

Determinants of Covenants

Theoretical Implications

Economists have argued that transactions subject to repeated bargaining problems should be governed by long-term contracts (Klein, Crawford, and Alchian 1978; Williamson 1979). Say a coal mine operator seeks to expropriate rents by raising prices once a utility has built a plant near the mine shaft. To limit opportunistic behavior and ensure allocational efficiency, a contractual relationship between the two parties is critical. A venture partnership presents many of the same problems: once the funds have been raised, the limited partners must have very limited recourse to these funds. One way to accomplish this is to insist on terms and conditions that limit the general partner's ability to behave opportunistically.

In the financial and organizational literatures the determinants of contractual provisions are treated in two hypotheses. Both assume that observed contracts are optimal within a contractual environment. So the two hypotheses are viewed as complements and can be at work simultaneously. Our tests examine the relative importance of each hypothesis in determining contractual outcomes.[2]

The costly contracting theory predicts that negotiation and enforcement of explicit provisions are costly. Covenants are included only when the benefits of restricting activity are greater than the costs. Williamson (1985) advances similar arguments about factors that influence contractual completeness. The optimal set of restrictions will differ across contracts because the ease of monitoring and incentives to pursue opportunistic behavior vary.

The costly contracting hypothesis was explored by Smith and Warner (1979) who argued that the complexity of debt contracts reflects the cost of

---

2. Grossman and Hart (1986) suggest an alternative approach to the question of covenant inclusion. These authors argue that ownership is the ability to exclude someone from access to a particular asset. Ownership should be assigned to the party who will be least likely to engage in wasteful ex post renegotiating. Contractual covenants can be loosely interpreted as a mechanism that reserves ownership of particular activities for the limited partners. (Under partnership law, the general partner is assumed to have those rights not explicitly reserved by the limited partners.)

contracting. Crocker and Reynolds (1993) take the cost, that is, the degree of specificity in payment terms, to be related to the level of technological and production uncertainties, such as in U.S. government jet engine procurement contracts. Malitz (1986) shows costs to be more common for issuers with characteristics that may proxy for a greater need of monitoring in specific classes of bond covenants.

The second hypothesis contends that relative supply and demand conditions in the venture capital market affect the covenants and restrictions in long-term contracts. If the demand for the services of experienced venture capitalists changes rapidly while the supply of those venture capitalists is fixed in the short run, the price of venture capital services should rise. Of course, venture capitalists' expected total compensation should increase.

The price of venture capital services is the compensation that general partners of the fund receive. This compensation has two components. The first component is monetary compensation paid to fund managers. The venture capitalist may also receive private benefits from certain activities. For ease of explication, we focus on private benefits that enhance the venture capitalist's reputation in a certain area. For example, venture capitalists may seek to invest in leveraged buyouts because if they succeed, they can raise a specialized LBO fund. The benefits of these reputation-building activities accrue exclusively to the venture capitalist. Because the expected return to the limited partners is likely to be diminished by these activities, they should seek to prohibit them.

The numbers of venture capitalists and investors are small, so the allocation of private benefits will be affected by relative supply and demand conditions. A sudden increase in demand for venture capital investing services—that is, if institutional investors suddenly increase their allocation to venture capital funds—should increase their price. Competition among venture capitalists does not lead to allocating all the gains to the investor because venture capital funds are imperfect substitutes for each other. Only a small number of venture capitalists may be raising a fund at any particular time, and these firms are likely to be differentiated by size, industry focus, location, and reputation. Many venture organizations will limit both how often they raise funds and the size of these funds, in the belief that excessive growth reduces returns. Meanwhile managers who allocate alternative investments for institutions often operate under limitations about the types of funds in which they can invest (e.g., rules that prohibits investments into first funds raised by venture organizations), and they are pressured to meet allocation targets by the end of the fiscal year. Institutional investors have few alternatives to investing in new partnerships: the market for secondary interests in existing venture partnerships is illiquid and very thin.

It might appear puzzling that much of the adjustment takes place through both the insertion and deletion of covenants and explicit monetary compensation. Why should the entire adjustment not take place through the adjustment of compensation? One possibility is that these adjustments in the consumption of private benefits are an optimal response. The combination of expected fund returns and reputation-building activity by the venture capitalist define a Pareto frontier of possible contracts. The level of expected returns cannot be increased without curtailing reputation-building activity, and vice versa. If venture capitalists optimize the mixture of compensation, then increases in demand are likely to lead to both increased monetary compensation and reduced restrictiveness. In many cases it may be easier and cheaper to adjust contractual restrictiveness.

A related explanation is suggested by the literature on agency issues among institutional investors (Lakonishok, Shleifer, and Vishny 1992). These covenants represent a less visible way to make price adjustments than explicit modifications of the split in capital gains. Deviations from the standard 80 to 20 percent division of profits are likely to attract widespread attention in the institutional investor community (for an example, see Asset Alternatives 1994b, 2003). The inclusion or deletion of covenants, however, is much less likely to attract notice. Investment officers responsible for choosing venture capital investments may find that concessions made in this manner attract less scrutiny from regulators or superiors.

Although they are featured prominently in practitioners' accounts of contracting, supply and demand theories of contractual design have received little attention in academic circles. Hubbard and Weiner (1991) present a model that derives predictions about the relative importance of transaction costs and "market power" in determining contractual provisions. They test those predictions in a sample of natural gas contracts. While they find some monopsonistic effects on the initial contract prices (by using absolute and relative size of the transacting parties as a proxy for market power), they find little support for market power in other contractual provisions.[3]

---

3. The costly contracting and supply-and-demand hypotheses are not mutually exclusive. The supply-and-demand hypothesis assumes that certain activities of the general partner impose costs on limited partners and need to be controlled by restricting those activities. A third possibility is that contractual provisions are benign and persist because there are no costs or benefits to their inclusion. This suggestion appears to run counter to the protracted and costly bargaining over covenants that precedes the signing of venture partnership agreements and many other types of contracts.

Empirical Implications of Costly Contracting

The costly contracting theory predicts that contracting parties should balance the benefits of restricting activities with the cost of negotiating the provisions, writing the contractual clauses, and monitoring compliance. Fund- and firm-specific factors that increase the benefits of restrictions or decrease monitoring costs should lead to a greater number of restrictions.

Monitoring costs may be related to fund size. A large fund should be easier to monitor because it makes more investments and provides more opportunities to evaluate the policies of the venture capitalists. If that were the case, we would expect that larger funds would have more covenants and restrictions. The benefits of restricting certain activities may also be greater in larger funds. Because larger funds may have greater scope to make investments that do not necessarily benefit the limited partners (e.g., substantial investments in leveraged buyouts or other venture funds), restrictions on these types of investments may be important.

Investors may not need to restrict the activities of venture organizations that have reputations as fair and reasonable players. Reputational concerns make opportunistic behavior less attractive and reduce the need for covenants. The likelihood of including covenants that restrict activities of the general partner should be significantly reduced for reputable venture capital organizations.

The sensitivity of compensation to performance may also reduce restrictions. Jensen and Meckling argue that agency costs decline as the financial rewards of managers become more closely tied to the firm's future prospects.[4] Increasing the sensitivity of the venture capitalists' compensation to performance should reduce incentives to make investments that do not maximize limited partners' returns. The perceived need for covenants should thus fall.

The relative benefits of covenants may also increase as the scope for opportunistic behavior rises. Investments in early-stage and high-technology companies may increase the venture capitalist's ability to engage in opportunistic activities. These investment classes potentially involve the greatest asymmetric information and allow venture capitalists more opportunity to exploit their knowledge. Accounting performance may shed little light on the performance of a young firm; assessing the health of a high-technology

---

4. Jensen and Meckling (1976). While the more visible portion of venture capitalists' return, their share of profits, is bunched between 20 and 21 percent, other aspects of compensation vary. Consequently the sensitivity of pay to performance varies considerably, as discussed in chapter 5.

firm is likely to require a detailed understanding of the technical position of the company and its competitors. Restrictions on activities of the general partners may thus be more likely. Monitoring compliance with the covenants in these types of funds, however, may be more difficult. Consequently we have an ambiguous prediction about the relationship between the type of fund and the number of covenants.

A final empirical implication of the costly contracting view is that the number of covenants may change over time if investors learn about the venture capital industry. Because venture limited partnerships have become widespread only during the past twenty years, and the market has only gradually learned about the incentives and activities of venture capitalists, early contracts may be significantly different from more recent agreements. In particular, early contracts may have far fewer covenants and restrictions than later contracts. If all potential future outcomes cannot be foreseen, the cost of writing and monitoring specific contracts may be very high. As the process and incentives become better understood, contracts could include more specific restrictions.[5]

Empirical Implications of Supply and Demand Hypothesis

The supply and demand hypothesis suggests that when the demand for venture capital services is high, relative to a fixed supply of venture capital providers, the number of restrictions should decline. The bulk of the covenants prevent behavior that enriches venture capitalists at the investors' expense. Thus the general partner's "compensation" increases with reductions in the number of restrictions. Several factors proxy for shifts in relative demand.

While it is impossible to directly measure the supply of and demand for venture capital services, we can measure capital inflows relative to the existing venture pool. If the short-run supply of venture services is fixed, changes in inflows may primarily reflect changes in demand. When the annual influx of funds is a large fraction of the existing venture pool (demand is high), the average number of covenants should fall.

---

5. The structure of railroad sidetrack agreements in the late nineteenth and early twentieth centuries is examined in Pittman (1991). The author argues that the provisions in these contracts evolved in response to specific opportunistic behavior that took place. Similarly evidence that few debt contracts prior to the leveraged buyout boom of the mid-1980s included event covenants related to buyouts or recapitalizations is presented in Lehn and Poulsen (1991). After the risk of expropriation became known, these types of risks were addressed with new types of covenants.

The presence of an investment manager may affect the likelihood of including restrictive covenants in venture agreements. Investment managers not only select the funds in which pension funds invest, they also negotiate the terms and conditions of the partnership agreement. Investment managers typically place the funds of several pensions into a single venture fund. This bundling allows investment managers to insert restrictions that otherwise would not be included in the partnership agreement (e.g., see Huemer 1992). Raising a fund without the participation of these investment managers should indicate that the demand for the experienced venture capitalists' services is high. Therefore funds without gatekeepers should have fewer covenants.[6] Anecdotal evidence supporting this hypothesis is found in discussions of the fund-raising strategies of venture capital firms. Some established venture organizations, such as Greylock, explicitly refuse to take money from investment managers.

The demand for top-performing venture capital organizations should also be high relative to the supply of their services. While older, better performing venture organizations do add general partners to their funds, they tend to limit growth in the belief that large organizations lose their ability to operate effectively. Although direct measures of past performance are difficult to find, several proxies for performance can be tested. First, older venture organizations are likely to be better, on average, than new firms because poorly performing organizations are unable to raise new funds. Older firms therefore should have fewer covenants. Second, funds with higher compensation should have fewer covenants. The level of compensation also proxies for high demand for the venture organization's services.

The supply and demand hypothesis also predicts that pay sensitivity should be negatively related to the number of covenants. If the venture capitalist is taking more compensation in the form of private benefits at the expense of potential returns, limited partners want to tie the venture capitalist's monetary compensation more closely to fund returns.

---

6. An alternative interpretation is that funds selected by investment managers have a greater potential for agency problems. A particular concern is that the investment manager and general partners may engage in collusive behavior. To address these potential problems, limited partners may demand more covenants. It is very difficult to design a test that can distinguish between these two interpretations, but there are at least two reasons why the agency hypothesis is problematic. First, it is unclear why the investment manager would want to engage in collusive behavior with the venture capitalists. Investment managers receive all their compensation from the limited partners. These fees are typically independent of the returns generated by the venture funds that they have selected and of the value of the funds' assets. Second, investment managers are very sensitive to reputational concerns. Most of their clients are pension funds and endowments whose trustees are under a considerable amount of regulatory and public scrutiny. If an investment manager is revealed to have behaved in a questionable manner, the repercussions are likely to be severe.

Two difficulties with these predictions must be discussed. First, age and total compensation may be related to reputation. The greater the venture capitalists' reputational capital, the less likely they are to engage in opportunistic behavior that might destroy future returns to their reputation. Larger and more highly compensated venture capital firms may have fewer restrictions because they have less incentive to exploit investors, not because their funds are in greater demand.

Second, the costly contracting hypothesis may generate a similar time-series pattern. In particular, it may be that the costs of opportunism for the venture capitalists vary over time. During periods when there is a particularly heavy inflow of funds, fewer covenants are needed, because the cost of opportunistic behavior (e.g., forgone future fund-raising) is greater.

This interpretation, while seemingly plausible, is problematic for two reasons. First, venture partnerships typically raise funds only every several years. A year of rapid growth in the venture pool tends to be followed by another year of rapid growth, but there is no correlation across several years.[7] Thus it is unclear why worries about future fundraising should be particularly intense in high-growth years. Second, this hypothesis assumes that limited partners can rapidly identify opportunistic behavior by venture capitalists. In fact venture capital investments are long-term by nature, and it is often difficult for outsiders to assess the status of the private firms in a venture capitalist's portfolio. Consequently it takes a long time for opportunistic behavior to be identified.[8]

A First Look at the Covenants

We construct a random sample of 140 partnership agreements. We use these partnership agreements in the files of two gatekeepers and one limited partner. In chapter 22 we assess the completeness and representativeness of our sample.

These partnership agreements are complex, often extending for 100 pages or more. Our procedure for coding the documents was as follows:

---

7. The average venture organization that raised a fund between 1968 and 1987 and raised a follow-on fund did so 2.9 years later. Using data from 1968 to 1994, the flow into venture capital funds (expressed as a percentage of the venture pool in the previous year) has a correlation coefficient with its one-year lag of 0.873 (with a p-value of 0). The correlation coefficient with its three-year lag is -0.105 (with a p-value of 0.634).

8. To cite one example, Hambrecht and Quist raised a fund in 1981 that was plagued by a wide array of organizational problems and had exceedingly poor returns. The venture organization was nonetheless able to raise one dozen funds with nearly half-a-billion dollars in capital over the remainder of the decade (see King 1990).

First, we reviewed the earlier literature and identified the broad areas involved in partnership agreements (i.e., Bartlett 1988, 1994; Dauchy and Harmon 1986; Halloran et al. 1995; Sahlman 1990; Venture Economics 1989b, 1992). A research assistant culled the contractual provisions in these areas from a subsample of forty contracts. We then used these forty descriptions to design a coding form that captures the key features of the agreements. The coding of the 140 contracts was done by an MBA candidate who had previously received a law degree and spent several years practicing contract law.

Each covenant was related to a particular type of opportunistic activity that the general partners might undertake for their own personal benefit but may impose costs on the limited partners. Our description of the covenants focuses on the potential agency costs that might arise if the covenants were not included. The formal tests later in the chapter will examine how the number of covenants varies with potential agency problems in the fund and with the relative supply and demand for venture capital services.

We created fourteen classes of restrictions in partnership agreements. These covenant classes include all restrictions found in at least 5 percent of the agreements in our sample and no more than 95 percent of agreements (between 7 and 133 out of the 140 contracts). This way we could enhance the tractability of the analyses by eliminating several classes that are either standardized or else exceedingly rare.

Many variants of each covenant are found in partnership agreements. To do justice to the complexity of restrictions, we provide qualitative descriptions of the fourteen classes. In the descriptions and the analyses, we divide the covenants into three broad families: those relating to the overall management of the fund, the activities of the general partners, and the permissible types of investments.

Covenants Relating to Overall Fund Management

The first set of restrictions limits the amount invested in any one firm. Such investment restrictions are intended to prohibit the general partners from attempting to salvage an investment in a poorly performing firm by investing significant resources in follow-on funding. The general partners typically do not receive a share of profits until the limited partners have received the return of their investment. The venture capitalists' share of profits can be thought of as a call option: the general partners may gain disproportionately from increasing risk of the portfolio at the expense of diversification. This limitation is frequently expressed as a maximum percentage of capital invested in the fund (typically called committed capital) that can be invested in any one firm. Alternatively, the limit may be expressed as a percent of the current value of the fund's assets. In a few cases the aggregate size of the partnership's two or three largest investments is capped.

The second covenant class limits the use of debt. As option holders, general partners may be tempted to increase the variance of their portfolio's returns by leveraging the fund. Increasing the riskiness of the portfolio would increase the value of their call option at the investors' expense. Partnership agreements often limit the ability of venture capitalists to borrow funds themselves or to guarantee the debt of their portfolio companies (which might be seen as equivalent to direct borrowing). Partnership agreements may limit debt to a set percentage of committed capital or assets, and in some instances also restrict the maturity of the debt to ensure that all borrowing is short term.[9]

The third restriction relates to coinvestments with the venture organization's earlier and/or later funds. Many venture organizations manage multiple funds formed several years apart. These can lead to opportunistic behavior.[10] Consequently, partnership agreements for second or later funds frequently require that the fund's advisory board review such investments or that a majority (or supermajority) of the limited partners approve these transactions. Contracts also address these problems by requiring that the earlier fund invest simultaneously at the same valuation. Alternatively, the investment may only be allowed if one or more unaffiliated venture organizations simultaneously invest at the same price.

A fourth class of covenant relates to reinvestment of profits. For several reasons, venture capitalists may reinvest capital gains rather than distribut-

---

9. A related provision—found in virtually all partnership agreements—is that the limited partners will avoid unrelated business taxable income. Tax-exempt institutions must pay taxes on UBTI, which is defined as the gross income from any unrelated business that the institution regularly carries out. If the venture partnership is generating significant income from debt-financed property, the limited partners may have tax liabilities (see Bartlett 1995). In the analysis below we code funds as having a restriction on debt only if there are limitations beyond a clause concerning UBTI.

10. Consider, for instance, a venture organization whose first fund has made an investment in a troubled firm. The general partners may find it optimal for their second fund to invest in this firm in the hopes of salvaging the investment. Distortions may also be introduced by the need for the venture capitalists to report an attractive return for their first fund as they seek investors for a third fund. Many venture funds will write up the valuation of firms in their portfolios to the price paid in the last venture round. By having the second fund invest in one of the first fund's firms at an inflated valuation, they can (temporarily) inflate the reported performance of their first fund.

ing the profits to the limited partners.[11] The reinvestment of profits may require approval of the advisory board or the limited partners. Alternatively, such reinvestment may be prohibited after a certain date, or after a certain percentage of the committed capital is invested.

Covenants Relating to Activities of the General Partners

Five frequently encountered classes of restrictions curb the activities of the general partners. The first limits the ability of the general partners to invest personal funds in firms. This is because general partners who invest in selected firms might be prone to devote excessive time to these firms and not terminate funding if the firms encounter difficulties. The size of the investment that the general partners can make in any of their fund's portfolio firms is therefore often limited to a percentage of the fund's total investment or, less frequently, to the net worth of the venture capitalist. In addition the venture capitalists may be required to seek permission from the advisory board or limited partners. An alternative approach employed in some agreements is to require the venture capitalists to invest a set dollar amount or percentage in every investment made by the fund.[12]

A second restriction addresses the reverse problem: the sale of partnership interests by general partners. Rather than seeking to increase their personal exposure to selected investments, general partners may try to sell their share of the fund's profits to other investors. While the general partnership interests are not entirely comparable with the limited partners' stakes (e.g., the general partners will typically only receive distributions after the return of the limited partners' capital), other investors may seek to invest in these securities. Limited partners are faced with the possibility that such sales will reduce the general partners' incentives to monitor their

---

11. First, many partnerships receive fees on the basis of either the value of assets under management or adjusted committed capital (capital less any distributions). Distributing profits will reduce these fees. Second, reinvested capital gains may yield further profits for the general (as well as the limited) partners. A third reason why venture capitalists may wish to reinvest profits is that such investments are unlikely to be mature at the end of the fund's stated life. The presence of investments that are too immature to liquidate is a frequently invoked reason for extending the partnership's life beyond the typical contractual limit of ten years. In these cases the venture capitalists will continue to generate fees from the limited partners (though often on a reduced basis).

12. Another issue relating to coinvestment is the timing of the investments by the general partners. In some cases venture capitalists involved in the establishment of a firm will purchase shares at the same time as the other founders at a very low valuation, then immediately invest their partnership's funds at a much higher valuation. Some partnership agreements address this problem by requiring venture capitalists to invest at the same time and price as their funds.

investments. Partnership agreements may therefore prohibit the sale of general partnership interests outright, or else require that these sales be approved by a majority (or super majority) of the limited partners.

A third area for restrictions on the general partners is fund-raising. The raising of a new fund will raise the management fees that venture capitalists receive and likely reduce the attention that they pay to existing funds. Partnership agreements may prohibit fund-raising by general partners until a certain percentage of the portfolio has been invested or until a certain date.[13]

Some partnership agreements restrict general partners' outside activities. Because outside activities may reduce the attention paid to investments, venture capitalists may be required to spend "substantially all" (or some large fraction) of their time managing the investments of the partnership. Alternatively, the general partners' involvement in businesses not in the venture fund's portfolio may be restricted. These limitations are often confined to the first years of the partnership, or until a set percentage of the fund's capital is invested, when the need for attention by the general partners is presumed to be the largest.

A fifth class of covenant relates to the addition of new general partners. By adding less experienced general partners, venture capitalists may reduce the burden on themselves. The quality of the oversight provided, however, is likely to be lower. As a result many funds require that either the advisory board or a set percentage of the limited partners approve the addition of new general partners.

Although many issues involving the behavior of the general partners are addressed through partnership agreements, some others typically are not. One area that is almost never discussed in the sample is the vesting schedule of general partnership interests. If general partners leave a venture organization early in the life of the fund, they may forfeit all or some of their share of the profits. If venture capitalists do not receive their entire partnership interest immediately, they are less likely to leave soon after the fund is formed. A second issue is the division of profits among the general partners. In some funds most profits accrue to the senior general partners, even if the younger partners provide the bulk of the day-to-day management. While these issues are addressed in agreements between the general partners, they are rarely discussed in the contract between the general and limited partners.

---

13. Alternatively, fund-raising may be restricted to a fund of a certain size or focus. For instance, the venture organization may be allowed to raise a buyout fund, which would presumably be managed by other general partners.

Covenants Restricting the Types of Investment

The third family of covenants limit the types of assets in which the fund can invest. These restrictions are typically structured in similar ways: the venture fund is allowed to invest no more than a set percentage of capital or asset value in a given investment class. An exception may be made if the advisory board or the set percentage of the limited partners approve. Occasionally more complex restrictions will be encountered, such as the requirement that the sum of two asset classes not exceed a certain percentage of capital.

Two fears appear to motivate these restrictions on investments. First, compared to other investors in a particular asset class, the general partners may be receiving compensation that is inappropriately large. For instance, the average money manager who specializes in investing in public securities receives an annual fee of about 0.5 percent of assets (Lakonishok, Shleifer, and Vishny 1992), while venture capitalists receive 20 percent of profits in addition to an annual fee of about 2.5 percent of capital. Consequently limited partners seek to limit the ability of venture capitalists to invest in public securities. Similarly the typical investment manager receives a one-time fee of 1 percent of capital for investing an institution's money in a venture fund (Venture Economics 1989a). Partnership agreements often also include covenants that restrict the ability of the general partners to invest capital in other venture funds.

A second concern is that the general partners will opt for classes of investments in which they have little expertise just to gain some experience. For instance, during the 1980s many venture funds began investing in leveraged buyouts (LBOs). Those that developed a successful track record proceeded to raise funds specializing in LBOs; many more, however, lost considerable sums on these investments.[14] Similarly many firms invested in foreign countries during the 1980s. Only a handful proved sufficiently successful to raise funds specializing in these investments (for a practitioner discussion, see Kunze 1990).

Empirical Analysis

Univariate Comparisons

The fourteen primary covenant classes in the sample are presented in table 4.1. The percentage of contracts that include each provision over three

---

14. The poor performance of venture-backed LBOs, such as Prime Computer, has been much discussed in Gallese (1990); quantitative support of these claims is found in analyses of the returns of funds with different investment objectives by Venture Economics (e.g., 1998).

Table 4.1
Classes of covenants in 140 venture partnership agreements, by five-year periods

Covenant class	Percentage of contracts with each covenant		
	1978–82	1983–87	1988–92
On management of fund			
Restrictions on size of investment in any one firm	33.3	47.1	77.8
Restrictions on use of debt by partnership	66.7	72.1	95.6
Restrictions on co-investment by organization's earlier or later funds	40.7	29.4	62.2
Restrictions on reinvestment of partnership's capital gains	3.7	17.6	35.6
On activities of general partners			
Restrictions on co-investment by general partners	81.5	66.2	77.8
Restrictions on sale of partnership interests by general partners	74.1	54.4	51.1
Restrictions on fund-raising by general partners	51.9	42.6	84.4
Restrictions on other actions by general partners	22.2	16.2	13.3
Restrictions on addition of general partners	29.6	35.3	26.7
On types of investment			
Restrictions on investments in other venture funds	3.7	22.1	62.2
Restrictions on investments in public securities	22.2	17.6	66.7
Restrictions on investments in LBOs	0.0	8.8	60.0
Restrictions on investments in foreign securities	0.0	7.4	44.4
Restrictions on investments in other asset classes	11.1	16.2	31.1
Total number of partnership agreements in sample	27	68	45
Average number of covenant classes	4.4	4.5	7.9
Average number of covenant classes (weighted by fund size)	4.4	4.6	8.4

five-year periods gives an initial impression of persistent heterogeneity in the distribution of these covenants. The differences are particularly striking in light of the concentration of capital providers and advisors in the venture capital industry: relatively few limited partners provide the bulk of capital, and partnership documents are prepared by a modest number of law firms. Note the marked increase in the number of covenant classes in agreements executed after 1987. This effect is driven by the pronounced increase in provisions about the management of the fund and types of investment. In fact all nine covenant classes in these two families increase in frequency during the sample period. Weighting observations by fund size makes little difference in this analysis or in those reported below.

This increase contrasts with the decline in four of the five covenants about the activities of general partners. The overall pattern is consistent with the costly contracting hypothesis. During the early period when venture capital limited partnerships are a relatively recent phenomenon, restricting the activities of general partners is important. Because potential agency problems relating to the management of the fund or investments are difficult to predict, restrictions are general in nature. As investors learn about what agency costs are probable, specific restrictions concerning fund management and investments are written. General restrictions on venture capitalists' activities, which may have limited their flexibility undesirably, are consequently dropped.

We will analyze below how the number of restrictions varies with eight variables. Four of these measure potential agency problems. The first two relate to fund focus. General partners of early-stage and high-technology funds may have more scope to engage in opportunistic behavior. The costly contracting hypothesis predicts that limited partners in these funds demand covenants that restrict potential agency problems. We determine the fund's focus by examining the contracts and offering documents that are used to promote the funds.[15]

A third proxy for potential agency costs is fund size.[16] All else being equal, limited partners should add more restrictions to larger funds. There should be increasing returns to scale in negotiating and monitoring compliance with covenants. Larger funds, however, are raised by more established venture firms that may not wish to risk their reputational capital by engaging in opportunistic behavior. We determine fund size using the Venture Economics funds database.

---

15. In many cases the information will be in the offering document, but not in the partnership agreement. Where we do not have the offering document, we use the information about the fund focus recorded in the Venture Economics funds database.

16. One concern is that fund size is a proxy for the reputational capital of the venture organization, not the individual venture capitalists. Ideally we would have a measure of the cumulative experience of the venture capitalists associated with the fund. Unfortunately, constructing such a measure is problematic. Many venture capitalists have diverse backgrounds: for instance, as founders of entrepreneurial firms, corporate managers, or university researchers. It is unclear how individual experience should be aggregated. Even if such a measure could be designed, only about half of the private placement memoranda provide detailed information on the general partners' backgrounds. Obtaining biographical information on venture capitalists elsewhere is often very difficult. To address this concern, we examine whether the venture capitalists in older, larger venture organizations had more prior experience. We look at 267 venture organizations established between 1978 and 1985 that had a board seat on at least one firm that went public in the seven years after the fund closed. To assess experience, we look at the boards on which the venture capitalists served prior to the closing of the fund. (We total the inflation-adjusted market capitalization of all IPOs on whose boards these venture capitalists served.) Older and larger venture organizations tend to have more experienced venture capitalists. The correlation coefficients, 0.29 and 0.25 respectively, are significant at the 1 percent confidence level.

Our fourth measure is the elasticity of compensation to performance, or pay sensitivity. Both the supply and demand hypothesis and costly contracting hypothesis predict that fund managers who have compensation more closely tied to performance have fewer restrictive covenants. As pay is more closely related to the fund's monetary returns, the need for restrictive covenants is reduced. We compute compensation measures using the detailed information on the management fees, division of profits, and timing of payments from the partnership agreements. For measures that cannot be computed in advance, we use historical averages. We first calculate the elasticity of compensation to performance.[17] We then compute the net present value of the base and variable compensation, with the assumption that assets with the venture capitalists' management grow by 20 percent annually.

The second set of variables controls for relative supply and demand conditions in the venture capital market. The first measure is the inflow of new capital into venture funds in the year the fund is established. Because the supply of venture capital services is fixed in the short run, a large growth in capital commitments suggests that demand for venture capital services is high relative to supply, causing the number of covenants to decline and total compensation to rise. While fund-raising activity was relatively sluggish before and after, the years 1982 through 1986 were characterized by a dramatic growth in this capital pool. We measure the growth of this pool by computing the ratio of total capital committed to venture funds in the year the fund closed to the amount raised in the previous ten years.[18]

An alternative measure of the relative demand for the general partners' services is the presence or absence of investment managers. The absence of investment managers should be an indication of high demand. To determine whether an investment manager advised a client to invest in the fund, we examine the lists of names and addresses of limited partners that are typi-

17. We use the increase in the net present value of compensation associated with an increase in the asset growth rate from 20 to 21 percent. This is near the mean of venture performance during the 1980s (Venture Economics 1998). The procedure is described in detail in chapter 5.

18. The calculations are made using the Venture Economics funds database. We use inflation-adjusted dollars throughout. Because we are concerned that the results may be sensitive to the definition of the venture growth rate, we also employ three alternative measures. These are (1) the ratio of total capital committed to venture funds in the year the fund closed to the amount raised in the previous five years (to correct for the fact that much of the capital of older funds already has been returned to the limited partners), (2) the ratio of new capital to the number of active venture organizations (defined as those that had raised a fund in the previous ten years), and (3) the absolute growth in venture capital pool in the year the fund closed.

cally appended to the partnership agreement. This is usually indicated when an investment manager advises the limited partner.[19] In addition we obtain the names of the venture funds in which five major investment managers have allocated funds.

A third proxy for the venture capital supply and demand conditions is the total compensation they receive. Venture capitalists may increase both their monetary compensation and their consumption of private benefits in response to increased demand. As described above, we calculated total compensation, assuming a 20 percent growth rate, and express it as a fraction of the fund's capital.

The final measure that we employ is the age of the venture organization. We can anticipate more experienced venture capitalists to have greater demand for their services. Older firms have been able to raise a series of funds and should have higher ability on average. Using the Venture Economics funds database, we compute the time from the closing of the venture organization's first fund to the closing of this fund.[20]

Table 4.2 summarizes the univariate comparisons of the number of restrictions. Fund focus and the presence of an investment manager are dummy variables that equal one for firms with each characteristic. In the other cases, funds are divided by whether they are above or below the median of each measure. We compare the mean and median number of restrictions.

We find significant differences in the number of restrictions when we divide the contracts by three measures suggested by the supply and demand hypothesis: the growth rate of the venture pool in the year of the fund's closing (measured in four different ways), the presence of an investment manager as an advisor to one or more limited partners, and total compensation of the general partners. Funds established at times when the venture pool grew rapidly, where an investment manager was not involved, or in which the venture capitalists were highly compensated have significantly fewer restrictions. The differences are significant whether we compare means or medians. When we divide the funds by indicators that we expect to be associated with a greater need for monitoring—for instance, whether the

19. Because the investment manager will typically handle the continuing administrative work concerning the partnership (e.g., liquidating stock distributions and responding to any proposed modifications of the partnership agreement), the address of the limited partner will be listed as care of the investment manager.

20. In a closing an investor or group of investors signs a contract that binds them to supply a set amount of capital to a private equity fund, and they often provide a fraction of that capital immediately.

Table 4.2
The number of covenant classes in 140 venture partnership agreements for various subgroups

Focus of covenant	Number of covenants for funds where this is…		p-Value, test of no difference
	True	False	
On early-stage investments	5.0	5.3	0.567
	[5]	[5]	[0.524]
On high-technology investments	5.3	5.2	0.790
	[5]	[5]	[0.877]
On presence of investment manager	5.8	3.8	0.001
	[6]	[3]	[0.001]
	Number of covenants for funds that are…		p-Value, test of no difference
	Above median	Below median	
On size of venture fund	5.2	5.2	0.691
	[5]	[5]	[0.752]
On sensitivity of general partner compensation to performance	4.7	5.9	0.717
	[5]	[6]	[0.534]
On rate of growth of venture pool in year of fund's closing[a]	4.0	7.2	0.000
	[4]	[8]	[0.000]
On total compensation of the general partners	4.2	6.4	0.017
	[4]	[6]	[0.033]
On age of venture organization in year of closing	5.5	5.0	0.414
	[5]	[5]	[0.464]

Note: The first two columns compare the mean and median [in brackets] number of covenant classes for funds in the sample that fall into various categories. In the first panel, firms are divided by their focus and the presence of an investment manager; in the second panel, by whether they are above or below the median on several measures. The third column presents the p-values of t-tests and Wilcoxon signed-rank tests [in brackets] of the null hypotheses that these distributions are identical.
a. The rate of the growth of venture pool is significant at the one percent level using three alternative definitions.

fund focuses on early-stage and high-technology investments—we find no significant differences in the number of covenants.[21]

Regression Analyses

We examine these patterns using regression analyses in table 4.3. The dependent variable is the number of covenant classes included in the partnership agreement (out of a total of fourteen). We employ two econometric specifications, ordinary least squares (OLS) and Poisson. The latter may more accurately reflect the nonnegative, ordinal nature of the dependent variable.[22] Because the dummy variables for funds with an early-stage and high-technology focus are highly correlated, we use only one of these variables at a time. Since we are missing data in some cases, we employ only 124 out of the 140 observations.[23]

In the OLS and Poisson regressions the coefficients of the variables measuring the growth rate of the venture pool and the presence of one or more investment managers are significant. Consistent with the supply and demand hypothesis, there are fewer restrictions for funds established at times when the venture capital pool is growing rapidly and where investment managers do not advise the limited partners.

We next test whether the independent variables that proxy for agency problems or supply and demand conditions jointly differ from zero. We include p-values in the table from tests of the null hypothesis of no difference. Using both specifications, we can reject the null hypothesis for supply and demand proxies at the 1 percent level. The variables that measure the costly contracting hypothesis, however, do not differ from zero. As these

21. Our results are not driven by all-or-nothing covenant inclusion. Most covenant classes are positively correlated with other covenant classes, and many of the correlations are significant. The correlation coefficients are reasonably small, however. For example, the average correlation coefficient among restrictions on the fund's management is 0.169, and 33 percent are significant at the 1 percent confidence level. The highest correlation is among the restrictions on investments: 90 percent of the correlation coefficients are significant at the 1 percent level; the average correlation coefficient is 0.432. The largest correlation across covenant classes is between restrictions concerning fund management and investment activity. The average correlation coefficient is 0.258: 55 percent are significant at the 1 percent level, with 80 percent significant at the 5 percent level.

22. The standard errors in the OLS regression are heteroskedasticity-consistent, while those in the Poisson regression are not adjusted in this manner. The usefulness of Poisson regressions in these settings is discussed in Maddala (1983).

23. In some cases we do not know the size of the fund. In other cases, we cannot calculate the base compensation since it is set in a budget negotiated annually between the limited and general partners or else is based on the debt taken on by the firms in the venture capitalists' portfolio.

Table 4.3
Regression analysis of the number of covenant classes in venture partnership agreements

| Specification | Independent variable[a] | | | | | | | | Adjusted R^2 | Root MSE | χ^2-Statistic | p-Value |
	Early-stage focus?	Sensitivity of pay to profits	Size of venture fund	Venture pool growth	Investment manager?	Total compensation	Age of venture fund	Constant				
OLS[b]	0.19 [0.34]	−51.67 [1.63]	0.005 [1.45]	−5.06 [5.83]	1.47 [2.23]	−13.19 [1.33]	−0.06 [1.11]	12.51 [2.85]	0.22	2.658		
Poisson[c]	0.01 [0.16]	−8.30 [1.60]	0.001 [1.42]	−0.98 [5.05]	0.27 [2.82]	−2.23 [1.74]	−0.01 [1.67]	2.89 [4.92]			53.19	0.000

	p-Value, test of whether agency proxies are zero[d]	p-Value, test of whether market power proxies are zero[d]
OLS	0.231	0.000
Poisson	0.214	0.000

Note: The regressions use 124 partnership agreements for which complete data are available.
a. The dependent variable is the number of covenant classes (out of a total of 14) included in the partnership agreement.
b. Coefficients of an ordinary least squares regression [with absolute heteroskedasticity-consistent t-statistics in brackets].
c. Poisson regression [with absolute t-statistics in brackets].
d. The p-values of F- and χ^2-tests that the sets of variables that proxy for agency costs (early-stage focus, sensitivity of pay to performance, and size of the venture fund) and for the venture organization's market power (venture pool growth, presence of an investment manager, total compensation, and age of the venture organization) are equal to zero.

regressions suggest, the relative demand for venture capital services is a critical determinant of the number of covenants.[24]

We examine the robustness of the analysis to the use of alternative dependent variables. To explore whether results can be driven by one covenant (or one set of restrictions), we consider each of the three covenant families separately. Table 4.4 presents three regressions that employ as dependent variables the number of restrictions relating to fund management, the activities of the general partners, and the investment type. We present only the regressions using an OLS specification; results using a Poisson specification are similar.

The results in table 4.4 support both the supply and demand and costly contracting hypotheses. The results show that fund size is important in determining the number of covenants on the management of the fund and the type of investment. The potential agency problems on fund management and investments are likely to increase with the size of the fund, while the potential for agency problems involving general partners does not. (The number of investments is likely to increase linearly with fund size, while the number of general partners typically only increases slowly with size.) In these two regressions the costly contracting proxies are jointly different from zero. The coefficients of the venture pool growth and investment manager variables have the sign predicted by the supply and demand hypothesis in all three regressions (and are significant at the 5 percent confidence level in two). The measures of supply and demand are jointly significant in all three regressions. Formal tests of the significance of these variables are presented in lower portion of table 4.4.

An alternative empirical approach examines first differences to determineif changes in the explanatory variables are related to changes in the

---

24. We undertake several modifications of these regressions to address concerns about their robustness. First, we add a variable that indicates the date that the fund closed to control for any trend in the number of covenants. While the primary results are robust to the addition of this variable, the trend term is positive and highly significant. This might indicate that the market has been learning about potential agency costs over time and continues to include more specific restrictions. Second, we address the concern that two of the independent variables—the amount and performance sensitivity of the compensation—are determined at the same time as the dependent variable. While a venture organization will typically announce a target fund size in advance, the compensation will be negotiated at the same time as the terms and conditions of the partnership. We rerun the regressions omitting these measures. Third, we reestimate the regressions using three alternative measures of the venture pool growth because we are concerned that the results may reflect the particular measure that we employ. Finally, we employ a dummy variable for a fund with a high-technology (rather than an early-stage) focus. In all cases the independent variables associated with the supply and demand hypothesis remain jointly significant at the 1 percent confidence level. Those addressing the costly contracting hypothesis are in each case insignificant at conventional confidence levels.

Table 4.4
Regression analysis of the number of covenant classes in venture partnership agreements, divided into three families

Dependent variable[a]	Independent variable[b]									
	Early-stage focus?	Sensitivity of pay to profits	Size of venture fund	Venture pool growth	Invest-ment manager?	Total compen-sation	Age of venture fund	Constant	Adjusted R^2	Root MSE
Covenants on management of fund	0.04 [0.17]	-17.78 [1.82]	0.003 [3.41]	-1.38 [3.06]	0.35 [1.48]	-3.74 [1.08]	-0.03 [1.11]	4.04 [2.76]	0.14	1.024
Covenants on activities of general partners	0.10 [0.40]	-1.34 [0.09]	0.001 [0.44]	-0.56 [1.38]	0.59 [2.02]	-3.16 [0.93]	-0.06 [2.27]	3.60 [2.12]	0.10	1.205
Covenants on types of investment	0.05 [0.18]	-32.56 [2.02]	0.003 [2.42]	-3.12 [6.92]	0.53 [1.99]	-6.28 [1.16]	0.02 [0.84]	4.87 [2.11]	0.32	1.345

	p-Value, test if agency proxies are zero[c]	p-Value, test of whether market power proxies are zero[c]
Covenants on management of fund	0.005	0.011
Covenants on activities of general partners	0.954	0.000
Covenants on types of investment	0.042	0.000

Note: The regressions use 124 partnership agreements for which complete data are available.

a. The dependent variable is the number of covenant classes in each family included in the partnership agreement.

b. Coefficients of an ordinary least squares regression presented with absolute heteroskedasticity-consistent t-statistics in brackets.

c. The p-values of F-tests that the sets of variables proxy for agency costs (early-stage focus, sensitivity of pay to performance, and size of the venture fund) and for the venture organization's market power (venture pool growth, presence of an investment manager, total compensation, and age of the venture organization) are equal to zero.

number of covenants. The first-difference analysis eliminates many unobserved organization-specific characteristics that may be correlated with the explanatory variables. Table 4.5 shows how the number of covenant classes changes in subsequent funds of the same venture organization. We divide the funds by whether there were changes in the presence of a gatekeeper, the type of focus of the fund, and the rate of growth of the venture industry in the year of the fund's closing. The effects are in the expected direction. For example, the number of covenants increases by 2.4 when a gatekeeper supplies capital to the current fund but not to the previous fund. Declining growth rates in the venture pool also lead to an increase in the number of covenants. Both results are consistent with the supply and demand hypothesis. In addition, early-stage and high-technology funds have more scope to engage in opportunistic activities, so restricting their activities is more valuable. The second panel tests the significance of these differences. The differences in the number of covenants are significant at the 5 percent confidence level in the growth-rate analysis; those relating to fund focus are of borderline significance.

The first-difference regressions are presented in table 4.6. Unlike the earlier regressions, a change in the focus of the fund to either early-stage or high-technology investments increases the number of covenants significantly, by approximately two. This is consistent with the costly contracting hypothesis. Changes in the gatekeeper status do not significantly affect the number of covenants, which may reflect the smaller sample size in these first-difference analyses. Finally a decline in the growth rate of the venture pool increases the number of covenants in the contracts. These results are generally consistent with both the costly contracting and supply and demand hypotheses.

Conclusions

In this chapter we examined the use of contractual covenants in venture capital partnership agreements. Two complementary explanations for the presence of these restrictions were analyzed: differences in the need for oversight and differences in supply and demand conditions for venture capital services. The evidence from a sample of 140 contracts indicates that both factors are important determinants of contractual restrictiveness. The proxies for supply and demand conditions are consistently significant in univariate and regression analyses. When the covenants are broken down into families, proxies for potential agency problems lead to covenants that restrict the management of the fund and investment activities, while the

Table 4.5
Change in number of covenant classes in current and previous venture partnership agreements

	Change in number of restrictions		
	Mean	Standard error	Observations
Gatekeeper status			
Gatekeeper invested in this fund but not in previous fund	+2.4	1.1	14
Gatekeeper invested in this and in previous fund	+1.4	0.5	45
No gatekeeper invested in this fund	+1.5	0.9	16
Stage focus			
Early-stage but previous fund was not early-stage	+4.3	2.4	6
This and previous fund specialize in early-stage investments	+1.4	1.0	10
This and previous fund do not specialize in early-stage investments	+1.6	0.5	49
Previous fund specialized in early-stage investments and this one does not	+0.6	1.4	10
Technology focus			
High-tech fund but previous fund was not high-tech	+3.6	1.5	11
This and previous fund specialize in high-tech investments	+2.3	0.9	16
This and previous fund do not specialize in high-tech investments	+1.2	0.5	41
Previous fund specialized in high-tech investments and this one does not	−0.4	1.7	7
Growth rate of venture pool at time of fund's closing			
Greater than at time of last fund's closing	−0.9	0.7	15
Between 0% & 10% below last fund's closing	+1.8	0.9	21
Between 10% & 20% below last fund's closing	+2.4	0.8	20
More than 20% below last fund's closing	+2.7	0.8	19

	Test statistic	p-Value
Cases where gatekeeper invested in this fund but not in previous fund	0.87	0.389
Cases with an early-stage focus in this fund but not in previous fund	1.85	0.068
Cases with a high-tech focus in this fund but not in previous fund	1.94	0.057
Cases where various venture pool growth rate changes differ	3.46	0.021

Note: The observations are divided by whether there is a change in whether the fund has a gatekeeper among its investors, a change in fund focus (to or from a focus on early-stage or high-technology investments), and a change in the growth rate of the venture capital pool in the year of the fund's closing. There are a total of 14 covenant classes. The second panel presents the results of *t*-tests and an *F*-test of the significance of these differences. The sample consists of 75 second and later venture funds where information is available on an earlier fund of the venture organization.

Table 4.6
Regression analysis of the change in the number of covenant classes in venture partnership agreements

Dependent variable[a]	Independent variable							
	Change in whether early-stage focus	Change in whether high-tech focus	Change in gatekeeper presence	Change in growth rate of venture pool	Constant	Adjusted R^2	F-Statistic	p-Value
Change in number of restrictions	1.90 [2.07]		-0.10 [0.13]	-3.77 [2.46]	1.30 [2.85]	0.08	3.15	0.030
Change in number of restrictions		2.01 [2.33]	-0.39 [0.52]	-3.28 [2.16]	1.17 [2.58]	0.09	3.56	0.018

Note: The table presents the coefficients of ordinary least squares regressions [with absolute t-statistics in brackets]. The sample consists of 75 second and later venture funds where information is available on an earlier fund of the venture organization.

a. The dependent variable is the difference in the number of covenant classes (out of a total of 14) included in the current and previous partnership agreements.

b. Independent variables are the change in fund focus (either to or from a focus on early-stage or high-technology investments), the change in whether the fund has a gatekeeper among its investors, and the change in the growth rate of the venture capital pool in the year of the fund's closing.

supply and demand proxies affect all three groups. The results are robust to a variety of modifications.

This research differs from earlier empirical analyses of contract structure. Earlier analyses have either focused exclusively on the costly contracting hypothesis or found weak support for the claim that supply and demand conditions affect contractual form. Our results suggest that the relative neglect of the supply and demand hypothesis is unwarranted. The paucity of academic work on supply and demand effects contrasts with the weight placed on this factor in practitioner accounts. We hope that further theoretical and empirical work will take our description of the supply and demand hypothesis and examine the role of shifts in supply and/or demand in determining contractual forms.

5   How Are Venture Capitalists Compensated?

In addition to the terms and conditions discussed in chapter 4, venture capital limited partnership agreements clearly define the compensation over the fund's life to be paid to the venture capitalists. Typically these agreements designate a percentage of the fund's capital or assets as an annual management fee and a percent of the profits to be paid out as investment returns are realized. Compensation is based on actual returns from the venture fund's investments. While compensation in the different funds raised by a venture organization may differ, the individual partnership agreements are rarely renegotiated, unlike executive employment contracts.[1]

Contractually specified compensation is particularly important in the venture capital setting. As discussed in chapter 2, the limited partners in venture capital funds cannot utilize many of the methods of disciplining managers found in corporations and must avoid direct involvement in the fund's activities. Removing a venture capitalist is a difficult and costly procedure, as compensation can become a contentious issue between limited and general partners of venture funds (see Venture Economics 1989b; Asset Alternatives 2003).

At first glance, the compensation terms in these models resemble one another. Figure 5.1 shows the distribution of the percentage of profits allocated to the general partners after provision for the return of invested capital, or of invested capital plus a premium. The share in our sample varies from 0.7 to 45 percent, but 81 percent of the funds are between 20 and 21 percent, inclusive. While superficially quite homogeneous, there are many subtle differences across the compensation provisions in these agreements. Many of these differences, we will show, reflect the diversity of the venture organizations entering into the agreements. In this chapter we explore some of these differences and their causes.

---

1. Similar schemes are found in funds devoted to leveraged buyout, mezzanine, real estate, and oil-and-gas investments as well as hedge funds.

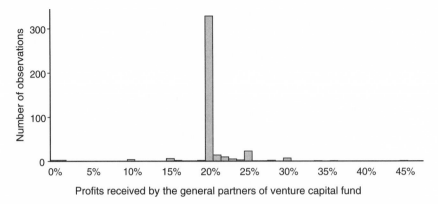

Figure 5.1
Share of profits received by 419 venture capital partnerships whose first closing was between
January 1978 and December 1992. The profit figure indicates the average share of capital
gains received by the venture capital organizations after any initial return of investment to the
limited partners.

Two models are given that might explain the variation in compensation
in these contracts, which have quite different empirical implications. We
then analyze a sample of 419 U.S. venture capital partnerships. We find that
compensation for older and larger venture capital organizations is more
sensitive to performance and more variable than the compensation of other
venture groups. The fixed component of compensation is higher for smaller,
younger funds and funds focusing on high-technology or early-stage investments. No relationship is found between the incentive compensation
and performance. The empirical results are consistent with the primary predictions of a model in which neither the venture capitalist nor the investor
initially knows the venture capitalist's ability, but this information is gradually revealed over time.

Determinants of Venture Capitalist Compensation

Information about a venture capitalist's ability should affect the time-series
and cross-sectional variation of compensation for venture capitalists for
both fixed and variable pay. In this section we discuss two stylized models
that generate predictions framing the compensation analyses. First, we
adapt the compensation model from Gibbons and Murphy (1992) to the
venture capital setting and derive the equilibrium compensation to explore
the learning model. We assume that initially there is symmetric uncertainty
about the ability of the venture capitalist. Then in a discussion of the sig-

naling model we assume the venture capitalists, but not the investors, to be initially informed about their ability. Appendixes A and B present the models in full detail.

The Learning Model

An abstraction of the learning model is the assumption that venture capitalists raise two funds (partnerships) in two consecutive periods. The outcome of investments in the first fund, including any investment returns, is realized prior to the second fund being raised. No projects shift from the first fund to the second. The fund return is a function of the venture capitalists' ability to select high-quality projects and add value after the investment, their effort, and noise. While the venture capitalists' ability either to select attractive projects or to add value after the investment is uncertain, both venture capitalists and investors know the distribution of abilities in advance. Investors cannot observe the effort level chosen in either fund because this information is private. The venture capitalists' compensation is assumed to be a linear function of fund returns.

Compensation contracts are written for each fund and are conditional on the information available from returns, if any exist. The compensation contract is set out before effort is chosen or investments are made. Investors in both funds can, but need not, be the same. Investors in the second fund, however, have verifiable information about the performance of the first fund. In appendix A of this chapter, we derive the equilibrium contract under the assumptions of the learning model.

The learning model has five implications for venture capitalist compensation:

• Level of pay-for-performance sensitivity over time. The sensitivity of compensation to performance is higher in the venture capitalists' second fund. Venture capitalists have an incentive to work hard in their first fund because, if they increase effort, investors will think they have higher ability. (This relation holds for fixed expectations about equilibrium effort choice.) Greater effort not only raises current income but also total compensation in the second period.[2]

---

2. The comparison of first- and second-fund compensation can be viewed as indicative of patterns among venture capitalists with and without established reputations. If a venture capital firm has established a good reputation, it needs explicit incentives in the form of high pay-for-performance sensitivity to induce effort. To empirically assess this claim, we will use venture organization age and size as proxies for reputation. Older and larger venture capital organizations are likely to have established reputations and therefore need higher pay sensitivities to

• Level of fixed fees over time. The learning model is ambiguous about the relative fixed fees in new and old venture firms. While the level of variable compensation unambiguously increases in established venture firms, fixed fees can rise, fall, or remain unchanged.

• Level of fixed fees and effort level. Because we assume a Nash bargaining solution, fixed fees incorporate the cost of effort such that the higher cost of effort, the higher are the fixed fees. All else being equal, higher investment and monitoring costs enable the venture capitalists to receive higher fixed fees.

• Variance in pay-for-performance sensitivity over time. This model also predicts lower cross-sectional variance for new and smaller venture organizations than for established organizations. Compensation schemes for small, young venture capital organizations are clustered because neither the venture capitalists nor the investors know the venture capitalists' abilities. As venture capitalists' abilities become known, compensation schemes are revised to reflect the updated information about ability. In any distribution of abilities, the cross-sectional variance of variable compensation is higher for larger, older venture capital organizations.

• Level of pay-for-performance sensitivity and performance. The learning model suggests that pay-for-performance sensitivity across periods will be unrelated to the performance of the venture capital fund. In the first period, when pay-for-performance is low, the venture capitalist is driven to work hard by the desire to establish a reputation. In the second period, higher explicit incentives are required because the potential for higher compensation in the next period is not there. Put another way, incentive compensation is endogenous and elicits the optimal effort given the perceived ability of the venture capitalist. In a cross section of venture capital funds, pay sensitivity should have no predictive power for performance.

The Signaling Model

The principal-agent literature demonstrates that the nature of contracts changes dramatically once informational assumptions are altered. In the

---

induce the desired effort level. New and smaller venture organizations work harder because they seek to establish a reputation that will allow them to command greater compensation in future funds. This implicit incentive means that less pay-for-performance sensitivity is necessary for small, young venture firms. An important issue that we do not model is whether reputation adheres to the venture organization or the individual venture capitalists. Although we show in the empirical analysis below that established venture capital organizations tend to be comprised of more experienced venture capitalists, exploring the ways in which reputation resides in and transfers among financial institutions is a fertile topic for future research.

learning model, investors and venture capitalists both have the same initial information about venture capitalists' abilities. Symmetric uncertainty leads to the central result. If before entering into a contract venture capitalists have hidden information, the contract that is possible in equilibrium changes state. Under certain circumstances high-ability venture capitalists will attempt to signal their type through the contracts they offer to investors in the first period.[3]

In the simple signaling model, the second fund's variable compensation is the same for high- and low-ability venture capitalists. This result accords with our assumption that marginal productivity after the first unit of effort and effort costs of both types of venture capitalists are identical. Because types are fully revealed in the first fund, second-period compensation differs only in the base compensation. High-ability venture capitalists receive higher fixed fees in subsequent funds. Once the high-ability venture capitalists have revealed their ability type, they desire more insurance, and hence receive higher fixed compensation and less variable compensation.

Deriving optimal first-period compensation schemes is more difficult. These classes of signaling models usually have a continuum of equilibrium points. Because low-ability venture capitalists set their compensation for their second fund under full information about ability, their optimal first-fund contract will be identical to the optimal second-fund contract. Low-ability venture capitalists act as if their type is completely known in their first fund.

High-ability venture capitalists offer a contract that maximizes their utility, subject to the constraint that low-ability venture capitalists are indifferent between accepting this contract and their own. As shown in appendix B of this chapter, the variable compensation for the high-ability venture capitalists in the first fund is more sensitive to performance than it is in the second fund. Likewise the fixed component of compensation is smaller in the first fund. The fixed component in a first-fund contract might even be negative, in which case high-ability venture capitalists would pay for the opportunity to invest in start-up companies in their first fund. For high-ability venture capitalists to separate from low-ability types, they must be willing to accept more risk. Linking compensation more closely to uncertain future returns increases the risk that the high-ability venture capitalists bear. The higher expected level of pay compensates these venture capitalists for the greater risk. Pay-for-performance sensitivity in the first fund for high-ability venture capitalists increases as the difference in ability increases. The

---

3. Although we examine the Riley (1979) information equilibrium, it is likely that other separating, as well as pooling, equilibria exist.

difference in second-period compensation is greater, and therefore low-ability venture capitalists have more to gain from imitating high-ability types.

The signal in this model is the level of risk that the venture capitalists bear. Variable compensation divides an uncertain payoff between venture capitalists and investors. Unlike signaling models in which the signal is explicitly nonproductive, such as education, the use of pay sensitivity as a signal has a second effect of inducing different effort choices in equilibrium.

Heinkel and Stoughton (1994) examine the case where investors evaluate portfolio managers on both the contracts offered and past performance. Their optimal contracts are complex but qualitatively resemble the learning model. This is because their model has both learning and signaling components. Adding a noisy signal of ability, like performance, creates incentives to work harder. Heinkel and Stoughton show that under their assumptions, the learning effect is stronger. In the model used here, however, investors do not have an opportunity to use past returns to update beliefs. Types are totally revealed to investors by the contracts offered in the first fund before the venture capitalists have any performance. In the learning model discussed earlier, both the venture capitalists and investors infer the venture capitalists' ability through realized returns. Our empirical analysis can be seen as a comparison of the power of these two effects, which are depicted in extreme form in our models. Our central empirical result—the greater pay-for-performance sensitivity of more established venture organizations—is consistent with the predictions presented in Heinkel and Stoughton (1994) and the learning model.

In our signaling model, where venture capitalists know their ability to select and oversee entrepreneurs before raising a fund, the predicted empirical patterns differ from those derived in the learning model, where venture capitalists and investors have equally poor initial information about ability:

• Level of pay-for-performance sensitivity over time. The signaling model predicts that new and smaller venture organizations that are confident about their high ability will increase their pay-for-performance sensitivity in early funds. Once the venture capitalists' ability has been revealed through their contract choice, the desire for insurance on the part of the risk-averse venture capitalists causes incentive compensation in subsequent funds to decline. Older and larger venture capital organizations with established reputations should receive less incentive compensation.

• Level of fixed fees over time. Fixed fees for older and larger venture capital firms should be higher because these organizations will demand insurance.

• Level of fixed fees and effort level. As in the learning model, higher investment and monitoring costs should lead the venture capitalists to receive higher fixed fees.

• Variance in pay-for-performance sensitivity over time. We also expect that the cross-sectional variance in pay-for-performance sensitivities will be smaller in older, larger organizations. In the model where each type's marginal product is equal, there is no variance in the variable compensation for the later fund. Thus both the level and the cross-sectional variance of pay-for-performance sensitivities should be higher for younger venture capital firms. Both of these predictions are the reverse of the predictions of the learning model.

• Level of pay-for-performance sensitivity and performance. The signaling model predicts that pay sensitivity should be positively related to performance. High-ability venture capitalists increase their pay-for-performance sensitivity to signal their quality. Young, high-ability venture capitalists will work hard because of the higher variable compensation and thus will have higher returns.

The Form of Compensation

We examine 419 venture partnership agreements and offering memoranda for funds formed between 1978 and 1992. The construction of the sample is described in chapter 22.

The form of venture capitalist compensation in these contracts is analyzed in three ways. First, we examine the most visible aspect of compensation, the percentage of profits received by the venture capitalists. Second, we examine the net present value (NPV) of the fixed management fees. Finally, we examine the elasticity of venture partnerships' compensation, defined as the percentage change that will occur in the NPV of total compensation in response to a 1 percent change in performance. The elasticity is a function of both the percentage of profits retained by general partners and the base compensation. Therefore it is the best measure of the sensitivity of compensation to performance.

The Percentage of Profits

As we indicated in figure 5.1, a great deal of bunching occurs in the share of profits. This concentration of profits is broadly consistent with a learning model in which information is revealed slowly. If investment ability is uncertain, venture capitalists negotiate very similar compensation terms.

But there are also substantial differences. Panel A of table 5.1 presents the mean level of variable compensation. We divide the observations in several ways. As discussed above, we use two measures of venture organization reputation. The first measure is the age of the venture organization, or the time from the closing of the first partnership that the venture organization raised to the closing of this fund. We use this measure for age because investors should know more about the ability of older venture organizations. These older venture organizations are likely to be of higher quality. Low-quality venture capitalists are eventually be unable to raise new funds. The average level of compensation will rise because we do not observe the low compensation of poor venture capitalists in later funds.

Venture organization age will not, however, capture the fact that venture capitalists beginning a new organization may have had considerable experience at another venture group or elsewhere. We consequently employ a second proxy for the experience of the venture capitalists, which is the size of the venture organization's previous funds. Venture organization size is a potentially useful measure of uncertainty concerning ability. Investors may provide larger sums to venture capitalists with proven track records, even if they have not raised any earlier funds. We total the capital invested in the organization's funds, using 1997 dollars, whose first closing was in the ten calendar years prior to the year that this fund closed. Because the size of the venture pool increased dramatically over these years, we employ a measure of relative size. We divide this sum by the total amount raised by venture organizations in these years, again using 1997 dollars.

Neither measure of experience is perfect. Ideally we would have a measure of the cumulative experience of the venture capitalists associated with the fund, but unfortunately, constructing such a measure is problematic. Many venture capitalists have diverse backgrounds, including experience as founders of entrepreneurial firms, corporate managers, or university researchers. It is unclear how individual experience should be aggregated. Even if such an experience measure could be designed, only about half of the private placement memoranda would provide detailed information on the backgrounds of the general partners. Obtaining biographical information on venture capitalists elsewhere is often very difficult. To address this concern, we examine whether the venture capitalists in older and larger venture organizations had more prior experience. We look at 267 venture funds established between 1978 and 1985, including some not in the sample, that had a board seat on at least one firm that went public in the seven years after the fund closed. To assess experience, we look at the boards on which the venture capitalists served prior to the closing of this fund.

Table 5.1
Share of profits received by venture capital organizations

	Percentage of profits received by VCs	Number of observations
Panel A: Mean share of profits received by venture capitalists		
Age of venture organization		
No earlier funds	20.5	146
Four years or less	20.7	88
Between four and eight years	20.6	94
More than eight years	21.4	91
Size of venture organization		
No earlier funds[a]	20.4	170
Between 0.0% and 0.2%	20.9	84
Between 0.2% and 0.7%	20.5	88
Greater than 0.7%	21.6	77
Objective of fund		
Focus on high-technology firms	21.2	199
Other industry focus (or no focus)	20.3	220
Focus on early-stage investments	21.1	173
Other stage focus (or no focus)	20.5	246
Date of closing		
January 1978–December 1984	20.5	100
January 1985–June 1986	20.9	111
June 1986–December 1988	20.7	120
January 1989–December 1992	20.9	85

Variables	Coefficient	*p*-Value
Panel B: Tests of significance involving pattern of profits		
Correlation, age of venture organization and % of profits	0.104	0.032
Correlation, size of venture organization and % of profits	0.109	0.026
Correlation, date of closing and % of profits	0.027	0.577
t-Test, high-technology focus and % of profits		0.004[b]
t-Test, early-stage focus and % of profits		0.047[b]
Variance test, organizations below and above 0.7% of pool		0.000[c]
Variance test, organizations below and above 10 years old		0.022[c]

Note: The sample consists of 419 venture capital partnerships whose first closing was between January 1978 and December 1992. The size of the venture organization is the ratio of the capital invested in the organization's funds, in constant dollars, whose first closing was in the ten calendar years prior to the year that this fund closed, to the total amount raised by all venture organizations in these years, again in constant dollars.

a. This category includes funds that raised a previous fund whose size cannot be determined.

b. *p*-value from a *t*-test comparing the percentage of profits received by funds with and without this investment focus.

c. *p*-value from an *F*-test comparing the variance of profits received by experienced and inexperienced venture organizations.

We total the inflation-adjusted market capitalization of all IPOs on whose boards these venture capitalists served. Older and larger venture organizations tend to have more experienced venture capitalists. The correlation coefficients, 0.29 and 0.25 respectively, are significant at the 1 percent confidence level.

The oldest and largest funds command about a 1 percent greater share of profits than less established funds. As the correlation analysis in panel B of table 5.1 demonstrates, these effects are significant at least at the 5 percent confidence level. Similarly firms with a focus on high-technology or early-stage investments receive a significantly higher percent of profits. No significant time effect appears. Again, consistent with the learning model, larger and older venture capital organizations have significantly greater variance in the share of profits that they receive.

Even if the differences between more and less established funds are statistically significant, they may not be economically meaningful. To address this concern, we examine a representative fund, using the assumptions outlined in appendix C. A 1 percent difference in the share of profits matters very little if the venture fund does not perform well. For instance, if the fund's investments grow only at an annual rate of 10 percent, an increase in the venture capitalists' profit share from 20 to 21 percent boosts the NPV of total compensation by only 0.3 percent. The small magnitude of this change occurs because the compensation in this case is dominated by the fixed fee. If, however, the fund's investments perform well, a very different picture emerges. For example, if the fund's investments grow at an annual rate of 50 percent, an increase in the profit share for the venture capitalists from 20 to 21 percent raises the NPV of total compensation by 4.2 percent.

Table 5.2 reports the results from several regression analyses. The first is an ordinary least squares (OLS) analysis. The dependent variable is the venture capitalists' share of profits. We express this variable as a number between 0 and 100, where 21.2 represents a profit share of 21.2 percent. Independent variables are the date of the closing, venture organization size and age, and dummy variables denoting whether the fund focuses on high-technology or early-stage firms. We include the dummy variables for fund focus to control for other factors that may influence base compensation and that may also be associated with fund reputation to isolate the effect of the reputation measures. These dummy variables take on a value of 1 if the fund has such a focus.

We are unsure, however, whether OLS is the proper specification, so we also employ three alternatives. First, we classify funds into those where venture capitalists' percentage of profits is in five ranges and run an ordered logit regression. We code funds receiving below 20 percent as 0, those between 20 and 21 percent as 1, those between 21 and 25 percent as 2, those between 25 and 30 percent as 3, and those above 30 percent as 4. Second, we perform a Tobit regression, where we examine whether the venture organization received more than 21 percent of the profits, and if so, how much more. The use of this specification is motivated by the fact that the vast majority of contracts fall into the range between 20 and 21 percent, or else are greater than 21 percent. In the final set of regressions we employ a maximum likelihood approach. We estimate if the venture capitalists received between 20 and 21 percent of the profits, and if not, what percentage was received. We assume that the percentage received by the venture capitalists, if not in the 20 to 21 percent range, has a normal distribution. This allows us to use funds receiving less than 20 percent as well as those getting more than 21 percent. It also allows us to estimate separate coefficients for the decision to deviate from the standard range and the extent of the deviation.

As reported in table 5.2, the venture organization's size and age are positive and significant in the first six regressions. While the regressions are noisy and the adjusted R^2s are low, the results are consistent with the learning model. In the final pair of maximum likelihood regressions, larger venture capitalists are more likely to deviate from the 20 to 21 percent range, and to receive a larger share of profits (at the 10 percent confidence level).

Base Compensation

We next examine fixed fees, also known as management fees. Because these fees are a significant fraction of venture capitalist's compensation, and are calculated in many different ways, omitting them may give a misleading impression. Fixed fees may be specified as a percent of the committed capital (i.e., the amount of money investors have committed to provide over the life of the fund), the value of fund's assets, or some combination or modification of these two measures. Both the base used to compute the fees and the percentage paid as fees may vary over the life of the fund. To examine management fees, we compute the NPV at the time of the partnership's closing of the fixed fees that are specified in the contractual agreement. We express the value as a percent of the committed capital. We discount relatively certain compensation, such as fees based on committed capital, at 10 percent, while applying a 20 percent discount rate to more uncertain compensation, such as fees based on net asset value. The results do not change

Table 5.2
Regression analyses of share of profits received by venture capital organizations

Independent variable	Dependent variable: Percentage of profits received by venture capital organization						Maximum likelihood	
	OLS	OLS	OLS	Ordered logit	Ordered logit	Tobit	Profits in target range	Actual profits
Date of closing	0.04 [0.80]	-0.002 [0.03]		0.01 [0.19]	-0.03 [0.73]	-0.21 [1.07]	0.05 [1.94]	0.12 [0.61]
Fund closed in 1978–1982			-0.01 [0.02]					
Fund closed in 1983–1987			-0.27 [0.80]					
Size of venture organization	50.67 [2.54]		48.19 [2.40]	42.57 [2.86]		189.78 [2.60]	-17.90 [2.05]	117.58 [1.86]
Age of venture organization		0.07 [2.47]			0.05 [2.11]			
Fund focus on high technology	0.93 [3.08]		0.94 [3.13]	0.61 [2.41]		1.57 [2.27]	0.10 [0.72]	4.18 [3.19]
Fund focus on early stages		0.75 [2.41]			0.35 [1.39]			
Constant	-58.52 [0.60]	23.53 [0.23]	20.26 [60.04]			433.26 [1.10]	-91.38 [1.93]	-210.63 [0.55]
Adjusted R^2	0.03	0.02	0.03					
F-statistic	5.07	3.49	3.83					
Log-likelihood				-306.07	-309.52	-328.16	-461.74	
χ^2-Statistic				12.42	5.52	9.78	22.07	
p-Value	0.002	0.016	0.005	0.006	0.137	0.020	0.001	
Number of observations	416	416	416	416	416	416	416	416

Note: The sample consists of 419 venture capital partnerships whose first closing was between January 1978 and December 1992. The first three regressions are ordinary least squares (OLS) analyses, with the capital gains received by the venture capital organizations after any initial return of investment to the limited partners as the dependent variable. The next two regressions are ordered logit analyses, with funds receiving below 20% coded as 0, those between 20% and 21% as 1, those between 21% and 25% as 2, those between 25% and 30% as 3, and those above 30% as 4. The sixth is a Tobit analysis of whether the percentage of profits is above 21%, and if so, by how much. The final two regressions are a maximum likelihood analysis of whether the fund receives between 20% and 21% of profits, and if not, what the level is, assuming a normal distribution for those observations not between 20% and 21%. Independent variables include the date of the closing, with January 1, 1978 coded as 1978.0, and so forth, the size of the venture capital organization, measured as the ratio of capital raised in the ten calendar years prior to the year in which the fund closed to the total amount raised by venture capital organizations in that time, the age of the venture organization at the time of the fund closing, in years, and dummy variables indicating whether the fund focused on high-technology or early-stage investments, with 1 denoting such a fund. [Absolute t-statistics are in brackets.]

significantly when we use other discount rates. When necessary, for example, in cases where fees are based on net asset value, we make a series of assumptions about fund performance, which are summarized in appendix C of this chapter.

Table 5.3 reports the mean NPV of the base compensation as a percentage of committed capital. Older and larger venture capital organizations receive lower base compensation than younger, smaller ones. Funds focusing on early-stage and high-technology investments have higher base compensation. The NPV of base compensation appears to have increased over time, rising by nearly 2 percent since 1984.

Regression results are presented in table 5.4. The dependent variable is the NPV of base compensation as a percent of committed capital. Fees totaling 20 percent of committed capital would again be expressed as 20. Independent variables include the date of the fund's closing, venture organization size and age, and dummy variables denoting whether the fund focuses on high-technology or early-stage investments, with 1 denoting such a fund. We find that larger and older venture organizations are associated with significantly lower fees, while funds specializing in early-stage or high-technology investments have significantly larger base compensation.

The results are consistent with the predictions of the learning model, which suggests that established firms will receive a greater share of their compensation in the form of variable payments. The signaling model, however, predicts that base compensation should be higher for older and larger venture capital organizations. Once they have established reputations, venture capitalists should demand insurance through higher base compensation. This prediction is not borne out in the data.

The Sensitivity of Compensation to Performance

An alternative measure of variable compensation is the elasticity of compensation to fund performance. This allows us to get a more complete picture of the sensitivity of compensation to performance, as we can assess the impact of both the base and variable compensation. To determine the elasticity, we calculate the NPV of the total compensation under reasonable assumptions.

We discount the payments back to the date of the partnership's formation. We undertake the calculation at two asset growth rates, 20 and 21 percent. By comparing these two values, we can examine the incremental value of a small amount of additional performance at a level of performance that is typical for this period. For example, Venture Economics (2003) esti-

Table 5.3
Base compensation and sensitivity of compensation to performance for venture capital organizations

	Mean base compensation	Mean sensitivity of compensation to performance
Panel A: Mean base compensation and sensitivity of compensation to performance[a]		
Age of venture organization		
No earlier funds	18.9	4.5
Four years or less	18.5	4.5
Between four and eight years	19.3	4.3
More than eight years	15.9	4.9
Size of venture organization		
No earlier funds[b]	18.8	4.5
Between 0.0% and 0.2%	19.9	4.4
Between 0.2% and 0.7%	18.2	4.5
Greater than 0.7%	15.1	5.1
Objective of fund		
Focus on high-technology firms	18.8	4.6
Other industry focus (or no focus)	17.8	4.6
Focus on early-stage investments	19.2	4.6
Other stage focus (or no focus)	17.6	4.6
Date of closing		
January 1978–December 1984	16.7	5.2
January 1985–June 1986	18.8	4.6
June 1986–December 1988	18.9	4.3
January 1989–December 1992	18.3	4.4

Variables	Coefficient	*p*-Value
Panel B: Tests involving base compensation		
Correlation, age of venture organization and base compensation	−0.238	0.000
Correlation, size of venture organization and base compensation	−0.330	0.000
Correlation, date of closing and base compensation	0.134	0.008
t-Test, high-technology focus and base compensation		0.041[c]
t-Test, early-stage focus and base compensation		0.001[c]
Variance test, organizations below and above 0.7% of pool		0.417[d]
Variance test, organizations below and above 10 years old		0.227[d]

Table 5.3
(continued)

Variables	Coefficient	p-Value
Panel C: Tests involving sensitivity of compensation to performance		
Correlation, age of venture organization and performance sensitivity	0.109	0.031
Correlation, size of venture organization and performance sensitivity	0.242	0.000
Correlation, date of closing and performance sensitivity	−0.274	0.000
t-Test, high-technology focus and performance sensitivity		0.950[c]
t-Test, early-stage focus and performance sensitivity		0.459[c]
Variance test, organizations below and above 0.7% of pool		0.042[d]
Variance test, organizations below and above 10 years old		0.043[d]

Note: The sample consists of 419 venture capital partnerships whose first closing was between January 1978 and December 1992.
a. We present base compensation as the mean net present value of the fixed fees as a percentage of committed capital, and sensitivity of compensation to performance as the mean percentage increase in the net present value of total compensation associated with an increase in the asset growth rate from 20% to 21%. We discount relatively certain compensation, such as fees based on committed capital, at 10%, and uncertain compensation, such as the venture capitalists' share of the capital gains, at 20%. The size of the venture organization is the ratio of the capital, in constant dollars, invested in the organization's funds whose first closing was in the ten calendar years prior to the year that this fund closed to the total amount, again in constant dollars, raised by all venture organizations in these years. Panels B and C test the significance of these patterns.
b. This category includes funds that raised a previous fund whose size cannot be determined.
c. p-Value from a t-test comparing the performance sensitivity in funds with and without this investment focus.
d. p-Value from an F-test comparing the variance of performance sensitivity in funds of experienced and inexperienced venture organizations.

mates that funds established between 1976 and 1992 still active in 1989 had a mean return of 15 percent as of September 2003, with an interquartile range of 17 percent. We once again discount relatively certain compensation, such as that based on committed capital, at 10 percent, while applying a 20 percent discount rate to more uncertain compensation, such as expected profits. Additional assumptions are described in appendix C. Figure 5.2 displays considerably greater dispersion in the sensitivity to performance than in the share of profits.

An alternative approach to measuring the elasticity of compensation to performance would be to view the venture capitalist's compensation as consisting of two securities: a bond—the base compensation—and an option on the percentage of the assets of the partnership, which would be the variable compensation. We could then compute the value of the bond and the option. While Sahlman (1990) computes the value of such an option in a simple case, undertaking such a calculation for several hundred funds with different payout structures would be prohibitively difficult.

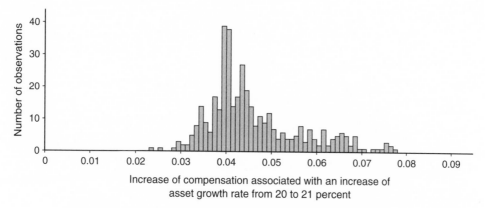

Figure 5.2
Sensitivity of venture capitalist compensation to performance. As in figure 5.1, the sample consists of 419 venture capital partnerships whose first closing was between January 1978 and December 1992. The figure indicates the percentage increase in compensation associated with an increase in the asset growth rates from 20 to 21 percent. We discount relatively certain compensation, such as fees based on committed capital, at 10 percent, and uncertain compensation, such as the venture capitalists' share of the capital gains, at 20 percent.

Table 5.3 reports the mean elasticity of compensation to performance. Older and larger venture organizations have significantly greater performance sensitivity. Funds specializing in high-technology and early-stage investments, which command both higher base and variable compensation, display no difference in the sensitivity of compensation to performance. The variance of the performance sensitivity is significantly higher for larger and older venture organizations.

Table 5.3 presents regression analyses of compensation sensitivity to performance. The dependent variable is the change in the NPV of total compensation associated with increasing the asset growth rate from 20 to 21 percent. Compensation for larger and older venture organizations displays greater performance sensitivity, while compensation for funds specializing in early-stage and high-technology firms does not.

Here are two observations about the level and pattern of elasticity measures. The first is the relatively large impact of an increase in performance on the pay of the venture capitalists. An increase in the asset growth rate from 20 to 21 percent leads to a 4 to 5 percent increase in compensation. This increase results from the highly leveraged position of the venture capitalists, who receive a share of the profits only after the return of the investors' committed capital. This sensitivity is magnified among the older and larger firms due to the greater sensitivity of their compensation to performance.

Second, our analyses have a significant bias against finding the patterns displayed in tables 5.3, 5.4, and 5.5. Several of the oldest and largest venture organizations do not charge a fixed annual fee based on committed capital or assets. Rather, they negotiate annual budgets with their limited partners. These organizations are reputed to have very low fee structures. This claim is corroborated through an examination of recent annual reports for eight such funds in the Harvard Management Company files. The funds charged an average fee of 1.6 percent of committed capital, considerably below the standard 2.5 percent. These funds are not included in our analyses of base compensation or performance sensitivity since their compensation is not fixed in advance. Were we able to include them, the level of base compensation would decline, and the level and variance of the performance sensitivity would increase for the oldest and largest funds.

The elasticity results are consistent with the predictions of the learning model but not the signaling one. As the abilities of venture capitalists become known with greater certainty, explicit incentives, typically in the form of variable performance compensation, replace implicit career concerns. The variance in compensation schemes rises over time as investors and venture capitalists learn about abilities. If early-stage and high-technology venture funds differ from other funds only in the level of effort necessary to monitor the portfolio, fixed fees should be higher, but performance sensitivity should not differ between the groups. This difference is what we find empirically.

Ex ante Compensation and Ex post Performance

Our two models also differ in their predicted relationship between ex ante sensitivity of compensation to performance and ex post performance. In other words, each model provides different predictions on whether performance-sensitive compensation negotiated at the time of the partnership agreement will be associated with higher returns. The learning model suggests that there will not necessarily be any relationship between pay sensitivity and performance. Reputational concerns lead young venture capitalists with little explicit incentive compensation to work hard and perform well. The signaling model, on the other hand, suggests a positive relationship between pay sensitivity and success. Higher ability venture capitalists signal their ability by taking more risk and then work harder. In this section we empirically examine this relationship. Consistent with the learning model, we do not find evidence of a relationship between pay sensitivity and performance.

Table 5.4
Regression analyses of the net present value of base compensation of venture capital organizations

Independent variable[b]	Dependent variable: Net present value of base compensation as a percent of committed capital[a]			
	With dummy for high-tech focus		With dummy for early-stage focus	
Date of closing	0.22	0.35	0.23	0.35
	[2.82]	[4.29]	[2.97]	[4.31]
Size of venture organization	−225.51		−214.99	
	[6.83]		[6.48]	
Age of venture organization		−0.25		−0.23
		[5.88]		[5.35]
Fund focus on high technology	0.86	1.02		
	[1.88]	[2.21]		
Fund focus on early stages			1.29	1.32
			[2.78]	[2.78]
Constant	−419.58	−680.11	−442.25	−681.20
	[2.70]	[4.17]	[2.85]	[4.19]
Adjusted R^2	0.13	0.10	0.14	0.11
F-Statistic	19.96	15.82	21.56	16.88
p-Value	0.000	0.000	0.000	0.000
Number of observations	393	393	393	393

Note: The sample consists of 419 venture capital partnerships whose first closing was between January 1978 and December 1992. [Absolute t-statistics are in brackets.]

a. The dependent variable is the net present value of the expected base compensation paid to venture capitalists as a percentage of committed capital. We assume an annual asset growth rate of 20%, and discount relatively certain compensation, such as fees based on committed capital, at 10%, and uncertain compensation, such as fees based net asset value, at 20%.

b. Independent variables include the date of closing, with January 1, 1978 coded as 1978.0, and so forth, the size of the venture capital organization, measured as the ratio of capital raised in the ten calendar years prior to the year in which the fund closed to the total amount raised by venture capital organizations in that period, the age of the venture organization at the time of the closing of the fund, in years, and dummy variables indicating whether the fund focused on high-technology or early-stage investments, with 1 denoting such a fund.

Table 5.5
Regression analyses of the sensitivity of compensation to performance for venture capital organizations

Independent variable[b]	Dependent variable: Sensitivity of compensation to performance[a]			
	With dummy for high-tech focus		With dummy for early-stage focus	
Date of closing	−0.10	−0.12	−0.10	−0.12
	[5.73]	[6.53]	[5.76]	[6.54]
Size of venture organization	36.72		36.15	
	[5.05]		[4.93]	
Age of venture organization		0.04		0.04
		[3.87]		[3.73]
Fund focus on high technology	0.02	−0.01		
	[0.18]	[0.09]		
Fund focus on early stages			−0.05	−0.06
			[0.44]	[0.53]
Constant	200.74	238.79	202.06	239.18
	[5.86]	[6.66]	[5.89]	[6.67]
Adjusted R^2	0.13	0.10	0.13	0.10
F-Statistic	19.74	15.94	19.80	16.05
p-Value	0.000	0.000	0.000	0.000
Number of observations	393	393	393	393

Note: The sample consists of 419 venture capital partnerships whose first closing was between January 1978 and December 1992. [Absolute t-statistics are in brackets.]

a. The dependent variable is the percentage increase in the net present value of total compensation associated with an increase in the asset growth rate from 20% to 21%. We discount relatively certain compensation, such as fees based on committed capital, at 10%, and uncertain compensation, such as the venture capitalists' share of the capital gains, at 20%.

b. Independent variables include the date of closing, with January 1, 1978, coded as 1978.0, and so forth, the size of the venture capital organization, measured as the ratio of capital raised in the ten calendar years prior to the year in which the fund closed to the total amount raised by venture capital organizations in that time, the age of the venture organization at the time of the closing of the fund, in years, and dummy variables indicating whether the fund focused on high-technology or early-stage investments, with 1 denoting such a fund.

Several data constraints limit our analysis. First, we do not have access to the internal rate of return (IRR) information for the funds in our sample. While this information is compiled by several monitoring organizations, it is considered proprietary information. Second, our sample consists primarily of funds from the 1980s and 1990s. Few of these funds had yet been concluded at the time of the analysis. The ten-year contractual life for most venture funds is often extended by several years. Consequently most of our funds have investments remaining in their portfolios. Because valuations of private firms are often very subjective, even if they were available, rates of return would be of limited value.

Thus we employ an alternative measure of performance, which is the ratio of the market value of the fund's stakes in firms that went public to the total amount raised by the fund. This measure is highly correlated with the fund's final IRR. As discussed in chapter 2, venture capitalists generate the bulk of their profits from firms that go public.

We identify potential venture-backed initial public offerings (IPOs) using three sources. The first is the listings of venture-backed IPOs published in Venture Economics' Venture Capital Journal. This is the same source used by Barry et al. (1990), and Megginson and Weiss (1991). Venture Economics' listings, however, do not include approximately 15 percent of all venture-financed firms (see chapter 22). We consequently use listings of security distributions by venture funds. Venture capitalists typically divest their successful investments by distributing shares to their partners. We obtain lists of the distributions received by a major pension fund and three investment managers. Most of the successful investments by 135 venture funds can be identified from these lists. The final source is the private placement memoranda used to raise new venture funds. In these offering memoranda, venture organizations often list successful past investments. We examine over 200 memoranda in the files of Venture Economics. We then examine the firms' IPO prospectuses and note each venture capital fund holding an equity stake of at least 5 percent. We identify 835 IPOs between 1972 and 1992 where one or more venture capitalists held such an equity stake. We then determine which venture capital funds in our sample of 419 partnerships held an investment in one of the IPO companies.

Venture capitalists typically do not sell their holdings at the time of the IPO, but hold them for approximately one-and-a-half years thereafter (see chapter 19). We do not know the precise date at which they liquidate these investments in most cases. We consequently value the venture capitalists' stakes at the market price eighteen months after the IPO date, using the

Securities Data Company Corporate New Issues and Center for Research in Security Prices databases.

These analyses, reported in table 5.6, employ all 234 funds begun before January 1987, which include those out of the sample of 419 with at least six years to take firms public. The dependent variable is the ratio of the dollar value of each fund's stake in IPOs, summing the amount in 1997 dollars, to the fund's total committed capital. Because older funds have had more time to harvest their portfolios, we normalize the ratio of the mean fund in each year to one. Independent variables include the date of the fund's closing, venture organization size, and the percent of profits accruing to the general partners. One concern in choosing the sample of firms to review is that different venture organizations may take companies public at different times. Chapter 16 shows that a new venture capital organization may take companies public earlier to impress potential investors in its second fund. Consequently IPOs in the first years of a fund's life may not provide a clear indicator of ultimate performance. We address this concern in unreported regressions by examining only the subset of funds begun before January 1983. For these funds, we can observe all IPOs over the first ten years of the fund's life. Neither the magnitude nor the significance of the relationship between compensation and performance differs appreciably when this subset is used.

In the first regression, we use an OLS specification. Because the dependent variable is bounded by zero, this may produce biased coefficients. We thus employ a Tobit specification in the second regression. Finally we employ a two-stage approach to control for factors that may explain the percentage of profits received by the venture capitalist. In each, the compensation measure has virtually no explanatory power. We explore several alternative approaches in unreported regressions. First, we use the measure of pay sensitivity defined above; then we add additional independent variables, such as venture organization age. In none of these regressions is there a significant relationship between compensation and performance. This result is consistent with the predictions of the learning model.

An interesting unanswered question is whether the variance of returns of high- and low-ability venture capitalists differs. The models presented constrain the variance of these two group's returns to be the same. It could be that experienced venture capitalists invest in less risky firms, or reduce these risks by engaging in active management of these firms. This question has not been empirically explored to date by financial economists, but is a topic that we are currently examining in a research project.

Table 5.6
Regression analyses of the performance of venture capital funds

| Independent variable[a] | Dependent variable: Dollar volume of IPOs relative to capital raised | | |
	OLS analysis	Tobit analysis	Two-stage least squares analysis
Date of closing	0.004	−0.05	−0.12
	[0.09]	[0.78]	[0.29]
Size of venture organization	11.79	23.77	0.01
	[1.07]	[1.70]	[0.11]
Venture capitalists' percentage of profits	0.004	0.001	17.92
	[0.15]	[0.04]	[0.76]
Constant	−6.92	91.27	−6.86
	[0.08]	[0.79]	[0.07]
Adjusted R^2	−0.008		
F-Statistic	0.41		0.40
Log-likelihood		−388.64	
χ^2-Statistic		4.06	
Root MSE			1.454
p-Value	0.744	0.255	0.757
Number of observations	234	234	234

Note: The sample consists of 234 venture capital partnerships whose first closing was between January 1978 and December 1986. The first regression is an ordinary least squares (OLS) analysis, with the ratio of the value of the fund's stakes in firms that had gone public in an initial public offering (IPO) by December 1992 to the total amount raised by the fund, as the dependent variable. The value of the firm is determined eighteen months after the IPO. To control for the different maturities of the portfolios, the ratio of the mean fund begun in each year is normalized as 1.0. The second regression employs a Tobit specification, the third, a two-stage least squares approach, for which only the second-stage regression is reported. [Absolute t-statistics are in brackets.]

a. Independent variables include the date of closing, with January 1, 1978 coded as 1978.0, and so forth, the size of the venture capital organization, measured as the ratio of capital raised in the ten calendar years prior to the year in which the fund closed to the total amount raised by venture capital organizations in that time, and the percentage of profits received by the venture organization.

Conclusions

Because they have few alternatives, investors in limited partnerships must rely on incentive schemes to control managers. The small number of general partners, and the accuracy with which their success can be measured, ensure that compensation schemes can effectively motivate management actions. The terms of the compensation schemes are clearly defined in the initial partnership agreements and are rarely renegotiated.

Evidence from 419 U.S. venture partnerships formed between 1978 and 1992 is generally consistent with the view that reputation is an important motivation for young, unseasoned venture capitalists. Using two proxies for reputation—the age and size of the venture organization—we find that the compensation of established funds is significantly more sensitive to performance and more variable than that of other funds. Older and larger firms have lower base compensation as well. Performance and pay sensitivity do not appear to be related.

The results indicate that venture capital entrants may not have superior information about their investment abilities, and may be concerned about establishing a reputation. This interpretation seems plausible. The venture capital industry may require skills that were not used in venture capitalists' previous employment. As discussed in chapter 2, venture capitalists argue that it is difficult to predict success of new partners in advance. Meanwhile investors are sophisticated institutions that closely track performance. It is reasonable to expect that neophyte venture capitalists do not know their own investment abilities any better than their investors do.

While we have only tested the learning model against the signaling model, other factors may help explain compensation patterns. A leading alternative is a human capital model. Leading venture capitalists may be able to extract higher pay than their less seasoned counterparts because more investors want to invest in their next funds. This trend might lead to a similar pattern of older venture organizations, whose venture capitalists often have extensive investment experience, receiving higher compensation as a return on their superior human capital. It is difficult to build a human capital model, however, that has the higher pay occurring only in the variable compensation. If venture capitalists are risk averse, they should demand more insurance. Established venture capital firms should raise new funds with higher base and variable compensation, if the venture capitalists extract higher pay with both components, or with higher base and lower variable compensation, if the demand for insurance predominates. As demonstrated above, older and larger venture capital organizations receive higher variable and lower base compensation. This pattern is not what a human capital model would suggest, but it is consistent with our learning model.

These empirical patterns raise several unanswered questions. First is why there is so much uniformity in the most visible aspect of compensation, the distribution of carried interest. Clustering of the visible portion of compensation is very common. For instance, many lawyers work for a 33 percent contingent fee and most real estate brokers in an area charge the same sales commission. An interesting theoretical model would attempt to explain this lack of variation within professions and the factors that lead to these focal equilibria. A second puzzle is how compensation arrangements in limited partnerships interact with the many restrictions in these arrangements. As chapter 4 discusses, there is considerably more variability in the use of covenants and restrictions in venture capital limited partnership agreements. These variations in covenants might be thought of as prices as well. Why the price of restrictions is more variable than explicit compensation terms is a fertile area for future research.

Appendix A: Derivation of the Learning Model

We assume that there is symmetric uncertainty about the ability of the venture capitalist, η. This can represent either the venture capitalist's skill in selecting portfolio companies (either through screening or through proactively identifying transactions), or an ability to add value after the investment. Venture capitalists and investors believe that η is distributed normally, with mean m_0 and variance σ_0^2. Neither side has private information about the venture capitalist's quality in advance of the project.

Venture capitalists raise two partnerships in two consecutive periods. The outcome of investments in the first fund and any investment returns are realized prior to the second fund being raised. No projects shift from the first fund to the second. The fund return in period t, π_t, is a function of ability, the venture capitalist's effort (e_t), and noise (ε_t):

$$\pi_t = \eta + e_t + \varepsilon_t. \tag{A1}$$

We use the simple additive production function to simplify the derivation of the optimal contract. We have also derived results for a multiplicative production function (i.e., ηe). In this alternative production function the feature of the learning model that distinguishes it from the signaling model presented below remains the same: early funds have lower pay-for-performance sensitivity. The multiplicative production function, however, leads to second-period compensation schemes in which high-ability venture capitalists have lower pay-for-performance sensitivity than the others. In reality, certain activities of the venture capitalist appear to be additive, such as providing contacts and advice, while others, like reputational spillovers, seem to be multiplicative.

In equation (A1), noise (ε_t) is distributed independently and identically normal with mean 0 and variance σ_ε^2. The number of projects in a venture fund is typically small enough that residual uncertainty about returns exists. At the time a venture capitalist raises the next fund, considerable uncertainty about abilities is likely to remain. While venture capitalists and investors have the same beliefs about ability before the funds are formed, investors cannot observe the effort level chosen in either fund. Effort choice is private information.

The venture capitalist's compensation, w_t, is a linear function of fund returns. Holmstrom and Milgrom (1987) show that when effort choice and output are continuous, but monitoring by the principal is periodic, linear sharing rules are optimal. An added motivation for using a linear scheme in the model is the prevalence of such agreements in venture partnership agreements. The venture capitalist receives some fixed payment, f_t, and variable compensation that represents a share, v_t, of the return on the fund:

$$w_t(\pi_t) = f_t + v_t \pi_t. \tag{A2}$$

$C(e_t)$ is the direct disutility, in monetary terms, of effort. Both the venture capitalist and the investor know $C(e_t)$. $C(e_t)$ is convex, and $C'(0) = 0$, $C'(\infty) = \infty$, and $C''' \geq 0$. $C''' \geq 0$ ensures uniqueness of the equilibrium contract. The investor is risk neutral, but the venture capitalist is risk averse, with a coefficient of risk aversion, r, and a constant per-period discount rate, δ. The venture capitalist's utility function is given by equation (A3):

$$U(w_1, w_2; e_1, e_2) = -\exp\left(-r\left[\sum_{t=1}^{2} \delta^{t-1}[w_t - C(e_t)]\right]\right). \tag{A3}$$

As in Gibbons and Murphy (1992), this utility function is not additively separable. The utility function displays constant absolute risk aversion and makes the derivation of two-period incentive schemes easier. Because investors in venture funds are primarily large institutions, such as pension funds and insurance companies, investor risk neutrality is reasonable. Venture capitalist risk aversion may result from wealth constraints or lack of investment portfolio diversification (for survey evidence, see Tyebjee and Bruno 1984).

Compensation contracts are written for each fund, conditional on the information available from returns, if any exist. The terms of the compensation contract are set out before effort is chosen or investments are made. Investors in both funds can, but need not be, the same investors as in the first fund. Investors in the second fund, however, have verifiable information about the performance of the first fund. We assume that one investor and one venture capitalist negotiate over the terms of the compensation and that a Nash (1950) bargaining solution is relevant. In other words, the compensation package evenly splits the expected gains from investment:

$$f_1(v_1) + v_1 E(\pi_1|\hat{e}_1) - C(\hat{e}_1) = \tfrac{1}{2}[E(\pi_1|\hat{e}_1) - C(\hat{e}_1)]; \tag{A4}$$

$$f_2(v_2) + v_2 E(\pi_2|\pi_1, \hat{e}_1, \hat{e}_2) - C(\hat{e}_2) = \tfrac{1}{2}[E(\pi_2|\pi_1, \hat{e}_1, \hat{e}_2) - C(\hat{e}_2)]. \tag{A5}$$

A Nash bargaining solution, which assumes equal bargaining power, is appropriate for venture capital settings where only a small number of potential players are involved in the negotiations (i.e., the number of investors and venture capitalists is not large). The model's theoretical predictions are robust to other divisions of the surplus.

The venture capitalist maximizes expected utility in both funds:

$$\max - E[\exp(-r[f_1 + v_1(\eta + e_1 + \varepsilon_1) - C(e_1)]$$

$$-r\delta[f_2 + v_2(\eta + e_2 + \varepsilon_2) - C(e_2)])]. \tag{A6}$$

The optimal schedule of incentives is derived starting in the second period. Conditional on first fund returns of π_1, venture capitalists choose effort to maximize

$$\max - E[\exp(-r[f_2 + v_2(\eta + e_2 + \varepsilon_2) - C(e_2)]) | \pi_1]. \tag{A7}$$

If the investor observes a return of π_1 and believes that the venture capitalist exerted $\hat{e}_1$ in the first fund, the investor's posterior estimate of the venture capitalist's ability will be

$$m_1(\pi_1, \hat{e}_1) = \frac{\sigma_\varepsilon^2 m_0 + \sigma_0^2(\pi_1 - \hat{e}_1)}{\sigma_\varepsilon^2 + \sigma_0^2}. \tag{A8}$$

The intuition behind equation (A8) is that the higher first-period returns are, the larger will be the revision in beliefs about ability. That is to say, the higher the variance of noise relative to the variance in abilities, the smaller will be the revision in beliefs. If equation (A7) is maximized with respect to e_2, we get the first-order condition for the optimal second-period effort:

$$C'(e_2) = v_2 \tag{A9}$$

Equation (A9) says that venture capitalists work until their marginal share of the expected increase in return equals their marginal effort cost. We substitute equation (A5) into equation (A7), and take the expectation, to get

$$\max - \exp\left[-\frac{r}{2}\left[m_1(r_1, \hat{e}) + e_2(v_2) - C(e_2(v_2)) - \frac{r}{2}v_2^2(\sigma_\varepsilon^2 + \sigma_1^2)\right]\right]. \tag{A10}$$

Note that $E\{\exp(-kx)\} = \exp(-k\mu + \frac{1}{2}k^2\sigma^2)$. Maximizing equation (A10) gives the first-order condition for v_2^*. Equation (A11) gives the expression derived from that solution:

$$v_2 = \frac{1}{1 + 2r(\sigma_\varepsilon^2 + \sigma_1^2)C''(e_2^*(v_2))} \tag{A11}$$

To get a value for v_1, equations (A5) and (A4) are substituted into equation (A6), to yield

$$\max - E\left[\exp\left(-r\left[\frac{1}{2}[(1 - 2v_1)(m_0 + \hat{e}_1(v_1)) + C(\hat{e}_1(v_1))]\right.\right.\right.$$

$$\left. + v_1[\eta + e_1(v_1) + \varepsilon_1] - C(e_1^*(v_1))\right]$$

$$- r\delta\left[\frac{1}{2}\left[(1 - 2v_2)\left[\frac{\sigma_\varepsilon^2 m_0 + \sigma_0^2(y_1 - \hat{e}(v_1))}{\sigma_\varepsilon^2 + \sigma_0^2} + \hat{e}_2(v_2)\right] + C(\hat{e}_2(v_2))\right]$$

$$\left.\left.\left. + v_2[\eta + e_2(v_2) + \varepsilon_2] - C(e_2(v_2))\right]\right)\right]. \tag{A12}$$

Taking the expectation of equation (A12) yields

$$\max - \exp\left\{-r\left[\frac{1}{2}((m_0 + \hat{e}_1(v_1) - C(\hat{e}_1(v_1))\right]\right.$$

$$- \frac{1}{2}r\delta[m_0 + e_2(v_2) - C(e_2(v_2))]$$

$$+ \frac{1}{2}r^2v_1^2[\sigma_\varepsilon^2 + \sigma_0^2] + \frac{1}{8}\frac{r^2\delta^2(1 - 2v_2)^2(\sigma_0^2)^2(\sigma_\varepsilon^2 + \sigma_0^2)}{(\sigma_\varepsilon^2 + \sigma_0^2)^2}$$

$$+ \frac{1}{2}r^2\delta^2v_2^2(\sigma_\varepsilon^2 + \sigma_0^2) + \frac{1}{2}\frac{r^2\delta v_1(1 - 2v_2)(\sigma_0^2)(\sigma_\varepsilon^2 + \sigma_0^2)}{\sigma_\varepsilon^2 + \sigma_0^2}$$

$$+ \frac{1}{2}\frac{r^2\delta^2v_2(1 - 2v_2)\sigma_0^2}{\sigma_\varepsilon^2 + \sigma_0^2} + r^2\delta v_1v_2\sigma_0^2\right\}. \tag{A13}$$

The v_1 that satisfies the first-order condition for equation (A13) will be the optimal variable compensation sensitivity. The first-order condition is

$$-\frac{1}{2} + \frac{1}{2}C'(e_1^*(v_1)) + rv_1(\sigma_\varepsilon^2 + \sigma_0^2)C''(e_1^*(v_1))$$

$$+ \frac{1}{2}r\delta(1 - 2v_2)\sigma_0^2 C''(e_1^*(v_1)) = 0. \tag{A14}$$

From equation (A12) we know that the venture capitalist's optimal effort level in period 1, e_1, must be given by

$$C'(e_1^*(v_1)) = v_1 + \delta(1 - 2v_2)\frac{\sigma_0^2}{\sigma_\varepsilon^2 + \sigma_0^2}. \tag{A15}$$

We substitute equation (A15) into equation (A14) and solve for the optimal variable compensation in period 1:

$$v_1 = \frac{1}{1 + 2r(\sigma_\varepsilon^2 + \sigma_0^2)C''[e_1^*(v_1)])}$$

$$- \delta(1 - 2v_2^*)\frac{\sigma_0^2}{\sigma_\varepsilon^2 + \sigma_0^2} - \frac{2r\delta v_2^* \sigma_0^2 C''[e_1^*(v_1)]}{1 + 2r(\sigma_\varepsilon^2 + \sigma_0^2)C''[e_1^*(v_1)]}. \tag{A16}$$

The level of fixed fees is determined by substituting equations (A11) and (A16) into equations (A5) and (A4), respectively, taking expectations, and solving, to yield f_1 and f_2:

$$f_1(v_1^*) = \frac{1}{2}[(1 - 2v_1^*)[m_0 + e_1^*(v_1^*)] + C(e_1^*(v_1^*))]. \tag{A17}$$

$$f_2(v_2^*|\pi_1) = \frac{1}{2}\left[(1 - 2v_2^*)\left[\frac{\sigma_\varepsilon^2 m_0 + \sigma_0^2(\pi_1 - e_1^*(v_2^*))}{\sigma_\varepsilon^2 + \sigma_0^2} + e_2^*(v_2^*)\right] + C(e_2^*(v_2^*))\right]. \tag{A18}$$

Appendix B: Derivation of the Signaling Model

We continue to employ the basic framework and notation of appendix A, except that we assume venture capitalists initially know their ability type η^H while investors do not. For ease of exposition we assume that venture capitalists can have two types, high ability (H) or low ability (L), with $\eta^H > \eta^L$. Effort after the first unit is equally productive for both types because we have assumed an additive return function. To determine the optimal contract that will be offered by high-ability venture capitalists, we first need to assume that we are constructing a separating equilibrium. Not only will other separating equilibria exist, but pooling equilibria are also likely to exist for various parameter values. Because we are interested in the case where high-ability types are able to distinguish themselves, we will only focus on the Riley (1979) separating equilibrium.

We again assume that venture capitalists and investors split the expected surplus from investments:

$$f_2^H + v_2^H[\eta^H + \hat{e}(v_2^H)] - C(\hat{e}(v_2^H)) = \tfrac{1}{2}[E(\eta^H + \hat{e}(v_2^H) - C(\hat{e}(v_2^H)))]; \tag{B1}$$

$$f_2^1 + v_2^L[\eta^L + \hat{e}(v_2^L)] - C(\hat{e}(v_2^L)) = \tfrac{1}{2}[E(\eta^L + \hat{e}(v_2^L) - C(\hat{e}(v_2^L)))]. \tag{B2}$$

The single-period maximization problem then becomes a problem of maximizing expected utility in the second period, assuming full information. Because we are constructing separating equilibria, information about abilities is totally revealed in the first period. Contracts signed in the second period reflect this information. For high-ability venture capitalists, we solve

$$\max - E[\exp(-r[f_2^H + v_2^H(\eta^H + e_2 + \varepsilon_2) - C(e_2)])]. \tag{B3}$$

The second fund's variable compensation for both high- and low-ability venture capitalists is

$$v_2^H = v_2^L = \frac{1}{1 + 2r\sigma_\varepsilon^2 C''[e_2^*(v_2)]} = v_2. \tag{B4}$$

The result in equation (B4) is not surprising because we assume that marginal productivity and effort costs of high- and low-ability venture capitalists are the same. Since types are fully revealed in the first period, second-period compensation differs only in the base component of compensation. This is true because the utility function we choose does not display any wealth effects. The level of expected income does not affect risk aversion. Fixed compensation for the two types is given by equations (B5) and (B6):

$$f_2^H(v_2^*) = \tfrac{1}{2}[(1 - 2v_2^*)[\eta^H + e_2^*(v_2^*)] + C(e_2^*(v_2^*))]; \tag{B5}$$

$$f_2^L(v_2^*) = \tfrac{1}{2}[(1 - 2v_2^*)[\eta^L + e_2^*(v_2^*)] + C(e_2^*(v_2^*))]. \tag{B6}$$

The difference in second-period fixed compensation is directly proportional to the difference between high- and low-ability venture capitalists:

$$f_2^H - f_2^L = \tfrac{1}{2}(1 - 2v_2^*)[\eta^H - \eta^L]. \tag{B7}$$

The optimization program for the high-ability venture capitalist in period one is given by equation (B8):

$$\max - E[\exp\{-r[\tfrac{1}{2}[(1 - 2v_1^H)[\eta^H + e_1(v_1^H) + C(e_1(v_1^H))]$$

$$+ v_1^H[\eta^H + e_1(v_1^H) + \varepsilon_1] - C(e_1(v_1^H))]\}]$$

$$\text{s.t.} - E[\exp\{-r[\tfrac{1}{2}[(1 - 2v_1^L)[\eta^L + e_1^*(v_1^L) + C(e_1^*(v_1^L))]$$

$$+ v_1^L[\eta^L + e_1^*(v_1^L) + \varepsilon_1] - C(e_1^*(v_1^L))]$$

$$+ \delta\{(1 - 2v_2^L)[\eta^L + e_2^*(v_2^L) + C(e_2^*(v_2^L))]$$

$$+ v_2^L[\eta^L + e_2^*(v_2^L) + \varepsilon_2] - C(e_2^*(v_2^L))\}]\}]$$

$$= -E[\exp\{-r[\tfrac{1}{2}[(1 - 2v_1^H)[\eta^H + e_1^*(v_1^H) + C(e_1^*(v_1^H))]$$

$$+ v_1^H[\eta^L + e_1^*(v_1^H) + \varepsilon_1] - C(e_1^*(v_1^H))]$$

$$+ \delta\{(1 - 2v_2^H)[\eta^H + e_2^*(v_2^H) + C(e_2^*(v_2^H))]$$

$$+ v_2^H[\eta^L + e_2^*(v_2^H) + \varepsilon_2] - C(e_2^*(v_2^H))\}]\}]. \tag{B8}$$

The interpretation of equation (B8) is straightforward. High-ability venture capitalists maximize their utility in the first period, subject to the constraint that low-ability venture capitalists are indifferent between offering their optimal contract, which reveals their type in period one, and offering the contract that high types offer. The choice of contract for high-ability venture capitalists in the first period will not influence the form of their second-period contract, so their program for the first period is to maximize their first-period utility, assuming that low-ability venture capitalists will not find it in their interest to mimic the high type's offer. The high-ability venture capitalist is concerned only about first-period utility because we are ruling out two-period contracts.

Taking the expectation of equation (B8), and remembering from equation (B4) that $v_2^H = v_2^L = v_2$, yields the following:

$$\max - \exp\left\{-r\left[\frac{1}{2}[\eta^H + e_1(v_1^H) - C(e_1)] - \frac{r}{2}(v_1^H)^2\sigma_\varepsilon^2\right]\right\}$$

$$\text{s.t.} - \exp\left\{-r\left[\frac{1}{2}[\eta^L + e_1^*(v_1^L) - C(e_1^*)] - \frac{r}{2}(v_1^L)^2\sigma_\varepsilon^2\right.\right.$$

$$\left.\left. + \delta\left\{\frac{1}{2}[\eta^L + e_1^*(v_2) - C(e_2^*)] - \frac{r}{2}(v_2)^2\sigma_\varepsilon^2\right\}\right]\right\}$$

$$= -\exp\left\{-r\left[\frac{1}{2}[(1 - 2v_1^H)\eta^H + 2v_1^H\eta^L + e_1^*(v_1^H) - C(e_2(v_2))]\right.\right.$$

$$-\frac{r}{2}(v_1^H)^2\sigma_\varepsilon^2 + \delta\left\{\frac{1}{2}[(1-2v_2)\eta^H + 2v_2\eta^L\right.$$

$$\left.+ e_2^*(v_2^H) - C(e_2^*(v_2))] - \frac{r}{2}(v_2)^2\sigma_\varepsilon^2\right\}\right]\right\}. \tag{B9}$$

Equation (B9) can be transformed into an equivalent optimization problem by removing the exponentials, to give the program in equation (B10):

$$\max \frac{1}{2}[\eta^H + e_1(v_1^H) - C(e_1)] - \frac{r}{2}(v_1^H)^2\sigma_\varepsilon^2$$

$$\text{s.t.} \frac{1}{2}[\eta^L + e_1^*(v_1^L) - C(e_1^*(v_1^L))] - \frac{r}{2}(v_1^L)^2\sigma_\varepsilon^2$$

$$+ \delta\left\{\frac{1}{2}[\eta^L + e_1^*(v_2) - C(e_2^*(v_2))] - \frac{r}{2}(v_2)^2\sigma_\varepsilon^2\right\}$$

$$= \frac{1}{2}\left\{(1-2v_1^H)\eta^H + 2v_1^H\eta^L + e_1^*(v_1^H) - C(e_2(v_2))\right\} - \frac{r}{2}(v_1^H)^2\sigma_\varepsilon^2$$

$$+ \delta\left\{\frac{1}{2}[(1-2v_2)\eta^H + 2v_2\eta^L + e_2^*(v_2^H) - C(e_2^*(v_2))] - \frac{r}{2}(v_2)^2\sigma_\varepsilon^2\right\}. \tag{B10}$$

Equation (B10) can be solved by forming the Lagrangian equation (B11), and taking the first-order conditions for v_1^H:

$$L = [\eta^H + e_1^*(v_1^H) - C(e_1^*)] - r(v_1^H)^2\sigma_\varepsilon^2$$

$$+ -\lambda\{(1-2v_1^H)\eta^H + 2v_1^H\eta^L + e_1^*(v_1^H) - C(e_2(v_2)) - r(v_1^H)^2\sigma_\varepsilon^2$$

$$+ \delta\{[(1-2v_2)\eta^H + 2v_2\eta^L + e_2^*(v_2) - C(e_2^*(v_1^H))] - r(v_2)^2\sigma_\varepsilon^2\}$$

$$- \{[\eta^L + e_1^*(v_1^L) - C(e_1^*(v_1^L))] - r(v_1^L)^2\sigma_\varepsilon^2$$

$$+ \delta[\eta^L + e_1^*(v_2) - C(e_2^*(v_2)) - r(v_2)^2\sigma_\varepsilon^2 r]\}\} \tag{B11}$$

The solution to these first-order conditions is shown in equations (B12) and (B13):

$$v_1^H = \frac{1 + 2\left(\dfrac{\lambda}{1-\lambda}\right)(\eta^H - \eta^L)C''[e_1(v_1^H)]}{1 + 2r\sigma_\varepsilon^2 C''[e_1^*(v_1^H)]}; \tag{B12}$$

$$\lambda = \frac{e_1' - C'(e_1)e_1' - 2rv_1^H\sigma_\varepsilon^2}{e_1' - C'(e_1)e_1' - 2rv_1^H\sigma_\varepsilon^2 + 2(\eta^L - \eta^H)}. \tag{B13}$$

Because the optimal v_1^H is above the unconstrained optimal v, both the numerator and the denominator in equation (B13) are less than 0. The absolute value of the denominator is greater than the absolute value of the numerator, and the Lagrangian multiplier is therefore between 0 and 1:

$$0 < \lambda < 1. \tag{B14}$$

Appendix C: Assumptions Used in the Calculation of Variable and Base Compensation

The fixed fee in venture capital fund contracts, also known as the management fee, changes in many funds over time. For instance, the management fees will often be reduced in later years, reflecting the expectation that the partnership's costs will decline in the last years of a venture capital fund's life. The fees may contain provisions for inflation adjustments. The base used to calculate the fee also often varies. Although most agreements compute the annual fee as a percentage of invested capital, in some cases the partnership's net asset value is used as the base. Funds will also often limit the maximum or the minimum fee, or both. A number of funds do not charge a stated fee but rather negotiate fees based on actual expenses. In most cases the contract will indicate a range in which fees are expected to fall; in other cases a budget is negotiated annually. Finally a number of firms charge fees not only on the funds raised by the partnership but also on the indebtedness of the companies in which they invest. This fee structure was commonplace in the 1960s, when Small Business Investment Companies (SBICs), many of which were commercial bank affiliates, made equity investments in firms and arranged for their credit lines.

To address the problems that arise from the disparities in venture capital partnership agreements, we make the following assumptions:

• We do not include in the analysis cases where a budget is negotiated each year, or where fees are charged on the indebtedness of companies in which they invest. These cases represent only 6 percent of the observations.

• We assume that all funds last for eleven years. Most funds have a contractual life of ten years (a few have shorter lives). Most further have provisions, which venture capitalists frequently exercise, for one or two extensions, each to extend the life of the contract for one or two more years. We repeat the analysis assuming that the partnerships have a thirteen-year life. Because most funds have fees in their final years that are considerably below the fees charged in earlier years, and the assets remaining in the funds at this point are typically quite small, we find that this change makes little difference.

• In some cases the fixed fees stipulated in the private placement memoranda are conditional on the ultimate amount raised. For example, fees could be set at 2.5 percent of committed capital up to $20 million, and 2 percent of all committed capital above that amount. In these cases we employ the ultimate amount raised by the partnership to compute the annual fee. If we do not know the ultimate amount raised, we use the midpoint between the minimum and maximum amount being sought. We know the actual amount raised for 94 percent of the funds.

• We assume that the venture fund's assets, before any deductions for fees, grow at one of three rates: 5, 20, or 35 percent. These values roughly correspond to the average returns and a one standard deviation range for funds active over the sample period. For instance, Venture Economics (1998) estimates that funds established prior to 1982 that were still active in 1989 had a mean return of 17.6 percent, with a standard deviation of 14.2 percent.

• We assume that the venture capitalist draws down funds from the limited partners in even amounts at the beginning of the year. Venture partnership agreements typically call for funds to be disbursed in a series of capital infusions. This structure reflects the staged nature of the venture investment process, wherein the bulk of the funds are not immediately needed. For example, if the contract calls for 40 percent of the funds to be disbursed at the close of the investment, and 30 percent to be disbursed at the first and second anniversaries, we treat these as three equal installments. If the contract only indicates a minimum and maximum time until the last investment will be required, we use the anniversary nearest the midpoint of this range. If no schedule of capital infusions is provided, we assume that the funds are drawn down in three equal amounts, at the closing and first and second anniversaries. For those funds in our sample with complete data, the mean time from the closing to the last drawdown is 2.4 years; the median, 2.0 years.

• We assume that distributions follow an identical pattern for all funds included in the sample. A major institutional investor has provided us with monthly valuation and distribution data through December 1992 for 140 domestic and foreign venture funds. For the 116 funds that we can confirm as independent U.S.-based venture partnerships, we compute the ratio of the distributions in each year of the fund's life to its valuation on the previous anniversary. We assume that each fund follows this average pattern in undertaking its distributions. In other words, since the average fund distributes

10 percent of the value of its assets between its fourth and fifth anniversary, each fund in our calculations does the same. If all distributions go to the limited partners prior to the return of committed capital, we replicate this pattern in our calculations, and if the fund specifies a hurdle based on net asset value, we employ such a test. We assume that the portfolios are completely liquidated on their eleventh anniversary. We explore the robustness of the results to other assumptions by repeating the calculations using two other rules. We alternatively assume that distributions, as a percentage of asset value, are twice as high as in the institutional investor's sample, and that no fund undertakes any distributions until the end of the eleventh year. The results in reported tables are robust to these assumptions.

• For those funds that compute fees on the basis of capital under management, less the cost basis of distributions and write-offs, we assume that the cost basis of distributions follows a pattern proportional to the distributions, such that if 10 percent of all distributions over the life of the partnership occur in one year, then 10 percent of the reduction in the cost basis occurs in that year. When we vary the pattern of distributions as described above, we vary the change in the cost basis accordingly.

• We assume that each year's fixed fees are paid in advance on each anniversary. These payments are almost always paid in advance on a quarterly basis, but this assumption simplifies the calculations considerably.

• If the fees are reduced after the fund is fully invested, we assume that this reduction occurs two years after the date of the last capital drawdown. If the fees are reduced after the fund is 75 percent invested, we assume that this reduction occurs one year after the date of the last capital infusion. We also assume that these events occur four and two years, respectively, after the last capital drawdown, and find that the changes have little impact.

• If the fees are reduced after the organization raises a new fund, we assume that this event occurs on the fund's sixth anniversary. We use this anniversary year because of historical patterns. Examining the venture funds raised before 1985, we find that the median organization raised its next fund four years and one month after the last closing. Because fund-raising has become more difficult in recent years, we use a slightly longer interval for our calculations. We also assume that the next fund is raised four years after this fund's closing. We find that the change has little impact. If fees are indexed for inflation, we assume that they rise at a 4 percent annual rate.

• In our calculations, we do not consider whether the fixed fee covers the legal, accounting, brokerage, and consulting fees, or whether these additional costs are borne in whole or in part by the limited partners. These charges are generally modest. An analysis of recent annual reports in the files of Harvard Management Company, which include a total of 141 reporting years covering 44 funds, suggests that these fees average less than 0.1 percent of net asset value. Our reluctance to include these fees stems from the disparate information contained in the partnership agreements and private placement memoranda. Although the treatment of these fees is always addressed in the partnership agreements, such relatively minor considerations are often ignored in placement memoranda. Rather than introduce biases due to incomplete reporting, we ignore this factor entirely. This choice will lead to a slight understating of fees. Similarly we ignore any reductions in fees due to the payment of board membership fees by portfolio companies to the general partners. This omission will lead to a slight overstating of fees.

· We alternately discount the venture capitalists' compensation at 10, 15, or 20 percent. We also discount fees that can be expected to be paid with relative certainty, including those based on committed capital, committed capital less the cost basis of distributions, or the minimum of committed capital and net asset value, at 10 percent, while applying a 20 percent discount rate to the more uncertain fees, based on net asset value or the maximum of asset value and capital under management. Distributions of capital gains are discounted at 20 percent.

6   Does the Venture Capital Structure Matter?

As noted in chapter 2, the structure of private equity organizations—in particular, the reliance on limited partnerships of finite life with substantial profit sharing—has been identified as critical to a venture group's success. This claim, however, has received little empirical scrutiny.

In this chapter we address this omission by comparing investments made by traditional venture capital organizations with those of venture funds sponsored by corporations. These corporate funds have similar missions and are staffed by individuals with backgrounds resembling those in independent organizations. But the organizational and incentive structures in corporate funds are very different: most are structured as corporate subsidiaries and have much lower incentive-based compensation. In this respect corporate funds differ dramatically from both independent venture organizations and funds associated with commercial and investment banks. Many bank-affiliated funds retain the autonomous partnership structure employed by independent venture organizations, although with a lower share of the profits accruing to the venture investors. A deeper discussion of bank-affiliated venture funds is presented in chapter 17.

This provides a natural test case for examining the impact of organizational structure on investment performance. The lengthy literature on the importance of the structure of independent, private-equity organizations suggest that corporate programs would prove less successful. Either their process of selecting or overseeing investments would be distorted or else the programs would prove unstable. It may be, however, that corporate programs enjoy benefits that offset some of these costs. A lengthy literature on complementarities in the strategy literature argues that corporations can benefit from closely related activities (for a review and formalization, see Athey and Stern 1998). Corporations may be better able to select ventures using the information from their related lines of business, or they can add value to the venture capital firms once the investments are made.

The experience of Xerox Technology Ventures illustrates both of these points. This corporate venture fund compiled excellent financial returns between 1988 and 1996 by aggressively exploiting the technology and knowledge of the corporate parent. Nevertheless, the corporate parent dissolved the fund before the ending date originally intended. The Xerox Technology group proved that contrary to both popular wisdom and academic arguments, corporate venture programs can be successful without the traditional partnership structure. However, they also showed that these efforts encounter difficulties, and the apparent importance of having a strong linkage between the fund's investment focus and the corporate parent's strategic focus.

More general evidence comes from our analysis of the VentureOne database of private equity financings, which compiles over thirty thousand cases of investments into entrepreneurial firms by venture capital programs. These cases appear to underscore the importance of the complementarities hypothesis outlined above. The successful portfolio companies—defined as those going public or being archived at a favorable valuation—received funds from corporate investors with a well-defined strategic focus. Investments are made at a premium, but this may reflect the indirect benefits that the corporation receives. Corporate programs with a well-defined strategic focus appear to be as stable as traditional independent venture organizations. Among the corporate funds without a strong strategic focus, we see significantly less success in the investments and less stability than among the focused funds.

We end with a more general discussion of the implications of these results for our understanding of the venture capital industry. It may be that—contrary to the emphasis in the finance literature—the structure of corporate venture funds is not a critical barrier to their success. Rather, the presence of a strong strategic focus may be critical for achieving a sustainable program. Alternatively, the corporate programs without a strong strategic focus may also have particularly weak incentive schemes and other problematic structural characteristics.

The History of Corporate Venture Capital Investment[1]

The first corporate venture funds began in the mid-1960s, about two decades after the first formal venture capital funds. The corporate efforts were

---

1. This history is based in part on Fast (1978), Gee (1994), and Venture Economics (1986), among other sources.

spurred by the successes of the first organized venture capital funds, which backed such firms as Digital Equipment, Memorex, Raychem, and Scientific Data Systems. Their success roused large companies to establish divisions that emulated venture capitalists. During the late 1960s and early 1970s more than 25 percent of the Fortune 500 firms attempted corporate venture programs.

These efforts were generally external but also internal. Many large corporations financed new firms alongside other venture capitalists. Some corporations simply provided funds for a venture capitalist to invest. Others invested directly in start-ups, giving them a greater ability to tailor their portfolios to their particular needs. In addition some large corporations attempted to tap the entrepreneurial spirit within their organizations. These programs allowed within-company entrepreneurs to develop their innovations, with the corporate parent providing financial, legal, and marketing support.

In 1973 the market for new public offerings—the primary avenue through which venture capitalists exit successful investments—sharply declined. Independent venture partnerships began experiencing significantly less attractive returns and encountered severe difficulties in raising new funds. At the same time corporations began scaling back their own initiatives. The typical corporate venture program begun in the late 1960s was dissolved after only four years.

Funds began flowing into the venture capital industry and the number of active venture organizations increased dramatically during the late 1970s and early 1980s. Corporations were once again attracted to the promise of venture investing in response. These efforts peaked in 1986, when corporate funds managed $2 billion, or nearly 12 percent of the total pool of venture capital.

After the stock market crash of 1987, however, the market for new public offerings again went into decline. The low returns of independent partnerships affected fund-raising, and corporations scaled back dramatically their commitments to venture investing. By 1992 the number of corporate venture programs had fallen by one-third and their capital under management represented only 5 percent of the venture pool.

Interest in corporate venture capital resurged in the mid-1990s, both in the United States and abroad. As in the 1970s, much of this interest was stimulated by the recent success of the independent venture sector: the rapid growth of funds and their attractive returns. Again, corporate funds were invested directly in a variety of internal and external ventures as well as in funds organized by independent venture capitalists. (By 2001, according to Venture Economics estimates, corporations accounted for 5 percent of total capital under management and 12 percent of total venture investment.)

From this brief history it should be clear that corporate involvement in venture capital has mirrored (sometimes in the extreme) the cyclical nature of the venture capital industry as a whole over the past three decades. At the same time, as numerous discussions suggest, certain basic noncyclical issues had a significant impact on corporate venture capital activity.

Primarily it appears that the frequent dissolutions of earlier corporate venture programs were due to three structural failings. First, these programs suffered from a lack of well-defined missions (Fast 1978; Siegel, Siegel, and MacMillan 1988). Typically they sought to accomplish a wide array of not necessarily compatible objectives, from providing a window on emerging technologies to generating attractive financial returns. The confusion over program objectives often led to dissatisfaction with the outcomes. For instance, when outside venture capitalists were hired to run a corporate fund under a contract that linked compensation to financial performance, management frequently became frustrated about their failure to invest in the technologies that most interested the firm.

A second cause of failure was insufficient corporate commitment to the venturing initiative (Hardymon, DiNino, and Salter 1983; Rind 1981; Sykes 1990). Even if top management embraced the concept, middle management often resisted. Research and development (R&D) personnel preferred that funds be devoted to internal programs; corporate lawyers disliked the novelty and complexity of these hybrid organizations. In many cases new senior management teams terminated programs, seeing them as expendable "pet projects" of their predecessors. Even if they did not object to the idea of the program, managers were often concerned about its impact on the firm's accounting earnings. During periods of financial pressure, money-losing subsidiaries were frequently terminated in an effort to increase reported operating earnings.

A final cause of failure was inadequate compensation schemes (Block and Ornati 1987; Lawler and Drexel 1980). Corporations have frequently been reluctant to compensate their venture managers through profit-sharing ("carried interest") provisions, fearing that they might need to make huge payments if their investments were successful. Typically successful risk taking was inadequately rewarded and failure excessively punished. As a result corporations were frequently unable to attract top people (i.e., those who combined industry experience with connections to other venture capitalists) to run their venture funds. All too often corporate venture managers adopted a conservative approach to investing. Nowhere was this behavior more clearly manifested than in the treatment of lagging ventures. As discussed in part II of this volume, independent venture capitalists often ceased funding to failing firms because they want to devote their limited energy to firms with the greatest promise. Corporate venture capitalists were frequently unwilling to write off unsuccessful ventures, lest they incur the reputational repercussions of failure. These general observations can be illustrated through the case of Xerox Technology Ventures.

The Case of Xerox Technology Ventures

The Xerox Corporation originated as a photography-paper business called the Haloid Company.[2] The Haloid Company's entrance into what would later become its principal business came in 1947 when it and Battelle Memorial Institute, a research organization, agreed to produce a machine based on the recently developed process named xerography. Invented by patent lawyer Chester Carlson, xerography involved a process by which images were transferred from one piece of paper to another by means of static electricity. Rapid growth and a redirection of the company's emphasis toward xerography characterized the Haloid Company in the 1950s. In 1961, in recognition of the spectacular growth of sales engendered by the first plain paper copier, the firm was renamed the Xerox Corporation.

In response to IBM's entrance into the copier field in the late 1960s, Xerox experimented with computers and with designing an electronic office of the future. It formed Xerox Computer Services, acquired Scientific Data Systems, and opened its Palo Alto Research Center (PARC) in California. These efforts were only the beginning of the copier giant's effort to become a force in the computer industry. Throughout the 1970s Xerox completed several acquisitions to further their project for an "architecture of information." Unfortunately, in assembling these noncopier companies and opening PARC, Xerox created a clash of cultures. Differences between its east coast operations and west coast computer people would severely affect the company.

The focus for much of this division was PARC. In the 1970s, PARC was remarkably successful in developing ingenious products that would fundamentally alter the nature of computing. The Ethernet, the graphical user interface (the basis of Apple Computer's and Microsoft's Windows software), the "mouse," and the laser printer were all originally developed at PARC.

---

2. The first sixteen paragraphs of this section are based on Hunt and Lerner (1995).

The culmination of much of PARC's innovation was its development of the Alto, a very early personal computer. The Alto's first prototype was completed in 1973, and later versions were placed into the White House, Congress, and various companies and universities. Nevertheless, the Alto project was terminated in 1980.

Inherent in the Alto's demise was Xerox's relationship with PARC. Xerox did not have a clear-cut business strategy for its research laboratory, and in turn many of PARC's technologies did not fit into Xerox's strategic objectives. For instance, the Alto's ability to adapt to large customers' computer systems was inconsistent with Xerox's strategy of producing workstations compatible only with its own equipment.

The establishment of Xerox Technology Venture (XTV) was driven by two events in 1988. First, several senior Xerox managers were involved in negotiating and approving a spin-off from Xerox, ParcPlace, which sought to commercialize an object-oriented programming language developed at PARC in the 1970s. The negotiation of these agreements proved to be protracted and painful, highlighting the difficulty that the company faced in dealing with these contingencies. More important, in 1988 a book documenting Xerox's failure to develop the personal computer, *Fumbling the Future*, appeared. Stung by the description in the book, Xerox Chairman David Kearns established the task force, with the mandate of preventing the repetition of such a failure to capitalize on Xerox innovations.

The task force reviewed Xerox's history with corporate venture programs. Xerox had invested since the early 1970s in venture-backed firms. For instance, it had joined a variety of venture capitalists in investing in Rolm, Apple, and a number of other firms. The investments, while successful financially, were made on an ad hoc basis. In the early 1980s Xerox established two venture funds with an external focus. These did not prove particularly successful, largely due to disputes within the firm over appropriate investments. The task force, in member (and future XTV president) Robert Adams's words, rapidly "concluded that we needed a system to prevent technology from leaking out of the company" (Armstrong 1993). The committee focused on two options: (1) to begin aggressively litigating those who tried to leave with new technologies, and (2) to invest in people trying to leave Xerox. Due to variations in employee noncompetition law across states (and particularly the weak level of protection afforded by the California courts), it was unclear how effective a policy of aggressive litigation would be. Furthermore such a policy might reduce Xerox's ability to recruit the best research personnel, who might not want to limit their future mobility.

Based on the task force's recommendation, chairman Kearns decided to pursue a corporate venture capital program. He agreed to commit $30 million to invest in promising technologies developed at Xerox. As he commented at the time, "XTV is a hedge against repeating missteps of the past" (Armstrong 1993). He briefly considered the possibility of asking an established venture capital firm to jointly run the program with Xerox, but he decided that the involvement of another party would introduce a formality that might hurt the fledgling venture.

Modeling XTV after venture organizations had several dimensions. The most obvious was the structure of the organization. While this was a corporate division, rather than an independent partnership like most venture organizations, the XTV partners crafted an agreement with Xerox that resembled typical agreements between limited and general partners in venture funds.

The spin-out process was clearly defined in the agreement to ensure that disputes did not arise later on and to minimize the disruption to the organization. The XTV officials insisted on a formal procedure to avoid the ambiguity that had plagued earlier corporate ventures. The agreement made clear that the XTV partners had the flexibility to respond rapidly to investment opportunities, as independent venture capitalists typically possess. They essentially had full autonomy when it came to monitoring, exiting, or liquidating companies. The partners were allowed to spend up to $2 million at any one time without getting permission from the corporation. For larger expenditures they were required to obtain permission from XTV's governing board, which consisted of Xerox's chief executive officer, chief financial officer, and chief patent counsel.

Similar to independent venture organizations, but unlike many corporate programs, the program also had a clear goal: to maximize return on investment. The XTV partners believed that the ambiguous goals of many of the 1970s corporate venture programs had been instrumental in their downfall. They hoped to achieve a return on investment that exceeded both the average returns of the venture capital industry and Xerox's corporate hurdle rate for evaluating new projects.

Not only was the level of compensation analogous to that of the 20 percent "carried interest" that independent venture capitalists received, and the degree of autonomy similar, but XTV operated under the same ten-year time frame employed in the typical partnership agreement. Under certain conditions, however, Xerox could dissolve the partnership after five years.

The analogy to independent venture organizations also extended to the companies in which XTV invested. These were structured as separate legal entities, with their own board and officers. XTV sought to recruit employees from other start-ups who were familiar with managing new enterprises. The typical CEO was hired from the outside, on the ground that such entrepreneurial skills, particularly in financial management, were unlikely to be found in a major corporation. XTV also made heavy use of temporary executives who were familiar with a variety of organizations.

The independence of management extended to technological decision making in these companies. The traditional Xerox product—for instance, the copier—was designed so that it could be operated and serviced in almost any country in the world. This meant not only constraints on how the product was engineered but also the preparation of copious documentation in many languages. These XTV ventures, however, could produce products for "leading-edge" users, who emphasized technological performance over careful documentation.

Like independent venture capitalists, XTV intended to give up control of the companies in which they invested. Transferring shares to management and involving other venture capitalists in XTV companies would reduce Xerox's ownership of the firm. Over the long run, after several rounds of financing, Xerox's goal would be to hold from 20 to 50 percent equity stake. XTV sought to have under a 50 percent equity stake at the time a spin-out firm went public. In this way it would not need to consolidate the firm in its balance sheet (i.e., it would not need to include the company's equity on its balance sheet, which would reduce Xerox's return on equity). The Xerox lawyers had originally only wanted employees to receive "phantom stock" (typically bonuses based on the growth in the new units' performance). Instead, XTV insisted that the employees receive options to buy real shares in the venture-backed companies, in line with traditional Silicon Valley practices. The partners believed that this approach would have a much greater psychological impact, as well as a cleaner capital structure to attract follow-on financings by outside investors.

Between 1988 and 1996, the organization invested in over one dozen companies. These covered a gamut of technologies, mostly involving electronic publishing, document processing, electronic imaging, workstation and computer peripherals, software and office automation. These not only successfully commercialized technology lying fallow in the organizations but also generated attractive financial returns.

One successful example of XTV's ability to catalyze the commercialization of technological discoveries was Documentum, which marketed an object-oriented document-management system. Xerox had undertaken a large number of projects in this area for over a decade prior to Documentum's founding but had not shipped a product. After deciding this was a promising area, XTV recruited Howard Shao and John Newton, both former engineering executives at Ingress Corporation (a relational database manufacturer) to lead up the technical effort.

Shao spent the first six months assessing the state of Xerox's knowledge in this area—including reviewing the several 300-plus page business plans prepared for earlier proposed (but never shipped) products—and assessing the market. He soon realized that while Xerox understood the nature of the technical problems, it had not grasped how to design a technologically appropriate solution. In particular, the Xerox business plans had proposed building document-management systems for mainframe computers rather than for networked personal computers (which were rapidly replacing mainframes at many organizations). With the help of the XTV officials, Shao and Newton led an effort to rapidly convert Xerox's accumulated knowledge in this area into a marketable product. Xerox's substantial know-how—as well as XTV's aggressive funding of the firm during the Gulf War period, when the willingness of both independent venture capitalists and the public markets to fund new technology-based firms abruptly declined—gave Documentum an impressive lead over its rivals.

Documentum went public in February 1996 with a market capitalization of $351 million.[3] XTV was able to exit a number of other companies successfully, whether through an initial public offering, a merger with an outside firm, or a repurchase by Xerox (at a price determined through arm's-length bargaining). A conservative calculation (assuming that Xerox sold its stakes in firms that went public at the time of the initial public offering, rather than the substantially appreciated prices thereafter, and valuing investments that Xerox has not yet exited or written off at cost, less a 25 percent discount for illiquidity) indicates that the $30 million fund generated capital gains of $219 million. Given the 80 to 20 percent split established in the XTV agreement, the proceeds to Xerox should have been at least $175 million, and those to the three XTV partners, at least $44 million.

Using the same assumptions, this suggests a net internal rate of return for Xerox (i.e., after fees and incentive compensation) of at least 56 percent. This compares favorably to independent venture capital funds begun in 1989, which had a mean net return of 13.7 percent (an upper quartile fund begun in that year had a return of 20.4 percent) (Venture Economics 1998). These calculations of Xerox's internal rate of return (IRR) do not include any ancillary benefits generated by this program for the corporation. For

---

3. The next two paragraphs are based on public security filings and press accounts.

instance, some observers argued that high expected value projects that might have otherwise not been funded through traditional channels due to their high risk were increasingly funded during this period, apparently out of the fear that they would otherwise be funded by XTV and prove successful.

Despite these attractive returns, Xerox decided to terminate XTV in 1996, well before the completion of its originally intended ten-year life.[4] The organization was replaced with a new one, Xerox New Enterprises (XNE), which did not seek to relinquish control of firms nor to involve outside venture investors. The XNE business model called for a much greater integration of the new units with traditional business units. The autonomy offered to the XNE managers and their compensation schemes were much closer to those in a traditional corporate division. As such XNE appears to represent a departure from the several of the key elements that the XTV staff believed were critical to their success, such as their considerable degree of autonomy and high-powered incentives.

The experience of XTV has several implications for corporate venture capital programs more generally:

• Corporate venture capital programs—contrary to the suggestions in writings by both venture capitalists and financial economists—need not be failures. Xerox's financial returns, as noted above, were exceedingly favorable when compared to returns from comparable independent venture funds.

• XTV's successes—such as Document Sciences and Documentum—were concentrated in industries closely related to the corporate parent's core line of business (i.e., document processing). This suggests that the fund's strong strategic focus was important to its success.

• Despite efforts by XTV's founders to model the fund as closely as possible after a traditional venture partnership, the fund was dissolved early. The Xerox Corporation was unable to commit to a structure akin to that of a traditional venture capital partnership. Xerox's experience underscores the challenges that these hybrid organizational forms face.

The Analysis

We now turn to assessing the experience of corporate venture programs more systematically. In this analysis, we use the VentureOne database (described in chapter 22). The investors in the VentureOne database are

---

4. This paragraph is based on *www.xerox.com/xne* and Turner (1997).

diverse. They include individuals, institutional investors such as pension funds, traditional independent venture funds (e.g., Kleiner, Perkins, Caufield & Byers), and funds sponsored by corporations, financial institutions, and government bodies. To understand the impact of organizational structure, we concentrate below on two types of funds: independent venture partnerships and corporate funds. By so doing, we sought to draw as sharp a contrast as possible between corporate and independent funds. We eliminated other hybrid venture funds, such as those affiliated with commercial and investment banks, because many of these closely resembled traditional venture organizations. The procedure we employed is described in detail in chapter 22.

It is worth emphasizing that it is not always easy to ascertain whether an investor was a corporate venture organization. Some U.S. and several European companies invest in companies through traditional venture capital partnerships. For example, Eastman Kodak not only makes direct equity investments but also invests through a partnership called Aperture Partners in which it is the sole limited partner. While we were able to identify many of these cases, we may have missed some such affiliations. In other cases independent venture organizations also cater to corporate investors. A prominent example is Advent, a Boston-based organization that organizes commingled funds for financial investors and other funds for single corporate limited partners. From the VentureOne data, it is usually difficult to determine whether the private equity group is investing its traditional partnerships or one of its corporate funds.

Finally, for the corporate venture capital investments, we characterized the degree of fit between the corporation and the portfolio firm. To do this, we examined the corporate annual reports for the 1983, 1989, and 1994 fiscal years. We classified investments as to whether there was a direct fit between one of the corporation's lines of business during the period and the portfolio firm, whether there was an indirect relationship, or whether there was no apparent relationship at all. In the analyses below, we denoted investments as having a strategic fit only if there was a direct relationship between a line of business of the corporate parent and the portfolio firm. The results are robust to expanding the definition and including indirectly related transactions as well: for example, when a corporate fund invests in a firm that is a potential supplier to or customer of the corporate parent. Not all investments were classified. In some cases, we were not able to determine the relationship. In others, we could not obtain the proximate annual reports. In particular, it was difficult to obtain the 1983 and 1989 annual reports for many of the foreign firms.

Table 6.1
Distribution of the sample, by year

Year	Number of investments			Number of rounds	Dollar amount
	Total	Corporate VC	Independent VC		
1983	1,841	53	1,013	436	2,386
1984	2,249	91	1,206	550	3,123
1985	2,593	139	1,382	625	3,128
1986	2,557	129	1,381	592	2,574
1987	2,675	152	1,397	642	3,295
1988	2,599	179	1,385	611	2,889
1989	2,866	202	1,490	720	3,299
1990	2,826	233	1,455	784	3,913
1991	2,890	249	1,472	757	3,448
1992	3,166	214	1,699	911	4,183
1993	3,118	198	1,586	931	4,872
1994	2,984	193	1,601	947	5,346
Total	32,364	2,032	17,067	8,506	42,457

Note: The table depicts the number of venture capital investments in the VentureOne sample by year between 1983 and 1994, as well as the number of financing rounds (a round may consist of several investments by different investors) and the aggregate amount of funding disbursed (in millions of 1997 dollars). Similar tabulations of the number of investments are presented for corporate and independent venture funds.

Summary Statistics

Table 6.1 provides an overview of the sample by year. After the deletions noted above, the sample consists of 32,364 investments. Investments by independent venture funds represent over one-half of the total transactions in the sample. Corporate venture investments represent a much smaller share, about 6 percent. Because on average about four investors participate in each financing round, the number of rounds—8,506—is significantly smaller. In the discussion below, we will analyze patterns on both the investment and round levels.

Table 6.2 provides a comparison of four categories of investments: the total sample, those by corporate and independent venture capital organizations, and corporate investments where there was a strategic fit between the parent and the portfolio firm. In general, the corporate investments closely resemble those of the other funds:

• Status at time of investment. Corporate funds tend to invest slightly less frequently in start-up and mature private firms. Instead, they are dis-

Table 6.2
Characteristics of firms at the time of investment

	Entire sample	Corporate VC only	Corporate VC and strategic fit	Independent VC only
Status at time of investment				
Start-up	9.8%	7.1%	6.4%	10.4%
Development	30.5	33.6	35.9	31.2
Beta	4.1	5.5	6.4	4.1
Shipping	45.5	44.4	42.9	44.8
Profitable	7.6	6.9	5.6	7.3
Re-start	2.4	2.5	2.8	2.3
Location of firm				
All western United States	59.7%	63.7%	59.6%	60.8%
California	51.6	53.7	51.3	52.7
All eastern United States	24.1	25.2	29.1	23.4
Massachusetts	12.8	14.0	16.5	12.6
Industry of firm				
Medical	25.5%	25.9%	24.2%	24.2%
Computer hardware	16.7	17.0	16.2	16.8
Communications	14.5	14.2	22.1	15.5
Computer software/on-line services	15.1	15.1	14.0	16.2
Other	28.1	27.9	23.5	27.3
Round of investment				
Mean	2.4	2.8	2.9	2.4
Median	2	3	3	2
Age of firm at time of investment				
Mean	3.9	4.0	4.2	3.8
Median	3.0	3.3	3.4	2.8
Amount invested in venture round				
Mean	6.6	6.7	6.5	6.1
Median	4.6	4.8	5.1	4.5

Note: The sample consists of 32,364 investments in privately held venture-backed firms between 1983 and 1994. The table presents the stage of the firm's development at the time of the investment, the geographic location of the firm, the industry of the firm, the ordinal rank of the venture round, the age of the firm at the time of the investment (in years), and the amount of the investment in the financing round (in millions of 1997 dollars). Separate tabulations are presented for investments by corporate venture firms, corporate funds where there was a strategic fit between the parent and portfolio firms, and independent venture funds.

proportionately represented among companies in the middle stages such as "development" or "beta."[5]

• Location of firm. The sample disproportionately includes investments in firms based in California. This reflects VentureOne's greater coverage of this region, particularly in the early years. While corporate venture investments as a whole are slightly more common in California than other venture investments, corporate investments with a strong strategic fit are more frequent elsewhere.

• Industry of the firm. Venture capital investments tend to focus on a few high-technology industries. This is even more true for corporate venture investments with a strategic focus.

• Maturity of firm and investment characteristics. Corporate venture funds tend to invest in later and larger financing rounds and in slightly older firms than other venture funds.

Success of Investments

We now consider the success of the investments by the various types of venture organizations. In accord with the importance of the independent venture organizations' partnership structure noted above, these investors should have the greatest success. From our suggestion that corporate investors may benefit from complementarities with their existing lines of business, corporate investments should also perform well where there is a strong strategic fit.

The measurement of returns presents some challenging issues. Ideally we would capture the direct and indirect returns to each class of venture investor. Unfortunately, because VentureOne does not compile the stake held by each investor, we cannot compute the direct financial returns for particular investors. Furthermore it is difficult to identify the indirect benefits—for example, an insight that leads to a redirected research program in a corporate laboratory—that corporate venture investors receive, much less quantify these benefits. As a result we employ two less satisfactory, but more tractable measures.

The first is the success of the firm receiving the funds. This is likely to be a reasonable measure for traditional venture groups. As noted above, traditional venture capitalists generate the bulk of their profits from firms that go public. This measure is also likely to have some validity for corporate ven-

---

5. See the appendix to this chapter for definitions of stages, regions, and industries.

Table 6.3
Status of firms in the spring of 1998

Status in the Spring of 1998	Entire sample	Corporate VC only	Corporate VC and strategic fit	Independent VC only
Panel A: Status of firms[a]				
Initial public offering completed	31.1%	35.1%	39.3%	30.6%
Registration statement filed	0.7	0.2	0.3	0.7
Acquired	29.0	29.0	27.5	30.3
Still privately held	20.6	21.1	18.3	19.7
Liquidated	18.7	14.6	14.7	18.7

	Probability of IPO	Probability of IPO, registration, or acquisition at $>2 \times$ value	Probability of not liquidated
Panel B: p-Value, tests of equality of firm status[b]			
Corporate VC vs. all others	0.000	0.002	0.000
Independent VC vs. all others	0.043	0.557	0.796
Corporate VC vs. independent VC	0.000	0.005	0.000
Corporate VC and strategic fit vs. independent VC	0.000	0.000	0.006

Note: The sample consists of 32,364 investments in privately held venture-backed firms between 1983 and 1994.
a. Panel A presents the status of the firms in the spring of 1998. Separate tabulations are presented for investments by corporate venture firms, corporate funds where there was a strategic fit between the parent and portfolio firms, and independent venture funds.
b. Panel B presents the p-values from Pearson χ^2-tests of the equality of three outcomes (completion of an initial public offering; IPO or filing of a registration statement or acquisition at twice [in inflation-adjusted dollars] the post-money valuation at the time of the investment; and not being liquidated) in different subsamples.

ture investors. If the venture fails, the key people and knowledge are likely to be scattered, and the benefits to the corporation are likely to be few. A more successful venture may or may not provide indirect benefits to the corporate parent, but at least should have attractive financial returns.

Table 6.3 presents the status of the firm in the spring of 1998 for four classes of investors as well as tests of the statistical significance of the differences between them. Firms backed by corporate venture groups are significantly more likely to have gone public than those financed by other organizations and are less likely to have been liquidated. These differences are particularly strong for the investments where there was a strategic tie between the corporate parent and the portfolio firm. These comparisons may be influenced, however, by differences among the firms backed by corporate and other venture investors.

To address this concern, we examine these patterns in a regression framework. We estimate logit regressions, alternatively using each investment and each financing round as observations. We seek to explain the probability that the investment had gone public by the spring of 1998 or the probability that the firm had gone public, filed a registration with the U.S. Securities and Exchange Commission (a preliminary step before going public), or been acquired for a valuation of at least twice the post-money valuation[6] of the financing.[7] As independent variables, we use the age of the firm at the time of the investment and the ordinal rank of the investment round. We also employ dummy variables denoting investments by corporate and independent venture capital funds, corporate venture investments where there was a strategic fit with the portfolio firm, firms based in California and Massachusetts, the status of the firm at the time of the investment, the year of the investment, the industry of firm, and a constant.

The results are consistent with the univariate comparisons above. Corporate venture investments are significantly more successful than other investments. (In most of the regressions, independent venture investments are also more successful, though the effect is smaller in magnitude and statistical significance.) When the dummy variable denoting corporate venture investments with a strategic fit is added to the regressions, the corporate venture dummy variable becomes insignificant (and frequently negative). Corporate venture investments in general do not perform better, only those with a strategic fit do so. These results appear consistent with the complementarities hypothesis above.

Our second proxy for the direct and indirect returns for corporate and other investors is the valuation assigned to the firm at the time of the investment. All else being equal, the higher the valuation (i.e., the higher price paid per share), the lower the direct financial returns to the investor (subject to the caveats in the discussion below). For each investment round where the data were available (about one-half of the entire sample), we computed the pre-money valuation, the product of the price paid per share in the financing round and the shares outstanding before the financing round.[8]

---

6. The post-money valuation is defined as the product of the price paid per share in the financing round and the shares outstanding after the financing round. In calculating the valuations, VentureOne converts all preferred shares into common stock at the conversion ratios specified in the agreements. Warrants and options outstanding are included in the total, as long as their exercise price is below the price per share being paid in the financing round.

7. The results are also robust to the use of a third dependent variable, the probability that the firm had not been liquidated by the spring of 1998.

8. As discussed at length in Lerner (1994), the pre-money valuation is a more appropriate dependent variable than the post-money valuation because it is independent of the amount invested in the firm during the current financing round. As we show in chapter 8, the amount invested may vary with many considerations, including the fund-raising environment.

Table 6.4
Logit regression analyses of firms in the spring of 1998

Independent variable[a]	Observations are investments				Observations are rounds	
	Did firm go public?		Did firm go public, register, or have favorable acquisition?		Did firm go public?	
Age of firm at time of financing	-0.02 [5.52]	-0.02 [0.50]	-0.02 [6.17]	-0.02 [6.13]	-0.02 [2.47]	-0.02 [2.50]
Round number	0.13 [11.39]	0.13 [11.18]	0.13 [11.48]	0.13 [11.29]	0.17 [7.13]	0.16 [6.95]
Corporate venture investment	0.15 [2.54]	-0.19 [1.31]	0.12 [2.15]	-0.23 [1.64]	0.20 [2.87]	0.03 [0.31]
Independent venture investment	-0.003 [0.09]	-0.002 [0.07]	0.07 [2.54]	0.07 [2.56]	0.14 [1.92]	0.13 [1.82]
Corporate investment and strategic fit		0.52 [3.15]		0.57 [3.55]		0.40 [3.32]
Firm based in California	0.30 [9.29]	0.29 [8.96]	0.23 [7.44]	0.22 [6.98]	0.25 [3.96]	0.26 [4.04]
Firm based in Massachusetts	0.36 [7.83]	0.36 [7.75]	0.24 [5.26]	0.23 [5.04]	0.25 [2.77]	0.25 [2.71]
Firm in development stage	0.44 [7.73]	0.42 [7.27]	0.38 [6.99]	0.35 [6.41]	0.37 [3.70]	0.36 [3.68]
Firm in beta stage	0.25 [2.83]	0.22 [2.50]	0.14 [1.60]	0.11 [1.24]	0.13 [0.70]	0.13 [0.69]
Firm in shipping stage	0.38 [6.28]	0.36 [5.95]	0.30 [5.20]	0.28 [4.82]	0.33 [3.12]	0.34 [3.23]
Firm in profitable stage	1.32 [17.08]	1.30 [16.61]	1.10 [14.77]	1.08 [14.27]	1.44 [10.52]	1.46 [10.65]
Firm in re-start stage	-0.56 [4.20]	-0.56 [4.19]	-0.43 [3.64]	-0.45 [3.71]	-0.45 [1.70]	-0.45 [1.68]
Log-likelihood	-14743.6	-14252.0	-15477.4	-14973.7	-3694.4	-3688.9
χ^2-Statistic	2409.9	2362.4	2065.5	2025.7	609.0	620.1
p-Value	0.000	0.000	0.000	0.000	0.000	0.000
Number of observations	24,515	23,740	24,515	23,740	6,445	6,445

Note: The sample in the first four regressions consists of 32,364 investments in privately held, venture-backed firms between 1983 and 1994; in the fifth and sixth regressions, 8,506 financing rounds of privately held, venture-backed firms between 1983 and 1994. The dependent variable in the first, second, fifth, and sixth regressions is a dummy variable that takes on the value of one if the firm had gone public by the spring of 1998. In the third and fourth regressions, the dummy takes the value of one if the firm had gone public, filed a registration statement, or been acquired at twice (in inflation-adjusted dollars) the post-money valuation at the time of the investment by the spring of 1998. [Absolute t-statistics are in brackets.]
a. Independent variables include the age of the firm at the time of the investment, the ordinal rank of the investment round, and dummy variables denoting investments by corporate and independent venture capital funds, corporate venture investments where there was a strategic fit with the portfolio firm, firms based in California and Massachusetts, the status of the firm at the time of the investment, the year of the investment (not reported), the industry of firm (not reported), and a constant (not reported). All dummy variables take on the value of one if the answer to the posed question is in the affirmative.

Table 6.5
Pre-money valuation at the time of financing

	Mean	Median
Panel A: Pre-money valuation at time of financing[a]		
Entire sample	20.1	12.9
Corporate VC only	28.5	17.4
Corporate VC and strategic fit	26.9	15.9
Independent VC only	18.1	11.7
Panel B: p-Value, tests of equality of pre-money valuations[b]		
Corporate VC vs. all others	0.0	0.0
Independent VC vs. all others	0.0	0.0
Corporate VC vs. independent VC	0.0	0.0
Corporate VC and strategic fit vs. independent VC	0.0	0.0

Note: The sample consists of 32,364 investments in privately held venture-backed firms between 1983 and 1994.
a. Panel A presents the mean and median pre-money valuation of the firms at the time of the financing in 1994 dollars. The pre-money valuation is defined as the product of the price paid per share in the financing round and the shares outstanding prior to the financing round. Separate tabulations are presented for investments by corporate venture firms, corporate funds where there was a strategic fit between the parent and portfolio firms, and independent venture funds.
b. Panel B presents the *p*-values from *t*-tests and Wilcoxon rank-sum tests of the equality of the mean and median valuations in different subsamples.

Table 6.5 presents the pre-money valuations for four classes of investors tabulated above, as well as tests of the statistical significance of these differences. Corporate venture funds appear to pay significantly more, with a mean pre-money valuation of $28.5 million versus an average of $18.1 million for the independent venture firms. Corporate investments in which there is a strategic fit are also priced at a premium, but the average price ($26.9 million) is lower than the other corporate investments.

Once again, we seek to corroborate these patterns through a regression analysis (table 6.6). We estimate a hedonic regression, seeking to explain the logarithm of the pre-money valuations (see chapter 9 for a detailed discussion of this methodology). We again use each investment and each financing round as observations. As independent variables we use the logarithm of the age of the firm at the time of the investment and the logarithm of the ordinal rank of the investment round. We employ dummy variables denoting investments by corporate and independent venture capital funds, corporate venture investments where there was a strategic fit with the portfolio firm, firms based in California and Massachusetts, the status of the firm at the time of the investment, the year of the investment, the industry of firm, and a constant.

We find results similar to those in the univariate comparisons. Corporate venture investments are associated with between 18 and 30 percent higher valuations, while those by independent funds are associated with between 7 and 18 percent lower valuations. The dummy variable denoting corporate venture investments with a strategic fit is inconsistent in sign and never significant.

These results suggest two possible interpretations. First, traditional venture investors and entrepreneurs could be exploiting the relative inexperience of the corporate venture investors, persuading them to invest in overvalued transactions (e.g., see AbuZayyad et al. 1996). Second, corporate investors are likely to enjoy some indirect benefits from their involvement with portfolio firms that independent venture firms do not enjoy. Standard bargaining models (Nash 1950) suggest that the additional surplus enjoyed by the corporation will lead to corporate venture capitalists investing at higher prices than others. Some of this value created by the investment will be shared with the young firm and its investors.

Disentangling these interpretations is difficult. Nevertheless, we are struck by the lack of a relationship between the price premium paid and the degree of strategic fit. We suggest that this may reflect the fact that corporations are also more savvy investors in companies close to their existing lines of business. While the indirect benefits to the parent may be greater in these instances resulting in a willingness to pay more, its understanding of the market is also likely to be better. As a result the corporation may be less likely to invest in overpriced transactions in these cases. In areas outside the corporation's experience, overpaying for investments may be a more common phenomenon. This appears to be supported by the data.

Duration of Programs

We finally consider the duration of the venture organizations. Table 6.7 presents several measures of the stability of these organizations. First, we examine the total number of investments in the sample. Similarly we examine the time span (in years) between the first and the last investment in the sample by each venture organization. (A venture organization that made a single investment would be coded as having a time span of zero.)

Both of these measures, however, are somewhat problematic. Many corporate venture programs have begun in recent years. As a result they would have made only few investments to date. This does not imply, however, that they will not continue to exist for a long time in the future. To control for this "vintage effect," we create a third measure: the time between the first

Table 6.6
Ordinary least squares regression analyses of pre-money valuation at the time of the financing

	Observations are investments		Observations are rounds	
Logarithm of age of firm	0.14 [11.32]	0.14 [11.26]	0.15 [6.01]	0.15 [6.00]
Logarithm of round number	0.68 [49.43]	0.69 [48.94]	0.68 [24.09]	0.68 [24.04]
Corporate venture investment	0.18 [7.39]	0.26 [4.38]	0.30 [9.43]	0.27 [6.76]
Independent venture investment	−0.07 [5.76]	−0.07 [5.75]	−0.18 [4.85]	−0.18 [4.91]
Corporate investment and strategic fit		−0.09 [1.37]		0.07 [1.22]
Firm based in California	0.20 [14.78]	0.20 [14.54]	0.14 [4.76]	0.14 [4.80]
Firm based in Massachusetts	0.06 [2.79]	0.06 [2.82]	0.03 [0.61]	0.03 [0.59]
Firm in development stage	0.40 [14.08]	0.38 [13.30]	0.37 [7.01]	0.37 [6.99]
Firm in beta stage	0.51 [13.24]	0.50 [12.81]	0.48 [6.11]	0.48 [6.10]
Firm in shipping stage	0.58 [18.86]	0.57 [18.26]	0.60 [10.28]	0.60 [10.30]
Firm in profitable stage	1.10 [29.06]	1.09 [28.61]	1.15 [15.51]	1.15 [15.54]
Firm in re-start stage	−0.85 [17.22]	−0.84 [17.00]	−0.72 [7.04]	−0.72 [7.04]
Adjusted R^2	0.39	0.39	0.43	0.43
F-Statistic	397.1	371.5	102.03	98.32
p-Value	0.000	0.000	0.000	0.000
Number of observations	15,895	15,406	3,544	3,544

Note: The sample in the first two regressions consists of 32,364 investments in privately held, venture-backed firms between 1983 and 1994 in third and fourth regressions, 8,506 financing rounds of privately held, venture-backed firms between 1983 and 1994. The dependent variable is the logarithm of the pre-money valuation of the firms at the time of the financing in 1994 dollars. The pre-money valuation is defined as the product of the price paid per share in the financing round and the shares outstanding prior to the financing round. Independent variables include the logarithm of the age of the firm at the time of the investment, the logarithm of the ordinal rank of the investment round, and dummy variables denoting investments by corporate and independent venture capital funds, corporate venture investments where there was a strategic fit with the portfolio firm, firms based in California and Massachusetts, the status of the firm at the time of the investment, the year of the investment (not reported), the industry of firm (not reported), and a constant (not reported). All dummy variables take on the value of one if the answer to the posed question is in the affirmative. [Absolute *t*-statistics are in brackets.]

Table 6.7
Duration of investment programs

	Number of investments		Time span		Ratio of active to possible time span	
	Mean	Median	Mean	Median	Mean	Median
Panel A: Duration of investment programs[a]						
Entire sample	22.3	4	4.6	3.8	51.7%	58.7
Corporate VC only	4.4	2	2.5	1.0	34.8%	21.8
Corporate VC and strategic fit	9.8	4	4.4	4.2	55.6%	71.5
Independent VC only	43.5	21	7.1	8.0	71.7%	90.4
Panel B: p-Value, tests of equality of investment program duration[b]						
Corporate VC vs. independent VC	0.000	0.000	0.000	0.000	0.000	0.000
Corporate VC and strategic fit vs. independent VC	0.000	0.000	0.000	0.000	0.001	0.000

Note: The sample consists of 19,099 investments by 855 corporate and independent venture funds in privately held firms between 1983 and 1994.

a. Panel A presents the mean and median number of investments during the sample period by each venture organization, the time-span between the first and last investments by the venture organization in the sample (in years), and the time-span between the first and last investments by the venture organization in the sample, expressed as a percentage of the time-span from the first investment by the venture organization to December 1994. Separate tabulations are presented for investments by corporate venture firms, corporate venture funds where there was a strategic fit with the portfolio firm in at least one-half of the investments, and independent venture funds.

b. Panel B presents the *p*-values from *t*-tests and Wilcoxon rank-sum tests of the equality of the mean and median measures of duration in different subsamples.

and last investments by the venture organization in the sample expressed as a percentage of the time from the first investment by the venture organization to December 1994. Using this approach, we coded as 1.0 both a long-standing venture group and a relatively recent program that remains active through the end of the sample period.

Unlike the earlier analyses, we confine the analysis (and that in table 6.8) to independent and corporate venture funds. Some of the other investors are reported in an inconsistent manner, which would make this type of analysis potentially misleading. For instance, when only a small number of individuals invest, the more prominent ones are identified by name. When a large number invest, all are lumped together as "individuals."

Stark differences appear between the corporate and independent funds. The corporations make a mean of 4.4 investments over 2.5 years, while the independent funds make 43.5 investments over 7.1 years. Even using the ratio of the active time span to the possible time span, the differences are dramatic: the average is 34.8 percent for the corporate funds as opposed to

Table 6.8
Double-censored regression analyses of pre-money valuation at the time of the financing

Independent variable[b]	Dependent variable[a]		Corporate and independent funds with ≥ 4 investments	
	All corporate and independent VC funds			
Date of first investment	−0.05 [10.15]	−0.05 [9.69]	−0.0003 [0.07]	0.001 [0.28]
Corporate venture fund	−0.32 [8.98]	−0.39 [10.77]	−0.11 [4.55]	−0.16 [6.03]
Corporate investment and strategic fit		0.35 [6.42]		0.15 [3.95]
Constant	103.85 [10.22]	96.77 [9.76]	1.47 [0.18]	−1.45 [0.18]
Log-likelihood	−586.2	−566.1	−52.2	−59.9
χ^2-Statistic	290.2	330.5	23.0	38.4
p-Value	0.000	0.000	0.000	0.000
Number of observations	855	855	450	450

Note: The sample consists of 855 corporate and independent venture funds that invested in privately held firms between 1983 and 1994. All dummy variables take on the value of one if the answer to the posed question is in the affirmative. [Absolute t-statistics are in brackets.]
a. The dependent variable is the time between the first and last investments by the venture organization in the sample, expressed as a percentage of the time from the first investment by the venture organization to December 1994. The first two regressions employ all observations; the second set, only those organizations with four or more investments in the sample.
b. Independent variables include the date of the venture organization's first investment (with an investment in May 1992 expressed as 1992.4, etc.), dummy variables denoting observations of corporate venture capital funds and of corporate venture funds where there was a strategic fit with the portfolio firm in at least one-half of the investments, and a constant.

71.7 percent for the independent funds. The differences are less extreme, but still significant, for the corporate programs where there was a strategic fit in at least one-half of the investments.

We then examine these patterns in a regression analysis. The first two regressions employ all corporate and independent venture organizations in the sample as observations; the second set, only those organizations with four or more investments in the sample.[9] As a dependent variable, we use the ratio of the time span that the fund was active to the time span from its first investment to December 1994. Independent variables include the date of the venture organization's first investment, dummy variables denoting observations of corporate venture capital funds and of corporate venture funds where there was a strategic fit with the portfolio firms in at least one-half of the investments, and a constant. To reflect the fact that the dependent variable must fall between 0 and 1, we employ a double-censored regression specification.

Once again, the corporate venture programs have a significantly shorter duration. The dummy variable for corporate venture programs in which at least one-half of the investments were strategic, however, has a positive co-efficient of almost equal magnitude. While corporate programs without a strategic focus are very unstable, those with such a focus appear to have a longevity equivalent to more traditional independent funds, at least by this measure.

We consider two explanations for the shorter time span of the corporate investments. One possibility is that this is a response to technological change. An extensive literature on the economics of innovation has high-lighted that new entrants often exploit technological breakthroughs in more innovative and aggressive ways than the established incumbents, and that these changes are often associated with dramatic shifts in market leader-ship.[10] In many cases product leaders have rapidly lost their commanding position after many years of dominance. Academics have attributed these patterns to a rational reluctance on the part of existing industry leaders to jeopardize their current revenues and profits as well as the myopic reluc-tance of many successful organizations to recognize that their leadership is waning. (In many instances, the continuing financial success of mature

---

9. This way we seek to examine whether groups that dissolve after only one or two invest-ments drive the results or whether this is a more general pattern. The results are also robust to the use of other cutoff points.

10. Two academic studies documenting these patterns (there are also many other more anec-dotal accounts) are Henderson (1993) and Lerner (1997).

product lines masks the organizations' failure to introduce new products.[11])
Corporate venture capital programs may be a response to these short-run
periods of technological discontinuity.[12] Once this transition period has
passed, the corporation may dissolve the effort.

Alternatively, the instability may reflect the manner in which corporate
programs are designed. One important argument in favor of the decade-
long partnership structure typically employed by independent venture
funds is that it allows venture capitalists to make long-run investments
without the fear of demands to liquidate their portfolios. (For a discussion
of how such fears can affect the behavior of hedge fund managers, who
typically do not have these protections, see Shleifer and Vishny 1997a.)
Corporate venture funds are typically structured as corporate divisions or
affiliates without the protections afforded by a legal partnership agreement.
Furthermore field research suggests that corporate venture groups are often
plagued by defections of their most successful investors, who become frustrated at their low level of compensation. These defections may also affect
the stability of the groups. This suggests that most corporate venture
groups should be unstable.

The evidence is difficult to reconcile with either hypothesis. If programs
were generally designed to address short-run technological discontinuities,
it should be the strategic programs that were of the shortest duration. This
is clearly not the case. The structural view suggests that most corporate
venture programs should rapidly be terminated, which is hard to reconcile
with the success of programs with strong strategic objectives. One possibility is that the organizations without a clear strategic focus also tend to be
the ones with a low degree of autonomy and low levels of incentive compensation. Thus the limited duration of the funds without a clear strategic
focus may reflect the importance of the organizational structure employed
by independent venture funds.

Conclusions

In this chapter we compared investments by corporate venture organizations with those of independent and other venture groups. Corporate ven-

---

11. For an overview, see Reinganum (1989).
12. For instance, the pharmaceutical industry aggressively employed corporate venture programs after being confronted with the biotechnology revolution in the 1980s. Henderson and
Cockburn (1996) show that the more successful firms responded by aggressively establishing
outside relationships to access new ideas in response.

ture investments in entrepreneurial firms appear to be at least as successful (by such measures as the probability of the portfolio firm going public) as those backed by independent venture organizations, particularly when there is a strategic overlap between the corporate parent and the portfolio firm. Although corporate venture capitalists tend to invest at a premium to other firms, this premium appears to be no higher in investments with a strong strategic fit. Finally corporate programs without a strong strategic focus appear to be much less stable, frequently ceasing operations after only a few investments, but strategically focused programs appear to be as stable as independent venture organizations. The evidence is consistent with the existence of complementarities that allow corporations to effectively select and add value to portfolio firms, but somewhat at odds with the suggestion that the structure of corporate funds introduces distortions and limits their effectiveness.

We suggested that the presence of a strong strategic focus is critical to the success of corporate venture funds. This subset of corporate funds appears to have been successful despite its very different structures from traditional funds. This result appears to challenge the emphasis in the finance literature on the importance of the partnership structure employed by independent private equity funds. But, as alluded to above, it may well be that corporate programs without a clear strategic focus are also the ones with a low degree of autonomy and low levels of compensation. To comprehensively distinguish between these hypotheses, we would need to have information on the compensation schemes and organization structures employed by these groups. This is a rich area for further exploration, which we hope to explore in future research.

Our discussion in this chapter is related to an extensive corporate finance literature about the relationship between organizational structure and corporate performance (e.g., reviewed in Jensen 1993). More specifically, a number of papers has examined the structure of financial institutions and investment performance. Among these are studies of the performance of initial public offerings underwritten by investment banks that are and are not affiliated with commercial banks (Kroszner and Rajan 1994), the performance of loans underwritten by savings and loan institutions structured as mutual and stock organizations (Cordell, MacDonald, and Wohar 1993), and the impact of mutual fund performance on investment choices and returns (Chevalier and Ellison 1997). As far as we are aware, however, no paper has analyzed the impact of the limited partnership structure on investment performance.

Our discussion here is also related to a body of literature on private equity partnerships more generally. These writings suggest reasons to be both positive and skeptical about the importance of the partnership structure. On the one hand, a set of articles document that investments by private equity organizations are associated with real changes in the firms that they fund, measured on both an accounting (Muscarella and Vetsuypens 1990) and a financial basis (see chapter 20). They suggest the structure of private-equity groups—whether measured through the sensitivity of compensation to performance (see chapter 5) or the extent of contractual restrictions (see chapter 4)—to be responsive to the changing investment mix and characteristics of the funds. On the other hand, it appears that other factors (see chapter 4) can also affect the structure of partnerships. Indeed, certain features of partnerships can lead to pathological outcomes. For instance, policies allowing venture capitalists to distribute shares in stock, designed to maximize investors' choices regarding the liquidation of their positions, have been exploited by some private-equity groups to inflate returns and to boost their compensation (see chapter 19). As we showed in this chapter, a clear strategic orientation may be more important than issues of partnership structure employed by independent private-equity funds.

Our analysis raises several puzzles that cannot be probed with the existing data. We end by highlighting two of these. First, why do corporations set up programs that appear likely to be unsuccessful? In the sample, for instance, we see repeated examples of funds being established that do not have a clear relationship to the corporate parent's lines of business. In many cases, carefully thought-through proposals appear to have been modified during the review process in ways that are likely to substantially reduce their likelihood of success. Understanding these processes and placing them in the context of the broader literature on the problems that can beset corporate decision making is an interesting area for future research.

Second, is there an optimal mixture between internally funded corporate research and outside ideas accessed through initiatives such as corporate venture programs? Some high-technology corporations, such as AT&T and IBM, have historically funded internal research laboratories at high levels. Other high-technology giants, such as Cisco Systems, have relied on acquisitions and strategic investments to identify and access product and process innovations. The "make-or-buy" decisions that corporate R&D managers face is an important but little-researched issue.

Appendix: Definition of Firm Categorizations

Definition of Investment Stages

Start-up: Company with a skeletal business plan, product, or service development in preliminary stages.

Development: Product or service development underway, but the company not generating revenues from sales.

Beta: For companies specializing in information technology, the phase when the product is being tested by a limited number of customers but is not available for broad sales. For life sciences companies, the beta phase is synonymous with a drug in human clinical trials or a device being tested.

Shipping: The product or service being sold to customers, with the company deriving revenues from those sales but expenses still exceeding revenues.

Profitable: The company sales revenue yielding a positive net income from selling products or services.

Restart: A recapitalization at a reduced valuation, accompanied by a substantial shift in the product or marketing focus.

Definition of Industry Groups

Computer hardware: Firms whose primary lines of business are personal computing, minicomputers or workstations, mainframe computers, CAD/CAM/CAE systems, data storage, computer peripherals, memory systems, office automation, source data collection, multimedia devices, and computer networking devices.

Computer software: Firms whose primary lines of business are compilers, assemblers, systems application, CAD/CAM/CAE/CASE, recreational and home, artificial intelligence, educational, and multimedia software, and on-line services.

Communications: Firms whose primary lines of business include modems, computer networking, fiber optics, microwave and satellite communications, telephone equipment, pocket paging, cellular phones, radar and defense systems, television equipment, teleconferencing, and television and radio broadcasting.

Medical: Firms whose primary lines of business include biotechnology, pharmaceuticals, diagnostic imaging, patient monitoring, medical devices, medical lab instruments, hospital equipment, medical supplies, retail medicine, hospital management, medical data processing, and medical lab services.

Definition of Regions

Eastern United States: Firms whose headquarters are located in Connecticut, Delaware, the District of Columbia, Maine, Maryland, Massachusetts, New Hampshire, New Jersey, New York, Pennsylvania, Rhode Island, Vermont, and West Virginia.

Western United States: Firms whose headquarters are located in Alaska, Arizona, California, Colorado, Hawaii, Idaho, Montana, New Mexico, Nevada, Oregon, Utah, Washington, and Wyoming.

II Venture Capital Investing

7 An Overview of Venture Capital Investing

Before considering the mechanisms employed by venture capitalists, let us review why firms backed by venture capitalists find it difficult to meet their financing needs through traditional mechanisms. Entrepreneurs rarely have the capital to see their ideas to fruition and must rely on outside financiers. However, those who control capital—for instance, pension fund trustees and university overseers—are unlikely to have the time or expertise to invest directly in young or restructuring firms.

While some entrepreneurs can turn to traditional financing sources, such as bank loans or the issuance of public stock, to meet their needs, a variety of factors limit access to capital for the most potentially profitable and exciting firms. The difficulties faced by most entrepreneurs can be sorted into four critical factors: uncertainty, asymmetric information, the nature of firm assets, and the conditions in the relevant financial and product markets. At any time these four factors determine the financing choices that a firm faces. As a firm evolves, however, these factors can change in rapid and unanticipated ways. In each case the firm's ability to change dynamically is a key source of competitive advantage, but also a major problem to those who provide the financing.

The first of these four problems, uncertainty, is a measure of the array of potential outcomes for a company or project. The wider the dispersion of potential outcomes, the greater is the uncertainty. By their very nature, young and restructuring companies are associated with significant levels of uncertainty. Uncertainty surrounds whether the firm's research program or new product will succeed. The response of firm's rivals may also be uncertain. High uncertainty means that investors and entrepreneurs cannot confidently predict what the company will look like in the future.

Uncertainty affects the willingness of investors to contribute capital, the desire of suppliers to extend credit, and the decisions of firms' managers. If managers are averse to taking risks, it may be difficult to induce them to make the right decisions. Conversely, if entrepreneurs are overoptimistic, investors want to curtail various actions. Uncertainty also affects the timing of investment. Should investors contribute all the capital at the beginning or should they stage the investment through time? Investors need to know how information-gathering activities can address these concerns and when they should be undertaken.

The second factor, asymmetric information, is distinct from uncertainty. Because of day-to-day involvement with the firm, an entrepreneur knows more about the company's prospects than investors, suppliers, or strategic partners. Various problems develop in settings where asymmetric information is prevalent. For instance, the entrepreneur may take detrimental actions that investors cannot observe: perhaps undertaking a riskier strategy than initially suggested or not working as hard as the investor expects. The entrepreneur might also invest in projects that build up a reputation at the investors' expense.

Asymmetric information can even lead to selection problems. Entrepreneurs may exploit the fact that they know more about the project or their abilities than investors do. Investors may find it difficult to distinguish between competent entrepreneurs and incompetent ones. Without the ability to screen out unacceptable projects and entrepreneurs, investors are unable to make efficient and appropriate decisions about where to invest.

The third factor affecting a firm's corporate and financial strategy is the nature of its assets. Firms that have tangible assets—for example, machines, buildings, land, or physical inventory—may find financing easier to obtain or may be able to obtain more favorable terms. The ability to abscond with the firm's source of value is more difficult when it relies on physical assets. When the most important assets are intangible, such as trade secrets, raising outside financing from traditional sources may be more challenging.

Market conditions also play a key role in determining the difficulty of financing firms. Both the capital and product markets may be subject to substantial variations. The supply of capital from public investors and the price at which this capital is available may vary dramatically. These changes may be a response to regulatory edicts or shifts in investors' perceptions of future profitability. Similarly the nature of product markets may vary dramatically, whether due to shifts in the intensity of competition with rivals or in the nature of the customers. If there is exceedingly intense competition or a great deal of uncertainty about the size of the potential market, firms may find it very difficult to raise capital from traditional sources.

Related Literature

Jensen and Meckling (1976) demonstrate that conflicts between managers and investors ("agency problems") can affect the willingness of both debt and equity holders to provide capital. If the firm raises equity from outside investors, the manager has an incentive to engage in wasteful expenditures (e.g., lavish offices) because he may benefit disproportionately from these but does not bear their entire cost. Similarly, if the firm raises debt, the manager may increase risk to undesirable levels. Because providers of capital recognize these problems, outside investors demand a higher rate of return than would be the case if the funds were internally generated.

Even if the manager is motivated to maximize shareholder value, informational asymmetries may make raising external capital more expensive or even preclude it entirely. Myers and Majluf (1984) and Greenwald, Stiglitz, and Weiss (1984) demonstrate that equity offerings of firms may be associated with a "lemons" problem (first identified by Akerlof 1970). If the manager is better informed about the investment opportunities of the firm and acts in the interest of current shareholders, then managers only issue new shares when the company's stock is overvalued. Indeed, numerous studies have documented that stock prices decline when equity issues are announced, largely because of the negative signal sent to the market.

These information problems have also been shown to exist in debt markets. Stiglitz and Weiss (1981) show that if banks find it difficult to discriminate among companies, raising interest rates can have adverse selection effects. In particular, the high interest rates discourage all but the highest risk borrowers, so the quality of the loan pool declines markedly. To address this problem, banks may restrict the amount of lending rather than increasing interest rates.

More generally, the inability to verify outcomes makes it difficult to write contracts that are contingent on particular events. This inability makes external financing costly. Many of the models of ownership (Grossman and Hart 1986; Hart and Moore 1990) and financing choice (Hart and Moore 1998) depend on the inability of investors to verify that certain actions have been taken or certain outcomes have occurred. While actions or outcomes might be observable, meaning that investors know what the entrepreneur did, they are assumed not to be verifiable: that is, investors could not convince a court of the action or outcome. Start-up firms are likely to face exactly these types of problems, making external financing costly or difficult to obtain.

If the information asymmetries could be eliminated, financing constraints would disappear. Financial economists argue that specialized financial intermediaries, such as venture capital organizations, can address these problems. By intensively scrutinizing firms before providing capital and then monitoring them afterward, venture capitalists can alleviate some of the information gaps and reduce capital constraints. Thus it is important to understand the tools employed by venture investors as responses to this difficult environment and that enable firms to ultimately receive the financing they cannot raise from other sources. It is the nonmonetary aspects of venture capital that are critical to its success.

The issue of whether entrepreneur should seek debt financing or venture capital financing might depend on the behavior of other entrepreneurs or the business climate as a whole. Landier (2001) develops a model that predicts the optimal financing choice of a firm by analyzing such factors. In an environment where entrepreneurs choose low-risk strategies, "good" entrepreneurs are likely to succeed, and "poor" entrepreneurs are likely to fail. This stigma of failure, because it signals the ability of the entrepreneur, is enough to maintain an entrepreneur's discipline. As a result outside monitoring and expertise on the part of the investor is not as necessary, and debt financing is the optimal financing choice. If high-risk strategies are the norm, however, the stigma of failure may not signal entrepreneur quality, so investors will need to closely monitor entrepreneurs, and venture capital will be the optimal financing choice. Landier asserts that exogenous variables, such as corporate culture and the actions of other entrepreneurs, determine whether an entrepreneur will choose a high-risk or low-risk business strategy.

The mechanisms that venture capitalists use to mitigate agency conflicts among entrepreneurial firms and outside investors have been explored in depth in a series of theoretical studies. These include the active monitoring and advice that is provided (Cornelli and Yosha 2003; Marx 1994; Hellmann 1998), the screening mechanisms employed (Chan 1983), the incentives to exit (Berglöf 1994), the proper syndication of the investment (Admati and Pfleiderer 1994), and the staging of the investment (Bergemann and Hege 1998). In virtually all cases a critical role of venture capitalists is generating information about the firm's prospects. This work has deepened our understanding of the factors that affect the relationships between venture capitalists and entrepreneurs.

The most common and potent feature of venture capital is the meting out of financing in discrete stages over time. Prospects for the firm are periodically reevaluated. The shorter the duration of an individual round of financing, the more frequently the venture capitalist monitors the entrepreneur's progress and the greater the need to gather information. Staged capital infusion keeps the owner/manager on a "tight leash" and reduces potential losses from bad decisions. Because venture capital financings are costly to negotiate and structure, funding is provided in discrete stages.

Although venture capitalists periodically "check-up" on entrepreneurs between capital infusions, entrepreneurs still have private information about the projects that they manage. Thus it is important to employ other mechanisms as well. Two of these are informal monitoring and controls over the compensation of the entrepreneur.

Gorman and Sahlman (1989) explore venture capitalists' oversight of portfolio firms through a survey. They show that between financing rounds, the lead venture capitalist visits the entrepreneur once a month on average and spends four to five hours at the facility during each visit. Nonlead venture capitalists typically visit the firm once a quarter for an average of two to three hours. Venture capitalists also receive monthly financial reports. Gorman and Sahlman show, however, that venture capitalists do not usually become involved in the day-to-day management of the firm. Major reviews of progress and extensive due diligence are confined to the time of refinancing. The checks between financings are designed to limit opportunistic behavior by entrepreneurs between evaluations.

Another mechanism utilized by venture capitalists to avoid conflicts is the widespread use of stock grants and stock options. Managers and critical employees within a firm receive a substantial fraction of their compensation in the form of equity or options. This tends to align the incentives of managers and investors. The close link between investors' and managers' returns is a natural response to the special circumstances facing entrepreneurial firms. Jensen and Meckling (1976) show that if managers have little ownership in the firm, conflicts with investors' interests become likely. These conflicts are likely to be particularly problematic in young, start-up firms. Linking incentives of all parties is critical to success.[1]

The venture capitalist also employs additional controls on compensation to reduce potential gaming by the entrepreneur. First, venture capitalists usually require vesting of the stock or options over a multiyear period. In this way entrepreneurs cannot leave the firm and take their shares. Similarly

---

1. By way of contrast, in Jensen and Murphy's (1990) examination of a large set of public companies, the typical sensitivity of pay for performance is quite low. Typically a CEO's personal wealth increases by only a dollar or two for each $1,000 increase in firm value. This may either reflect the diminished need for incentive compensation in this setting for the presence of agency problems.

the venture capitalist can significantly dilute the entrepreneur's stake in subsequent financings if the firm fails to realize its targets. This provides additional incentives for the entrepreneur. To maintain a stake, the entrepreneur will need to meet stated targets.

Kaplan and Strömberg (2002) focus on the relationship between the monitoring activities of venture capitalists and the contracts they structure with entrepreneurs. Venture capitalists utilize contracts to mitigate risk. Risks might be internal to the firm (e.g., management team quality), where the investor is less informed ex ante than the entrepreneur, or external to the firm (e.g., market size or customer adoption rates), where both parties are equally uninformed, and risks might involve some element of complexity (e.g., product or technology innovation). Internal and external risk can be managed through greater investor control and ownership, as well as greater contingent compensation for the entrepreneur. Complexity risk can be mitigated through less contingent compensation, and more vesting over time. The extent of investor's monitoring activities is correspondingly associated with the type of contract written: for example, as control increases, investors are more likely to strengthen management teams, and as cash flow rights increase, investors are more likely to provide value-added services.

On a related theme Kaplan and Strömberg (2003) chart how venture capitalists allocate various control and ownership rights contingent on observable measures of financial and nonfinancial performance by studying 213 investments in 119 portfolio companies by 14 venture capital firms. If a portfolio company performs poorly, venture capitalists obtain full control. As performance improves, the entrepreneur obtains more control rights. If the firm performs very well, the venture capitalists relinquish most of their control and liquidation rights but retain their cash flow rights.

Hsu (2002) studies the price entrepreneurs are willing to pay to be associated with reputable venture capitalists. He analyzes a sample of 149 high-tech start-ups, of which 51 received financing offers from multiple venture capitalists. Hsu shows that high investor experience is associated with a 15 percent discount in the relative firm valuation. He hypothesizes that the certification value of reputable venture capitalists may be more distinctive than the actual capital provided, which is equivalent across venture capitalists. These "extra-financial" venture capitalist functions can have financial consequences, which can explain why entrepreneurs accept valuation discounts from reputable investors.

Hochberg (2002) studies the influence of venture capitalists on the corporate governance of a firm following its IPO by conducting three tests on how governance and monitoring might differ for venture-backed and non-venture firms. Venture-backed firms are found to manage earnings less in the IPO year, as measured by the level of discretionary accounting accruals. Venture-backed firms also experience a stronger wealth effect when they announce adoption of a poison pill, which implies that investors are less worried that the poison pill will be utilized to entrench the management team at the expense of shareholders. Finally venture-backed firms are more likely to have independent boards and audit and compensation committees, as well as a separation of the roles of CEO and chairman.

Why can other financial intermediaries (e.g., banks) not undertake the same sort of monitoring? First, because regulations limit banks' ability to hold shares, they cannot freely use equity to fund projects. Though several papers focus on monitoring by banks (James 1987; Petersen and Rajan 1994, 1995; Hoshi, Kashyap, and Scharfstein 1991), banks may not have the necessary skills to evaluate projects with few collateralizable assets and significant uncertainty. In addition Petersen and Rajan (1995) argue that banks in competitive markets are unable to finance high-risk projects because they are unable to charge borrowers rates high enough to compensate for the firm's riskiness. Taking an equity position in the firm allows the venture capitalist to proportionately share in the upside, guaranteeing that the venture capitalist benefits if the firm does well. Finally venture capital funds' high-powered compensation schemes examined in chapter 4 give venture capitalists incentives to monitor firms more closely because their individual compensation is closely linked to the funds' returns.

In Gompers, Lerner, and Scharfstein (2003) we study the factors that lead to the creation of venture capital-backed entrepreneurs, a process we term "entrepreneurial spawning." One prominent example of a spawning firm is Xerox PARC, whose history in this area is discussed in chapter 6. Two hypotheses are contrasted. In one view, employees of established firms are trained and conditioned to be entrepreneurs by being exposed to the entrepreneurial process and by working in a network of entrepreneurs and venture capitalists. Alternatively, individuals become entrepreneurs because their large, bureaucratic employers are reluctant to fund their entrepreneurial ideas. We find that the most prolific spawning firms are companies that were once backed by venture capitalists. Less diversified firms are also more likely to spawn new firms, and spawning levels for these firms rise as their sales growth declines.

An Overview of Part II

The six chapters that follow examine the various roles played by venture capitalists in addressing these problems. Although they are not intended to be an exhaustive catalog of the interactions between venture capitalists and entrepreneurs, the chapters highlight the diversity and flexibility of the venture capitalist's role.[2]

In chapter 8, we examine the staging of venture capital investments. The research on conflicts between investors and managers suggests several factors that should affect the duration and size of venture capital investments. Venture capitalists should weigh potential agency and monitoring costs when determining how frequently they should reevaluate projects and supply capital. The duration of funding should decline and the frequency of reevaluation should increase when the venture capitalist expects conflicts with the entrepreneur to be likely. The nature of the firm's assets also has important implications for expected agency costs and the structure of staged venture capital investments. Intangible assets should be associated with greater agency problems. As assets become more tangible, venture capitalists can recover more of their investment in liquidation. This reduces the need to monitor tightly and should increase the time between refinancings. Industries with high levels of R&D should also have more frequent agency problems, and venture capitalists should shorten funding duration. Finally a substantial finance literature argues that firms with high market-to-book ratios are more susceptible to these agency costs; thus venture capitalists should increase the intensity of monitoring of these firms.

These suggestions are tested using a random sample of 794 venture capital financed companies. The results confirm the predictions of agency theory. Venture capitalists concentrate investments in early-stage companies and high-technology industries where informational asymmetries are significant and monitoring is valuable. Venture capitalists monitor the firm's progress. If they learn negative information about future returns, the project is cut off from new financing. Firms that go public (these firms yield the highest return for venture capitalists on average) receive more total financing, and a greater number of rounds than other firms (which may go bankrupt, be acquired, or remain private). Early-stage firms receive significantly less money per round. Increases in asset tangibility increase financing duration and reduce monitoring intensity. As the role of future investment opportunities in firm value increases (higher market-to-book ratios or R&D intensities), firms are refinanced more frequently. These results suggest the important monitoring and information-generating roles played by venture capitalists.

---

2. While part II of this volume will focus on the venture investment process, we will also highlight the interconnections with other parts of the venture cycle. The strength of the fundraising environment and the characteristics of the public markets at the time will affect how the venture capitalists deploy their assets.

As discussed in chapters 1 and 2, the venture industry appears to have gone through periods when there were dramatic shifts in the supply of capital available from institutional and individual investors and the demand from entrepreneurs. These shifts appear to affect not only the terms of venture capital partnerships but also the investments made by these funds. Understanding the venture cycle requires an understanding of the linkages between the various stages. The fund-raising environment and the terms and conditions of venture partnerships can have profound effects on the efficiency of venture investing.

While discussions of these issues have appeared in the trade press since at least the 1960s, the first extended discussion was in Sahlman and Stevenson (1986). The authors chronicle the exploits of venture capitalists in the Winchester disk drive industry during the early 1980s. Sahlman and Stevenson assert that a type of "market myopia" affected venture capital investing in the industry. During the late 1970s and early 1980s, nineteen disk drive companies received venture capital financing. Two-thirds of these investments came between 1982 and 1984, the period of rapid expansion of the venture industry. Many disk drive companies also went public during this period. While industry growth was rapid during this period (sales increased from $27 million in 1978 to $1.3 billion in 1983), Sahlman and Stevenson question whether the scale of investment was rational given any reasonable expectations of industry growth and future economic trends.[3] Similar stories are often told concerning investments in software, biotechnology, and the Internet. The phrase "too much money chasing too few deals" is a common refrain in the venture capital market during periods of rapid growth.

In chapter 9, we examine one facet of this issue: the impact of capital inflows into venture funds on valuations of these funds' new investments. Studies have shown that in a public market setting, capital inflows do affect securities' valuations. We study the relationship between demand shifts and asset prices in the U.S. private equity market by examining over 4,000 venture investments made between 1987 and 1995. We then attempt to identify the cause of this relationship. For example, are increased valuations driven by capital inflows or by improvements in investment prospects?

The analysis confirms that inflows into venture capital funds distort private firm valuations. The impact of inflows on prices is greatest in states with the most venture capital activity and industry segments with the

---

3. Lerner (1997) suggests, however, that these firms may have displayed behavior consistent with strategic models of "technology races" in the economics literature. Because firms had the option to exit the competition to develop a new disk drive, it may have indeed been rational for venture capitalists to fund a substantial number of disk drive manufacturers.

greatest growth of capital inflows. We also document an increase in the probability of refinancing during periods of high inflows.

In chapter 9, we also note that the relationship between inflows and prices does not appear to result from increased investment prospects. We witness an insignificant difference in the success rate of investments during periods of high and low capital inflows. This suggests that demand pressure drives up prices during "hot" periods.

The advice and oversight provided by venture capitalists is often embodied by their role on the firm's board of directors. In chapter 10, we analyze the decision of venture capitalists to provide this oversight. We examine whether venture capitalists' representation on the boards of the private firms in their portfolios is greater when the need for oversight is larger. This approach is suggested by Fama and Jensen (1983) and Williamson (1983), who hypothesize that the composition of the board should be shaped by the need for oversight. These authors argue that the board will bear greater responsibility for oversight—and consequently that outsiders should have greater representation—when the danger of managerial deviations from value maximization is high. If venture capitalists are especially important providers of managerial oversight, their representation on boards should be more extensive at times when the need for oversight is greater.

In chapter 10, we also examine changes in board membership around the time that a firm's chief executive officer (CEO) is replaced, an approach suggested by Hermalin and Weisbach's (1988) study of outside directors of public firms. The replacement of the top manager at an entrepreneurial firm is likely to coincide with an organizational crisis and to heighten the need for monitoring. An average of 1.75 venture capitalists are added to the board between financing rounds when the firm's CEO is replaced in the interval; between other rounds, 0.24 venture directors are added. No differences are found in the addition of other outside directors. This oversight of new firms involves substantial costs. The transaction costs associated with frequent visits and intensive involvement are likely to be reduced if the venture capitalist is proximate to the firms in a portfolio. Consistent with these suggestions, geographic proximity is an important determinant of venture board membership: organizations with offices within five miles of the firm's headquarters are twice as likely to be board members as those more than 500 miles distant. Over half of the firms in the sample have a venture director with an office within sixty miles of their headquarters.

Venture capitalists will usually make investments with other investors. One venture firm will originate the deal and look to bring in other venture capital firms. This syndication serves multiple purposes. First, it allows the venture capital firm to diversify its portfolio, thereby reducing the exposure to any single investment. If the venture capitalist were the sole investor in all the companies in a portfolio, then many fewer investments could be made. By syndicating investments, the venture capitalist can invest in more projects and diversify away some of the firm-specific risk.

For example, a venture capital firm may raise a fund of $100 million. In any one particular round, a portfolio company receives between $2 and $5 million. If the typical venture-backed company receives four rounds of venture financing, any one firm might require between $10 and $20 million of financing. If the venture capital firm originating the deal were to make the entire investment, the fund could only make five to ten investments. Hence the value of bringing in syndication partners for diversification is large.

A second potential explanation for syndication patterns is that involving other venture firms provides a second opinion on the investment opportunity. There is usually no clear-cut answer as to whether any of the investments that a venture organization undertakes will yield attractive returns. Having other investors approve the deal limits the danger that bad deals will get funded. This is particularly true when the company is early stage or technology based.

In chapter 11, we test this "second opinion" hypothesis in a sample of biotechnology venture capital investments. In the early rounds of investing, experienced venture capitalists tend to syndicate only with venture capital firms that have similar experience. The analysis argues that if venture capitalists were looking for a second opinion, then they would want to get a second opinion from someone of similar or better ability, certainly not from someone of lesser ability.

Over the past decade many countries have established public entities designed to spur venture capital growth. Their hope is that increased venture capital activity will lead to greater entrepreneurialism and innovation in these countries, as has been observed in the United States. In chapter 12, we explore the premise that venture capital spurs innovation by examining the influence of venture capital on patented inventions in the United States across twenty industries over three decades. We find that increases in venture capital activity in an industry are associated with significantly higher patenting rates. While the ratio of venture capital to R&D averaged less than 3 percent from 1983 to 1992, our estimates suggest that venture capital accounted for 8 percent of industrial innovations in that period. One dollar of venture capital thus appears to be three times more likely to stimulate patenting than one dollar of corporate R&D.

We also test whether patents can be considered a reasonable proxy of the level of innovation by comparing indicators of quality of patents between 122 venture-backed and 408 non-venture-backed companies. We note that venture-backed firms' patents are more frequently cited than other patents and are more aggressively litigated, implying that venture backing does not lead to lower quality patents.

In chapter 13, we explore the efforts of public institutions to subsidize small, high-technology firms. Public programs directly financed or implicitly guaranteed at least $2.4 billion to small businesses in 1995, compared to the $3.9 billion disbursed by venture capital funds in that year. We examine the largest U.S. initiative, the Small Business Innovation Research (SBIR) program, by studying the employment and sales growth of 1,435 firms between 1985 and 1995. Two-fifths of the sample received one or more awards, while the other firms closely match the awardees in firm size and industry. We find that SBIR awardees grow significantly faster than matched firms over a decade and are more likely to attract venture financing. The superior performance of awardees is confined to firms in regions with substantial venture capital activity, and is pronounced in high-technology industries. Those awardees receiving large subsidies do not perform better than those receiving small subsidies, suggesting that the SBIR awards play an important certification function.

Final Thoughts

While in chapter 12 we take an initial look at the impact of venture capital in the economy, many questions remain. A key motivation for policy makers abroad seeking to emulate the U.S. model is the perception that venture capital organizations are a key factor in the rising leadership of U.S. firms in high-technology industries, whether measured through patent counts or more qualitative measures. Demonstrating a causal relationship between innovation and job growth, on the one hand, and the presence of venture capital investment, on the other, remains a challenging empirical problem.[4] To what extent are the mechanisms described above uniquely suited to addressing the needs of entrepreneurial high-technology firms? To what extent is venture capital just one of many financing alternatives for these firms, with its own set of strengths and limitations?

On a more speculative level, it may be possible that the tremendous concentration of the firms backed by venture capitalists is also problematic in

---

4. See also Hellmann and Puri (2000). Many research opportunities remain, however, in this arena.

terms of social welfare. Several models argue that institutional investors frequently engage in "herding": making investments that are too similar to one another. These models suggest that a variety of factors—for instance, when performance is assessed on a relative, not an absolute, basis—can lead to investors obtaining poor performance by making too similar investments. (Much of the theoretical literature is reviewed in Devenow and Welch 1996.) Social welfare may suffer as a result if value-creating investments in less popular technological areas have been ignored. These topics will reward creative researchers in the years to come.

8 Why Are Investments Staged?

Staged capital infusions are the most potent control mechanism a venture capitalist can employ. Prospects for the firm are periodically reevaluated. The shorter the duration of an individual round of financing, the more frequently the venture capitalist monitors the entrepreneur's progress and the greater the need to gather information. The role of staged capital infusion is analogous to that of debt in highly leveraged transactions, keeping the owner/manager on a "tight leash" and reducing potential losses from bad decisions.

In this chapter we examine the staging of capital infusions by venture capitalists. We explore not only how these investments are structured but also why this approach is employed. The evidence indicates that the staging of capital infusions allows venture capitalists to gather information and monitor the progress of firms, maintaining the option to abandon projects periodically.

We develop predictions from agency theory that shed light on factors affecting the duration and size of venture capital investments. Venture capitalists weigh potential agency and monitoring costs when determining how frequently they should reevaluate projects and supply capital. Venture capitalists are concerned that entrepreneurs' private benefits from certain investments or strategies may not be perfectly correlated with shareholders' monetary return. Because monitoring is costly and cannot be performed continuously, the venture capitalist will periodically check the project's status and preserve the option to abandon. The duration of funding and hence the intensity of monitoring should be negatively related to expected agency costs. Agency costs increase as the tangibility of assets declines, the share of growth options in firm value rises, and asset specificity grows.

Our random sample of 794 venture capital financed companies confirms the predictions of agency theory. Venture capitalists concentrate investments in early-stage companies and high-technology industries where informational asymmetries are significant and monitoring is valuable. Venture capitalists monitor the firm's progress, and if they learn negative information about future returns, the project should be cut off from new financing. Firms that go public (these firms yield the highest return for venture capitalists on average) receive more total financing and a greater number of rounds than other firms (those that go bankrupt or are acquired). Early-stage firms also receive significantly less money per round. Increases in asset tangibility increase financing duration and reduce monitoring intensity. As the role of future investment opportunities in firm value increases (higher market-to-book ratios), duration declines. Similarly higher R&D intensities lead to shorter funding durations.

We also provide evidence about the relationship between investment and liquidity in the venture capital market. In periods when venture capitalists are able to raise more capital for new investments, they invest more money per round and more frequently in the firms they finance. Greater commitments to new venture capital funds may measure entry of new, inexperienced venture capitalists or free cash-flow agency costs.

Factors Affecting the Structure of Staged Venture Capital Investments

Agency and Monitoring Costs

Venture capitalists claim that the information they generate and the services they provide for portfolio companies are as important as the capital infused. Many entrepreneurs believe that venture capitalists provide little more than money. If the monitoring provided by venture capitalists is valuable, certain predictions can be made about the structure of staged capital infusions.

If monitoring and information gathering are important, venture capitalists should invest in firms in which asymmetric information is likely to be a problem. The value of oversight will be greater for these firms. Early-stage companies have short or no histories to examine and are difficult to evaluate. Similarly firms in industries with significant growth opportunities and high R&D intensities are likely to require close monitoring. A significant fraction of venture investment should therefore be directed toward early-stage and high-technology companies.

Total venture financing and the number of financing rounds should also be higher for successful projects than for failures if venture capitalists utilize information in investment decisions. Venture capitalists monitor a firm's progress and discontinue funding the project if they learn negative information about future prospects. Firms going public—which, as discussed in chapter 2, yield the highest return for venture investors—should thus receive greater total funding and more rounds of financing than firms that are acquired or liquidated.

The positive relationship between going public and level of investment is not obvious unless venture capitalists use information during the investment process. If venture capitalists only provide capital, firms that go public might quickly turn profitable and would need less venture capital financing and fewer rounds than companies that are acquired or liquidated.

If asymmetric information and agency costs do not exist, the structure of financing is irrelevant. As Hart (1993) points out, if entrepreneurs pursue shareholder value-maximizing strategies, financing is simple. Venture capitalists would give entrepreneurs all the money they need and entrepreneurs would decide whether to continue the project based on their information. In the case of start-ups, entrepreneurs would derive stopping rules that maximized shareholder value using methods described in Roberts and Weitzman (1981) and Weitzman, Newey, and Rabin (1981). Based on their private information, they would decide whether to continue the project or not.

The private benefits from managing the firms they create, however, may not always be perfectly correlated with shareholders' monetary returns. Entrepreneurs may have incentives to continue running projects they know have negative net present value (NPV). Similarly entrepreneurs may invest in projects that have high personal benefits but low monetary returns for investors. If venture capitalists could costlessly monitor the firm, they would monitor and infuse cash continuously. If the firm's expected NPV fell below the stopping point, the venture capitalist would halt funding the project.

In practice, venture capitalists incur costs when they monitor and infuse capital. Monitoring costs include the opportunity cost of generating reports for both the venture capitalist and entrepreneur. If venture capitalists need to "kick the tires" of the plant, read reports, and take time away from other activities, these costs can be substantial. Contracting costs and the lost time and resources of the entrepreneur must be imputed as well. Each time capital is infused, contracts are written and negotiated, lawyers are paid, and other associated costs are incurred. These costs mean that funding will occur in discrete stages.

Two well-known companies illustrate how venture capitalists use staged investment to periodically evaluate a firm's progress. Apple Computer received three rounds of venture capital financing. In the first round, venture capitalists invested $518,000 in January 1978 at a price of $0.09 per share. The company was doing well by the second round of venture financing in

September 1978. Venture investors committed an additional $704,000 at a price of $0.28 per share, reflecting the progress the firm had made. A final venture capital infusion of $2.331 million was made in December 1980 at $0.97 per share. At each stage the increasing price per share and the growing investment reflected resolution of uncertainty concerning Apple's prospects.

Federal Express represents a second example of how venture capitalists utilize staged capital infusions to monitor the firm. Federal Express also received three rounds of venture capital financing, but the firm's prospects developed in a much different manner. The first venture financing round occurred in September 1973 when $12.25 million was invested at a price of $204.17 per share. The firm's performance was well below expectations and a second venture financing round was necessary in March 1974. $6.4 million was invested at $7.34 per share, reflecting the poor performance of the company. Performance continued to deteriorate and a third round of financing was needed in September 1974. At this stage the venture capital investors intervened extensively in the strategy of the company. The $3.88 million investment was priced at $0.63 per share. Ultimately performance improved and Federal Express went public in 1978 at $6 per share, but the staged investment of the venture capitalist allowed the venture investors to intervene and price subsequent rounds so they could earn a fair rate of return.

Two related types of agency costs exist in entrepreneurial firms. First, entrepreneurs might invest in strategies, research, or projects that have high personal returns but low expected monetary payoffs to shareholders. For example, a biotechnology company founder may choose to invest in a certain type of research that brings great recognition in the scientific community but provides less return for the venture capitalist than other projects. Similarly, because entrepreneurs' equity stakes are essentially call options,[1] they have incentives to pursue high-variance strategies like rushing a product to market when further testing may be warranted.

Second, if the entrepreneur possesses private information and chooses to continue investing in a negative NPV project, the entrepreneur is undertaking inefficient continuation. For example, managers may receive initial results from market trials indicating little demand for a new product, but

1. The entrepreneurs' equity stakes are almost always junior to the preferred equity position of venture capital investors. The seniority of the venture capitalists' stake makes the entrepreneur's payoff analogous to levered equity, hence it is also equivalent to a call option. Similarly, if the firm is doing poorly and the option is "out of the money," entrepreneurs may have incentives to increase risk substantially.

entrepreneurs may want to keep the company going because they receive significant private benefits from managing their own firm.

The nature of the firm's assets may have important implications for expected agency costs and the structure of staged venture capital investments. The capital structure literature motivates a search for those factors. Much of this literature (see Harris and Raviv 1991) has emphasized the role of agency costs in determining leverage. Asset characteristics that increase expected agency costs of debt reduce leverage and make monitoring more valuable. Therefore factors reducing leverage should shorten funding duration in venture capital transactions.

Williamson (1988) argues that leverage should be positively related to the liquidation value of assets. Higher liquidation values imply that default is less costly. Liquidation value is positively related to the tangibility of assets because tangible assets (e.g., machines and plants) are, on average, easier to sell and receive a higher fraction of their book value than are intangible assets like patents or copyrights. In empirical research on capital structure, many researchers, including Titman and Wessels (1988), Friend and Lang (1988), and Rajan and Zingales (1995), use the ratio of tangible assets to total assets as a measure of liquidation value. All find that use of debt increases with asset tangibility.

In the context of staged venture capital investments, intangible assets would be associated with greater agency costs. As assets become more tangible, venture capitalists can recover more of their investment in liquidation, and expected losses due to inefficient continuation are reduced. This reduces the need to monitor tightly and should increase funding duration.

Shleifer and Vishny (1992) extend Williamson's model by examining how asset specificity might affect liquidation value and debt levels. They show that firms with assets that are highly industry and firm specific would use less debt because asset specificity significantly reduces liquidation value. Firms that have high R&D intensities are likely to generate assets that are strictly firm and industry specific. Bradley, Jarrell, and Kim (1984) and Titman and Wessels (1988) use the ratio of R&D to sales to measure uniqueness of assets in investigating the use of debt. Both find a negative relationship between leverage and R&D intensity. Similarly Barclay and Smith (1995) utilize the ratio of R&D to firm value to explore debt maturity.

Asset specificity would also influence the structure of staged venture capital investments. Industries with high levels of R&D intensity would be subject to greater discretionary investment by the entrepreneur and increase risks associated with firm- and industry-specific assets. These factors increase expected agency costs and shorten funding durations.

Finally, Myers (1977) argues that firms whose value largely depends on investment in future growth options would make less use of debt because the owner/manager can undertake investment strategies that are particularly detrimental to bondholders. Myers suggests that a firm's market-to-book ratio may be related to the fraction of firm value that is comprised of future growth opportunities. Empirical results support this prediction. Rajan and Zingales (1995) find a negative relationship between firm market-to-book ratios and leverage. Similarly Barclay and Smith (1995) find that debt maturity declines with a firm's market-to-book ratio.

Entrepreneurs have more discretion to invest in personally beneficial strategies at shareholders' expense in industries where firm value largely depends on future growth opportunities. Firms with high market-to-book ratios are more susceptible to these agency costs, thus increasing the value of monitoring and reducing funding duration.

Venture Capital, Liquidity, and Investment

The growth of inflows to new venture capital funds may also have effects on the structure of investment. As discussed in the introduction, the venture capital industry has gone through several fund-raising cycles. During periods of low fund-raising, venture capitalists might be liquidity constrained. Liquidity constraints and their effects on investment have been examined in several contexts (Fazzari, Hubbard, and Petersen 1988; Hoshi, Kashyap, and Scharfstein 1991; Petersen and Rajan 1994). Venture capitalists would like to make more and bigger investments (which are positive NPV), but they are unable to raise enough money to invest in all of these projects. If constraints restrict investment, greater commitments to new funds lead venture capitalists to invest more money per round and to invest more often.

Free cash-flow theory (Jensen 1986) also predicts that increases in commitments to venture capital funds would lead to larger investments and shorter time between investments. Venture capitalists would try to put the increased level of commitments to use. Free cash-flow agency costs have been documented by Blanchard, Lopez de Silanes, and Shleifer (1994), who provide evidence that cash windfalls adversely affect companies' investment behavior. Lawsuit winners appear to invest in bad projects rather than give cash to shareholders. If free cash-flow problems affect venture capitalists, more frequent and larger investment implies venture capitalists may be overinvesting.

Similarly growth of the venture capital pool may measure entry by inexperienced venture capitalists. These new entrants may overinvest and may not monitor companies as effectively as experienced venture capitalists. As in the case of free cash-flow agency costs, the increase in investment is excessive.

The Structure of Staged Investment

Summary Information and Statistics

A random sample[2] of 794 firms that received venture capital financing between January 1961 and July 1992 was gathered from the Venture Economics' Venture Intelligence Database (described in chapter 22). The firms were included in the sample if their first round of venture capital financing occurred prior to January 1, 1990.[3] This chapter utilizes a database of venture capital funds compiled by Venture Economics' Investors Services Group (described in chapter 22) to collect annual information on total venture capital funds under management, new capital commitments to the industry, and the amount of venture capital invested.

Because accounting data for private firms is unavailable, annual Standard Industrial Codes (SIC) industry averages from COMPUSTAT for each firm that received venture capital financing is used to control for industry effects. If the four-digit SIC group had fewer than four companies, the three-digit industry was used. Similarly, if the three-digit group had fewer than four companies, the two-digit SIC group averages is used. Variables were collected to calculate various measures of asset tangibility (the ratio of tangible assets to total assets), growth opportunities (market value of equity to book value), and research intensity (either the ratio of R&D expenditures to total assets or R&D expenditures to sales). The data were matched by date and industry to each firm and each round of financing. The inflation rate and real

---

2. The random sample was generated as follows: at the time the data were collected, approximately 7,000 firms were contained in the Venture Economics database. Each firm is given a number from 1 to 7,000 by Venture Economics. Then 800 unique random numbers were generated from 1 to 7,000 in a spreadsheet. These 800 numbers were used as firm reference numbers. Six firms were eliminated from the final sample because their data were suspect. The six firms had venture financing dates that were more than ten years apart. Apparently, for each of these six entries two firms with the same name had been venture financed and their records merged.

3. The current status of each firm was verified with Lexis/Nexis databases. COMPNY and NEWS databases were searched for all records concerning the firms. If no news stories or legal filings were found, the firm was assumed to be private. The data are limited in several respects. First, it is unclear how well each company is doing at each round of financing. Second, the data do not have information on other types of financing that the firms receive.

return on treasury bills and common stocks were collected for each month from 1961 to 1992 from Ibbotson Associates.

Table 8.1 provides summary information on the dates and amounts of total venture capital financing for the 794 firms. These 794 firms received 2,143 individual rounds of venture capital financing and represent roughly 15 percent of all venture capital over this period.[4] The coverage of the data appears to be better for the latter half of the sample period. This may reflect increasing completeness of the Venture Economics database over time.

Table 8.2 looks at the distribution of investments across various industries by the percentage of rounds invested. Industry trends can be discerned. Computer firms received significant amounts of financing from 1982 to 1984, but investment subsequently declined. After the oil embargoes of the 1970s, energy-related investments were popular, but these declined substantially after the early 1980s when domestic exploration declined. On the other hand, medical and health-related firms have been receiving increasing attention from venture capitalists.

What is evident from the industry results, however, is the focus on high-technology firms (e.g., communication, computers, electronics, biotechnology, and medical/health). The percentage of venture capital invested in high-technology firms never falls below 70 percent of annual investments. For firms in the sample, the average industry ratio of R&D to sales is 3.43 percent (median 3.82 percent). The average for all COMPUSTAT industries during the time period 1972 to 1992 was 1.30 percent (median 2.66 percent). Asymmetric information and agency costs are a major concern in R&D-intensive firms, which may require specialized knowledge to monitor. Industry investment composition suggests that venture capitalists specialize in industries in which monitoring and information evaluation are important.

Table 8.2 also examines the distribution of investment by stage. (Rounds are classified as early stage if the investment is seed, start-up, or early stage. The investment is classified as late stage if it is expansion, second, third, or bridge financing.) The table documents the relative decline in early-stage financing and the growing importance of later stage investments. This trend reflects the effects of a maturing industry. While the venture capital industry was growing rapidly in the early 1980s, more investment went to early-stage companies. As the industry matured, the investment mix reflected previous investments. Early-stage investments in the mid-1980s became

---

4. The sample represents slightly more that 15 percent because certain data on financing amounts were missing.

Table 8.1
Time series of random sample from the Venture Economics database

Year	Rounds of venture capital financing	Amount of venture capital investment	Number of new firms receiving venture capital
1961	1	$318	1
1962	1	$227	1
1968	1	$284	1
1969	3	$2,423	2
1970	6	$2,168	4
1971	8	$2,561	4
1972	4	$2,803	1
1973	9	$22,055	6
1974	9	$18,591	1
1975	14	$12,227	9
1976	17	$20,623	9
1977	23	$10,285	12
1978	35	$20,122	24
1979	44	$73,517	30
1980	55	$39,025	30
1981	77	$129,125	50
1982	126	$204,211	64
1983	170	$431,931	82
1984	208	$588,251	84
1985	179	$587,161	66
1986	204	$549,667	95
1987	219	$493,567	60
1988	225	$674,393	85
1989	234	$475,382	67
1990	142	$179,044	0
1991	109	$162,127	0
1992	16	$48,533	0

Note: The sample is 794 randomly selected companies from the set of firms that received their first venture capital investment prior to January 1, 1990. The table shows the number of rounds, total amount invested, and the number of new firms in each year in the sample of random firms. Amount of known investment is in thousands of 1997 dollars.

Table 8.2
Percentage of investment by industry and stage of development in each year

Industry	1975	1976	1977	1978	1979	1980	1981	1982	1983	1984	1985	1986	1987	1988	1989
Panel A: Percentage of rounds invested by industry															
Communications	28.6%	23.5%	18.2%	8.6%	18.2%	11.1%	13.3%	12.9%	14.9%	13.3%	12.4%	12.3%	11.9%	12.0%	11.5%
Computers	0.0%	0.0%	0.0%	2.9%	2.3%	3.7%	4.0%	8.9%	10.1%	10.1%	6.2%	3.9%	4.6%	4.4%	1.3%
Computer related	0.0%	5.9%	4.5%	11.4%	15.9%	11.1%	13.3%	21.8%	19.6%	16.1%	17.5%	14.2%	14.2%	11.1%	15.8%
Computer software	7.1%	0.0%	0.0%	0.0%	0.0%	0.0%	6.7%	10.5%	13.7%	9.6%	14.7%	13.2%	11.4%	9.3%	11.1%
Electronic components	0.0%	0.0%	4.5%	0.0%	2.3%	5.6%	2.7%	0.8%	3.6%	3.2%	4.5%	3.4%	4.6%	3.6%	3.0%
Other electronics	28.6%	35.3%	4.5%	2.9%	4.5%	11.1%	10.7%	8.9%	3.6%	7.8%	6.8%	4.4%	4.1%	4.9%	5.6%
Biotechnology	7.1%	0.0%	0.0%	2.9%	6.8%	3.7%	2.7%	5.6%	3.6%	3.7%	1.1%	4.4%	5.0%	6.7%	6.4%
Medical/health	0.0%	0.0%	9.1%	20.0%	4.5%	9.3%	2.7%	6.5%	10.1%	11.0%	16.4%	13.2%	14.6%	15.6%	12.0%
Energy	14.3%	0.0%	31.8%	5.7%	6.8%	7.4%	4.0%	3.2%	3.0%	0.0%	0.6%	1.5%	0.5%	1.3%	0.9%
Consumer products	0.0%	11.8%	4.5%	17.1%	13.6%	18.5%	10.7%	4.8%	6.0%	11.9%	9.6%	9.3%	11.4%	15.1%	13.7%
Industrial products	7.1%	17.6%	4.5%	14.3%	9.1%	9.3%	17.3%	9.7%	4.2%	6.0%	4.0%	7.8%	7.8%	9.8%	8.5%
Transportation	0.0%	0.0%	18.2%	0.0%	4.5%	0.0%	1.3%	2.4%	0.6%	0.9%	0.6%	2.0%	0.9%	1.8%	0.0%
Other	7.1%	5.9%	0.0%	14.3%	11.4%	9.3%	10.7%	4.0%	7.1%	6.4%	5.6%	10.3%	9.1%	4.4%	10.3%
Panel B: Percentage of rounds invested by stage of development															
Early stage	69.2%	92.9%	85.7%	63.3%	70.6%	66.7%	52.3%	59.5%	54.9%	55.3%	47.7%	43.1%	39.7%	40.0%	34.5%
Late stage	30.8%	7.1%	14.3%	36.7%	29.4%	33.3%	47.7%	40.5%	45.1%	44.7%	52.3%	56.9%	60.3%	60.0%	65.5%

Note: Data are 2,143 financing rounds for a random sample of 794 venture capital-backed firms. Panel A shows the industry composition of venture investments in the sample through time. Industry classifications are reported by Venture Economics. Panel B shows how the stage of firm development for venture investments varies in the sample. Early stage investments are seed, startup, early-, first-, and other early-stage investments. Late-stage financing is second-, third-, or bridge-stage investments.

late-stage investments in the late 1980s. Even with the decline, a substantial fraction of investment is in early-stage companies where monitoring is important.

The distribution of outcomes for firms that received venture capital financing is examined in table 8.3. Firms can go public (IPO), undergo a merger or acquisition, file for bankruptcy, or remain private as of July 31, 1992. In table 8.3 only those firms that had not received a venture capital infusion since January 1, 1988, are classified as venture-backed firms that remain private. Other firms may yet receive another venture capital investment or may achieve some other exit (IPO, merger, etc.) While this measure is imprecise, and it is impossible to be certain of the eventual status of all projects, the present classification gives some indication of relative outcomes. Such a determination is critical if research is to determine how investment structure affects a firm's success.

Table 8.3 shows that in the entire sample 22.5 percent of the firms go public, 23.8 percent merge or are acquired, 15.6 percent are liquidated or go bankrupt, and 38.1 percent remain private. In transportation, biotechnology, and medical/health, the proportion of firms that go public is quite high. This may reflect either the relative success of companies in this industry or their need for large capital infusions that an IPO provides. In electronic components, industrial products, and other (services), the proportion of IPOs is quite low and many more firms remain private. These results may understate the proportion of liquidations, however. First, some of the acquisitions/mergers may be distressed firms that provide little more than physical assets to their acquirer.[5] The return to the venture capitalist from these firms would be very low. Similarly a number of the firms classified as private may have been liquidated, but no record of the event could be located. Firms without any debt would have no need to file for bankruptcy.

Funding statistics by industry and outcome are presented in table 8.4. Average total funding received, number of rounds, and age at first funding show considerable variability across industries. High-technology ventures receive more rounds and greater total financing than low-technology ventures. The four industries with the highest total funding per firm are communications, computers, computer related, and biotechnology. Four of the five industries with lowest total funding per firm are energy, industrial products, transportation, and other (primarily services). A firm's age at first funding does not appear to follow any clear pattern even though one might

---

5. Initial public offerings and acquisitions may also be viewed as one large financing round. Examining the amount of venture capital invested classifying firms by outcome is still important for understanding the venture capitalists' return.

Table 8.3
Outcomes for 794 venture capital-backed firms by industry

Industry	IPOs	Mergers/ acquisitions	Liquidations/ bankruptcies	Private[a]
Communications	17 (24.6%)	17 (24.6%)	9 (13.0%)	26 (37.7%)
Computers	5 (20.0%)	7 (28.0%)	9 (36.0%)	4 (16.0%)
Computer related	20 (29.0%)	19 (27.5%)	15 (21.7%)	15 (21.7%)
Computer software	11 (21.6%)	9 (17.6%)	11 (21.6%)	20 (39.2%)
Electronic components	2 (11.8%)	6 (35.3%)	0 (0.0%)	9 (52.9%)
Other electronics	6 (20.0%)	9 (30.0%)	6 (20.0%)	9 (30.0%)
Biotechnology	9 (50.0%)	5 (27.8%)	2 (11.1%)	2 (11.1%)
Medical/health	17 (30.4%)	17 (30.4%)	12 (21.4%)	10 (17.9%)
Energy	4 (20.0%)	3 (15.0%)	2 (10.0%)	11 (55.0%)
Consumer products	19 (27.9%)	10 (14.7%)	6 (8.8%)	33 (48.5%)
Industrial products	4 (7.0%)	20 (35.1%)	6 (10.5%)	27 (47.4%)
Transportation	5 (41.7%)	2 (16.7%)	1 (8.3%)	4 (33.3%)
Other	8 (11.1%)	10 (13.9%)	9 (12.5%)	45 (62.5%)
Total	127 (22.5%)	134 (23.8%)	88 (15.6%)	215 (38.1%)

Note: The number of firms that had performed an initial public offering, merged, went bankrupt, or remained private as of July 31, 1992. (Percentage of outcome classification for each industry are in parentheses.)

a. These firms are still private and have not received venture capital financing since January 1, 1988.

think that high-technology companies need access to venture capital soon after incorporation. Biotechnology, electronic components, and medical/health companies are relatively young. Firms in computers, consumer products, and transportation are substantially older on average. Most firms are not start-ups; they are typically well over one year old when they receive their first venture capital infusion. These firms received other funding (personal, "angel," or bank financing) prior to receiving venture capital.

Table 8.4 also stratifies funding data by outcome. Examining the structure of funding by outcome can determine whether venture capitalists periodically evaluate a firm's prospects. The total amount and number of rounds of financing are greater for the sample of IPO firms than for either the entire sample or the subsamples that go bankrupt or are acquired/merged. The data indicate that venture capitalists stage capital infusions to gather information and monitor the progress of firms they finance. New information is useful in determining whether or not the venture capitalist should continue financing the project. Promising firms receive new financing while others either are liquidated or find a corporate acquirer to manage the assets of the firm.

The Duration and Size of Financing Rounds

The analysis in this section classifies each financing according to the company's stage of development at the time of financing as reported by Venture Economics (seed, start-up, first stage, etc.) This information is self-reported by venture capital firms. There are no clear divisions among the definitions of each stage, so divisions should be seen as relative measures of firm development rather than absolute measures. To overcome some of the potential reporting biases in the regression results, various stages are grouped into early rounds, middle rounds, or late rounds. All seed and start-up investments are classified as early rounds. These investments are usually made in very young companies. First-stage and early-stage investments are classified as middle rounds because even though the firms are still relatively young, they are further developed than seed or start-up companies. Finally second, third, expansion, or bridge stage funding is considered to be late-stage financing.

Table 8.5 summarizes average duration, amount of venture capital funding, and the rate at which the firm uses cash during that particular round (in dollars per year) for various types of investment. In general, the duration of financing declines for late-stage companies and the average amount of financing per round generally rises. Venture capitalists may know more

Table 8.4
Number of investments, age at first funding, and total funding received by industry and outcome

Industry	Number of rounds				Age at first funding			
	Full	IPO	Bankrupt	Acquired	Full	IPO	Bankrupt	Acquired
Communications	2.78 (2)	3.41 (2)	2.44 (2)	2.47 (2)	3.46 (0.92)	3.29 (1.34)	2.56 (1.87)	5.11 (1.34)
Computers	3.89 (3)	4.60 (6)	4.33 (4)	3.42 (3)	4.19 (1.33)	1.11 (0.17)	2.75 (1.84)	2.30 (1.29)
Computer related	3.66 (3)	4.0 (4)	3.47 (2)	3.32 (3)	4.29 (1.88)	3.74 (1.67)	4.10 (2.75)	4.10 (2.75)
Computer software	2.99 (3)	2.91 (2)	2.00 (1)	3.22 (3)	3.59 (1.92)	3.83 (3.67)	4.30 (2.59)	4.30 (2.59)
Electronic components	3.27 (2)	4.00 (4)	na	3.50 (3.5)	0.86 (0.00)	0.53 (0.53)	na	0.77 (0)
Other electronics	3.21 (2)	2.50 (2)	3.50 (2.5)	2.78 (2)	3.45 (2.38)	2.54 (3.17)	5.67 (3)	5.46 (3.92)
Biotechnology	3.69 (4)	3.56 (3)	4.00 (4)	4.60 (4)	1.21 (0.71)	0.89 (0.50)	0.37 (0.37)	2.08 (2)
Medical/health	2.98 (2)	3.94 (3)	1.91 (1)	2.53 (2)	1.97 (1.00)	2.30 (1.41)	0.58 (0.12)	1.59 (0.71)
Energy	1.91 (1)	2.25 (2)	2.00 (2)	1.67 (1)	2.85 (2.00)	7.01 (5.17)	2.13 (2.13)	2.00 (2)
Consumer products	2.14 (1)	2.16 (2)	2.33 (2)	1.20 (1)	5.90 (1.67)	7.63 (4.41)	0.98 (0.75)	17.92 (17.35)
Industrial products	2.09 (1)	3.75 (2)	2.17 (1.5)	1.65 (1)	3.79 (2.25)	5.94 (6.38)	18.97 (10.46)	4.66 (2.46)
Transportation	1.93 (2)	2.00 (2)	2.00 (2)	2.50 (2.5)	6.33 (5.67)	15.84 (5.27)	na	9.09 (9.09)
Other	1.60 (1)	1.63 (1)	1.78 (1)	1.80 (1)	5.83 (2.25)	12.48 (3.17)	1.00 (0.46)	10.11 (5.96)

Industry	Total funding				Number of firms			
	Full	IPO	Bankrupt	Acquired	Full	IPO	Bankrupt	Acquired
Communications	$8,399 ($3,745)	$7,962 ($4,962)	$3,224 ($2,269)	$5,325 ($1,642)	98	17	9	17
Computers	$18,339 ($8,794)	$23,243 ($23,243)	$17,596 ($6,808)	$6,086 ($2,828)	27	5	9	7
Computer related	$9,148 ($5,596)	$15,189 ($15,189)	$8,433 ($5,674)	$5,634 ($4,905)	90	20	15	19
Computer software	$5,148 ($2,374)	$8,606 ($8,606)	$3,379 ($1,702)	$6,931 ($1,820)	77	11	11	9
Electronic components	$11,891 ($3,953)	$14,099 ($14,099)	na	$7,845 ($2,818)	22	2	0	6
Other electronics	$5,932 ($4,539)	$7,229 ($7,183)	$7,690 ($7,690)	$3,586 ($2,128)	41	6	6	9
Biotechnology	$9,716 ($6,241)	$14,429 ($12,433)	$8,691 ($8,691)	$9,153 ($13,617)	29	9	2	5
Medical/health	$6,445 ($3,404)	$11,626 ($4,136)	$3,237 ($3,237)	$4,239 ($3,858)	90	17	12	17
Energy	$3,502 ($1,020)	$4,446 ($2,762)	$5,331 ($5,331)	$2,227 ($965)	22	4	2	3
Consumer products	$7,434 ($2,538)	$12,665 ($6,210)	$3,012 ($3,012)	$6,461 ($1,087)	103	19	6	10
Industrial products	$3,384 ($1,702)	$11,183 ($8,936)	$3,573 ($3,573)	$2,580 ($1,362)	89	4	6	20
Transportation	$5,654 ($3,690)	$7,339 ($2,837)	$4,539 ($4,539)	$6,667 ($6,667)	15	5	1	2
Other	$5,136 ($2,233)	$14,625 ($9,078)	$3,189 ($3,189)	$9,915 ($4,853)	96	8	9	10

Note: The sample is 794 venture capital-backed firms randomly selected from the Venture Economics database. The number of rounds, age at first funding, and total venture capital financing (in constant 1997 dollars) are tabulated for various industries and various outcomes. Firms can either go public in an IPO, go bankrupt, or be acquired. Average age at first funding is in thousands of dollars. Average age at first funding is in years. (Median values are in parentheses.)

Table 8.5
Duration, amount of investment, and cash utilization by stage of development

Type of funding[a]	Time to next funding[b]	Amount of funding[c]	Cash utilization ($000s per year)[d]	Number
Seed	1.63	$1,045	$641	122
	(1.17)	($329)	($281)	
Startup	1.21	$2,709	$2,255	129
	(1.00)	($1,246)	($1,246)	
Early stage	1.03	$1,196	$1,161	114
	(0.83)	($851)	($1,026)	
First stage	1.08	$2,188	$2,025	288
	(0.92)	($1,135)	($1,233)	
Other early	1.08	$2,476	$2,292	221
	(0.75)	($1,362)	($1,816)	
Expansion	1.26	$2,659	$2,111	377
	(0.88)	($1,135)	($1,289)	
Second stage	1.01	$2,845	$2,816	351
	(0.83)	($1,532)	($1,846)	
Third stage	0.86	$3,159	$3,673	181
	(0.75)	($1,362)	($1,816)	
Bridge	0.97	$3,066	$3,160	454
	(0.83)	($1,702)	($2,050)	

Note: The sample is 794 venture capital-backed firms randomly selected from the Venture Economics database.
a. Investment type is self-reported stage of development for venture capital-backed firms at time of investment. Median values are in parentheses.
b. Time to next funding is the duration (in years) from one reported financing round to the next.
c. Amount of funding is the average size of a given type of financing round (in thousands of 1997 dollars).
d. Cash utilization is the rate at which the firm is using cash between rounds of financing (in thousands of 1997 dollars per year).

about late-stage firms and may therefore be willing to invest more money and for longer periods of time. Late-stage companies would be associated with lower agency costs. Similarly the rate of cash utilization rises for late-stage firms. Cash utilization rates for later rounds might be higher because the need for investment in plant and working capital accelerates as the scale of the project expands.[6]

---

6. A second possibility is that only poorly performing firms receive later rounds of financing (profitable firms generate their own cash). The higher cash utilization rate indicates a selection bias caused by selecting poor performers. Evidence from the sample of 127 firms going public indicates that the selection bias is not a problem. Successful firms have higher cash utilization rates.

Regression results in table 8.6 present a clearer picture of the factors affecting venture capital staging patterns. The regressions include dummy variables to control for early and middle stage financings utilizing the Venture Economics classifications for type of investment. (The results are unchanged if firm development is measured by using round numbers—first investment, second investment, etc.—instead of dummies for early-, middle-, and late-stage firms.) The regressions also include industry accounting variables to control for the nature of the firm's assets and investment opportunities. Because private firm balance-sheet data are unavailable, industry averages from COMPUSTAT should be viewed as instruments for the private firms' true values. To the extent that any of the coefficients on the industry variables are significant, significance levels for firms' true values are probably even higher.

From the previous discussion, firms that are subject to greater agency costs should be monitored more often, and funding durations should be shorter. The ratio of tangible assets to total assets for the industry should be related to the liquidation value of the firm. The coefficient on the ratio of tangible assets to total assets should be positive in regressions for the duration of financing rounds. Tangible assets lower expected agency costs of inefficient continuation. The market-to-book ratio should rise as the fraction of growth options in firm value rises. Because potential agency costs associated with investment behavior rise with growth options, the coefficient on the market-to-book ratio should be negative. Two measures of research and development intensity are included: R&D expenditure to sales and R&D expenditure to total assets. R&D intensive firms are likely to accumulate physical and intellectual capital that is very industry and firm specific. As asset specificity increases, so do expected losses in liquidation. Therefore coefficients on R&D measures should be negative in the duration regressions.

Also included is firm age when it receives venture financing. Older firms may have more information available for venture capitalists to evaluate. Therefore, holding stage of development and all else constant, informational asymmetries are smaller and the funding duration should be longer (i.e., the coefficient on age should be positive in the duration regressions).

Finally the effects of venture capital market growth on financing are measured through the amount of money (in constant dollars) raised by venture capital funds in the year prior to the financing of the firm. If venture capitalists cannot make all the investments they would like because they have insufficient capital, more liquidity should decrease the duration of financing

Table 8.6
Regressions for duration and amount of funding per round controlling for firm and industry factors

Independent variable[b]	Dependent variable: Duration of financing round[a]					
	(1)	(2)	(3)	(4)	(5)	(6)
Panel A: Regressions for duration of financing round						
Constant	-0.030 (-0.19)	0.361 (2.50)	0.407 (2.86)	0.417 (2.93)	0.070 (0.39)	0.082 (0.42)
Investment in early-stage firm	0.051 (0.63)	0.040 (0.49)	0.037 (0.44)	0.047 (0.56)	0.036 (0.44)	0.031 (0.38)
Investment in middle-stage firm	-0.054 (-0.93)	-0.058 (-1.00)	-0.103 (-1.72)	-0.094 (-1.55)	-0.102 (-1.71)	-0.106 (-1.75)
Capital-committed to new venture funds in previous year	$-0.60 \times$ E-04 (-4.97)	$-0.56 \times$ E-04 (-4.56)	$-0.52 \times$ E-04 (-4.10)	$-0.55 \times$ E-04 (-4.41)	$-0.54 \times$ E-04 (-4.22)	$-0.56 \times$ E-04 (-4.36)
Industry ratio of tangible assets to total assets[c]	0.405 (4.01)				0.400 (3.84)	0.398 (3.23)
Industry market-to-book ratio		-0.047 (-1.87)			0.000 (0.00)	-0.019 (-0.41)
Industry ratio of R&D expense to sales[d]			-3.390 (-2.52)		-2.268 (-1.79)	
Industry ratio of R&D expense to total assets				-0.795 (-2.69)		-0.194 (-1.67)
Age of the firm at time of venture financing round	0.016 (3.58)	0.016 (3.68)	0.016 (3.49)	0.017 (3.56)	0.016 (3.52)	0.017 (3.60)
Logarithm of the amount of venture financing this round	0.011 (0.71)	0.012 (0.73)	0.016 (0.68)	0.011 (0.65)	0.010 (0.59)	0.009 (0.52)
Pseudo-R^2	0.045	0.037	0.045	0.046	0.053	0.051
Model χ^2	56.00	42.25	48.64	49.47	62.74	60.38

Panel B: Regressions for size of each financing round

Constant	6.580 (38.00)	6.756 (39.02)	6.902 (46.39)	6.929 (46.27)	6.379 (26.97)	6.108 (22.39)
Investment in early-stage firm	-0.635 (-4.14)	-0.608 (-4.22)	-0.703 (-4.83)	-0.703 (-4.83)	-0.748 (-5.14)	-0.760 (-5.23)
Investment in middle-stage firm	-0.224 (-2.29)	-0.216 (-2.20)	-0.308 (-3.06)	-0.309 (-3.06)	-0.314 (-3.13)	-0.328 (-3.26)
Capital committed to new venture funds in previous year	0.0001 (3.94)	0.0001 (4.21)	0.0001 (3.91)	0.0001 (3.98)	0.0001 (3.10)	0.0001 (3.08)
Industry ratio of tangible assets to total assets[c]	0.352 (2.23)				0.612 (3.64)	0.810 (4.16)
Industry market-to-book ratio		-0.051 (-0.64)			0.041 (0.49)	0.084 (1.03)
Industry ratio of R&D expense to sales[d]			1.578 (0.72)		3,618 (1.56)	
Industry ratio of R&D expense to total assets				-0.099 (-0.21)		1.372 (2.43)
Age of the firm at time of venture financing round	-0.019 (-2.58)	-0.019 (-2.58)	-0.014 (-1.82)	-0.014 (-1.86)	-0.014 (-1.90)	-0.014 (-1.89)
R^2	0.031	0.028	0.039	0.031	0.041	0.044
F-Statistic	9.33	8.40	8.50	8.40	8.03	8.55

Note: The sample is 2,143 funding rounds for 794 venture capital-backed firms for the period 1961 to 1992. Panel A are maximum-likelihood estimates for Weibull distribution duration models. Panel B estimates are ordinary least squares. (t-statistics for coefficients are in parentheses.)

a. The dependent variables are the time in years from funding date to the next funding date and the logarithm of the round's funding amount in thousands of 1992 dollars.

b. Independent variables include a dummy variable that equals 1 if the funding round is either seed or startup (early stage) and a dummy variable that equals 1 if the round is either early, first, or other early (middle stage). Liquidity in the venture capital industry is controlled using new capital commitments to venture capital partnerships in the previous year in constant 1992 dollars.

c. Tangibility of assets is measured by the average ratio of tangible assets to total assets for company's in the firm's industry. Market-to-book is the average industry ratio of market value of equity to book value of equity.

d. Research and development intensity is proxied by the average industry ratios of R&D to sales or R&D to assets. The age of the venture capital-backed firm is months from incorporation to financing date.

(firms receive follow-on funding sooner) and increase the amount of funding per round.

The dependent variable in panel A of table 8.6 is the duration of a particular venture financing round, the time in years from one particular financing to the next. The estimation of regressions with duration data introduces certain methodological issues. First, the data are right censored: we only observe the duration of financing when a subsequent financing occurs. A subsequent financing might not be observed for two reasons: firms may be in the middle of an ongoing financing round or firms might not receive another investment because they went bankrupt, went public, or were acquired. Models of unemployment (Lancaster 1979, 1985) deal with similar censoring. Duration data techniques are used, as in the unemployment estimation surveyed in Kiefer (1988).

A firm is assumed to have a certain probability of receiving financing in each period. The instantaneous probability of receiving financing is called the hazard rate, $h(t)$. $h(t)$ is defined as

$$h(t) = \frac{\text{Probability of receiving funding between } t \text{ and } t + \Delta t}{\text{Probability of receiving funding after } t}. \tag{1}$$

To estimate the duration model, assumptions about the distribution of the hazard rate must be made. The two most common distributions used in duration models are the Weibull and exponential distributions. The Weibull distribution offers two advantages. First, the time dependency of the hazard rate can be estimated. Second, the likelihood function for the Weibull model can be easily modified to allow for censored data. Other distributional assumptions (e.g., exponential or normal) were estimated and did not affect the qualitative results, although the Weibull model gave better fit. The model estimated in tables 8.6 and 8.8 is

$$h(t) = h_0(t)e^{\beta_0 + \beta_1 X_1 + \cdots + \beta_K X_K};$$
$$h_0(t) = t^{1/(\sigma - 1)}, \tag{2}$$

where $h_0(t)$ is the baseline hazard function.

Coefficients $\beta_0, \beta_1, \ldots$ are estimated via maximum likelihood estimators. These coefficients yield estimates of the probability that the firm receives financing in a particular month given values of the independent variables (including time from last investment). The resulting estimates from the Weibull regressions can be presented in multiple ways. Tables 8.6 and 8.8 present the model in log-expected time parameterization; that is, for given values of the independent variables, the model gives the logarithm of the

Table 8.7
Regressions for total venture capital funding and number of rounds of financing

Independent variable[b]	Dependent variable: Logarithm of total venture financing received[a]					
	(1)	(2)	(3)	(4)	(5)	(6)
Panel A: Regressions for total funding						
Constant	11.017	7.075	7.290	7.427	4.714	4.771
	(12.38)	(38.22)	(67.40)	(68.38)	(4.41)	(4.47)
Firm exited via IPO	1.043	1.018	0.882	0.905	0.664	0.666
	(6.18)	(6.01)	(4.88)	(4.96)	(4.31)	(4.32)
Firm bankrupt or liquidated	−0.023	−0.024	−0.102	−0.047	−0.085	−0.077
	(−0.11)	(−0.12)	(−0.49)	(−0.22)	(−0.48)	(−0.44)
Firm exited via merger or acquisition	−0.125	−0.129	−0.003	−0.009	0.124	0.123
	(−0.76)	(−0.78)	(−0.02)	(−0.05)	(0.84)	(0.83)
Industry ratio of tangible assets to total assets[c]	−3.660				1.118	1.036
	(−3.90)				(1.12)	(1.04)
Industry market-to-book ratio		0.311			0.402	0.420
		(2.90)			(3.52)	(3.69)
Industry ratio of R&D expense to sales[d]			13.033		3.600	
			(4.02)		(1.24)	
Industry ratio of R&D expense to total assets				5.709		2.540
				(1.95)		(1.02)
Number of rounds of venture financing received					0.396	0.399
					(15.19)	(15.43)
R^2	0.073	0.064	0.067	0.048	0.337	0.336
F-Statistic	13.40	11.60	11.05	7.82	44.37	44.26

Independent variable[b]	Dependent variable: Number of financing rounds received[a]			
	(1)	(2)	(3)	(4)
Panel B: Poisson regressions for number of rounds				
Constant	2.904	0.945	0.796	0.888
	(10.51)	(13.88)	(18.82)	(21.55)
Firm exited via IPO	0.255	0.239	0.186	0.203
	(4.35)	(4.06)	(2.91)	(3.18)
Firm bankrupt or liquidated	0.054	0.052	0.017	0.052
	(0.71)	(0.68)	(0.23)	(0.68)
Firm exited via merger or acquisition	0.027	−0.006	−0.010	−0.004
	(0.43)	(−0.09)	(−0.16)	(−0.06)
Industry ratio of tangible assets to total assets[c]	−2.054			
	(−6.96)			
Industry market-to-book ratio		0.021		
		(0.54)		
Industry ratio of R&D expense to sales[d]			7.416	
			(6.25)	
Industry ratio of R&D expense to total assets				2.907
				(2.73)

Table 8.7
(continued)

Independent variable[b]	Dependent variable: Number of financing rounds received[a]			
	(1)	(2)	(3)	(4)
Pseudo-R^2	0.020	0.006	0.019	0.007
Model χ^2	60.25	18.55	50.07	18.81

Note: The sample is 794 venture capital-backed firms for the period 1961 to 1992. Estimates in panel A are from ordinary least squares regressions. Estimates for equations in panel B are from Poisson regressions. (t-statistics for regression coefficients are in parentheses.)
a. The dependent variables are the total venture capital funding that the firm received in thousands of 1992 dollars and the number of distinct rounds of venture financing.
b. Independent variables include a dummy variable that equals 1 if the firm completed an initial public offering, a dummy variable that equals 1 if the firm filed for bankruptcy, and a dummy variable that equals 1 if the firm was acquired by or merged with another company.
c. Tangibility of assets is measured by the average ratio of tangible assets to total assets for companies in the firm's industry. Market-to-book is the average industry ratio of market value of equity to book value of equity.
d. Research and development intensity is proxied by the average industry ratios of R&D to sales or R&D to assets.

expected time to refinancing. The interpretation of coefficients is straight-forward: positive coefficients imply longer financing duration on average. Conversely, negative coefficients imply shorter expected durations.

The results of table 8.6 are generally consistent with the implications of an informational and agency-cost explanation for staged venture capital infusions. In panel A, financing duration declines with decreases in the industry ratio of tangible assets to total assets, increases in the market-to-book ratio, and greater R&D intensity. The coefficients are significant between the 7 and 1 percent confidence levels. These factors are associated with greater agency costs of investment and liquidation and therefore lead to tighter monitoring.

The age of the venture-backed firm at the time of financing is positively and significantly related to financing duration. More information may be available for venture capitalists to evaluate older projects. One might also expect that larger financing rounds lead to longer funding duration. That is not the case. None of the coefficients on amount of venture financing are significant. The results indicate that industry- and firm-specific factors are important in determining the financing duration independent of the invest-ment size.

Finally, in regressions 5 and 6, all industry accounting variables are used together to determine which of the asset measures are relatively more important. The ratio of tangible assets to total assets remains the most significant variable, while market-to-book drops out completely. Higher R&D intensities still reduce funding duration, but size and significance of the coefficients are reduced when the other asset measures are included. The results indicate that tangible assets may be particularly important in lowering expected agency costs.

Panel B examines factors affecting size of the venture round. The dependent variable is the logarithm of the size of the financing round in thousands of 1992 dollars. The ratio of tangible assets to total assets has the greatest effect on the amount of financing. Increases in tangibility increase the amount of financing per round. More R&D intensive industries also appear to receive more financing per round controlling for tangibility.

Panel A also shows that the durations of early- and middle-stage financings are not significantly different from late-stage financings. The stage of development does, however, affect the amount of financing per round. Results from regressions in panel B show that average early-stage investments are between $1.30 and $2.03 million smaller than comparable late-stage investments. Similarly middle-stage investments are on average $0.70 to $1.21 million smaller than late-stage investments. The increasing size of investment per round reflects the growing scale of a firm. Greater investment is needed to expand the firm.

The duration of financing and the amount of funding per round is also sensitive to the growth in the venture capital industry. Greater commitments of capital to new venture funds reduce duration of financing and increase financing amount per round. A one standard deviation increase in new commitments to venture capital funds decreases funding duration by two months and increases the average funding by almost $700,000.

If venture capitalists are capital rationed, larger cash commitments allow venture capitalists to invest more often in positive NPV projects and with larger cash infusions. If venture capitalists are susceptible to free cash-flow agency costs, they might waste the extra cash by investing more, and more often, in bad projects. Similarly the growth in new and inexperienced fund managers during the mid-1980s could have led to a deterioration in investment quality and monitoring. Sahlman and Stevenson's (1986) case study of the computer disk drive industry shows that venture capital investment in certain industries during the early and mid-1980s might have been excessive. This period coincides with the dramatic increase in commitments to venture capital funds and might indicate that either free cash-flow agency costs or venture capitalist inexperience is a more likely explanation for the investment sensitivity to fundraising during this period of rapid entry.

Table 8.8
Regressions for duration controlling for firm and industry factors with the sample split into high- and low-technology companies

	Dependent variable: Duration of financing round[a]					
Independent variable[b]	(1)	(2)	(3)	(4)	(5)	(6)
Panel A: Regressions for duration of financing round for high-technology industries						
Constant	−0.036 (−0.17)	0.464 (2.56)	0.542 (2.99)	0.549 (3.03)	0.022 (0.09)	−0.056 (−0.22)
Investment in early-stage firm	0.066 (0.68)	0.065 (0.66)	0.042 (0.42)	0.046 (0.45)	0.036 (0.36)	0.029 (0.30)
Investment in middle-stage firm	−0.022 (−0.32)	−0.009 (−0.13)	−0.085 (−1.15)	−0.084 (−1.14)	−0.101 (−1.38)	−0.109 (−1.48)
Capital committed to new venture funds in previous year	−0.63 × E-04 (−4.50)	−0.59 × E-04 (−4.01)	−0.54 × E-04 (−3.59)	−0.57 × E-04 (−3.82)	−0.59 × E-04 (−3.81)	−0.61 × E-04 (−3.93)
Industry ratio of tangible assets to total assets[c]	0.514 (3.47)				0.553 (3.60)	0.633 (3.55)
Industry market-to-book ratio		−0.059 (−0.66)			0.037 (0.39)	−0.003 (−0.03)
Industry ratio of R&D expense to sales[d]			−2.418 (−1.83)		−0.986 (−0.51)	
Industry ratio of R&D expense to total assets				−0.541 (−1.88)		−0.315 (−1.68)
Age of the firm at time of venture financing round	−0.001 (−0.17)	−0.001 (−0.09)	−0.005 (−0.70)	−0.005 (−0.70)	−0.006 (−0.74)	−0.005 (−0.64)
Logarithm of the amount of venture financing this round	0.001 (0.07)	0.003 (0.13)	−0.002 (−0.08)	−0.002 (−0.08)	−0.004 (−0.21)	−0.005 (−0.22)
Pseudo-R^2	0.036	0.029	0.032	0.032	0.041	0.040
Model χ^2	31.07	20.75	21.85	21.99	33.63	33.81

Panel B: Regressions for duration of financing round for low-technology industries

Constant	−0.078 (−0.29)	0.399 (1.50)	0.382 (1.54)	0.400 (1.62)	0.130 (0.45)	0.208 (0.62)
Investment in early-stage firm	−0.050 (−0.35)	−0.095 (−0.66)	−0.087 (−0.61)	−0.068 (−0.48)	−0.093 (−0.65)	−0.098 (−0.69)
Investment in middle-stage firm	−0.148 (−1.45)	−0.194 (−1.88)	−0.210 (−2.03)	−0.179 (−1.72)	−0.196 (−1.89)	−0.195 (−1.88)
Capital committed to new venture funds in previous year	−0.43 × E-04 (−1.86)	−0.38 × E-04 (−1.89)	−0.37 × E-04 (−1.68)	−0.40 × E-04 (−1.72)	−0.38 × E-04 (−1.68)	−0.38 × E-04 (−1.62)
Industry ratio of tangible assets to total assets[c]	0.433 (2.90)				0.393 (2.55)	0.337 (2.17)
Industry market-to-book ratio		−0.076 (−1.41)			−0.053 (−0.91)	−0.078 (−1.43)
Industry ratio of R&D expense to sales[d]			−4.270 (−2.18)		−2.006 (−1.89)	
Industry ratio of R&D expense to total assets				−1.067 (−2.41)		−0.388 (−1.66)
Age of the firm at time of venture financing round	0.026 (4.07)	0.028 (4.34)	0.030 (4.44)	0.031 (4.54)	0.029 (4.34)	0.030 (4.41)
Logarithm of the amount of venture financing this round	0.022 (0.79)	0.018 (0.63)	0.017 (0.61)	0.014 (0.50)	0.019 (0.66)	0.017 (0.59)
Pseudo-R^2	0.086	0.075	0.088	0.091	0.100	0.100
Model χ^2	39.27	33.29	39.38	40.34	46.19	45.82

Note: The sample is 2,143 funding rounds for 794 venture capital-backed firms for the period 1961 to 1992. The age of the venture capital-backed firm is months from incorporation to financing date. All regressions are maximum-likelihood estimates for Weibull distribution duration models. (*t*-statistics for coefficients are in parentheses.)

a. The dependent variable is the time in years from funding date to the next funding date.

b. Independent variables include a dummy variable that equals 1 if the funding round is either seed or startup (early stage) and a dummy variable that equals 1 if the round is either early, first, or other early (middle stage). Liquidity in the venture capital industry is controlled using new capital commitments to venture capital partnerships in the previous year in constant 1992 dollars.

c. Tangibility of assets is measured by the average ratio of tangible assets to total assets for company's in the firm's industry. Market-to-book is the average industry ratio of market value of equity to book value of equity.

d. Research and development intensity is proxied by the average industry ratios of R&D to sales or R&D to assets.

Total Venture Financing and Number of Rounds

Data on total venture capital invested and the number of rounds provide another measure of monitoring intensity. Table 8.7 presents results for both variables. Included in the regressions are three dummy variables for the outcome of venture financing: a dummy variable that equals one if the firm went public, another dummy variable that equals one if the firm was liquidated or filed for bankruptcy, and a third dummy variable that takes the value one for all firms that are acquired or merge with another company. Coefficients on these dummies provide information about the impact of monitoring for projects of varying success.

The dependent variable in panel A is the logarithm of the total amount of venture financing that the firm received. Firms that go public, the results show, receive between $3.36 and $5.67 million more venture capital financing than firms that remain private. There is no difference in the total funding for those firms that are acquired and those that are liquidated compared to firms that remain private. Even controlling for the number of financing rounds, firms that eventually go public receive more total financing.

The results in panel B for the number of financing rounds confirm these results. Because the dependent variable is nonnegative and ordinal, Poisson regressions are estimated for the number of rounds received. Firms that go public receive more financing rounds than those that remain private, while firms that are acquired or go bankrupt do not receive more rounds on average than those that remain private.

A plausible explanation for these results is that venture capitalists gather information about the potential profitability of projects over time. If venture capitalists receive favorable information about the firm and it has the potential to go public, the venture capitalist continues to fund the project. If the project is viable but has little potential to go public, the venture capitalist quickly searches for a corporate buyer. Firms that have little potential are liquidated.

Industry factors appear to have an important impact on total funding received. Panel A shows that firms in industries with more tangible assets receive less total financing. Firms in industries with high market-to-book ratios receive more total financing. Similarly R&D intensive industries receive significantly greater amounts of financing.

The most important factor influencing total venture financing is the number of financing rounds the firm has received. In fact, when the number of financing rounds is included in regressions with industry variables, tangibility of assets and R&D intensity are no longer significant. The coefficient on industry market-to-book ratio is unchanged, however. Even controlling for the number of financing rounds, firms in industries with high market-to-book ratios receive more total venture funding. If market-to-book measures the potential profitability of investment and growth opportunities, investment should be relatively higher in industries that have more growth opportunities. Similarly firms in high market-to-book industries may have less access to debt financing and may therefore rely more on venture capital.

Panel B shows that tangibility of assets and R&D intensity do indeed work through the number of financing rounds. Firms in industries with a greater fraction of tangible assets receive fewer rounds of venture financing. Similarly firms in R&D intensive industries receive more rounds of financing.

Overall, the evidence suggests that venture capitalists are concerned about the lack of entrepreneurial incentive to terminate projects when it becomes clear that projects will fail. Venture capitalists minimize agency costs by infusing capital more often. As asset tangibility and liquidation value increase, venture capitalists can recover more of their money if liquidation occurs, and the need to monitor declines. By gathering information, venture capitalists determine whether projects are likely to succeed and continue funding only those that have high potential.

Alternative Explanations

While the results from the above section are consistent with predictions from agency theory, alternative explanations may explain the results. Cost of monitoring may affect investment structure through the efficacy of interim monitoring. Tangible assets may be easy to monitor without formal evaluation. A venture capitalist can tell if a machine is still bolted to the floor. If costs of monitoring are very low, the venture capitalist may choose to have long financing rounds to avoid costs of writing new contracts. At the same time, venture capitalists could monitor the firm more often between capital infusions. Easier interim monitoring would reduce expected agency costs between financing rounds, and hence increase funding duration.

Both monitoring and agency costs are important. Conversations with practitioners, however, indicate that they normally make continuation decisions when a new financing round occurs. Venture capitalists evaluate a firm based upon performance progress, not whether a machine is still bolted down. Future work should examine the importance of monitoring costs in determining investment structure and the frequency of monitoring.

The relation between funding duration and the nature of firm assets may also be driven by differences between high-technology and low-technology firms. High-technology firms may naturally pass through more milestones. Because industry measures like the ratio of tangible assets to total assets, market-to-book, and R&D intensity are highly correlated with high-technology and low-technology status, shorter funding duration may be correlated with these measures. The coefficients in table 8.6 would measure the amount of information revealed over time and the number of benchmarks used to evaluate the firm. The more information that is revealed, the more often the project is reevaluated.

If the alternative of technology-driven milestones were true, then coefficients on asset measures would be driven by the difference between high-technology and low-technology industries. If we rerun the duration regressions within technology groups, the effect of asset tangibility, industry market-to-book ratios, and R&D intensities should be much less important. Table 8.8 presents Weibull distribution maximum likelihood estimates for each technology cohort. In panel A, the sample is high-technology firms, including communications, computers, computer related, software, electronic components, other electronics, biotechnology, and medical equipment companies. The sample in panel B is low-technology firms, including medical services, energy, consumer products, industrial products, transportation, and other (primarily services) companies.

The coefficients on industry-asset measures are surprisingly similar for the high-technology and low-technology cohorts, and both have estimates that are close to the estimates for the entire sample. It is impossible to reject the hypothesis that the coefficients for the tangibility of assets, market-to-book ratio, and the R&D intensity are equal across types of industries. The similarity of the coefficients shows that the relation between duration and asset measures is consistent within industrial classifications as well. In unreported regressions, finer industry divisions had no qualitative effect on the coefficients.

The one major difference between the two groups is the effect of firm age. The age of the firm receiving financing does not have an effect on the financing duration for high-technology firms but has a significantly positive effect in the low-technology cohort. Firm age may be more important in measuring potential asymmetric information for low-technology firms but may have only a small impact on asymmetric information for high-technology companies.

While alternative explanations may help explain some of the results, conversations with venture capitalists indicate that they are concerned about the entrepreneur's continuation decisions and strategy choices. Results in the section on staged investment are consistent with venture capitalists' stated concern that entrepreneurs have private information about the future viability of the firm, that they always want to continue the firm, and that entrepreneurs may want to enrich their reputation through activities at investors' expense.

Conclusions

Corporate control is a fundamental concern of investors. If individuals knew all potential outcomes, state-contingent contracts would be able to solve any potential agency cost. But such complete knowledge does not exist, and investors must minimize potential agency costs. Mechanisms in financial contracts among venture capitalists and entrepreneurs directly account for potential agency costs and private information associated with high-risk, high-return projects.

This chapter has demonstrated that the staging of venture capital investments can be understood in an agency and monitoring framework. Results from a sample of venture capital-backed companies are consistent with the predictions presented. Venture capitalists are concerned that entrepreneurs with private information and large private benefits will not want to liquidate a project even if they have information that the project has a negative NPV for shareholders. Entrepreneurs may also pursue strategies that enrich their reputation at shareholders' expense. Agency costs increase with declining asset tangibility, increasing growth options, and greater asset specificity. Venture capitalists monitor entrepreneurs with increasing frequency as expected agency costs rise.

The evidence indicates that venture capitalists use their industry knowledge and monitoring skills to finance projects with significant uncertainty. Venture capitalists concentrate investment in early-stage companies and high-technology industries. Results also demonstrate that the duration of financing is related to the nature of the firm's assets. Higher industry ratios of tangible assets to total assets, lower market-to-book ratios, and lower R&D intensities are associated with longer funding duration. Firms that go public have received significantly more financing and a greater number of rounds than have firms that are acquired or liquidated.

This chapter raises several interesting questions for future research. Because large firms also engage in projects that compete with investments by venture capitalists, comparing the structure and timing of investment of large corporations with those of venture capitalists might shed light on the comparative advantage of each. What implication does the structure of venture capital investment have on the future performance of new business and established firms? Can the structure of investment increase the probability that an entrepreneurial project ends up like Apple Computer, Genentech, or Microsoft? Cross-sectional and time-series effects of firm- and industry-specific factors on the outcome of investment (e.g., IPO, merger, bankruptcy, or remaining private) need to be examined.

The effect of growth in the venture capital industry on investment should be investigated further. Do free cash-flow costs, liquidity constraints, or the entry of inexperienced venture capitalists better describe venture capitalists' response to changes in capital commitments to new funds through the 1980s? Does the fund-raising ability of the venture capitalist affect only the size of the investment, or does it lead to softer benchmarks as well?

The data in this chapter are limited because they examine only venture capital equity financing. Most venture capital backed firms receive some financing before they tap venture capital. What are these sources and how significant are they? "Angels," wealthy individuals who invest in entrepreneurial ventures, are one source. Family and friends are also major contributors. Bank lending may be important in certain industries, but very high-risk companies might not have access to debt financing. Future work should examine appropriate sources of capital for new firms and how those sources change as the firm evolves. Determining the relationship among sources of capital for start-up enterprises would be pivotal in understanding the genesis of new firms.

9   Do Fund Inflows Impact Private Equity Valuations?

Introduction

One of the enduring questions in the finance literature is whether exogenous shifts in the demand for individual securities affect their valuations. The efficient market hypothesis implies, as Myron Scholes stated in 1972, that "the shares a firm sells are not unique works of art but rather abstract rights to an uncertain income stream for which close counterparts exist either directly or indirectly." Over the past decades this assertion has inspired a variety of analyses. Examples include analyses of the impact on stock prices of inclusion in the Standard & Poors' 500 Index (Dhillon and Johnson 1991; Harris and Gurel 1986; Shleifer 1986), the effects of eased restrictions on foreign investors on valuations in developing country stock markets (Henry 2000; Kim and Singhal 2000; Stulz 1997), and the relationship between mutual fund purchases and stock market returns, both on an individual security (Wermers 1999) and an aggregate level (Warther 1995). While the analyses are not without their controversial aspects, several suggest that capital inflows have a real effect on valuations.

The bulk of these analyses focus on the valuation of public securities. This focus is surprising since numerous practitioner accounts suggest that the relation between asset prices and demand shifts is particularly pronounced in *private* markets. This chapter examines these relations in the venture capital market. As the capital under management in this asset class has grown from $3 billion in 1980 to $364 billion in 2002, observers have claimed that increasing capital inflows have led to higher security prices, or colloquially, "too much money chasing too few deals."[1] This chapter seeks to understand how the pricing of investments, in venture capital is affected by inflows to

---

1. Three representative accounts over the decades are Noone and Rubel (1970), Sahlman and Stevenson (1986), and Asset Alternatives (1996).

funds.[2] Further, unlike earlier studies, we are able to examine the impact of inflows in particular segments of the industry (e.g., funds dedicated to specific geographic regions and investment stages) on the pricing of those particular types of transactions.

We proceed in two parts. First, we seek to document a relation between commitments to venture capital funds and the valuation of new investments. Second, we explore the cause of this relation. We examine whether this relation is driven by demand pressures or by improvements in investment prospects. For example, does more money committed to the venture industry drive up the valuation of investments, or do increases in expected cash flows or a reduction in the riskiness of investments lead to both higher valuations and greater venture commitments?

The data set consists of over 4,000 venture investments between 1987 and 1995 developed by the consulting firm VentureOne, as well as detailed information on capital inflows from two specialized information vendors. While studies of publicly traded securities can examine daily changes in prices, gaps of one to two years between refinancings of venture-backed firms are typical. A price index based purely on the changes in valuations between financings for the same company would therefore be incomplete and misleading. We consequently employ a hedonic approach, regressing the valuation of firms on their characteristics such as age, stage of development, and industry, as well as inflows into venture capital funds. The tests also control for public market valuations through industry portfolio valuations and industry book-to-market and earnings-to-price ratios.

Results show a strong positive relation between the valuation of venture capital investments and capital inflows. Other variables also have significant explanatory power, for instance, the marginal impact of a doubling in public market values is a 15 to 35 percent increase in the valuation of private equity transactions. A doubling of inflows into venture funds led to between a 7 and 21 percent increase in valuation levels. The results are robust to the use of a variety of specifications and control variables.

We undertake a variety of diagnostic analyses. These examine whether the relation between inflows and pricing is an artifact of our inability to fully control for firm characteristics, shifts in the value of comparable

2. In a related analysis, Kaplan and Stein (1993) examine the evolution of buyout pricing during the 1980s, a period in which a considerable expansion of funds established to make equity investments in buyouts. They show that the valuation of 124 buyout transactions mirrored marketwide movements in earnings–price ratios. Once these movements are controlled for, there is no significant time trend.

public firms, or changes in the required return on such investments. Our first approach is to add a variety of control variables that address several alternative hypotheses, such as price changes in comparable public firms only affect private valuations with a delay. Industry book-to-market and earnings-to-price ratios control for potential changes in market risk premia.

Second, we examine first differences. Many venture-backed firms receive multiple financing rounds, often at sharply divergent valuations. Using changes in the valuations and firm characteristics limits the impact of unobserved heterogeneity across firms. Also two-stage regressions are used to control for the probability of refinancing. During periods of high inflows to venture funds, firms are more likely to be refinanced, but the impact of inflows on valuations remains positive.

Third, we employ an instrumental variables approach to control for any omitted variable bias that unduly inflates the significance of venture inflows. We identify a variable that should be related to shifts in commitments to the private equity industry, but otherwise largely uncorrelated with the expected success of venture capital investments: inflows into leveraged buyout funds. This approach increases the significance of the inflow measure substantially.

Fourth, we examine the impact of capital inflows in different market segments. The effect of inflows should not be uniform. Interaction terms suggest that the impact of venture capital inflows on prices is greatest in states with the most venture capital activity. In a related analysis we decompose inflows to venture capital funds by location or stated fund objective. The segmentation of valuations and inflows into region and investment focus effectively increases the number of independent observations. The evidence suggests that the influx of capital into funds with a particular focus has a greater impact on the valuation of investments meeting those criteria.

The final analysis examines whether increases in venture capital inflows and valuations simultaneously reflect improvements in the environment for young firms. We look at the ultimate success of venture-backed firms. Results show that success rates, whether measured through the completion of an initial public offering or an acquisition at an attractive price, did not differ significantly between investments made during the early 1990s, a period of relatively low inflows and valuations, and those of the boom years of the late 1980s. As we discuss below, the interpretation of these results is not without ambiguities. Nevertheless, the analysis may help allay concerns about simultaneous shifts in the supply of entrepreneurial opportunities. Overall, the evidence is consistent with the demand pressure explanation.

Theoretical Considerations

Here we examine two sets of predictions for the relations between inflows to venture capital funds and valuations. First, we explore the empirical implications of the view that financial markets are perfect. We then consider the alternative suggestion, that exogenous increases in inflows into venture funds affect valuations due to the segmentation of this market from other financial sectors.

Finance theory teaches that the value of a firm should equal the discounted value of its expected future cash flows. The value of a firm should increase if investors learn that its future profitability will be higher. Similarly, if they learn that the firm will be less risky than originally foreseen (i.e., its cost of capital declines), the valuation should rise. Since close substitutes exist for virtually any asset, either directly or indirectly through combinations of securities, demand curves should be flat. The movement in equity market prices, whether of publicly or privately held firms, should be driven by changes in the expected cash flows or in the firm's cost of capital.

If markets are perfect, inflows of money into venture capital funds should be unrelated to the valuations of private companies. While one might argue that an asset class such as venture capital is different from the individual securities discussed by Scholes (1982), Shleifer (1986), and Harris and Gurel (1986), the analogy to the literature on individual securities is not unreasonable. The capitalization of venture capital funds did not exceed 1 percent of that of public equity markets during the years under study, and was typically much smaller. Most venture-backed private firms have close substitutes among public firms. As long as the inflow of capital is exogenous (i.e., unrelated to future expected returns on venture investments), then the price of private firms should not be affected because substitutes will always exist. Neither the firm's cost of capital nor its expected cash flows should change with the inflow of capital.

If the inflow of capital to venture funds is not exogenous, however, then the empirical patterns may be more complex. In particular, more favorable expected conditions for young, high-technology companies may trigger both increases in valuations and growth in commitments to venture capital funds. In this case, prices paid for investments and venture inflows would increase simultaneously, even if there were no causal relationship between the two. We discuss below how the empirical tests control for this possibility.

The alternative view is motivated by the possibility that the venture capital market is segmented from other asset classes. In this case exogenous increases in venture capital commitments may have a dramatic effect on prices. Because partnership agreements typically require that venture funds invest almost exclusively in private companies, increases in the supply of venture capital may result in greater competition to finance companies and rising valuations. The increase in commitments to the venture industry may also have different effects on different segments of the private equity market. For example, if capital is raised by funds in a geographically concentrated area and if investment by these funds is localized, then competition should lead to greater price increases where the inflows of capital are greatest.

These industry and geographic patterns may be distinguished from positive news about an industry's prospects leading to a simultaneous increase in inflows and valuations. The favorable news reflected in the higher public market prices and inflows would likely have symmetric effects on early- and later-stage companies as well as on firms in various geographic regions. Better industry prospects would improve the expected cash flow of all firms in an industry, independent of their stage of development. It should also be acknowledged that various other factors should be related to the valuation of the private companies, whether or not inflows affect pricing. Earnings might be a useful indicator of firm value. Firm value may also be related to the company's sales, employment level, or age. Considerable uncertainty exists about private companies. Many are years away from the positive cash flows that investors value. Signals such as these can separate firms that are expected to be relatively more successful from others. We use these as control variables in the regressions that follow.

Empirical Analyses

Construction of the Sample

VentureOne's database is used to identify the valuation data (described in chapter 22). As shown in table 9.1, of the 7,375 venture rounds identified by the firm between 1987 and 1995,[3] the valuations of the firm at the time of

---

3. The VentureOne database also includes a variety of other transactions including initial and follow-on public offerings by venture-backed firms, investments in leveraged buyouts and publicly traded firms by venture funds, and so forth. In tabulating venture capital rounds, we eliminate these transactions and only include equity investments by professional venture organizations in privately held firms.

Table 9.1
Number of observations, by year

Year	Number of financing rounds	Rounds with valuation data	Percentage with valuation data	Rounds with valuation data Rounds with sales data	Percentage with sales data	Rounds with employment data	Percentage with employment data
1987	693	255	36.8%	166	65.1%	191	74.9%
1988	634	314	49.5%	207	65.9%	221	70.4%
1989	751	369	49.1%	262	71.0%	276	74.8%
1990	797	420	52.7%	269	64.0%	275	65.5%
1991	785	440	56.1%	283	64.3%	297	67.5%
1992	941	626	66.5%	334	53.4%	332	53.0%
1993	952	647	68.0%	364	56.3%	358	55.3%
1994	955	570	59.7%	349	61.2%	428	75.1%
1995	867	428	49.4%	268	62.6%	315	73.6%
All years	7,375	4,069	55.2%	2,502	61.5%	2,693	66.2%

Note: The table shows the number of professional venture financings of privately held firms in the VentureOne database, as well as the number and percentage with valuation data. Of the rounds with valuation data, the table also displays the number and percentage for which we obtained sales and employment data for the beginning of the year of the financing.

the financing can be calculated in 4,069 cases (55 percent).[4] Forty-five percent of observations have valuation data in the first three years of the sample, compared to 61 percent in the 1990 to 1994 period. Consistent with the
discussion in chapter 22 about forms of selection bias, the completeness of
observations for 1995 is again lower, 49 percent (see table 9.2).

To address the omissions of valuation data, in unreported analyses we
repeat the regressions reported in table 9.6 through 9.8 using a Heckman
sample selection approach. We first estimate the probability that Venture-
One has been able to obtain information about the valuation in the financing round, and then seek to explain the determinants of the valuation. This
correction has little impact on the magnitude or the significance of the independent variables in the analyses of the determinants of valuations.[5]

Table 9.3 provides an overview of the patterns of valuations in the sample. Not surprisingly, more mature firms receive higher valuations, with the
exception of the dramatically depressed valuations for firms undergoing re-
starts (financial and product market restructurings). Semiconductor, data
processing, and communications companies have on average the highest
valuations, while industrial equipment and instrumentation companies have
the lowest. Firms based in the western United States, particularly in California, appear to be priced at a premium.

We complement VentureOne data in four ways. First, we examine a variety of sources to determine missing information such as the firm's start date
(details in chapter 22). Second, until recently VentureOne has not archived
employment and sales data on firms. Instead, they merely updated the database entries. We consequently use the reference sources cited in chapter 22

---

4. Throughout this chapter we use what is known in the venture industry as the pre-money
valuation, equal to the product of the price paid per share in the financing round and the shares
outstanding prior to the financing round. As discussed at length in Lerner (1994), the pre-
money valuation is more appropriate for hedonic pricing analyses. The pre-money valuation is
independent of the amount invested in the firm during the current financing round. As discussed in chapter 8, the amount invested may vary with many considerations, including the
fundraising environment. In calculating the valuation, VentureOne converts all preferred shares
into common stock at the conversion ratios specified in the agreements. Warrants and options
outstanding are included in the total, as long as their exercise price is below the price per share
being paid in the financing round.

5. These tabulations of completeness raise the question whether VentureOne captures the
total number of venture rounds, or whether the denominator substantially understates the
total number of financings. In recent years the total number of financing rounds identified by
VentureOne has been within 10 percent of the total identified by Venture Economics (which
compiles this information using the annual reports of venture capital funds). Before 1990, however, the Venture Economics tabulations indicate a substantially larger number of rounds than
VentureOne does. This may partially reflect the incompleteness of the early VentureOne data,
but it also reflects the tendency of the older Venture Economics entries to record a single venture as multiple financings, discussed in chapter 10.

Table 9.2
Comparisons of financing rounds with and without valuation data

	Rounds with valuation data	Rounds without valuation data	p-Value from test of equality[a]
Stage of firm at time of round			
Start-up stage	9%	18%	0.000
Development stage	31%	28%	0.001
Beta stage	5%	2%	0.000
Shipping stage	43%	44%	0.734
Profitable stage	8%	8%	0.184
Restart stage	2%	1%	0.008
Industry of firm			
Data processing industry	9%	8%	0.256
Computer software industry	17%	17%	0.450
Communications industry	16%	13%	0.001
Consumer electronics industry	1%	1%	0.133
Industrial equipment industry	4%	4%	0.780
Medical industry	31%	27%	0.000
Instrumentation industry	2%	2%	0.562
Components industry	3%	3%	0.651
Semiconductor industry	4%	3%	0.008
Other industry	13%	22%	0.000
Location of firm			
Eastern states	24%	28%	0.000
Western states	57%	50%	0.000
Elsewhere	19%	22%	0.000
Time and other characteristics[b]			
Date of financing	January 1992	June 1991	0.000
VW industry public equity index	2.31	2.19	0.000
EW industry public equity index	2.53	2.26	0.000
VW industry B/M ratio	0.37	0.39	0.000
EW industry B/M ratio	0.80	0.70	0.155
VW industry E/P ratio	0.03	0.03	0.924
EW industry E/P ratio	-0.15	-0.15	0.847
Age of firm (years)	4.0	4.1	0.262
Venture capital inflow in prior four quarters (1995$ mil)	3,165	3,429	0.000

Table 9.2

(continued)

Note: The sample consists of 7,375 professional venture financings of privately held firms between January 1987 and December 1995 in the VentureOne database. The table summarizes the characteristics of the 4,069 financing rounds in the sample for which VentureOne was able to determine the valuation of the financing round, and the 3,306 where VentureOne was not able to do so.

a. The p-values from t- and χ^2-tests of the null hypothesis of the two populations are identical.

b. Industry public equity indexes are normalized to 1.00 on January 1, 1987. The value-weighted (VW) and equally weighted (EW) industry public equity indexes are measured at the beginning of the month of financing and the VW and EW book-to-market (B/M) and earnings-to-price (E/P) ratios are measured at the beginning of the quarter of financing.

Table 9.3

Pre-money valuations of financing rounds, by firm characteristic

	Pre-money valuation		
	Mean	Standard error	N Observed
Stage of firm at time of round			
Start-up stage	2.7	0.1	366
Development stage	14.3	0.6	1231
Beta stage	21.1	1.6	217
Shipping stage	20.1	0.6	1706
Profitable stage	33.4	2.0	332
Restart stage	3.9	0.5	73
Industry of firm			
Data processing industry	20.0	1.3	376
Computer software industry	14.4	0.8	706
Communications industry	19.0	1.0	636
Consumer electronics industry	16.2	2.4	44
Industrial equipment industry	12.9	1.2	164
Medical industry	17.8	0.7	1260
Instrumentation industry	13.9	1.5	63
Components industry	15.5	1.7	112
Semiconductor industry	31.5	2.8	169
Other industry	15.9	1.2	528
Location of firm			
Eastern states	16.0	0.7	983
Western states	19.1	0.5	2321
Based elsewhere	15.1	0.8	765

Note: The sample consists of 4,069 professional venture financings of privately held firms between January 1987 and December 1995 in the VentureOne database for which VentureOne was able to determine the valuation of the financing round. The pre-money valuation is defined as the product of the price paid per share in the financing round and the shares outstanding prior to the financing round, expressed in millions of 1995 dollars.

to determine firms' sales and employment at the end of the calendar year prior to each financing with valuation data. When either sales or employment were not available from these sources, we contacted the firms for this information. (The VentureOne database provides the contact information for these firms.) Each firm received a faxed letter. Nonrespondents were contacted at least twice by telephone. The final two columns of table 9.1 summarize our success rate. In all, we identified historical sales data for 61 percent of the observations with valuation data in the VentureOne database and employment data for 66 percent.

Third, we develop several measures of public market valuations at the beginning of the month or the quarter of each financing. Rather than employing an overall market index, we construct industry indexes. We first associate each of the 103 VentureOne industry classes with a three-digit Standard Industrial Classification (SIC) code. This is based on an examination of all firms in each VentureOne class that had gone public. The Securities Data Company's Corporate New Issues database provides the primary three-digit SIC code assigned to these firms at the time they went public. In most cases the overwhelming majority of firms in each VentureOne class are assigned to a single three-digit SIC code. When no SIC code represents a majority, we also examine the distribution of the three-digit SIC codes of the active privately held firms listed in the *Corporate Technology Directory*. In cases that remain ambiguous, we consult with VentureOne officials regarding their classification criteria. In some cases, multiple VentureOne classifications were assigned to the same three-digit SIC code. For example, numerous classifications were matched to SIC code 737, "Computer and Data Processing Services."

For each of the 35 three-digit SIC codes, we identify all active companies that have a primary classification to that SIC code in Compustat. For each of these firms, we extract their monthly returns, shares outstanding, and market price at the beginning of each month from the Center for Research in Security Prices database. From Compustat, we identify the net income during and shareholders' equity at the beginning of each quarter.

These variables are used to create two sets of valuation measures. First, we construct monthly equal- and value-weighted industry stock price indexes for each VentureOne code. These industry stock price indexes should be a measure of industry investment opportunity. Including them in the regression controls for the portion of the increase in venture capital prices that is attributable to better investment opportunities. All firms in each three-digit industry with a return in that month are included and portfolios are rebalanced monthly. A concern is that these public market indexes might not perfectly measure future investment opportunities in an industry. In partic-

ular, an industry stock price index could be higher in 1995 than in 1988 because of (1) increases in price levels in the economy as a whole, (2) upward
revisions by investors of the expected future cash flows for that particular
industry, or (3) a decrease in the systematic riskiness of the industry leading
to declines in the industry cost of capital. Increases in expected future cash
flows and decreases in systematic industry risk would both lead to higher
industry prices (and private valuations) and increases in investment inflows
without the inflows driving up the prices. We also controlled for price levels
using the gross domestic product (GDP) deflator to alleviate the concern
that industry stock prices might just measure increases in nominal prices.

Second, we measure valuation levels using two market multiples. Price-
earnings and market-to-book ratios are frequently used by practitioners as
an approximate measure of equity market values. These ratios may be better
measures of future investment opportunities in an industry than the industry
indexes are. For each of the public firms assigned to the 35 industries, we
compute (1) the ratio of net income in the four previous quarters to the equity market value at the beginning of the quarter of the financing and (2) the
ratio of shareholders' equity to the market value of the equity at the beginning of the quarter. If multiple classes of common and preferred stock were
outstanding, the combined value of all classes is used. In many industries,
numerous small firms with significant negative earnings introduce a substantial skewness to the distribution of these ratios. Consequently both the
simple averages of these ratios and the averages weighted by equity market
capitalization at the beginning of the quarter are used.

Finally we tabulate the inflow of capital to funds devoted to investments
in venture capital and leveraged buyout transactions. Data are obtained
from the records of the consulting firm Asset Alternatives (the publisher of
the newsletter *Private Equity Analyst*). Many institutions defer making commitments of capital until the last quarter, meaning that financings display a
strong seasonal pattern. Consequently the total inflation-adjusted amount of
funds raised in the previous four quarters is tabulated.[6]

---

6. The tabulation of venture capital raised by year (displayed in table 9.4) differs from those
presented in chapter 4. The latter tabulation was based on the records of Venture Economics
whose methodology differs from that of Asset Alternatives in two ways. First, many funds raise
capital through multiple closings. In a closing an investor or group of investors signs a contract
that binds them to supply a set amount of capital to a private equity fund, and often provides a
fraction of that capital immediately. The Venture Economics database treats the total amount
ultimately raised by the fund as having been raised on the date of the first closing; the Asset
Alternatives database treats each closing as a separate event. Second, some private equity funds
make investments into both venture capital and buyout transactions. While there does not appear to be a systemic pattern, Venture Economics and Asset Alternatives differ in how they
classify some of the hybrid funds.

Table 9.4
Pre-money valuations of financing rounds, by year

Year	Pre-money valuation[a] Mean	Standard error	Inflow into venture industry (1995$ mil)	Average of value-weighted indexes	Average of book-to-market ratio
1987	19.0	1.6	4,969	1.18	0.50
1988	16.5	1.2	3,995	1.09	0.54
1989	16.6	1.1	4,082	1.33	0.54
1990	18.0	1.2	2,221	1.25	0.49
1991	15.8	1.0	1,542	1.51	0.58
1992	15.8	1.0	2,108	1.80	0.49
1993	16.4	0.8	3,065	2.06	0.43
1994	20.1	1.1	4,825	2.16	0.38
1995	20.9	1.4	4,517	2.47	0.41

Note: The sample consists of 4,069 professional venture financings of privately held firms between January 1987 and December 1995 in the VentureOne database for which VentureOne was able to determine the valuation of the financing round.

a. The pre-money valuation is defined as the product of the price paid per share in the financing round and the shares outstanding prior to the financing round, expressed in millions of 1995 dollars. The mean level of the 35 value-weighted industry stock indexes is used to control for the public market valuations of firms in the sample (January 1, 1987, is normalized as 1.00 for each index, with an adjustment for inflation), and the mean level of the book-to-market ratio is for the 35 industries (each industry ratio measure is the market value-weighted average of each active firm).

Basic Pricing Patterns

Before examining the determinants of the valuations of venture investments econometrically, we present the basic patterns. Table 9.4 makes clear that the highest inflation-adjusted valuations between 1987 and 1995 occurred in 1987, 1994, and 1995. These were also the years with the greatest inflows to private equity funds in constant dollars. The table also presents the value-weighted average book-to-market ratios and inflation-adjusted equity indexes for 35 industries whose construction is described above. Here the correlation with the pricing of venture investments is less clear; the greatest public market valuations were confined to the final years of the sample.

Two figures graphically depict the pricing patterns. Figure 9.1 presents the average of the public market indexes and the private equity valuations on a quarter-by-quarter basis, as well as the annual inflow into venture funds. For clarity, we present both market indexes and the inflows on a scale

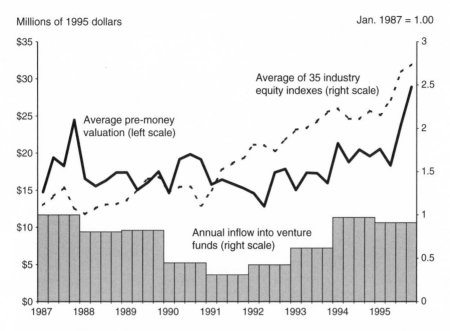

Figure 9.1
Quarterly pre-money valuations of financing rounds, average public market equity values, and inflows into the venture capital industry. The sample consists of 4,069 professional venture financings of privately held firms between January 1987 and December 1995 in the VentureOne database for which VentureOne was able to determine the valuation of the financing round. Thirty-five value-weighted industry stock indexes were used to control for the public market valuations (with January 1, 1987, normalized as 1.00 for each index and with an adjustment for inflation) and the total annual inflow to the venture capital industry (with 1987 normalized as 1.00).

that is normalized to 1.00 in 1987. Figure 9.2 presents the valuation of early- and later-stage investments on a biannual basis. The more dramatic rise of pricing levels for later-stage investments in both the first and last years of the sample is apparent.

A natural question is the extent to which the changes in valuations over time are driven by the changing mixture of firms being financed. The higher valuations in 1987, 1994, and 1995 may reflect different firms being funded during periods of rapid growth in commitments to venture funds. Venture capital organizations do not proportionately add partners as they increase capital under management. (For a discussion and evidence, see chapter 4.) Typically the number of investments that each partner can oversee is limited. Each investment requires extensive due diligence, attendance at monthly board meetings, and frequent informal interactions. Consequently

Millions of 1995 dollars

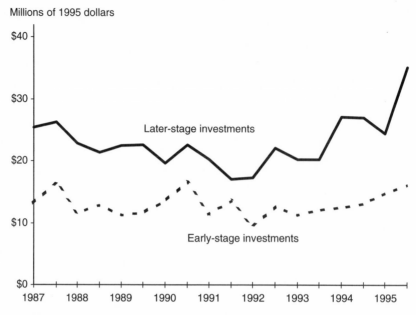

Figure 9.2
Pre-money valuations of later- and early-stage financing rounds. The sample consists of 4,069 professional venture financing of privately held firms between January 1987 and December 1995 in the VentureOne database for which VentureOne was able to determine the valuation of the financing round. The figure presents the mean pre-money valuation for firms in the shipping or profitable stages (later-stage investments), as well as those in all other stages (early-stage investments), in each half-year period.

venture funds that are rapidly growing tend to increase the average amount that they invest in each firm and shift from early- to later-stage investments, which can absorb more capital. This suggests the desirability of examining the share of firms being funded each year that are of the types that command high valuations. Examples include firms with higher sales, those that are already profitable, and those in the semiconductor industry. Regression analyses also control for these characteristics.

Table 9.5 presents some univariate evidence on these issues:

• The relation between sales and employment, on the one hand, and venture capital inflows, on the other, is economically and statistically insignificant. For example, the correlation coefficient between inflows and sales is only 0.006.

• Start-ups, which command the lowest valuations on average, actually comprise a greater percentage of the sample during periods with high inflows into venture capital funds. Also the probability that firms in the sample are shipping products or are profitable varies negatively with inflows. This is exactly the opposite pattern than we would have expected were the valuation pattern a consequence of the mixture of transactions.

• For medical-related and data processing firms, the probability of being funded is significantly negatively correlated with venture capital inflows. During years with the greatest venture capital inflows, there are more transactions with firm in the data processing industry and less with firms in the medical industry.

Thus the pattern of valuations over time does not appear to be determined by the changing mix of transactions. We must look elsewhere for an explanation of the time-series variation.

Basic Econometric Analysis

As the findings above suggest, the econometric analysis of the valuation of venture capital investments poses estimation challenges that are somewhat different from traditional studies of the pricing of publicly traded assets. Most pricing studies examine changes in the prices of an essentially constant basket of securities (except, of course, for new offerings and delistings). This environment is quite different. The average time between refinancings in our sample, and hence price observations, is 16.4 months.

One approach would be to examine only the changes in prices for firms that have a previous observed valuation. This is reminiscent to the "matched model" approach employed in pricing analyses. As Berndt and Griliches (1993) argue, this method can lead to misleading estimates. In particular, if the process through which new firms are valued is different from that in the refinancing of existing firms, this analysis can give a biased impression. For instance, in the pharmaceutical industry political pressures have often limited companies' abilities to raise the prices of existing pharmaceutical products, but such pressures have had much less impact on the initial pricing of new drugs. Furthermore this approach eliminates those companies that only receive one financing. These firms, which are typically the concerns that are liquidated or merged, may differ systematically from other firms.

Consequently we examine the pricing pattern using a hedonic regression approach. This method, first developed by Frederick Waugh to examine the pricing of vegetables in Boston's Fanueil Hall in 1927, includes all price observations in a regression analysis. The analysis includes firms receiving

Table 9.5
Characteristics of the sample firms receiving venture financing, by year

Year	Firm sales	Firm employment	Firm in start-up stage	Firm in shipping stage	Firm in profitable stage	Firm in data processing industry	Firm in communications industry	Firm in medical industry	Firm in semiconductor industry
1987	10.9	90.0	13%	35%	4%	20%	13%	20%	5%
1988	9.6	79.3	17	37	6	21	14	21	7
1989	9.4	79.5	11	38	8	14	15	24	5
1990	7.2	66.1	6	47	5	12	16	26	6
1991	8.1	59.6	6	47	7	11	15	32	4
1992	7.8	67.0	7	45	8	6	14	36	3
1993	7.5	78.7	9	42	13	4	16	36	3
1994	5.7	57.8	8	42	9	5	17	34	3
1995	7.7	77.7	8	38	7	4	18	35	3
Correlation coefficient	0.006	0.016	0.055	−0.059	−0.065	0.044	0.002	−0.056	0.022
p-Value	0.763	0.398	0.000	0.000	0.000	0.000	0.847	0.000	0.064

Note: The sample consists of 4,069 professional venture financings of privately held firms between January 1987 and December 1995 in the VentureOne database for which VentureOne was able to determine the valuation of the financing round. The table summarizes the mean characteristics of the firms financed in each year included in the sample, as the correlation coefficient between these measures and the inflow into venture capital funds in the four quarters prior to the financing (in millions of 1995 dollars), and the p-value of the test of the null hypothesis that the correlation coefficient equals zero. Sales (in millions of 1995 dollars) and employment are at the beginning of the year of the financing.

their first or follow-on financings. The price is the dependent variable, and the characteristics of the firm and the environment are the independent variables. The regression approach enables us to incorporate even those firms that received just one financing round.

An important assumption of hedonic pricing models is that the researcher can either measure the factors that are important for determining the price of the firm or good or identify reasonable proxies for these measures. If the qualities that determine the price are not quantifiable or measurable, then the hedonic regression model will have little explanatory power. Alternatively, the omitted variables may introduce biases that lead to mistaken interpretations of the results.

Tables 9.6 and 9.7 present the basic analysis.[7] We employ an ordinary least squares (OLS) specification and a log-log framework, meaning that the logarithm of the valuation is regressed on the dummy variables and the logarithms of the continuous, nonnegative variables. The log-log specification makes sense because many of the factors should be multiplicative. For instance, an increase in public market values should lead to a greater dollar increase in the valuation of an already substantial firm than that of a smaller one. As opposed to table 9.4, we employ the nominal value of the valuation, correcting for inflation by including the GDP deflator as an additional independent variable.

We use a variety of independent variables. First, dummy variables capture the firm's industry, stage of development, and location. Second, we control for public market valuations of firms in the same industry. Table 9.6 includes the value of corresponding equal- and value-weighted industry indexes at the end of the month prior to the financing. Table 9.7 shows the regressions using the value of the two market multiples at the end of the quarter prior to the financing. Third, we employ venture capital inflows (in constant dollars) in the four quarters prior to the investment. Finally, regressions include the firm's age, employment, and sales. Because employment and sales data are missing in some cases, and the two measures are highly correlated, we present regressions that do not use either variable and then ones that use each in turn.

---

7. The regressions in these and all other tables (with the exception of the Heckman sample selection regressions reported in the third and fourth columns of table 9.10) employ *t*-statistics computed with heteroskedasticity-consistent standard errors (White 1980). Because in many cases there are several observations of the same firm (due to multiple financing rounds), the observations may not be independent. We address this issue in the final two paragraphs of this section.

Table 9.6
Ordinary least squares regression analyses of pre-money valuations of financing rounds

Independent variable[a]	No firm size measure		Using firm sales		Using firm employment	
Stage of firm						
Start-up stage	−0.85 [6.67]	−0.87 [6.77]	−0.89 [5.35]	−0.90 [5.42]	−0.76 [5.35]	−0.77 [5.45]
Development stage	−0.14 [1.11]	−0.16 [1.26]	−0.08 [0.52]	−0.11 [0.65]	−0.02 [0.16]	−0.05 [0.37]
Beta stage	0.13 [0.96]	0.10 [0.75]	0.22 [1.26]	0.18 [1.02]	0.25 [1.62]	0.18 [1.20]
Shipping stage	0.16 [1.37]	0.15 [1.23]	0.18 [1.16]	0.15 [0.95]	0.19 [1.47]	0.14 [1.12]
Profitable stage	0.52 [3.98]	0.50 [3.83]	0.46 [2.80]	0.41 [2.49]	0.45 [3.17]	0.38 [2.70]
Restart stage	−1.22 [8.66]	−1.25 [8.82]	−1.30 [7.71]	−1.35 [7.98]	−1.28 [8.49]	−1.35 [8.98]
Industry of firm						
Data processing industry	0.32 [3.64]	0.27 [2.99]	0.27 [2.37]	0.17 [1.48]	0.35 [3.35]	0.24 [2.36]
Computer software industry	−0.04 [0.51]	−0.02 [0.26]	−0.09 [1.04]	−0.07 [0.80]	−0.04 [0.56]	−0.02 [0.19]
Communications industry	0.34 [4.76]	0.29 [3.98]	0.28 [3.14]	0.19 [2.05]	0.34 [4.13]	0.23 [2.83]
Consumer electronics industry	0.25 [1.47]	0.25 [1.48]	0.27 [1.48]	0.26 [1.46]	0.23 [1.56]	0.22 [1.58]
Industrial equipment industry	−0.21 [2.01]	−0.24 [2.29]	−0.23 [1.72]	−0.28 [2.13]	−0.18 [1.49]	−0.23 [1.91]
Medical industry	0.39 [5.86]	0.37 [5.38]	0.43 [4.89]	0.37 [4.04]	0.46 [5.91]	0.38 [4.69]
Instrumentation industry	0.01 [0.13]	−0.02 [0.13]	0.04 [0.32]	−0.01 [0.08]	0.09 [0.76]	0.04 [0.29]
Components industry	−0.04 [0.38]	−0.05 [0.49]	−0.06 [0.49]	−0.08 [0.66]	−0.07 [0.54]	−0.08 [0.66]
Semiconductor industry	0.60 [5.55]	0.60 [5.48]	0.45 [3.74]	0.44 [3.58]	0.49 [4.56]	0.49 [4.46]
Location and other characteristics						
Eastern states	0.10 [1.92]	0.09 [1.78]	0.17 [2.62]	0.15 [2.42]	0.16 [2.77]	0.15 [2.54]
Western states	0.30 [6.48]	0.29 [6.39]	0.33 [5.72]	0.33 [5.61]	0.32 [5.97]	0.32 [5.90]
Log of firm age (in years)	0.43 [13.90]	0.43 [13.90]	0.30 [7.11]	0.30 [7.04]	0.19 [4.55]	0.18 [4.27]
Log of firm sales			0.19 [7.44]	0.20 [7.68]		

Log of firm employment	0.16 [4.21]			0.27 [13.73]	0.30 [14.31]
Log of value-weighted industry index		0.27 [5.20]		0.31 [6.42]	
Log of equal-weighted industry index	0.15 [4.17]		0.26 [5.61]		0.35 [7.93]
Log of inflow of venture capital	0.18 [4.94]	0.14 [3.10]	0.16 [3.46]	0.07 [1.67]	0.09 [2.03]
Constant	−0.19 [0.58]	−0.06 [0.14]	−0.16 [0.37]	−0.11 [0.27]	−0.26 [0.65]
R^2	0.32	0.34	0.34	0.38	0.38
F-Statistic	98.94	69.47	70.80	76.33	76.39
p-Value	0.000	0.000	0.000	0.000	0.000
Number of observations	3,896	2,433	2,433	2,622	2,622

Note: The sample consists of 4,069 professional venture financings of privately held firms between January 1987 and December 1995 in the VentureOne database for which VentureOne was able to determine the valuation of the financing round. The pre-money valuation is defined as the product of the price paid per share in the financing round and the shares outstanding prior to the financing round. The logarithm of the pre-money valuation, expressed in millions of current dollars, is used as the dependent variable. [Absolute heteroskedasticity-consistent t-statistics are in brackets.]

a. The independent variables include dummy variables controlling for the firm's status, industry, and location, and the logarithms of the firm's age (in years), of sales (in millions of 1995 dollars), and employment at the beginning of the year of the financing, of two indexes for the public market valuations of publicly traded firms in the same industry as the firm at the beginning of the month of the financing (with January 1, 1987 normalized as 1.00 for each index), and of the inflow into venture capital funds in the four quarters prior to the financing (in millions of 1995 dollars).

Table 9.7
Ordinary least squares regression analyses of pre-money valuations of financing rounds, with alternative measures of public market valuations

Independent variable[a]	Using book to market		Using earnings to value	
	Value-weighted	Equal-weighted	Value-weighted	Equal-weighted
Stage of firm				
Start-up stage	−0.97 [5.76]	−0.98 [5.78]	−0.87 [6.05]	−0.87 [6.07]
Development stage	−0.18 [1.07]	−0.18 [1.08]	−0.15 [1.11]	−0.16 [1.13]
Beta stage	0.09 [0.51]	0.10 [0.56]	0.06 [0.37]	0.06 [0.37]
Shipping stage	0.07 [0.42]	0.07 [0.47]	0.14 [0.27]	0.04 [0.27]
Profitable stage	0.33 [1.91]	0.33 [1.95]	0.27 [1.81]	0.27 [1.82]
Restart stage	−1.43 [8.19]	−1.41 [8.05]	−1.45 [9.26]	−1.45 [9.26]
Industry of firm				
Data processing industry	0.23 [1.93]	0.28 [2.29]	0.31 [3.01]	0.31 [3.00]
Computer software industry	0.01 [0.08]	−0.03 [0.30]	0.08 [1.05]	0.08 [1.06]
Communications industry	0.24 [2.68]	0.30 [3.00]	30 [3.66]	0.30 [3.68]
Consumer electronics industry	0.32 [1.79]	0.38 [2.07]	0.29 [2.05]	0.29 [2.05]
Industrial equipment industry	−0.21 [1.57]	−0.15 [1.04]	−0.14 [1.18]	−0.14 [1.18]
Medical industry	0.48 [5.50]	0.46 [5.27]	0.52 [6.70]	0.52 [6.65]
Instrumentation industry	0.07 [0.54]	0.11 [0.75]	0.13 [1.09]	0.13 [1.08]
Components industry	−0.03 [0.25]	0.01 [0.08]	−0.02 [0.18]	−0.03 [0.22]
Semiconductor industry	0.46 [3.77]	0.49 [3.95]	0.51 [4.64]	0.50 [4.57]
Location and other characteristics				
Eastern states	0.16 [2.55]	0.16 [2.46]	0.16 [2.66]	0.16 [2.70]
Western states	0.33 [5.69]	0.33 [5.68]	0.32 [5.95]	0.32 [6.00]
Log of firm age (in years)	0.28 [6.63]	0.28 [6.59]	0.16 [3.80]	0.16 [3.84]
Log of firm sales	0.21 [7.78]	1.84 [7.85]		
Log of firm employment			0.30 [14.02]	0.30 [14.00]
Log of gross domestic product deflator	1.96 [5.92]	1.84 [5.44]	2.48 [8.05]	2.53 [8.05]
Log of equal-weighted industry book-to-market ratio	−0.004 [1.27]			
Log of value-weighted industry book-to-market ratio		−0.36 [1.80]		
Log of equal-weighted industry earnings-to-market value ratio			0.01 [0.43]	
Log of value-weighted industry earnings-to-market value ratio				0.54 [0.82]
Log of inflow of venture capital	0.20 [4.31]	0.19 [4.06]	0.14 [3.07]	0.13 [2.92]
Constant	−9.62 [5.74]	−8.84 [5.11]	−12.18 [7.92]	−12.40 [7.93]

Table 9.7
(continued)

Independent variable[a]	Using book to market		Using earnings to value	
	Value-weighted	Equal-weighted	Value-weighted	Equal-weighted
R^2	0.34	0.34	0.38	0.38
F-Statistic	68.69	68.75	74.62	75.15
p-Value	0.000	0.000	0.000	0.000
Number of observations	2,433	2,433	2,622	2,622

Note: The sample consists of 4,069 professional venture financings of privately held firms between January 1987 and December 1995 in the VentureOne database for which VentureOne was able to determine the valuation of the financing round. The pre-money valuation is defined as the product of the price paid per share in the financing round and the shares outstanding prior to the financing round. The logarithm of the pre-money valuation, expressed in millions of current dollars, is used as the dependent variable. [Absolute heteroskedasticity-consistent t-statistics are in brackets.]

a. The independent variables include dummy variables controlling for the firm's status, industry, and location, and the logarithms of the value-weighted and equally-weighted average ratios of book-to-market equity value and earnings-to-market equity value of publicly traded firms in the same industry as the firm, of the gross domestic product deflator at the beginning of the quarter of the financing, of the firm's age (in years) at the beginning of the year of the financing, of the firm's sales (in millions of 1995 dollars) and employment at the beginning of the year of the financing, and of the inflow into venture capital funds in the four quarters prior to the financing (in millions of 1995 dollars).

Significantly higher valuations are associated with profitable firms. There is a monotonic relation between stage of development and valuation. Startups and firms undergoing restructurings have lower valuations. These firms have considerably more uncertainty about whether they will ultimately be successful. Older and larger firms are associated with higher valuations than less developed firms. Greater age and size are also likely to be proxies for superior future prospects.

The regressions also suggest that firms in the eastern and western United States are associated with higher valuations, as are those in the computer hardware, communications, medical, and semiconductor industries. The geographic patterns are consistent with firms situated in high-technology complexes enjoying a variety of benefits, which are reflected in higher valuations. As Krugman (1991) discusses, benefits include the presence of specialized intermediaries such as patent lawyers, an ample supply of the highly skilled employees that they require, and technological spillovers.[8] We

---

8. Inferences are robust to employing dummy variables for the states with the greatest venture capital investment, for example, California and Massachusetts, or using the pool of venture funds based in each state at the beginning of 1987. It is also possible that the East and West Coast dummies proxy for intense competition for attractive investments. We discuss this alternative later.

have no prior reason to believe any industry patterns should emerge, but they may reflect the greater expected future cash flows for firms in these industries.

Public market valuations have an uneven impact. Industry indexes are consistently significant. A 10 percent increase in public market values is associated with a marginal increase in private equity valuations of between 1.5 and 3.5 percent. The coefficient on the average industry book-to-market ratio is, as expected, negative. An industry whose average book-to-market ratio is high has lower private equity valuations in the subsequent quarter. An industry with a high book-to-market ratio is commonly interpreted as having low future growth prospects. However, this variable is only marginally significant. The earnings-to-price ratio of firms in the same industry at the end of the previous quarter is consistently insignificant, and its sign is opposite of what would be expected. Using the median industry earnings-price ratio, which may be less influenced by outliers, the coefficient takes on the expected negative sign but remains statistically insignificant. The results are also robust to using the inflation-adjusted valuation as the dependent variable and the inflation-adjusted industry stock index as an independent variable.

Finally inflows to venture capital funds are significantly related to the valuations of these funds' investments in private firms. A 10 percent increase in venture inflows is associated with a marginal increase in valuations of between 0.7 and 2.1 percent. This result is consistent with the suggestion that demand pressures affect prices. The magnitude and significance of the coefficient on venture capital inflows falls when employment is used as a control variable, but to a much less extent when sales is employed. This is puzzling given the low correlation between inflows and the employment of firms financed. It appears to reflect the fact that the firms in which the employment is known are not entirely representative of the sample as a whole. Furthermore this may partially reflect the smaller sample size. Were we to have full data on employment of these firms, the coefficient would be likely to be more significant. However, many of the regressions below continue to use both sales and employment as control variables as a check of the robustness of the relation between inflows and valuations.

One concern with these analyses is the potential impact of autocorrelation across the different financings of the same firm. While regressions control for heteroskedasticity, the estimates may still be biased if the residuals are correlated. We address this concern repeating the estimation of several of the regressions reported in table 9.6 employing generalized least squares

(GLS). McCullagh and Nelder (1989) show that this approach simultaneously controls for first-order autocorrelation across the subsequent financings of the same firm and heteroskedasticity across the observations of the different firms. Unfortunately, the estimation can only employ observations in which firms have had two or more financings with valuation data. As a result we compare the standard errors in these regressions to those in heteroskedasticity-corrected regressions only using cases for which there is more than one observation of each firm.

In the table 9.6 regressions we used White's heteroskedasticity adjustment. We compare the regressions to the GLS regressions. The comparison is restricted to the regression observations in which the firm had two or more financings with valuation data. The comparison shows that the correction for first-order autocorrelation has little impact on the results. While the standard errors are generally (but not universally) higher, the effects are modest. Consider the leftmost regression in table 9.6. The standard errors for the location dummy variables are 1.6 percent higher on average in the GLS regressions, and those of the sector dummies are 0.1 percent higher. The standard error on the venture inflow measure is actually very slightly lower once the GLS correction is made. The results of the other regressions in table 9.6 are similar. In each case the average standard error increases by less than 10 percent when the GLS specification is substituted for the heteroskedasticity-adjusted OLS regressions, with the sample in each case held constant.

Using Control Variables to Assess Robustness

While results show a relation between venture inflows and prices, specification errors may cause a spurious correlation. Here we seek to assess the robustness of results. None of these adjustments appear to alter the basic patterns seen above. Venture inflows continue to have a large, positive effect on valuations.

One possibility is that additional factors not captured in the basic specification affect the value of the venture-backed firms. The firms used to construct the public market benchmarks, while matched by industry, differ systematically from the firms backed by venture capitalists in at least two ways. They are, on average, considerably larger, and they have already successfully accessed the public capital markets. Fama and French (1992) have shown that the stock market returns of small firms differ significantly from those of other concerns.

We address this concern by adding additional control variables to the basic specification. The first of these, as shown in the top panel of table 9.8, is an index of the performance of small-capitalization stocks. We employ Ibbotson and Associates' monthly index of the total return on the two smallest deciles of firms traded on the New York and American Stock Exchanges. While this small-capitalization stock index has considerable explanatory power, the influx of funds into venture capital funds remains highly significant.

A variety of additional factors are added in unreported regressions. For instance, small private firms might be more sensitive to business cycles. To address this suggestion, we add indexes measuring the level of the GDP deflator, the real GDP, and the changes in these measures in the past three and six months. We also explore the impact of credit market conditions. Some firms may consider bank loans to be an alternative to venture financing. In situations where bank loans are more expensive or less available, entrepreneurs may be willing to settle for lower equity valuations (i.e., pay a higher cost of equity capital). The difference in the average yields of bonds rated by Moody's as Aaa and those rated Baa proxies for the premium that firms with weaker balance sheets must pay to borrow money. The number of small business failures and incorporations as tabulated by the U.S. Small Business Administration's Office of Advocacy captures changing conditions and expectations for small businesses as a whole. In each case the impact of venture capital inflows on prices changes little in magnitude or significance.

A second possibility is that the pricing of investments by private equity firms reflects equity valuation levels in the public market, but only with a substantial lag. Negotiations between venture investors and entrepreneurs can be protracted, for example, if the venture investor needs to find a syndication partner before finalizing the transaction. Consequently the price of the investment might be tentatively agreed upon well before the date of the closing.

To address this possibility, we include the lagged industry price index as an additional independent variable. Alternative regressions employ the index value six, twelve, and eighteen months prior to the financing. Panel B of table 9.8 reports the results of the regression employing the index value twelve months prior to the financing. These controls have little impact on the coefficient or the significance of the variable measuring the inflow of funds into the venture industry.

A third possibility is that prices may be affected by differences between first and later round investors. In particular, in chapter 11 we show that

Table 9.8
Ordinary least squares regression analyses of pre-money valuations of financing rounds, with controls for additional hypotheses

Panel A: Adding a small capitalization stock index[a]		
Log of value-weighted industry index	0.06 [1.20]	
Log of equal-weighted industry index		0.02 [0.39]
Log of small capitalization stock index	0.24 [2.77]	0.27 [2.42]
Log of inflow of venture capital	0.14 [3.80]	0.14 [3.33]
Panel B: Adding a lagged price index[b]		
Log of value-weighted industry index	0.07 [0.80]	
Log of equal-weighted industry index		0.11 [1.36]
Log of value-weighted industry index from 12 months previously	0.23 [2.20]	
Log of equal-weighted industry index from 12 months previously		0.17 [2.00]
Log of inflow of venture capital	0.14 [3.02]	0.13 [2.48]
Panel C: Adding a dummy variable for later venture rounds[c]		
Log of value-weighted industry index	0.27 [5.64]	
Log of equal-weighted industry index		0.30 [7.02]
Second or later venture round?	0.47 [11.91]	0.46 [11.53]
Log of inflow of venture capital	0.07 [1.74]	0.09 [2.05]

Note: The sample consists of 4,069 professional venture financings of privately held firms between January 1987 and December 1995 in the VentureOne database for which VentureOne was able to determine the valuation of the financing round. The pre-money valuation is defined as the product of the price paid per share in the financing round and the shares outstanding prior to the financing round. The logarithm of the pre-money valuation, expressed in millions of current dollars, is used as the dependent variable. The independent variables in all regressions include dummy variables controlling for the firm's status, industry, and location, and the logarithms of two indexes for the public market valuations of publicly traded firms in the same industry as the firm at the beginning of the month of the financing (with January 1, 1987, normalized as 1.00 for each index), of the firm's age (in years) at the beginning of the year of the financing, and of the inflow into venture capital funds in the four quarters prior to the financing (in millions of 1995 dollars). In panel B, the logarithm of the firm's sales (in millions of 1995 dollars) at the beginning of the year of the financing is an additional independent variable. In panel C, the logarithm of the firm's employment at the beginning of the year of the financing is included. Also, panels A, B, and C respectively add as independent variables the logarithm of a small capitalization stock index, the logarithm of the relevant price index twelve months prior to the investment, and a dummy variable denoting second and later rounds of venture capital investment. Only selected coefficients are presented. [Absolute heteroskedasticity-consistent *t*-statistics are in brackets.]

established venture groups tend to syndicate second and later venture rounds with less established investors. These later rounds are associated with a substantial premium, which partially reflects the fact that these later-round investors are rarely asked to join the board or provide other value-added services.

To examine the possibility that these changing syndication patterns affect valuations, we control for the round of venture investment.[9] In the regression reported in panel C of table 9.8, we add a dummy variable indicating whether the transaction was a second or later venture round. While the dummy is strongly positive, suggesting that first-round investors are being compensated for their services by buying equity at lower prices, the measure of venture inflows remains positive and significant at least at the ten percent confidence level. Similar results appear when we employ additional independent variables to more finely indicate the round of venture investment.

First Difference Analysis

One persistent concern is that the analyses above cannot capture many of the firm-specific determinants of pricing. One way to address this concern is to undertake a first difference analysis. By examining the changes in valuation across venture rounds, we are able to minimize the distortionary effects of unobservable firm characteristics. While this analysis is not without its limitations, the first-difference analysis can provide another check on the validity of the results.[10]

The first two columns of table 9.9 present the results of several OLS analyses. The observations include all venture rounds in which the valuation is known in the current and subsequent financing rounds. The dependent variable is the difference between the logarithm of the valuation in the subsequent and current rounds. To maximize the sample size, the table presents the results from regressions that do not use employment or sales data. The other results are similar.

9. The reader may be confused about the addition of this control variable since we have already controlled for the firm's stage of development. Although most firms receive their initial venture capital financing while still in the start-up or development stages, a significant minority receive their first venture financing after a number of years of operations. For instance, as we report in chapter 8, the average consumer products company was nearly six years old at the time of its first venture financing. These older firms are likely to be shipping product or even to be profitable at the time of their initial financing round.

10. Problems with "matched model" estimations discussed in the second paragraph of the basic econometric analysis.

Table 9.9
Ordinary least squares and Heckman sample selection regression analyses of changes in pre-money valuations between financing rounds

Independent variable	OLS estimates		Heckman equation estimates	
Stage of firm in prior round				
Start-up stage	0.84 [7.29]	0.84 [7.27]	0.81 [6.53]	0.80 [6.48]
Development stage	0.58 [5.12]	0.57 [5.08]	0.55 [4.74]	0.54 [4.67]
Beta stage	0.40 [2.98]	0.40 [2.96]	0.38 [3.00]	0.38 [2.97]
Shipping stage	0.32 [2.85]	0.31 [2.81]	0.30 [2.80]	0.29 [2.74]
Profitable stage	0.29 [2.42]	0.29 [2.38]	0.30 [2.37]	0.29 [2.33]
Restart stage	0.80 [4.11]	0.79 [4.10]	0.79 [5.05]	0.78 [5.00]
Industry of firm				
Data processing industry	−0.05 [0.75]	−0.06 [0.78]	−0.05 [0.83]	−0.06 [0.88]
Computer software industry	−0.01 [0.19]	−0.01 [0.21]	−0.01 [0.22]	−0.01 [0.23]
Communications industry	0.07 [1.15]	0.06 [1.09]	0.07 [1.24]	0.07 [1.17]
Consumer electronics industry	−0.03 [0.29]	−0.03 [0.32]	−0.03 [0.24]	−0.04 [0.26]
Industrial equipment industry	−0.20 [2.28]	−0.20 [2.29]	−0.20 [2.37]	−0.20 [2.38]
Medical industry	0.01 [0.22]	0.01 [0.17]	0.01 [0.24]	0.01 [0.19]
Instrumentation industry	−0.02 [0.19]	−0.02 [0.20]	−0.02 [0.19]	−0.03 [0.22]
Components industry	−0.06 [0.68]	−0.06 [0.70]	−0.06 [0.58]	−0.06 [0.60]
Semiconductor industry	0.06 [0.68]	0.06 [0.66]	0.06 [0.70]	0.05 [0.68]
Location of firm				
Eastern states	−0.01 [0.24]	−0.01 [0.24]	−0.02 [0.33]	−0.02 [0.33]
Western states	0.001 [0.02]	0.002 [0.04]	−0.01 [0.13]	−0.01 [0.13]
Events between prior and current round				
Firm began active product marketing	0.01 [0.26]	0.01 [0.25]	0.01 [0.26]	0.01 [0.24]
Firm underwent restart	−1.72 [12.69]	−1.72 [12.71]	−1.72 [16.99]	−1.72 [17.00]
Log of time between rounds	0.01 [0.27]	0.0003 [0.01]	0.001 [0.06]	−0.01 [0.21]
Change in log of value-weighted index	0.02 [0.27]		0.03 [0.44]	
Change in log of equal-weighted index		0.05 [0.75]		0.05 [1.01]
Change in log of venture capital inflow	0.08 [2.03]	0.08 [2.15]	0.08 [2.50]	0.09 [2.66]
Constant	0.13 [1.06]	0.13 [1.05]	0.19 [1.30]	0.20 [1.34]
R^2	0.23	0.23		
F-Statistic	19.56	19.76		
χ^2-Statistic			961.17	961.27
p-Value	0.000	0.000	0.000	0.000
Number of observations	1,941	1,941	4,064	4,064

Table 9.9
(continued)
Note: The sample consists of 4,069 professional venture financings of privately held firms between January 1987 and December 1995 in the VentureOne database for which VentureOne was able to determine the valuation of the financing round. The pre-money valuation is defined as the product of the price paid per share in the financing round and the shares outstanding prior to the financing round. The difference between the logarithm of the pre-money valuation in the subsequent and current venture rounds, expressed in millions of current dollars, is used as the dependent variable. The independent variables include dummy variables controlling for the firm's status, industry, and location at the time of the current round, dummies that indicate a change in status between the current and subsequent round, the logarithm of the time between the two financing rounds (expressed in years), and the differences in the logarithms of the two indexes of the valuations of publicly traded firms in the same industry as the firm (with January 1, 1987, normalized as 1.00 for each index) and of the inflows into venture capital funds in the four quarters prior to the financing (in millions of 1995 dollars). The third and fourth columns present the coefficients from the second equation in a two-equation system. (The initial equation controls for the probability that the current round is followed by another venture financing. The χ^2-statistic and the number of observations refer to the entire two-equation system.) [Absolute heteroskedasticity-consistent t-statistics are in brackets in the first two columns, and absolute t-statistics are in brackets in the third and fourth columns.]

The greatest write-ups are associated with firms with the lowest valuations in the current rounds, namely those in the start-up, development, or re-start phase. These are also the firms that are in greatest risk of not receiving another financing round. Many of the firms that disappear from the VentureOne database have either been terminated or else joined the ranks of the "living dead," ongoing firms whose future growth prospects are so modest that they are not attractive candidates for an IPO or an acquisition. Thus it is not surprising that the low-valued firms that receive subsequent financing are associated with the greatest markups. The very fact that they have been refinanced implies that they have made substantial progress. Neither is it surprising that firms encountering difficulty between the current and subsequent financing and undertaking a re-start round experience a dramatic drop in valuations. The change in price reflects new information that becomes available on these firms. Few clear patterns emerge by industry or location.

With respect to changes in the external environment, quite stark results emerge. Changes in public market valuations, whether measured using equal- or value-weighted indexes or (in unreported regressions) using the market multiples, have little impact on pricing. However, changes in venture inflows have a significant impact. The valuation of a firm financed in two consecutive years will increase by an additional 8 percent if the venture capital inflow doubles in that period. The first differences results provide additional evidence that venture inflows could be driving up prices through greater investment competition.

The third and fourth columns of table 9.9 present Heckman sample selection analyses. Using each financing round as an observation, we estimate a two-equation system. The first equation measures the probability that there will be a subsequent financing round. If there is a subsequent round, the second equation measures the change in the valuation, again expressed as the difference between the logarithm of the valuation in the subsequent and current rounds. In the unreported first-stage probit analysis, several patterns emerge. The probability of refinancing is higher during periods of large venture capital inflows.[11] This is broadly consistent with the impact of inflows on valuations. Those firms that are either already profitable (who typically go public thereafter) or undergoing a "re-start" (many of which are abandoned) are less likely to obtain subsequent venture financing. The probability of another venture financing falls when we examine firms financed at the end of the sample period, and this reflects the fact that we do not observe financings subsequent to the end of 1995. Results from the second-stage regressions, reported in the third and fourth columns of table 9.9, are similar to the OLS analysis. The coefficients on the variables explaining the change in valuations in the first two regressions, including the influx into venture capital, remain statistically significant in this analysis.

Decomposition of Price Movements

We now examine whether influxes of capital affect certain types of firms particularly strongly. We undertake two types of analyses. First we examine whether the pricing of particular investments is especially sensitive to the influx of venture capital or to public market values. Next we examine whether the influxes into venture capital funds based in different locations and with particular investment foci have differential effects on the valuation of these types of transactions.

If the increase in valuations associated with periods of high venture inflows is caused by competition for investments between venture funds, then it is likely that the increase will not be uniform. First, while regions like Silicon Valley and Route 128 are characterized by a concentration of entrepreneurial ventures, the representation of venture capitalists is even more disproportionate. For instance, several hundred venture organizations have offices on Sand Hill Road near the Stanford University campus. In

---

11. In a similar vein, we show in chapter 8 that a one standard deviation increase in venture capital commitments leads to a two-month reduction in the time between venture financings.

chapter 10, we show that many venture capitalists invest locally, implying that the regions with the most venture funds are likely to experience the greatest competition for transactions. Second, as discussed above, the typical venture organization has seen an increase in capital managed per partner as fund size grew. Because of the pressure to deploy capital in larger transactions, we might expect that high venture inflows should disproportionately inflate the valuation of later-stage investments. Finally, because venture funds often invest locally and have at least somewhat well-defined mandates, the growth of venture funds of a particular type should have a disproportionate effect on valuations of that particular class of investment.

The first panel of table 9.10 presents two representative regressions using interaction terms. Each uses the base specification (i.e., without employment or sales) and measures public market values with the equity indexes. The results using the sales, employment, and market multiple variables are similar. The reported regressions interact venture capital inflows and the public market indexes, with a dummy variable indicating whether the firm is located in the two states with the largest venture pools, California or Massachusetts, or the financing is a later-stage transaction, a firm in the shipping or profitable stages at the time of the investment. The regressions employ an OLS specification and the equal- and value-weighted industry indexes. Rather than presenting the coefficients of all the variables, we present selected results.

Neither firm characteristic is significant when interacted with public market values. Shifts in public market values appear to affect all transactions equally, regardless of stage or region. This supports the suggestion that the industry public market indexes measure the expected future profitability of the industry and hence affect the prospects of all firms. It is not the case that later-stage companies' "closeness" to the public markets causes greater sensitivity to public market price movements because of financing substitutability. However, consistent with the discussion above, venture capital inflows appear to have increased the valuations of California and Massachusetts firms more than other firms. The coefficient on the interaction between the venture capital inflow and the pool of venture capital based in the state is also significant. This finding is robust to measuring the pool in absolute or per capita terms. In each case, we use the venture pool at the beginning of 1987 to avoid simultaneity problems. The coefficient on the interaction between inflows and later-stage investments has the predicted positive sign but is statistically insignificant.

Panels B and C of table 9.10 give two representative analyses of how influxes of funds located in particular regions and focusing on certain stages affect the valuations of firms in those segments. The regressions examine the pricing of two classes of venture transactions: firms based in the eastern United States and later-stage investments. We compare how valuations change with the influx of funds based in that region or specializing in that class of investment, as well as with influxes to other types of funds.[12] By segmenting flows and valuations, we increase the number of independent observations that we can observe. In the former case, the coefficient is significantly greater on influxes into funds based in this particular region. Similar results hold in several unreported analyses employing other geographic partitions. A similar pattern emerges from the analysis of later-stage investments, but the difference is smaller in magnitude and statistically insignificant. This may partially reflect the imprecision with which funds report their investment targets. Many venture organizations, which originally specialized in early-stage investments, continue to report such a focus long after they have raised substantial funds and shifted to later-stage transactions. It is possible that these firms are reluctant to alert their limited partners, who might reasonably worry that the funds' returns will suffer during this transition. This analysis provides at least some corroboration of the suggestion that the influx of funds influences the pricing of venture investments.

Addressing Omitted Variable Bias

In settings where an important control variable is missing from a regression, Judge et al. (1985) show that omitted variable bias may lead to the coefficients of correlated independent variables being inflated. This effect may be happening here. In particular, we may have omitted an important explanatory variable that would control for the changes in the quality of investments presented to venture capitalists. This omission may cause us to falsely impute significance to the measure of venture capital inflows. To address this problem, we employ an instrumental variable. The instrumental variable should be correlated with the inflows to the venture capital industry but otherwise be unrelated to the venture capitalist's opportunity set.

The reason for worrying about this problem is as follows. The changes in opportunities facing venture capitalists are difficult to observe. Venture investors fund only a minute fraction of businesses begun each year, so it

---

12. These classifications are from annual compilations of venture capital fund-raising by Asset Alternatives and (in earlier years) Venture Economics.

Table 9.10
Ordinary least squares regression analyses of pre-money valuations of financing rounds, dividing the sample by firm characteristics

Panel A: Adding interaction terms to the base regression		
Log of value-weighted industry index	0.19 [2.97]	
Log of equal-weighted industry index		0.21 [3.22]
Log of inflow of venture capital	0.11 [2.29]	0.13 [2.71]
Log of industry index * firm in later stages	0.02 [0.36]	−0.04 [0.68]
Log of venture inflow * firm in later stages	0.09 [1.27]	0.07 [0.95]
Log of industry index * firm in California or Massachusetts	−0.06 [0.87]	−0.06 [0.93]
Log of venture inflow * firm in California or Massachusetts	0.02 [2.48]	0.02 [2.54]
Panel B: Exclusively examining firms based in the eastern United States		
Log of value-weighted industry index	0.16 [1.52]	
Log of equal-weighted industry index		0.19 [1.91]
Log of inflow of venture funds based in eastern United States	0.38 [3.09]	0.41 [3.28]
Log of inflow of venture funds based elsewhere in United States	−0.12 [0.98]	−0.13 [1.07]
p-Value, test of equality of two venture inflow variables	0.030	0.020
Panel C: Exclusively examining later-stage firms		
Log of value-weighted industry index	0.19 [3.05]	
Log of equal-weighted industry index		0.20 [3.53]
Log of inflow of venture funds focusing on later-stage investments	0.11 [2.67]	0.10 [2.05]
Log of inflow of venture funds focusing on other investment stages	0.08 [3.16]	0.09 [2.60]
p-Value, test of equality of two venture inflow variables	0.661	0.872

Note: The sample consists of 4,069 professional venture financings of privately held firms between January 1987 and December 1995 in the VentureOne database for which VentureOne was able to determine the valuation of the financing round. The pre-money valuation is defined as the product of the price paid per share in the financing round and the shares outstanding prior to the financing round. The logarithm of the pre-money valuation, expressed in millions of current dollars, is used as the dependent variable. In all regressions the independent variables include dummy variables controlling for the firm's status, industry, and location, and the logarithms of two indexes for the public market valuations of publicly traded firms in the same industry as the firm at the beginning of the month of the financing (with January 1, 1987, normalized as 1.00 for each index), of the firm's age (in years) at the beginning of the year of the financing, and of the inflow into venture capital funds in the four quarters prior to the financing (in millions of 1995 dollars). In panel B, the logarithm of the firm's sales (in millions of 1995 dollars) at the beginning of the year of the financing is an additional independent variable. In panel C, the logarithm of the firm's employment at the beginning of the year of the financing is used. In panel A, interactions between the market valuation, venture inflow, and firm characteristic variables are also used as independent variables (with a total of 3,896 observations used in the regressions). Later-stage firms are defined as those in shipping or profitable stages at the time of the investment. In panels B and C, the regression is restricted to firms in the eastern United States (a total of 641 observations) and in the later stages of investment (a total of 1,579 observations), respectively. The relative impact of fund-raising by venture funds located or specializing in that particular sector and other funds is compared. [Absolute heteroskedasticity-consistent *t*-statistics are in brackets.]

is unlikely that the count of business starts can control for shifts in high-quality technological opportunities. Public market indexes may inaccurately measure the shifts in value of private equity financed firms since the types of firms in each public index may be somewhat different from the corresponding firms attracting venture financing. For instance, in certain years there were many private venture-backed Internet service providers and biotechnology firms, but few publicly traded ones. If the shifts in the number of opportunities are being measured inaccurately and inflows to the venture industry are correlated with these changes, our estimations may be misleading. In particular, inflows to the venture industry may be falsely identified as having a significant effect on pricing levels.

To address this problem, we employ the influx of capital to funds specializing in leveraged buyout (LBO) investments. This is an attractive instrument for two reasons. First, it is clear that inflows to venture and buyout funds are correlated. Using annual data between 1980 and 1995, the correlation coefficient is 0.66 (with a p-value of 0.006). Like commitments to venture funds, influxes to buyout funds soared during the 1980s, dropped sharply in the early 1990s, and then recovered dramatically in the middle of the decade. These parallels reflect the manner in which institutional investors allocate their portfolios. Typically a single group that specializes in "alternative investments" manages investments in venture and buyout funds. When the institution's investment policy committee increases the allocation to alternatives, the inflows to venture and buyout funds are both likely to increase.

In fact there is relatively little correlation between the success of venture and buyout investments. Most successful investments by both venture and buyout investors are exited through IPOs. IPOs of firms backed by venture and buyout firms have not been strongly associated. Between 1991 and 1995[13] the correlation between the number and dollar volume of venture- and buyout-backed IPOs was actually *negative* (-0.24 and -0.19 respectively), though neither coefficient is significant at conventional confidence levels. Thus LBO inflows should not be correlated with the success of venture investments. These two considerations suggest that this is an appropriate instrument for venture capital inflows.

Table 9.11 repeats the OLS analyses from table 9.6, now estimated using the inflow into LBO funds as an instrumental variable. In each the impact of venture inflows is equal or larger in magnitude and statistically more

---

13. Venture-backed IPOs are compiled by both VentureOne and Venture Economics; but only Venture Economics tracks buyout offerings. They did not begin doing so on a systematic basis until the early 1990s.

Table 9.11
Instrumental variable regression analyses of pre-money valuations of financing rounds

Independent variable	No firm size measure		Using firm sales		Using firm employment	
Stage of firm						
Start-up stage	−0.85 [6.61]	−0.86 [6.72]	−0.88 [5.29]	−0.89 [5.37]	−0.76 [5.28]	−0.77 [5.40]
Development stage	−0.13 [1.04]	−0.15 [1.19]	−0.07 [0.46]	−0.10 [0.60]	−0.01 [0.08]	−0.04 [0.32]
Beta stage	0.14 [1.01]	0.11 [0.79]	0.23 [1.30]	0.19 [1.05]	0.25 [1.66]	0.19 [1.23]
Shipping stage	0.17 [1.45]	0.16 [1.30]	0.19 [1.24]	0.16 [1.02]	0.20 [1.56]	0.15 [1.19]
Profitable stage	0.53 [4.05]	0.51 [3.89]	0.47 [2.88]	0.42 [2.56]	0.47 [3.28]	0.40 [2.78]
Restart stage	−1.21 [8.57]	−1.24 [8.74]	−1.28 [7.63]	−1.33 [7.92]	−1.26 [8.40]	−1.33 [8.91]
Industry of firm						
Data processing industry	0.32 [3.63]	0.26 [2.97]	0.27 [2.36]	0.17 [1.46]	0.35 [3.32]	0.24 [2.34]
Computer software industry	−0.04 [0.53]	−0.02 [0.27]	−0.09 [1.06]	−0.07 [0.81]	−0.05 [0.58]	−0.02 [0.20]
Communications industry	0.34 [4.75]	0.29 [3.96]	0.28 [3.13]	0.19 [2.04]	0.34 [4.11]	0.23 [2.81]
Consumer electronics industry	0.25 [1.46]	0.25 [1.47]	0.27 [1.48]	0.26 [1.46]	0.23 [1.56]	0.22 [1.58]
Industrial equipment industry	−0.21 [2.04]	−0.24 [2.33]	−0.23 [1.76]	−0.29 [2.17]	−0.19 [1.54]	−0.24 [1.95]
Medical industry	0.39 [5.86]	0.37 [5.37]	0.43 [4.89]	0.37 [4.03]	0.46 [5.91]	0.38 [4.68]
Instrumentation industry	0.01 [0.13]	−0.02 [0.14]	0.04 [0.30]	−0.01 [0.10]	0.09 [0.73]	0.03 [0.27]
Components industry	−0.04 [0.40]	−0.06 [0.51]	−0.06 [0.52]	−0.09 [0.69]	−0.07 [0.57]	−0.09 [0.68]
Semiconductor industry	0.60 [5.54]	0.60 [5.47]	0.45 [3.73]	0.44 [3.57]	0.49 [4.55]	0.49 [4.46]
Location and other characteristics						
Eastern states	0.10 [1.90]	0.09 [1.77]	0.17 [2.62]	0.15 [2.42]	0.16 [2.76]	0.15 [2.54]
Western states	0.30 [6.47]	0.29 [6.38]	0.33 [5.72]	0.33 [5.61]	0.32 [5.95]	0.31 [5.89]
Log of firm age (in years)	0.43 [13.91]	0.43 [13.90]	0.30 [7.17]	0.30 [7.10]	0.20 [4.64]	0.18 [4.35]
Log of firm sales			0.18 [7.39]	0.20 [7.65]		

	(1)	(2)	(3)	(4)	(5)	(6)
Log of firm employment					0.27 [13.60]	0.29 [14.23]
Log of value-weighted industry index	0.16 [4.29]		0.27 [5.24]		0.31 [6.42]	
Log of equal-weighted industry index		0.15 [4.28]		0.27 [5.69]		0.35 [7.96]
Log of inflow of venture capital	0.21 [5.60]	0.22 [5.85]	0.19 [3.87]	0.20 [4.17]	0.12 [2.67]	0.13 [2.81]
Constant	−0.47 [1.38]	−0.53 [1.53]	−0.42 [0.95]	−0.50 [1.12]	−0.52 [1.25]	−0.60 [1.44]
R^2	0.32	0.32	0.34	0.34	0.37	0.38
F-Statistic	98.94	98.36	69.24	70.65	76.26	76.39
p-Value	0.000	0.000	0.000	0.000	0.000	0.000
Number of observations	3,896	3,896	2,433	2,433	2,622	2,622

Note: The sample consists of 4,069 professional venture financings of privately held firms between January 1987 and December 1995 in the VentureOne database for which VentureOne was able to determine the valuation of the financing round. The pre-money valuation is defined as the product of the price paid per share in the financing round and the shares outstanding prior to the financing round. The logarithm of the pre-money valuation, expressed in millions of current dollars, is used as the dependent variable. The independent variables include dummy variables controlling for the firm's status, industry, and location, and the logarithms of the firm's age (in years), of sales (in millions of 1995 dollars) and employment at the beginning of the year of the financing, of two indexes for the public market valuations of publicly traded firms in the same industry as the firm at the beginning of the month of the financing (with January 1, 1987, normalized as 1.00 for each index), and of the inflow into venture capital funds in the four quarters prior to the financing (in millions of 1995 dollars). The inflow into leveraged buyout funds in the four quarters prior to the financing (in millions of 1995 dollars) is used as an instrument for the inflow into venture funds. [Absolute heteroskedasticity-consistent t-statistics are in brackets.]

significant. The results are similar when the other reported OLS regressions are re-estimated. The instrumental variable estimations underscore the suggestions that capital inflows may be associated with greater competition for investments.

Demand Pressure or Better Prospects

In the analyses above we implicitly treated inflows to venture funds as exogenous. Inflows were used as an independent variable in the regressions. This assumption may be questioned. In particular, inflows to venture funds may be a response to information that suggests that entrepreneurial firms are likely to do well in the future. This same information could lead venture capitalists to assign higher valuations to firms in which they invest. We could be implying a causal impact to fund inflows on the pricing of venture investments when both are actually correlated with the future prospects of these firms. We address this concern by examining the success rates of venture-backed firms over time.

Before addressing this issue empirically, our concerns can be at least partially assuaged by the examination of the determinants of inflows into venture funds presented in chapter 3. The importance of exogenous policy shifts in determining the inflow to venture funds at least partially addresses our concerns about using inflows as an independent variable.

Another way to address these concerns is to examine the ultimate success of the firms funded by venture capitalists. If inflows to venture funds and high valuations are rational responses to information about the changing prospects of young firms, investments during these "hot" periods should be more successful. If venture capitalists just simply made fewer investments during "cold" periods, this pattern would not occur. But in general, as a comparison of tables 9.1 and 9.4 make clear, there is much greater variation in the inflows of capital to venture funds than in the number of firms receiving venture investments.

This analysis faces two challenges. Ideally we would compare the rates of return, adjusted to reflect the risks associated with the varying maturity of these firms, from the investments in various time periods. Unfortunately, many of the firms remain privately held, or else were acquired for an undisclosed price. Thus we employ two proxies. The first of these is the percentage of firms that have been taken public or filed to go public with the SEC. The second measure that we employ is the percentage of investments that either resulted in an IPO or were acquired for at least twice the valuation of that round. While VentureOne is not able to obtain the valuation for all acquired firms, it is able to do so for many of the larger and hence more visible transactions.[14]

A second concern is that many of these firms remained privately held at the time we assessed their status, March 1996. Some of these will ultimately be successful. As a result we only examine the outcome of venture investments made between 1987 and 1991. This may lead to a bias: the later years (e.g., 1990 to 1991) should have a lower share of companies reaching successful exits simply because they have had less time to mature to the point of being taken public or sold.

Table 9.12 presents the results of this analysis. We compare the success of investments in the years with high influxes to venture funds with those in other years. The observations include the 1,798 professional venture financings of privately held firms between January 1987 and December 1991 in the VentureOne database for which VentureOne was able to determine the valuation of the financing round. The first panel compares whether the firm had gone public or had filed to go public as of March 1996. The second panel measures if the firm had gone public, filed to go public, or been acquired at more than twice the valuation of the original venture round as of March 1996. Each panel divides the observations in two ways. We compare financings in 1987 and 1988 to those between 1989 and 1991, and those made between 1987 and 1989 to those from 1990 and 1991.

In each case the probability of a successful exit is slightly higher in the earlier period with high inflows to venture funds. However, none of these differences are statistically significant at conventional confidence levels. Because many of the firms funded in the later years were still quite immature in March 1996, over time the difference between the success rate of the two classes of investments should narrow. While as discussed above, the interpretation of these patterns is not unambiguous, they help allay fears that shifts in venture inflows and valuations were driven by changes in future prospects.

Conclusions

In this chapter we revisited the questions of whether flows of capital into an asset class affect the valuation of those assets and whether those changes in valuation reflect shifts in the demand for those securities or changes in future prospects. Unlike virtually every previous analysis, which focuses on

---

14. We also explore the robustness of the results to the use of other definitions of successful acquisitions, such as those five or ten times the valuation at the time of the venture financing. These alternative definitions have little impact on the results.

Table 9.12
Analyses of the success of venture backed firms

Year of investment	Average fund inflow in period	Investments with successful outcomes
Panel A: Successful outcome is an initial public offering (or IPO Filing)		
1987–1988	4,482	33.6%
1989–1991	2,615	30.1%
p-Value, χ^2-test of equality of success probabilities		0.141
1987–1989	4,348	32.5%
1990–1991	1,881	29.7%
p-Value, χ^2-test of equality of success probabilities		0.209
Panel B: Successful outcome is an IPO (or IPO Filing) or acquisition at 2 or more times original valuation		
1987–1988	4,482	35.5%
1989–1991	2,615	31.7%
p-Value, *t*-test of equality of success probabilities		0.106
1987–1989	4,348	34.5%
1990–1991	1,881	31.1%
p-Value, *t*-test of equality of success probabilities		0.115

Note: The sample consists of 1,798 professional venture financings of privately held firms between January 1987 and December 1991 in the VentureOne database for which VentureOne was able to determine the valuation of the financing round. The first panel examines the percentage of the financings that were taken public (or had filed to go public) as of March 1996. The panel presents two divisions of observations: one comparing investments made in 1987 and 1988 with those made between 1989 and 1991, the other comparing those from 1987 through 1989 to those made in 1990 and 1991. The table also presents the average annual fund inflow in these periods (in millions of 1995 dollars), and the *p*-value from a χ^2-test of the equality of the probability of a successful outcome. The second panel examines the percent of investments that were taken public, had filed to go public, or had been acquired at more than twice the valuation of the original venture round.

public markets, this analysis examines the U.S. private equity market, where practitioner accounts suggest these effects are particularly strong.

We address two primary questions in this chapter. First, the analysis shows that inflows to venture capital funds have had a substantial impact on the pricing of private equity investments. This effect is robust to the addition of a variety of variables to control for alternative hypotheses, an analysis of first differences, and the use of instrumental variables. Consistent with predictions, the impact of venture capital inflows on prices is greatest in states with the most venture capital activity and segments with the greatest growth in venture inflows. The increase in the probability of refinancing in the Heckman sample selection regressions during periods of high inflows is also broadly consistent with the valuation patterns.

Second, the relation between increased fund-raising and prices does not appear to be due to greater perceived investment prospects. The regulatory- and tax-driven nature of venture fund-raising and the insignificant difference in success rates of investments in "hot" and "cold" fund-raising periods suggest that demand pressure drives prices up during high inflow periods.

These findings have a variety of implications. First, the results suggest that it would be fruitful to examine the impact of fund inflows on valuations in other investment classes in which fund inflows fluctuate widely due to regulatory and tax factors. Real estate and developing country capital markets are two particular areas that may enhance our understanding of this phenomenon.

Second, the results raise a series of public policy questions. Several economists, such as Stiglitz (1994), have expressed concerns about the destabilizing influence of shifts in foreign capital inflows ("hot money") on developing countries' equity markets. It may be that some of the same detrimental effects are at work here. As mentioned in part I, the U.S. venture capital market is characterized by highly variable capital inflows, which affect not only the volume of investments but also the valuations of these transactions. Numerous industry observers have expressed concern about the impact of these shifts on the pace and direction of technological innovation. During periods with high inflows, venture capitalists' standards for funding firms are alleged to be lowered, only to be raised dramatically when inflows decline.[15] A careful examination of the effects of financing patterns on the rate and pattern of innovation is a fertile area for future research.

---

15. For a discussion of the detrimental impacts of these cycles on both private and social welfare, see National Advisory Committee on Semiconductors (1989).

10   How Do Venture Capitalists Oversee Firms?

In this chapter we examine another aspect of venture capitalists' role as overseers of private firms: their role on the boards of directors. We analyze whether venture capitalists' representation on the boards of the private firms in their portfolios is greater when the need for oversight is larger. To do this, our analysis examines the periods when the need for oversight is likely to be particularly high: the transition between chief executive officers (CEOs) of the firm. The role of venture capitalists in the firm should be particularly sensitive to such events, with increasing involvement around such events.

Venture capitalists' oversight of new firms involves substantial costs. The transaction costs associated with frequent visits and intensive involvement are likely to be reduced if venture capitalists are proximate to the firms in their portfolios. Consistent with these suggestions, geographic proximity is an important determinant of venture board membership: organizations with offices within five miles of the firm's headquarters are twice as likely to be board members as those more than 500 miles distant. Over half the firms in the sample have a venture director with an office within sixty miles of their headquarters. This has important implications due to the uneven regional distribution of venture capitalists. Petersen and Rajan (1994, 1995) demonstrate that the concentration of bank credit can lead to highly different financing patterns across markets. The presence or absence of venture capitalists may likewise lead to significant differences in the availability and pricing of venture capital across regions.

The Determinants of Board Composition

The Sample and Descriptive Statistics

As in chapters 11 and 15 that follow, we narrow our discussion to a single industry, biotechnology. This way we can focus on a group of industry-specific information sources. Through these data sources, we can thoroughly analyze the behavior of firms that ultimately went public and include in the sample many firms that were acquired or terminated before going public.[1]

This analysis is based on the database of venture capital financings assembled by Venture Economics, which is discussed in chapter 22. This section also describes the steps taken to correct the sample using other data sources. Table 10.1 summarizes the sample, disaggregated by year and round of investment. The table presents the number of financing rounds, as well as the cumulative and average size of these transactions. (All size figures are in millions of 1997 dollars.) Observations are concentrated in the latter half of the sample. While no trend appears in the size of transactions over time, the greater size of later financing rounds is apparent.

Information about the boards of these firms is found in several locations. IPO prospectuses report board members at the time of the offering and in many cases indicate former board members in the "certain transactions" and "principal and selling shareholders" sections. When these listings do not mention former directors, the firm's original and amended articles of incorporation, which are usually reproduced in its S-1 registration statement, are checked. Information is often available about the boards of private firms that are acquired by public firms or file for an abortive IPO in the acquirers' proxy, 10-K, or 10-Q statements, or in the (ultimately withdrawn) registration statements. In addition, in the fall of 1990 we gathered material on these firms in the files of the North Carolina Biotechnology Center (NCBC). The NCBC solicits information from public and private firms on an annual basis. Their files include promotional material (used to produce an industry directory) and surveys conducted for the U.S. Office of Technology Assessment. These materials detail both the firms' managements and their boards.

The IPO prospectuses provide biographies of directors. Other sources, however, often only list directors' names. Directors are identified using Pratt's Guide to Venture Capital Sources (Venture Economics 1996), biographical material in other prospectuses (many individuals serve on more than one board), general business directories (Marquis's Who's Who in Finance and Industry 1993, Standard and Poor's Register of Corporations,

---

1. Because an industry sample allows the use of other data sources to verify and correct the data set, the investment patterns here may not be representative of venture capital as a whole. The IPOs of firms in the biotechnology sample closely resemble the 433 venture-backed IPOs examined by Barry et al. (1990) in several critical respects. These include the inflation-adjusted IPO size, the length of venture capitalist involvement with the firm, and the number of venture capitalists serving as directors of the firm.

Table 10.1
Corrected financings sample

Year	Number of rounds	Aggregate size (1997$ mil)	Average size (1997$ mil)
Panel A: Financings segmented by year			
1978	7	22.03	3.14
1979	8	69.58	8.69
1980	16	157.81	9.87
1981	41	180.10	4.61
1982	46	249.50	5.55
1983	62	291.31	4.86
1984	46	182.60	4.24
1985	55	190.65	3.89
1986	79	345.08	4.73
1987	102	460.18	4.84
1988	102	392.84	4.13
1989	89	430.12	5.51
Panel B: Financings segmented by round number			
First round	270	673.82	2.70
Second round	186	881.19	5.04
Third round	113	832.24	7.85
Later round	84	584.57	7.59

Note: The table presents the number of financing rounds of private biotechnology firms in the corrected Venture Economics sample, the total dollars disbursed, and the average size of each round (in millions of 1997 dollars). The sample consists of 653 financing rounds of 271 bio-technology firms between 1978 and 1989. Financing rounds are segmented by year and by round number.

Because we could not determine the size of some financing rounds, the aggregate size does not equal in all cases the product of the number of rounds and the average round size.

Directors and Executives 1993), and BioVenture View's BioPeople (1993). These sources are supplemented with information from the NCBC "actions" (1990a) database (a compilation of trade magazine stories) and Mead Data Central's databases.

Panel A of table 10.2 presents the distribution of board members by round of investment. Each case where the board members at the time of the investment or within three months of the investment date are known is used. Following Baysinger and Butler (1985), directors are divided into quasi-insiders, outsiders, and insiders. Quasi-insiders are those parties who do not work directly for the firm, but have an ongoing relationship with the concern. Affiliated academic professionals who hold full-time teaching or clinical positions are counted as quasi-insiders rather than insiders, even if

Table 10.2
Board membership of private biotechnology firms

Financing round	Mean number of board members			
	Venture capitalists[a]	Other outsiders[b]	Insiders[c]	Quasi-insiders[d]
Panel A: Board membership by round number				
First round	1.40	0.86	1.28	0.52
Second round	1.87	0.86	1.40	0.56
Third round	2.09	1.02	1.61	0.67
Later round	2.12	1.27	1.73	0.54
Panel B: Professional affiliation of board members at time of last financing round (in %)				
Outside directors				
Venture capitalist				36.2
Corporate partner				6.4
Other investor				3.1
Executive with other health-care or biotechnology firm				3.5
Retired health-care or high-technology executive				3.6
Academic without firm affiliation				0.9
Lawyer, consultant, or investment banker without firm affiliation				1.4
Other or unidentified				5.1
Inside directors				
Senior manager				20.3
Junior manager				7.1
Quasi-inside directors				
Academic affiliated with the firm				8.9
Lawyer affiliated with the firm				0.5
Investment or commercial banker affiliated with the firm				1.0
Former manager of the firm				0.6
Relative or other				1.3

Note: The sample consists of 653 financing rounds of 271 biotechnology firms between 1978 and 1989; The board membership by round is presented for each of the 362 rounds where membership can be determined.

a. Venture capitalists are defined as individuals who are general partners or associates at venture capital organizations that are either unaffiliated with any other organization or else affiliated with a financial institution. Full-time affiliates of a venture capital organization are counted as venture capitalists, even if they work for a venture-backed firm.

b. Other outsiders include corporate investors, other investors (individuals who (alone or in a partnership) held a 5% stake in the organization at some time, never were an officer of the firm, and never were an affiliate of a company that signed a collaborative arrangement with the firm or of a venture investor), and individuals that do not have another relationship with the firm.

c. Insiders are either senior (the chief executive officer, president, and chairman of the board) or junior managers employed directly by the firm.

d. Quasi-insiders are those parties who do not work directly for the firm but have an ongoing relationship with the concern. The second panel reports the professional affiliation of board members at the time of the last financing round in the sample.

they hold an official title in the firm and draw substantial compensation. Outside directors include investors and disinterested outsiders. Included in this category are representatives of corporations who have invested in or financed research at the firm.[2] The analysis distinguishes between venture capitalists and other outsiders.[3]

The number of board members increases in each round, from a mean of four in the first round to just fewer than six in the fourth and later rounds. In the fourth and later rounds, venture capitalists control a mean of 2.12 board seats. This sample corresponds closely to the interindustry population of 433 venture-backed IPOs of Barry et al. (1990). In their mean firm, venture capitalists control two out of six board seats. The distribution of the directors is presented in more detail in panel B. In table 10.2 only one observation of each firm is used: the directors at the time of the last round of venture financing in the sample period.

Board Membership and Chief Executive Officer Turnover

This section follows an approach suggested by Fama and Jensen (1983) and Williamson (1983), who hypothesize that the composition of the board should be shaped by the need for oversight. These authors argue that the board will bear greater responsibility for oversight—and consequently that outsiders should have greater representation—when the danger of managerial deviations from value maximization is high. If venture capitalists are especially important providers of managerial oversight, their representation on boards should be more extensive at times when the need for oversight is greater.

This chapter examines changes in board membership around the time that a firm's CEO is replaced, an approach suggested by Hermalin and

---

2. In corporations that channel their funds through a corporate venture capital subsidiary, the corporate venture capitalist may sit on the board. Such officials are counted as other outsiders rather than as venture capitalists. If the analysis above is repeated with these individuals recorded as venture capitalists, neither the magnitude nor the significance of the results changes markedly.

3. The analysis includes venture organizations that are either unaffiliated with any other organization or else affiliated with a financial institution. Venture capitalists are defined as individuals who are general partners or associates at partnerships focusing on venture capital investments (i.e., equity or equity-linked securities with active participation by the fund managers in the management or oversight of the firms). These individuals are counted as venture capitalists even if they officially work for the firm. (Most partnership agreements between general and limited partners require that salaries be paid out of the management fee and not by the fund. Venture capitalists can get around this restriction by being paid by a firm in their portfolio.)

Weisbach's (1988) study of outside directors of public firms. The replacement of the top manager at an entrepreneurial firm is likely to coincide with an organizational crisis and to heighten the need for monitoring. The need for monitoring should be greater in these cases. As with public firms (Weisbach 1988), the replacement of the CEO frequently occurs when the firm is encountering difficulties. In addition, since the uncertainty about the new person's ability is likely to be high, the CEO's activity may be more intensively monitored.[4]

The analysis only uses as cases of CEO turnover instances where the firm's top executive was replaced. It is important to avoid instances that may generate a spurious correlation between the addition of board members and CEO turnover: for example, cases where neither a CEO has been hired nor a complete board assembled when the firm begins operations. Consequently instances where a venture capitalist that originally held the title of "chairman and chief executive officer" relinquishes the second title are not included. Similarly eliminated are cases where a firm run by an "acting CEO" or by one or more vice presidents hires a full-time chief.

Cases of CEO turnover are identified using the sources described above. Forty cases of CEO turnover meeting these criteria are identified. Few of these changes are retirements: the median age of the exiting CEOs at the time of the last financing round in which they are in office is 40. (The median age of the CEOs holding office at the time of the last financing round in the sample is 43.) Only one replaced CEO is between the ages of 64 and 66 at the time of exit, the criterion used by Weisbach (1988) to identify CEO retirements.

Table 10.3 summarizes the changes in board membership between venture rounds. First presented are the 180 second or later venture rounds where the board membership at the time of the current and previous financing round is known and there was no CEO turnover in this interval. (Also included are cases where there is an observation of board members up to three months after the financing.) There is a slight increase in the representation of each class of board member.

---

4. Robert Kunze (1990, pp. 213–14) of Hambrecht and Quist notes that the replacement of the CEO "is the single most critical development in the life of a baby company. The time spent hiring the new chief executive officer, the shock to the organization when the changeover takes place, the lack of direction in the interim, the quality of the new person hired, and the speed with which he or she seizes command, all impact heavily on the health and potential of the company. In the best of circumstances replacing a chief executive officer is a wrenching experience and companies can easily fail at this juncture."

Table 10.3
Changes in board membership between financing rounds

	Venture capitalists	Other outsiders	Insiders	Quasi-insiders
Panel A: Mean changes in board membership between financing rounds				
180 rounds without CEO turnover	+0.24	+0.28	+0.10	+0.06
40 rounds with CEO turnover	+1.75	+0.33	+0.23	+0.25
Panel B: Tests of equality of changes in board membership between financing rounds				
p-Value, *t*-test	0.000	0.750	0.339	0.140
p-Value, Wilcoxon test	0.000	0.519	0.094	0.297

Note: The sample consists of 220 second or later financing rounds where the board membership at the time of the current and previous round can be determined. The first panel indicates the change in board membership since the last financing round, divided by whether CEO turnover occurred. Venture capitalists are defined as individuals who are general partners or associates at venture capital organizations that are either unaffiliated with any other organization or else affiliated with a financial institution. Full-time affiliates of a venture capital organization are counted as venture capitalists, even if they work for a venture-backed firm. Other outsiders include corporate investors, other investors (individuals who (alone or in a partnership) held a 5% stake in the organization at some time, never were an officer of the firm, and never were an affiliate of a company which signed a collaborative arrangement with the firm or of a venture investor), and individuals that do not have another relationship with the firm. Insiders are managers employed directly by the firm. Quasi-insiders are those parties who do not work directly for the firm, but have an ongoing relationship with the concern. The second panel presents *p*-values from *t*-tests and nonparametric Wilcoxon tests of whether the change in board membership differs in rounds with CEO turnover. The *t*-tests do not assume that the two distributions have the same variance.

Then the forty rounds in the sample where the board membership at the time of the current and previous financing is known and there was CEO turnover in this interval are presented.[5] In these rounds the representation of each class of board member increases at a greater rate than between rounds without CEO turnover. The increase in insiders and quasi-insiders is not surprising, as in some cases the departing CEO will remain a board member, whether the person continues as a lower-level employee or becomes a former employee (who are classified as quasi-insiders). By far the largest increase (1.75) is in the number of venture directors. The analysis presents *t*-tests and Wilcoxon tests of whether the change in the number of directors is the same in rounds with and without CEO turnover. Because in each case an *F*-test rejects the equality of variances, the *t*-tests do not assume that the distributions have the same variance. Nonparametric

---

5. A supplemental test examines whether the forty rounds coinciding with CEO replacements differ from the other 180: for example, if they tend disproportionately to be early venture rounds. The distribution of rounds with and without CEO turnover is virtually identical.

Wilcoxon tests are employed because the change in the number of board members is an ordinal number. Panel B presents the *p*-values from these tests. The increase in the representation of venture board members is significantly larger when there is CEO turnover. The differences in the changes of other directors are insignificant.

These patterns are then examined econometrically. Following Hermalin and Weisbach (1988), a Poisson specification is employed, with the number of new directors as the dependent variable. (In these regressions, a goodness-of-fit test cannot reject the Poisson specification.) Two separate regressions are run, using as dependent variables the number of new directors who are venture capitalists and other outsiders. All 216 second and later venture rounds where both the board membership and funds provided at the time of the current and previous rounds are used. As independent variables, the regression employs a dummy variable indicating if there was CEO turnover between the current and previous venture round (with 1.0 indicating such a change) and two control variables. The first controls for the difference between the funds provided in the current and previous venture round (expressed in millions of constant dollars). An increase in funding may lead to the involvement of new investors, who may be offered a board seat. The second controls for the number of directors who have exited the board since the previous round. As Hermalin and Weisbach note, if firms routinely fill vacated board seats, a regression without such a control may be biased.

As panel A of table 10.4 reports, the coefficient of the CEO turnover variable in the venture capitalist regression, 1.88, is highly significant. At the mean of the other independent variables, the exit of the CEO increases the number of new venture directors from 0.25 to 1.59. This coefficient in the other outsiders regression is of the opposite sign and insignificant. In panel B, the coefficients of the CEO turnover variable in the venture capitalist and other outsider regressions are compared. Table 10.4 presents the *p*-value from the χ^2-test of the null hypothesis of no difference. The null hypothesis is rejected at the 1 percent level of confidence. This difference is robust to modifications of these regressions. For instance, an independent variable that controls for the time between the current and previous venture round is added, and separate independent variables are created for each class of director who leaves the board. Also the number of new investors is used as an independent variable instead of the increase in the funds provided.

Hermalin and Weisbach (1988) propose an alternative explanation for the addition of outside directors around a CEO succession. They suggest that corporate insiders who are passed over for the top position leave after a

Table 10.4
Poisson regression analysis of the addition of board members between financing rounds

	Dependent variable	
	Venture board members	Other outsiders
Panel A: Poisson regression analysis of the addition of board members between financing rounds		
CEO turnover	1.88 [8.86]	−0.04 [0.13]
Change in dollars invested	0.02 [0.89]	−0.06 [2.28]
Number of departing board members	0.15 [2.06]	0.19 [1.41]
Constant	−1.43 [8.94]	−1.13 [8.00]
Log-likelihood	−175.29	−157.20
χ^2-Statistic	112.50	7.56
p-Value	0.000	0.056
Number of observations	216	216
Panel B: Tests of the equality of coefficients in the venture capitalist and other outsider regressions		
p-Value, χ^2-test of null hypothesis that CEO turnover coefficients are equal		0.000

Note: The sample consists of 216 second or later financing rounds where the board member-ship at the time of and the amount invested in the current and previous round can be deter-mined. In the first panel, separate regressions are estimated using the number of new directors who are venture capitalists and other outsiders as the dependent variable. Independent vari-ables include a dummy indicating if there was CEO turnover between the previous and current round, the difference in the amount invested in the current and previous round (expressed in millions of 1989 dollars), and the number of board members who departed the board between the previous and current round. The second panel tests whether the coefficients of the CEO turnover variable in the two regressions are equal. [Absolute *t*-statistics are in brackets.]

new CEO is selected. The firm—facing a shortage of qualified insiders—then fills the board seats with outsiders. This explanation is unlikely to ap-ply here. Managers who depart private firms voluntarily often must pay a heavy financial penalty: selling their shares back to the firm at the same dis-counted price that they originally paid (typically a small fraction of the cur-rent value). Consequently voluntary departures of senior executives from private venture-backed firms are infrequent.

Board Membership and Geographic Proximity

The distance between venture capitalists and the private firms on whose boards they sit is then examined. The cost of providing oversight is likely to be sensitive to the distance between venture capitalists and the firms in which they invest. If the provision of oversight is a significant and costly role for venture capitalists, then proximity should be an important determi-nant of which venture investors serve on the board.

First, the geographic proximity of venture directors is examined. To compute this measure, the zip codes in which the firm has its headquarters and the venture capital organization has its office nearest the firm are used. To determine the former, the specialized industry directories cited above and the records of Venture Economics are employed. The latter information is available for each venture organization in several sources (Clay 1991, National Register 1992, and Venture Economics 1996). If possible, the edition of *Pratt's Guide* published in the year of the firm's final financing round in the sample is used. (Pratt's information is gathered through a survey of venture organizations conducted in January of the year of publication.) Since the Venture Economics database lists the name of the fund, the associated venture organization must be determined. The name of the venture organization is often obvious (e.g., Mayfield, VII, LP, is managed by the Mayfield Fund). In other cases, an unpublished Venture Economics database identifies the venture organization. To compute the distance between the zip codes, a computer program developed by the Center for Regional Economic Issues at Case Western Reserve University is used. The program computes the mileage between the centers of pairs of zip codes.

Panel A of table 10.5 presents the distance from each firm's headquarters to its most proximate, farthest, and median venture director at the time of the last venture round in the sample. The results suggest that for the majority of the firms, the nearest venture director is quite close. More than half the firms have a venture director with an office within sixty miles of their headquarters, while 25 percent of the firms have a venture director within seven miles. Panel B examines the probability that a venture investor is a director at the time of the final round in the sample. The probability that a venture investor with an office within five miles of the firm serves as a director is 47 percent; for a venture capitalist whose nearest office is more than 500 miles away, the probability is 22 percent. An F-test is used to examine whether these probabilities are equal. The null hypothesis of no difference is rejected at the 1 percent confidence level.

To correct for other determinants of board membership, a probit regression is estimated. As observations, the regression uses each venture investor in the firm as of the last round in the sample. The dependent variable is a dummy indicating whether a representative of the venture organization served on the firm's board at the time of the last round in the sample (with 1.0 denoting a board member). As independent variables, the distance from the investor's nearest office to the firm's headquarters (in thousands of miles) is used and several control variables. A venture organization with a larger equity stake in a firm should be more likely to have a director, as it has more at risk. The stake that venture organizations held in the firms is determined through the Venture Economics database, as well as information from Recombinant Capital and U.S. Securities and Exchange Commission filings. Larger and older venture capitalists are more likely to serve as board members: experienced venture capitalists can be more effective monitors or can more effectively certify the firm to potential investors. To determine the age and size of the venture organization, *Pratt's Guide* and several other sources (Clay 1991, National Register 1992, and Venture Economics 1996) are used. The age of each venture organization is expressed in years; size is the ratio of the capital committed to the venture organization at the time of the investment to the total pool of venture capital. A ratio is employed because the size of the venture pool changes dramatically over this period. Separate regressions use venture capitalist age and size as control variables, because these two measures are highly correlated.

Panel C of table 10.5 presents the results. The coefficient for distance is highly significant in explaining the service of venture capitalists on boards, even after controlling for ownership and experience. Since the venture organization's stake cannot always be computed, this variable is omitted in the third and fourth regressions. The results are robust to the use of the larger sample.[6]

Conclusions

In this chapter we examined the role of venture capitalists as directors of private venture-backed firms. Our analysis showed that the representation of venture capitalists increases around the time of CEO turnover, as might be expected if these individuals are intensively monitoring managers. Unlike other outside directors, the representation of venture capitalists increases around such events. Our analysis included an examination of the geographic proximity of venture directors. Because the provision of oversight is costly, venture capitalists can seek to minimize this cost by overseeing local firms. Most firms have a nearby director, and proximity is an important determinant of board membership. These findings complement earlier empirical studies of how venture capitalists address agency problems as well as analyses of the ties between banks and the firms to which they lend.

Our results suggest several avenues for further investigation. The first is the impact of venture capitalists' involvement in firms after going public.

---

6. In unreported regressions the logarithm of distance is used as an independent variable, which proves to have even more explanatory power.

Table 10.5
Relationship between proximity and board membership for venture investors

	Distance from venture capitalist's nearest office to firm headquarters (miles)			
	Mean	First quartile	Median	Third quartile
Panel A: Proximity of venture capitalist directors				
Nearest venture director	359	7	59	418
Median distance venture director	584	32	287	965
Farthest venture director	993	73	419	1,951

	Distance from venture capitalist's nearest office to firm headquarters (miles)			
	<5	5–50	50–500	>500
Panel B: Relationship between proximity of venture investor and probability of board membership				
Probability of joining board	46.7%	30.7%	34.9%	21.8%
p-Value, F-test of null hypothesis of no relationship				0.000

	Dependent variable: Venture investor served on board			
	Using venture capitalist age and stake	Using venture capitalist size and stake	Using venture capitalist age	Using venture capitalist size
Panel C: Regression analysis of board membership				
Venture office to firm (000 miles)	−0.18 [3.72]	−0.20 [4.04]	−0.16 [4.16]	−0.20 [4.71]
Stake held by venture organization	4.21 [6.96]	4.19 [6.61]		
Age of venture organization (years)	0.01 [1.54]		0.01 [2.18]	
Organization's share of total venture pool		18.64 [2.17]		18.62 [2.77]
Constant	−0.86 [7.33]	−0.87 [7.57]	−0.51 [5.80]	−0.48 [6.07]

Log-likelihood	−319.48	−297.36	−413.19	−384.85
χ^2-Statistic	82.68	85.58	27.12	35.66
p-Value	0.000	0.000	0.000	0.000
Number of observations	580	548	700	661

Note: The distance between the headquarters of the firm and the nearest office of each venture capitalist that served as a board member at the time of the last venture round in the sample. The sample consists of 700 pairs of venture capital organizations and private biotechnology firms. The second panel presents the relationship between probability of a venture investor serving as a board member and its distance to the firm, and the p-value from an F-test of this pattern. The final panel presents a probit regression analysis of the relationship between venture investor proximity and board membership. The dependent variable is a dummy indicating if a representative of the venture organization served on the board at the time of the last venture round in the sample. (1.0 denotes a director.) Independent variables include the distance from the venture organization's nearest office to the headquarters of the firm (in thousands of miles), the age of the venture organization (in years), and its size (the ratio of its committed capital to the total venture capital pool). All variables are calculated at the time of the last venture round in the sample. [Absolute t-statistics are in brackets.]

Barry et al. (1990) and Lin and Smith (1998) document the continuing role of venture capitalists as directors and shareholders in the years after going public. In some cases venture capitalists terminate their relationships with the firm quickly, but in a significant number of cases venture capitalists retain a board seat even after distributing their holdings to the limited partners of their funds. Where venture capitalists are specialized providers of oversight, it might be expected that these firms are less prone to agency problems.[7]

A second avenue for empirical analysis concerns regional differences in the geographic proximity of venture capitalists. Regions differ greatly in their concentration of venture capitalists (see table 1.4). For example, Petersen and Rajan (1994, 1995) found differences across credit markets with different degrees of lending concentration. Similarly firms located in regions where venture capital is relatively scarce may face different price schedules for or availability of this form of financing.

---

7. An alternative possibility is that a relationship between firm success and venture involvement exists but is driven by reverse causality. Venture capitalists may choose to remain on the boards of successful companies, out of the belief that board membership highlights their past accomplishments to outsiders or else out of hubris.

11 Why Do Venture Capitalists Syndicate Investments?

In this chapter we explore three hypotheses about why investors share transactions with each other. The first two suggest that syndication may be a mechanism through which venture capitalists resolve informational uncertainties about potential investments. While these three hypotheses do not exhaust the rationales for syndication, they lend themselves to empirical examination.

• Syndicating first-round venture investments may lead to better decisions about whether to invest in firms. Sah and Stiglitz (1986) show that hierarchical organizations, in which investments are made only if several independent observers agree, may be superior to ones in which projects are funded after one affirmative decision. Another venture capitalist's willingness to invest in a potentially promising firm may be an important factor in the lead venture capitalist's decision to invest.

• Syndicating later round financing may avoid opportunistic behavior. Admati and Pfleiderer (1994) develop a rationale for syndication in later venture rounds, based on informational asymmetries between the initial venture investor and other potential investors. A venture capitalist involved in the firm's daily operations understands the details of the business. The venture capitalist may exploit an informational advantage, overstating the proper price for the securities in the next financing round. Under the model's assumptions, the only way to avoid opportunistic behavior is if the lead venture capitalist maintains a constant share of the firm's equity.

• Syndication may help venture capitalists exploit informational asymmetries and collude to overstate their performance to potential investors. Lakonishok, Shleifer, Thaler, and Vishny (1991) suggest that pension funds "window dress." Because institutional investors may examine not only quarterly returns but also end-of-period holdings, money managers may adjust their portfolios at the end of the quarter by buying firms whose shares have appreciated and selling "mistakes." Venture capitalists may similarly make investments in the late rounds of promising firms, even if the financial returns are low. This strategy allows them to represent themselves in marketing documents as investors in these firms.

This chapter examines these three concepts using a sample of 651 investment rounds prior to going public at 271 biotechnology firms. Experienced venture capitalists primarily syndicate first-round investments to venture investors with similar levels of experience. In later rounds, established venture capitalists syndicate investments to both their peers and less experienced capital providers. When experienced venture capitalists invest for the first time in later rounds, the firm is usually doing well (i.e., the firm's valuation has increased over the prior venture round). Finally the ownership stake of venture capitalists frequently stays constant in later venture rounds.

Syndication is a topic of more general interest as well: cooperation among financial institutions is an enduring feature of the equity issuance process. Syndicated underwritings in the United States date back at least as far as an 1870 offering by Pennsylvania Railroad. By the 1920s these arrangements were quite intricate: separate syndicates in many cases handled the purchase, inventory, and sale of securities (Galston 1925). Although the Securities Act of 1933 regulated these arrangements, comanaged offerings and selling syndicates continue to be prominent in equity issues to this day. Despite its persistence, syndication has been little scrutinized in the corporate finance literature. The neglect may be due to the complex motives for these arrangements as well as the difficulty of analyzing these patterns empirically.

Venture capital syndications differ in two ways from public sales of registered securities, which suggest that securities sales by private firms are an attractive arena to study the economics of syndication. First, the process through which private firms sell securities is little regulated by the SEC. Thus financial intermediaries have few constraints on their ability to work together. Second, the securities are purchased directly by the venture capital fund and must be held for at least one year under SEC Rule 144. By contrast, financial intermediaries take on relatively limited risks when they underwrite a public security issue: the underwriters ascertain the demand schedule for the new security before the price is determined.

Syndication is of more general interest for another reason: corporate finance has devoted relatively little attention to interactions among incumbent and entrants. By way of contrast, industrial organization has long focused on relationships. Because interactions and returns are measurable, finance is a natural testing ground. This chapter joins the relatively few studies of the relationship between incumbent and entrant financial institutions.[1]

Rationales for Syndication

Syndication may lead to a superior selection of investments. Sah and Stiglitz (1986) contrast decision making in hierarchies and polyarchies: that is, settings in which projects are undertaken only if two reviewers agree that the project is worthy and those in which the approval of either is sufficient. The authors show that it may be more efficient to undertake only those projects approved by two reviewers.

Venture capitalists, upon finding a promising firm, typically do not make a binding commitment to provide financing. Rather, they send the proposal to other investors for their review. Another venture capitalist's willingness to invest in the firm may be an important factor in the lead venture investor's decision to invest (Pence 1982). Practitioners often emphasize this motivation for syndication:

Venture capitalists prefer syndicating most deals for a simple reason—it means that they have a chance to check out their own thinking against other knowledgeable sources. If two or three other funds whose thinking you respect agree to go along, that is a double check to your own thinking (George Middlemas, Inco Securities, quoted in Perez 1986).

A syndicate of two or more venture groups provides more capital availability for current and follow-on cash needs. Syndication also spreads the risk and brings together more expertise and support. These benefits pertain only to start-up financing requiring the venture capitalist's first investment decision. There are different strategies and motivations for syndication in follow-on financing (Robert J. Kunze, Hambrecht, and Quist 1990).

If financing is the primary motivation for syndication, venture organizations should be careful in their choice of first-round syndication partners. Established firms should be unlikely to involve either new funds or small, unsuccessful organizations as co-investors. The choice of syndication partners should be less critical in later rounds. Having decided to provide capital to the firm, venture capitalists should be much less concerned about confirming their judgment. This suggests that (1) experienced venture capitalists are likely to invest with one another in the first round and (2) seasoned

---

1. Others include, for example, Beatty and Ritter (1986), Hayes, Spence, and Marks (1983), Lakonishok, Shleifer, and Vishny (1992), and Sirri and Tufano (1998).

venture capitalists should invest with both experienced and inexperienced investors in later rounds.[2]

Avoiding information asymmetry is the rationale for syndication in later rounds developed by Admati and Pfleiderer (1994). Syndication should occur, they argue, even when venture capitalists are risk neutral and without capital constraints. They begin by considering a situation where an informed entrepreneur raises funds from outside investors directly. In keeping with Brennan and Kraus (1987), the entrepreneur can communicate all private information with a set of contingent claims. If an unforeseen state of the world occurs, however, the signaling equilibrium breaks down. As a result the entrepreneur may be unable to raise the full amount needed.

A lead venture capitalist, who becomes involved in the firm's operations, can solve this information problem. Other, less informed investors will invest if the venture capitalist does. The venture capitalist, however, may exploit an informational advantage. For instance, if one believes that the firm's prospects are particularly attractive, one may reserve fewer shares for outside investors. If troubled by the firm's prospects, one may allow outside investors to provide more of the capital. Under this assumption, as Admati and Pfleiderer show, the only way to ensure optimal behavior in the face of this "adverse selection" problem is if the lead venture capitalist maintains a constant equity stake. Consider the example where the lead venture capitalist obtains one-half of a company's two million shares in the first round. (The entrepreneur retains the other 50 percent.) If the second round involves the issuance of another million shares, the venture capitalist should buy only one-half of these. The remaining half-million shares should be purchased by other venture capitalists. This model provides the rationale for syndication in later rounds, as this way venture capitalists will hold a constant equity stake across rounds.

Lakonishok et al.'s (1991) discussion of "window dressing" by money managers suggests a third rationale for venture syndication. They note that pension funds, which typically assess their money managers once a quarter, must examine several aspects of performance. Because market-adjusted performance is a noisy indicator of a money manager's skill, plan sponsors also examine the portfolio of securities held at the end of the quarter. In response, money managers may adjust their portfolios just before the

---

2. Another hypothesis that would generate a similar empirical pattern is Welch's (1992) model of "cascades" in equity sales. While Welch focuses on the sale of equity in IPOs, the same pattern could appear here: upon observing the decision of early venture capitalists to invest in the firm, less sophisticated venture investors rush in to invest in later rounds.

quarter's end. This may include buying firms that have performed particularly well in that quarter or selling "mistakes" that incurred losses.

Venture capital funds may exhibit similar behavior. In their private placement memoranda for new funds, venture organizations discuss the performance of their previous funds. The performance data are often difficult for outsiders to confirm. For instance, in computing historical returns in these documents, venture capitalists may make generous assumptions about the valuation of securities.[3] Thus potential investors also may examine venture organizations' prior investments. The private placement memoranda discuss successful past investments, often leaving ambiguous whether the venture organization was an early or late investor. (Similar listings of previous investments are found in marketing documents aimed at managers of new firms seeking financing.) An investment in a promising firm shortly before it goes public may consequently benefit a venture organization, even if the financial return is low. Early venture investors may curry favor with their colleagues by permitting them to invest in later-round financings of promising firms. The early-round investors may do so in the hope that the syndication partners will in turn offer them opportunities to invest in later rounds of their deals.

This hypothesis suggests that venture capitalists should offer shares in the best deals to those firms most able to reciprocate: well-established venture firms. Venture capitalists should be less likely to offer shares to less established venture organizations.

A final rationale for syndication that is not examined is diversification through risk sharing (Wilson 1968). Venture capitalists have much at stake in the performance of their funds. First, venture capitalists typically receive as compensation between 20 and 30 percent of their funds' profits. Fund performance also affects the ability to raise new funds. Under certain assumptions venture capitalists may wish to diversify their holdings to ensure that they do not conspicuously underperform their peers. To address this behavior, many contracts establishing venture capital partnerships contain explicit prohibitions against investing in other venture funds (see chapter 4).

---

3. Venture funds frequently do not sell shares of firms that have gone public, but rather distribute them to their limited partners. (Limited partners usually include tax-exempt and tax-paying entities, which may have different preferences on the timing of sales.) The transfer of the securities from the venture capitalist to the limited partners may take several weeks. During this period the firm's share price may fall sharply, either because the venture capitalists themselves sell their shares of the thinly traded security or because the market anticipates forthcoming sales by the limited partners. In calculating returns, venture funds may employ not the price on the date that the shares reached the limited partners but the price on the date that the distribution was announced (see chapter 19).

By investing in many syndicated investments, however, a venture fund can achieve much the same effect.

It is unclear whether risk aversion will lead to a greater tendency to syndicate by less or more established funds. A new venture organization may believe that a follow-on fund is difficult to raise unless it performs very well (see chapter 16). The fund may make high-risk solo investments. Alternatively, an established venture organization may believe that its reputation will allow it to raise a later fund even after a disastrous performance. Its fund may thus be willing to invest alone in risky but promising projects. To analyze empirically the relationship between risk aversion and syndication, we would need to know about the utility functions of the venture capitalists, the status of their current funds, and their future fund-raising plans.[4]

An Analysis of Syndication Patterns

The Sample

In Venture Economics' Venture Intelligence Database between 1978 and 1989, 271 privately held biotechnology firms received venture capital before going public. (For a detailed description of the database, see chapter 22.) Table 11.1 describes the sample. Even in the first round, there was extensive syndication. In each later venture round, two or more new investors typically invested in the firm. The mean number of investors rose from 2.7 (including nonventure investors[5]) to 5.3. Because some early round investors did not invest in subsequent rounds, the number of investors in a given round was often less than the sum of the number of investors in the previous round and the number of new investors.

The amount invested per venture and nonventure investor was quite stable. The size of each financing round increased (on an absolute and per

---

4. One test is to examine funds that specialize in start-ups, traditionally the most risky of venture investments. These venture capitalists, it might be anticipated, have relatively little risk aversion. A *t*-test is used to compare the number of syndication partners (by round of investment) for these funds and all others. The specialist funds are identified using a database of funds assembled by Venture Economics (described in chapter 22). Although these funds have slightly fewer syndication partners, the differences are not statistically significant.

5. Venture investors are defined as either (1) traditional limited partnerships where general partners invest the limited partners' capital and oversee these investments or (2) corporate venture capital programs that are established enough to be listed in *Pratt's Guide* (Venture Economics 1996). Nonventure investments include private placements by other corporations or financial institutions as well as by partnerships established solely to invest in a single firm. Investments that are made by an agent and marketed to retail investors are also designated as nonventure investments.

Table 11.1
Description of the sample

	Round of external financing		
	First	Second	Third+
Number of observations	269	184	198
Mean number of investors in each round			
Venture investors	2.2	3.3	4.2
Nonventure investors	0.5	0.9	1.1
Mean number of new investors in each round			
Venture investors	2.2	1.5	1.3
Nonventure investors	0.5	0.7	0.7
Amount invested per investor ($mil)			
Venture investors	0.5	0.6	0.6
Nonventure investors	0.9	0.9	1.3

Note: The sample consists of 651 financing rounds of privately held biotechnology firms between 1978 and 1989. The table indicates the number of observations, the mean number of venture and nonventure investors, and the mean number of such investors investing in the firm for the first time. The table also reports the mean amount invested by venture and nonventure investors, in millions of nominal dollars.

Because some early-round investors do not invest in subsequent rounds, the number of investors in a given round is often less than the sum of the investors in the previous round and the new investors.

investor basis) as the firm matured. This reflects the growing number of investors and the increasing representation of nonventure investors.

Syndication Partners in First and Later Rounds

Our analysis focuses first on the syndication partner choices in the sample. Established venture capitalists disproportionately syndicated first-round investments with other established firms. In later rounds, they appeared more willing to syndicate investments with less seasoned firms.[6]

There was no obvious way to distinguish between established and marginal venture capital organizations, however. While many influential venture capital organizations such as Greylock and TA Associates date back to the 1960s, others of today's leading venture capitalists did not close

---

6. One question suggested by this analysis is which firms do not syndicate at all. The age and size of venture organizations investing alone are compared to those organizations investing jointly. Larger and older venture organizations are only slightly more likely to invest alone than others are. The *t*-tests comparing syndicating and solo investors are statistically insignificant and not reported in the tables.

their first fund until the 1980s. Meanwhile a substantial number of venture organizations have had protracted lives without ever becoming major factors in the industry. Our analysis does not thus simply characterize venture capitalists by age, it also considers the relative size of the organization's fund. Recall that more established venture organizations are able to access capital from investors for larger and more frequent funds. Venture capitalists generally prefer larger funds because of the substantial economies of scale in operating a large venture fund (or several large funds). The organization's size is expressed as a percentage of the total venture capital pool because venture capital expanded dramatically in the years after 1978: it is by relative rather than absolute size that we measure this experience.[7]

In table 11.2 we divide all venture capitalists into quintiles based on size. Size is computed as the ratio of venture organization's committed capital (the total amount provided by investors) to the total venture pool in the year of investment. Venture organizations typically operate several funds (i.e., partnerships) at any given time. In the table we aggregate all funds sponsored by a venture capital organization for the purpose of analysis. We use committed capital rather than the value of assets because venture capitalists follow divergent practices as to when they write up or write off their investments.

The syndication partners in each size quintile of venture organizations are then examined. First-, second- and later-round investments are considered separately. Were funds equally likely to syndicate with a venture organization of any size, each cell would be equal: 20 percent of the syndications will be with the largest quintile of organizations, 20 percent with the middle quintile, and so forth.

The results are presented figure 11.1 and table 11.2. The tabulations are not symmetric around the diagonal axis because there are an uneven number of observations for each quintile. For instance, there are forty-four syndicated first-round investments between venture capitalists in the largest quintile and those in the middle quintile. The number of syndicated investments involving the largest quintile of organizations is slightly larger

---

7. Neither age nor relative size provides an indication of industry expertise. One might expect certain venture capitalists to develop special expertise in a complex industry such as biotechnology. While we might expect that many early round investments would involve a specialist in biotechnology, it is not obvious that these specialists will be particularly likely to coinvest with each other. In many cases early round syndications between two established venture organizations will pair one group with industry-specific experience and another without such experience, which is expected to contribute general management and financial expertise. Established venture organizations can be expected to be involved as syndication partners, even when they do not have specialized industry expertise (Kunze 1990).

Table 11.2
Syndication partners in venture financings of privately held biotechnology firms

Venture capital size quintiles	Size quintile of syndication partner				
	Largest	Second	Middle	Fourth	Smallest
Panel A: First-round financings					
Largest quintile	14%	35	20	17	14
Second quintile	27%	25	14	19	16
Middle quintile	22%	20	20	23	16
Fourth quintile	18%	25	21	16	20
Smallest quintile	12%	17	12	16	43
Panel B: Second-round financings					
Largest quintile	21%	22	24	18	15
Second quintile	25%	22	20	15	17
Middle quintile	26%	19	21	21	13
Fourth quintile	22%	18	23	21	18
Smallest quintile	18%	18	14	18	32
Panel C: Later-round financings					
Largest quintile	19%	23	26	18	14
Second quintile	20%	20	25	21	17
Middle quintile	19%	21	24	21	15
Fourth quintile	17%	21	25	20	17
Smallest quintile	15%	18	22	20	24

Note: The sample consists of 651 financing rounds between 1978 and 1989. Venture organizations are divided into quintiles on the basis of committed capital, relative to all venture organizations active in biotechnology in the year of the investment. Each row of the table indicates, for one size quintile, the distribution of syndication partners (i.e., the percentage of syndication partners in each size quintile).

Rows may not add to 100%, due to rounding. Because certain size quintiles undertook more or fewer syndicated investments, the table is not symmetric along the diagonal axis.

than the number involving the middle quintile. Thus co-investments with middle-quintile firms make up 20 percent of the joint investments by the largest quintile of organizations. These forty-four transactions with the largest quintile comprise 22 percent of the co-investments by middle-quintile venture capitalists.

The smallest quintile of venture capitalists is disproportionately likely to undertake early round transactions with each other. The bottom quintile of venture organizations syndicates 43 percent of their first-round investments with other bottom-quintile venture capitalists. With each subsequent round, this pattern becomes less pronounced. The percentage of the bottom quintile's syndications with each other in second and later rounds was 32 and 24

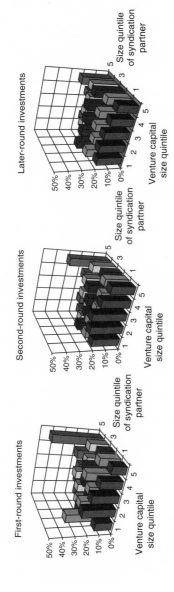

Figure 11.1
Syndication partners in venture financing of privately held biotechnology firms. The sample consists of 651 financing active between 1978 and 1989. Venture organizations are divided into quintiles on the basis of committed capital, relative to all venture organizations active in biotechnology in the year of the investment. The quintile of the largest venture capital firms is denoted as 1; the smallest as 5. First-, second-, and later-round investments are considered separately. The vertical axis indicates, for each size quintile, the percentage of syndication partners in each of the five quintiles.

Table 11.3
Tests of the randomness of the distribution of syndication partners in venture financings of privately held biotechnology firms

	Firms divided into quintiles by venture organization	
	Size	Age
First-round financings		
Pearson χ^2-statistic	48.08	26.87
p-Value	0.000	0.043
Second-round financings		
Pearson χ^2-statistic	18.93	7.83
p-Value	0.273	0.954
Later-round financings		
Pearson χ^2-statistic	6.44	16.07
p-Value	0.983	0.448

Note: The sample consists of 651 financing rounds between 1978 and 1989. Venture organizations are divided into quintiles on the basis of committed capital and age, relative to all venture organizations active in biotechnology in the year of the investment. The table indicates the test statistic and significance level for a Pearson χ^2-test, whose null hypothesis is that 20% of the observations are in each cell. Separate tests are performed for the first, second and later investment rounds.

percent. Some patterns, however, are not readily explicable. It is not obvious, for instance, why top-tier firms syndicate first-round investments more frequently with second-quintile organizations (35 percent) than other top-quintile firms (14 percent).

Table 11.3 examines the statistical significance of these patterns and tests the null hypothesis that the probability of each cell is 20 percent using a Pearson χ^2-test. For the first-round analysis reported in table 11.2, the null hypothesis is rejected at the 1 percent level of confidence. In the other rounds, the null hypothesis cannot be rejected at conventional confidence levels.

Similar results appear when venture organizations are segmented by age: 36 percent of the first-round syndication partners of the quintile of youngest firms are also in the youngest quintile. Although the full results are not reported for age, the pattern is similar. Table 11.3 tests for deviations from the equally likely distribution. Again, the null hypothesis of equal probabilities is rejected (at the 5 percent level of confidence) in the first round. In later rounds, the null hypothesis cannot be rejected.

For the analyses reported in tables 11.2 and 11.3 we used age and size proxies. The results suggest sharp divisions between more and less

Table 11.4
Experience of venture capitalists investing in the second and later rounds

Measures of venture experience	Average difference, experience of new investor and previous investor	p-Value, t-test of no difference
Venture organization size (% of total pool)	−0.12%	0.008
Age of venture organization (in years)	−1.42	0.006
Prior biotech investments by venture organization	−0.76	0.001

Note: The sample consists of 651 financing rounds between 1978 and 1989. The experience level of each venture organization investing in a firm for the first time in the second or later round is compared to the experience level of previous venture investors in the firm. Venture organizations are compared on the basis of size (committed capital in the year of the investment as a percentage of the total pool of venture capital), age (in years), and the number of biotechnology firms in which the organization had previously invested. The differences are expressed as the experience level of the new investor minus that of the previous investor.

established venture capitalists. If the unwillingness of experienced venture capitalists to invest with small and young organizations in the first round stems from a mistrust of inexperienced investors' judgment, then a second pattern should appear as well. Experienced venture capitalists should be reluctant to invest in the later rounds of deals begun by their less seasoned counterparts. Inexperienced venture investors should be brought into later round financings by experienced organizations, and not vice versa.

To prove this claim, we examined venture organizations investing for the first time in the second or later venture rounds. We contrasted the characteristics of new investors with those of venture organizations that invested previously in a firm. Funds are compared along three measures of experience: the size of the venture capital organization (committed capital in the year of the investment as a percentage of the total committed capital in the venture pool), age of the venture organization in years, and the number of biotechnology firms in which the organization had invested before this transaction.

The later-round venture investors should be less experienced than the previous investors. In table 11.4 we compare the characteristics of the new investors to those of the previous venture financiers and presents the p-values from t-tests comparing these firms. The results are consistent with the hypothesis and significant at the 1 percent confidence level. The typical later-round syndication involves less experienced venture capitalists investing in a deal begun by established organizations.

Table 11.5
Equity stakes in privately held venture-backed biotechnology firms

	Round of external financing		
	First	Second	Third+
Total stake held by outside investors after investment round	33.9%	51.1%	57.0%
Share of equity sold in round purchased by previous investors		30.0%	52.7%

Note: The sample consists of 332 financing rounds between 1978 and 1989 where the size of the ownership stake for each investor can be determined. The table indicates the mean percentage of the firm's equity held by outside investors after each venture round, as well as the percentage of the equity sold in the round purchased by previous investors in the firm.

In computing the equity stake, all preferred shares are converted into common at the conversion ratios then in force. (These are typically stipulated in the amended by-laws prepared after each venture round.) Outstanding warrants and options are only counted if their exercise price is below the per-share price of the venture round.

Changes in Equity Holdings across Venture Rounds

Next we took Admati and Pfleiderer's model and examined their prediction that the stakes held by venture capitalists remain relatively constant across venture rounds. Table 11.5 lists investors' aggregate equity holdings and their equity purchases in the financing rounds. In the second round, first-round investors purchase 30 percent of the shares sold. New investors buy the remaining shares. The existing investors' purchase corresponds quite closely to their previous ownership position of 33 percent prior to the round. In the third round, when previous investors hold 51 percent of the equity, existing shareholders purchase about half the shares. In later rounds, current shareholders purchase over half the shares. These results confirm the prediction of Admati and Pfleiderer that venture shareholders strive to maintain a constant equity share.

Similarly the equity ownership of individual venture organizations shows relatively little variation. Table 11.6 shows the change in equity held by each venture investor before and after each venture round, computing:

$$[(\textit{Stake after round-Stake before round})/\textit{Stake before round}]. \tag{1}$$

In 21 percent of the cases, the share of the firm held by the venture capitalist changes by less than 5 percent after the venture round. In 70.5 percent of the cases, the change is less than 25 percent.[8]

---

8. In 70 percent of the cases a venture capitalist with a 10 percent stake in a company before a venture round would have an equity stake of between 7.5 and 12.5 percent thereafter.

Table 11.6
Changes in venture equity stakes in privately held biotechnology firms

Change in ownership	Number of observations	Percent
$<-25\%$	72	8.3
$<-5\%$ and $>-25\%$	298	34.2
$<5\%$ and $>-5\%$	183	21.0
$<25\%$ and $>5\%$	134	15.3
$<50\%$ and $>25\%$	94	11.1
$<75\%$ and $>50\%$	23	2.6
$<100\%$ and $>75\%$	27	3.1
$>100\%$	40	4.6

Note: The sample consists of 188 second or later financing rounds between 1978 and 1989 where the size of the ownership stake of each venture capitalist before and after the venture round can be determined. The table indicates the change in the equity ownership of each venture organization around each financing round: the difference between the new and old stake divided by the old stake is calculated (a total of 871 observations). All funds of a given venture organization are considered together.

In computing the equity stake, all preferred shares are converted into common at the conversion ratios then in force. (These are typically stipulated in the amended by-laws prepared after each venture round.) Outstanding warrants and options are only counted if their exercise price is below the per-share price of the venture round.

Later-Round Syndications of Investments in Promising Firms

Last we examined suggestions of "window dressing" in the syndication of venture investments. The implication is that experienced venture capitalists will invest in the later rounds of deals, particularly those likely to go public.

We used each second- and later-round venture investment as an observation and ran a pair of probit regressions. For the pair we used the same independent variables but different dependent variables:

$$(INVEST?)_{ij} = \alpha_{0j} + (\Delta VALUE)_i \alpha_{1j} + (VCSIZE)_i \alpha_{2j} + \varepsilon_{ij}. \tag{2}$$

The dependent variables are dummy variables. They indicate if (1) one or more experienced venture capitalists invested in the firm for the first time in the round and (2) one or more inexperienced venture capitalists invested for the first time. In both cases the dependent variable is coded 1.0 when a new investor is present. Experienced and inexperienced firms are defined as those above and below the median size of those venture organizations investing in biotechnology in that year, using the amount of capital committed to the venture organization as a measure of size.

We used two independent variables. We identified the most promising deals by the change in the per share valuation of the firm between the current and previous venture round. The firms whose valuations increased sharply are considered to be superior performers and are thus the most likely to go public. The size of the largest previous venture investor is also used as an independent variable to control for the reluctance of established firms to invest in deals begun by less established firms.

The partition of venture capitalists into experienced and inexperienced is crude: much of the information about their characteristics is discarded. In unreported regressions, the analysis is repeated with specifications that capture more detail. First, four separate regressions are run, examining if venture capitalists in each of four size quartiles invested for the first time in the transaction. The Poisson specification is used, where the dependent variable is the number of new venture capitalists in each size quartile who invested in the firm. The results are robust to these changes.

To verify their robustness, we fitted the results to the venture organization's age rather than relative size:

$$(INVEST?)_{ij} = \beta_{0j} + (\Delta VALUE)_i \beta_{1j} + (VCAGE)_i \beta_{2j} + \varepsilon_{ij}. \tag{3}$$

The two dependent variables are the experienced or inexperienced venture capitalist that joins as a new investor. Experienced and inexperienced firms are now defined as those above or below the median age of those venture organizations investing in biotechnology in that year. Instead of size, the age of the oldest previous investor is used as an independent variable.

In table 11.7 the coefficients 0.14 and 0.15 in the first and third regressions show that established venture capitalists invest significantly more often for the first time in later rounds when valuations have increased sharply.[9] Valuation changes are insignificant (even negative) in the probability of investments being made by less established firms.

---

9. Although it could be argued that the price per share increases because other experienced venture capitalists invested in the firm, there are strong arguments to the contrary. Venture capital partnership agreements will frequently specify that new venture investors be involved in situations where venture capitalists may be tempted to price investments at too high valuations. An example is when a venture fund makes a later-round investment in a company already held by the venture capitalist's earlier fund (Venture Economics 1992). Venture capitalists may be tempted to undertake a follow-on financing at a high valuation. This is because they can then write up the value of their first fund's investment, in the hopes of impressing potential investors in the third fund. (The potential investors will find it difficult to independently assess the value of a privately held firm.) The investors in the second fund can demand a co-investment by another venture capitalist who does not stand to benefit from the write-up of current holdings because they expect that such an investor will demand a lower valuation.

Table 11.7
Probability of venture capitalists investing for the first time in a second or later financing round

	Dependent variable			
	Organization above median size invested	Organization below median size invested	Organization above median age invested	Organization below median age invested
Change in valuation between previous and current round (%)	0.14 [2.21]	−0.04 [0.83]	0.15 [2.67]	−0.03 [0.57]
Size of oldest previous investor (% of total venture pool)	21.86 [2.12]	12.33 [1.50]		
Age of oldest previous investor (in years)			0.03 [2.15]	0.02 [2.66]
Constant	0.33 [1.85]	−0.49 [3.15]	0.41 [1.12]	−0.62 [3.58]
Log-likelihood	−101.9	−128.2	−110.6	−128.4
χ^2-Statistic	8.86	2.86	6.99	7.79
p-Value	0.01	0.24	0.03	0.02
Number of observations	199	199	199	199

Note: The sample consists of 199 second or later financings of privately held biotechnology companies between 1978 and 1989 in which the valuations of the firm in the current and previous rounds are available. The dependent variable is a dummy variable indicating if one or more venture investors above or below the median size or age of venture organizations active in biotechnology in that year were first-time investors in this round. (Rounds with new investors are coded as 1.0.) The independent variables are the percentage change in the valuation of the firm from the previous to the current venture round, the age (or size) of the most experienced venture organization that had previously invested in the firm, and a constant. A probit regression is employed. [t-statistics are in brackets.]

The change in the firm value is computed using the price per share in the previous venture round and the price per share in the current round. Number of shares and valuation are corrected for any stock splits, reverse splits and stock dividends.

Conclusions

In this chapter we examined the structure of private investments in the bio-technology industry. We found that in the first round, established venture capitalists tend to syndicate, and in later rounds, less established venture organizations begin to invest alongside established groups. Our results are consistent with the view that syndication is a mechanism by which established venture capitalists obtain information on whether to invest in risky start-up firms. Often established funds join as new investors in later rounds after the firm's valuation has increased sharply. This pattern fits the notion of "window dressing" in the syndication of later-round investments. We also presented evidence consistent with Admati and Pfleiderer's constant equity share hypothesis.

Although we limited our syndication analysis to one environment, the results may be more broadly applicable. Many of these behaviors can be seen in public security issuances. For instance, in IPOs of firms specializing in complex technologies, the decision to go public and the terms of the offering are often decided in consultation with two co-lead investment bankers. Decision sharing is an important motivation in many of these comanaged offerings (e.g., see the description of Microsoft's IPO in Wallace and Erickson 1992).

Our analysis does not address how reputation affects the risk aversion of venture capitalists and their consequent willingness to syndicate. We leave this as a research opportunity. Also open to further research is the question whether more established venture organizations are willing to accept lower returns when variance is kept low. They may then participate in many syndicated deals. Another research opportunity, due to the industrial organization literature, is investigating the response to entrants. The 1980s and 1990s saw the entry of many new firms into venture capital. While a few entrants participated in many syndicated first-round transactions, many more were relegated to later-round syndications. The process through which some of the entrants joined the core of established venture organizations remains unclear. Nor is it clear whether the syndication of later-round investments by established venture capitalists helped establish the stature of the new organizations. (One of the few empirical examinations of entry in the finance literature is Beatty and Ritter 1986.)

12   Does Venture Capital Spur Innovation?

In the 1990s there was a dramatic expansion of public programs around the globe to encourage the formation of venture capital funds. These programs shared a common rationale: that venture capital spurred innovation in the United States, and could do so elsewhere (e.g., see the European Commission's *Green Paper on Innovation* 1995).

The rationales for these programs, however, have not been scrutinized, even though there appear to be several successes:

• In the United States many pioneering independent venture firms were founded in the 1960s. Their founders often received their initial experience in funds as part of the Small Business Investment Company program. The initial formation of high-technology firms and business intermediaries in the Silicon Valley and Route 128 regions has been attributed to this program.

• The Israeli government initiated two programs to encourage the formation of venture capital funds in 1991. Many analysts claim that the Yozma and Inbal initiatives led to not only an increase in venture capital under management (from $29 million in 1991 to over $550 million in 1997), but to a burst of investment by foreign high-technology companies in Israeli R&D and manufacturing facilities.

• Singapore began aggressively promoting venture capital funds in 1985. The impact on venture capital activity has been dramatic—in 1996, over 100 funds managed over $7.7 billion, up from two funds and $42 million in 1985—and a number of observers have argued that these programs have led to a more general increase in high-technology R&D activity.

In this chapter we take a first step toward systematically assessing policies that promote venture capital. We examine not the success of the initiatives themselves, but rather the reasonableness of an essential premise behind the efforts: that venture capital funds spur technological innovation.

We explore the experiences of twenty industries in the U.S. manufacturing sector over a three-decade period. First we examine, using reduced-form regressions, whether controlling for R&D spending, venture capital funding has an impact on the number of patented innovations. We find that venture capital is associated with a substantial increase in patenting. The results are robust to a variety of specifications of how venture capital and R&D affect patenting and to different definitions of venture capital.

We next consider the limitations of this approach. We present a stylized model of the relationships between venture capital, R&D, and innovation. This model suggests that simple reduced-form regressions may overstate the effect of venture funding. Both venture funding and patenting could be positively related to a third unobserved factor: the arrival of technological opportunities.

To study the impact of technology on venture funding, we first consider the role of the 1979 U.S. Department of Labor policy shift that led to a sharp increase in the funds committed to venture capital. This type of exogenous change should identify the role of venture capital, because it is unlikely to be related to the arrival of entrepreneurial opportunities. We exploit this shift in instrumental variable regressions. Second, we use R&D expenditures to control for the arrival of technological opportunities that were anticipated by economic actors at the time but were unobservable to econometricians. In the framework of our model, we show that the causality problem disappears if we estimate the impact of venture capital on the patent-R&D ratio rather than on patenting itself.

Even after we address these causality concerns, we find that venture funding has a strong positive effect on innovation. The estimated parameter can vary according to the techniques we employ, so we focus on a conservative middle ground, where a dollar of venture capital is about three times more powerful in stimulating patenting than a dollar of traditional corporate R&D. Our estimates suggest that although venture capital averaged less than 3 percent of corporate R&D from 1983 to 1992, its share of U.S. industrial innovations in this decade was much greater—about 8 percent.

One natural concern is that changes in the legal environment may be confounding our results. In earlier work (1998) we have showed how the creation of a centralized appellate court for patent cases in 1982 nearly coincided with an increase in the rate of U.S. patent applications. To obtain our finding, we employed in our regressions dummy variables for each year. In this way we could control for changes in the propensity to file for patents or in applications granted. Year-to-year effects allowed us to control for changes in the overall legal environment unless the 1982 policy shift boosted patenting disproportionately in particular industries, which does not appear to have been the case (Kortum and Lerner 1998).

Last we address concerns about the relationship between the dependent variable in our analyses (patents) and what we really wish to measure (innovations). Venture capital can spur patenting and have no effect on innovation if venture-backed firms simply patent more of their innovations to impress potential investors or to avoid expropriation of their ideas by these investors. To investigate this possibility, we compare indicators of the quality of patents between 122 venture-backed and 408 non-venture-backed companies based in Middlesex County, Massachusetts. Venture-backed firms' patents are more frequently cited by other patents and are more aggressively litigated: venture backing does not appear to lead to lower-quality patents. Furthermore the venture-backed firms are frequent litigators of trade secrets, which may indicate that they are not simply patenting more in lieu of relying on trade secret protection.

It is important to acknowledge the limits of our analysis. We follow a somewhat crude "production function" approach to assess the contribution of venture capital. In so doing, we face many of the fundamental issues raised by Griliches (1979) in his critique of attempts to assess the contributions of R&D to productivity. Due to the lack of previous research in this area, the work we present in this chapter should be seen as a first cut at quantifying venture capital's impact on innovation. We hope to stimulate additional investigations of the relationship between the institutions through which innovative activities are financed and the rate and direction of technological change.[1]

The Data

Our annual data covers patents issued to twenty manufacturing industries between 1965 and 1992. The dependent variable is the U.S. patents issued to U.S. inventors by industry and date of application. The main explanatory variables are measures of venture funding collected by Venture Economics and industrial R&D expenditures collected by the U.S. National Science Foundation (NSF).

---

1. In addition to the literature on the contribution of R&D to productivity (Griliches 1979) and on the relationship between R&D and patenting (reviewed in Griliches 1990), in this chapter we consider the empirical literature on the relationship between cash flow and R&D expenditures at the firm level (e.g., Bernstein and Naidri 1986; Himmelberg and Petersen 1994). But as far as we are aware there is only one other study examining the relationship between innovation and the presence of particular financial institutions: Hellmann and Puri (1998) compare the survey responses of 170 venture-backed and non-venture-backed firms.

The Industry Data Set

Patent Applications   We collected our patent data by industry from Kortum (1992) and updated the data using information on U.S. patent awards by technology class in a variety of databases prepared by the U.S. Patent and Trademark Office (USPTO). We compiled from these databases the number of successful patents applied for by U.S. inventors in each year. Because of variations in the speed with which the USPTO handles patent applications (in particular, the periodic slowdowns associated with budget crises), it is preferable to compile the number of successful applications filed each year rather than the patents awarded. This information is not known until all patents filed in a given year are issued. Thus, while we can be confident about essentially how many successful patent applications were filed in 1980, the number of successful applications filed in 1995 is still quite uncertain.

Concerns about data incompleteness determined the last year of the analysis. While we can project from preliminary data (e.g., the number of patent applications filed in 1992 that were awarded through 1996) how many applications filed in each year will ultimately be granted, we do not wish to have to make large imputations. Consequently we only extend the analysis through 1992.

In addition to defining the time frame of the analysis, we have to consider which patents to include in the analysis. USPTO databases compile not only awards to U.S. inventors but also those to foreign firms and individuals seeking protection in the U.S. market. Because we seek a proxy for the innovative output of the United States, we drop patents that were not originally filed in the United States.

The USPTO does not compile total patent applicants by industry, and many of these firms have multiple lines of business. Thus, although we know the names of the applicants, we must rely on a concordance that relates the primary classification to which the patent is assigned to the most likely industry of the inventing firm. This concordance, based on a study of Canadian patenting behavior, employs the International Patent Classification to which the patent is assigned to determine the industry where it is likely to be used.

One challenge with both compilations of patent awards is the need to adjust the number of recent patent awards. While we exclude from the sample patent applications from recent years, a few patents applied for in the early 1990s will not be awarded until the first decade of the twenty-first century. We adjust the observed counts of patent awards between 1987 and 1992 upward to reflect the number of patents that can expected to be awarded based on historical patterns. The patent data are summarized in table 12.1.

Venture Capital Disbursements   The consulting firm Venture Economics compiles investments by venture capital funds (also known as disbursements). We obtained Venture Economics tabulations that list total disbursements by the industry of the firm receiving the financing. The industry codes are classified according to a proprietary scheme developed by Venture Economics. We mapped these codes into our industry classification scheme, with the help of a concordance between the Venture Economics and the Standard Industrial Classification (SIC) codes.

One complex issue is what constitutes a venture capital investment. Until the late 1970s, there were no distinct funds set up to make investments in leveraged buyout transactions. Rather, venture capital groups would invest into a wide variety of transactions: seed and early-stage financings, expansion rounds of rapidly growing entrepreneurial firms, buyouts, and other special situations (e.g., purchases of blocks of publicly traded securities). Since the 1970s, most buyout investing by private equity funds has been done through specialized funds dedicated to these transactions (e.g., Kohlberg, Kravis, and Roberts). Some venture capital funds, however, have continued to invest in buyouts (this was a particularly common phenomenon in the mid-1980s) and other special situations. Meanwhile some groups frequently classified as buyout specialists (e.g., Welch, Carson, Anderson, and Stowe) also make a considerable number of venture capital investments.

We focus our analysis on the relationship between innovation and investments in growing firms where the types of information problems that venture capitalists address are most critical. While many buyouts create value by eliminating inefficiencies and improving cash flows, these types of transactions are outside the focus of this chapter. The standard tabulation of venture capital investments prepared by Venture Economics includes investments by venture capital funds into venture transactions and buyouts as well as venture investments by groups classified as buyout funds. We undertake a special tabulation of the venture capital investments only, whether made by groups classified as venture capital or buyout funds. To ensure compatibility with the other data series, we include only investments into firms based in the United States (whether the venture fund was based domestically or not). Similarly, to test the robustness of our results, we compile the seed and early-stage investments by these funds. We collect

Table 12.1
Patenting activity of U.S. manufacturing industries, by industry and five-year period

Industry	SIC codes	1965–69	1970–74	1975–79	1980–84	1985–89	1990–92
1: Food and kindred	20	1,790	1,957	1,365	1,201	1,555	1,138
2: Textile and apparel	22,23	3,246	3,004	2,639	2,339	3,787	2,923
3: Lumber and furniture	24,25	3,028	3,052	2,877	2,160	3,149	2,539
4: Paper	26	2,738	2,312	1,924	1,626	2,493	1,859
5: Industrial chemicals*	281,282,286	22,124	22,353	18,507	15,612	15,882	11,673
6: Drugs*	283	2,099	2,873	3,561	4,399	8,262	6,281
7: Other chemicals	284,285,287–289	14,559	14,403	11,760	10,461	11,283	8,405
8: Petroleum refining and extraction*	13,29	892	794	850	827	744	450
9: Rubber products	30	8,504	8,169	6,726	5,823	9,028	6,641
10: Stone, clay, and glass products	32	2,677	2,671	2,366	2,062	2,790	2,147
11: Primary metals	33	2,245	2,183	1,689	1,340	1,710	1,156
12: Fabricated metal products	34	19,805	19,484	18,479	14,894	18,359	13,211
13: Office and computing machines*	357	5,487	5,752	4,931	4,922	6,638	5,905
14: Other nonelectrical machinery*	351–356,358–359	60,790	61,139	52,426	42,634	48,135	35,534
15: Communication and electronic*	366,367	30,838	28,380	24,679	24,302	30,417	25,793
16: Other electrical equipment*	361–365,369	23,768	22,403	19,213	16,995	19,736	14,197
17: Transportation equipment*	371,373–375,379	10,829	12,119	9,715	7,096	8,579	6,610
18: Aircraft and missiles*	372,376	1,634	1,434	1,200	905	1,113	835
19: Professional and scientific instruments*	38	18,690	19,244	17,287	15,683	21,026	17,235
20: Other manufacturing	21,27,31,39	13,769	15,050	15,054	12,237	16,582	13,521
Total		249,512	248,775	217,247	187,518	231,268	178,053

Note: Patent applications refer to the number of ultimately successful patent applications filed in each year. Industries marked with an asterisk had an R&D-to-sales ratio above the median in 1964. These industries define a "high R&D" subsample used for some of the later regressions.

both the dollar amount invested and the number of companies funded in each year. An updated tabulation of this venture capital data can be found in table 12.2.

R&D Expenditures   We compile information on privately and federally funded R&D performed by industry from the U.S. National Science Foundation (NSF). Both data series have been compiled since 1957 as part of the "Survey of Research and Development in Industry," using an industry scheme based on two- and three-digit SIC codes. Occasionally data series for smaller industries are suppressed in particular years. In these cases it is necessary to extrapolate based on the relative level of R&D spending in previous years.[2] We slightly collapse the NSF industry scheme to ensure comparability with the patent classification discussed above, for a total of twenty industries. The R&D data are summarized in table 12.3.

Gross Industry Product   The Department of Commerce's Bureau of Economic Analysis has estimated gross product by industry for the two-digit SIC classes, as well as some important three-digit classes, using the current definitions of these industries. Not all three-digit SIC codes necessary for this analysis are compiled in their database. For the missing industries, we collect this information from the printed volumes of the *Annual Survey of Manufacturers* (ASM). While the ASM does not report gross product by industry, it does compile a related value-added measure. In each case we examine the distribution of value added across the three-digit industry classes, and then assign the two-digit industry's gross product in a proportionate manner. Where necessary, we adjust the categories reported in these volumes to reflect today's classification structures. (For instance, prior to 1972, guided missiles were included in SIC 19, "ordnance and accessories." When that category was disbanded, they were moved to SIC 37, "transportation equipment.")

The Firms Data Set

To assess the behavior of firms at a more disaggregated level, we examined firms whose headquarters are in a single county, Middlesex County in

---

2. The NSF will not report data when one or two firms account for the majority of the R&D in an industry or when firms representing more than one-half the R&D spending do not respond to the survey. Ideally we would also have compiled expenditures by universities relevant to each industry. Associating the classes of academic research with particular industries, however, proved problematic.

Table 12.2
Distribution of firms in the analysis of venture-backed and non-venture-backed firms

SIC class	United States		Middlesex County		Sample	
	Percent of establishments	Percent of employees	Percent of establishments	Percent of employees	Percent of firms	Percent of employees
20: Food and kindred products	5.5%	8.0%	3.7%	4.3%	2.6%	8.3%
21: Tobacco products	0.0	0.2	0.0	0.0	0.0	0.0
22: Textile mill products	1.7	3.6	1.1	1.7	0.6	0.1
23: Apparel and other textiles	6.4	5.7	2.9	1.6	1.5	0.3
24: Lumber and wood products	9.3	3.9	2.2	0.7	1.3	0.1
25: Furniture and fixtures	3.2	2.8	1.7	0.5	0.8	0.0
26: Paper and allied products	1.7	3.5	1.9	3.7	0.6	0.1
27: Printing and publishing	16.8	8.6	17.7	9.4	3.2	2.8
28: Chemicals and allied products	3.3	4.8	3.8	3.3	9.1	3.2
29: Petroleum and coal products	0.6	0.6	0.5	0.1	0.2	0.0
30: Rubber and miscellaneous plastics	4.1	4.9	3.5	3.5	2.5	0.7
31: Leather and leather products	0.5	0.7	0.4	0.1	0.2	2.7
32: Stone, clay, and glass products	4.3	2.9	2.1	1.0	0.8	0.1
33: Primary metal industries	1.8	4.0	1.0	1.4	1.3	0.5
34: Fabricated metal products	10.1	8.2	9.3	4.8	5.1	1.3
35: Industrial machinery	13.8	10.6	14.8	14.5	19.1	24.8
36: Electronic equipment	4.6	8.6	11.1	16.8	14.7	12.3
37: Transportation equipment	2.9	9.9	1.4	5.1	0.8	0.3
38: Instruments	2.7	5.3	9.7	19.4	16.4	24.9
39: Miscellaneous manufacturing	4.8	2.2	4.3	1.8	2.3	1.9
7372 & 7373: Software	1.9	0.9	7.0	6.4	17.2	15.4

Note: We compare the number of firms and employees across manufacturing industries (two-digit Standard Industrial Code classes). We compare all firms in the United States, all those in Middlesex County, Massachusetts, and the 530 in the sample. The U.S. and Middlesex County figures are based on U.S. Department of Commerce (1991). These present the number of establishments (one firm may have multiple establishments). Not all firms with fewer than twenty employees are included. The county figures are only for those employees actually working in the county. The sample columns present the number of firms, and include all employees of these firms, whether or not they work in Middlesex County.

Table 12.3
R&D expenditures by U.S. manufacturing industries, by industry and five-year period

Industry	1965–69	1970–74	1975–79	1980–84	1985–89	1990–92
1: Food and kindred	3,271	3,741	4,333	5,643	7,231	4,032
2: Textile and apparel	962	909	869	1,002	1,376	781
3: Lumber and furniture	269	945	1,204	1,111	936	670
4: Paper	2,419	2,871	3,554	4,019	3,980	3,520
5: Industrial chemicals	14,780	13,582	14,376	18,587	22,023	15,518
6: Drugs	6,384	9,033	12,365	17,870	25,730	21,395
7: Other chemicals	3,191	4,105	4,504	6,776	10,826	7,086
8: Petroleum refining and extraction	7,135	7,423	8,784	13,657	12,207	7,270
9: Rubber products	3,089	3,738	3,559	4,330	4,054	3,572
10: Stone, clay, and glass products	2,430	2,535	2,734	3,625	4,898	1,521
11: Primary metals	4,293	4,231	5,070	4,916	4,222	2,006
12: Fabricated metal products	2,812	3,664	3,578	4,343	4,390	2,278
13: Office and computing machines	10,802	17,045	23,398	35,485	53,779	33,061
14: Other nonelectrical machinery	8,455	10,226	12,543	15,849	14,596	9,445
15: Communication and electronic	16,902	20,262	22,106	37,661	50,187	20,711
16: Other electrical equipment	12,483	13,903	13,764	13,597	8,560	7,722
17: Transportation equipment	19,713	25,133	30,340	34,324	46,152	28,489
18: Aircraft and missiles	19,104	16,631	17,043	27,177	34,692	18,113
19: Professional and scientific instruments	6,958	10,259	14,748	24,186	30,321	21,101
20: Other manufacturing	1,580	2,094	2,417	3,094	2,342	1,763
Total	$147,032	$172,328	$201,288	$277,251	$342,501	$210,055

Note: All figures are in millions of 1992 dollars.

Massachusetts. We include in the sample all 130 manufacturing firms based there that were publicly traded between January 1990 and June 1994, as well as a random sample of 400 such firms that were privately held. By taking the sample of firms in one region, rather than use a diverse array of locations, we were able to examine the innovative activities in more depth.[3]

---

3. In particular, we can examine not only patent filings but also intellectual property litigation. In both the federal and state court systems, intellectual property cases are often not identified as such by the courts' internal tracking systems. They are often recorded simply as "miscellaneous tort" or "contract" disputes, depending on the circumstances of the case. We do not use the firms' 10-K filings with the U.S. Securities and Exchange Commission to identify litigation for two reasons. First, we wish to include in our sample privately held firms, which need not make such filings. Second, although firms are required to report any material litigation in these filings, they are often highly selective in the suits that they actually disclose.

Middlesex County includes much of the Route 128 high-technology complex as well as concentrations of more traditional manufacturers. The first four columns of table 12.3 contrast the mix of industrial establishments and employment in the U.S. and Middlesex County in 1990. The comparison indicates that the mixture of traditional industry in the county is fairly representative of the nation as a whole. Technology-intensive sectors, however, are disproportionately represented.

We included all firms in Compustat with headquarters in Middlesex County that file financial data with the U.S. Securities and Exchange Commission for any quarter between the first quarter of 1990 and the second quarter of 1994. Following this analysis, we confined our analysis to manufacturing firms (Standard Industrial Codes 20–39), but also included firms in SIC codes 7372 and 7373 that make packaged software and operating systems for mainframe computers.[4] We excluded shell companies that are established merely to make an acquisition and SWORDs, publicly traded subsidiaries that finance R&D. After these deletions, the sample consists of 130 firms.

Publicly traded firms are likely to have different characteristics than other companies. Thus we sought to include a representative sample of private firms as well. There is no single directory that lists all the firms in the county. Conversations with economic development officials, however, indicated that two directories taken together provide comprehensive coverage of manufacturing firms. *George D. Hall's Directory of Massachusetts Manufacturers*, which is prepared with the cooperation of the Associated Industries of Massachusetts, provides the most detailed listing of traditional manufacturers, and the *Corporate Technology Directory* specializes in high-technology firms. We drew 200 firms based in Middlesex County each from these directories. In both publications the information is collected via a survey (in *Hall's*, through consultation with the records of the Associated Industries of Massachusetts). All firms are required to have been in business by the end of 1989, though some exit (e.g., through bankruptcy or liquidation) during the sample period.

In the fifth and sixth columns of table 12.3 we compare the firms in the sample with those in the nation and county. To classify the public firms in our sample into industries, we used the primary SIC provided by Compustat; for the other firms, we used the SIC code of the first-listed line of busi-

---

4. Our rationale is that while software manufacturers are classified as service providers, their relationship with customers is more akin to that of manufacturers. The analyses below are robust to the deletion of these observations.

ness in the *Hall's* and *Corporate Technology* directories. (Both directories list lines of business in order of importance, as reported by the firm.[5])

From Compustat or the two business directories, we were able to determine the sales and employment in 1990, as well as the year in which the firm was founded. From CRSP, we could determine if and when the firm went public. We determined whether the firm was venture-backed from Venture Economics. We also used the number of patents that the firm was awarded in the period 1969 through 1994 (as well as citations to these awards), which we identify using Mead's LEXIS/PATENT/ALL file and the USPTO's CASSIS CD-ROM database. (We included awards to subsidiaries, R&D limited partnerships, and earlier names, which we identify through the data sources cited below.)

We finally identified all litigation involving these firms in the federal and state judicial districts that include their headquarters: the Federal District for Massachusetts and the Commonwealth of Massachusetts' Middlesex Superior Court. Both systems include every lawsuit that was open during the sample period, even if the suit was settled almost immediately after the initial complaint was filed. We identified 1,144 cases that were open on January 1, 1990, or were filed between January 1, 1990, and June 30, 1994. After eliminating cases that were unlikely to involve intellectual property issues, we examined the remaining case files.[6] The docket records also allowed us to compute the total number of docket filings by the plaintiffs, defendants, and other parties in the dispute between January 1, 1990, and June 30, 1994. (This approach to characterizing disputes was also used in the Georgetown antitrust study; see White 1988.) The records do not provide information on the extent of activity at the appellate level. Thus they tend to understate the magnitude of litigation in cases that are appealed.

---

5. The comparison of the sample with the federal and county data is not precise for three reasons. First, the tabulation of the sample firms shows the distribution of firms; the U.S. and county columns present the pattern of establishments. (Many firms will have multiple establishments.) Second, firms with less than twenty employees are only sampled in *County Business Patterns*, and thus are underrepresented. The two directories appear to have quite comprehensive coverage of smaller firms, who generally welcome the visibility that a listing provides. Consequently industries with many small firms may have greater representation in the sample. Finally the tabulation of employment in the sample firms includes employees that work in Middlesex County and elsewhere. The county tabulation presents the distribution of employees working in Middlesex County, regardless of where the parent firm has its headquarters.

6. In addition we could not examine nine dockets that may or may not have involved intellectual property issues. These cases had been either lost or sealed. (While most of the case files were accessible at the clerk of the court's offices at the two courthouses, we found many case files in off-site storage archives, in courthouses elsewhere in the county or state, or in the possession of judges' docket clerks.)

Table 12.4
Characteristics of venture-backed and non-venture-backed firms

	Mean	Median	Standard deviation	Minimum	Maximum
Panel A: 122 Venture-backed firms					
Firm sales in 1990 ($mil)	173	11	1,199	0	12,942
Firm employment in 1990	526	106	2,103	8	20,184
Year firm was founded	1,977	1,981	15	1,880	1,989
Publicly traded at end of 1989[a]	0.30			0.00	1.00
Patent awards, 1969–89	10	0	41	0	375
R&D/sales ratio of industry in 1990[b]	0.11	0.10	0.08	0.00	0.38
Panel B: 408 Non-venture-backed firms					
Firm sales in 1990 ($mil)	44	2	477	0	9268
Firm employment in 1990	184	19	940	2	11,768
Year firm was founded	1,967	1,974	25	1,842	1,989
Publicly traded at end of 1989[a]	0.11			0.00	1.00
Patent awards, 1969–89	13	0	149	0	2,644
R&D/sales ratio of industry in 1990[b]	0.06	0.04	0.06	0.00	0.38

Note: The sample consists of 530 firms based in Middlesex County, Massachusetts. The tabulation presents the summary statistics for the 122 firms that had received venture capital financing prior to January 1990, and the 408 that did not.
a. The "publicly traded at end of 1989" variable is a dummy that takes on the value 1.0 if the firm was publicly traded.
b. The average ratio of R&D-to-sales of all publicly traded firms that reported R&D data in 1990 with a primary assignment in Compustat to the same four-digit SIC code as the firm.

Table 12.4 lists the features of the venture-backed and non-venture-backed firms used in the sample. The 122 venture-backed firms are significantly larger in sales and employment than the 408 non-venture-backed firms, and they are more likely to be publicly traded. They tend to have been founded later, and as a result have accumulated a smaller stock of patents. The venture-backed firms are concentrated in high-technology industries. The average ratio of R&D to sales of all public firms that reported R&D data in 1990 with a primary assignment in Compustat to the same four-digit SIC code as the venture-backed firms is higher than the ratios of the companies matched to the non-venture-backed firms.

Challenges of the Data

Before discussing the use of these data, we should acknowledge two challenges that these measures posed. First, since the U.S. Patent and Trademark

Office (USPTO) does not compile patent statistics by industry and many firms have multiple lines of business, patenting in each industry can be only be indirectly inferred. Our dependent variable is therefore problematic. We rely on a concordance that relates a patent's industry to the primary technological classification to which it is assigned by the patent examiner.[7]

Second, the industrial R&D data we used overlook the activities of many smaller firms and undoubtedly include some research financed by venture capital organizations. The data therefore do not allow a clean division. We can only distinguish conceptually between R&D financed by corporations and R&D financed by venture capital organizations. Similarly, while the bulk of venture financing supports innovative activities at technology-intensive firms, some is used for other purposes. For instance, some of the venture financing goes to low-technology concerns or is channeled to marketing activities. It should be noted that by leaving some venture funding in our measure of corporate R&D, it is less likely that we will find an impact of venture capital on patenting conditional on the R&D measure.

We aggregated venture funding and patents into essentially the industry scheme used by the NSF in tabulating its survey of industrial R&D. We consolidated a few NSF industries that account for little R&D.[8] The resulting 20 industries are listed in table 12.1.

Table 12.5 summarizes the time-series dimension of the main data series. The table indicates the rapid growth of the venture capital industry. The

---

7. This concordance relies on industry assignments of patents issued by Canada (the majority of which are issued to U.S. inventors) to determine the likelihood of a particular industry assignment given a patent's technological classification (Kortum and Putnam 1997). Industry counts for the United States are based on the International Patent Classification assigned to each patent issued by the USPTO. The patent assignments differ depending on whether the assigned industry corresponds to the user or the manufacturer of the patented invention. We focus on the industry of use series, but our results about the impact of venture capital are robust to replacing industry of use with industry of manufacture. In either case the industry assignment of patents may not correspond precisely to the industry doing the R&D or receiving the venture capital funding that led to the underlying invention.

8. We focus on the manufacturing industries, since survey evidence (summarized in Cohen 1995) suggests that the reliance on patenting as a means of appropriating new technological discoveries is much higher in these industries (e.g., as opposed to trade secrecy or first-mover advantages). Patenting is thus likely to be a better indicator of the rate of technological innovation in the manufacturing sector. The time period is determined on the one end by the availability of data on venture capital investment and on the other end by our inability to observe the detailed technological classifications of U.S. patent applications before they are issued (applications are held confidential until issue).

Table 12.5
Patenting activity of, R&D expenditures by, and venture capital disbursements for U.S. manufacturing industries, by year

Year	Successful patent applications	R&D expenditures ($mil)	Venture capital disbursements		Ratio of venture capital to R&D	
			Number of firms	Amount ($mil)	All VC	Early-stage only
1965	50,278	25,313	8	13	0.05	0.02
1966	48,740	27,573	3	2	0.01	0.00
1967	48,900	29,515	9	24	0.08	0.07
1968	49,980	31,387	25	37	0.12	0.08
1969	51,614	33,244	66	149	0.45	0.38
1970	53,950	32,883	63	126	0.38	0.24
1971	54,776	32,360	57	224	0.69	0.41
1972	49,777	33,593	52	209	0.62	0.44
1973	45,807	36,169	74	235	0.65	0.30
1974	44,465	37,323	42	81	0.22	0.13
1975	44,082	35,935	41	118	0.33	0.24
1976	44,026	38,056	47	83	0.22	0.10
1977	41,550	39,605	57	138	0.35	0.21
1978	42,648	42,373	116	255	0.60	0.37
1979	44,941	45,318	152	301	0.66	0.28
1980	41,726	48,700	231	635	1.30	0.80
1981	39,137	52,012	408	1,146	2.20	1.39
1982	38,039	55,033	466	1,388	2.52	1.29
1983	34,712	58,066	656	2,391	4.12	1.97
1984	33,905	63,441	709	2,347	3.70	1.95
1985	36,732	66,860	646	1,951	2.92	1.42
1986	41,644	68,476	639	2,211	3.23	1.62
1987	46,434	67,700	713	2,191	3.24	1.57
1988	51,355	69,008	660	2,076	3.01	1.54
1989	55,103	70,456	669	1,995	2.83	1.56
1990	58,358	69,714	557	1,675	2.40	1.11
1991	58,924	69,516	422	1,026	1.48	0.71
1992	60,771	70,825	469	1,571	2.22	1.05

Note: All dollar figures are in millions of 1992 dollars. The ratios of venture capital disbursements to R&D expenditures are computed using all venture capital disbursements and early-stage venture disbursements only.

ratio of venture capital to R&D jumped sharply in the late 1970s and early 1980s, and fell a bit thereafter. Patenting declined from the early 1970s to the mid-1980s but then rose sharply.[9]

Tables 1.2, 12.1, and 12.2 summarize the industry dimension of the data on patents, venture capital, and R&D, respectively. It should be noted that disbursements are concentrated in certain industries. The top three industries—drugs, office and computing, and communication equipment—represent 54 percent of the venture disbursements. The comparable figure for R&D expenditures is 39 percent.

Table 12.6 presents venture capital disbursements as a percentage of R&D spending. When normalized by total R&D, a number of low-tech industries, such as textiles and apparel, appear to be relatively reliant on venture funding. Note also the high degree of persistence over time in the set of industries in which venture funding is a substantial fraction of R&D. This pattern is maintained when looking only at early stage financing, as in panel B.

Reduced-Form Regressions

We start our empirical analysis by investigating whether, conditional on R&D spending, venture capital funding influences innovation. We estimate and report on patent production functions in the next two subsections. In undertaking this analysis, we employ many of the conventions of the literature on innovation production functions, reviewed in Griliches (1990).[10] In the last subsection we estimate a simpler linear specification that is addressed in detail at the end of the chapter. Throughout this section we treat venture financing as exogenous, deferring the discussion of its determinants until the next section.

---

9. A natural concern is the extent of correlation between the venture capital and private R&D measures. While the two variables are positively correlated, the extent of correlation is less than the aggregate numbers in table 12.5 might lead one to believe. In particular, the correlation coefficient between the logarithms of the dollar volume of venture financings and private R&D in each industry is 0.43. The partial correlation, once the year and industry are controlled for, is 0.31. The correlation between the number of companies receiving venture financing and private R&D is even lower.

10. As in this literature we initially ignore the impact of such factors as the uncertainty about technological success on the propensity to patent innovations. Later in the chapter we show that the results are robust to the use of alternative measures that at least partially address these problems.

Table 12.6
Ratio of venture capital disbursements to R&D expenditures for U.S. manufacturing industries, by industry and five-year period

Industry	1965–69	1970–74	1975–79	1980–84	1985–89	1990–92
Panel A: All venture capital disbursements/R&D spending						
Food and kindred	0.14	0.50	0.16	0.44	2.93	3.18
Textile and apparel	0.57	1.68	1.59	2.72	3.24	10.59
Lumber and furniture	1.44	1.77	0.72	2.32	21.39	4.40
Paper	0.06	0.28	0.10	0.08	0.56	0.03
Industrial chemicals	0.00	0.00	0.01	0.22	0.15	0.10
Drugs	0.01	0.17	1.10	3.49	7.26	6.16
Other chemicals	0.03	0.98	0.09	0.13	1.43	0.38
Petroleum refining and extraction	0.16	0.08	1.04	2.63	0.90	0.17
Rubber products	0.04	0.07	0.42	0.64	0.20	0.21
Stone, clay, and glass products	0.00	0.02	0.19	0.93	2.01	2.62
Primary metals	0.00	0.19	0.21	0.51	1.59	0.94
Fabricated metal products	0.00	0.00	0.00	0.03	0.01	0.03
Office and computing machines	0.62	2.37	1.23	9.17	4.63	1.85
Other nonelectrical machinery	0.75	0.16	0.30	4.27	4.58	1.48
Communication and electronic	0.26	0.93	0.37	4.64	5.27	5.03
Other electrical equipment	0.00	0.06	0.38	0.57	1.25	0.53
Transportation equipment	0.00	0.04	0.01	0.03	0.10	0.15
Aircraft and missiles	0.00	0.00	0.00	0.07	0.05	0.04
Professional and scientific instruments	0.19	0.84	0.77	3.35	4.78	2.87
Other manufacturing	0.46	1.34	0.90	3.65	7.51	5.81
Panel B: Early-stage venture capital disbursements/R&D spending						
Food and kindred	0.14	0.22	0.05	0.14	1.69	2.17
Textile and apparel	0.36	0.90	0.79	0.67	1.46	3.05
Lumber and furniture	0.00	0.74	0.51	1.19	11.23	2.07
Paper	0.00	0.28	0.00	0.08	0.21	0.01
Industrial chemicals	0.00	0.00	0.00	0.21	0.04	0.07
Drugs	0.01	0.14	0.92	2.53	4.40	3.39
Other chemicals	0.00	0.62	0.03	0.10	0.55	0.21
Petroleum refining and extraction	0.13	0.08	0.56	1.40	0.59	0.11
Rubber products	0.00	0.05	0.32	0.41	0.17	0.00
Stone, clay, and glass products	0.00	0.02	0.00	0.50	1.37	1.46
Primary metals	0.00	0.15	0.12	0.46	1.35	0.17
Fabricated metal products	0.00	0.00	0.00	0.00	0.01	0.00
Office and computing machines	0.55	1.32	0.73	4.21	1.74	0.87
Other nonelectrical machinery	0.68	0.08	0.12	2.08	2.11	0.49
Communication and electronic	0.19	0.46	0.16	2.68	2.69	1.97

Table 12.6
(continued)

Industry	1965–69	1970–74	1975–79	1980–84	1985–89	1990–92
Other electrical equipment	0.00	0.04	0.20	0.33	0.69	0.27
Transportation equipment	0.00	0.03	0.00	0.00	0.04	0.01
Aircraft and missiles	0.00	0.00	0.00	0.02	0.01	0.04
Professional and scientific instruments	0.10	0.65	0.26	1.95	2.86	1.39
Other manufacturing	0.31	1.12	0.36	2.34	3.54	1.84

Note: All dollar figures are in millions of 1992 dollars. The ratios of venture capital disbursements to R&D expenditures are computed using all venture capital disbursements and early-stage venture disbursements only.

The Patent Production Function

We estimate a patent production function of the form: $P_{it} = (R_{it}^{\rho} + bV_{it}^{\rho})^{\alpha/\rho} u_{it}$ Patenting (P) is a function of privately funded industrial R&D (R) and venture disbursements (V), while an error term (u) captures shifts in the propensity to patent or technological opportunities, all indexed by industry (i) and year (t). We focus on the parameter b, which captures the role of venture capital in the patent production function. For any $b > 0$, venture funding matters for innovation, while if b equals zero, the patent production function reduces to the standard form, $P_{it} = R_{it}^{\alpha} u_{it}$. The parameter α captures returns to scale, meaning the percentage change in patenting brought about by a 1 percent increase in both R and V. The parameter ρ measures the degree of substitutability between R and V as means of financing innovative effort. When ρ equals one, the function reduces to $P_{it} = (R_{it} + bV_{it})^{\alpha} u_{it}$. As ρ goes to zero, the patent production function approaches the Cobb-Douglas functional form, $P_{it} = R_{it}^{\alpha/(1+b)} V_{it}^{\alpha b/(1+b)} u_{it}$.

Estimates

Nonlinear least squares estimates of the patent production function are shown in table 12.7. The dependent variable is the logarithm of the number of (ultimately successful) patent applications filed by U.S. inventors in each industry and year. The two independent variables of interest are privately financed R&D in that industry and year and either the dollar volume of venture disbursements or the number of firms in the industry receiving

Table 12.7
Nonlinear least squares regression analysis of the patent production function

	Using firms receiving venture backing		Using venture disbursements	
	Uncon-strained	Constrained ($\rho = 1$)	Uncon-strained	Constrained ($\rho = 1$)
Returns to scale parameter (α)	0.22	0.23	0.20	0.20
	[0.02]	[0.02]	[0.02]	[0.02]
Venture capital parameter (b)				
Firms receiving funding	58.51	39.57		
	[67.31]	[10.97]		
Venture disbursements			58.71	46.94
			[77.52]	[13.66]
Substitution parameter (ρ)	1.08	1.00	1.04	1.00
	[0.24]	—	[0.26]	—
Federally funded industrial R&D	0.01	0.01	0.01	0.01
	[0.01]	[0.01]	[0.01]	[0.01]
R^2	0.99	0.99	0.99	0.99
R^2 relative to dummy variable only case	0.26	0.26	0.27	0.27
Number of observations	560	560	560	560
Likelihood ratio statistic		0.2		0.0
p-Value, likelihood ratio test		0.65		0.99

Note: The dependent variable is the logarithm of the number of patents. Year and industry dummy variables are included in each regression. [Standard errors are in brackets.]

venture backing.[11] We use as controls the logarithm of the federally funded R&D in the industry, as well as dummy variables for each industry (to control for differences in the propensity to patent) and year.

The results suggest that venture funding matters. The magnitude of b estimated in the unconstrained equation is substantial, in fact implausibly large, an issue we will return to below. Although the estimates are imprecise, a likelihood ratio test overwhelmingly rejects the special case of b equal to zero (with a p-value of less than 0.005).

We also find that R&D and venture capital are highly substitutable, with the point estimate of ρ close to one. A likelihood ratio test does not come

---

11. The parameter b is generally not invariant to the units in which venture activity is measured. To facilitate comparisons across regressions, we scale the measure based on the number of companies funded by venture capitalists to have the same overall mean as the dollar disbursements measure (in 1992 dollars). For both measures of venture finance, we add a minuscule amount (the equivalent of $1,000) to each observation so that we can consider the Cobb-Douglas limiting case in which the log of venture funding is what matters.

close to rejecting the restriction that $\rho = 1$. On the other hand, $\rho = 0$ (the Cobb-Douglas special case) is strongly rejected (with a p-value of less than 0.005). As a consequence the remainder of the chapter focuses on the restricted equation $\ln P_{it} = \alpha \ln(R_{it} + bV_{it}) + \ln u_{it}$, in which R&D and venture funding are perfect substitutes. In the restricted equation, b has the interpretation of the potency of a dollar of venture funding relative to a dollar of R&D (this interpretation of b holds for either measure of venture funding).

The results for the restricted equation are shown in the second and fourth columns of table 12.7. Together, variation in R&D and venture funding explain over one-fourth of the variation in the logarithm of patenting not captured by industry or time effects.[12] The returns-to-scale parameter α is about one-fourth, small but not implausible. What does strain credibility, however, are the point estimates of b in the two regressions, implying as they do that venture funds are about 40 times as potent as R&D. Below we explore a number of reasons why these estimates might be biased upward.

A Linear Specification

Before turning to the more difficult issues arising from the endogeneity of venture funding, we consider estimating b through a linear approximation of the patent production function (again with $\rho = 1$). Such an approximation is valid when venture funding is small relative to R&D. The linear specification has the advantage of simplicity. It is also inherently conservative in its empirical implications for the potency of venture capital. It interprets the observed average impact of V/R on patenting as the maximum marginal impact (i.e., the marginal impact as V/R approaches zero). Since our task is to evaluate the null hypothesis that venture capital is impotent, we find this inherent conservatism reassuring.

After linearizing the equation we get $\ln P_{it} = \alpha \ln R_{it} + \alpha b(V_{it}/R_{it}) + \ln u_{it}$. This approximation is analogous to that employed by Griliches (1986) in his analysis of the impact of basic research, which like venture capital represented a small fraction of total R&D expenditures, on productivity growth. Note that in this equation, the potency of venture funding is calculated

---

12. In all of the regression tables we present two measures of the goodness of fit: the overall R^2 and the R^2 when compared against a regression with just year and industry dummies. The latter is computed as $(\text{SSR}_{\text{dummy only}} - \text{SSR}_{\text{new regression}})/\text{SSR}_{\text{dummy only}}$, where SSR refers to the sum of squared residuals of the various regressions.

Table 12.8
Ordinary least squares regression analysis of the linear patent production function

	Levels with year and industry effects		Long differences with period effects	
Privately funded industrial R&D (α)	0.25	0.24	0.24	0.22
	[0.06]	[0.06]	[0.07]	[0.07]
Venture capital/privately funded R&D (αb)				
Firms receiving funding	2.13		2.42	
	[0.63]		[1.21]	
Venture disbursements		1.73		2.29
		[0.69]		[1.04]
Federally funded industrial R&D	0.01	0.01	0.03	0.02
	[0.01]	[0.01]	[0.02]	[0.02]
R^2	0.99	0.99	0.81	0.82
R^2 relative to dummy variable only case	0.21	0.20	0.24	0.25
Number of observations	560	560	60	60
Implied potency of venture funding (b)	8.49	7.26	9.98	10.39
	[2.62]	[3.16]	[5.82]	[6.21]

Note: For the levels specifications they are based on the Newey-West autocorrelation-consistent covariance estimator (with a maximum of three lags). The standard errors for the parameter b are calculated using the delta method. [Standard errors are in brackets.]

by dividing the coefficient on V/R by the coefficient on $\ln R$. Table 12.8 presents regressions employing the linear specification. The basic equations are in the first two columns. Consider the second regression, which estimates the coefficient on venture capital as 1.73. Because this is an estimate for the product of α and b, we must divide by our estimate of α, 0.24, to obtain the implied potency of venture funding, $b = 7.26$. The implied estimates of potency and the associated standard errors (calculated using the delta method) are shown in the last two rows. In both regressions the estimate of potency is significantly positive.[13] The estimates suggest that a dollar of venture capital is over seven times more powerful in stimulating patenting than a dollar of corporate R&D. Although these estimates are large, they are substantially more modest than the estimates of b from the nonlinear regressions.

---

13. Our error term consists of shocks to the propensity to patent and technological opportunities, which are likely to be persistent over time. To avoid inflating the statistical significance of the results, we calculate the standard errors using the autocorrelation-consistent covariance estimator of Newey and West (1987), with a maximum lag of three years.

These linear results appear to be quite robust. We explored changing the specification,[14] the measures of venture capital,[15] and the sample,[16] adding additional controls,[17] and using lags of the explanatory variables.[18]

Addressing the Causality Problem

The empirical results in the preceding section suggest that there is a strong association between venture capital and patenting and that corporate R&D and venture funding are highly substitutable in generating innovations. The mechanisms behind this relationship and the extent to which our estimates of the impact of venture funding may be inflated by unobserved factors, however, are not addressed by our reduced-form regressions.

---

14. If the errors in the patent production function follow a random walk, then the equation should be estimated in differences rather than in levels. The difference regressions are shown in the last two columns of table 12.8. In order to reduce the errors-in-variables problem, which tends to be magnified in a first-difference approach (Griliches and Hausman 1986), we compute averages of the logarithm of each variable over a four-year period. We then compute the change in the industry measures at eight-year intervals. Since we difference out the industry effects, we drop industry dummies from these regressions, but maintain a set of period dummies (not shown). The results of the long difference regressions are very similar to those of the levels regressions except that the precision of the estimates declines.

15. It might be thought that the financing of start-ups and very young companies would pose the greatest information problems, and that the contributions of the venture capitalists would be most valuable here. In regressions reported in the first two columns of table 12.9, we replace the venture funding measures with the count and dollar volume of only seed and early-stage financings. The estimated potency of a dollar of venture funding increases by 45 to 80 percent.

16. Our analysis may be distorted by the inclusion of numerous industries with very little innovative activity. In regressions reported in the last two columns of table 12.9, we drop industries whose R&D-to-sales ratio was below the median in 1964, the year before the beginning of the analysis. (These industries appear with a star in table 12.1.) Once again, there is an increase in the estimated potency of venture funding relative to our baseline regressions.

17. In unreported regressions, we also control for the logarithms of gross industry product or of industry employment. The effect of adding these controls is to reduce the coefficient α on the logarithm of R&D, although a remains significantly positive. Both the magnitude and significance of the coefficient on V/R are essentially unchanged by the addition of either control.

18. Another robustness check concerns possible lags between R&D spending, venture financing, and patenting. The empirical literature suggests that R&D spending and patent filings are roughly contemporaneous (Hall, Griliches, and Hausman 1988). Furthermore there is an institutional reason why there should not be long lags between venture capital and patenting: the ten-year life-spans of venture partnerships lead to pressure on companies to rapidly commercialize products after obtaining venture financing. Nevertheless, to explore this issue empirically, in unreported regressions we repeat the analyses in table 12.8, including one-year and two-year lagged values of the R&D and venture capital variable along with the contemporaneous variables. We find that the contemporaneous variables have the bulk of the explanatory power (and their coefficients are significantly positive), while the lagged variables have coefficients that are smaller (and insignificantly different from zero).

To explore these issues, we build a theoretical model of venture capital, corporate research, and innovation. The model illustrates under what conditions the preceding approach is appropriate and when it may be problematic. The final two subsections present refinements of our empirical approach, motivated by the model. We do not seek to determine which single model is the best representation of the impact of venture capital on innovation. Rather, we seek to demonstrate the robustness of the preceding results by showing that they hold up across a variety of models.

Modeling the Relationship

We consider an industry in which inventions can be pursued through either corporate R&D funding or venture capital. We make four major assumptions. First, we assume that the production function for innovations I in each industry i and time period t is essentially the one we settled upon empirically:

$$I_{it} = (R_{it} + bV_{it})^{\alpha} N_{it} = H_{it}^{\alpha} N_{it}, \tag{1}$$

where $0 < \alpha < 1$. For expositional ease, we denote total innovative effort by H_{it}. The final term N_{it} represents a shock to the invention production function, which we interpret as the exogenous arrival of innovative opportunities.

Second, we assume that innovations, on average, translate into patents in a proportional manner. Thus $P_{it} = I_{it}\varepsilon_{it}$, where P_{it} is the number of patented innovations generated in a particular industry and year and ε is an independent shock determining the propensity to patent innovations. Combining this equation with equation (1), we obtain

$$P_{it} = H_{it}^{\alpha} N_{it} \varepsilon_{it}. \tag{2}$$

The unobserved factor driving patenting thus is $N\varepsilon$, the product of technological opportunities and the propensity to patent.

Third, we assume that the expected value of a new innovation for a given time period and industry is Π_{it}. We take a simple partial equilibrium approach and do not model the determinants of Π, although we have in mind that it evolves with the size of the market, as in Schmookler (1966). We assume that individual firms are small relative to the industry, and therefore take Π as given. The expected value of a new invention incorporates the fact that some, but not all, innovations will be worth patenting.

Finally, we make assumptions regarding the marginal costs of innovating, and these deserve discussion at some length. In addition to the direct expenditures on R&D and venture disbursements, we assume that there are associated indirect expenses. These might include the costs of screening opportunities, recruiting managers and researchers, and undertaking the crucial regulatory approvals to sell the new product. We argue that at each point of time, there is likely to be a spectrum of projects: some will be appropriate for a corporate research laboratory, while others will be more suited for funding by a venture capitalist in an entrepreneurial setting. Raising venture activity as a fraction of total innovative effort pushes venture capitalists into areas farther from their comparative advantage, raising their costs, while corporate researchers are able to specialize in areas they have the greatest advantage in exploiting.

More specifically, we assume that given total research effort H, and venture financing V, the venture capitalist's costs of managing the last venture-backed project is $v_t f_V(V_{it}/\lambda_{it} H_{it})$, while the corporation's costs of managing the last corporate-backed project is $f_R(V_{it}/\lambda_{it} H_{it})$. We assume that the venture capitalists' function f_V is strictly increasing while the corporations' f_R is strictly decreasing in $V/\lambda H$. The term λ_{it} governs the extent to which opportunities are conducive to venture finance. We interpret a rise in λ to mean that technological opportunities have become more radical in nature, a shift that will lower the management costs of pursuing such projects in an entrepreneurial rather than a corporate setting. The v_t term represents the venture capitalist's cost of funds, which we enter explicitly to enable us to consider the impact of the 1979 clarification of the prudent man rule (a fall in v).

From this set of assumptions we derive several equilibrium conditions. The equilibrium level of venture capital and corporate R&D will equate the marginal cost of additional spending to the marginal benefit. Assuming that we are not at a corner solution where V or R is equal to zero,[19] the conditions are

$$\Pi_{it} \frac{\partial I_{it}}{\partial V_{it}} = \alpha \Pi_{it} N_{it} b H_{it}^{\alpha-1} = v_t f_V \left(\frac{V_{it}}{\lambda_{it} H_{it}} \right), \tag{3}$$

$$\Pi_{it} \frac{\partial I_{it}}{\partial R_{it}} = \alpha \Pi_{it} N_{it} H_{it}^{\alpha-1} = f_R \left(\frac{V_{it}}{\lambda_{it} H_{it}} \right). \tag{4}$$

---

19. An attractive feature of the model is that it can also address the empirically relevant case of $V = 0$. In that case

$\alpha \Pi_{it} N_{it} b R_{it}^{\alpha-1} \leq v_t f_V(0),$

where $R_{it} = [\alpha \Pi_{it} N_{it} / f_R(0)]^{1/(1-\alpha)}$.

Through a series of mathematical manipulations,[20] we obtain the expressions

$$H_{it} = \left[\frac{\alpha \Pi_{it} N_{it}}{g_1(v_t)}\right]^{1/(1-\alpha)},$$ (5)

$$\frac{V_{it}}{R_{it}} = \lambda_{it}\left[\frac{g_2(v_t)}{1 - b\lambda_{it}g_2(v_t)}\right],$$ (6)

where g_1 is an increasing function and g_2 a decreasing one. According to equation (5), total innovative effort is decreasing in the cost of venture funds v and can be stimulated by positive shocks to either the value of inventions or the arrival of technological opportunities. Venture funding relative to corporate R&D, equation (6), increases by the degree to which these opportunities are radical in nature, λ, and decreases in the cost of venture funds.

A shock to λ favors venture capital relative to corporate R&D, while a jump in N not only stimulates both forms of financing but also can create a jump in patenting conditional on the amount of innovative effort. To complicate matters, we suspect that the two shocks λ and N are positively correlated. A burst of innovative opportunities will often be associated with a radical shift in the technology. Small venture-financed entrepreneurs will often be better able to exploit technological opportunities than large corporations. Because of this potential correlation between a shock to the patent equation and a shock that favors venture finance, we are skeptical of our reduced form regression results.

Implications for the Estimation

The next set of equations allows us to illustrate the issues that we face in estimating the linear form of the patent production function:

$$\ln P_{it} = \alpha \ln R_{it} + \alpha b\left(\frac{V_{it}}{R_{it}}\right) + \ln N + \ln \varepsilon_{it},$$ (7)

with industry dummies, year dummies, and federally funded R&D included as controls. If technological opportunities N are totally captured by our

---

20. Specific steps were to (1) define $x \equiv \alpha \Pi_{it} N_{it} H_{it}^{\alpha-1}$, (2) combine equations (12.3) and (12.4) to get $b/v = (1/x)f_V(f_R^{-1}(x)) \equiv h(x)$, where $h(x)$ is a strictly decreasing function, (3) solve for $x = h^{-1}(b/v) \equiv g_1(v)$, (4) plug into equation (12.4) to get $V/H = \lambda f_R^{-1}(g_1(v)) \equiv \lambda g_2(v)$, (5) use $x \equiv g_1(v)$ to solve for H, and (6) recalling that $H = R + bV$, solve for V/R.

Table 12.9
Ordinary least squares regression analysis of the linear patent production function: Robustness checks

	Using early-stage financing		Using high R&D industries only	
Privately funded industrial R&D (α)	0.24	0.24	0.38	0.37
	[0.06]	[0.06]	[0.09]	[0.09]
Venture capital/privately funded R&D (αb)				
Firms receiving funding	3.74		6.98	
	[1.30]		[1.68]	
Venture disbursements		2.50		5.14
		[1.09]		[1.59]
Federally funded industrial R&D	0.02	0.01	−0.07	−0.07
	[0.01]	[0.01]	[0.04]	[0.04]
R^2	0.99	0.99	0.99	0.99
R^2 relative to dummy variable only case	0.21	0.19	0.45	0.43
Number of observations	560	560	280	280
Implied potency of venture funding (b)	15.44	10.50	18.22	13.76
	[5.35]	[4.74]	[5.95]	[5.69]

Note: Standard errors [in brackets] are based on the Newey-West autocorrelation-consistent covariance estimator (with a maximum of three lags). In all regressions the standard errors for the parameter b are calculated using the delta method. Year and industry dummy variables are included in each regression.

controls, our estimates in tables 12.7, 12.8, and 12.9 should be valid. Variation in Π_{it}, according to equation (5), will lead to variation in H and hence R, which identifies α. Variation in the cost of funds to venture capitalists v_t, interacted with differences across industries in λ, will cause variation in V/R, which identifies b.

The more likely scenario, however, is one where variation in technological opportunities is only partially explained by the controls. Variations in H, and hence R, will be correlated with the disturbance. Similarly variations in V/R will be correlated with the disturbance (if λ and N are correlated). Simply regressing patents on R&D and venture funding can yield biased estimates of both α and b, and will likely overstate the potency of venture capital.

We consider two approaches to get around potential biases in our estimates of the potency of venture funding. First, we attempt to find good instruments. Our instrument for venture funding relative to corporate R&D relies on the Department of Labor's 1979 clarification of the prudent man rule. We argue that this clarification has lowered the cost of funds to venture capitalists, much like a drop in v_t in our model. We propose an instrument based on the interaction of this 1979 change with the historical differences across industries in venture funding relative to corporate R&D.[21]

Our second approach is to use R&D to control for the unobservable term N, which is the source of our identification problems when estimating the patent production function. The basic idea is similar to that of Olley and Pakes (1996) and more recently Levinsohn and Petrin (2003), who use capital investment and purchased materials, respectively, to control for unobservables in a standard production function. Combining equations (2) and (5) while noting that $R_{it} = H_{it}/(1 + bV_{it}/R_{it})$, we solve for the patent–R&D ratio

$$\frac{P_{it}}{R_{it}} = \left[\frac{\alpha \Pi_{it}}{g_1(v_t)} \right]^{-1} \left(1 + b\frac{V_{it}}{R_{it}} \right) \varepsilon_{it}. \tag{8}$$

The striking feature of equation (8) is that normalizing patents by R&D eliminates technological opportunities N from the right side of the equation. We no longer identify α (which was not essential in any case), but we can now estimate the potency of venture funding b without worrying (subject to some caveats in how we treat Π) about correlation between V/R and the disturbance in the equation.

Instrumental Variables Estimation

We now turn to a more complete discussion of our instrument choice and to the results we obtain using instrumental variables techniques to estimate equation (7). We start with our instrument for V/R. It is based on the Department of Labor's clarification of a rule that, prior to 1979, limited the ability of pension funds to invest in venture capital. One might initially think of capturing this shift empirically through a dummy variable taking on the value of zero through 1979 and one thereafter. The problem with this simple approach is that patenting rates across all industries may change over time for a variety of reasons, including swings in the judicial enforcement of patent-holder rights and antitrust policy. We are unlikely to be able to disentangle the shift in venture fundraising from that in the propensity to

---

21. This approach also faces another challenge, which we explore in depth below. Even if our instrument for V/R is convincing, we are still faced with the endogeneity of total innovative effort. To address this issue, we consider demand-side instruments that are correlated with the value of inventions, Π_{it}, but potentially unrelated to technological opportunities.

patent. As table 12.5 shows, the filing of successful patent applications actually fell in the years after 1979. But this was also a period during which firms' ability to enforce intellectual property rights were under attack (Kortum and Lerner 1998).

The 1979 policy shift, however, should have had a predictably greater impact on patenting in some industries than others. Industries with a high level of venture capital prior to the policy change should have experienced a greater increase in funding, and thus a greater burst in patenting. In certain circumstances we can therefore use the level of venture financing prior to the shift, interacted with a dummy variable taking on the value zero through 1979 and one thereafter, as an instrumental variable.[22]

The observed relationship is likely to derive from two features of the venture industry. First, the supply of venture capitalists is quite inelastic, at least in the short run. As described in chapter 4, during periods with increasing inflows into venture capital, both the amount raised in the average new venture fund and the dollars managed per partner increase. They suggest that the highly specialized skills of venture capitalists can only be developed through years of experience undertaking these investments. Second, individual venture capitalists tend to specialize in particular industries. For instance, venture capitalists often have educational backgrounds that match the areas in which they invest, such as a doctorate in biochemistry or a master's degree in electrical engineering.

We can motivate the proposed instrument more formally by returning to the model. From equation (6) we see that the impact on V_{it}/R_{it} of a change in v_t (we argue above that v declined dramatically in the late 1970s) is increasing in V_{it}/R_{it} itself. In particular, the derivative of V/R with respect to a change in v in 1979 is $D_i = (-g_2'/g_2)(V_{i79}/R_{i79})(1 + bV_{i79}/R_{i79})$. Historically differences between industries in venture funding relative to R&D have been highly persistent over time. Hence the industry-specific average of V/R from 1965 through 1978, denoted A_i, should be highly correlated with D_i. To exploit this result, we propose an instrument that takes on the value of zero up through 1979 (before the effect of the policy shift is

---

22. The empirical relevance of this instrument is based on the observation that the increase in the ratio of venture capital activity to R&D following the 1979 shift was positively correlated with the level of V/R prior to the shift. A regression of y_i (the industry-specific change in the average ratio of venture capital disbursements to R&D spending between the 1985 to 1990 period and the 1965 to 1975 period) on x_i (the average ratio in the 1965 to 1975 period) yields an R^2 of 0.42. The observed relationship is likely to derive from the inelastic supply of venture capitalists and the industry specialization of individual venture capitalists.

seen) but in each year after 1979, and for each industry i, takes on the value A_i.[23]

The validity of the instrument, however, requires that λ_{it} not deviate for too long from its industry-specific mean. To ensure this property, we assume that $\ln \lambda_{it}$ can be decomposed into the sum of a permanent industry component λ_i (which accounts for the persistent differences between industries in V/R) and a transitory component ω_{it}. If the transitory component is independent across time, then from 1980 on it will not be correlated with A_i. Under this assumption our instrument will not be correlated with technological opportunities ($\ln N_{it}$) as these vary from their industry-specific means (industry and year dummies will always be included in the regressions). More generally, if ω_{it} is a moving average process of order m, then the instrument is still valid as long as it is amended by calculating A_i as the industry-specific average of V/R from 1965 only up to only m years prior to 1980. We consider this extension in two of the regressions below, for the case of $m = 5$.

As noted above, we must also contend with the endogeneity of R&D expenditures. There is no point in instrumenting for V/R while ignoring the potential correlation between R&D expenditures and the disturbance in the patent equation. The endogeneity problem, however, would be irrelevant if we already knew the value of the parameter α. Thus, before undertaking the daunting task of searching for a valid instrument for R&D, we simply fix the parameter α at some pre-assigned values and instrument for V/R.

The results are shown in panel A of table 12.10. Here we have instrumented for V/R in the linear specification of the patent production function, while fixing $\alpha = 0.2$ or $\alpha = 0.5$ (which straddle our estimates from tables 12.7 and 12.8).[24] We still obtain large and statistically significant estimates

---

23. Note that our instrument for V/R is based on an average of the level of venture capital financing, A_i, over a number of years. Venture capital disbursements in each industry are "lumpy": a single large later-round financing may account for a substantial fraction of the total financing in a given industry and year. By better capturing the mean level of financing activity in a given industry, the instrument may alleviate errors-in-variables problems, and may even lead to an increase in the coefficient on venture capital.

24. All of the instrumental variable (IV) regressions that we report are based on the linear specification used in tables 12.8 and 12.9. We also experimented with nonlinear IV estimation based on the specification in the second and fourth regressions in table 12.7. A feature of nonlinear IV is ambiguity about what functions of the underlying instruments should be included in the instrument set. In some cases we obtained estimates of the potency of venture capital similar to the estimates reported in table 12.10, but these estimates were not robust to dropping or adding powers of the underlying instruments. Since a comparison of table 12.7 and table 12.8 suggests that the linear specification is more conservative in its implications about the potency of venture funding, we decided to focus on that specification.

Table 12.10
Instrumental variable (IV) regression analysis of the linear patent production function

	IV: 1965–78 period $\alpha = 0.20$		IV: 1965–78 period $\alpha = 0.50$	
Panel A: IV regressions, constraining α				
Privately funded industrial R&D (α)	0.20	0.20	0.50	0.50
	—	—	—	—
Venture capital/privately funded R&D (αb)				
Firms receiving funding	3.06		2.51	
	[0.92]		[1.06]	
Venture disbursements		3.38		1.72
		[1.13]		[1.10]
Federally funded industrial R&D	0.01	0.01	0.02	0.02
	[0.01]	[0.01]	[0.01]	[0.01]
R^2	0.99	0.98	0.98	0.98
R^2 relative to dummy variable only case	0.19	0.14	0.07	0.07
Number of observations	560	560	560	560
Implied potency of venture funding (b)	15.28	16.89	5.02	3.45
	[4.59]	[5.63]	[2.12]	[2.21]

	IV's: 1965–78 period and industry GDP		IV's: 1965–75 period and industry GDP	
Panel B: IV regressions, instrumenting for R&D				
Privately funded industrial R&D (α)	0.52	0.48	0.52	0.54
	[0.10]	[0.12]	[0.10]	[0.13]
Venture capital/privately funded R&D (αb)				
Firms receiving funding	2.48		2.12	
	[1.13]		[1.14]	
Venture disbursements		1.81		0.13
		[1.40]		[1.70]
Federally funded industrial R&D	0.02	0.02	0.02	0.02
	[0.01]	[0.01]	[0.01]	[0.02]
R^2	0.98	0.98	0.98	0.98
R^2 relative to dummy variable only case	0.07	0.07	0.05	−0.04
Number of observations	560	560	560	560
Implied potency of venture funding (b)	4.81	3.74	4.08	0.25
	[2.67]	[3.56]	[2.58]	[3.21]

Note: Standard errors [in brackets] are based on the Newey-West autocorrelation-consistent covariance estimator (with a maximum of three lags). The standard errors for the parameter b are calculated using the delta method. Year and industry dummy variables are included in each regression.

of the potency of venture funding. The magnitude of the estimated parameter, however, is sensitive to the assumed value of α. We find that venture capital is about fifteen times as potent as corporate R&D if $\alpha = 0.2$, but only three to five times as potent as R&D if $\alpha = 0.5$. In light of our uncertainty about the actual value of α, and given its substantial impact on the results, we attempt to instrument for R&D as well as venture capital.

The perfect instrument for R&D would be a measure of shifts in industry demand that affect the value of an invention Π_{it}, but are unrelated to technological opportunities. Since this ideal instrument is not available, we settle on an instrument that we can measure—the value of the gross industry product Y_{it}—which under certain assumptions is the same as the ideal instrument. The value of industry product is almost certainly relevant since the amount of R&D in an industry will be stimulated by an increase in the size of the market. Its validity as an instrument is less of a sure thing. In particular, the instrument will only be valid if technological opportunities (and the innovations stimulated by those opportunities) do not affect the size of the market.[25]

The regressions reported in panel B of table 12.10 use instruments for both venture funding relative to R&D and for R&D itself. The last two regressions in the panel also apply a modification of the instrument for V/R, as suggested above, to allow for the transitory component in entrepreneurial opportunities ω_{it} to be correlated for up to five years. Using the value of industry product as an instrument for R&D approximately doubles the estimate of α. The effect is to lower our estimates of the potency of venture funding, much like in the last two regressions in panel A (in which α is constrained to be 0.5). The large increase in α when we instrument for R&D can be understood in two ways. One possibility is that our earlier estimates of α are biased downward (due to errors in our measure of R&D). A second possibility is that gross industry product is not a valid instrument because it is positively correlated with technological opportunities. Since we cannot resolve these issues within the context of our instrumental variable approach, we pursue instead a very different technique for dealing with the endogeneity of venture funding.[26]

---

25. Such a feedback will not exist if the price elasticity of industry demand is equal to one. In this case a fall in quality-adjusted prices associated with a process or product innovation will be just offset by the increase in demand, leaving the value of industry output unchanged.

26. If we accept $\alpha = 0.5$, we can resolve the puzzle of the high estimates of venture-capital potency shown in table 12.7. Redoing those nonlinear regressions under the restriction that $\alpha = 0.5$ (and $\rho = 1$) yields much lower estimates of the potency of venture capital, in the range of four to five.

Controlling for Technological Opportunities

Our second approach for dealing with the endogeneity problem is to use R&D to control for unobserved technological opportunities. The basic idea follows from equation (8): conditional on the ratio of venture capital to R&D and the expected value of an innovation, the patent–R&D ratio does not depend on technological opportunities. Taking logarithms of equation (8) and linearizing around $V/R = 0$, we have

$$\ln P_{it} - \ln R_{it} = b\left(\frac{V_{it}}{R_{it}}\right) - \ln \Pi_{it} + \ln \varepsilon_{it}. \tag{9}$$

(The term $\ln[g_1(v_t)/\alpha]$ is subsumed in year effects. Industry effects are also included.) One approach to estimating this equation is to subsume any variation in the expected value of inventions in the disturbance. This approach implicitly assumes, however, that shocks to venture funding relative to R&D are uncorrelated with shocks to the expected value of an invention.

Our other approach begins with equation (9) but uses industry output as a proxy for the expected value of an invention, $\ln \Pi_{it} = a_0 + a_1 \ln Y_{it}$. Assuming $a_1 = 1$, we obtain the equation,

$$\ln P_{it} - (\ln R_{it} - \ln Y_{it}) = b\left(\frac{V_{it}}{R_{it}}\right) + \ln \varepsilon_{it}. \tag{10}$$

The dependent variable can be thought of as the logarithm of the ratio of patents P to R&D intensity, R/Y. Note that our use of the value of industry output as a proxy for the expected value of an invention does not require that the value of industry output be independent of technological opportunities. Thus we are able to avoid the most problematic assumption that was required in our instrumental variable approach.

The results from estimating equations (9) and (10), shown in table 12.11, are largely consistent with our findings in tables 12.8, 12.9, and 12.10. In all cases venture funding is significantly more potent than corporate R&D. The estimates of b are more modest, suggesting that venture funding is between one and a half times and three times as potent as corporate R&D.[27]

---

27. We can generalize by including $-a_1 \ln Y_{it}$ on the right-hand side of equation (9). Restricting $a_1 = 0$, we get back the specification shown in the first two columns of table 12.11, while restricting it to be 1 yields the specification in the last two columns. If we estimate a_1, we get a value of about 0.4, while the corresponding estimate of b remains statistically significant and within the range reported in table 12.11. We have also run regressions corresponding to the nonlinear versions of equations (9) and (10). The estimates of b are somewhat larger than those reported in table 12.11: 3.23 [0.74], 1.86 [0.58], 4.55 [0.91], and 4.81 [0.84].

Table 12.11
Ordinary least squares regression analyses of the patent–R&D ratio

	Dependent variable			
	$\ln P_{it} - \ln R_{it}$		$\ln P_{it} - (\ln R_{it} + \ln Y_{it})$	
Venture capital/privately funded R&D (b)				
Firms receiving funding	2.39		2.96	
	[0.82]		[0.87]	
Venture disbursements		1.45		2.70
		[0.55]		[0.85]
R^2	0.97	0.97	0.97	0.97
R^2 relative to dummy variable only case	0.04	0.02	0.06	0.07
Number of observations	560	560	560	560

Note: Standard errors [in brackets] are based on the Newey-West autocorrelation-consistent covariance estimator (with a maximum of three lags). Year and industry dummy variables are included in each regression.

Patenting or Innovation?

While the analyses above suggest a strong relationship between venture capital and patenting on an industry level, one major concern remains. In particular, it might be thought that the relationship between venture capital disbursements and patent applications is not indicative of a relationship between venture disbursements and innovative output. It may be that the increase in patenting is a consequence of a shift in the propensity to patent innovations stimulated by the venture financing process itself. In the terms of equation (7), there may be a positive correlation between the ε_{it} and V_{it}/R_{it} terms.

Two reasons might lead venture-backed firms—or companies seeking venture financing—to patent inventions that other firms would not. First, they may fear that the venture investors will exploit their ideas. Firms seeking external financing must make extensive disclosures of their technology. While potential investors may sign nondisclosure agreements (and may be restrained by reputational concerns), there is still a real possibility that entrepreneurs' ideas will be directly or indirectly transferred to other companies. Alternatively, venture or other investors may find it difficult to discern the quality of firms' patent holdings. In order to enhance their attractiveness (and consequently increase the probability of obtaining financing or the valuation assigned in that financing), firms may apply for patents on technologies of marginal worth.

The industry-level data does not provide us much guidance here, but we can explore these possibilities by examining a broader array of behavior by venture-backed and non-venture-backed firms. Using a sample of 530 Middlesex County firms, we examine three measures of innovative activity:

• Trajtenberg (1990) has demonstrated a strong relationship between the number of patent citations received and the economic importance of a patent. Using only those firms that received any patent awards prior to 1990, we compute the ratio of the number of U.S. patent citations during the period between 1990 and June 1994 to U.S. patents awarded between 1969 and 1989. Citations per patent provides a largely external measure of the average importance of the firms' patent awards.

• The second and third measures of the intellectual property activity of firms are the frequency and extent of patent and trade secret litigation in which the firm has engaged. Models in the law-and-economics literature suggest parties are more likely to file suits and pursue these cases to trial when (1) the stakes of the dispute are high relative to the costs of the litigation, or (2) the outcome of the case is unclear (Cooter and Rubinfeld 1989). Thus, litigation may serve as a rough proxy for economic importance, a suggestion verified empirically by Lanjouw and Schankerman (1998). We present these tabulations separately for patent and trade secret suits. These measures may provide a rough indication of the importance of both patents and trade secrets to the firm.

Table 12.12 presents univariate comparisons. There are substantial differences between the 122 venture-backed and 408 non-venture-backed firms: the venture firms are more likely to patent, have previous patents cited, and engage in frequent and protracted litigation of both patents and trade secrets. All the tests of differences in means and medians in these three categories are significant at least at the 5 percent confidence level, as well as when we employ regression specifications. These findings help allay fears that differences in the propensity to patent drove our findings in the preceding sections. At the same time it is important to acknowledge that while the firm-level analysis allows us to examine whether the innovative behavior of venture-backed and non-venture firms differ on measures other than patent counts, it does not allow us to address endogeneity issues as in the industry-level analysis.

Table 12.12
Comparisons of intellectual property activities of venture-backed and non-venture-backed firms

	Mean		p-Value compared	
	Venture-backed firms	Non-venture firms	Means	Medians
Patents, 1990 to mid-1994	12.74	2.40	0.029	0.000
Citations/patent	6.44	4.06	0.016	0.004
Intellectual property suits				
Number of suits	0.79	0.18	0.000	0.000
Number of docket filings	30.29	4.21	0.000	0.000
Patent suits only				
Number of suits	0.36	0.08	0.000	0.000
Number of docket filings	15.35	2.04	0.000	0.000
Trade secret suits only				
Number of suits	0.34	0.08	0.000	0.000
Number of docket filings	6.43	1.86	0.007	0.000

Note: The sample consists of 530 firms based in Middlesex County, Massachusetts, of which 122 are venture-backed.

Conclusions

In this chapter we examined the impact of venture capital on technological innovation. From patenting patterns across industries over a three-decade period the effect appears to be positive and significant. We obtained robust results in taking different measures of venture activity, subsamples of industries, and representations of the relationship between patenting, R&D, and venture capital. We averaged across our preferred regressions to come up with an estimate for b (the impact on patenting of a dollar of venture capital relative to a dollar of R&D) of 3.1. This estimate suggests that venture capital accounted for 8 percent of industrial innovations in the decade ending in 1992.[28] Given the rapid increase in venture funding since 1992, and assuming that the potency of venture funding has remained constant, the results imply that by 1998 venture funding accounted for about 14 percent of U.S. innovative activity.[29]

---

28. We get the estimate of $b = 3.1$ by averaging the estimates in the regressions reported in panel B of table 12.10, table 12.11, and note 27. The ratio of venture capital disbursements to R&D (V/R) averaged over the years 1983 to 1992 is 2.9 percent (see table 12.5). Our calculation of the share of innovations due to venture capital is $b(V/R)/(1 + b(V/R))$.

29. Based on estimates of venture capital disbursements to all industries in 1998 (from Venture Economics) and preliminary estimates of R&D performed and funded by industry (from the National Science Foundation), we calculate that V/R increased at a 14 percent annual rate from 1992 to 1998. Given that V/R was 2.22 percent in 1992, we project that it had risen to 5.1 percent by 1998. Applying the same venture funding potency b of 3.1, we get the 14 percent number noted in the text.

In our earlier work (1998) we argued that the surge in patenting in the United States over the past two decades could be explained by changes in the management of innovative activities. Interpreted broadly, the growth of the venture capital is one such management change. While our results helped answer some questions, they pose some additional questions:

• What are the sources of the venture capitalists' advantage in funding innovation? Is the key source of advantage the process by which projects are chosen ex ante, or rather is it the monitoring and control after the investment is made?

• Why haven't industrial R&D managers adopted some of the same approaches to financing innovation? Jensen (1993), for one, has argued that agency problems have hampered the effectiveness of major corporate industrial research facilities over the past several decades. What barriers have limited the diffusion of the venture capitalists' approaches?

• Is it possible to disentangle the distinct effects of the rise of venture capital from other innovations in the management of R&D in large corporations, where during the 1990s the R&D facilities were increasingly redirected toward more applied problems? (For an overview, see Rosenbloom and Spencer 1996.)

13 Can the Government Be an Effective Venture Capitalist?

Despite economists' interest in interactions between governments and firms, the public subsidization of small firms has attracted virtually no scrutiny. This chapter seeks to address this omission by examining the largest such program in the United States, the Small Business Innovation Research (SBIR) program, which provided over $13 billion to small high-technology firms between 1983 and 2003.

Addressing this omission is important for three reasons:

1. Theoretical models of interactions between the public and private sectors can be empirically examined. This interaction has been a topic of enduring interest in the economics literature for several decades.

2. Public programs to subsidize small high-technology firms have represented a significant but little studied area of public expenditures. (Table 13.1 lists the programs in the United States over the past several decades. See OECD 1996 for tabulations of efforts in Europe and Asia.) For instance, the sum of the financing provided through, and guaranteed by, the programs listed in table 13.1 in 1995 was at least $2.4 billion, compared to the $3.9 billion disbursed by private venture capital funds in that year.

3. A number of public programs are reputed to have had a positive and significant impact on economic growth. Some of America's most dynamic companies received support through federal programs while privately held. These companies include Apple Computer, Chiron, Compaq, Federal Express, and Intel. In addition to funding firms, publicly sponsored funds during the 1960s provided early experience for many of the individuals who later went on to lead independent venture organizations. Overseas, much of the recent growth in high-technology firms in such nations as Israel, Singapore, and Taiwan has been attributed to government venture capital initiatives (see OECD 1996).

Economic analyses suggest at least two sets of rationales for governments to offer subsidies to small high-technology firms. First, the social

Table 13.1
U.S. public venture capital initiatives, 1958–1997

Sponsoring organization	Program name	Brief description	Span
Small Business Administration	Small Business Investment Company Program	Provides capital to federally sponsored funds that make debt and equity investments in growth firms	1958–1997
Department of Commerce	State Technical Services Program	Supported various government programs to help high-technology companies (especially new firms)	1965–1969
Department of Housing and Urban Development Model Cities Administration	Venture Capital Development Assistance	Demonstration projects in selected cities financed businesses begun by residents of targeted neighborhoods	1967–1971
At least 30 states	At least 43 state venture funds or SBIC programs	Make investments into funds supporting new enterprises, which often focus on high-technology firms	1970–1997
Department of State Agency for International Development	At least 13 developing country venture funds	Provided loans to financial intermediaries that made equity and debt investments in new enterprises in over 30 countries	1971–1993
Small Business Administration	Specialized Small Business Investment Company Program	Provides capital to federally sponsored funds that make debt and equity investments in growth firms owned by disadvantaged individuals	1972–1997
Department of Commerce National Bureau of Standards	Experimental Technology Incentives Program	Catalyzed new public programs (across agencies) to encourage industrial research and venture capital	1972–1979
National Science Foundation	Federal Laboratories Validation Assistance Experiment	Funded assessments by national laboratory personnel of prototype products and processes developed by entrepreneurs	1972–1975
National Science Foundation and Small Business Administration	Innovation Centers Experiment	Provided assistance to high-tech entrepreneurs through incubation centers, subsidies, and technical assistance	1973–1981

Agency	Program	Description	Years
Department of Energy Office of Energy-Related Inventions	Energy Related Inventions Program	Provides financing to individual inventors and small firms to commercialize energy-conserving discoveries	1975–1997
Small Business Administration	Small Business Development Centers Program	Funds university-based centers to assist small businesses and encourage technology transfer	1976–1997
Department of Commerce	Corporations for Innovation Development Initiative	Designed to fund state and regional corporations to provide equity financing to new firms; only one such corporation funded	1979–1981
Department of Commerce Minority Business Development Agency	Technology Commercialization Program	Financed minority technology-oriented entrepreneurs, as well as centers to assist such entrepreneurs	1979–1982
At least 15 states	At least 107 business incubators	Provide office and manufacturing space, support services, and often financing to start-up businesses	1980–1996
11 federal agencies	Small Business Innovation Research Program	Provides awards to small technology-oriented businesses (also predecessor programs at 3 agencies, 1977–1982)	1982–1997
Department of Energy Office of Energy Research	At least 6 contractor-organized venture funds	Make equity investments in spinouts from national laboratories (funds organized by prime or subcontractors at laboratories with Department's encouragement)	1985–1997
At least 30 states	State Small Business Innovation Research Programs	Makes SBIR-like grants, often in conjunction with federal SBIR awards	1987–1997
Department of Commerce National Institute of Standards and Technology	Advanced Technology Program	Awards grants to develop targeted technologies to firms and consortia; some emphasis on small businesses	1988–1997
Department of Defense Defense Advanced Research Projects Agency	Experimental venture capital investment program	Designed to make investments in private high-technology firms in exchange for equity or royalties; program only made one investment	1989–1991
Department of State Agency for International Development	Enterprise Fund Program	Oversees 12 federally funded venture funds investing in Eastern Europe, the former Soviet Union, and Africa	1990–1997

Table 13.1
(continued)

Sponsoring organization	Program name	Brief description	Span
Overseas Private Investment Corporation	Venture capital fund guarantees	Guarantees full or partial return of capital to investors in at least 16 private venture funds in developing countries	1990–1997
Department of Housing and Urban Development Community Relations and Involvement Office	Tenant Opportunity Program	Funds new businesses and other initiatives by public housing residents (other aspects of program had begun in 1987)	1993–1997
Department of Energy Office of the Under Secretary	Defense Programs Small Business Initiative	Provides funding, technological assistance, and national laboratory access to small high-technology businesses	1993–1997
11 federal agencies	Small Business Technology Transfer Program	Finances cooperative research projects between small high-technology firms and non-profit research institutions	1994–1997
Department of Defense Cooperative Threat Reduction Program	Defense Enterprise Fund	Finances an independent venture fund investing in defense conversion projects in the former Soviet Union	1994–1997
Department of the Treasury	Community Development Financial Institutions Fund	Invests in and provides assistance to community development venture capital and loan funds	1995–1997
Department of Defense	"Fast Track" Program	Provides 4:1 matching funds for private financing raised by SBIR awardees	1995–1997
Department of Agriculture Rural Business and Cooperative Development Service	Intermediary Relending Program (as amended)	Permits program managers to guarantee returns of investors in rural venture funds	1997

Source: Eisinger (1988), Organisation for Economic Co-operation and Development (1996), U.S. Small Business Administration (1996), and various news stories in the LEXIS/NEXIS database and government reports.

Note: The table summarizes programs sponsored by state and federal organizations in which equity investments or equity-like grants were made into privately held companies, or into funds that made such investments. If a program had multiple names, the name is reported in May 1997. The name of a program terminated prior to this date is recorded at the time of the termination. If an organization sponsoring a program changed its name, or if responsibility for the program was transferred between organizations, the name of the sponsoring organization is reported in May 1997. If the program was terminated prior to this date, the sponsoring organization is recorded at the time of the program's termination.

returns from the firms' R&D expenditures may exceed their private returns. Second, in making such awards, knowledgeable government officials may certify firms to private investors and address the informational asymmetries that might have otherwise precluded investments. An extensive literature on regulatory capture, however, suggests that government involvement may be distorted by the desire of interest groups—or of the politicians themselves—to maximize their own private benefits.

This chapter assesses the long-run success of firms participating in the SBIR program. It examines the employment and sales growth of 1,435 firms over a ten-year period (1985 to 1995). Two-fifths of the sample received one or more awards in the first three cycles of the program; the others are matching firms chosen to closely resemble the awardees. The analysis relies heavily on a unique data set of awardees compiled by the U.S. General Accounting Office (GAO).

Over this period the SBIR awardees enjoyed substantially greater employment and sales growth than the matching firms. The growth of the awardees does not appear to have been due to the receipt of procurement contracts by these firms or other alternative explanations. These firms were also more likely to subsequently receive venture capital financing. The growth, however, was not uniform. The superior performance was confined to awardees in areas with substantial new firm creation, as measured by early-stage venture capital disbursements. The relationship between SBIR awards and growth was much stronger in high-technology industries. SBIR awardees receiving large subsidies did not perform better than those receiving smaller subsidies did. The results suggest that these awards play an important certification function. At the same time distortions in the award process may adversely affect the program's effectiveness, especially in regions with fewer high-technology firms and among firms receiving large subsidies.

The analysis has two important limitations. The most critical of these is the inability to assess the impact of these programs on social welfare. Only with much more detailed data could the relative costs and benefits of the initiative be fully assessed. Second, the analysis' focus on a single program limits its ability to show the impact of alternative program designs.

The Subsidization of Small High-Technology Firms

Theoretical Motivations

The economics literature suggests at least two sets of rationales for governments to offer subsidies to small high-technology firms. Other works, however, argue that government involvement may be distorted by the desire of interest groups or politicians to maximize their own benefits. These suggest a more skeptical view of such programs.

Public finance theory emphasizes that subsidies are an appropriate response to activities that generate positive externalities. Such investments as R&D expenditures and pollution control equipment purchases may have positive spillovers that benefit other firms or society as a whole. But because the firms making these investments are unlikely to capture the entire surplus, public subsidies may be an appropriate response.

An extensive literature (reviewed in Griliches 1992 and Jaffe 1996) has documented the presence of R&D spillovers. These spillovers take several forms. The profits associated with new innovations may accrue to competitors who rapidly introduce imitations, to developers of complementary products, or to consumers of the new products. Whatever the mechanism of the spillovers, the consequence is the same: firms will tend to invest below the socially optimal level of R&D. After reviewing a wide variety of studies, Griliches argues that the social rate of return exceeds the private rate by a considerable amount. He estimates that the social rate of return is between 150 and 200 percent of the private rate of return. Few studies have examined how these gaps vary with firm characteristics. A number of case-based analyses (Jewkes, Sawers, and Stillerman 1958; Mansfield et al. 1977), however, suggest that spillover problems are particularly severe among small firms, which are often unable to effectively defend their intellectual property or to extract most of the rents in the product market.

A second rationale for public subsidies for small high-technology firms lies in the fact that they may convey information to other potential investors. As discussed in chapter 7, informational asymmetries may make raising external capital very expensive for entrepreneurs, or even preclude it entirely. If these information gaps between the entrepreneurs and investors could be eliminated, financing constraints would disappear. Financial economists argue that specialized financial intermediaries, such as venture capital organizations, can address these problems by intensively scrutinizing firms before providing capital and then monitoring them afterward. Nonetheless, venture capitalists back only a tiny fraction of the technology-oriented businesses begun each year. Tables 1.2 and 1.3 in chapter 1 show historical venture capital disbursements by industry and state. For example in 2001, the third highest recorded year for venture capital investments, 1,172 companies received initial investments by venture capitalists (data from NVCA/Venture Economics). By way of comparison, the Small Business Administration estimates that close to one million businesses have been started annually in recent years. If federal awards could effectively certify firms to their potential investors, these problems could be addressed.[1]

The arguments outlined above implicitly assume that once a market failure is identified, the government can dispassionately address it. An extensive political economy and public finance literature, however, has emphasized the distortions that may result from government subsidies, as interest groups or politicians seek to direct subsidies in a manner that benefits themselves. As articulated by Olson (1965) and Stigler (1971), and formally modeled by Peltzman (1976) and Becker (1983), the theory of regulatory capture suggests that direct and indirect subsidies will be captured by groups who stand to gain substantial benefits and whose collective political activity is not too difficult to arrange (i.e., when free-riding by coalition members is not too large a problem). As Stigler (1971) points out, even very small firms (which have historically dominated industries such as trucking and the licensed professions) can organize to benefit from public largesse. Many of the initial works in this literature treated politicians and government bureaucrats as passive implementers of policies desired by private coalitions. Other models (summarized in Laffont and Tirole 1993) have incorporated voters, politicians, and/or bureaucrats as distinct actors, often in a principal-agent relationship.

These distortions may manifest themselves in several ways. One possibility (e.g., discussed in Eisinger 1988) is that firms may seek transfer payments that directly increase their profits. Politicians may acquiesce to such transfers to politically connected companies. A more subtle problem is discussed by Cohen and Noll (1991) and Wallsten (2000): officials may seek to select firms based on their likely success, regardless of whether the government funds are needed. In this case they can claim credit for the firms' ultimate success, even if the marginal contribution of the public funds was very low.

Empirical Implications

These contrasting views have different empirical implications for the relative performance of small high-technology firms receiving public subsidies. Following are four sets of predictions about the impact of public subsidies on firm performance.

---

1. Consistent with this view, several directories of high-technology firms denote companies that have won SBIR awards, and at least 167 press releases concerning SBIR awards were issued by firms in 1996.

Overall Impact of Subsidies   The first rationale is that subsidies are required to encourage small firms to undertake research because of spillover problems. In this regard subsidy recipients should perform at least slightly better than their peers, even if much of the surplus created by their R&D accrues to other firms in their industry or to consumers. Similarly, if public awards can certify firms to investors, the awardees may be able to attract additional capital and grow more rapidly. If, on the other hand, these awards are captured by politically connected firms, the funds may be squandered and not translate into long-run growth. The final view delineated above—that federal agencies are selecting firms that are likely to grow rapidly in any case—also suggests that SBIR firms should perform better than a set of matched firms.

Variation in Subsidy Impact across Regions   The externality and certification views suggest no clear implications for where the regional benefits of the program should be greatest. The more political economy-based views, however, raise the possibility of different geographic impacts. In particular, it may be that in regions without large numbers of high-technology firms and venture capital organizations, these awards may be captured by other firms than the intended population: politicians may encourage awards to politically connected firms with few growth prospects (e.g., consulting and contract research firms). Presumably these types of distortions in the selection process are much less likely in regions with active communities of high-technology firms and venture investors, as these groups are likely to have a considerable degree of political influence. This suggests that the relative impact of the program may be greater in regions with concentrated populations of venture capitalists and high-technology firms.[2]

Variations of Subsidy Impact with Industry Characteristics   Industries vary tremendously in their degree of transparency to outside investors. In some cases the financial statements traditionally analyzed by bankers and accountants provide much valuable information. In other instances the firms' primary assets are intangible intellectual property, which does not show up on balance sheets and may yield returns only after many years. These differences can again be exploited in the empirical analysis:

---

2. A natural question is why any awards are made in regions with few high-technology firms. While this issue has not been discussed at great length in the public finance literature, a substantial body of work on political institutions documents that even in programs that disproportionately benefit particular regions (e.g., Air Force procurement contracts), some federal funds are spread across a wide number of states to insure congressional support. See Carsey, Rundquist, and Fox (1997) for a review of this literature.

• The certification hypothesis suggests that if public awards convey information to investors, these signals are likely to be particularly valuable in technology-intensive industries where traditional financial measures are of little use. Specialists at the National Institute of Health or Department of Defense may have considerable insight into which biotechnology or advanced materials companies are the most promising, while the traditional financial statement analysis undertaken by bankers would be of little value. In these cases, the signal that a government award provides might be particularly significant.

• The hypothesis that federal officials are selecting firms likely to perform in a superior fashion suggests a different pattern. Even though the insights of federal officials may give them an advantage relative to private investors (and thus make an award a valuable signal), they may not find the selection of successful firms in high-technology industries to be easy. Federal officials should be equally able—or even more likely—to choose successful firms in low-technology industries. This hypothesis suggests that when comparing SBIR awardees to a sample of matching firms, the superior performance of awardees should not be confined to high-technology industries.

Predicting firm success in high-technology industries is very difficult. For instance, Audretsch (1995, table 4.11) analyzes the growth of 7000 start-ups over a ten-year period. Both firm and industry characteristics have considerable explanatory power in his regressions analyzing the success of firms in low- and medium-technology industries. In a regression analysis of high-technology firms, however, the coefficients are individually and jointly statistically insignificant. Thus, if the crucial criterion for selecting awardees is the ultimate success of the firm, it is not clear that federal officials will be particularly successful in high-technology industries. The relative success of low-technology awardees, where identifying firms that will ultimately be successful is substantially easier, may be even greater.

Variations of Subsidy Impact with the Amount of Subsidies Received
If the main role of public subsidies is to address the externality posed by small firms' inability to capture the bulk of the surplus generated by their innovations, there should be a positive relationship between the amount of subsidy received and the impact on the firm. As long as firms undertaking R&D capture at least some of the benefits from their research, they should grow more quickly as subsidies increase. The certification hypothesis suggests that there may not be a positive relationship between the amount of

subsidies and firm growth. In particular, the marginal value of the signal that the tenth subsidy provides should be considerably lower than that of the first. Meanwhile the pursuit of these awards may become increasingly costly to the firm as the size (or number) of subsidies increase and management attention is diverted from commercialization.

The Structure and Implementation of the SBIR Program

The Small Business Innovation Development Act, enacted by Congress in July 1982, established the SBIR program. The program mandated that all federal agencies spending more than $100 million annually on external research set aside 1.25 percent of these funds for awards to small businesses. When the program was reauthorized in 1992, Congress increased the size of the set-aside to 2.5 percent. In 1997, this represented annual funding of about $1.1 billion.

While the eleven federal agencies participating in the program are responsible for selecting awardees, they must conform to the guidelines stipulated by the act and the U.S. Small Business Administration (SBA). Awardees must be independently owned, for-profit firms with less than 500 employees, at least 51 percent owned by U.S. citizens or permanent residents. Promising proposals are awarded phase I awards (originally no more than $50,000, today $100,000 or smaller), which are intended to allow firms to determine the feasibility of their ideas. (Typically about ten phase I applications are received for every award made.) Approximately one-half of the phase I awardees are then selected for the more substantial phase II grants. Phase II awards of at most $750,000 (originally, one-half million dollars) are transferred to the small firm as a contract or grant. The government receives no equity in the firm and does not own the intellectual property that the firm develops with these funds. Table 13.2 displays the annual expenditures on the SBIR program, the number of phase II awards, and the percentage set aside.

Conversations with federal program managers, as well as assessments by the GAO (1985, 1987b, 1995), suggest that the program is to a certain extent insulated from the political pressures to make awards to particular firms encountered in other programs. In particular, three factors limit the pressures to select politically connected firms:

1. The awards are reasonably small in size, not exceeding $750,000. Consequently an award is less likely to be the subject of an intense lobbying activity than that of a program making larger disbursements.

Table 13.2
Volume of SBIR awards

| | SBIR awards | | |
Year	$ Amount	Number of phase II awards	Size of external R&D set aside
1983	0.07	0	0.2%
1984	0.15	388	0.6%
1985	0.27	407	1.0%
1986	0.40	564	1.25%
1987	0.45	768	1.25%
1988	0.49	711	1.25%
1989	0.52	749	1.25%
1990	0.53	837	1.25%
1991	0.53	788	1.25%
1992	0.55	916	1.25%
1993	0.71	950	1.5%
1994	0.71	961	1.5%
1995	0.86	1,263	2.0%
1996	0.89	1,191	2.0%
1997	1.08		2.5%

Source: U.S. Small Business Administration (1996) and personal communications with SBA officials.
Note: The table indicates the amount of SBIR awards (in billions of 1995 dollars), the number of phase II awards, and the share of external R&D spending that all agencies spending more than $100 million on external R&D were required to set aside for the program. The subsidy was phased in over a number of years. The Department of Defense was allowed an extra year to reach the 1.25% target, and consequently had lower set-aside levels between 1983 and 1986. 1997 award total is estimated.

2. The awards are not made by a single body in each agency, but rather allocated according to each subunit's external R&D spending. Within the Department of Defense, for instance, hundreds of mid-level officials (whose primary responsibility is overseeing other research and development efforts) decide on SBIR awards. Thus it is harder to influence the selection process than in programs where a single committee is responsible for making all the awards.

3. The scoring systems used to rank applicants largely focus on the technological merit of the proposals, rather than more subjective assessments of commercial potential. This may leave evaluators with less discretion to choose well-connected applicants.

Despite the presence of these protections, it is not clear that the program always makes awards in a manner that addresses the externalities induced by spillover problems or certifies firms to outside investors. Firms that have participated in the SBIR program, former program managers, and other observers suggest several deviations:

1. The program managers have faced pressure from congressional officials to make geographically diverse awards. The share of funds going to firms in California and Massachusetts—which has consistently been about 40 percent—has attracted scrutiny from congressmen unhappy about the awards' geographic concentration. One indication of the political sensitivity of the allocation of SBIR awards may be the fact that in almost every recent fiscal year, all fifty states have received at least one SBIR award (SBA 1996). In private conversations, several former program managers indicated that interest from congress members representing districts with few awards went beyond questions about the overall distribution of awards to include in some cases inquiries about the status of particular SBIR applications.

2. Particular companies have demonstrated an ability to capture a disproportionate number of awards. Evaluations of the SBIR program (e.g., GAO 1992) suggest that these "SBIR mills"—many of which have staffs in Washington that focus on identifying opportunities for applications—appear to commercialize projects at a significantly lower rate than other firms.

3. Many program officers focus on making awards to firms that are most likely to meet agency needs, with little regard to the impact of awards on the pace of technological innovation or even to the long-run sustainability of the awardees as businesses.

4. The contravening pressure exists to back firms that are likely to be successful. As Wallsten (2000) discusses, the Small Business Administration and program officers at many agencies compile stories of successful awardees, which are frequently presented in speeches and reports. This may lead to pressures to select firms that would succeed even without the award.

Challenges of the Evaluation

While both government agencies and academic economists have sought to assess the efficacy of federal programs to aid technology-intensive industries, they have tended to focus on different questions. Most federal evaluations of these programs have consisted of case studies and surveys of the commercial activity directly attributable to the awards. Examples of such evaluations include Myers, Stern, and Rorke (1983), Price Waterhouse (1985), GAO (1987a, 1989, 1992, 1995), and Wessner (1999).

Such surveys of direct commercial impacts, however, are subject to several biases. In the case of the SBIR program, small business advocates conducted a protracted lobbying campaign to expand the program. Executives active in this effort could have overstated the benefits from the awards. At the same time some firms could have downplayed the commercial benefits of the program, lest they attract unwelcome attention from reporters and politicians seeking to expose "corporate welfare." Finally, because many firms pursued SBIR projects closely related to their core technologies, the direct impact of an SBIR award could not be easily determined.

Studies of federal technology programs by academic economists, beginning with Levy and Terleckyj (1983), have tended to focus on the short-run effects of these efforts. In particular, they often ask whether federal funds substitute for or stimulate private R&D spending. For instance, Irwin and Klenow (1996) show that semiconductor manufacturers substantially reduced their own R&D spending while participating in the Sematech consortium. In the study most closely related to this one, Wallsten (2000) shows that the subset of SBIR awardees that were publicly traded reduced their own spending on R&D in the years immediately following the award.

However valuable a framework when examining the macroeconomic impact of public expenditures, it is less clear that this analytic approach is appropriate when assessing public programs for small high-technology firms. In many cases small high-technology firms are organized around one key scientist or engineer and his research laboratory or product development team. It may not be possible to accelerate the project's progress by "scaling up" the project through the addition of more researchers or technicians. In this case it is rational for the firm to not increase its rate of spending, but rather to use the funds to prolong the time until it needs to seek additional capital. To interpret a short-run reduction in internal research spending by awardees as an indication of program ineffectiveness is problematic. So the long-run impact of the awards is the crucial question.

Based on the discussion above, the need for an assessment of the long-term performance of the SBIR awardees is clear. However, the problem still is identifying the appropriate metric. Ideally both the social and private impacts of the program should be measured. While a small number of participants in the SBIR program (e.g., along the lines of Mansfield et al. 1977) can be studied for information on social benefits, no such effort is possible for a large sample.[3]

---

3. These analyses were complemented, however, with eleven interviews of Massachusetts firms that had received at least one phase II award from the Department of Defense, as well as numerous informal conversations with SBIR program managers.

It is even difficult to determine an appropriate measure of private benefits. Ideally the relationship between program participation and firms' valuations should be examined, but only 2 percent of the SBIR awardees in the first three program cycles were publicly held at the time of their initial phase I awards. For these reasons our analysis focuses instead on two alternative measures: sales and employment growth. The valuations assigned to private firms by venture capitalists can be shown to be highly correlated with these two measures (see chapter 9). The supplemental analysis discussed in the following section under the subsection "Variation in Subsidy Impact across Regions" shows that the changes in valuations for the subset of publicly traded firms are consistent with the employment and sales results.

Empirical Analysis

The Construction of the Data Set

The database we use was prepared by the GAO. The GAO was mandated in the legislation establishing the SBIR program to periodically evaluate the initiative. In late 1985 the agency generated a sample of 933 firms that received SBIR awards in the first three program cycles from the twelve federal agencies participating in the program at the time. This sample includes all firms that had received phase II awards to that date, as well as a sampling of the firms that had only received the preliminary phase I awards. GAO surveyed these firms in early 1986 and mid-1988. Of these firms, 835 responded to at least one survey. Of these, 541 received phase II awards in the first three program cycles, while 294 only received phase I awards.

In addition to the 294 firms that only received phase I awards, two matching samples of 300 firms each that did not receive SBIR awards in the first three program cycles are constructed. In each case the firms selected closely resemble the phase II awardees using Corporate Technology Information Services' *Corporate Technology Directory* (1996), the most comprehensive directory of U.S. high-technology firms. This directory employs a highly detailed industry and geographic classification scheme, which allows quite precise matches.

One set is matched on industry and firm size. The primary industry classification of each phase II awardee was recorded in the 1986 edition of the *Corporate Technology Directory*, or in the first subsequent volume in which the firm was listed. (In all, 74 percent of the phase II awardees are listed.) The set includes a random selection of 300 of these awardees. Each selected firm is matched with a firm listed in the 1986 *Corporate Technology Directory* in the same classification with the closest sales level.[4] The sample excludes as possible matches firms that were units or subsidiaries of other concerns or firms that had received any SBIR awards in the first three program cycles (determined through SBA 1986).

The second set is matched on geographic location and firm size. Following the same procedure as above, a random sample of 300 firms (pulled from the 541 phase II awardees) is matched to firms listed in the 1986 *Corporate Technology Directory* in the same city and state with the closest sales level to each firm. If there are no matches within the same city, a firm from the next city with the same three-digit zip code (in the same state) listed in the volume is selected. The Venture Economics and VentureOne databases are used to determine whether the awardees or matching firms had received venture financing (the databases are described in chapter 22).

The samples are summarized in tables 13.3 and 13.4. The firms are similar in most respects. The matching firms had slightly greater sales in 1985; the awardees, greater employment. The awardees are slightly more likely to be located in California or Massachusetts (35 percent vs. 30 percent).

A final step in constructing the sample is determining the employment and sales of the SBIR phase II awardees and the matching firms at the end of 1995.[5] SEC filings are used for publicly traded firms; a variety of printed and electronic databases are used for private firms.[6] For firms where employment and sales cannot be ascertained, the news stories compiled in various electronic databases are checked. Many of the firms, for which 1995 sales and employment data cannot be obtained from the published and online directories, went out of business. In cases where firms were liquidated prior to the end of 1995, the firm's 1995 employment and sales is recorded as zero.

Acquired firms pose another challenge. In many cases their operations were folded into those of the acquirer, precluding a determination of the

---

4. While the Standard Industrial Classification (SIC) scheme places all software firms in class 7372, this directory distinguishes between firms that manufacture educational software used for teaching typing and for music instruction. If there are no matches within the class, a firm in a related industry is chosen: for instance, if there is no appropriate match for a firm classified as a plastic composite laminate manufacturer, the firm is matched to another composite laminate manufacturer.

5. In a few cases firms did not disclose 1985 sales. Furthermore SBIR awardees were only requested to report ranges for 1985 sales. Consequently, in all cases where firms did not report sales, or where reported sales were in one of the ranges above $1 million, 1985 sales are determined using the 1986 editions of the same sources used to determine 1995 sales.

6. Where possible, the *Corporate Technology Directory* is used, one of the few business directories with a rigorous procedure to identify (and correct) problematic responses. The analyses below are repeated, eliminating observations that relied on other commercial data sources. These omissions had little impact on the magnitude of the results.

Table 13.3
Construction of sample of SBIR phase II awardees and matching firms

	Number of firms
General Accounting Office survey	
Sample size	933
Respondents to 1986 General Accounting Office Survey	750
Respondents to 1988 General Accounting Office Survey	729
Respondents to either General Accounting Office Survey	835
Of respondents to either General Accounting Office Survey	
Received one or more phase II awards in first three program cycles	541
Did not receive phase II award in first three program cycles	294
Matching firms selected through 1986 Corporate Technology Directory	
Industry and sales matched	300
Location and sales matched	300
Final sample	
Phase II awardees from survey	541
Matching firms from survey and *Corporate Technology Directory*	894

Note: 835 of a total of 933 firms responded to either the 1986 or the 1988 General Accounting Office Survey. Of those firms which responded to the survey, 541 had received one or more phase II awards in the first three program cycles. To construct the sample of matching firms, 600 firms were chosen which matched both sales and either industry or location of the awardees, and added to the 294 firms from the survey which had not received awards, bringing the total number of matching firms to 894.

original firm's level of activity in 1995. Consequently the analysis does not include the employment and sales of firms that were acquired, unless the companies continued to operate as separate subsidiaries through the end of 1995. Another exception is where the purchase of the firm was an asset sale as part of a bankruptcy; then case employment and sales are recorded as zero. In cases where there is only a range available for sales, the midpoint of this range is used.

Overall Impact of Subsidies

First, the SBIR phase II awardees are compared with the three groups of matching firms. Panel A of table 13.5 shows that the mean sales increase from the end of 1985 to the end of 1995 was greater for the awardees ($4.0 million vs. $1.1 million, both in constant 1995 dollars). Panel B displays a similar employment increase (a boost of 26 vs. 6 employees). For the mean SBIR awardee, this represents a 98 percent boost in sales (in inflation-adjusted dollars) and a 56 percent increase in employment. Note that in both cases the differences in means are statistically significant.

Table 13.4

Comparison of SBIR phase II awardees and matching firms

	Mean	Standard deviation	Minimum	Maximum
Panel A: SBIR phase II awardees				
Year founded	1977.5	6.9	1935	1985
1985 sales	4.1	8.4	0.1	87.9
1985 employment	46.6	85.8	0	600
Number of phase II awards in first 3 cycles	2.8	3.5	1	30
Located in California?	0.21		0	1
Located in Massachusetts?	0.14		0	1
Number of early-stage venture financings, 1983–1985				
State	230.0	293.3	0	770
Zip code	3.2	8.1	0	46
Panel B: Matching firms				
Year founded	1976.6	9.6	1899	1985
1985 sales	4.2	8.9	0.1	86.9
1985 employment	33.2	68.9	0	650
Number of phase II awards in first 3 cycles	0	0	0	0
Located in California?	0.20		0	1
Located in Massachusetts?	0.10		0	1
Number of early-stage venture financings, 1983–1985				
State	216.2	286.4	0	770
Zip code	2.2	6.6	0	46

Note: Panel A provides summary statistics on the 541 firms that received SBIR phase II awards in the first three program cycles; panel B, the 894 matching firms in the sample. All sales figures are in millions of 1995 dollars.

Both distributions are highly skewed: among the SBIR phase II awardees, for instance, only about one-fifth of the observations are above the mean level of employment growth. This skewness is consistent with evidence on the financial and operating performance of other small firms, such as portfolio companies of venture capitalists or those completing initial public offerings. At each reported percentile, the changes in employment and sales are more positive for the awardees. The differences between the awardees and the matching firms are relatively modest, however, until the top one-third of the distribution. The null hypothesis of the equality of medians was tested—and rejected—thus demonstrating that a few outliers did not cause the differences.

Unreported analyses compare the sales and employment growth *between* the three subsets of matching firms. These patterns do not appear to be a

Table 13.5
Growth of SBIR phase II awardees and matching firms

	SBIR phase II awardees	Matching firms	p-Value from comparison
Panel A: Change in sales, 1985–1995			
Mean	4.03	1.14	
90th percentile	8.29	3.68	
75th percentile	1.40	0.33	
Median	−0.07	−0.40	
25th percentile	−0.64	−1.00	
10th percentile	−4.01	−7.19	
Standard error	1.29	0.81	
p-Value, comparison of means			0.046
p-Value, comparison of medians			0.000
Observations	493	836	
Panel B: Change in employment, 1985–1995			
Mean	26.20	5.78	
90th percentile	66	29	
75th percentile	10	2	
Median	−1	−3	
25th percentile	−8	−10	
10th percentile	−45	−50	
Standard error	10.32	4.47	
p-Value, comparison of means			0.038
p-Value, comparison of medians			0.000
Observations	499	846	

Note: The table summarizes the change in the sales and employment of the 541 firms that received SBIR phase II awards in the first three program cycles and the 894 matching firms in the sample. All sales figures are in millions of 1995 dollars.

consequence of peculiarities in one of the groups of matching firms. The growth of sales and employment differs little between the 294 firms that received SBIR phase I awards and the 600 firms taken from the *Corporate Technology Directory*. For instance, the mean employment for the phase I awardees increased by 4.2 jobs, while for the *Directory* firms, the average increase was 6.5. (The average employment increase was 6.2 among the *Directory* firms matched by industry, and 6.8 among those matched by geography.) Joint *F*-tests of the null hypothesis that the three groups do not differ, as well as pairwise comparisons of means and medians, do not identify any significant differences. The differences between the SBIR phase II awardees presented in tables 13.5 and 13.6 remain significant, at least at the

Table 13.6
Growth of SBIR phase II awardees and matching firms, by location

	SBIR phase II awardees	Matching firms	p-Value
Panel A: Firms located in zip code with an early-stage venture financing, 1983–1985			
Change in sales, 1985–1995			
Mean	7.71	1.06	
Median	−0.06	−0.42	
Standard error	3.09	1.23	
p-Value, comparison of means			0.026
p-Value, comparison of medians			0.001
Observations	189	271	
Change in employment, 1985–1995			
Mean	47.43	3.35	
Median	−1	−4	
Standard error	22.99	7.99	
p-Value, comparison of means			0.039
p-Value, comparison of medians			0.001
Observations	190	277	
Panel B: Firms located in zip code without an early-stage venture financing, 1983–1985			
Change in sales, 1985–1995			
Mean	1.74	1.18	
Median	−0.07	−0.40	
Standard error	0.81	1.04	
p-Value, comparison of means			0.718
p-Value, comparison of medians			0.000
Observations	304	565	
Change in employment, 1985–1995			
Mean	13.14	6.96	
Median	−2	−3	
Standard error	8.80	5.39	
p-Value, comparison of means			0.527
p-Value, comparison of medians			0.057
Observations	309	569	

Note: The table summarizes the change in the sales and employment of the 541 firms that received SBIR phase II awards in the first three program cycles and the 894 matching firms in the sample. Firms are divided by whether their headquarters in 1985 was in a zip code with one or more seed or early-stage venture financings between 1983 and 1985. All sales figures are in millions of 1995 dollars.

ten percent confidence level, when the phase II awardees are only compared to the phase I awardees or to the *Directory* firms.

An alternative explanation for the superior long-run growth of the SBIR awardees is that winners cultivate relationships with politicians or federal program managers and are consequently likely to receive subsequent procurement contracts. To examine this possibility, the analysis above is restricted to the two agencies that made significant numbers of SBIR awards but are unlikely to undertake procurement contracts with awardees: the National Science Foundation (NSF) and the Department of Health and Human Services (HHS). (HHS's external research, and consequently their SBIR awards, overwhelmingly came from the basic research-oriented National Institutes of Health.) The gap between the firms that received phase II awards from these agencies and those that only received phase I awards is even greater than the dispersion in the sample as a whole. For instance, firms that received phase II awards from NSF and HHS in the first three program cycles grew by 32.6 employees between 1985 and 1995; those that only received phase I awards grew by 2.1 employees. These results suggest that the growth of the awardees is not a consequence of them subsequently obtaining procurement contracts.[7]

Variation in Subsidy Impact across Regions

Next the regional disparities in these growth patterns are examined. To measure new venture activity in the region where the firm was located, seed and early-stage financings by private venture capital funds in the years 1983 to 1985 are tabulated. The Venture Economics database (described in chapter 22) is used to determine the dollar volume and number of early-stage financings in each five-digit zip code.[8]

---

7. The awardees from HHS are compared to matching firms specializing in biotechnology and medical devices that received no SBIR awards, with similar results. An alternative explanation for the superior growth of the SBIR awardees is that winners of SBIR awards are more likely to win subsequent SBIR awards. While this may have been true in the initial years of the program (e.g., GAO 1987b), conversations with federal officials suggest that it has been much less of an issue in recent years. Not only were SBIR awards to firms that had received multiple previous grants more likely to be scrutinized by the GAO, resulting in a reluctance to make such grants, but the 1992 reauthorization of the SBIR program (Public Law 102–564) added additional criteria for the evaluation of SBIR applications of firms that have received awards in the past.

8. Five-digit zip codes are a fine gradation: the city of Cambridge, Massachusetts, for instance, is divided into six five-digit zip codes; the code 021 encompasses the city of Boston and the nearby suburbs. Additionally the analyses are also repeated using the *number* of seed and early-stage financings in the zip code. These alternative measures have little impact on the results. In an analysis later in this section, the use of broader geographic divisions is explored.

Panels A and B of table 13.6 present comparisons similar to those in table 13.5, but also divide firms by whether their headquarters at the end of 1985 was in a zip code with at least one early-stage venture financing in the years 1983 to 1985. The differences between the SBIR phase II awardees and the matching firms in the zip codes with venture capital activity are pronounced. For instance, employment increased by 47 for these awardees, as opposed to increasing by 3 for the others. For the average SBIR awardee in a zip code with venture activity—which in 1985 had $5.1 million in sales (again in 1995 dollars) and 57 employees—inflation-adjusted sales over the next decade grew by 151 percent and employment by 83 percent. The differences are much smaller in other areas (employment rose by 13 for the awardees, as opposed to by 7 for the matching firms). The differences in means are statistically significant only among the firms in regions with venture activity. Medians display a similar pattern. The difference in median sales, however, is also highly significant when awardees and nonawardees are compared in areas without venture capital activity.

Table 13.7 examines the growth of employment and sales in a regression framework. The table examines the change in employment and sales, as well as the percentage change in these variables.[9] The independent variables are: 1985 sales or employment, the volume (in millions of dollars) of early-stage venture capital activity in the firm's zip code between 1983 and 1985, a dummy variable indicating whether the firm received any phase II awards in the first three SBIR funding cycles, and an interaction between the venture capital activity and SBIR awardee variables.

Panel A examines the change in sales and the percentage change in sales (both in constant 1995 dollars) in ordinary least squares (OLS) regressions. Because the firms are of very different sizes, a heteroskedasticity problem is likely to exist. Consequently the firms are divided into groups on the basis of 1985 sales, and heteroskedasticity-consistent standard errors are calculated. (A similar procedure was used in all the OLS regressions reported in this table.) Panel B undertakes a similar analysis of the change in employment.

The regressions strongly support the suggestion that the superior performance of SBIR awardees is not uniform. The presence of a SBIR award alone has little relationship with sales and employment growth. Rather, only the interactions between the SBIR indicator and venture activity in the zip code are consistently significant. The SBIR awards are associated with firm growth in areas with considerable venture financing activity, but no

---

9. Because some of the firms had minimal employment and sales in 1985, the percentage change variable is calculated as $100 * (1995 \text{ value} - 1985 \text{ value})/(1985 \text{ value} + 1)$.

Table 13.7
Regression analyses of the change in employment and sales between 1985 and 1995

	Change	Percent change
A. OLS regressions, with change and percentage change in sales as the dependent variables[a]		
1985 sales	−0.18 [2.67]	−2.28 [2.46]
Value of early-stage financings in zip code	0.07 [2.12]	1.90 [2.56]
Any phase II SBIR awards in first three cycles?	1.88 [0.80]	25.05 [0.80]
Value of financings ∗ any phase II awards in first three cycles	0.16 [4.75]	2.41 [3.43]
Constant	1.63 [1.26]	60.34 [2.07]
Root mean square error	25.37	564.93
Adjusted R^2	0.02	0.01
Number of observations	1,329	1,329
B. OLS regressions, with change and percentage change in employment as the dependent variables[b]		
1985 employment	−0.19 [3.32]	−0.46 [5.13]
Value of early-stage financings in zip code	0.29 [0.85]	0.39 [0.31]
Any phase II SBIR awards in first three cycles?	14.70 [1.00]	−12.54 [0.41]
Value of financings ∗ any phase II awards in first three cycles	1.43 [11.84]	5.11 [5.45]
Constant	10.83 [3.80]	110.08 [4.89]
Root mean square error	173.04	930.47
Adjusted R^2	0.02	0.002
Number of observations	1,345	1,345
C. Median regressions, with change and percentage change in sales as the dependent variables[c]		
1985 sales	−0.62 [5.37]	−1.69 [5.02]
Value of early-stage financings in zip code	0.003 [4.09]	0.11 [0.43]
Any phase II SBIR awards in first three cycles?	0.39 [18.42]	18.96 [3.08]
Value of financings ∗ any phase II awards in first three cycles	0.01 [10.67]	0.27 [0.69]
Constant	−0.03 [1.89]	−17.38 [4.37]
Sum of absolute weighted deviations	7918.87	160923.20
Pseudo R^2	0.07	0.01
Number of observations	1,329	1,329
D. OLS regressions, with change and percentage change in sales as the dependent variables, using only firms located in zip codes without early-stage venture financings[d]		
1985 sales	−0.20 [3.91]	−1.75 [4.23]
Was state's venture capital financings above mean?	−1.07 [0.65]	−36.75 [0.94]
Any phase II SBIR awards in first three cycles?	−0.53 [0.37]	−8.50 [0.21]
State venture dummy ∗ any phase II awards in first three cycles	2.56 [1.98]	84.57 [6.10]
Constant	2.38 [1.26]	69.61 [1.89]
Root mean square error	21.62	571.10
Adjusted R^2	0.01	0.002
Number of observations	869	869

Table 13.7
(continued)

	Industry intangible to total asset ratio	
	Above median	Below median
E. OLS regressions for firms in industries with high and low intangible to total asset ratios, with change in sales as the dependent variable[e]		
1985 sales	−0.13 [1.64]	−0.29 [4.89]
Value of early-stage financings in zip code	0.12 [1.62]	0.02 [1.67]
Any phase II SBIR awards in first three cycles?	3.26 [0.96]	−0.07 [0.04]
Value of financings ∗ any phase II awards in first three cycles	0.44 [5.73]	−0.08 [1.01]
Constant	0.90 [0.98]	3.19 [1.61]
Root mean square error	24.97	25.67
Adjusted R^2	0.05	0.002
Number of observations	789	531
p-Value, F-test of equality of SBIR coefficients in two regressions		0.000

	Industry R&D/sales ratio	
	Above median	Below median
F. OLS regressions for firms in industries with high and low R&D to sales ratios, with change in employment as the dependent variable[e]		
1985 employment	−0.15 [1.63]	−0.19 [7.51]
Value of early-stage financings in zip code	0.10 [0.21]	0.60 [1.67]
Any phase II SBIR awards in first three cycles?	10.13 [0.60]	19.50 [1.14]
Value of financings ∗ any phase II awards in first three cycles	3.60 [6.71]	−1.19 [2.31]
Constant	16.08 [1.69]	3.98 [0.60]
Root mean square error	207.27	116.07
Adjusted R^2	0.03	0.02
Number of observations	735	600
p-Value, F-test of equality of SBIR coefficients in two regressions		0.000

	Change	Percent change
G. OLS regressions, with change and percentage change in sales as the dependent variables, and additional independent variables for multiple SBIR awardees[f]		
1985 sales	−0.19 [2.64]	−2.28 [2.28]
Value of early-stage financings in zip code	0.07 [2.13]	1.90 [2.56]
Any phase II SBIR awards in first three cycles?	0.11 [0.08]	19.83 [0.60]
Multiple phase II SBIR awards in first three cycles?	4.02 [1.66]	15.61 [0.99]
Value of financings ∗ any phase II awards in first three cycles	0.48 [2.69]	8.71 [2.22]
Value of financings ∗ multiple phase II awards in first three cycles	−0.58 [2.24]	−10.93 [1.93]
Constant	1.67 [1.27]	60.35 [2.05]
Root mean square error	25.23	562.73
Adjusted R^2	0.02	0.01
Number of observations	1,329	1,329
p-Value, F-test of insignificance of multiple awardee variables	0.018	0.144

Table 13.7
(continued)

	Change	Percent change
H. OLS regressions, with change and percentage change in employment as the dependent variables, and additional independent variables for multiple SBIR awardees[f]		
1985 employment	−0.19 [3.05]	−0.42 [5.86]
Value of early-stage financings in zip code	0.29 [0.85]	0.38 [0.30]
Any phase II SBIR awards in first three cycles?	11.72 [0.79]	0.59 [0.02]
Multiple phase II SBIR awards in first three cycles?	8.05 [0.78]	−23.99 [2.44]
Value of financings ∗ any phase II awards in first three cycles	3.96 [7.41]	13.46 [4.40]
Value of financings ∗ multiple phase II awards in first three cycles	−4.39 [4.19]	−14.25 [3.16]
Constant	10.75 [4.08]	108.89 [4.74]
Root mean square error	171.81	928.16
Adjusted R^2	0.03	0.01
Number of observations	1,345	1,345
p-Value, *F*-test of insignificance of multiple awardee variables	0.000	0.007

Note: The dependent variables in the regressions are the change and percentage change in sales (in millions of 1995 dollars) and employment between the end of 1985 and the end of 1995. The percentage change is computed as 100*((1995 value−1985 value)/(1985 value + 1)). The independent variables are sales (in millions of 1995 dollars) and employment at the end of 1985, the volume (in millions of dollars) of seed and early-stage venture capital transactions between 1983 and 1985 in the zip code in which the firm was located in 1985, a dummy variable measuring whether the firm received one or more phase II SBIR awards in the first three program cycles, and an interaction between the venture capital and SBIR variables. The sample (in all regressions except panel D) consists of 541 firms that received SBIR phase II awards in the first three program cycles and 894 matching firms. Absolute *t*-statistics (computed using heteroskedasticity-consistent standard errors in all but panel C) are in brackets.

a. Ordinary least squares (OLS) regressions with change and percentage change in sales as the dependent variables.

b. Similar OLS employment regressions.

c. Median regression specification used to analyze the change and percentage change in sales.

d. Firms based in zip codes used without a seed and early-stage venture capital transaction between 1983 and 1985. This regression uses a dummy variable denoting whether the state had above the mean level of *per capita* venture financings instead of the dollar volume of disbursements in the zip code.

e. Change in sales and employment, estimating separate OLS regressions for firms whose industries are above or below the median in intangible to total assets and R&D to sales ratios at the end of 1985. *F*-tests examine the null hypothesis that the coefficients on the SBIR variables are the same across the subsamples.

f. Dummy variable added to the basic OLS specification to denote whether the firm had received more than one SBIR award in the first three program cycles. The interaction between this and the venture capital activity in the firm's zip code is between 1983 and 1985. *F*-tests examine the null hypothesis that the two new variables do not differ from zero.

relationship emerged elsewhere. These patterns are consistent with suggestions that politically connected firms with few growth prospects can capture
awards in regions without large numbers of high-technology firms or venture capital organizations.

While the coefficient of the interaction variable is consistently significant,
the overall goodness-of-fit in the regressions is disappointing. The poor fit
reflects the fact that much of the success and failure of small firms is driven
by idiosyncratic, firm-specific factors, difficult to control for in a large-sample
study. This pattern raises the concern, however, that a few extreme outliers
might drive the results. A median regression specification is employed to
address this issue, which reduces the influence of outliers. As panel C of
table 13.7 reports, these modifications have some impact on the results: the
magnitude and statistical significance of the coefficient of the SBIR awardee
dummy variable increases, while the interaction term becomes less important. This pattern is consistent with the median analysis of sales reported in
table 13.6, which suggests a significant difference between awardees and
nonawardees across all regions.

If the geographic disparities are a consequence of political pressures, then
we might expect to also see differences among the firms located in zip codes
without venture capital. Political pressures to allocate SBIR funds to firms
located in states with high levels of venture capital activity (even if concentrated elsewhere) should be considerably less than in states with very
little venture activity at all. Put another way, state and congressional officials are much more likely to conduct a concerted lobbying campaign for
awards to firms in Idaho than in northeastern California.

Regression analyses confined to the SBIR awardees and matching firms
that were located in zip codes without a seed or early-stage venture capital
financing round between 1983 and 1985 address this suggestion. The awardees and matching firms located in those states with above and below
the mean level of *per capita* venture capital disbursements during this three-
year period are compared. Panel D of table 13.7 presents two regression
analyses, which employ the change in sales as a dependent variable, as well
as the percentage change. The independent variables are 1985 sales of the
firm, a dummy variable indicating whether the firm received any phase II
awards in the first three SBIR funding cycles, a dummy variable denoting
whether the state received above the mean amount of *per capita* venture
capital disbursements in the years 1983 through 1985, and an interaction
between the dummy variables denoting SBIR awardees and above-average
venture capital activity in the state.

The political pressure hypothesis suggests that the disparity between awardees and matching firms should be greater in the states with high levels of venture capital activity. In states with low levels of venture activity, the distortions in the award process may lead to the selection of firms that could not benefit from the funds. Consistent with this suggestion, the interaction between the SBIR awardee dummy and that denoting above-average venture capital activity is significantly positive. Consider, for instance, the coefficient of 2.56 on the interaction term in the leftmost regression. This implies that the difference in the sales growth of the SBIR awardees and the matching firms (in zip codes without venture capital activity) is $2.6 million greater in states with above the mean level of venture activity.

Several additional unreported analyses examine the robustness of the geographic regressions. First, there is concern that the results could be an artifact of the two measures of firm success used, employment and sales. Consequently the changes in valuations are examined under a quite stark assumption: that the valuation of privately held or acquired firms is nominal when compared to the publicly traded firms. If this supposition holds, changes in public market valuations could provide a reasonable indication of the overall change in these firms' valuations. The value of those SBIR awardees and matching firms that were publicly traded in 1985 and 1995 are summed (determining these valuations through the databases of the Center for Research in Securities Prices and the several *Moody's* stock guides). Then the difference between the total valuation at the beginning and end of this period is examined. The difference in the growth of the SBIR awardees and the matching firms is dramatic. The increase in the public market valuation of the 541 SBIR phase II awardees between 1985 and 1995 was $9.5 billion. The valuation of the 894 matching firms, on the other hand, only increased by a total of $3.0 billion during this period. Consistent with the results involving employment and sales, the increase in the valuation was the greatest for the awardees that were located in a zip code with an early-stage venture financing in the years 1983 to 1985. The 209 awardees located in such zip codes increased in value by $8.7 billion; the 332 awardees located in other zip codes increased in value by under $800 million.

The matching approach is another issue of concern. As discussed above, the analysis includes two constructed populations of matching firms. An alternative approach would be to undertake a single matched set, based on both region and industry: that is, rather than matching a Cambridge genome sequencing company to either another Cambridge firm or another genome firm, a matching firm in the same industry and region* could be selected. The analysis does not employ this procedure due to fears that it would introduce systematic biases. In particular, an attempt to do such a matching on two criteria showed dramatic variations in the quality of the matches. While quite precise matches can be obtained in California and Massachusetts, in some other regions the matching firms have very different characteristics (e.g., they tend to be much larger than the awardees). This is a consequence of the fact that there are few potential matches in many states. For example, in Hawaii, Idaho, and Kentucky there are only a handful of entries in the 1986 *Corporate Technology Directory*. Such a procedure would bias the results in ways that would be very difficult to address in the subsequent analyses. In order to address concerns that one of the sub-populations of matching firms included in the analysis might still be biased in some not readily apparent manner, various tests are performed. The equations are re-estimated using only the phase II SBIR awardees and the *Corporate Technology Directory* matching firms, as well as only the phase II and phase I SBIR awardees. Similarly only the *Corporate Technology Directory* firms matched on industry and those matched on location are used. The smaller sample sizes lead to lower significance levels, but have little effect on the magnitudes or signs of the coefficients. Additionally, controls are added for the age of the firm, whether it was venture-backed by the end of 1985, and for the two-digit Standard Industrial Classification (SIC) code of the firm, in case the results are shaped by some unobserved differences between the SBIR awardees and the matching firms. These have little impact on the coefficients or significance levels.

Third, the use of alternative econometric specifications is explored. Because the dependent variable in the regressions analyzing the percentage change in sales and employment is bound at −100 percent (corresponding to the liquidation of a firm), these analyses are repeated employing a Tobit specification. This has little impact. The magnitude and significance of the coefficients changes little when systems of two equations are estimated, with the second equation examining the propensity of firms to win phase II awards in the first three program cycles. A two-stage Heckman regression is estimated also, looking first at whether the firm survived and then at the extent of its growth. The interaction terms remain strongly significant. An alternative way to control for outliers is to divide the dependent variable in each regression into ten deciles, namely by creating ten equal-sized groupings based on the change in sales and employment. The results with this ordered logit specification very closely resemble those in the median regressions reported above.

Industry Patterns

The next analysis examines whether these patterns are especially pronounced in certain industries. As discussed above, the contrasting explanations for the growth of the SBIR awardees—the suggestions that SBIR awards certify firms to investors and that federal officials attempt to select successful firms for SBIR awards, whether the funds are needed or not—implies different empirical patterns. To address these concerns, the firms are divided into those in higher and lower technology industries, and the regressions in panels A and B of table 13.7 are re-estimated.

To divide the firms, the characteristics of the firm's industry are examined. Because the financial condition of the private firms cannot be observed, the characteristics of the average public firm in the same industry are used. The ratios of intangible assets to total assets, R&D spending to sales, and market to book equity values are computed for all firms with a primary assignment in Compustat to the same four-digit SIC class as a company in the sample during the fiscal year ending in 1985 or at the end of the fiscal year ending in 1985. If there are fewer than four firms assigned to a four-digit SIC code, all firms with a primary assignment to the same three-digit SIC code are used. Then the average of these ratios is computed.

Panels E and F of table 13.7 present the results of the two analyses.[10] Separate regressions for the observations from industries above and below the median on these proxies are reported. Table 13.7 also presents the *p*-values from *F*-tests of the null hypothesis that the two coefficients measuring the impact of SBIR awards (the dummy variable and the interaction term) are identical in the two regression analyses. In the regression employing the change in sales as the dependent variable (panel E), the SBIR dummy variable is positive and the interaction term is positive and significant for the firms in industries with more intangible assets. Among the other firms the two variables are negative and insignificant. The null hypothesis of no difference is rejected. In panel F, where the change in employment is used as the dependent variable and firms are divided by industry R&D to sales ratios, a similar pattern holds for firms with R&D spending above the median. The null hypothesis of no difference is once again rejected. This pattern is consistent with the view that SBIR awards provide certification to firms.

---

10. The results dividing firms on the basis of the third measure (the ratio of market-to-book equity values) are similar. The analyses are also robust to checks we describe earlier in the final paragraphs of "Variation in Subsidy Impact across Regions."

Number of Awards

The fourth empirical analysis examines how the impact of the awards changes with the number of awards. The distribution of awards in the first three program cycles is quite skewed. While the median SBIR phase II awardee firm received one phase II award in the first three program cycles, four firms received a total of 90 awards. (The mean firm received 2.8 awards in this period.) Two independent variables that control for firms that received multiple SBIR awards are added. As discussed above, if the main role of public subsidies is to address the externality created by small firms' inability to capture the bulk of the rents from their innovations, more awards should translate into faster growth. As long as the firms capture some of the surplus generated by the research, they should continue to benefit from additional subsidies. The certification hypothesis suggests a more ambiguous relationship, with the marginal value of subsequent awards declining sharply. Furthermore the pursuit of these awards might introduce increasing distortions as the size (or number) of subsidies increases.

Panels G and H of table 13.7 present four regressions. The regressions are identical to those in panels A and B, with the addition of a dummy variable denoting firms that received more than one phase II award in the first three program cycles and an interaction between this new dummy and the measure of venture activity in the firm's zip code. These panels also present the p-values from F-tests of the null hypothesis that these two new variables are jointly equal to zero. The dummy denoting frequent awardees is never significantly positive, and in one regression is negative in sign. The interaction term between the multiple awardee dummy and the amount of venture activity in the zip code is significantly negative in all regressions. The joint test of the two variables rejects the null hypothesis of no difference from zero in three out of the four regressions.[11] The pronounced superior performance of the SBIR awardees in regions with venture activity is confined to firms receiving modest subsidies. Additional awards appear to have minimal positive benefits, and the pursuit of these awards may even have detrimental effects on the firms.

---

11. The results are robust to using other cutoff points to denote multiple SBIR awardees, such as firms that received more than five phase II awards. Unreported analyses also examine the robustness of the results to the controls as we described earlier in "Variation in Subsidy Impact across Regions."

SBIR Awards and Venture Capital Financing

An important group to whom SBIR awards may provide information is the venture capital community. As discussed above, venture capitalists fund only a handful of the high-technology businesses begun each year. While the number of companies funded in this manner is small, the amount of capital provided is significant. Furthermore these firms account for a disproportionately large share of the companies going public each year (see chapter 19) and of successful patent applications (see previous chapter). The importance of venture capitalists suggests an alternative test of the certification hypothesis. Here the relationship between the receipt of SBIR awards and venture capital financing is examined instead of the overall growth of the SBIR awardees and the matching firms.

The interpretation of the results may be quite different, depending on the relative timing of the awards and the venture financing. If the SBIR awards play a certification function, then we might expect to see awardees disproportionately receiving venture capital financing in the years after the awards. The awards themselves might serve as a signal to venture capitalists, or alternatively might allow the firm to attract high-quality managers or individual investors who in turn attract venture investors. It would be harder to argue that the awards play a certification role if awardees were no more likely to receive venture financing than matching firms. The reverse relationship would also be problematic, if venture capital financing *predicted* the receipt of an SBIR award. This might suggest—in the spirit of the models of political capture delineated earlier in this chapter—that venture capitalists use the SBIR program as a subsidy for firms already in their portfolios. Rather than refinancing firms, they may push them to obtain public funds.

Table 13.8 examines these issues in univariate and regression analyses. Panel A presents the probability that the awardees and the matching firms received venture financing in the years before and after the first three program cycles. First, the probability that the firms received venture financing through the end of 1981, the year immediately previous to the first SBIR awards is presented. While the probability that SBIR awardees received venture financing is greater, the difference is not statistically significant. The probability that the firms received venture financing for the first time after 1987 is presented, when the results of the first three award cycles were largely known. (Awardees were typically notified of whether they received a phase II award within a year of completing their phase I project.) This calculation excludes firms that had already attracted venture financing or were

Table 13.8
Univariate and regression analyses of SBIR awards and venture financings

	SBIR phase II awardees	Matching firms	*p*-Value
Panel A: Univariate analysis of probability of venture capital financing for first time[a]			
Funding prior to 1981	2.2%	1.3%	0.210
Funding after 1987	2.5%	0.9%	0.020
Dependent variable	Did firm receive SBIR award in first 3 cycles?	Did firm receive venture funding after 1987?	
Panel B: Logit regression analyses[b]			
Value of early-stage financings in zip code	0.01 [2.04]	−0.02 [0.77]	
Was firm based in California?	−0.001 [0.00]	0.11 [0.16]	
Was firm based in Massachusetts?	0.25 [1.27]	0.62 [0.88]	
Did firm receive venture capital prior to 1981?	0.34 [0.73]		
Any phase II SBIR awards in first three cycles?		1.39 [2.60]	
1985 employment		0.002 [0.54]	
χ^2-Statistic	173.33	24.01	
p-Value	0.000	0.020	
Log-likelihood	−431.46	−81.35	
Number of observations	1,435	1,193	

Note: Panel A summarizes the probability that the SBIR awardees and the matching firms received venture capital financing. The panel presents the probability that the firms received venture financing for the first time before the end of 1981 and after 1987. (Firms that received venture capital financing or went public in 1987 or before are excluded from the second analysis.) Panel B presents two logit regression analyses. The dependent variable in the first regression is a dummy coded as 1.0 if the firm received an SBIR phase II award in the first three program cycles. The dependent variable in the second regression is a dummy coded as 1.0 if the firm received venture financing for the first time after 1987. The independent variables are the volume (in millions of dollars) of seed and early-stage venture capital transactions between 1983 and 1985 in the zip code in which the firm was located in 1985, dummy variables denoting companies based in California and Massachusetts in 1985, dummy variables denoting the firm's two-digit Standard Industrial Classification code (not reported), a dummy variable denoting whether the firm received venture financing prior to the end of 1981 (in the first regression only), a dummy variable measuring whether the firm received one or more SBIR phase II awards in the first three program cycles (in the second regression only), and the firm's employment at the end of 1985 (in the second regression only). The sample consists of 541 firms that received SBIR phase II awards in the first three program cycles and 894 matching firms. (Firms that received venture capital financing or went public in 1987 or before are excluded from the second regression.) The first regression employs a fixed-effect logit specification; the second, a standard logit specification. [Absolute *t*-statistics are in brackets.]

publicly traded by the end of 1987. The difference between the awardees and the matching firms is larger in magnitude and statistically significant. These patterns are robust to the selection of other break points (e.g., 1980, 1982, and 1986). Thus the univariate comparisons suggest that the awards might certify firms to venture capitalists.

One concern with these univariate results is that they may reflect unobserved differences between the firms. In order to address these concerns, these patterns are examined in logit regression analyses. First, each of the 1,435 firms is observed to determine whether the presence of a venture capital investor can explain the probability of a firm receiving an SBIR award. The dependent variable is a dummy that takes on the value of one if the firm receives an SBIR phase II award in the first three program cycles. Independent variables are a dummy denoting whether the firm received venture financing through the end of 1981 and controls for whether the firm was located in Massachusetts or California, the extent of venture capital activity in the zip code, and the two-digit SIC code. Because the data set was constructed by matching the universe of SBIR awardees to a sample of nonawardees, a simple logit analysis may lead to inconsistent and biased estimates (Palepu 1986). To address this problem, a fixed-effects logit regression is estimated (Chamberlain 1980). As the leftmost regression in panel B reports, once the firm and industry characteristics are controlled for, the presence of an earlier venture capital round does not predict whether the company receives an SBIR award. The results are robust to modifications in the set of regressors.

Then, the probability that the firm received venture capital financing for the first time in the years after the three SBIR award cycles is examined (i.e., after 1987). The analysis excludes any firms that received venture financing or went public in earlier years.[12] Once again the analysis controls for the characteristics of the firm (including now the employment level at the end of 1985). Additionally a dummy variable is added denoting whether the firm received any phase II SBIR awards in the first three program cycles. In the reported regression—as well as in others using modifications of the dependent and independent variables—the SBIR awardee variable is significantly positive. SBIR awardees were more likely to receive venture financing. At the mean of the other independent variables, the predicted probability of a nonawardee obtaining venture financing is 0.8 percent, while that of an SBIR awardee is 3.1 percent.

---

12. The sample also shrunk because of missing employment data and because some independent variables completely determined the outcome.

Conclusions

In this chapter we examined the long-run performance of high-technology firms receiving funds from a major public venture capital initiative, the SBIR program. We compared the growth of awardees to a set of matching firms. During the period examined, the SBIR awardees enjoyed substantially greater employment and sales growth. While the awardees and matching firms did not differ significantly in the likelihood of receiving venture capital in the years prior to the awards, in subsequent years the awardees were significantly more likely to receive such financing.

We showed that this pattern is not uniform. The superior growth of SBIR awardees is confined to firms based in zip codes with substantial venture capital activity. These patterns are more pronounced in high-technology industries. No increase of performance is associated with larger subsidies. These patterns are consistent with the awards playing an important role in certifying firm quality, but also with some distortions of the award process. These findings raise questions about the practice of awarding large numbers of SBIR awards to a few firms, as well as about congressional efforts to ensure greater geographic dispersion of awards.

Two important limitations should be acknowledged, which in turn point to future research opportunities.[13] First, our analysis did not seek to assess the social benefits of the program.[14] Numerous studies have suggested

13. Another issue is that political pressures and economic changes may have led to a deterioration of the SBIR program's effectiveness over time. For instance, as discussed above, the set-aside for SBIR awards has increased dramatically. This may have led to more efforts to influence the award process. The pool of venture capital also greatly increased during the 1980s. The expansion of the private equity market may have obviated the need for such a program, and the long-run competitive advantage that SBIR awards confer today may be much lower. No performance differential can be seen in the relative success of firms that received SBIR awards in the first and third program cycles (venture disbursements had increased sharply between 1982 and 1984). But questions about the changes in the effectiveness of the program over longer time-spans will only be answerable in the future.

14. While a rough calculation indicates that this program has had an attractive return for the federal government, these estimates must be approached with a degree of skepticism. For instance, given the typical SBIR awardee ten years later has $2.9 million in additional sales and 20 more employees than a matching firm, under plausible assumptions (30 percent corporate and individual tax rates, $50,000 annual salary per employee, and 15 percent before-tax profit margins), the federal government would receive in additional taxes in one year an amount almost equal to the (nominal) amount of a phase II award. If this level of enhanced sales and employment were sustained for a little more than two years, the government's rate of return would exceed the ten-year Treasury bond rate. Any more sustained increase in the firm's activity would make the government's return even more attractive. The returns would increase if there were significant spillovers to other firms and consumers, or decrease if much of the growth was at the expense of other firms (resulting in a smaller marginal impact on aggregate economic activity or employment).

that, because of knowledge spillovers, social rates of return to R&D are often much higher than the private returns which the firms performing the research enjoy. Our analysis focused exclusively on private returns, as roughly measured through sales and employment growth. The differentials between the private and social benefits of the SBIR awards might be particularly large because many projects involve very early-stage technologies (where spillovers to other firms may be more frequent) or those important to national defense or public health. The detailed case studies prepared by the National Science Foundation (Tibbetts 1996) suggest that awards in many cases led to substantial spillovers. At the same time the gains in employment and sales of the typical awardee could have come at the expense of small losses at many competitors. Furthermore many academic critics (e.g., Mervis 1996) argue that the SBIR set-aside has led to a reduction in funding for academic research, which may have even greater social benefits. While challenging, a detailed computation of the social costs and benefits must be a crucial element in assessing these programs.

A second important unanswered question relates to the design of public venture capital programs such as the SBIR initiative. Because our study focused on a single program that has been essentially unchanged since its inception, it was difficult to assess whether the program could be altered in significant ways. For instance, the evidence suggests that a key benefit of SBIR awards is the certification that they provide, so a program that offers much more modest subsidies can also be effective in certifying the quality—and spurring the growth—of small high-technology firms. Our crucial assumptions, however, were that such recognition would be sufficient to motivate firms to seek awards and that the integrity of the selection process could be insured. The recent wave of experimentation with public venture capital programs, both in the United States and abroad, suggests that a cross-program analysis of these and other questions can yield important insights.

III Exiting Venture Capital Investments

14   An Overview of Exiting Venture Capital Investments

In this part of the book we examine the process through which private equity investors exit their investments. Successful exits are critical to ensuring attractive returns for investors and, in turn, to raising additional capital. But private equity investors' concerns about exiting investments—and their behavior during the exiting process itself—can sometimes lead to severe problems for entrepreneurs.

While exiting is the last phase of the venture capital cycle that we discuss, it is extremely important to the health of the other parts of the cycle. The need to ultimately exit investments shapes every aspect of the venture capital cycle, from the ability to raise capital to the types of investments that are made.

Perhaps the clearest illustration of the relation between the private and public markets was seen during the 1980s and early 1990s. In the early 1980s, many European nations developed secondary markets. These sought to combine a hospitable environment for small firms (e.g., they allowed firms to be listed even if they did not have an extended record of profitability) with tight regulatory safeguards. These enabled the pioneering European private equity funds to exit their investments. A wave of fund-raising by these and other private equity organizations followed in the mid-1980s. After the 1987 market crash, initial public offering activity in Europe and the United States dried up. But while the U.S. market recovered in the early 1990s, the European market remained depressed. Consequently European private equity investors were unable to exit investments by taking them public. They were required either to continue to hold the firms or to sell them to larger corporations, often at relatively unattractive valuations. While U.S. private equity investors—pointing to their successful exits— were able to raise substantial amounts of new capital, European private equity fund-raising during this period remained depressed. The influence of exits on the rest of the private equity cycle suggests that this is a critical issue for funds and their investors. Many European nations again set up emerging stock exchanges in the late 1990s in the hopes of promoting increased venture capital activity. Given the recent collapse of the *Neuer Markt* and other new emerging market exchanges in Europe, however, the problems with the exit environment facing European private equity investors in the early-to-mid 1990s have reappeared and are likely to persist in the years to come.

The exiting of venture capital investments also has important implications for social welfare. As discussed in part I, the typical private-equity fund is liquidated after about one decade. Thus, if private-equity investors cannot foresee how a company will be mature enough to take public or to sell at the end of a decade, they are unlikely to invest in the firm. If it was equally easy to exit investments of all types at all times, this might not be a problem. But interest in certain technologies by public investors appears to be subject to wide swings. For instance, in recent decades "hot-issue markets" have appeared and disappeared for computer hardware, biotechnology, multimedia, and Internet companies. Concerns about the ability to exit investments may have led to too many private-equity transactions being undertaken in these so-called hot industries. At the same time insufficient capital may have been devoted to industries not in the public limelight. Promising technologies might not be developed if they are currently out of favor.

Concerns about exiting may also adversely affect firms once they are financed by venture capitalists. Less scrupulous investors may occasionally encourage companies in their portfolio to undertake actions that boost the probability of a successful initial public offering, even if they jeopardize the firm's long-run health: for example, increasing earnings by cutting back on vital research spending. In addition many private-equity investors appear to exploit their inside knowledge when dissolving their stakes in investments. While this may be in the best interests of the limited and general partners of the fund, it may have harmful effects on the firm and the other shareholders.

As discussed in part I, some institutions and features have evolved to improve the efficiency of the venture capital investment process, while others have sprung up primarily to shift more of the economic benefits to particular parties. Many of the features of the exiting of private-equity investments can be understood as responses to environmental uncertainties. An example is the provision for "lockup" that prohibits corporate insiders and private equity investors from selling at the time of the offering. This helps avoid situations in which the officers and directors exploit their inside knowledge that a newly listed company is overvalued by rapidly liquidating their positions.

At the same time, other features of the exiting process can be seen as attempts to transfer wealth between parties. An example may be the instances in which private-equity funds distribute shares to their investors immediately prior to a drop in price. Even if the price at which the investors ultimately sell the shares is far less, the private-equity investors use the share price before the distribution to calculate their fund's rate of return and to determine when they can begin profit sharing.

The efficiency and attractiveness of exiting venture capital investments will be determined by the relative strength of these two forces. Over time, an attractive environment for exits can exist only when formal or informal safeguards prevent opportunitistic behavior.

Related Literature

Venture-backed offerings were the focus of much of the initial empirical research into IPOs. Much of this research focused on the structure of IPOs, contrasting differences between venture-backed and nonventure IPOs.

Barry et al. (1990) focus on establishing a broad array of facts about the role of venture capitalists in IPOs, using a sample of 433 venture-backed and 1,123 nonventure IPOs between 1978 and 1987. Barry et al. document that venture capitalists hold significant equity stakes in the firms they take public (on average, the lead venture capitalist holds a 19 percent stake immediately prior to the IPO, and all venture investors hold 34 percent), and they hold about one-third of the board seats. They continue to hold their equity positions in the year after the IPO. Finally, venture-backed IPOs have less of a positive return on their first trading day. The authors suggest that this implies that investors need less of a discount to purchase these shares (i.e., the offerings are less "underpriced"), because the venture capitalist has monitored the quality of the offering. In their paper, however, they explicitly eschew undertaking formal hypothesis testing, preferring to generate a broad array of facts about venture investments.

Megginson and Weiss (1991) argue that because venture capitalists repeatedly bring firms to the public market, they can credibly stake their reputation on the quality of the issuing firm. Put another way, they can certify to investors that the firms they bring to market are not overvalued. Certification requires that venture capitalists possess reputational capital, that the acquisition of such a reputation is costly, and that the present value of lost reputational capital by cheating is greater than the one-time gain from behaving in a duplicitous manner.

The certification model yields several empirical implications. First, because venture capitalists repeatedly take firms public, they build relationships with underwriters and auditors. These relationships may lead to the average venture-backed IPO having higher quality underwriters and auditors than nonventure IPOs. Megginson and Weiss also argue that these relationships and the existence of reputation should lead to greater institutional holdings of the venture-backed firm after IPO. Megginson and Weiss claim that the retention of large stakes of equity both before and after the IPO is a "bonding mechanism" that increases the effectiveness of the venture capitalist's certification. Any benefit to issuing overpriced shares would be minimized because the venture capitalist sells few or no shares at IPO.

Megginson and Weiss test these ideas using a matched set of 320 venture-backed and 320 nonventure IPOs between 1983 and 1987. First, they examine the quality of the underwriters who bring the firms to market. They show that the underwriters of venture-backed firms are significantly more experienced than the underwriters of comparable nonventure offerings. Megginson and Weiss also find that institutional holdings of venture-backed firms after the IPO are higher than comparable nonventure companies. Third, Megginson and Weiss gather evidence on expenses associated with going public. Venture-backed IPOs have significantly lower fees than nonventure IPOs. Fourth, Megginson and Weiss demonstrate that venture capitalists retain a majority of their equity after the IPO. Megginson and Weiss argue that this is a commitment device. Finally, Megginson and Weiss present evidence that the underpricing of venture capital-backed IPOs is significantly less than the underpricing of nonventure IPOs.

Hellmann (2002) analyzes the use of various types of convertible securities in venture capital, as well as how these securities assign cash flow rights to investors in the case of exit through an IPO versus through an acquisition. He argues that a convertible preferred instrument that automatically converts to equity in the event of an IPO, but allows the investor to extract additional cash flows in the case of an acquisition, ensures that the venture capitalist will behave optimally.

Hellmann develops a model that makes a number of predictions regarding the use of convertible securities. If the external funding requirement is low, simple convertible preferred equity is ideal, while if the external funding requirement is high, participating preferred equity is optimal. The model also shows that control rights do not matter for transactions with low external financing requirements, while contingent control is optimal for those with higher external financing requirements. Finally Hellmann notes the stronger the venture capitalist's control rights, the more likely an exit will occur through acquisition, versus through an IPO.

Lee and Wahal (2002) propose a variant of the "grandstanding" hypothesis discussed in chapter 16 when analyzing first-day returns of 6,413 venture-backed and nonventure IPOs. Throughout the entire sample period of 1980 through 2000, the average first-day returns are larger for venture-backed IPOs. The difference in first-day returns of the IPOs, 37 percent of which were venture-backed, ranges from 2 percent from 1980 to 1998 to 25 percent in 1999 to 2000. The authors posit that venture capital firms have an incentive to underprice IPOs. The publicity surrounding a successful offering will enable the venture capital group to raise more capital for future funds than it otherwise would have been able to do. Lee and Wahal confirm this hypothesis by reporting a positive relationship between first-day returns and future fund-raising by venture capital firms, which persists even after controlling for the age, size, and history of the venture capital firm.

Kraus (2002) tests the certification role of venture capitalists in relation to IPO underpricing (an analysis similar in spirit to chapter 17) by examining a set of 124 venture-backed and 184 nonventure IPOs on Germany's *Neuer Markt* between March 1997 and May 2001. Kraus notes that while venture-backed IPOs appear less underpriced than nonventure IPOs when examined within the first trading month, this underpricing disappears when controlling for hot-issue markets, uncertainty, and underwriter reputation. Venture-backed companies underwritten by top banks also seem to be underpriced more than nonventure comparable companies. Kraus suggests that these results might provide evidence for different perceptions by investors on venture-backed firms, as well as the relationship between venture capitalists and underwriters.

Cumming and MacIntosh (2002) compare full and partial venture capital exits, such as IPOs, acquisitions, secondary sales, buybacks, and write-offs, across the United States and Canada. In both countries the greater the information gaps between the venture capitalist and the buyer, the more likely the venture capitalist will employ a partial exit to signal quality. The authors also note in the United States and Canada, the differences in the extent of exit across exit types, as well as the differences in risk and return of venture capital investments, can be traced to differences in the institutional, regulatory, and market contexts of these countries.

Another area of related research is the performance of venture capital funds. Kaplan and Schoar (2003) study three issues relating to the performance of private equity partnerships using a data set of fund returns compiled by Venture Economics. Their first analysis finds considerable heterogeneity in returns across funds and time periods.

The authors also note substantial persistence across consecutive LBO and VC funds. GPs who outperform the industry in one fund are likely to outperform in the next fund, while those who underperform in one fund are likely to underperform with the next fund. These results contrast with those of mutual funds, where persistence is difficult to identify and is more often found in cases of underperformance rather than overperformance.

Kaplan and Schoar's third analysis relates fund performance to capital flows, fund size, and fund survival. Capital flows are positively correlated to past performance, but in a manner that differs from that of the mutual fund industry. New partnerships are most likely to be formed after the industry has performed well, but funds raised in boom times are likely to underperform and not raise follow-on funds. The marginal dollar invested in private equity during boom times is likely to go to funds that perform poorly and fail to raise future funds, thereby depressing returns for the industry as a whole. During boom times, however, the performance of established funds is less affected. This persistence of established fund performance might be attributed to heterogeneity of skills across GPs, as well as access to superior deal flow and deal terms.

Cochrane (2001) estimates the returns of venture capital investments while correcting for selection bias. He notes that many analyses of returns focus only on investments that go public, get acquired, or go out of business. Such calculations may produce biased returns by concentrating only on the portfolio's winners and outright failures. Cochrane develops a maximum likelihood estimate that measures the probability of going public or being acquired as the value of a portfolio company increases, as well as the probability of going out of business as the value of a portfolio company decreases. Returns generated by a portfolio of investments can be estimated by calculating the explicit returns of firms that have gone public, been acquired, or gone out of business, as well as the estimated returns for firms that are still private by applying the maximum likelihood estimator.

The exiting of venture capital investments has attracted very little theoretical attention. (The few exceptions include Berglöf 1994, Black and Gilson 1998, and the Hellmann 2002 paper discussed above.) The complex institutional features and the many conflicting incentives suggest that this remains a rich environment for such analyses.

An Overview of Part III

In the six chapters that follow we examine the timing of the decision to take firms public and to liquidate the venture capitalists' holdings (which frequently occurs well after the IPO), as well as the relative performance of venture-backed and nonventure offerings. Consistent with discussion above, we suggest that venture capitalists can add significant value to the firms in which they invest, although distortions may affect the timing of decisions to exit venture capital investments.

Several potential factors affect when venture capitalists choose to bring firms public. One of these is the relative valuation level of publicly traded securities. In chapter 15 we examine when venture capitalists choose to finance a sample of biotechnology companies in another private round versus taking the firm public. Using a sample of 350 privately held venture-backed firms, our analysis shows that venture capitalists take firms public at market peaks, relying on private financings when valuations are lower. Seasoned venture capitalists appear more proficient at timing IPOs. The results are robust to the use of alternative criteria to separate firms and controls for firms' quality. The results are not caused by differences in the speed of executing the IPOs or in the willingness to withdraw the proposed IPOs.

Another consideration may be the reputation of the venture capital firm. In chapter 16 we argue that young venture capital firms have incentives to grandstand: that is, they take actions that signal their ability to potential investors. Specifically, young venture capital firms bring companies public earlier than older venture capital firms in an effort to establish a reputation and successfully raise capital for new funds. For example, the effect of recent performance in the IPO market on the amount of capital raised is stronger for young venture capital firms, providing them with a greater incentive to bring companies public earlier. Young venture capital firms have been on the IPO company's board of directors fourteen months less and hold smaller percentage equity stakes at the time of IPO than the more established venture firms. The IPO companies that they finance are nearly two years younger and more underpriced when they go public than companies backed by older venture capital firms. Much of the difference in underpricing and the venture capitalists' percentage equity stake is associated with a shorter duration of board representation, indicating that rushing companies to the IPO market imposes costs on the venture firm. The results suggest that the relation between performance and capital raising affects the incentives and actions of venture capitalists.

In chapter 17 we study a potential conflict of interest surrounding venture capital firms affiliated with investment banks by examining the underwriting of IPOs by investment banks that hold equity in a firm through a venture capital subsidiary. We contrast two hypotheses. Under rational discounting, all market participants fully anticipate the conflict. The so-called naïve investor hypothesis suggests that investment banks are able to utilize superior information when they underwrite securities. The evidence supports the rational discounting hypothesis. Initial public offerings that are underwritten by affiliated investment banks perform as well or better than issues of firms in which none of the investment banks held a prior equity position. Investors do, however, require a greater discount at the offering to compensate for potential adverse selection. We also provide evidence that investment bank-affiliated venture firms address the potential conflict by investing in and subsequently underwriting less information-sensitive issues.

The typical venture capital firm does not sell their equity at the time of the IPO. The negative signal that would be sent to the market by an insider "cashing out" would prevent a successful offering. In addition most investment banks require that all insiders, including the venture capitalists, do not sell any of their equity after the offering for a prespecified "lockup" period (usually six months). In chapter 18 we explore the role of the lockup period in the IPO process by analyzing a sample of 2,794 IPO's and testing for three possible explanations: (1) lockups serve as a signal of firm quality, (2) lockups serve as a commitment device to alleviate moral hazard problems, and (3) lockups serve as a mechanism for underwriters to extract additional compensation for the issuing firm. Our results support the commitment hypothesis: insiders of firms that are associated with greater potential informational asymmetries about firm value lock up their shares for a longer period of time. We also find that insiders of firms that have experienced larger excess returns, which are backed by venture capitalists or go public with high quality underwriters, are more likely to be released from the lockup restrictions. In addition we find that the average abnormal return at lockup expiration is −2 percent. The price drop associated with this expiration is substantially higher for firms that are venture-backed.

Once the lockup period is over, venture capitalists can return money to investors in one of two ways. They can liquidate their position in a portfolio company by selling shares on the open market after it has gone public and then paying those proceeds to investors in cash. More frequently, however, venture capitalists make distributions of shares to investors in the venture capital fund. In the late 1990s many institutional investors received a flood of these distributions and grew increasingly concerned about the incentives of the venture capitalists when they declare these transfers.

In chapter 19 we examine how investors might be affected by these distributions of equity. From the records of four institutions, we construct a representative set of over 700 transactions by 135 funds over a decade-long period. We use the features of the venture funds making the distributions, the firms whose shares are being distributed, and the changes associated with the transactions in a way that can discriminate between the various alternative explanations for these patterns.

The results are consistent with venture capitalists possessing inside information and of the (partial) adjustment of the market to that information. After significant increases in stock prices prior to distribution, abnormal returns around the distribution are negative and significant, comparable to the market reaction to publicly announced secondary stock sales. The sign and significance of the cumulative excess returns for the twelve months following the distribution appear to be negative in most specifications, but are sensitive to the benchmark used. Distributions that occur in settings where information gaps may be greatest—especially where the firm has been taken public by a lower tier underwriter and the distribution is soon after the IPO—have larger immediate price declines. Postdistribution price performance is related to factors that predict event window returns.

Whatever the short-run behavior around the time of IPO and distribution, the ultimate question is whether the transition from venture capital financing to the public marketplace is good for the company and the new investors. As one of the quotes reproduced in the introduction suggests, many popular discussions of venture capitalists and the decision to go public suggest that public investors are consistently taken advantage of during this process. These issues are examined in the final section of this chapter.

In chapter 20 we investigate the long-run performance of over 4,000 venture-backed and nonventure IPOs between 1972 and 1992. The analysis shows that venture-backed firms do not underperform the market after going public. The poor performance of IPOs relative to market benchmarks appears to be confined to the smallest nonventure offerings. In fact venture-backed offerings appear to earn positive risk-adjusted returns subsequent to going public. Far from duping the public, venture capitalists appear to bring companies public that have considerable staying power.

Final Thoughts

In part III we thus paint two depictions of the IPO process. First, we show that the decision to go public is influenced by a wide variety of factors, including the need to impress potential investors and relative valuation levels. Venture investors do not appear averse to exploiting their superior information at certain times. But then, as we step back and take a broader view, a somewhat different picture emerges. When the evolution of venture-backed firms over the half-decade after the offering is viewed, there is no evidence that the transition is one with persistent inefficiencies.

The relationship between venture capital and the public markets is a rich area that will reward further exploration. We have already highlighted the need for theoretical analyses of the role that venture capitalists play in the decision to go public. Two empirical opportunities should also be highlighted.

The first of these is the assessment of venture capital as a financial asset. Many institutions, primarily public and private pension funds, have increased their allocation to venture capital and private equity in the belief that the returns of these funds are largely uncorrelated with the public markets. It is natural to see how they come to this conclusion. Firms receiving capital from private equity funds very often remain privately held for a number of years after the initial investment. These firms have no observable market price. To present a conservative assessment of the portfolio valuation, private equity managers often refrain from marking portfolio firm values to market, preferring to maintain the investments at book value. But as discussed throughout this volume, there appear to be many linkages between the public and private equity market values. Thus the stated returns of private equity funds may not accurately reflect the true evolution of value and the correlations reported by Venture Economics (1998) and other industry observers may be deceptively low. To ignore the true correlation is fraught with potential dangers. While the Cochrane (2001) paper discussed above—as well as Gompers and Lerner (1997b) and Jones and Rhodes-Kropf (2003)—represents a first step toward understanding these issues, much more work remains to be done.

Second, as the discussion at the beginning of this chapter and in chapter 2 suggested, policy makers in many nations have postulated that healthy domestic IPO markets will stimulate venture capital investments in their countries. Assessing these claims requires disentangling a complex web of interconnected events. Nevertheless, careful analyses of the evolution of venture capital activity across a wide range of nations would be a valuable exercise.

15　Do Market Conditions Affect the Decision to Go Public?

In this chapter we examine the ability of venture capitalists to time initial public offerings (IPOs) by going public when equity values are high and using private financings when values are lower. Recall that venture capitalists generate the bulk of their profits from firms that go public. Successful timing of the IPO market provides significant benefits to venture capitalists, even through they rarely sell shares at the time of the offering (Barry et al. 1990). Taking companies public when equity values are high minimizes the dilution of the venture investors' ownership stake. Models of sequential stock sales (Allen and Faulhaber 1989; Grinblatt and Hwang 1989; Welch 1989) suggest a second rationale for timing the IPO. The deliberate underpricing of a new issue, which may be easier to accomplish in a hot market, "leaves a good taste" with investors. These investors are then more willing to purchase shares in follow-on offerings.

Venture capitalists have several mechanisms to ensure that firms go public at times that they perceive as optimal. Venture investors usually have several board seats and powerful control rights, including the right to put their shares to the firm's management (Barry et al. 1990; Sahlman 1990). Probably more important is their activity as informal advisors to managers. Since 30 percent of the firms backed by venture capitalists over the past two decades have gone public, the venture investors have usually experienced many more IPOs than the firm's managers. Consequently the venture capitalists may take the lead in deciding when and how a firm should go public.

The chapter uses a sample of 350 privately held biotechnology firms financed by venture capitalists between January 1978 and September 1992. Not only is the timing of their IPOs examined but also that of their private financings. Venture capitalists successfully time IPOs by being more likely to take companies public when their valuations are at their absolute and short-run peaks. Experienced venture capitalists appear to be more proficient in timing IPOs than their less experienced counterparts.

The chapter focuses on the biotechnology industry because the development of a bioengineered pharmaceutical or agricultural product typically takes more than a decade. Biotechnology firms remain in an R&D phase until well after going public. These firms mature slowly and do not incur large up-front costs in building manufacturing facilities. Venture capitalists provide funds in stages, with each financing round accompanied by a formal review of the firm's status. Each round involves an explicit decision to go public or remain private. Therefore venture investors in biotechnology firms have the flexibility to try to time their IPOs according to market conditions. For IPOs in other industries the demand for capital and the changing need for oversight by active investors may be more important to the decision to go public than market conditions. Thus the sample provides an opportunity for a more precise test of the ability to time IPOs.[1] The analysis suggests that the positive correlation between IPO volume and public equity market valuations is due not only to greater financing activity when investment opportunities are good but also to the substitution of public for private equity.

The sample also enables us to isolate the impact of investor characteristics on IPO timing. The 1978 to 1992 period was characterized by diverse venture investors. Freed by a 1979 Department of Labor policy statement to enter into venture partnerships, pension funds invested heavily during the sample period. This led to extensive entry on the part of new venture partnerships. The pool of venture capital under management increased sixfold from 1978 to 1990 (adjusted by the gross domestic product deflator). The wide range of experience among venture capitalists during the sample period makes it easier to identify the influence of venture experience.

Empirical Analysis

The Sample and Summary Statistics

In contrast to earlier studies of IPO timing and performance, both public and private financings are examined. Venture Economics' Venture Intelligence Database (described in chapter 22) is used to identify a sample of 750 financings by privately held firms that had already received venture capital.

---

1. Ibbotson and Jaffe (1975) and Ritter (1984) document "hot issue" markets, while Ritter (1991) and Loughran and Ritter (1995) show that the poor long-run returns from investments in IPOs are due both to their poor performance relative to the market and their concentration around equity market peaks. The "impresario hypothesis" of Shiller (1990) and Shiller and Pound (1989) suggests that IPOs are subject to fads, which underwriters exploit by rushing firms to the market.

Table 15.1
Distribution of the sample

Year	Public financings (IPOs) by private venture-backed firms		Private financings by private venture-backed firms	
	Number of IPOs	Total $ raised	Number of rounds	Total $ raised
1978	0	0	4	11
1979	1	7	4	35
1980	1	67	8	106
1981	4	249	9	66
1982	4	100	18	154
1983	18	414	40	247
1984	2	40	30	146
1985	2	9	36	138
1986	17	519	52	280
1987	12	231	61	382
1988	1	26	68	379
1989	6	65	75	413
1990	4	74	87	503
1991	34	1,252	86	458
1992[a]	30	993	36	201
Total	136	4,044	614	3,521

Note: The table indicates by year the number and cumulative size (in millions of 1997 dollars) of public and private financings by privately held biotechnology firms which had already received venture capital. The gross amount raised is reported for both public and private financings, before any deductions for offering costs.
a. Through September 30 only.

As table 15.1 indicates, these include 136 IPOs and 614 private financings. The public financings raised a total of $4.0 billion in 1997 dollars; the private financings, $3.5 billion. (Both figures are gross amounts, before deducting expenses associated with the equity sales.) The firms in this sample went public after as few as one venture financing round or as many as eight.

To assess the ability of venture capitalists to time public and private financings, the equity values of publicly traded biotechnology firms around these transactions are examined. This section describes the construction of the index.

Ideally publicly traded biotechnology companies would be used as a benchmark throughout this period. Because companies dedicated to biotechnology did not begin going public until the late 1970s, however, "comparable" companies must be employed in the early years. For the 1978 to

1982 period, thirteen companies identified in the 1977 business press (primarily the analyst reports summarized in Wall Street Transcript, but also the Wall Street Journal, Business Week, and Fortune) as well-positioned to capitalize on the then current developments in biological science are employed. Beginning on January 1, 1983, the index uses thirteen "dedicated" biotechnology firms that went public between 1979 and 1982. The pre-1983 sample has the same distribution as the dedicated biotechnology firms: seven firms specialize in human pharmaceuticals or diagnostics, three firms whose products relate to agricultural or animal science, two producers of research equipment, and one specialty chemical producer.

The portfolio is invested equally in the comparable firms on January 1, 1978. At the end of each year the portfolio is rebalanced so that an equal dollar amount of each security is held. The portfolio is not rebalanced daily, because for many securities the spread between the bid and ask prices is significant relative to the share price. An index with daily rebalancing would be biased upward because of the "bid-ask bounce" documented by Blume and Stambaugh (1983). On January 1, 1983, the investment in the comparable portfolio is liquidated and the proceeds used to buy equal dollar amounts of the dedicated portfolio. As companies are acquired or delisted, the most seasoned, publicly traded dedicated biotechnology company is added to the index. The indexes constructed using the comparable and dedicated portfolios are highly correlated. During 1982 and 1983 (the year before and after the switch), the correlation coefficient of the daily returns is over 0.96.

Figures 15.1 and 15.2 display the number of IPOs and private financings in each month and the biotechnology equity index. The IPOs coincide with the peaks in equity valuations, while no clear pattern appears in the private financings. In particular, the high valuations of 1983, 1986, and 1991–92 were accompanied by intense IPO activity. The level of private financing activity, however, changed little. These patterns suggest that venture capitalists are able to time the market, taking companies public at times when industry valuations are highest.

The Timing of Financings

First, the timing of all external financings in the sample is examined. Panel A of table 15.2 presents the main results. As figures 15.1 and 15.2 suggest, IPOs are far more likely to occur when the equity values are high. The mean equity index at the time of IPOs is 4.05, as opposed to 3.05 at the time of private financings. (The index is normalized as one on January 1, 1978.) Us-

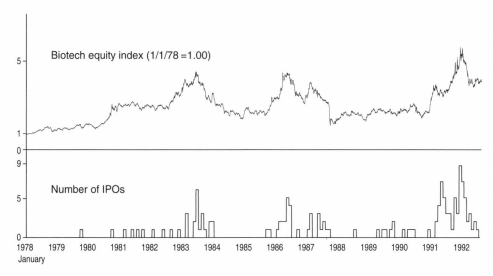

Figure 15.1
Timing of initial public offerings by privately held venture-backed biotechnology companies, January 1978 through September 1992. The top graph depicts an index of biotechnology equity, computed using the value of an investment in (between 1978 and 1982) 13 companies identified in the 1977 business press as well-positioned to capitalize on biotechnology developments and (from 1983 onward) 13 biotechnology companies. Acquired or delisted firms are replaced with the most seasoned publicly traded biotechnology firm. January 1, 1978, is normalized as one. The lower plot represents the *number* of biotechnology IPOs in each month. The data are compiled from Venture Economics, Recombinant Capital, SEC filings, company contracts, and CRSP.

ing a nonparametric Wilcoxon test, panel B of table 15.2 shows that the difference is statistically significant at the 1 percent level of confidence.

This test is repeated (as are the others shown below), adjusting the index in two ways. The increase in the equity index is partially due to inflation, and also to the need to provide a return to investors in excess of inflation. The index is detrended by the gross domestic product (GDP) deflator and by inflation plus a 5 percent annual premium. The differences in the index around IPOs and private financings remain significant. In the case of the inflation-adjusted series, the mean index at the time of the IPOs is 2.10; the mean index at the time of private financings, 1.69. (January 1, 1978, is once again normalized as one.) In the case of the inflation-adjusted series with the 5 percent annual premium, the mean index at the time of the IPOs is 1.26, the mean index at the time of private financings, 1.03. In both cases nonparametric Wilcoxon tests allow us to reject the null hypotheses of the equality of the distributions at the 1 percent level of confidence. The

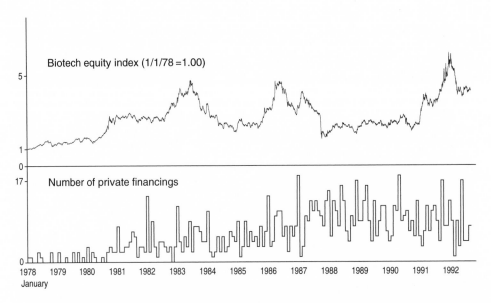

Figure 15.2
Timing of private financings by privately held venture-backed biotechnology companies, January 1978 through September 1992. The top graph depicts an index of biotechnology equity, computed using the value of an investment in (between 1978 and 1982) 13 companies identified in the 1977 business press as well-positioned to capitalize on biotechnology developments and (from 1983 onward) 13 biotechnology companies. Acquired or delisted firms are replaced with the most seasoned publicly traded biotechnology firm. January 1, 1978, is normalized as one. The lower plot represents the *number* of biotechnology private financings in each month. The data are compiled from Venture Economics, Recombinant Capital, SEC filings, company contracts, and CRSP.

modified indexes remain significant at the 1 percent level of confidence when used in probit regressions akin to that reported in table 15.3.

An IPO is also likely to coincide with a short-term maximum in equity values. The buy-and-hold returns from an equal-weighted investment in thirteen biotechnology securities are examined in the three months before and after the financing. The thirteen comparable securities are used prior to 1983 and thirteen publicly traded dedicated firms thereafter. The index is extended back into late 1977 and forward to the end of 1992 so that we can include observations that are near the beginning and the end of the sample period. If a firm is acquired or delisted during the period, the investment is rolled over into the most seasoned publicly traded dedicated biotechnology firm.

Such an investment gains an average of 9.9 percent in the event window (-60, -1) before an IPO. (The event window of sixty trading days is

Table 15.2
Biotechnology equity prices around public and private financings by privately held venture-backed biotechnology companies

		Mean raw "buy-and-hold" return from biotech equities around financing date	
	Mean level of biotechnology index	Trading days −60 to −1	Trading days 0 to 59
Panel A: Biotechnology equity prices			
136 initial public offerings	4.05	9.9%	−4.6%
614 private financings	3.05	4.6%	6.1%
Test			*p*-Value
Panel B: Tests of differences in means and medians			
Wilcoxon test, median equity index on date of IPO = median equity index on date of private financing			0.00
t-Test, mean return in [−60, −1] window before IPO = mean return in [−60, −1] window before private financing			0.00
t-Test, mean return in [0, 59] window after IPO = mean return in [0, 59] window after private financing			0.00
t-Test, mean return in [−60, −1] window before IPO = mean return in [0, 59] window after IPO			0.00
t-Test, mean return in [−60, −1] window before private financing = mean return in [0, 59] window after private financing			0.27

Note: The sample consists of 750 IPOs and private financings between January 1978 and September 1992 by firms that had already received venture capital. The table presents the level of a biotechnology equity index,[a] and the mean return from biotechnology equities in the three months before and after the financing. The table also compares the means and medians of these variables.
a. The index and change in equity values are computed for the period 1978 to 1982 using 13 companies identified in the 1977 business press as well positioned to capitalize on biotechnology developments and (from 1983 onward) 13 biotechnology companies. Acquired or delisted firms are replaced with the most seasoned publicly traded biotechnology firm. The index is normalized to one on January 1, 1978. For the private financings where only the month and year of the transaction are known, the twelfth trading day of the month is used.

Table 15.3
Estimated probit regressions of the decision of privately held venture-backed biotechnology firms to employ public or private financing

	Dependent variable: Did firm go public?[b]		
Level of biotechnology index[a]	0.50 [9.33]		
Raw return from biotech equities in [−60, −1] window		0.74 [2.80]	
Raw return from biotech equities in [0, 59] window			−0.65 [3.64]
Constant	−2.65 [13.16]	−0.96 [16.78]	−0.90 [16.71]
Log-likelihood	−307.55	−351.14	−348.23
χ^2-Statistic	95.00	7.83	13.66
p-Value	0.00	0.00	0.00
Number of observations	750	750	750

Note: The sample consists of 750 IPOs and private financings between January 1978 and September 1992 by firms that had already received venture capital. The dependent variable is 1 for firms that went public and 0 for firms that employed private financings. Independent variables include three alternative measures of market timing: the level of a biotechnology equity index at the time of the financing, the changes in equity prices in the three months before the financing, and the changes in equity prices in the three months after the financing. [Absolute t-statistics are in brackets.]
a. The index and change in equity values are computed for the period 1978 to 1982 using 13 companies identified in the 1977 business press as well positioned to capitalize on biotechnology developments and (from 1983 onwards) 13 biotechnology companies. Acquired or delisted firms are replaced with the most seasoned publicly traded biotechnology firm. The index is normalized to one on January 1, 1978. For the private financings where only the month and year of the transaction are known, the twelfth trading day of the month is used.
b. Regressions use alternative measures of market timing.

chosen to be consistent with Mikkelson and Partch 1988 and several other studies.) An identical investment made at the close of the IPO date has lost 4.6 percent of its value by day 59. Panel B indicates that the mean returns differ significantly at the 1 percent level of confidence.

Private financings display no such differences in the months before (+4.6 percent) and after (+6.1 percent) the transaction. Panel B shows that the mean returns in the three months prior to the IPOs are significantly greater than in the three months prior to the private financings. The mean returns are also significantly lower in the three months after IPOs. In some older entries in the database where the firm did not subsequently go public, only the month and year of the private financings are known. In these cases the twelfth trading day of the month is used. The results are robust to alternative approaches, including the assumption that the undated private financings took place on the first or last trading date of the month. They also are robust to using the changes in the index in the three months before and after the public and private financings, but not including the returns from the month of the financing.

One concern with the tests of the equality of means is their assumption of independence. The bunching of the IPOs and private financings implies that many of the sixty trading-day windows over which returns are calculated overlap. To address concerns about whether the bunching of returns may lead to an overstating of significance levels, the *t*-tests in table 15.2 are examined in a regression framework. The return is regressed on a constant and a dummy variable to indicate if the observation is from one of the two classes being compared: for example, if this is an observation of the returns in the sixty trading days prior to a private financing. Instead of assuming independence, however, we employ a generalized least squares (GLS) approach, akin to that used by Hansen and Hodrick (1980) and Meulbroek (1992a). In their analyses these authors employ monthly observations of forward and futures prices several months ahead. Through the use of GLS estimation, they correct their standard errors for the degree of overlap in the observations. Although the overlap here rises from the clustering of observations rather than the sampling procedure, a similar approach is used to examine the robustness of the results. A variance-covariance matrix Ω is created, and standard errors computed from the matrix $(X'\Omega^{-1}X)^{-1}$. The off-diagonal elements of the variance-covariance matrix Ω are constrained to be zero if the sixty trading day windows over which the equity index is calculated do not overlap and to be proportional to the extent of the overlap otherwise. In this way, nearby observations are assigned less weight in the analysis. Returns in the sixty trading days before and after IPOs remain significantly different at the 1 percent level of confidence. Returns in the sixty trading days prior to public and private financings do not differ at conventional confidence levels. Returns in the sixty trading days after public and private financings differ at the 5 percent level of confidence. In another analysis, the sixty trading-day returns are detrended for inflation and inflation plus a 5 percent annual premium. These corrections make little difference.

These patterns are then examined using the probit regression shown in table 15.3. Each financing by a privately held firm that has already received venture capital is employed as an observation. The dependent variable is a dummy indicating whether the firm received public or private financing (where 1 denotes an IPO, and zero a private financing):

$$IPO_{it} = \alpha_{0j} + \alpha_{1j}TIMING_{ijt} + \varepsilon_{ijt}. \tag{1}$$

The three measures of timing are the value of the biotechnology index at the time of the financing, the raw returns from an investment in biotechnology securities in the three months before the financing, and the raw returns in the three months after the financing.

Each of the variables is significant in explaining the decision to go public. As the coefficient of 0.50 suggests, a higher level of the equity index increases the probability of a public financing. The magnitude of this coefficient can be assessed by examining the effect of a 10 percent increase in the level of the equity index on the predicted probability that a public financing is employed. At the mean of all independent variables, the regression coefficients imply that the probability of an IPO is 15 percent. A 10 percent increase in the level of the equity index (i.e., from the mean of 3.23 to 3.56) boosts the probability of an IPO to 19 percent, or an increase of 27 percent. Increases in biotechnology equity values in the three months prior to the financing boost the chance of an IPO (the coefficient of 0.74) as do decreases in the three months after an IPO (−0.65).

The Impact of Venture Capitalist Experience

Next, to examine whether seasoned and inexperienced venture capitalists differ in their proficiency in taking firms public at market peaks, we repeat the analyses in tables 15.2 and 15.3. We divide the firms by the amount of experience the venture capitalists had.

The age of the oldest venture capital partnership having financed the firm is used as a proxy for venture capitalist experience. This approach differs slightly from Barry et al. (1990). Those authors used the venture capitalist with the largest equity stake in the firm at the time of the IPO to characterize the venture investors. The problem with this method is that the relative valuation of each round is not always known, because the largest shareholder cannot always be determined. Later in this chapter we use alternative measures of venture capital experience. In point of fact, however, these measures show little difference. Venture capitalists tend to syndicate investments either to their peers or to their less experienced counterparts. They are not likely to invest in deals begun by their less seasoned counterparts (see chapter 11). So the lead venture capitalist is usually the oldest one.

To establish that our partition of firms is economically meaningful, we divide the 136 IPOs in the sample by the age of the oldest venture capital organization investing in the firm. We characterize venture capital organizations by using several reference volumes (Clay 1991, National Register 1992, Venture Economics 1996). If the name of the venture capital fund recorded in the Venture Economics database does not match an entry in these directories of venture organizations, then to establish a match, we use an unpublished database from Venture Economics that lists venture capital funds and organizations. Data about the IPOs is collected from prospectuses, S-1 registration statements, and the Securities Data Company (SDC) Corporate New Issues database (1992).

IPOs divided in this manner differ in several respects. Table 15.4 shows that the reputation of the underwriter differs significantly at the 1 percent level of confidence, using the Carter-Manaster (1990) rankings of underwriter prestige. In this scheme, nine denotes the most prestigious underwriters and zero the least prestigious. These rankings are determined by positioning of companies in "tombstones," the advertisements that underwriters use to publicize offerings. If the book underwriter is not included in the Carter-Manaster ratings, the ranking of the comanaging underwriter is used. For twelve cases, there is no comanaging underwriter, or else it is not ranked. These are all small regional investment banks with limited underwriting experience (National Register 1992). These underwriters are assigned a rank of zero. Although Hambrecht and Quist is the most frequent underwriter for firms backed by experienced venture capitalists, D.H. Blair dominates the less experienced group.

Also presented are the other intermediaries involved in the offering. A partition frequently used to divide accounting firms in underpricing studies is the Big Six (previously the Big Eight), the largest U.S. accounting firms as measured by revenue (Balvers, McDonald, and Miller 1988; Beatty 1989). While the firms backed by more experienced venture capitalists are more likely to have a Big Six accounting firm, the difference is not significant. The most frequently used accountants and law firms are also reported.

The offerings also differ in magnitude. The equity stake retained by managers and employees after the offering is significantly larger for firms backed by the less experienced venture capitalists. In addition the dollars raised in the IPOs by firms with seasoned venture investors is larger (though only at the 10 percent level of confidence). Both results are consistent with Leland and Pyle (1977), who argue that lower quality managers must retain larger equity stakes and raise less money to obtain any external financing.

Firms backed by seasoned venture capitalists are significantly less likely to employ a unit offering. These bundled offerings include at least one share of stock and one warrant. Unit offerings are usually employed by small firms with uncertain prospects, by which only some of the funding are provided up front (see Schultz 1993). Unit offerings thus limit the danger of managers squandering invested capital. The remaining funds are provided

Table 15.4
Characteristics of IPOs by venture-backed biotechnology firms, divided by the age of the oldest venture investor in the firm

	Firms divided by age of oldest venture capital provider		p-Value, t-test of difference of means
	Above median	Below or equal to median	
Underwriter characteristics			
Carter-Manaster ranking[a]	6.6	4.8	0.00
Most frequent firm (number)	Hambrecht and Quist (6)	D. H. Blair (14)	
Auditor characteristics			
Percentage of firms in "Big Six"	98.5%	96.1%	0.56
Most frequent firm (number)	Ernst and Young (26)[e]	Ernst and Young (21)[e]	
Issuer's law firm characteristics			
Most frequent firm (number)	Cooley, Godward, Castro, Huddleston, and Tatum (11)	Bachner, Tally, Polevoy, and Misher (5)	
Offering characteristics			
Percentage of equity retained by employees and management[b]	7.2%	11.8%	0.00
Funds raised (1997$ mil)	33.7	25.6	0.08
Percentage of IPOs that are unit offerings[c]	4.4%	25.0%	0.00
Initial return[d]	10.3%	15.4%	0.31

Note: The sample consists of 136 IPOs between January 1978 and September 1992. The table compares the underwriter ranking, the presence of a "Big Six" accounting firm as the firm's auditor, and the most frequently represented underwriters, law firms, and accounting firms. The remaining columns describe these offerings: the share of equity retained by employees and management after the IPO, the mean inflation-adjusted offering size, the percentage of offerings in which units rather than common stock were sold, and the percentage change from the offering price to the first-day close. The table also compares the means of these variables for firms whose oldest venture capitalist is above and below the median age.
a. Carter and Manaster's (1990) ranking of lead underwriter prestige is employed, with nine representing the most prestigious underwriters, and zero the least. If the book underwriter is not included in the Carter-Manaster ratings, the ranking of the co-managing underwriter is used. If there is no co-managing underwriter, or it is also not ranked, these underwriters are assigned a rank of zero.
b. This measure includes all shareholdings by full-time managers and employees, but not venture capitalists or other financiers working as consultants at the firm.
c. This is the gross amount paid by the public, before allowance for direct and indirect underwriting fees. The gross domestic product deflator is used.
d. The closing price, when not available, is calculated as the mean of the bid and ask.
e. Includes predecessor entities Ernst and Whinney and Arthur Young.

only if the warrants are exercised. Because the warrants are typically out-of-the-money at the time of the IPO (i.e., they can be exercised at a price higher than the per share price of the IPO), the exercise of the warrants is usually conditional on the stock price rising. The first-day returns from the IPOs are lower for the firms backed by experienced venture capitalists, consistent with Barry et al. (1990), but the difference is not significant.

After separating firms whose oldest venture investor is above or below the median age, the analysis in table 15.2 is repeated. Panel A of table 15.5 shows the differences between private and public equity. Both classes of firms appear to time IPOs. The effectiveness of this timing, however, appears greater for the more experienced venture capitalists, as the tests in panel B confirm. The average firm backed by experienced venture capitalists went public when the index was at 4.31; for the firms below the median, the level was 3.80. Similarly the index run-up in the three months before the IPO and the run-down in the three months after are both larger.

Table 15.6 repeats the probit regression estimation of the decision to go public. Firms backed by venture capitalists above or below the median age are separated. Again, the probability that the firm went public is the dependent variable, with the three measures of market timing as independent variables. In each of the three pairs of regressions, the timing variable is greater in magnitude and significance in the seasoned venture capital regression.

Panel C shows that the regression coefficients differ significantly. First we estimated a pooled regression, allowing firms above and below the median to have distinct coefficients for the timing variable and constant. Then we constrained the coefficient of the timing variable to be the same in both regressions. The table presents the p-values from χ^2-tests of this constraint. In two of the three cases the null hypothesis of no difference at the 5 percent level of confidence is rejected. These findings suggest that firms backed by established venture capitalists are more successful at timing their IPOs.

Robustness to Alternative Measures and Control Variables

We undertake several analyses to assess the robustness of the results to alternative measures of venture experience and the presence of control variables. These analyses, however, have little effect on the qualitative and quantitative results.

First, to test the results to see if they may be an artifact of the criteria used to divide the venture capitalists, we used, as an alternative, size to divide venture capitalists into experienced and inexperienced investors. This way

Table 15.5
Biotechnology equity prices around public and private financings for privately held venture-backed bio-technology companies, divided by the age of the oldest venture investor in the firm

	Mean level of biotechnology index[a]	Mean raw "buy-and-hold" returns from biotech equities around financing date	
		Trading days −60 to −1	Trading days 0 to 59
Panel A: Biotechnology equity prices			
136 initial public offerings:			
Firms whose oldest venture investor is above the median age	4.31	12.5%	−6.8%
Firms whose oldest venture investor is below the median age	3.80	7.4%	−2.4%
614 private financings:			
Firms whose oldest venture investor s above the median age	3.08	5.1%	6.6%
Firms whose oldest venture investor is below the median age	3.03	4.0%	5.1%

	p-Value
Panel B: Tests of differences in means and medians	
Tests using firms whose oldest venture investor is above the median age	
Wilcoxon test, median equity index on date of IPO = median equity index on date of private financing	0.00
t-Test, mean return in [−60, −1] window prior to IPO = mean return in [−60, −1] window prior to private financing	0.00
t-Test, mean return in [0, 59] window after IPO = mean return in [0, 59] window after private financing	0.00
Tests using firms whose oldest venture investor is below the median age	
Wilcoxon test, median equity index on date of IPO = median equity index on date of private financing	0.00
t-Test, mean return in [−60, −1] window prior to IPO = mean return in [−60, −1] window prior to private financing	0.20
t-Test, mean return in [0, 59] window after IPO = mean return in [0, 59] window after private financing	0.01
Tests comparing firms whose oldest venture investor is above and below the median age	
Wilcoxon test, median equity index on date of IPO is same for both sets of firms	0.00
t-Test, mean return in [−60, −1] window prior to IPO is same for both sets of firms	0.03
t-Test, mean return in [0, 59] window after IPO is same for both sets of firms	0.07

Note: The sample consists of 750 IPOs and private financings between January 1978 and September 1992 by firms that had already received venture capital. The table presents the level of a biotechnology equity index, and the changes in equity prices in the three months before and after the financing. The table also compares the means and medians of these variables for firms whose oldest venture capitalist is above and below the median age.

Table 15.5
(continued)
a. The index and change in equity values are computed for the period 1978 to 1982 using 13 companies identified in the 1977 business press as well positioned to capitalize on biotechnology developments and (from 1983 onward) 13 biotechnology companies. Acquired or delisted firms are replaced with the most seasoned publicly traded biotechnology firm. The index is normalized to one on January 1, 1978. For the private financings where only the month and year of the transaction is known, the twelfth trading day of the month is used.

venture capitalists who raise new (but large) partnerships can be counted as seasoned investors. We computed the ratio of funds under management by the partnership to the total pool of venture capital under management in the year of the investment, using the annual values reported in Pratt's Guide (Venture Economics 1996). When this information is incomplete, we used the unpublished Venture Economics database. The results using this partition are consistent with those we reported above.

In a related set of regressions we divided firms by relative, rather than absolute, age and size. The mean age and size of the venture partnerships that financed biotechnology firms dipped in the mid-1980s, reflecting the extensive entry into venture capital. Our analysis identified the age of the oldest venture capitalist providing funds to each biotechnology firm in each year, and then divided the firms by whether their oldest investor was older or younger than the oldest investor in the median firm in that year. (The procedure for size is similar.) We found little difference between these results and those in tables 15.5 and 15.6. As these tests are not independent, relatively older venture partnerships are often the older ones on an absolute scale as well. Our analysis shows, however, that these results are not an artifact of a particular approach to dividing firms.

The independent variables can also be recast, using the change in the market index over two- and four-month windows. Using the longer window tends to slightly strengthen the results; the shorter window tends to weaken them. Although there are only a small number of cases in the sample where venture capitalists exited viable firms through mergers or sales, we examined the impact of including these cases. We recast the dependent variable to measure IPOs and acquisitions of firms at prices higher than that of the last venture round. This change had little impact.

Finally, we added controls for the quality of the firms going public. Because more experienced venture capitalists are thought to fund higher quality firms, which may bias the results, we used three sets of control variables for firm quality:

Table 15.6
Estimated probit regressions of the decision of privately held venture-backed biotechnology firms to employ public or private financing, with observations divided by the age of the oldest venture investor in the firm

	Dependent variable: Did firm go public?[b]		
Panel A: Estimated probit regressions using firms whose oldest venture investor is above the median age			
Level of a biotechnology index[a]	0.65 [7.75]		
Raw return from biotech equities in $[-60, -1]$ window		0.93 [2.53]	
Raw return from biotech equities in $[0, 59]$ window			-1.44 [3.94]
Constant	-2.79 [10.10]	-0.87 [10.89]	-1.04 [12.90]
Log-likelihood	-160.40	-191.14	-187.52
χ^2-Statistic	67.95	6.48	9.11
p-Value	0.00	0.01	0.00
Number of observations	375	375	375

	Dependent variable: Did firm go public?[b]		
Panel B: Estimated probit regressions using firms whose oldest venture investor is below the median age			
Level of biotechnology index[a]	0.31 [4.92]		
Raw return from biotech equities in $[-60, -1]$ window		0.48 [1.23]	
Raw return from biotech equities in $[0, 59]$ window			-0.54 [2.32]
Constant	-2.39 [8.09]	-1.07 [12.84]	-0.78 [10.65]
Log-likelihood	-145.46	-157.32	-155.58
χ^2-Statistic	25.33	1.52	5.60
p-Value	0.00	0.29	0.02
Number of observations	375	375	375

	p-Value
Panel C: χ^2-Tests of differences in regression coefficients	
Tests comparing firms whose oldest venture investor is above and below the median age	
Coefficient of "level of biotechnology index" variable is identical in both regressions	0.01
Coefficient of "change in biotech equity values in $[-60, -1]$ window" variable is identical in both regressions	0.21
Coefficient of "change in biotech equity values in $[0, 59]$ window" variable is identical in both regressions	0.03

Note: The sample consists of 750 financing rounds between January 1978 and September 1992 by firms that had already received venture capital. The dependent variable is 1 for firms that went public and 0 for firms that employed private financings. Independent variables include three alternative measures of market timing: the level of a biotechnology equity index at the time of the financing, and the changes in equity prices in the three months before and after the financing. [Absolute t-statistics are in brackets.] The table also compares the regression coefficients for firms whose oldest venture capitalist is above and below the median age.
a. The index and change in equity values are computed for the period 1978 to 1982 using 13 companies identified in the 1977 business press as well positioned to capitalize on biotechnology developments and (from 1983 onward) 13 biotechnology companies. Acquired or delisted firms are replaced with the most seasoned publicly traded biotechnology firm. The index is normalized to one on January 1, 1978. For the private financings where only the month and year of the transaction is known, the twelfth trading day of the month is used.
b. Regressions use alternative measures of market timing.

1. The age of the firm. In order of preference, we used the incorporation date reported in SEC filings, the self-reported founding date in industry directories (Corporate Technology 1996; Mega-Type 1992; Oryx 1992), a questionnaire response (NCBC 1990b), or the date reported by Venture Economics.

2. A private placement from a corporation with a related line of business. Strategic investments are frequently used in high-technology industries, particularly biotechnology, to cement long-term agreements (Pisano 1989). We defined related lines of business as those with any of the following Standard Industrial Classification identifiers in the Million Dollar Directory (Dun's 1996) in the year of the transaction: SIC 283, Drugs; SIC 287, Agricultural Chemicals; and SIC 384, Medical Instruments and Supplies.

3. The firm's intellectual property position. Intellectual property protection was important to biotechnology firms in the 1980s. (See Lerner 1994 for an overview.) Product market competition was embryonic, and the alternative methods of protecting intellectual property ineffective. The disposition of a single patent could shift the valuation of a biotechnology firm by as much as 50 percent. Patents associated with these 350 firms are identified by using U.S. Patent and Trademark Office databases (USPTO/OPDLP 1989, 1990), as well as those assigned to their wholly owned subsidiaries and their research and development limited partnerships. Awards to joint ventures and spin-offs are counted to the extent that the firm had an interest in the venture. The analysis uses two alternate variables. The first variable is the number of the patents awarded at the time of the financing round. The second is the number of successful patent applications awarded and in progress at the time. Because patent applications are held confidential by USPTO until the time of award, only observations made prior to 1990 are used in the second analysis.

In unreported regressions, while the age and patents variables have significant explanatory power, the timing variables remain significantly larger in the regressions that employ the firms backed by seasoned venture capitalists.

Alternative Explanations

Speed of IPO Execution

One explanation for established venture capitalists' apparent superiority in timing IPOs is better execution. The failure of less experienced venture capitalists to take their firms public at market peaks may reflect their limited

Table 15.7
Time from the filing of the original S-1 statement to the effective date of initial public offering, divided by the age of the oldest venture provider

	Mean	Median
Panel A: Months from S-1 filing to IPO effective date		
Firms whose oldest venture investor is above the median age	2.0	1.6
Firms whose oldest venture investor is below the median age	1.9	1.7

	p-Value
Panel B: Tests of differences in means and medians[a]	
t-Test, mean months from S-1 filing to IPO effective date is same for both sets of firms	0.52
Wilcoxon test, median months from S-1 filing to IPO effective date is same for both sets of firms	0.54

Note: The sample consists of 136 IPOs by venture-backed biotechnology firms between January 1978 and September 1992. The table also compares the mean and median time for firms whose oldest venture capitalist was above and below the median age.
a. The tests compare firms whose oldest venture investor is above and below the median age.

skill in planning and executing an offering, not their inability to perceive when the market is hot. In particular, SEC reviews of proposed IPOs can be protracted. Similarly organizing a selling syndicate demand for the offering may be time-consuming.

This claim is tested by examining the time from the receipt of the original S-1 statement by the SEC to the effective date of the IPO. The filing date is found in SDC's Corporate New Issues database (1992). When it is not available from this source, the date of the "received" stamp on the original S-1 filing is used.

Table 15.7 summarizes the results. The mean time from filing to offering does not differ significantly for the firms financed by seasoned or inexperienced venture capitalists (2.0 months for more experienced; 1.9 months for the less experienced), nor do the medians differ appreciably. The results provide no support for the claim that the superior timing of the IPO market by seasoned firms is due to better execution.

Willingness to Withdraw Offerings

A second explanation relates to withdrawn offerings. The legal procedure for canceling a proposed IPO is straightforward. Firms may write a letter to the SEC to withdraw proposed security offerings before their effective date. Often firms do not withdraw failed IPOs. When a registration statement has been on file at the SEC for nine months, the SEC writes a letter to the firm and then declares the offering abandoned (17 Code of Federal Regulatory §230.479).

Although the formalities associated with an IPO withdrawal are few, the repercussions may be severe. A firm that withdraws its IPO may later find it difficult to access the public marketplace. Even if the stated reason for the withdrawal is poor market conditions, the firm may be lumped with other businesses whose offerings did not sell because of questionable accounting practices or gross mispricing. These reputational considerations may be less severe for a firm associated with a major venture capitalist. A greater willingness to withdraw IPOs in the face of deteriorating market conditions may explain the apparent superiority of experienced venture capitalists in timing offerings.

To analyze these claims, withdrawn or abandoned IPO filings are examined. These offerings are identified using the SDC Corporate New Issues database. (SDC employs a data collection procedure similar to the Investment Dealers' Digest listings used by Mikkelson and Partch 1988 to identify withdrawn seasoned security offerings.) Because the coverage of abandoned IPOs is less than comprehensive, these records are supplemented with the "no go IPOs" section of Going Public (Howard 1992) and a database of failed IPOs compiled by a federal agency. (The official responsible for the creation of this database has requested anonymity.) Fourteen withdrawn or abandoned IPOs by these firms in this period were found.

Our results in examining the probability that an IPO filing is completed successfully are provided in table 15.8. The data we used are all filings of S-1 registration statements by privately held firms in the Venture Economics sample. (These include the 136 successful IPOs and the fourteen withdrawn offerings.) A probit regression is estimated:

$$COMPLETE_{it} = \beta_0 + \beta_1 MAXAGE_{it} + \varepsilon_{it}. \qquad (2)$$

The dependent variable is a dummy; it takes the value 1 if the offering was successfully completed. The independent variable measures the age (in years) of the oldest venture capitalist to have financed the firm. We found no evidence that older venture capitalists are more willing to withdraw IPOs: the coefficient 0.01 is of the opposite sign and insignificant.

The right-hand column in table 15.8 reports the results when the regression was rerun, controlling for the quality of the firm. Superior quality offerings are less likely to be withdrawn, no matter who is the venture investor. The independent variables used are the age of the firm, the presence of a private placement from a related corporation, and the number of patent awards at the time of the financing. No evidence was found that firms

Table 15.8

Estimated probit regressions of the successful completion of an IPO by privately held venture-backed biotechnology firms who filed S-1 registration statements

	Dependent variable: Did firm go public?	
Age of oldest venture investor (in years)	0.01 [0.46]	0.01 [0.76]
Age of firm at time of filing (in years)[a]		−0.08 [1.48]
Patents awarded at time of filing[b]		0.10 [1.04]
Did firm receive private placement from related corporation?		−0.32 [1.08]
Constant	1.22 [4.63]	1.58 [4.44]
Log-likelihood	−46.62	−44.67
χ^2-Statistic	0.21	3.71
p-Value	0.64	0.44
Number of observations	150	150

Note: The sample consists of 150 filings between January 1978 and September 1992. The dependent variable is 1.0 for firms that went public and 0.0 for firms that withdrew or abandoned their offerings. Independent variables include the age of the oldest venture investor, the age of the firm at the time of the filing, the number of patents awarded to the firm at the time of the filing, and a dummy variable indicating whether the firm had previously received a private placement from a corporation with a related line-of-business at the time of the filing. [Absolute t-statistics are in brackets.]

a. Corporations with related lines of business are defined as those with any of the following Standard Industrial Code identifiers in the *Million Dollar Directory* (Dun's, 1992) in the year of the transaction: SIC 283, Drugs; SIC 287, Agricultural Chemicals; and SIC 384, Medical Instruments and Supplies.

b. All patents assigned to firms, their wholly owned subsidiaries, and their research and development limited partnerships are included. Awards to joint ventures and spin-offs are counted to the extent that a firm had an interest in the venture.

backed by seasoned venture capitalists are inclined to withdraw their offerings, even after controlling for quality.

Equity valuations after the filing of S-1 statements are another measure of performance. Mikkelson and Partch (1988) examine stock prices after the announcement of seasoned security issues. In the weeks after the announcement of an ultimately withdrawn seasoned issue, they found both the market returns and the issuer's net-of-market returns to be negative. No such pattern appeared after the filing of successful offerings. We examined the returns from an equally weighted investment in thirteen biotechnology securities between the close of the S-1 filing date and the close of the twentieth trading day, using the same procedure. The index rose by 2 percent after the filing of successful offerings and declined by 9 percent after the filing of ultimately withdrawn offerings. The difference is significant at the 1 percent level of confidence, as are those computed using other windows.

Conclusions

In this chapter, we explored the differences between private and public equity using a sample of 350 privately held venture-backed firms. We saw that venture capitalists take firms public at market peaks, relying on private financings when valuations are lower. Seasoned venture capitalists appear more proficient at timing IPOs. The results are robust to the use of alternative criteria to separate firms and controls for firms' quality. The results are not caused by differences in the speed of executing the IPOs or in the willingness to withdraw the proposed IPOs.

Two limitations deserve further discussion. First, the design of our study used a setting conducive to the identification of market timing. In some industries the need for oversight, or lumpy demands for capital, as the firm matures may affect the decision to go public more dramatically. In some time the heterogeneity between new and seasoned venture capitalists may not be as pronounced. Practitioner accounts, however, underscore the importance of IPO timing across industries and time. An example is an investment manager's discussion (McNamee 1991, p. 26) of market conditions around peak periods for computer and electronics IPOs:

The whole problem can be summed up in the phrase "IPO window." The IPO window occurs when sellers try to bail out and buyers try to get rich without doing any work.... It is when the AEA (American Electronics Association) puts up a billboard on Highway 101 near Great America that says, "The buy side has lost its mind, let's bag them quick, before they catch on." Sometime late in the IPO window, we get to watch venture capitalists behave like Keystone Kops.

Such narratives are not confined to the 1980s, 1990s and early 2000s. Jeffery (1961) described similar patterns in the market for new securities of high-technology firms in the 1950s. In the business press, Stern and Pouschine (1992) discuss the timing of "reverse LBOs" (IPOs of firms that have previously undergone leveraged buyouts) by LBO funds. Venture capitalists may also time the market when they sell or distribute shares in firms that have gone public (as discussed in chapter 19).

Second, an interpretation of the seasoned venture capitalists' more effective timing of IPOs is their superior proficiency. They may be better at recognizing when valuations are at a peak. There remain, however, several alternate interpretations. Less experienced venture capitalists may also wish to take firms public at market peaks but may be unable to command the attention of investment bankers. The reason is that underwriting services are rationed in key periods. In the next chapter we show that inexperienced venture capitalists do not have to wait until the market is optimal to take firms public; they can signal their quality to potential investors in follow-on funds. The mechanisms by which managers and venture capitalists decide to go public and obtain access to investment bankers is an area worthy of further study.

Another research opportunity relates to the implications of the timing of the decision to go public. IPOs have been shown to coincide with declines in operating performance (Jain and Kini 1994) and broad shifts in the incentives offered managers (Beatty and Zajak 1994). Do early initial public offerings affect the subsequent performance of the firm? To what extent are these factors related to the maturity of the firm and the market conditions at the time of the IPO? An investigation of these interactions among these financing choices and operational performance may yield some interesting results.

16   Does Reputation Affect the Decision to Go Public?

In this chapter we study the evidence about the relation between performance and capital raising and its implications for fund managers. Young venture capital firms have incentives to grandstand; that is, they take actions that signal their ability to potential investors. In the effort to establish a reputation and successfully raise capital for new funds, young venture capital firms commonly bring companies public earlier than older venture capital firms.

Empirical tests for a sample of 433 venture-backed initial public offerings (IPOs) from January 1, 1978, through December 31, 1987, and a second sample consisting of the first IPO brought to market by 62 venture capital funds support predictions of the grandstanding hypothesis. For example, the effect of historical performance in the IPO market on the amount of capital raised is stronger for young venture capital firms, providing them with greater incentive to bring companies public earlier. Similarly young venture capital firms raise new funds closer to the IPO. Young venture capital firms have been on the IPO company's board of directors fourteen months less than older venture firms, hold smaller percentage equity stakes at the time of IPO than the stakes held by established venture firms, and the IPO companies they finance are nearly two years younger and more under-priced when they go public than companies backed by older venture capital firms. Much of the difference in underpricing and the venture capitalists' percentage equity stake is associated with a shorter duration of board representation, indicating that rushing companies to the IPO market imposes costs on the venture firm. The results suggest that the relation between performance and capital raising affects the incentives and actions of venture capitalists.

Reputation and its effect on attracting capital are important topics in recent corporate finance research. Theoretical work by Diamond (1989) shows that reputation can be important in accessing debt and equity markets.

Empirical research by Sirri and Tufano (1998) and Chevalier and Ellison (1997) demonstrates that past performance is a strong indicator of the ability to attract investors. The venture capital industry is particularly well suited for examining reputation and capital raising because most venture capital organizations raise money in limited partnerships. These partnerships have finite lifetimes, so a venture firm must periodically completely recapitalize itself by raising a new limited partnership. A venture capital organization would cease operations without raising a new fund. This puts pressure on young venture capital firms to establish a reputation and raise a new fund within a short, predetermined time.

Incentives to Grandstand

As discussed above, limited partnerships have predefined lifetimes, usually ten years with an option to extend the fund for up to three years. Venture capitalists must therefore liquidate investments and distribute proceeds to investors within that time, and make no new investments after the first four or five years of a fund. The predetermined lifetime of a particular fund means that venture capital firms must periodically raise follow-on partnerships to remain active in venture capital financing. Venture capital firms may have two or three overlapping funds, each starting three to six years after the previous fund.

As documented in chapter 4, most limited partners in venture capital funds are institutional investors whose role in the day-to-day operations of the fund is restricted by law if they are to retain limited liability. Limited partners receive periodic updates about the status of projects and new investment activity within the portfolio managed by the venture capitalist, but they do not participate in policy decisions. Evaluating a venture capitalist's ability is therefore difficult. Investors must search for signals of ability when evaluating venture capitalists.

Theoretical and empirical research on other types of investment funds demonstrates the importance of reputation and fund performance in raising capital. Lakonishok, Shleifer, Thaler, and Vishny (1991), Patel, Zeckhauser, and Hendricks (1991), and Sirri and Tufano (1998) examine fund-raising and investment patterns of various types of institutional fund managers and find that past performance influences fund-raising ability. Stein (1988, 1989) and Rajan (1994) develop models in which investors' horizons lead to managerial decisions that do not maximize shareholder value. They show that incentives to boost performance in the short run lead to activities that lower firm value. Chevalier and Ellison (1997) show that the relative performance of mutual fund managers affects growth in capital contributions to their funds. They find that investors have an incentive to increase the riskiness of their portfolio if funds underperform the market in the first nine months. This incentive is particularly strong for new mutual funds.

In our analysis we use a formal model of grandstanding developed by Gompers (1993). Through this model we demonstrate that in contrast to established venture capital firms, new venture capital firms are willing to incur costs by taking companies public earlier than would maximize their returns. We assume that venture capitalists have different abilities to select or create companies that have a high probability of going public. The most effective way they can signal their ability or the value of their portfolio companies is therefore to bring one of the portfolio companies public in an IPO.[1] As discussed in chapter 2, almost all of the returns for investors in venture capital are earned on companies that go public.

If investors believe that high-ability venture capitalists are more likely to fund companies that go public, then taking a portfolio company public would be interpreted as a sign that the venture capitalist is skilled at financing start-up companies. After an IPO, investors increase their assessment of the venture capitalist's ability. Because investors know more about older venture capital firms, an additional IPO will not affect their beliefs about an old firm's ability as much as it will their beliefs about a young venture firm's ability.

Since the amount of capital that venture capitalists can raise is an increasing function of their perceived ability and the costs of earlier IPOs (e.g., greater underpricing or smaller equity stakes) are not trivial, only young venture capital firms are willing to incur those costs. Old venture capital firms with good reputations do not need to signal, because investors have evaluated their performances over many years and have evidence of their high ability. Only new venture capital firms will benefit from signaling in the IPO market. If firms are believed to be of low quality (through their inability to bring companies public), they will be unable to raise new funds. Diamond (1989) shows how reputation can similarly affect the debt market. In his model, young borrowers choose risky projects. If they survive for a certain length of time and acquire reputations as reliable borrowers, their investment behavior changes and they choose safe projects. Age becomes a proxy for reputation. Reputation can work in a similar way in the venture capital industry.

---

1. By convention, most investments in a venture capital portfolio are held at book value until the next round of financing or an IPO occurs. Limited partners are often concerned that a venture capital fund may make a small investment in a company at a higher price to write up the value of all previous investments in that company to the new price even though that price may not be justified. For most investors the only meaningful price is therefore one established in the public market.

The grandstanding hypothesis predicts that the relation between bringing companies public and fund-raising ability should be strong for young venture capital firms. Each additional IPO attracts relatively more capital from investors for a young venture capital firm than for an old venture capital firm. An additional IPO changes investors' estimates of a young venture capitalist's ability more than it does their estimate of an old venture capitalist's ability. That is, each additional IPO for a young venture capital firm attracts significantly more capital than each additional IPO for an older venture capital firm. Because the reputation of established venture capital firms is affected less by doing an IPO, the incentive to raise new funds immediately following an IPO is small. If we consider the average time from an IPO to the closing of the venture capital firm's next fund, young venture firms will raise money sooner than older venture firms will.

The relation between reputation and capital raising is consistent with industry wisdom. Established venture capital firms with long track records can raise large funds quickly and with little effort. When Greylock Management Company, one of the nation's oldest and most prestigious firms, began their eighth venture fund early in 1994, they collected more than $175 million in only a few months ($150 million had originally been targeted). All of the investors in Greylock's new fund were previous Greylock investors.

If venture capital firms in their first fund have shown no returns, they will find it difficult to raise new money. These are the firms that have the strongest incentives to grandstand. For example, Hummer Winblad Venture Partners formed its first venture capital fund in 1989. When Hummer Winblad tried to raise a second fund in 1992, it found it extremely difficult to attract investors despite nearly a half-year of marketing. The lack of interest stemmed largely from the lack of successes; Hummer Winblad had never taken a firm public. After Powersoft, one of their investments, went public on February 3, 1993, Hummer Winblad raised a $60 million second fund in a few months.

An additional prediction of the grandstanding hypothesis is that companies brought to market by young venture capital firms should be less mature. Two measures of IPO maturity are examined. The age of the offering company at the time of issue is one measure of an early IPO. As new venture capital firms grandstand, the companies they back are younger at the offering date than companies backed by older venture firms. In the companies they rush to market (compared to older venture capital firms) they will have shorter relationships and will have served on the boards of IPO companies for less time.

A big cost incurred by new venture capital firms doing early IPOs is underpricing. Muscarella and Vetsuypens (1989) show that the older the firm is at IPO (controlling for various factors), the lower is the return on the first trading day. As in Rock's (1986) IPO model, older firms have long track records reducing asymmetric information and thus avoiding underpricing. Various models of IPOs (Welch 1989; Grinblatt and Hwang 1989; Allen and Faulhaber 1989) show underpricing to be a costly signal of a company's quality. In general, the greater the uncertainty surrounding a company, the greater will be the underpricing. A company that goes to market early is younger and has less information available for evaluation by potential investors and so is usually more underpriced. The real loss in underpricing for the venture capital firm is that it transfers wealth from existing shareholders, including the venture capitalist, to new shareholders. Companies brought to market by young venture capital firms are therefore likely to be more underpriced at the IPO than those brought to market by more experienced venture capitalists.

Additional costs incurred by bringing a company to market early are reduced prospects for future growth and a smaller equity stake for the venture capitalist. Compared with the equity stakes of old venture capital firms, the venture capitalists investing in a company with a young lead venture capital firm will hold a smaller percentage of the offering company's equity at the IPO date.

The grandstanding hypothesis predicts high costs of signaling for the young venture capital firm because the company goes public earlier than if it had been financed by a more established venture capitalist. The costs associated with an IPO are examined in regressions. The factors of age of the IPO company and the length of the venture capitalist's board service are used to explain some of the difference in underpricing and percentage equity stakes at IPO between young and established venture capital providers. The objective is to test if the early timing of the IPO increases underpricing and reduces equity stakes of a young venture backer. The age of the offering company and the length of board service should be thus negatively related to underpricing and positively related to the size of the venture capitalist's equity stake.

Empirical Results

Data Set and Descriptive Statistics

Two samples are used to test the predictions of the grandstanding hypothesis. The first sample, collected and described by Barry et al. (1990), consists of 433 venture-backed IPOs taken public between January 1, 1978, and December 31, 1987. Kemper Financial Services and Brinson Partners, two investment advisors, supplied a second data set that includes all IPOs for sixty-two venture capital funds between August 1, 1983, and July 31, 1993. This second, supplemental data set is useful for addressing potential selection biases in the first sample. These two data sets are described in more detail in chapter 22.

Dates and sizes of new funds are from Venture Economics, a consulting firm that tracks investments and fundraising by venture capital firms. Venture capitalists most often syndicate their investments with other venture capitalists. When this occurs, one investor usually takes the role of lead venture capitalist. This investor ordinarily has significant control over the decisions of the firm and more actively monitors the company through board service. The firm that has been on the board the longest is classified as the lead venture capitalist; this classification differs from that of Barry et al. (1990) who classify the lead venture capitalist as the firm that owns the largest equity stake and has a board seat. If two firms have been on the board the same length of time, the larger equity holder is designated as the lead. Gorman and Sahlman (1989) find that the venture capital firm originating the investment is usually the firm that acquires a board seat first and has the most input into the decisions of the offering company. The originating firm does not always end up owning the largest stake at IPO.

To test the grandstanding hypothesis, we divide the sample of venture-backed companies into two groups: those backed by experienced venture capital firms and those backed by young venture capital firms. We use the age of the lead venture capital firm at IPO as a proxy for reputation, although it is an imperfect measure of reputation since experienced partners sometimes leave to start new venture capital firms. This effect can bias the results away from any noticeable difference between new and old venture capital firms. All lead venture capital firms under six years in business at the IPO date are classified as young and those six years or more as old. The results are not sensitive to specifying cutoff between young and old venture capitalists at between four and ten years.[2]

Table 16.1 presents summary information for the IPOs backed by young and old venture capital firms. Younger venture capital firms bring companies public closer to the firms' next fund, an average (median) of sixteen

---

2. The use of a dummy variable addresses potential nonlinearities in the reputation measure. Typical funds invest all their capital in the first five years and harvest investments during the last five. The firm is likely to run out of cash in the fifth year and must raise a new fund before then. After a second fund has been raised, the pressure to grandstand is greatly reduced or eliminated. To check the robustness of the results, regressions are run using the natural logarithm of the venture capital firm's age instead of the dummy variable. Results are qualitatively similar using the logarithm of age specification.

Table 16.1
Comparison of the characteristics for initial public offerings backed by young and old venture capital firms

	Venture capital firms less than six years old at IPO	Venture capital firms six years old or greater at IPO	p-Value test of no difference
Average time from IPO date to next follow-on fund in months	16.0 [12.0]	24.2 [24.0]	0.001 [0.002]
Average size of next follow-on fund (1997$ mil)	87.9 [68.0]	136.6 [113.4]	0.018 [0.024]
Average age of venture-backed company at IPO date in months	55.1 [42.0]	79.6 [64.0]	0.000 [0.000]
Average duration of board representation for lead venture capital firm in months	24.5 [20.0]	38.8 [28.0]	0.001 [0.000]
Average underpricing at the IPO date	0.136 [0.067]	0.073 [0.027]	0.001 [0.036]
Average offering size (1997$ mil)	18.3 [13.0]	24.7 [19.1]	0.013 [0.000]
Average Carter and Manaster underwriter rank	6.26 [6.50]	7.43 [8.00]	0.000 [0.000]
Average number of previous IPOs	1 [0]	6 [4]	0.000 [0.000]
Average fraction of equity held by all venture capitalists prior to IPO	0.321 [0.287]	0.377 [0.371]	0.025 [0.024]
Average fraction of equity held by lead venture capitalist after IPO	0.122 [0.100]	0.139 [0.120]	0.098 [0.031]
Average market value of lead venture capitalist's equity after IPO (1997$ mil)	9.5 [4.3]	14.7 [8.7]	0.033 [0.000]
Average aftermarket standard deviation	0.034 [0.030]	0.030 [0.028]	0.080 [0.324]
Number of observations	99	240	

Note: Sample is 433 venture-backed companies that went public between January 1, 1978, and December 31, 1987. Medians are in brackets. Significance tests in the third column are p-values of t-tests for difference in averages and p-values of two-sample Wilcoxon rank-sum tests for difference in medians in brackets.

months (twelve) prior to the next fund compared to twenty-four (twenty-four) months prior for old venture capital firms. The Venture Economics funds database shows that experienced venture capital firms raise new funds every two to four years, while young venture capital firms raise new money only every five or six years. If IPOs occur randomly, the average IPO for an old venture capital firm should be closer to its next fund than the average IPO for a new venture capital firm. Because it takes approximately one year to solicit money and close a new fund, the eight- to twelve-month difference indicates that young venture capital firms could be bringing companies public right before or during the time they raise money whereas established firms do not. The average size of a new venture capital firm's next fund ($87.9 million) is also smaller than the size of an old venture firm's next fund ($136.6 million).

Summary statistics in table 16.1 for the maturity of the IPO company also support the predictions of the grandstanding hypothesis. The average (median) age of the offering company is 56 (42) months for IPOs backed by young venture capitalists and 80 (64) months for IPOs backed by old venture capitalists. Similarly young venture capital firms sit on boards of directors for shorter periods of time. For these firms the average (median) is 25 (20) months versus 39 (28) months for established venture firms.

Table 16.1 also shows that unseasoned venture capital firms bring to market IPOs that are underpriced. The average (median) underpricing at the IPO date is 13.6 percent (6.7 percent) for IPOs brought to market by young venture capital firms compared to 7.3 percent (2.7 percent) for older venture capital firms. The average offering size is also significantly smaller for IPOs brought to market by young venture capital firms. Old venture capital firms tend to use high quality underwriters (the established venture capital firms may have access to more established underwriters through previous IPOs or other business dealings). As expected, on average, old venture capital firms have financed more companies that have gone public (6.0) than have unseasoned venture capital firms (1.0).

The summary statistics in table 16.1 show that venture capitalists receive a significantly smaller share of the equity in companies that go public when the lead venture capital firm is under six years old. The average (median) equity stake of all venture capital investors is 32.1 percent (28.7 percent) of the equity prior to the IPO when the lead venture capital firm is under six years old compared to 37.7 percent (37.1 percent) when the lead venture capital firm is older.

The market value of the lead venture capitalist's equity stake is also significantly lower for new venture capital organizations. IPO prospectuses indicate the number of shares sold in the IPO and the number of shares held after IPO by the lead venture capitalist. In calculating the market value of shares sold, the venture capitalist is assumed to receive the IPO offering price for all shares sold in the IPO. Shares held after IPO are valued at the first price listed on the Center for Research in Security Prices (CRSP) data tapes. The first price listed on CRSP is usually on the IPO date, but it is never more than several days from the listed IPO date. Table 16.1 shows that the average (median) market value of a young lead venture capital firm's equity stake is $9.5 ($4.3) million while the market value of an established lead venture capital firm's equity stake is $14.7 ($8.7) million. These summary statistics are consistent with the grandstanding hypothesis. Young venture capital firms bring companies public early and bear real costs through underpricing and low equity stakes, although the company going public also bears some of the cost.

An alternative explanation for the differences in firm age and board service is a selection bias created by classifying as young venture capital firms all firms that are under six years old. The age of the venture capital firm might be correlated with the age of the IPO company without a causal relationship. By definition, no young venture capital firm will have been on the board of the IPO company for more than 71 months. As a result companies brought to market by young venture capital firms will have shorter venture capitalist board representation, on average, though the IPO process was the same for young and old venture capital firms.

This potential selection bias is not important because the length of time that the typical investment is held from first funding to IPO is significantly less than 71 months. Chapter 8 shows that the average (median) time from first-round venture financing to IPO date for a sample of 127 venture-backed IPOs is 34 (31) months. While the date of initial funding is unknown for the sample, in virtually all cases of first-round financing the venture capital firm receives a seat on the board of directors.[3] Old venture capital firms are on the board for an average (median) of 39 (28) months, while new venture capital firms are on the board 25 (20) months.

To determine the extent of the selection bias, the second set of IPOs provided by Kemper Financial Services and Brinson Partners is used. (This sample, for the period August 1, 1983, to July 31, 1993, is also described in chapter 22.) The sample consists of nineteen venture capital firms in their first fund and forty-three venture capital firms in their second fund or later.

---

3. Gompers (1995) examines conversion features and covenants in fifty venture capital convertible preferred private placements. Every contract included provisions for board representation by the syndicate of venture capital investors.

Table 16.2
Comparison of the characteristics for initial public offerings backed by young and old venture capital firms

	First-fund venture capital firms	Second- or later-fund venture capital firms	p-Value test of no difference
Average age of venture-backed company at IPO date in months	31.6 [33.5]	53.5 [50.0]	0.001 [0.001]
Average duration of board representation for lead venture capital firm in months	25.8 [30.0]	40.2 [40.0]	0.005 [0.005]
Average time from IPO date to next follow-on fund in months	12.9 [6.0]	29.0 [24.0]	0.028 [0.001]
Average underpricing at the IPO date	0.185 [0.215]	0.078 [0.038]	0.004 [0.005]
Average offering size (1997$ mil)	37.2 [29.0]	36.9 [29.5]	0.949 [0.943]
Average Carter and Manaster underwriter rank	8.19 [8.00]	8.16 [9.00]	0.939 [0.329]
Average aftermarket standard deviation	0.036 [0.035]	0.031 [0.028]	0.884 [0.245]
Number of observations	19	43	

Note: Sample is the first IPO for each of 62 venture capital funds for two institutional investors from August 1, 1983, through July 31, 1993. Medians are in brackets. Significance tests in the third column are p-values of t-tests for difference in averages and p-values of two-sample Wilcoxon rank-sum tests for difference in medians in brackets.

Funds that had not performed an IPO prior to July 1993 are excluded. From the complete fund histories, the first IPO brought to market by each fund is identified. The characteristics of the first IPO for first-fund venture capital firms are compared to the first IPO of second- or later-fund venture capital firms. Because a successful venture fund may have only two or three IPOs, the first IPO is a strong signal of ability to take companies public. Comparing first IPOs for various funds eliminates any selection bias but sacrifices sample size.

Table 16.2 presents summary statistics for the 62 IPOs. The results support conclusions from the larger sample and are consistent with the grandstanding hypothesis. First IPOs for first-fund venture capital firms are significantly younger (32 vs. 54 months) and more underpriced (18.5 percent vs. 7.8 percent) than first IPOs for second- or later-fund venture capital firms. First-fund venture capital firms have also been on the board for a shorter period of time, and they can raise money significantly sooner following the IPO (13 vs. 29 months). Neither the offering size nor average underwriter rank differs significantly. Average after-market standard deviation, however, is higher for the first-fund sample. Selection biases do not appear to drive the results.

Regression Results

Regressions are performed on the following variables: (1) the size of the lead venture capitalist's next fund, (2) the time from IPO to the lead venture capitalist's next fund, (3) length of board service, (4) the age of the offering company at IPO, (5) underpricing, and (6) the equity stake of all venture capitalists prior to IPO.

Mundlak (1961, 1978) demonstrates that if industry effects are present, fixed-effects regression models are appropriate. We therefore employ industry dummy variables to control for these effects:

$$Y_{i,j} = \beta' X_{i,j} + \alpha_i + \varepsilon_{i,j}. \tag{1}$$

If firm j in industry i goes public, the dependent variable $Y_{i,j}$ (e.g., underpricing, age at IPO, or time to next fund) is a function of the independent variables $X_{i,j}$ (e.g., offering size, IPO market liquidity, or underwriter rank.) and α_i, a term that represents industry effects. The sample is divided into nineteen industries based on SIC codes, with dummy variables for each industry to control for unmeasured industry effects.

Size of Next Fund and Time to Next Fund

Table 16.3 presents the results from regressions for the size of the lead venture capitalist's next fund and the length of time from the IPO to the firm's next fund. The dependent variable in the first set of regressions is the logarithm of the amount of capital raised in the lead venture capitalist's next fund in constant dollars. In accord with the grandstanding hypothesis, the amount of capital a venture firm can raise is positively related to the number of companies the firm has taken public. Capital raising should likewise be sensitive to IPOs for young venture capital firms.

In the first regression the table shows that the number of companies that the lead venture capitalist has taken public is positively related to the amount of capital raised. The coefficient of 0.039 means that each additional IPO translates into roughly $8 million more capital committed to the firm's next fund. Underwriter rank for the most recent IPO is also positively related to the amount of capital raised. High-quality underwriters tend to take large, promising companies public. If underwriter rank is related to the

Table 16.3
Regressions for the size of the lead venture capitalist's next fund and the time from IPO until the firm raises its next fund

Independent variables	Dependent variable							
	Logarithm of size of next fund				Years until venture firm raises next fund			
Venture firm less than six years old	0.036 [0.17]	−1.925 [−2.38]			−0.70 [−3.12]	−0.44 [−1.76]		
Logarithm of venture firm age			0.092 [0.76]	0.836 [1.83]			0.310 [2.43]	0.286 [1.76]
Number of IPOs in previous four months	0.0013 [0.89]	0.0018 [1.04]	0.0014 [0.80]	0.0013 [0.69]	−0.0014 [−0.67]	−0.0013 [−0.28]	−0.0029 [−1.26]	−0.0021 [−0.85]
Venture capital under management						0.0018 [2.51]		0.004 [0.51]
Number of IPOs for lead venture firm	0.039 [2.70]	0.037 [2.61]	0.033 [2.20]	0.036 [1.74]				
Number of IPOs for lead venture firm if under six years old		0.189 [1.86]						
Number of IPOs for lead venture firm multiplied by log of venture firm age				−0.015 [−0.41]				
Underwriter rank	0.0985 [1.93]	0.0171 [0.27]	0.896 [1.79]	0.295 [2.20]				
Underwriter rank if lead venture firm is under six years old		0.2297 [2.23]						
Underwriter rank times log of venture firm age				−0.106 [−1.68]				
First-day return (underpricing)	−0.216 [−0.46]	−0.225 [−0.48]	−0.175 [−0.37]	−0.242 [−0.51]				
Constant	3.307 [7.18]	3.914 [7.27]	3.219 [7.15]	1.809 [1.91]	2.14 [9.58]	1.77 [6.93]	1.34 [3.83]	1.91 [6.98]

R^2	0.121	0.169	0.125	0.147	0.083	0.081	0.042	0.036
p-Value of F-test	0.011	0.004	0.009	0.012	0.007	0.011	0.032	0.136
Number of observations	119	119	119	119	181	171	164	154

Note: The sample is 433 venture-backed IPOs from 1978–1987. The dependent variables are the time from IPO until the lead venture capital organization raises its next fund (in years) and the logarithm of the size of that next fund (in millions of 1992 dollars). Independent variables include a dummy variable that equals one if the lead venture organization is less than six years old, the logarithm of the venture capital firm's age in months, the cumulative number of IPOs (both venture and non-venture backed) in the previous four months, the capital under management at the lead venture capital firm, the number of previous IPOs in which the lead venture capital firm was an investor, the Carter and Manaster (1990) underwriter rank, and the first-day return on the IPO. [t-statistics are in brackets.]

quality of the IPO company, then the relation between rank and capital raised will be positive. Taking high-quality firms public is a strong signal of ability. Industry reports and fund offering memoranda touting recent IPO successes clearly indicate that venture capitalists understand this relation.

The second regression includes interaction terms between the young venture capital firm dummy variable, the number of IPOs brought to market, and underwriter rank. The significantly positive coefficients on both interaction terms show that the amount of capital raised by young venture capital firms is more sensitive to both the number of IPOs they have financed and the underwriter rank of the most recent IPO, consistent with the predictions of the grandstanding hypothesis. Because older venture capital firms have established reputations, beliefs about their ability are not sensitive to an additional IPO or the quality of the underwriter for that IPO. New venture capital firms have considerably more to gain (in reputation and fund-raising ability) by doing an IPO. The limited lifetime of venture funds and the strong relation between recent IPO performance and fund-raising provide powerful incentives for young venture capital firms to bring companies to market earlier than older venture firms. The third and fourth regressions in table 16.3 show that the results are robust to using the logarithm of age specification for venture capital firm reputation.

The second set of regressions in table 16.3 indicates that new venture capital firms raise money for follow-on funds significantly sooner after the date of the IPO (between five and nine months sooner) despite the older venture capital firms having started more funds during the time period. The results also indicate that larger venture capital firms wait longer to raise a new fund. Firms with more capital have less incentive to grandstand because they have more money in reserve for future investment opportunities. Although five to nine months may not seem like a large difference between young and established venture firms, the evidence is consistent with the existence of reputational concerns and the predictions of the grandstanding hypothesis. Reputation affects fund-raising in the venture capital market.

Length of Board Service and Age at IPO

The regressions in table 16.3 indicate that the sensitivity of fund-raising to recent IPO performance is stronger for young venture capital firms than it is for older ones. This relation provides an incentive for young firms to rush companies to the IPO market. Table 16.4 examines the effects of venture capital firm reputation on two measures of IPO timing. The first is the length of time that the lead venture capital firm has served on the board of

Table 16.4
Regressions for the length of board service and age of issuing company at IPO

Independent variables	Dependent variable							
	Full sample of 433 IPOs				Sample of first IPOs for 62 funds			
	Duration of board service (months)		Age of IPO firm (months)		Duration of board service (months)		Age of IPO firm (months)	
Venture firm less than six years old	−14.35 [−3.26]		−26.83 [−3.91]		−13.00 [−2.58]		−20.76 [−3.25]	
First-fund venture firms		−12.59 [−2.95]		−28.81 [−3.43]		−14.94 [−2.55]		−19.40 [−2.85]
Number of IPOs in previous four months	0.037 [0.95]	0.091 [2.23]	−0.030 [−0.48]	0.106 [1.55]	−0.082 [−1.47]	−0.045 [−0.71]	−0.037 [−0.53]	−0.018 [−0.24]
Logarithm of IPO offering size	−4.630 [−1.87]	−0.781 [−0.28]	−15.20 [−3.81]	−16.92 [−3.38]	2.718 [0.64]	4.736 [1.04]	6.475 [1.22]	6.674 [1.25]
Underwriter rank		1.059 [0.75]		2.816 [1.15]		2.466 [1.10]		3.312 [1.25]
Equity stake of all venture firms prior to IPO	0.265 [2.71]		0.035 [0.22]					
Venture capital under management		−0.020 [−1.41]		−0.037 [−1.41]		−0.004 [−0.19]		0.075 [3.31]
Constant	109.13 [2.66]	24.46 [0.57]	326.65 [4.90]	319.15 [4.15]	0.77 [0.01]	−55.65 [−0.68]	−54.84 [−0.61]	−96.81 [1.01]
R^2	0.171	0.232	0.207	0.235	0.168	0.192	0.189	0.351
p-Value of F-test	0.004	0.004	0.000	0.000	0.018	0.078	0.007	0.001
Number of observations	245	191	332	191	58	51	61	53

Note: The first sample is 433 venture-backed IPOs from 1978–1987. The second sample consists of the first IPOs for 62 venture capital funds from two institutional investors. The dependent variables are the length of time that the lead venture capitalist has been on the IPO company's board of directors (in months) at the time of IPO and the age of the offering company at the time of IPO (in months). Independent variables include a dummy variable that equals one if the lead venture firm is less than six years old, a dummy variable that equals one if the lead venture capital organization has only raised one venture capital fund at the time of the IPO, the cumulative number of IPOs (both venture backed and non-venture backed) in the previous four months, the logarithm of IPO offering size, the Carter and Manaster (1990) underwriter rank, the percentage of the IPO company's equity held by all venture investors immediately prior to IPO, and the capital under management at the lead venture capital firm. Regressions for the sample of 433 IPOs include industry dummy variables to control for any fixed effects. Coefficients on industry dummies are not reported. [t-statistics are in brackets.]

directors. In general, young venture capital firms that take companies public earlier will have served on the board of directors for a shorter length of time than the older venture firms. The second measure of early IPOs is age of the issuing company. The first two regressions indicate that young venture capital firms (those under six years old) have served on the board of directors between 12 and 14 months less than established venture capital firms. Similarly companies backed by a new venture capital firm are between 26 and 28 months younger than companies backed by more established venture capital firms. These results are consistent with the grandstanding hypothesis that companies backed by young venture capital firms go public sooner, controlling for other factors.

Table 16.4 also presents results from the sample of first IPOs for the sixty-two funds to examine potential selection biases. The results show that first-fund venture capitalists have been on the board of their first IPO 13 to 14 months less than second- or later-fund venture capitalists. The first company brought public by a new fund is 19 to 20 months younger on average than the first IPO of a second- or later-fund venture firm. These results are nearly identical to the results for the entire sample, indicating that selection bias is not a problem.

The differences in board service (14 months) and IPO firm age (28 months) are important. They represent a 30 percent difference in firm age and board service between the new venture capital firm sample and the old venture capital firm sample. Moreover these companies are very young, and 14 to 28 months is a substantial fraction of their existence. Because young companies often grow by 50 to 100 percent per annum in their first years of operation, the small differences in board service and IPO company age mean that new venture-backed companies have only half the level of sales and earnings of old venture-backed companies when they go public. This is a significant reduction in firm size. (As seen below, in economic terms the effect of board service on the size and market value of equity stakes is quite large.)

Underpricing

Table 16.5 presents underpricing regressions. Muscarella and Vetsuypens (1989) and Ritter (1987) view underpricing as a cost that companies bear when they go public because of the uncertainty surrounding the true value of the offering. Younger companies have more uncertainty and hence greater underpricing. Two specifications are used to control for the reputation of the venture capital firm. In all regressions, IPOs backed by young

Table 16.5
Regressions for underpricing of the IPO

Independent variables	Dependent variable					
	First-day return—underpricing					
Venture firm less than six years old	0.076 [3.82]	0.088 [3.49]	0.031 [0.98]			
Logarithm of venture firm age				−0.040 [−3.89]	−0.052 [−4.07]	−0.020 [−1.18]
Number of IPOs in previous four months	−0.001 [−4.91]	−0.001 [−4.90]	−0.001 [−3.70]	−0.001 [−4.82]	−0.001 [−4.78]	−0.001 [−3.70]
Logarithm of IPO offering size	0.037 [3.26]	0.062 [4.49]	0.072 [4.05]	0.036 [3.19]	0.061 [4.50]	0.071 [4.03]
Standard deviation of stock return	1.77 [3.28]	2.22 [3.35]	1.40 [1.95]	1.75 [3.24]	2.15 [3.29]	1.37 [1.94]
Logarithm of IPO company age		0.002 [0.15]	−0.008 [−0.49]		0.002 [0.17]	−0.007 [−0.45]
Logarithm of length of board service		−0.015 [−1.64]	−0.004 [−1.23]		−0.018 [−1.69]	−0.005 [−1.31]
Underwriter rank			−0.022 [−2.50]			−0.22 [−2.51]
Venture capital under management			−0.0001 [−1.68]			0.0001 [1.94]
Constant	−0.548 [−2.89]	−0.910 [−3.66]	−0.861 [−2.97]	−0.424 [−2.29]	−0.744 [−3.15]	−0.767 [−2.80]
R^2	0.248	0.339	0.363	0.249	0.352	0.365
p-Value of F-test	0.000	0.000	0.000	0.000	0.000	0.000
Number of observations	337	241	190	337	241	190

Note: The sample is 433 venture-backed IPOs from 1978–1987. The dependent variable is underpricing of the IPO (i.e., the first-day return on the IPO firm). Independent variables include a dummy variable that equals one if the venture organization is less than six years old, the logarithm of the lead venture capital firm's age in months, the cumulative number of IPOs (both venture backed and non-venture backed) in the previous four months, the logarithm of IPO offering size, the standard deviation of the stock returns from day 2 to day 20 after the IPO, the natural logarithm of the IPO company's age in months, the logarithm of the number of months that the lead venture capitalist has been on the company's board of directors, the Carter and Manaster (1990) underwriter rank, and the capital under management at the lead venture capital firm. All regressions include industry dummy variables to control for any fixed effects. Coefficients on industry dummies are not reported. [t-statistics are in brackets.]

venture capital firms are associated with greater underpricing (whether new venture capital firms are defined as firms less than six years old or using the logarithm of venture firm age). When the logarithm of the length of board service and the age of the offering company at IPO are included, the size and significance of the reputation coefficients show little change. Of the two variables that represent early IPOs, length of board service has the larger impact on underpricing, although it is only marginally significant. When underwriter rank is included in the regressions (third and sixth columns), the size and significance of the coefficients on the reputation variables are greatly reduced. Although companies brought to market by established venture firms are higher priced, the difference is largely due to higher underwriter reputation. The factors that contribute to the better pricing are greater IPO market liquidity, smaller offering size, and less uncertainty.

Venture Capitalists' Equity Stakes

Table 16.6 reports results for regressions by examining a direct measure of the cost of grandstanding: the fraction of the company's equity held by all venture capitalists prior to the IPO. The percent of equity held by venture capital investors should be lower where young venture firms incur costs by rushing companies to the IPO market.

The regressions show that young venture capital firms (using either firms that are under six years old or the logarithm of age to control for reputation) receive a significantly smaller fraction of the company's equity. The offering size has little impact on the venture capitalists' equity stake. The most important factor in the percentage of equity held prior to the IPO is the length of board service for the lead venture capital firm. Interestingly, when length of board service is included, the size and significance of the venture capital reputation variables are reduced, indicating that shorter relationships (and hence earlier IPOs) are the cause of reduced equity stakes as predicted by the grandstanding hypothesis. The longer the venture capital firm has been on the board of directors, the larger is its equity stake. The results in table 16.6 indicate that the 12 to 14 month shorter board service by young lead venture capital firms estimated in table 16.4 accounts for more than half of the smaller equity stake of young venture firms (nearly 3 percent of the 4.7 percent difference).

To test whether early IPOs have differential costs on young and old venture firms, interaction terms between reputation measures and IPO maturity are included in the regressions of tables 16.5 and 16.6, but these interaction terms are insignificant.

Table 16.6
Regressions for the percentage equity held by all venture capital firms prior to IPO

Independent variables	Percentage of equity held by all venture firms prior to IPO			
	Dependent variable			
Venture firm less than six years old	−4.73 [−2.27]	−2.83 [−0.70]		
Logarithm of venture firm age			0.973 [1.70]	0.536 [0.24]
Number of IPOs in previous four months	0.010 [0.44]	0.008 [0.25]	0.009 [0.40]	0.006 [0.019]
Logarithm of IPO offering size	2.918 [1.96]	0.144 [0.06]	3.266 [2.14]	0.256 [0.12]
Logarithm of IPO company age		−2.65 [−1.25]		−2.39 [−1.13]
Logarithm of length of board service		8.14 [4.04]		8.27 [4.12]
Underwriter rank		0.784 [0.71]		0.797 [0.73]
Venture capital under management		0.010 [0.85]		0.011 [0.92]
Constant	−7.93 [−0.31]	16.65 [0.45]	−17.08 [0.68]	11.44 [0.32]
R^2	0.125	0.270	0.118	0.268
p-Vaiue of F-test	0.005	0.003	0.005	0.002
Number of observations	338	190	338	190

Note: The sample is 433 venture-backed IPOs from 1978–1987. The dependent variable is the percentage of the offering company's equity held by all venture capital suppliers prior to the IPO (as listed in the IPO prospectus). Independent variables include a dummy variable that equals one if the lead venture organization is less than six years old, the logarithm of the venture capital firm's age in months, the cumulative number of IPOs (both venture backed and non-venture backed) in the previous four months, the logarithm of IPO offering size, the natural logarithm of IPO company age in months, the logarithm of the number of months that the lead venture capitalist has been on the IPO company's board of directors, the Carter and Manaster (1990) underwriter rank, and the capital under management at the lead venture capital firm. All regressions include industry dummy variables to control for any fixed effects. Coefficients on industry dummies are not reported. [t-statistics are in brackets.]

Alternative Explanations

Some writers have argued that venture-backed firms go public earlier than nonventure firms because venture capitalists certify the quality of offerings (see Barry et al. 1990; Megginson and Weiss 1991). Venture capitalists, in this view, repeatedly bring companies to the IPO market and can credibly commit not to offer overpriced shares. These arguments are similar to findings about the correlation of reputation of underwriters and underpricing of public offerings (Carter and Manaster 1990). Certification by venture capitalists is potentially consistent with grandstanding. However, Megginson and Weiss (1991) do not directly test for differences between types of venture capitalists. We believe that the grandstanding hypothesis has important implications for the IPO timing of young and old venture capital firms. Venture capital certification can lower underwriting costs and underpricing on average, but young venture capital firms will still have incentives to bring IPOs to market earlier than established venture capital firms to establish a track record and raise new capital.

Another explanation of earlier venture-backed IPOs is that investors recycle money within asset classes. Venture capitalists can bring companies public to provide liquidity for previous investments. If investors reinvest the profits from previous venture capital investments into new venture capital funds, the venture capital firm will receive capital sooner and return cash to investors.

The grandstanding hypothesis, however, considers the incentive that young venture capital firms have to perform early IPOs. The certification hypothesis predicts that older venture capital firms will be associated with IPOs that are earlier or at least not later than those of new venture firms. If certification affects the cost but not the timing of IPOs, then there should be no difference between the two groups. The recycling hypothesis also predicts no difference in IPO timing between old and young venture capital firms. Clearly, the results above support the existence of grandstanding and are evidence that young venture firms take their companies public earlier.

Grandstanding also predicts that young venture capital firms will incur the costs of early IPOs because their performance is more critical to fundraising than that of an older firm. Neither the certification nor the recycling hypothesis predicts that the length of board service at IPO explains the differences in underpricing and equity stakes between young and old venture firms. The results confirm that a portion of the underpricing and equity stake differences is due to length of board service, and thus the predictions of the grandstanding hypothesis.

Conclusions

Reputational concerns affect the IPO timing decisions of young venture capital fund managers. Young venture capital firms raise money for a new fund sooner after an IPO, and the size of a young firm's next fund is dependent on the number of IPOs it has financed previously. Companies backed by new venture capital firms are younger at IPO than those backed by established venture capital firms, and the young venture capitalists have been on their boards for a shorter time. They bear the costs of early IPOs by receiving smaller equity stakes. These differences are consistent with the predictions of grandstanding.

Signaling appears to cause real wealth losses. Limited partners bear a large fraction of the costs from early IPOs. More than 400 new venture capital firms entered the industry after 1978. The tremendous entry of new venture capital firms and the incentives to grandstand potentially explain some of the declining returns on venture capital in the 1980s.

The fixed fee compensation based on the size of the fund (2 to 3 percent of assets under management per annum), plus the 20 percent of the fund's profits from investing, provide the venture capitalist with an incentive to grow the firm's capital under management by starting large follow-on funds. Chapter 5 shows that the present value of the annual fee is typically as large as the present value of the profits. Annual fixed fees are four to six times larger than the fees received by public market money managers documented by Lakonishok, Shleifer, and Vishny (1992). The desire to increase the size of the funds in turn increases the incentive to grandstand. Reduced fixed fees and increased profit sharing in large funds might better align the incentives of venture capitalists with the goals of investors.

Future research should examine the effects of venture capital on the long-run prospects of entrepreneurial projects and its relation to underpricing and investment characteristics. Entrepreneurs have little information on the IPO market, and the venture capitalist's role in that process, in particular. While space does not permit us to address the reasons entrepreneurs seek financing from young venture capital firms who then rush them to the IPO market, the issue can be examined by attention to the following: the venture capitalist and entrepreneur relationship, the decision to seek venture financing, the factors in deciding to go public, and the adverse effects of grandstanding on the life cycle and performance of companies such as by a comparison of venture capital financing on pre- and post-IPO sales, earnings, and asset growth rates. Mikkelson, Partch, and Shah (1997) examine accounting performance in a sample of venture-backed and nonventure IPOs and find no long-run differences, but costs of early IPOs could exist. Assessing these other costs would be an important addition not only to the literature on venture capital investments but also to the knowledge about the decision to go public.

17 Do Investment Bank-Affiliated Venture Capitalists Exhibit Conflict of Interest?

The costs and benefits of universal banking have been debated for over seventy years. The desirability of altering the Glass-Steagall Act—the landmark 1933 law that, among other things, restricted underwriting by commercial banks—has attracted increasing attention. The wave of mergers in the financial sector in the past decade has intensified the scrutiny of these issues.

In this chapter we examine the potential conflicts of interest in venture capital settings analogous to universal banks. We first review the distinct contributions to the literature by financial economists on this question. Early work has focused on banks during the pre–Glass-Steagall era. Kroszner and Rajan (1994) and Puri (1994) find that securities underwritten by affiliates of commercial banks did not perform worse than similar offerings underwritten by investment houses and may have actually outperformed the investment bank offerings. Kroszner and Rajan (1994) find that universal banks of the 1920s may have chosen to address potential conflicts of interests by underwriting less information-sensitive issues. Puri (1996) examines similar data and argues that the public is willing to pay a premium for issues underwritten by universal banks; that is, banks, by their greater access to information, are able to more effectively certify the quality of the new issues. Kroszner and Rajan (1997) subsequently find that the organizational structure of the underwriting activity at a bank affects the market's perception of the offering.

We provide an alternative test that partially addresses the hurdles faced by these studies of pre–Glass-Steagall banks. We use venture capital-backed initial public offerings (IPOs) to investigate the importance of conflicts of interest in the issuance of public securities. Investment banks often have venture capital subsidiaries that invest in private firms. If the investment banker underwrites an offering for a firm in which it is already a venture investor, potential conflicts of interest may result. These conflicts are analogous to the conflicts of interest that might affect a bank that underwrites the security of a firm in which it holds a debt obligation.

The availability of stock price information allows us to calculate actual returns for the issuing firms. Similarly the detailed financial disclosure available for our sample allows us to determine the precise financial relationship between the underwriter and the issuer. As a result, unlike historical studies, we can examine more directly the consequences of potential conflicts.

We seek to determine (1) whether underwriters that hold an equity stake in issuing firms are able to take advantage of unsuspecting buyers (Kroszner and Rajan's 1994 so-called naïve investor hypothesis) or (2) whether the market correctly anticipates the conflict of interest (Kroszner and Rajan's 1994 so-called rational discounting hypothesis). We observe how venture-backed IPOs perform after issuance and how this performance is related to the potential conflicts arising from the relationship between the underwriter and the venture investors. We find that IPOs in which underwriters hold prior venture investments perform no worse, and some even better, than offerings in which no underwriter has a venture stake. We also find that when a potential conflict of interest exists, the reputation of the underwriting bank seems to mitigate some of the negative impact. The evidence is consistent with predictions of rational discounting.

We also examine the market's reaction at the time of the offering to determine whether the market anticipates any conflict of interest. The market does appear to account for some potential conflict of interest at the time of the offering. Issues underwritten by investment banks that are also venture investors are sold at a greater discount ("underpriced").

We also find evidence that venture capital subsidiaries of investment banks are sensitive to potential conflicts when they make investment decisions. IPOs by firms in which underwriters are also venture investors appear to be more common for firms in which asymmetric information is less of a problem. The companies with such investments have larger market capitalizations, employ higher quality underwriters, and have greater venture shareholdings. All of these may proxy for high-quality firms with fewer potential conflicts of interest.

The results of the analysis call into question the restrictions on underwriting by commercial banks instituted by the Glass-Steagall Act of 1933. In a structure that is in many ways analogous to universal banking, we find that the market correctly anticipates conflicts and that underwriters react to them.

In addition to pre–Glass-Steagall banking, this chapter also relates to the literature on underwriter reputation and long-run performance (Ritter 1991;

Nanda, Yi, and Yun 1995; Carter, Dark, and Singh 1998), underwriter reputation and underpricing (Carter and Manaster 1990), and venture capital reputation and underpricing (Barry et al. 1990; Megginson and Weiss 1991). None of these studies, however, consider the potential conflicts of interest that can arise because of a venture capital-investment banker affiliation.

The Universal Banking Debate

Roe (1990) and Kroszner (1996) document the populist sentiment against financial capitalism that developed in the United States in the late nineteenth and early twentieth century. The stock market crash of 1929 ended the post–World War I euphoria for investing and fanned the public sentiment against financial institutions. Most of the criticism centered on the role that banks played in the collapse of the stock market. It was argued that banks had an incentive to take advantage of investors by issuing securities in companies with outstanding loan balances at times when the firms' future prospects were not as positive as the public believed. Issuing overpriced securities allowed the firms to liquidate the outstanding balances owed to the banks.

The public outcry led to legislation in the 1930s that was meant to curb bank underwriting activities (Roe 1990). The Securities Acts of 1933 and 1934 required greater disclosure of information by firms. The Glass-Steagall Act of 1933 had myriad effects on the banking sector in the United States. Most important for our argument in this chapter, Section 20 of the Act barred commercial banks that were members of the Federal Reserve System and their affiliates from holding, trading, or underwriting corporate securities. (The act also created the deposit insurance system and regulated the rates that banks could pay on deposits.)

In the 1990s the debate about whether the United States should remove the restrictions on commercial banks imposed by the Glass-Steagall Act intensified. Advocates of repeal pointed to the efficiency of universal banking. The main argument was that universal banking could provide improved information gathering and monitoring, conflict resolution among claimants on the firm, diversification benefits, and more effective signaling (Calomiris and Ramirez 1996).

The problem with universal banking, however, was how to prevent conflicts of interest. Through monitoring and advising a firm, the universal bank could learn that the firm's securities are overpriced relative to their true value. Because of their ownership interest in the firm, they will have a strong incentive to take advantage of this information and even be tempted to sell the securities to the public. The banker is therefore subject to an adverse selection problem, as is detailed by Myers and Majluf (1984). It is more likely that a firm is overvalued when the bank chooses to issue securities that are of the same or a lower priority than its claim. Rajan (1992) develops a model in which banks are affected by both the good and bad aspects of being informed: they increase efficiency through the generation of information but have an incentive to take advantage of new investors.

Venture Capital as a Testing Ground for Universal Banking

Challenges to the Previous Research

While in the introduction we argued that the research on security underwriting by universal banks prior to Glass-Steagall does not show adverse effects of conflicts of interest, several factors hamper extrapolation of these results to the desirability of repealing the Glass-Steagall Act.

First, studies using data from the 1920s cannot discern if banks that issued securities through bank affiliates also had lending relationships with the issuing firms. Kroszner and Rajan (1994) do not know whether a firm had any bank loans and Puri (1994) can only determine whether a firm issuing securities had an outstanding loan agreement with *some* bank at the time of the offering. Many securities law reforms have sought to improve the information flow from companies to investors. A series of legislative initiatives and U.S. Securities and Exchange Commission (SEC) regulations required the release of substantial amounts of information that were often not available in the 1920s. Second, long-run returns to these securities are difficult or impossible to measure since prices of bonds in the 1920s and 1930s are hard to find on a systematic basis. Previous studies have only been able to look at default rates.

Last, the sample period for previous studies is short, usually limited to the latter half of the 1920s. Two factors may hamper this analysis. The first is cross-sectional correlation. A short sample period might bias the significance of the results if certain types of issues are clustered in time. Second, the Great Depression of the 1930s is a potential confounding factor.

Our sample has several advantages. First, we are able to precisely characterize the relationship between an underwriter and a company issuing equity in our sample. This characterization is both qualitative (is there a relationship?) and quantitative (how much of the firm does the underwriter own?). Second, we can observe not only delistings, but also risk-adjusted long-run and short-run returns. Finally, our twenty-year sample period allows us to overcome the potential clustering problems present in earlier work.

Venture Capital as a Testing Ground

The venture capital industry offers a testing ground for the importance of conflict of interest in the issuance of public securities. Most venture funds are run by independent firms that have no affiliation with another institution or organization. Others, however, have relationships with financial institutions or corporations. For the purpose of our study, the venture capital industry can be divided into those venture capital firms that are independent and those that are either captive subsidiaries of or are affiliated with an investment bank. This classification allows us to determine whether the market treats affiliated offerings differently from unaffiliated offerings.

The investment banks with venture capital affiliates are analogous to universal banks in many respects. First, an investment bank that is underwriting a security for a company in which it holds a venture capital investment will have substantial private information on the company: venture capitalists sit on boards and advise managers. If the investment bank has private information about the firm, it may attempt to time security market issues that increase the value of its existing investment. If it is selling a large fraction of their stake at the time of the IPO, the venture group will receive cash for its shares at a very attractive price. Chapter 19 notes that even if they do not sell any equity, the venture capitalists are typically free to liquidate their stakes within six months of the IPO. Furthermore they suffer less dilution of their equity holdings when the IPO is priced at a premium. The investment banks that have venture capital subsidiaries suffer from potential conflicts of interest similar to those associated with universal banks.

Lerner (1992) illustrates this potential conflict through his discussion of the IPO of the biotechnology firm Regeneron Pharmaceuticals. ML Venture Partners II, an affiliate of the lead underwriter of the offering (Merrill Lynch), was the lead venture capital investor, holding 23.8 percent of the firm at the time of offering. On the evening prior to the IPO, Merrill Lynch increased the offer price and the number of shares that it was selling. The price of Regeneron fell from an offer price of $22 to $14.75 in its first ten days of trading. Many industry analysts and the shareholder lawsuits that followed pointed to the perceived conflict of interest as the major reason for the price decline.

Hypotheses

Investment banks face conflicting pressures in valuing IPOs. On the one hand, an investment bank acts as an agent for the firm issuing securities in an initial public offering. As an agent, the investment bank has an incentive to declare a high price and raise as much money for the company for as little equity as possible. In addition its fee is based on the size of the offering. On the other hand, the investment bank is concerned about losing its ability to place shares in future offerings if it develops a reputation for pricing offerings too high. The investment bank also has long-term clients on the purchasing side—for example, large mutual and pension funds—that provide substantial amounts of business for the bank. The investment bank does not want these clients to be hurt by offering the issue at too high of a price. These concerns will limit how high the investment banker will set the price of any particular offering. In other words, the investment bank maximizes the offering price subject to the possibility that selling overpriced shares will tarnish its reputation. When an investment bank is also an investor in the firm, the ability to directly gain by selling overpriced shares (either at the time of the offering or shortly thereafter) may provide an additional incentive to sell equity at a higher price.

What happens both at the time of issuance and in the long run depends on the market conditions that prevail. Kroszner and Rajan (1994) propose two hypotheses concerning conflicts of interest and market performance. In the naïve investor hypothesis, investors do not take these conflicts into account when assessing offerings (nor do they measure past performance). Consequently an investment bank has an incentive to charge a high price when it holds an equity stake. The issues taken public by an investment bank that has invested in the company should perform significantly worse in the long run. The poor performance should be manifested in lower stock returns and higher liquidation rates.

Under the second hypothesis, rational discounting, the market correctly anticipates that underwriters who hold an investment interest will be subject to potential conflicts of interest. This condition may lead underwriters with venture capital subsidiaries to only bring the least information-sensitive portfolio firms to market. The market may choose not to purchase issues that are difficult to evaluate if there is a conflict. Underwriters that are also venture investors would therefore only bring less speculative issues to market.

If the market correctly anticipates the conflict of interest, then there should be no difference in long-run performance between issues brought public by an independent underwriter and those brought public by an investment bank that holds an investment in the company. If the investment bank with venture investments only underwrites their best firms, yet the market still perceives some conflict, then issues underwritten by an investment bank with an investment in the firm may actually perform better. The market may be overly cautious about the firm's quality. While we would not expect this "overperformance" to continue in equilibrium, it may occur as the market learns that underwriters are aware of and addressing the potential conflict.

The two hypotheses also have different predictions about the first-day return, namely underpricing. In many models of the IPO process, offerings are sold at a discount to initial investors in equilibrium. The extent of this underpricing is dependent on the severity of the potential adverse selection problem (Rock 1986). Investors are concerned that they will be allocated more shares of poor offerings than shares of good offerings if others know things about the firm that they do not. In the naïve investor hypothesis, investors do not differentiate between issues by independent investment banks and those that have a conflict. Because there is no perceived increase in adverse selection, underpricing will be the same. In the rational discounting hypothesis the presence of a conflict of implies that the adverse selection problems are intensified. Thus issues through investment banks that are investors should be more underpriced.

The Construction of the IPO Sample

We limit the sample of venture-backed IPOs to the offerings completed between December 1972 and December 1992.[1] We identify potential venture-backed IPOs using three sources. The first is the listings of venture-backed IPOs published in Venture Economics' *Venture Capital Journal*. The second is listings of the securities distributions by venture funds in which two institutional investors and three investment advisors had invested. Both of these listings are discussed in chapter 22. The final source used to identify IPOs for the sample are over four hundred offering documents by venture capitalists in the files of Venture Economics.[2]

---

1. We do not go back any further because the Corporate Reports Department at Harvard Business School only began receiving microfiched prospectuses from Disclosure at the end of 1972 and few earlier IPOs are included on the CRSP tapes.

2. Not all firms identified in these sources are venture-backed IPOs. We consequently examine IPO prospectuses to determine if any venture capital organizations were investors in the firm and if any individuals affiliated with these organizations were on the board.

The sample includes all firms with a venture investor listed in the database or a director affiliated with a listed venture organization at the time that the director joined the board. For each director, we record the associated venture organization[3] and the dates of board service; for each investor, we code the venture organization, the particular venture fund investing in the firm, and the size of the stake before and after the offering. This process leads to the identification of 885 IPOs in which a venture capitalist served as a director or a venture capital fund was a blockholder.

We gather the information about each IPO from SDC's Corporate New Issues database and SEC filings. From SDC we also obtain the return of the firm's stock price on the first day of trading. Where this item is missing or where there is a unit offering (which may lead to confusion about the return), we check the *Daily Stock Price Record* (Standard and Poor's, 1993 and earlier). Subsequent returns for the five years after the offering or through the end of 1995 are obtained from the Center for Research in Securities Prices (CRSP) databases. We then rank the reputation of the IPO's managing underwriter. For offerings prior to 1985 we use the scale in Carter and Manaster (1990), as described in chapter 15. For offerings from 1985 and subsequent years, we use Carter, Dark, and Singh's (1998) updating of these rankings.[4]

Last we characterize the quality of the venture organizations involved in these IPOs. First, we compute the mean age of the venture organizations that were directors or investors. Older venture organizations are likely to be better on average than new firms because poorly performing organizations will be unable to raise new funds. We determine the age of each venture organization at the time of the IPO using the Venture Economics funds database described above. For the mean age of the venture organi-

---

3. In some cases a venture capitalist will remain on a firm's board even if he switches to another venture capital organization. In these instances the individual is coded as representing the venture capital organization with which he was affiliated at the time that he joined the board.

4. If an investment bank is not listed in the preferred tabulation, but is listed in their tabulation from the other period, we use the available ranking. A number of investment banks active in underwriting venture-backed firms in the 1970s were merged or acquired during that decade, and consequently were not included in either ranking. The rankings of most of these can be deduced from Hayes (1971), which discusses the major groupings of investment banks. These three sources yield the underwriter ranking for 98 percent of the sample. We assigned an approximate ranking to the remaining investment banks after conversations with a number of Harvard Business School faculty who had undertaken field research into the financial services industry during the 1970s and 1980s. One potential concern is the endogeneity of underwriter ranking: we rank underwriters using "tombstones" printed contemporaneously with the IPOs we analyze. We are confident, however, that this has minimal effect on the results. Hayes examines the hierarchy in the underwriting business during the first seventy years of this century and found a great deal of persistence in relative rankings.

zations with board representation, we compute a simple average. We do not weight organizations with multiple board seats more heavily than those with only one seat. We use a slightly different approach for venture investors. The average of venture investors' ages is weighted, with each organization's weight proportional to its stake in the firm.[5]

We finally examine whether any of the venture investors served as underwriters of the offering. We determine whether the venture organizations in the sample had affiliations with investment banks during the sample period by the various annual volumes of *Pratt's Guide*—which has a list of each venture organization's affiliations—as well as searches of news stories in the LEXIS/NEXIS database and unpublished records in the files of Venture Economics.[6] In all, we found 282 venture capital firms affiliated with investment banks, approximately 25 percent of the venture capital organizations active during the past 25 years. In 386 of the 885 IPOs, an investment bank-affiliated venture fund had invested in the company. In 127 of these, a lead or co-lead underwriter had made an earlier venture investment in the firm.

Empirical Results

Our empirical analysis has four components. First, we examine the offerings' characteristics. This is followed by an analysis of long-run performance after issuance. Both the long-run stock price performance and the probability that a firm is liquidated are examined. The third set of analyses focuses on underpricing of the IPO. Finally, we examine whether the potential for conflict of interest induces affiliated investment banks to underwrite less information-sensitive issues.

Summary Statistics

The characteristics of the venture capital-backed IPOs are presented in table 17.1. The table verifies prior evidence on venture-backed issues. As shown

---

5. If we cannot determine the age of a venture organization, we do not use it in these averages. In alternative specifications we proxied for reputation by using the mean reputation rank of the underwriters for previous IPOs in which the venture capitalists had been an investor and the value of equity held in prior IPOs. The results using alternative reputation measures are qualitatively similar.

6. One complication is introduced by the fact that in seven cases, investment banks made direct investments into the firm prior to the initial public offering, but not through a venture fund that they sponsored. We treat these direct investments by investment banks in firms as if they had been made by a venture fund affiliated with the investment bank.

Table 17.1
Summary statistics for venture capital-backed IPOs

	Mean	Median
Characteristics of offering		
Market value of equity (1992$ mil)	$160.7	$98.9
Offer price per share (1992$)	$14.67	$13.00
Underwriter rank	7.54	8.75
Percentage of firm owned by venture capitalists before IPO	33.7%	30.5%
Percentage of firm owned by venture capitalists after IPO	23.4%	21.1%
Percentage of their stake sold by venture capitalists in the IPO	5.9%	0%
Mean age of the venture organizations who were directors (years)	11.8	11.7
Mean age of the venture organizations who were investors (years)	11.8	11.7
Underpricing	9.3%	3.7%
Five-year buy-and-hold return	+61.5%	−11.3%
Five-year excess buy-and-hold return versus size and book-to-market portfolios	+25.2%	−34.8%
Characteristics of the investment banking relationship		
Number of IPOs in which any of the investment bankers was also a venture capital investor in the firm		127
Number of IPOs in which the book investment banker was also a venture capital investor in the firm		71
Number of IPOs in which all of the investment bankers were also venture capital investors in the firm		23

Note: The sample is 885 venture capital-backed IPOs from 1972 through 1992 for which a venture capitalist could be identified as a five percent equity holder in or a director of the company prior to the offering.

in chapter 20, venture-backed IPOs tended to be larger than other IPOs. The mean (median) market value of the firm at its first CRSP-listed closing price was $161 ($99) million in 1992 dollars, while the average offering price was $14.67 per share. This is nearly twice the size of comparable non-venture IPOs referenced in chapter 20.

Venture capital equity ownership was substantial at the time of the offering. Venture capitalists owned 33.7 percent of the equity prior to the offering. The venture capital investors sold little of their equity in the offering, on average 5.9 percent (with a median of 0 percent). The low percentage of equity sold by venture investors at the time of the offering might reflect the perceived adverse selection problem if venture capitalists were thought to be cashing out.

The measures of reputation differ very little whether they are calculated as the average of the directors or the weighted average of all venture capital investors in the firm. The typical venture capital firm serving as director or investor was nearly twelve years old at the time of the offering.

Underpricing and long-run performance both have skewed distributions. The average underpricing—the percentage change from the offering price to the closing price on the first day of trading—was +9.3 percent, while the median underpricing was +3.7 percent. These results are similar to that found in Barry et al. (1990) and Megginson and Weiss (1991). Five-year performance (both nominal and relative) was even more highly skewed. The average five-year nominal buy-and-hold return (measured from the first CRSP-recorded closing price) was +61.5 percent, while the median return was −11.3 percent.[7]

To measure relative performance, we calculate the five-year buy-and-hold excess return. This is the difference between the five-year buy-and-hold return of the issuing firm and the five-year buy-and-hold return of the portfolio of firms with the same size and book-to-market ratio. The use of a size and book-to-market benchmark is advocated by Barber, Lyon, and Tsai (1998). Barber et al. argue that using size and book-to-market adjustments minimizes the misspecification in the long horizon performance tests.[8] The average excess return was +25.2 percent and the median excess return was −34.8 percent. The mean excess return was positive, demonstrating that, as chapter 20 shows, the average venture-backed IPO outperforms the matched size and book-to-market benchmark. The skewness of the excess returns is apparent.

Finally, the sample of 885 IPOs displays considerable heterogeneity in the relationships between the underwriters and the venture investors. For 758 of the issues, the underwriters were totally unaffiliated with any of the venture capital investors. In 127 of the cases, at least one of the investment bankers was a venture investor in the firm, creating the possibility of a conflict of interest. For 71 of the 127 issues, the book underwriter—the investment bank responsible for tallying orders from institutional and individual investors and ultimately allocating the shares to the investors—was a venture investor. Because the book manager has the most control over the IPO, the possibility for a conflict of interest at the time of offering is increased. Finally, in 23 of the issues, all of the investment bankers held venture investments in the firm. This final case would be associated with the highest possibility of conflict of interest. This dispersion in investment banker/

---

7. Returns for firms that delist from CRSP prior to their fifth anniversary are truncated at the delisting date and include the delisting return (when available). Benchmark returns are also truncated at the delisting date.

8. The matching portfolios exclude all firms that have issued equity in IPOs or seasoned equity offerings within the past five years. For a detailed description of their construction, see chapter 20.

venture capitalist relationships gives us the ability to examine whether such conflicts affect valuations.

Table 17.2 tabulates the time series distribution of our sample. Several trends are noticeable. First, the number of venture-backed IPOs increased dramatically during the 1980s and 1990s. This increase parallels both the growth in the venture industry and their increasing activity in the public markets. Second, the average offering size (in 1992 dollars) steadily declined over the time period. This likely reflects an increasing ability to bring smaller issues public as the IPO market expanded.

The final four columns show that considerable variation in these measures. Average underpricing ranges from as low as −1.8 percent (an actual decline in prices at the time of offering) to +27.9 percent. Long-run returns show equally dramatic variation. We also show the number of issuing firms that were delisted for bankruptcy, liquidation, or violations of capital requirements within the first five years of offering. The use of liquidations as a measure of long-run performance is in the spirit of Kroszner and Rajan (1994) and Puri (1994). In the early part of the sample, no firms were liquidated within five years. During the late 1980s and early 1990s, a small portion of the issuing firms are delisted within five years of their IPO.

Long-Run Performance and Conflict of Interest

We next explore the relation between long-run performance and conflict of interest. Table 17.3 tabulates our two measures of long-run performance to determine whether conflict of interest affects performance. We divide IPOs into those that have a potential conflict because an underwriting investment bank also holds an equity stake and those that do not.

The investment banking relationship classifications show little or no evidence of an unanticipated conflict of interest. Offerings underwritten by investment banks that had the strongest potential for conflict of interest (those in which all the underwriters or the book manager were venture investors) actually performed better than other issues, not worse as the naïve investor hypothesis would predict.

In table 17.4, we investigate the long-run excess returns in multivariate regressions. The dependent variable is the five-year buy-and-hold excess return. Independent variables include dummy variables denoting the underwriters' relationship with the venture investors as well as the venture firm and underwriter reputation measures. We also include the natural logarithm

Table 17.2
Summary statistics by year of offering

Year	Number	Market value (1992$ mil)	Underpricing (%)	Five-year return (%)	Excess return (%)	Liquidations within five years
1972	1	178.4	na	2.0	−9.1	0
1973	11	227.6	6.2	45.6	−21.3	0
1974	3	275.5	−1.8	181.4	−113.8	0
1975	0	na	na	na	na	na
1976	8	299.6	1.7	259.2	17.1	0
1977	5	138.1	13.3	346.7	269.5	0
1978	8	231.6	21.7	604.0	390.1	0
1979	6	234.8	27.9	1.7	−120.7	0
1980	23	459.5	18.5	67.9	14.9	1
1981	49	146.6	16.3	16.3	−21.9	5
1982	23	261.5	9.3	43.9	−54.0	2
1983	109	263.1	10.8	−11.2	−26.4	6
1984	46	119.6	1.7	−0.8	−23.4	8
1985	45	113.1	3.7	14.1	5.5	6
1986	94	143.0	6.8	83.0	83.4	13
1987	76	127.8	6.3	23.0	18.3	7
1988	35	132.8	7.4	120.6	90.0	5
1989	37	118.2	10.0	148.0	117.9	2
1990	40	121.9	10.9	2.0	−54.4	1
1991	104	145.1	13.0	106.5	59.6	3
1992	151	117.0	11.2	72.5	44.3	9

Note: The sample is 885 venture capital-backed IPOs from 1972 through 1992 for which a venture capitalist could be identified as a five percent equity holder in or a director of the company prior to the offering. The market value of the firm is determined by the first CRSP-listed closing price and is expressed in constant 1992 dollars. Underpricing is the percentage return on the first day calculated from the offering price to the close of the first trading day. The five-year return is the buy-and-hold return calculated over five years or until delisting. The excess return is the five-year buy-and-hold return on the IPO firm minus the five-year buy-and-hold return on a matched size and book-to-market portfolio which excludes all firms that have issued equity in initial public offerings or seasoned equity offerings within the past five years. The number of liquidations within the first five years after issue is also tabulated.

Table 17.3

Summary statistics for five-year excess returns and liquidation fraction sorted by investment banking relationship

	Five-year excess return		Liquidation fraction (%)
	Mean (%)	Median (%)	
All underwriters are venture investors in the firm	112.6	−24.1	0.0
Not all underwriters are venture investors in the firm	23.1	−35.0	8.2
	[0.082]	[0.530]	[0.153]
Book underwriter is a venture investor in the firm	31.6	−33.4	2.8
Book underwriter is not a venture investor in the firm	24.7	−35.0	8.4
	[0.817]	[0.905]	[0.094]
Any underwriter is an investor in the firm	20.5	−50.0	6.3
No underwriter is an investor in the firm	25.9	−34.1	8.3
	[0.815]	[0.271]	[0.453]

Note: The sample is 885 venture capital-backed IPOs from 1972 through 1992 for which a venture capitalist could be identified as a five percent equity holder in or a director of the company prior to the offering. The excess five-year return is calculated as the five-year buy-and-hold return on the IPO firm minus the five-year buy-and-hold return on the matched size and book-to-market portfolio which excludes all firms that have issued equity in initial public offerings or seasoned equity offerings within the past five years. The fractions of firms liquidated in the first five years are also tabulated. {p-Values for t-tests for differences in means, Wilcoxon rank-sum tests for differences in medians, and Pearson chi-squared tests for differences in incidence rates are in brackets.}

of firm size (market value in constant 1992 dollars) and the natural logarithm of the firm's book-to-market ratio.[9] If size and book-to-market portfolios properly adjust for risk, these coefficients should be insignificant. We also include the percentage of the firm that is held by the venture capitalists prior to the IPO. If the quality of monitoring or certification is related to how much of the company is owned by the venture investors, higher percentages of equity should be related to better performance. The percentage of the venture investors' equity sold at the time of the IPO is also included. If venture investors try to take advantage of investors, the higher the fraction of their equity that they sell at the time of the IPO, the poorer the performance of the offering firm should be. Finally, we include the percent revision in the offering price between the initial filing and the IPO. By including the revision variable, we control for the possibility that these price revisions are related to underwriters systematically taking advantage of investors.

---

9. Following the convention of Fama and French (1992) and Barber, Lyon, and Tsai (1998), we exclude all firms with negative book values from the regression analysis. In unreported regressions we employ dummy variables for the year of the offering.

Table 17.4

Regression analyses of five-year excess returns

Independent variables	Dependent variable: Five-year excess return					
Natural logarithm of firm size (constant 1992$)	−0.200 [−1.94]	−0.200 [−1.94]	−0.197 [−1.91]	−0.191 [−1.84]	−0.162 [−1.45]	−0.162 [−1.46]
Natural logarithm of firm book-to-market ratio	−0.032 [−0.98]	−0.033 [−0.39]	−0.025 [−0.30]	−0.023 [−0.27]	−0.062 [−0.71]	−0.048 [−0.56]
Average age of venture organizations that are investors	0.021 [1.64]	0.021 [1.65]	0.021 [1.59]	0.022 [1.62]	0.027 [1.94]	
Average age of venture organizations serving as directors						0.024 [1.85]
Underwriter ranking	0.111 [2.24]	0.110 [2.21]	0.109 [2.18]	0.110 [2.21]	0.086 [1.77]	0.091 [1.70]
All underwriters are venture investors in the firm	0.914 [1.78]	0.152 [0.05]			1.297 [2.35]	1.218 [2.20]
Book underwriter is a venture investor in the firm			0.001 [0.03]			
Any underwriter is an investor in the firm				−0.128 [−0.55]		
Underwriter is a venture investor * underwriter ranking		0.105 [0.23]				
Percentage of the firm owned by venture investors before IPO					0.004 [1.01]	0.003 [0.85]
Percentage of venture capitalists stake sold in the IPO					1.248 [1.87]	1.334 [1.99]
Revision to the IPO price (%)					−0.035 [−0.62]	−0.037 [−0.65]
Constant	0.054 [0.12]	0.059 [0.13]	0.097 [0.21]	0.076 [0.17]	−0.303 [−0.61]	−0.239 [−0.49]
Adjusted R^2	0.011	0.010	0.007	0.007	0.015	0.014
p-Value of F-test	0.018	0.032	0.061	0.054	0.014	0.015
Number of observations	814	814	814	814	766	766

Note: The sample is 885 venture capital-backed IPOs from 1972 through 1992 for which a venture capitalist could be identified as a five percent equity holder in or a director of the company prior to the offering. The dependent variable is the excess five-year return which is calculated as the five-year buy-and-hold return on the IPO firm minus the five-year buy-and-hold return on the matched size and book-to-market portfolio which excludes all firms that have issued equity in initial public offerings or seasoned equity offerings within the past five years. All regressions employ an ordinary least squares specification. [t-statistics are in brackets.]

The results support the rational discounting hypothesis: there is no difference in long-run performance conditioning on a relationship between the venture capitalists and the underwriter. On the contrary, when all the underwriters are venture investors in the company, long-run performance is better. The other two underwriter affiliation variables are insignificant.

Reputation of the venture investors is positively related to performance, although the results are only marginally significant. More important is the underwriter reputation: firms taken public with higher quality underwriters perform better in the long run. High-quality underwriters appear to be concerned about the negative consequences to their reputation of overpricing issues. This result seems to hold independent of whether the underwriter is also a venture investor. Interactions of the underwriter reputation with the investment bank-venture capital relationship variable were consistently insignificant.

While the share of the firm held by venture investors and the revision in the offering price are not related to long-run performance, the fraction of the venture investors' equity stake sold at the time of offering is significant. The relation, however, is opposite to that predicted by the naïve investor hypothesis. The more of their stake the venture investors sell, the better the company performs in the long run. One possible explanation for this result is the reputational concerns of the venture investors combined with the need to return capital to investors. As discussed in chapter 16, venture capitalists need to return money to their investors in order to raise new funds, but they do not want to sell a lot of equity at the time of offering if the firm might decline in value. The negative reputational impact of cashing out at the expense of new investors might hurt their ability to take firms public in the future. Therefore venture capitalists might only sell equity in the offering when they were certain that future news concerning the company will be positive.

Table 17.5 presents a comparable analysis of the factors that are associated with liquidations within the first five years of the IPO. The results show no evidence of a conflict of interest for underwriters who are also venture investors. However, the opposite relation seems to be true: the stronger is the relation between the underwriter and venture investor, the lower the likelihood of liquidation. The regressions in table 17.5 do not include the dummy variable that indicates if all the underwriters were venture investors because it perfectly predicts liquidations. No issue in which all underwriters were venture investors was liquidated within five years.

Table 17.5
Regression analyses of the incidence of liquidation within the first five years of offering

Independent variables	Dependent variable: Liquidation in the first five years				
Natural logarithm of firm size (constant 1992$)	−0.779 [−4.12]	−0.414 [−3.17]	−0.806 [−4.23]	−0.901 [−4.30]	−0.903 [−4.61]
Natural logarithm of firm book-to-market ratio	−0.166 [−1.35]	−0.192 [−2.07]	−0.169 [−1.37]	−0.080 [−0.61]	−0.088 [−0.66]
Average age of venture organizations that are investors	−0.004 [−0.18]	−0.030 [−1.82]	−0.005 [−0.23]	−0.004 [−0.17]	
Average age of venture organizations serving as directors					−0.028 [−1.27]
Underwriter ranking	−0.002 [−0.03]	−0.087 [−1.63]	−0.008 [−0.11]	0.071 [0.84]	0.084 [1.01]
Book underwriter is a venture investor in the firm	−0.761 [−1.03]	0.923 [0.32]		−0.829 [−1.12]	−0.779 [−1.05]
Any underwriter is an investor in the firm			0.243 [0.59]		
Underwriter is a venture investor * underwriter ranking		−0.245 [−0.64]			
Percentage of the firm owned by venture investors before IPO				−0.010 [−1.46]	−0.008 [−1.20]
Percentage of venture capitalists stake sold in the IPO				−3.534 [−1.94]	−3.599 [−1.96]
Revision to the IPO price (%)				0.205 [1.74]	0.210 [1.76]
Constant	0.715 [1.07]	0.841 [1.68]	0.804 [1.19]	1.393 [1.89]	1.464 [2.01]
Log-likelihood	−193.16	−328.2	−193.58	−184.81	−156.18
p-Value of χ^2-statistic	0.000	0.000	0.000	0.000	0.000
Number of observations	814	814	814	766	766

Note: The sample is 885 venture capital-backed IPOs from 1972 through 1992 for which a venture capitalist could be identified as a five percent equity holder in or a director of the company prior to the offering. The dependent variable is a dummy variable that equals one if the firm was liquidated within the first five years of its initial public offering. All regressions employ a logit specification. [t-statistics are in brackets.]

Unlike long-run returns, neither the reputation of the venture capital investors nor the reputation of the underwriter has an impact on the probability of liquidation. Size (market value at the time of the IPO) is the most important factor related to liquidation. Large firms are liquidated far less frequently. This makes sense if large firms at IPO raise more money and have better investment prospects.

While the percentage of the firm owned by the venture investors prior to IPO has no effect on liquidation probability, the fraction of their stake they sell at IPO does. Once again, the result is the opposite of what we would expect if the naïve investor hypothesis were true. If the venture investors sell a larger fraction of their holdings, the firm is less likely to be liquidated.

In summary, the long-run performance tests support rational discounting. The status of an investment bank as a venture investor is generally unrelated to the firm's performance.

Underpricing

The discount of the offering at the time of the IPO provides an alternative way to examine the market's reaction to potential conflicts of interest. As discussed in the third section, the rational discounting hypothesis suggests that issues in which an underwriter is also a venture investor would have to be underpriced more to induce investors to buy the issue because of the greater adverse selection.

In table 17.6 we tabulate the average and median underpricing. We once again sort the IPOs on the basis of underwriter status. Underpricing does seem to be related to the underwriter status. As a conflict of interest becomes more likely—that is, as we move from no underwriter being a venture investor to any underwriter being a venture investor to all underwriters being venture investors—the average underpricing increases. The differences, however, are statistically insignificant.

Regression results for underpricing are presented in table 17.7. While significance levels are low, there does appear to be a monotonic relationship between venture capital/underwriter affiliation and underpricing. A closer relationship is associated with greater underpricing. The market appears to require greater underpricing to compensate for perceived conflicts of interest. None of the venture firm reputation variables are associated with reduced underpricing. Unlike the long-run excess returns, the reputation of the venture capitalist has no effect on underpricing. In all the regressions, however, size of the issuing firm is positively related and its book-to-market ratio is negatively related to the firm's first day return. Large issuing firms and high-

Table 17.6
Summary statistics for underpricing sorted by investment banking relationship

	Underpricing	
	Mean (%)	Median (%)
All underwriters are venture investors in the firm	13.1	2.9
Not all underwriters are venture investors in the firm	9.2	3.8
	[0.250]	[0.829]
Book underwriter is a venture investor in the firm	11.6	5.9
Book underwriter is a venture investor in the firm	9.1	3.7
	[0.216]	[0.322]
Any underwriter is a venture investor in the firm	10.3	5.9
No underwriter is a venture investor in the firm	9.1	3.5
	[0.435]	[0.115]

Note: The sample is 885 venture capital-backed IPOs from 1972 through 1992 for which a venture capitalist could be identified as a five percent equity holder in or a director of the company prior to the offering. Underpricing is calculated as the percentage return on the first day of trading from the offering price to the closing price on the first day. {p-Values for t-tests for differences in means and Wilcoxon rank-sum tests for differences in medians are in brackets.}

growth (low book-to-market) companies are associated with more underpriced offerings. (It might be thought that information problems would be greater here.) The reputation of the underwriter has a significant impact on the first day return. IPOs underwritten by higher reputation investment banks have lower underpricing, as shown by Barry et al. (1990).

The role of reputation is particularly pronounced when there is a potential conflict of interest. Interactions between underwriter affiliation and underwriter reputation are consistently negative. When a potential conflict of interest is present, reputation may be a check on incentives to take advantage of investors. This highlights the role that reputation may play in ameliorating conflicts of interest.

Portfolio Company Selection

In this section we examine whether the venture capital subsidiaries of investment banks choose to invest in and underwrite less information-sensitive issues in order to limit potential conflicts of interest. Kroszner and Rajan (1994) do a similar analysis of public issues during the pre–Glass-Steagall period. We are able to obtain more detailed information on the venture-backed offerings and can therefore classify the types of offerings with greater detail.

Table 17.7
Regression analyses of the underpricing of initial public offerings

Independent variables	Dependent variable: First-day return					
Natural logarithm of firm size (constant 1992$)	0.048 [7.10]	0.048 [7.09]	0.048 [7.08]	0.048 [7.06]	0.038 [5.43]	0.039 [5.46]
Natural logarithm of firm book-to-market ratio	−0.031 [−5.67]	−0.031 [−5.62]	−0.031 [−5.62]	−0.031 [−5.61]	−0.023 [−4.25]	−0.023 [−4.25]
Average age of venture organizations that are investors	0.0004 [0.47]	0.0004 [0.49]	0.0004 [0.42]	0.0004 [0.45]	−0.001 [−0.86]	
Average age of venture organizations serving as directors						0.001 [0.65]
Underwriter ranking	−0.013 [−3.90]	−0.013 [−3.84]	−0.013 [−3.94]	−0.013 [−3.94]	−0.013 [−3.81]	−0.014 [−4.10]
All underwriters are venture investors in the firm	0.045 [1.34]	0.165 [1.65]			0.049 [1.39]	0.047 [1.34]
Book underwriter is a venture investor in the firm			0.014 [0.72]			
Any underwriter is an investor in the firm				0.002 [0.16]		
Underwriter is a venture investor * underwriter ranking		−0.017 [−1.80]				
Percentage of the firm owned by venture investors before IPO					0.0002 [0.88]	0.0002 [0.65]
Percentage of venture capitalists stake sold in the IPO					0.053 [1.24]	0.055 [1.33]
Revision to the IPO price (%)					0.031 [8.68]	0.031 [8.60]
Constant	−0.087 [−2.96]	−0.087 [−2.98]	−0.084 [−2.87]	−0.084 [−2.86]	−0.013 [−0.42]	−0.021 [−0.66]
Adjusted R^2	0.125	0.128	0.123	0.123	0.205	0.205
p-Value of F-test	0.000	0.000	0.000	0.000	0.000	0.000
Number of observations	812	812	812	812	765	765

Note: The sample is 885 venture capital-backed IPOs from 1972 through 1992 for which a venture capitalist could be identified as a five percent equity holder in or a director of the company prior to the offering. The dependent variable is underpricing of the initial public offering as calculated by the percentage return from the offering price to the closing price of the first day of trading. All regressions employ an ordinary least squares specification. [t-statistics are in brackets.]

Table 17.8
Summary statistics for venture capital-backed IPOs sorted by investment banker affiliation

Characteristic	Any investment banker is a venture capital investor	Investment bank-affiliated venture capital investor, but not an underwriter	No investment bank-affiliated venture capital investor
Market value of equity (1992$ mil)	191.6 [138.5]	148.0 [98.0]	159.5 [92.1]
Offer price per share (1992$)	17.44 [14.42]	13.58 [12.50]	14.60 [12.75]
Underwriter rank	8.10 [8.75]	7.73 [8.75]	7.27 [8]
IPO firm book-to-market ratio	0.293 [0.256]	0.272 [0.257]	0.292 [0.249]
Percentage of firm owned by venture capitalists before IPO	38.1 [37.7]	38.1 37.9	30.15 [25.3]
Market capitalization of previous venture-backed IPOs (in 1992$ mil) in which the venture directors were serving on the board at the time of the IPO	114.1 [66.7]	103.8 [54.6]	94.9 [65.7]
Mean age of the venture organizations who were directors (years)	13.08 [12.78]	12.11 [12.31]	11.23 [10.90]
Mean age of the venture organizations who were investors (years)	12.44 [12.08]	11.80 [11.63]	11.50 [11.20]
Mean reputational rank of the underwriters in the other IPOs in which the venture capitalists were involved as directors	7.66 [7.80]	7.70 [7.83]	7.33 [7.83]
Mean reputational rank of the underwriters in the other IPOs in which the venture capitalists were involved as investors	7.67 [7.85]	7.63 [7.74]	7.40 [7.83]
Number of observations	127	259	499

Note: The sample is 885 venture capital-backed IPOs from 1972 through 1992 for which a venture capitalist could be identified as a five percent equity holder in or a director of the company prior to the offering. [Medians in brackets.]

Table 17.8 presents summary statistics which classify issuers into three groups: if any of the underwriters was a venture investor, if an investment bank-affiliated venture capital firm invested in the company but was not an underwriter, and if no investment bank-affiliated venture capital firm invested in the firm. Firms in which an investment bank both invested as a venture capitalist and underwrote the offering are larger, have higher offering share prices, and have older venture capital investors than either those in which an investment bank-affiliated venture firm chose not to underwrite the offering or those in which there are no investment bank-affiliated

Table 17.9
Regression analyses of affiliation between underwriters and venture investor at the time of the initial public offering

Independent variables	Dependent variables		
	Is any underwriter a venture capital investor?	Is there an investment bank-affiliated venture capital investor?	If an investment bank-affiliated venture capital firm invested, does the investment bank also underwrite?
Logarithm of market value of equity (1992$ mil)	0.548 [4.49]	0.412 [4.18]	0.425 [2.52]
Logarithm of IPO firm book-to-market ratio	0.239 [1.98]	0.186 [2.11]	0.141 [0.99]
Mean age of the venture organizations who were directors (years)	0.052 [3.22]	2.029 [1.98]	0.030 [1.31]
Percentage of firm owned by venture capitalists before IPO	0.010 [2.06]	0.176 [4.60]	−0.003 [−0.52]
Constant	−4.883 [−7.63]	−2.0635 [−5.42]	−2.675 [−3.15]
Log-likelihood	−314.31	−417.52	−190.99
p-Value of χ^2-statistic	0.000	0.000	0.051
Number of observations	784	784	305

Note: The sample is 885 venture capital-backed IPOs from 1972 through 1992 for which a venture capitalist could be identified as a five percent equity holder in or a director of the company prior to offering. The dependent variable is a dummy variable that equals one if any underwriter was a venture investor in the firm, if there is an investment bank-affiliated venture investor in the firm (regardless of whether they underwrite the offering), and if an investment bank chooses to underwrite an issue in which it holds an investment interest through a venture capital affiliate. All regressions employ a logit specification. [t-statistics are in brackets.]

venture investors. These results are consistent with the belief that investment bankers are concerned about potential conflicts of interest and only choose to both invest in and underwrite offerings that are less information sensitive: that is, larger and higher priced firms with more reputable venture capital investors.

Table 17.9 presents three logit regressions. First, we determine what factors influence an investment bank to both invest in and underwrite the offering of a particular company. The first column shows that firms in which an underwriter is also a venture investor tend to be larger, have higher book-to-market ratios (i.e., are less likely to be "glamour" stock), have more reputable venture investors, and have higher equity ownership by the venture capitalists. The second column indicates that this pattern is a consequence of the types of firms in which investment bank-affiliated venture investors choose to invest. The regression examines whether or not the firm had received capital from an investment bank-affiliated venture capitalist, regardless of whether the investment bank underwrote the offering or not. The regression shows that investment banks invest in companies that have lower asymmetric information. In the third regression we examine which firms go public with an underwriter who is an venture investor, conditional on the firm having received an earlier investment by an investment bank-affiliated venture fund. We find that the only factor associated with the likelihood that an investment bank will underwrite an offering in which it is an investor is firm size: investment banks are unwilling to underwrite smaller offerings. The significant variables in the three regressions proxy for potentially lower asymmetric information. As in the earlier period studied by Kroszner and Rajan (1994), investment banks appear to internalize the conflict of interest and choose to simultaneously invest in and underwrite only those issues in which the potential to exploit asymmetric information is small. Again, this result is consistent with the predictions of the rational discounting hypothesis.

Conclusions

The evidence from venture affiliates of investment banks suggests that in a context analogous to a universal bank, the market appears to "rationally" discount for potential conflicts of interest. Offerings underwritten by an investment bank that is also a venture investor do not perform any worse than other issues. The market appears to require a greater discount at the offering to compensate for potential adverse selection. Some of this greater discount required is reduced by the reputation of the investment bank. Investment banks tend to choose to invest in and underwrite firms with lower asymmetric information.

While this study concurs with the conclusions of earlier historical studies, because of the greater information available for our sample, we are able to perform sharper and more detailed tests of Kroszner and Rajan's (1994) rational discounting and naïve investor hypotheses. Unlike earlier work, we can quantitatively document the precise ownership relationship between the underwriter and the firm issuing equity and have very detailed performance measures. Our analysis also controls for other factors that potentially confound previous studies, including size, book-to-market ratios, and reputation.

Our evidence strongly supports the rational discounting hypothesis, while rejecting the naïve investor hypothesis. The ability of the market to correctly anticipate conflicts of interest and incorporate them into the price of the security argues in favor of removing restrictions on investment and commercial banking imposed by the Glass-Steagall Act. The large number of institutional investors with large research staffs and the increase in disclosure requirements imply that the market has the ability to understand the incentive effects of universal banking (Gompers and Metrick 2001).

18   Why Do IPO Lockups Exist?

An initial public offering (IPO) often represents the first opportunity that a firm's founders and initial investors have to begin the process of realizing the value for their ownership stake in the firm.[1] We explore one particular aspect that regulates this cashing out by insiders, namely the structure of, the price reaction to, and the compliance with investment banker lockups at the time of the IPO. By focusing on the decisions of investment banks and firm insiders, our results provide insights into the role that investment banks play in intermediation and amelioration of potential conflicts between management and dispersed shareholders. Investment bankers serve an important function in the process of issuing equity to the public in an IPO. They lead "road shows" where the company management and the investment bankers meet with potential investors. They collect stated interest in the firm's offering and create a book of those demands. They price the offering and issue securities to investors on the first day of trading and potentially certify the quality of the offering (Carter and Manaster 1990). Similarly they often provide price stabilization and make a market in the company's stock for aftermarket trading (Aggarwal 2000; Ellis, Michaely, and O'Hara 2000). In addition the investment bank usually requires that the firm's management and pre-public investors agree to refrain from selling their stock in the aftermarket for a period of time after the IPO. This agreement is usually referred to as a "lockup." We explore the motivations for these lockups as well as price reaction at the time of lockup expiration and the trading activity of insiders before the lockup expires.

In this chapter we provide three contributions on going public and financial markets. First, we explore why pre-public insiders agree to long holding periods after the IPO. We test three potential explanations: (1) lockups as a signal of quality, (2) as a commitment device to alleviate moral hazard

---

1. See Habib and Ljungqvist (1999). Baker and Gompers (2000) show that the vast majority of insiders do not sell any of their own shares at the time of the IPO.

problems, and (3) as a means for investment banks to extract additional compensation from issuing firms. Our analysis supports the hypothesis that to deal with the problem of moral hazard, investment banks impose longer lockups as information asymmetry rises in the aftermarket. The problem firms include small firms, firms with low book-to-market ratios, firms that go public with lower quality underwriters, and firms that are not backed by venture capitalists. We conduct several tests of the signaling hypothesis and find no support for the idea that insiders signal their "quality" by locking themselves for a longer period of time than insiders at lower quality firms. Similarly we find little evidence in support of the possibility that lockups are imposed by investments banks as a means to extract additional compensation from the firm's insiders.

Second, we also explore the price reaction at the time of the lockup expiration. The parameters of the lockup are well specified (in terms of length and number of shares locked) and known at the time of the IPO. If markets were perfectly anticipatory, there should not be an abnormal price reaction at the time of the expiration. Indeed, even if demand curves for stocks slope downward, investors should correctly forecast the number of shares that insiders will sell at lockup expiration on average, and hence the average abnormal return should be zero. We find, however, a significant drop of 2 percent around the lockup expiration. Our evidence is consistent with downward-sloping demand curves and costly arbitrage. In addition we examine cross-sectional differences in the magnitude of the price decline and find that these are consistent with the prediction of the commitment hypothesis.

Third, because the lead underwriter has the ability to release locked-up shares early, we examine insider equity sales prior to expiration of the lockup. Under the commitment hypothesis only insiders of firms that have greatly diminished asymmetric information risk should be allowed to sell equity prior to the expiration of the lockup. Consistent with this prediction we find that early release is associated with greater price increases between IPO and lockup expiration, venture capital backing, and higher underwriter reputation.

Our analyses in this chapter are related to several independent studies in finance. An enduring issue in the corporate finance literature has been the impact of trading by informed insiders on securities prices. Two cases initiated by the U.S. Securities and Exchange Commission (SEC) in the early 1960s stimulated an interest in this relationship and its implications for social welfare (Manne 1966) that continues to this day. An extensive body of research has examined trading by corporate insiders. Notably Seyhun (e.g., 1986, 1988) has documented short- and long-run price impacts of trading by officers, directors, and other insiders.

We add to this literature in examining the role of reputation in the going-public process and the mitigation of adverse selection. Because the going-public process is potentially subject to Myers and Majluf (1984) adverse selection problems, it may be in the firm's interest to agree to resolve the adverse selection problem by incurring a costly signal (Leland and Pyle 1977). Agreeing not to undertake any sale of equity for a pre-specified period of time can function as such a signal (Welch 1989).

Finally several recent papers also focus on varying aspects of IPO lockups. Field and Hanka (2001) focus on explaining the price decline at lockup expiration.[2] Ofek and Richardson (2000) attempt to explain the price decline at lockup expiration and find no one explanation that is consistent with the data. They show, however, that transaction costs eliminate the ability of a trader to profit from the price decline. A third paper examining the price decline at lockup expiration, Bradley et al. (2001), focuses primarily on the role of venture capital backing on the price decline at lockup expiration.

IPO Lockup Contracts

Regulations Governing Lockups

When the issuing firm and the investment bank enter into an agreement to offer securities in an IPO, they sign an underwriter agreement. As Bartlett (1995) explains, these agreements typically include a covenant such as:

The Selling Securityholders agree that, without your (the investment bank's) prior written consent, the Selling Securityholders will not, directly or indirectly, sell, offer, contract to sell, make any short sale, pledge or otherwise dispose of any shares of Common Stock or any securities convertible into or exercisable for or any rights to purchase or acquire Common Stock for a period of 180 days following the commencement of the public offering of the Stock by the Underwriters.

Bartlett argues that the lockup, which is typically 180 days in length, keeps the stock from hitting the market all at once and creating a surplus.

---

2. Field and Hanka document the extent of early release by employing a small sample of insider transactions prior to lockup expirations (186 firms over a one-year period). In the third section of this chapter we provide a thorough analysis of all insider transactions conducted by our sample firms. This extensive database and our competing hypotheses provide a framework within which we are able to explore both the extent of early release as well as the determinants of early insider sales.

The agreement to not sell or sell-short their equity holdings is governed only by this underwriter agreement. It is not mandated by any SEC or state securities laws that regulate insider trading.[3] It is important to note that the underwriter can release any of the securities subject to the lockup agreements at any time without notice. We provide evidence that early release is used extensively in our sample period.

The sale of restricted securities, that is, stock purchased in a private placement directly from an issuer before the company is public, is governed by SEC Rule 144. Rule 144 allows for the sale of restricted securities in limited quantities in the aftermarket. Specifically, a person who has beneficially owned shares of common stock for at least one year (two years before February 1997) is entitled to sell, within any three-month period, a number of shares that does not exceed the greater of 1 percent of the number of shares of common stock then outstanding or the average weekly trading volume during the four calendar weeks preceding the filing of a notice on Form 144 with respect to the sale.

Finally, as Bettis, Coles, and Lemmon (1999) emphasize, insider trading is likely to be regulated by the firm itself. A large proportion of their sample firms have a policy in place restricting insider trading by employees as well as pre-specified blackout periods in which the company prohibits trading by insiders. Bettis and colleagues point out that insiders who are governed by these self-imposed company restrictions are sometimes granted permission to trade during the blackout periods for liquidity or diversification reasons.

Why Do Lockups Exist?

The central question addressed in this chapter is why IPO lockups exist. We explore three potential explanations for the existence of lockups. First, if the quality of a particular company cannot be observed by public investors, high-quality firms will be worried that potential investors will not pay a high price for their shares. Supposedly investors cannot distinguish between high-quality and low-quality firms. Leland and Pyle (1977) develop a model in which the fraction of equity retained by insiders at the time of IPO serves as a signal of quality. Insiders in high-quality firms are willing to hold more

---

3. Specifically, Section 10(b) of the Securities Exchange Act of 1934, and Rule 10b-5 of the Act are the primary provisions used by the SEC to prevent insider trading where insiders are officers, directors, or anyone else owning 10 percent or more of the outstanding company shares. Section 16b of the 1934 Act bans short-swing (within a six-month period) profit taking by insiders. In addition, under the Insider Trading and Securities Fraud Enforcement Act of 1988, corporations, brokerage firms or other "controlling persons" who supervise a person who violates the insider trading rules may also be liable.

of their stock after the IPO and hence remain more undiversified because they can thereby commit to the quality of their companies.

Courteau (1995) extends Leland and Pyle's model to voluntary lockups. She builds a model in which insiders use the IPO lockup as a similar signaling device. High-quality firms signal their quality by agreeing to longer lockups. Because insiders hold undiversified portfolios, restricting sale of stock for a longer period of time imposes a cost on them. If firms use lockups to signal, then higher quality firms would agree to longer lockups. Insiders at low-quality firms would be unwilling to bear the cost of committing to long lockups.[4]

The signaling hypothesis gives several predictions about the structure of lockups depending on the motivation for the signal. That is, firms may want to signal their quality either to get a higher offering price at the IPO or to get a better price at a subsequent seasoned offering (e.g., Allen and Faulhaber 1989; Grinblatt and Huang 1989; Welch 1989). Our empirical tests are designed as in Michaely and Shaw (1994). In particular, we would expect that firms that signaled their quality through longer lockups would be more likely to raise their offering price in order to garner greater proceeds at the time of the IPO or else they would be more likely to issue equity in a subsequent seasoned equity offering.

A second hypothesis for the existence of lockups is that these agreements serve as a commitment device to alleviate moral hazard problems. In this case it is the level of asymmetric information between managers and shareholders in the aftermarket about the firm's true valuation that is critical. In this setting everyone can observe a firm's quality (i.e., the potential level of information about firm value), but outside shareholders do not know managers' private information. Firms that shareholders fear would take advantage of asymmetric information about firm value would have to accept longer lockups imposed by the investment bank in order to convince the public to buy stock in the offering. During the period of time in which insiders are prohibited from selling equity, information about the firm's future prospects will be revealed through SEC filings, news stories, and analyst reports. As a result investors may be more willing to buy into the

---

4. Other authors have explored alternative mechanisms by which managers can overcome this asymmetric information problem. Carter and Manaster (1990) show that firms going public with high-quality underwriters have lower underpricing. Carter and Manaster argue that the investment bank is able to credibly certify the quality of the offering because it stakes its reputational capital on the future performance of the offering. Investors require less of a discount to buy into the offering because the adverse selection problem is diminished. Barry et al. (1990) and Megginson and Weiss (1991) examine a similar certification phenomenon with venture capital-backed companies.

offering knowing that insiders' ability to take advantage of them is reduced. Hence the lockup provision would be a commitment device.

The commitment hypothesis yields predictions that differ from the signaling alternative. Those firms that, ex ante, suffer from a greater potential for insiders to take advantage of shareholders would need longer lockups to induce investors to buy into the offering. This includes younger firms, firms with low book-to-market ratios, firms with greater stock price volatility, and firms with low cash flow margins. All these firms would have potentially higher levels of asymmetric information associated with their valuations. In addition firms that have other forms of certification or reputation will not need longer lockups; namely reputation is an alternative commitment device. For example, a firm that can convince Kleiner Perkins to invest in it or Goldman Sachs to underwrite its offering is less likely to engage in opportunistic insider sales. Goldman Sachs and Kleiner would be unwilling to risk their reputations by being associated with companies whose insiders are more likely to take advantage of investors. This implies that venture backing and higher reputation underwriters will be associated with shorter lockups.[5]

The commitment hypothesis also has implications for the types of firms that investment bankers will release from the lockup provision early and allow sales by insiders prior to the lockup expiration. Early release, by itself, does not mean that lockups are not a commitment device. Early release should be associated with firms that have alternative certification or commitment devices (i.e., venture capital backing or high underwriter rank), or else these firms will have received positive news about the company's prospects. This positive news is likely to lead to increases in the stock price prior to releasing insiders from the lockup. If the firm has received a series of positive news announcements and the stock price has risen, the information asymmetry problem concerning firm value should be dramatically reduced, and the chance that the insiders will take advantage of investors is lessened. Hence insiders can be released from their lockup commitments.

In addition, if the lockup is a commitment device, then the level of the price reaction at lockup expiration will be affected by returns between the IPO and lockup expiration, venture capital backing, and underwriter ranking. While we cannot explain the average level of price drop, if the commitment story is true, we can explain cross-sectional variation in abnormal

---

5. Indeed, it may be argued that underwriters may choose to write lockups that reflect their reputation. Specifically, the shorter the lockup, the more reputation is at stake, since any adverse information occurring shortly after the lockup expiration will imply that the underwriter may not have done the due diligence appropriately. In a separating equilibrium, high-quality underwriters would impose shorter lockups on higher quality firms.

returns at lockup expiration. The stock price reaction at lockup expiration should be lower for firms that are more informationally transparent. This includes firms with lower price volatility, high underwriter status, profitable firms, and firms that have been able to tap the seasoned equity offering (SEO) market.

A third potential explanation for the use of lockups is that investment banks want to extract additional compensation from issuing firms. The lockup agreement only allows insider equity sales prior to lockup expiration if the lead underwriter consents. In this case insiders would be forced to do a block trade through the lead underwriter or actually perform an SEO. In either instance the underwriter would make additional fees by either making a market in the firm's shares for the block transaction or else it would make fees from underwriting the SEO.

The underwriter market power story predicts that controlling for firm quality, lockups should be longer for firms underwritten by high-quality underwriters. The high-quality underwriters would extract more compensation by imposing longer lockups due to their greater prestige. Companies going public would be willing to agree to longer lockups if the higher tier underwriters offer greater services. We would also expect that the probability of doing an SEO that retains the same lead underwriter at the IPO would be higher within the lockup period. That is, controlling for the length of time from IPO to SEO, firms doing a seasoned equity offering within the lockup period should be more likely to use the same underwriter.

Data Sources and Sample Description

We employ an initial sample of 2,871 initial public offerings conducted over the period 1988 to 1996 obtained from the Securities Data Company (SDC) database. To be included in the sample, firms must be listed on CRSP sometime after the offering but before the lock up expiration. We exclude IPOs by closed-end funds, REITS, ADRs, and any carveouts. Daily stock returns and volume data are obtained from CRSP while accounting data was obtained from Compustat. Information regarding the length of the lockup, number of shares locked, primary and secondary shares offered, and offer price are from SDC. In those cases where SDC has a missing lockup data field we search the individual firm prospectus for the relevant information. In the initial analysis, 255 firms were lacking lockup length data. Of these, the appendix (at the end of the chapter) details how we were able to find information on 178 of those firms, giving us a final sample of 2,794 IPOs.

Table 18.1 provides descriptive statistics for the 2,794 IPOs. In panel A we provide the annual number of IPOs for the period 1988 to 1996. The volume of IPOs for the first three years in the sample is quite low relative to the volume of IPOs in 1991 through 1996. Panel B shows means, medians, as well as 10th and 90th percentile information, on various firm characteristics for the sample. Market value of equity is given in millions of 1992 dollars at the offering price. Book-to-market ratio is the ratio of book equity to market equity in the first reporting period following the IPO (Compustat item 60) divided by the market capitalization at the IPO. Underpricing is the percent return on the first day from the offering price to the closing price. Percent of offering which is primary shares is the fraction of the offering that is new shares. Underwriter rank is the Carter, Dark, and Singh (1997) underwriter reputation rank taking values from 1 (lowest rank) to 9 (highest rank). Days of lockup is the length of the underwriter lockup period. Fraction of post-IPO insider shares locked is the percentage of shares held by insiders after the IPO subject to the lockup restriction, for which we could find information. To eliminate the influence of outliers, when the number of shares locked exceeds the number of post-IPO shares held by insiders, we set the number of shares locked equal to 99 percent of post-IPO shares held by insiders (Field and Hanka 2001). Sales is the value of sales in the first reporting period after the IPO in millions of 1992 dollars (Compustat item 12). Employment is the number of employees in the first reporting period after the IPO (Compustat item 29). Return on assets is the ratio of net income to total assets (Compustat items 258 and 6).

Initial analysis of the lockup length shows considerable standardization. The 10th and 50th percentile lockups are all 180 days. This type of contract standardization is common in certain agreements. For example, Chen and Ritter (1999) find that investment bankers set gross spreads at 7 percent in the majority of the IPO deals in their sample. As noted earlier in chapter 5, 82 percent of venture partnership agreements allocate 20 percent of profits to the general partners of the venture funds. Insiders also appear to lockup a significant portion of their equity. The median firm locks-up 93 percent of post-IPO insider shares, while even the 25th percentile firm locks 52 percent of its post-IPO insiders' shares.

Panel C provides the distribution of the time to lockup expiration in calendar time starting with the lowest (less than 90 days) to the highest (1,095 days). It can be seen that while most lockups occur at monthly frequency, the majority of the contracts, 64 percent, are based on 180 days. There also appears to be a clustering of lockup lengths corresponding to annual intervals.

Panel D presents additional information on length of the underwriter lockup, percent of shares held by insiders after the IPO that are subject to the lockup, and underpricing. The panel separates IPO firms on the basis of firm characteristics. Rows 2 and 3 provide cross-sectional differences in these characteristics by sorting the IPO sample into two size groups (market capitalization above and below the median firm size of $70 million). The groups reveal that smaller IPOs are locked-up for a longer period of time. On average, smaller IPOs are locked for 321 days while larger IPOs are locked for 187 days. If smaller firms are potentially more plagued by asymmetric information about firm mispricing, then insiders at smaller firms would have to agree to longer lockups in order to sell equity to the public. No discernable pattern appears in relation to the fraction of post-IPO insiders' shares subject to lockup. In addition underpricing of smaller IPOs is significantly lower.

The next two rows present cross-sectional differences based on underwriter reputation, and rows 6 and 7 document the relationship between venture backing and these IPO characteristics. Both comparisons reveal that offerings with higher tier investment banks or those having venture capital investors have significantly shorter lockups on average. This is consistent with firms with less asymmetric information about their potential valuation not requiring strong commitment via long lockups. Underpricing is higher for both the high-reputation investment banker and the venture capital-backed IPOs.[6]

In the last set of rows we split the sample into two equal subperiods: earlier and later IPOs. It is readily apparent that no significant time trend in lockup provisions exists. General lockup length and the fraction of the firm's equity that is locked are comparable. IPO underpricing, however, has increased in the latter time period (Ritter 2001).

The Determinants of Lockup Length

Testing the Predictions of the Commitment Hypothesis

We next explore the determinants of the lockup length. We report regression results in table 18.2, which broadly support the commitment story. The

---

6. The positive association between underwriter rank and underpricing is consistent with the findings in Beatty and Welch (1996) and Krigman, Shaw, and Womack (2001). As the latter authors point out, the negative relationship between underwriter prestige and underpricing that was documented for the 1980s has reversed over the 1990s. Since our sample begins in the late 1980s, it is not surprising that we find a positive relationship.

Table 18.1
Descriptive statistics

Panel A: Number of IPOs, 1988–1996

Year	1988	1989	1990	1991	1992	1993	1994	1995	1996	Total
IPOs	111	108	104	272	355	435	368	414	627	2,794

Panel B: Means and 10th and 90th percentile information on firm characteristics

	10th percentile	Median	Mean	90th percentile
Market value of equity (1992$ mil)	14.5	69.7	121.4	258.9
Book-to-market ratio	0.14	0.35	0.47	0.89
Underpricing (%)	−2.1	7.7	14.6	40.6
Percent of offering as primary shares	66.1	100	89.6	100
Average underwriter rank	3.0	8.0	6.8	9.0
Days of lockup	180	180	254	540
Fraction of post-IPO insiders shares locked (%)	51.7	93.1	83.9	99.0
Sales (1992$ mil)	1.1	34.4	119.8	306.2
Employment	34	257	918	6,500
Return on assets (%)	−36.4	3.4	−7.7	15.4

Panel C: Distribution of time to expiration (in calendar days) of lockups

Lockup days	<90	90–91	91–179	180	181–360	360–366	367–540	541–549	550–720	721–1,095
Number of observations	7	84	172	1,793	96	236	183	32	4	187
Percent of observations	0.25	3.00	6.16	64.17	3.44	8.45	6.55	1.15	0.14	6.69

Panel D: Length of underwriter lockup, percent of shares subject to lockup, and underpricing

Sample	Number of observations	Days locked	Fraction of post-IPO insider shares locked (%)	Underpricing (%)
Full sample	2,794	254 [180]	57.0 [60.9]	14.7 [7.7]
Market value ≥ median	1,397	187 [180]	60.6 [64.6]	16.3 [9.8]
Market value < median	1,397	321 [180]	53.1 [56.6]	13.0 [5.6]
(p-Values for difference in means)		0.00	0.00	0.00
Underwriter rank ≥ 8	1,413	193 [180]	59.2 [63.2]	14.7 [14.7]
Underwriter rank < 8	1,381	316 [180]	54.6 [60.9]	14.6 [14.6]
(p-Values for difference in means)		0.00	0.00	0.89
Venture capital backed	1,177	202 [180]	58.5 [62.6]	15.3 [8.0]
Not venture capital backed	1,617	292 [180]	55.6 [59.6]	14.2 [7.5]
(p-Values for difference in means)		0.00	0.00	0.22
IPO on or before 7/01/92	810	269 [180]	55.7 [59.1]	11.6 [6.0]
IPO after 7/01/92	1,984	248 [180]	57.5 [61.5]	15.9 [8.7]
(p-Values for difference in means)		0.00	0.05	0.00

Note: The sample is 2,794 initial public offerings (IPOs) from January 1, 1988 through December 31, 1996 for which we could find lockup information. Market value, in millions of dollars, is in 1992 constant dollars. Market value is calculated using the offering price and shares outstanding obtained from CRSP. Book-to-market ratio is the ratio of book equity to market equity in the first reporting period following the IPO (Compustat item 60) divided by the market capitalization at the IPO. Underpricing is the percent return on the first day from the offering price to the closing price. Percent of offering as primary shares is the fraction of the offering that is new shares. Underwriter rank is the Carter, Dark, and Singh (1997) underwriter reputation rank taking values from 1 (lowest rank) to 9 (highest rank). Days of lockup is the length of the underwriter lockup period. Fraction of post-IPO insider shares locked is the percentage of shares held by insiders after the IPO subject to the lockup restriction, for which we could find information. To eliminate the influence of outliers, when the number of shares locked exceeds the number of post-IPO shares held by insiders, we set the number of shares locked equal to 99 percent of post-IPO shares held by insiders. Sales is the value of sales in the first reporting period after the IPO in millions of 1992 dollars (Compustat item 12). Employment is the number of employees in the first reporting period after the IPO (Compustat item 29). Return on assets is the ratio of net income to total assets (Compustat items 258 and 6). Both means and medians [in brackets] are presented. We report *p*-values for the test that the reported means are unequal (assuming unknown but equal variances).

Table 18.2
Regression results for length of lockup

Dependent variable: Log of length of the lockup (in days)		
Constant	6.33	6.54
	[15.96]	[203.10]
Venture capital-backed?	−0.10	−0.11
	[5.54]	[7.47]
Log of the market value of equity (1992$ mil)	−0.13	−0.16
	[10.37]	[19.47]
Percent of post-IPO insider shares locked	0.0002	
	[0.42]	
Book-to-market ratio	−0.24	−0.26
	[5.45]	[8.61]
Cash flow margin (%)	−0.003	
	[1.72]	
Underwriter ranking	−0.05	−0.05
	[9.52]	[12.15]
Percentage of offering that is primary shares	0.0026	
	[4.67]	
Percentage of company's shares issued in the IPO	0.001	
	[1.24]	
Annual time dummy	−0.003	
	[0.58]	
Adjusted R^2	35.4	36.2
Number of observations	1,663	2,634

Note: Regression results where the dependent variable is the log of the lockup length in days. The independent variables are: the log of the market value of the IPO in 1992 constant dollars. Market capitalization is the product of the offering price and shares outstanding that were obtained from CRSP. The Carter, Dark, and Singh (1997) underwriter reputation rank of the lead investment bank taking values from 1 (lowest rank) to 9 (highest rank). Percentage of post-IPO insider shares locked is the fraction of shares held by insiders after the IPO that are subject to the lockup restriction. To eliminate the influence of outliers, when the number of shares locked exceeds the number of post-IPO shares held by insiders, we set the number of shares locked equal to 99 percent of post-IPO shares held by insiders. Book-to-market ratio is the ratio of book equity to market equity in the first reporting period following the IPO (Compustat item 60) divided by the market capitalization at the IPO. A dichotomous variable takes the value 1 if the firm was financed by a venture capitalist. The cash flow margin of the offering firm calculated as the ratio of operating cash flow to sales (Compustat items 308 and 12). The percent of total shares offered as primary shares and the percentage of the company's shares, both primary and secondary, issued in the IPO relative to shares outstanding. An annual time indicator variable takes the values 1988 through 1996. To eliminate the possible influence of outliers, for each variable, we replace observations whose values are either lower than the first or higher than the 99th percentiles by the sample median. [t-statistics are in brackets.]

dependent variable is the logarithm of the length of the lockup in days. The independent variables are the Carter, Dark, and Singh underwriter ranking of the lead investment bank, the log of the market value of the IPO in 1992 constant dollars, the fraction of the post-IPO insider equity subject to lockup, the firm's book to market ratio, a dummy variable indicating whether the firm was financed by a venture capitalist, the cash flow margin of the offering firm defined as the ratio of the operating cash flow to sales, and the percent of offering that is primary shares. We also include an annual time indicator variable to control for possible year effects.

We find that larger firms, firms with higher quality underwriters, and firms backed by venture capitalists all have shorter lockups on average. Each of these variables is likely associated with less informational asymmetry about firm value. Firms with high-quality underwriters or venture backing are unlikely to take advantage of outside investors and therefore have less need for the commitment of a longer lockup. Lower book-to-market ratios are associated with longer lockup length. Lower book-to-market ratios are generally associated with high risk, high growth companies that are potentially subject to greater asymmetric information. Similarly we find that higher cash flow margins are negatively related to lockup length.

We also find that the fraction of the offering that is primary shares is positively related to the lockup length. In other words, firms that have secondary sales in their IPO have shorter lockups. We interpret this as being consistent with the commitment story. Firms that can sell a higher proportion of secondary shares in their IPO are likely to have lower information asymmetry problems. If informational asymmetries were high in these firms, the public would not buy into offerings that had a large secondary component. The public would worry that the insiders were "cashing out." Finally, the insignificance of the annual time trend is consistent with the evidence in table 18.1, panel D, that there are no systematic variations in lockup length over our sample period.[7]

To ascertain that having secondary shares sold at the IPO indicates lower likelihood of information asymmetry problems, we also conduct a logit

---

7. As an alternative to the annual dummy, we included the annual volume of IPOs to better capture differences in lockup length that are due to "hot" versus "cold" markets. This variable is insignificant as well. However, in unreported results we repeated the analysis on lockup length including IPOs through the end of 2000 to address concerns that IPO lockups have become more standardized at 180 days. While the fraction of lockups that are exactly 180 days increased, a large portion of this increase in 180 day lockups was due to changes in the composition of IPOs in the most recent period, namely increasing average size, increasing underwriter ranking, and greater fraction of venture capital IPOs. The regression results for the length of the IPO in table 18.2 remain qualitatively identical.

analysis in which we model the probability of a sale of secondary shares. We find that all of our proxies for lower information asymmetry are positively related to the probability of secondary sales at the IPO. That is, secondary sales are significantly higher for venture capital-backed companies, higher underwriter status, high cash flow margins, and high tangibility of assets. This provides support for our earlier argument that firms in which we observe secondary sales are less informationally sensitive and do not require long lockups.

Finally, if investment banks extract additional compensation by imposing lockups on issuing firms, a hypothesis which we examine in greater detail in the sixth section, we would expect that the length of the lockup, controlling for firm and market characteristics, should be positively related to the reputation of the underwriter. We find just the opposite: higher underwriter reputation is associated with shorter lockups. Overall, we find evidence indicating that the lockup is a commitment device. Firms that are potentially subject to greater information asymmetry problems utilize longer lockups.

Testing the Predictions of the Signaling Hypothesis

As was pointed out in the introduction, our tests of the signaling hypothesis hinge on the motivation for the signal. Firms may want to signal their type either to get a higher offering price at the IPO or to get a better price at a subsequent seasoned offering. First, high-quality firms might incur a costly signal in order to separate themselves from low-quality firms and get a higher offering price at the IPO. Recall that lockup length and amount locked are all specified in the prospectus well ahead of the initial public offering. Consequently one implication of this signaling story is that investors are unable to separate firms *prior* to the submission of the prospectus. Yet, during the period *subsequent* to the submission of the prospectus to the SEC, investors do observe the signal, and therefore high-quality firms should be able to revise their offering price prior to the IPO. We test this implication by calculating, for each firm, the percentage revision in the offering price from the midpoint of the initial offer range. If high-quality firms managed to separate themselves from low-quality firms we should observe positive revisions (from the initial pooling price) for longer lockup firms as these companies are now able to obtain a higher offering price.

For each IPO we obtain the offering range from SDC and calculate the percentage revision from the midpoint of the range. Table 18.3, panel A, presents our initial results. We are able to obtain price revisions for 2,786 firms, which are then split into positive and negative revision subsets. To

Table 18.3
Tests of the signaling hypothesis

Price revision from midpoint of offering range		Positive	Negative		*p*-Value for difference in means
Panel A: Incidence of lockups[a]					
Number of IPOs		1,039	1,094		
Length of lockup (in days)		211	234		1.00
Post-IPO insider shares locked (%)		85.2	84.2		0.19

	Number of IPOs	Lockup length (in days)	Post-IPO insider shares locked (%)	Frequency of SEOs (%)	Frequency of dividend initiations (%)
Panel B: Incidence of SEOs and dividend initiations within four years of the IPO[b]					
Lockup length > median	738	482	83.4	17.6	2.3
Lockup length < median	263	115	73.7	30.8	3.0
p-Value for difference in means			0.00	1.00	0.74

Note: The sample is 2,794 initial public offerings (IPOs) from January 1, 1988, through December 31, 1996, for which we could find lockup information. We obtain the IPO initial offering ranges from SDC. Price revision is the percent change from the mid-point of the range to the IPO offering price. Percentage of post-IPO insider shares locked is the fraction of shares held by insiders after the IPO that are subject to the lockup restriction. To eliminate the influence of outliers, when the number of shares locked exceeds the number of post-IPO shares held by insiders, we set the number of shares locked equal to 99 percent of post-IPO shares held by insiders.

a. We split IPOs with available price revision into those with positive (negative) price revisions and report averages of lockup lengths and percent of post-IPO insider shares locked. The last column in the panel provides a one-tail *t*-test and its associated *p*-value for the test that the reported average lockup length for the positive revision sample is higher than the average length of the negative revision sample (assuming unknown but equal variances).

b. We collect, from SDC, all SEOs done by our sample firms. The dividend initiation sample is derived by collecting, from CRSP, all ordinary cash dividends initiated by our sample firms. The sample is sorted into a subsample of IPOs whose lockup length is higher than the median lockup length (180 days) and a subsample whose lockup length is shorter than the median length. The last row in the panel provides *p*-values for the *t*-test that the average frequencies of SEOs and dividend initiations and percent shares locked for the longer lockup subsample are higher the average length of the negative revision sample (assuming unknown but equal variances).

increase the power of our tests, we further exclude from the analysis firms whose offering price equals the midpoint of the initial range. There are 1,039 firms with positive price revisions and 1,094 firms with negative price revisions. We find, contrary to the signaling prediction, that firms that experienced a positive price revision are actually associated with a shorter lockup length. The last column provides a one-tail t-test and its associated p-value which strongly rejects the null hypothesis. Since it might be argued that the amount of shares locked is used as an additional signal, we verify that the latter variable is unrelated as well to the price revision. The last row in panel A provides the percent of post-IPO insider shares locked for both subsamples. The sample averages are virtually identical at 85 percent, confirming the conclusion that the choice of lockup length is inconsistent with the signaling prediction.[8]

An alternative motivation for a firm to signal its quality by setting a long lockup length is to get a better price in a subsequent seasoned equity offering (Welch 1989). We should therefore find firms with longer lockup having higher incidence of equity offerings. Furthermore, as in Michaely and Shaw (1994), high-quality firms should have higher incidence of dividend initiations as well.

Table 18.3, panel B, presents our initial results. We first split the sample into a subsample of IPOs whose lockup length is higher than the median lockup length (738 firms) and a subsample whose lockup length is shorter than the median length (263 firms). We deliberately exclude firms whose lockup length equals the median length (180 days) so as to make our test more powerful in detecting differences in quality due to differences in lockup length. We collect from SDC all seasoned equity offerings conducted by our sample firms within four years of their IPO. The dividend initiation

---

8. In unreported results we conducted three additional robustness tests. First, we defined positive (negative) offering price revisions as positive (negative) revisions that exceed the high (low) end of the initial range. The resulting sample of positive revisions now included 556 firms whose lockup length was, still, shorter than that of the subsample of 636 firms whose offering price was below the low end of the initial filing range. Second, we examined separately the subsample of firms whose offering price equaled the midpoint of the initial range. The signaling hypothesis implies that, in a separating equilibrium, we should not observe firms taking costly signal with no revision from the initial (pooling) price range. We found, however, that for this sample of 653 firms, the average lockup length was 353 days, which is significantly larger than the average length for the subsample of firms that experienced a positive price revision form the initial midpoint. Third, we modeled the probability of a positive/negative price revision within a logit framework, allowing for both firm characteristics and lockup length to determine the direction of the revision. Consistent with the evidence in panel A, we found that lockup length was not positively associated with offering price revision as predicted by the signaling null.

sample is derived by collecting, from CRSP, all ordinary cash dividends initiated by our sample firms also within four years of the IPO.

Comparison of the frequency of equity offerings reveals that firms with lockup lengths shorter than the median actually have a much higher probability of conducting a subsequent equity offering (30.8 vs. 17.6 percent), contrary to the signaling prediction. This difference is large and significant, both economically and statistically. The same is true when we examine the frequency of dividend initiations: shorter lockup firms actually have a higher probability of initiating dividends (3 vs. 2.3 percent). Finally, we also present differences in the percentage of shares locked across the two samples, since we want to rule out any confounding effects due to the possible role of shares locked as an additional signal. We find that firms that impose long lockups actually lock a *higher* percentage of their post-IPO shares (83.4 vs. 73.7 percent) again refuting the notion that insiders incur two costly signals that, ex post, lead to a higher frequency of equity offerings and dividend initiations.

As a robustness check, in unreported results, we have also conducted a logit analysis in which we modeled the probability of an SEO (dividend initiation) as a function of both firm characteristics and lockup length. Our goal was to ascertain that the conclusions drawn form panel B are robust to variations in firm characteristics which capture differences in information asymmetry. While the signaling prediction is that lockup length should be positively related to the probability of either event, we actually observed a statistically significant negative relationship. We therefore conclude that our empirical results are inconsistent with the predictions of the signaling hypotheses and that it is unlikely that length of lockup is used by insiders to signal higher firm quality.[9]

Insider Selling Prior to Lockup Expirations

In this section we explore the extent of insider equity sales prior to lockup expiration. Because the lockup agreement is not mandated by the SEC, but is

---

9. We also explored the sensitivity of our results to the omission of IPO underpricing as an additional signal employed by the firm. Empirically, we found a strong *positive* relationship between lockup length and underpricing controlling for various firm characteristics and proxies for informational asymmetries. The observed complementarity of the two signals suggests that, controlling for information asymmetry and in a separating equilibrium, high-quality firms lock themselves for a longer period of time and have high underpricing. When we repeated the tests in table 18.3, conditioning on underpricing, we found stronger evidence against the signaling predictions. This result is not surprising in light of the evidence in the literature that underpricing is not used as a signal to convey firm quality (e.g., Michaely and Shaw 1994).

only an agreement between the lead underwriter and the IPO firm, insiders can sell equity if the lead underwriter chooses to "break" the lockup. If the lockup is truly a commitment mechanism, we expect that only firms that have greatly reduced information asymmetry will be released from the lockup restrictions. As noted earlier, the commitment hypothesis predicts that firms with higher post-IPO abnormal returns, as well as firms that are associated with higher tier investment banks and venture capitalists will be more likely to be released early.

We obtain our insider holdings data for the period January 1988 through May 1999, from Primark's Cleansed Insider Data Files. The information provided from this source is derived from individual reports mandated by the SEC (Form 3, Initial Statement of Beneficial Ownership of Securities; Form 4, Statement of Changes in Beneficial Ownership; and Form 5, Annual Statement of Changes in Beneficial Ownership of Securities) and is supplemented by data from proxy statements. We determine which of these early sales occurred prior to lock up expiration and retain those transactions that passed their cleansing checks and updates (indicators R and H). Early sales associated with employee benefit plans, derivative transactions, section 16(b) transactions (e.g., gifts), and other sales that are clearly unrelated to an early release are deleted. We eliminate insider sales when a comparison of aggregate sales on a given day exceed the reported share volume from CRSP and insiders' early sales that take place around seasoned equity offerings (obtained from SDC). The final sample consists of 1,436 events by 429 IPOs.

Table 18.4 presents a summary of insider sales prior to lockup expiration. We find that 15 percent of the firms have insider sales prior to the expiration of the lockup.[10] The average number of insider transactions, conditional on having insider sales prior to lockup expiration, is 6, while the median is 2. The average and median sale occur 60 percent of the way from the IPO to the lockup date. It is also noteworthy that the amount of sales is quite small. Average (median) sales relative to shares locked is 5.2 percent (0.8 percent). It can be seen that the average 30-day abnormal return (measured relative to the Nasdaq index) is 4.76 percent.[11]

Table 18.5 presents summary statistics on firms that are released from lockups and those that are not released. The sample of insider sales consists of 1,436 events by 429 IPOs. We report descriptive statistics both for the sample IPOs in which insider sales occurred versus the remaining IPOs in

---

10. We include firms that do not appear in the database as firms with no insider sales.

11. In a sample of 334 IPOs, Field and Hanka (2001) find 17 percent of firms with insider sales prior to lockup expiration.

Table 18.4
Summary statistics on insider early sales prior to lockup expirations

	10th percentile	25th percentile	Median	Mean	75th percentile	90th percentile
Average number of early sales	1	1	2	6	5	14
Average time since IPO as fraction of lockup length (%)	24	50	69	64	84	95
Shares locked relative to shares outstanding (%)	29	48	60	62	69	76
Shares sold early relative to shares locked (%)	0.05	0.17	0.83	5.22	3.32	9.75
Shares locked relative to post-IPO insiders' shares (%)	50	80	92	83	98	99
30-day abnormal return prior to early sale (%)	−16.05	−7.97	2.28	4.76	13.56	28.80
Daily share turnover 30 days prior to early sale (%)	0.25	0.45	0.74	1.21	1.36	2.26

Note: We obtain our insider holdings data for the period January 1988 through May 1999, from Primark's Cleansed Insider Data Files. The information provided from this source is derived from individual reports mandated by the SEC (Form 3, Initial Statement of Beneficial Ownership of Securities, and Form 4, Statement of Changes in Beneficial Ownership of Securities). We determine which of these early sales occurred prior for lock up expiration and retain those transactions that passed their cleansing checks and updates (indicators R and H). Early sales associated with employee benefit plans, derivative transactions, Section 16(b) transactions (e.g., gifts), and other sales that are clearly unrelated to an early release are deleted. We eliminate insider sales when a comparison of aggregate sales on a given day shows them to exceed the reported share volume from CRSP and insiders' early sales that take place around seasoned equity offerings (obtained from SDC). The final sample consists of 1,436 events by 429 IPOs. Firms that do not appear in our insider holdings database are considered as firms with no transactions. We calculate the 10th, 25th, 50th, 75th, 90th percentiles, and the mean for various early sale characteristics for those IPOs for which insider sales data is available. In row 1 we report distribution characteristics on the average number of early sales. For example, the mean number of insider sales, prior to lockup expiration, by one of the 429 IPOs is 6. Row 2 provides the average time of sale since the IPO. For each sale we calculate the ratio of the time since the IPO relative to the length of the lock up. If, for a given IPO, insiders sold shares in multiple events, we average the resulting ratios. For example, the mean time since the IPO for a sale to occur is at 64 percent of the specified lockup length. In row 3 we calculate the ratio of shares locked to shares outstanding for each IPO in which a sale occurred. To eliminate the influence of outliers, when the number of shares locked exceeds the number of post-IPO shares held by insiders, we set the number of shares locked equal to 99 percent of post-IPO shares held by insiders. Row 4 provides information on the percent of insider shares sold relative to shares locked. Specifically, for each IPO we calculate the ratio of all shares sold early to the shares locked. In row 5 we calculate the percentage of shares held by insiders after the IPO that are subject to the lockup restriction. In row 6 we calculate, for each IPO, the average 30-day buy and hold abnormal return measured relative to the Nasdaq index. For example, the mean abnormal return preceding a sale is 4.76 percent. Row 7 provides information on average daily turnover measured over the period beginning 30 days preceding a sale through a day before the transaction. Both daily volume and shares outstanding are from CRSP. If a firm had more than one insider sale we average the resulting turnover measures.

Table 18.5
Characteristics of firms with and without early insider sales prior to lockup expiration

Did early sales occur?	Yes	No	*p*-Value of difference
Number of IPOs	429	2,317	
Average number of insider sales	6	—	
Sale time as fraction of lockup length (%)	64	—	
Shares locked relative to shares outstanding (%)	62	—	
Shares locked relative to post-IPO insiders' shares (%)	83	—	
Sum of shares sold early relative to shares locked (%)	5.22	—	
30-day abnormal return (%)	4.76	0.03	0.00
Daily share turnover over 30 days prior to sale (%)	1.27	0.01	0.00
Market capitalization (1992$ mil)	137	118	0.06
Underwriter rank	6.7	6.8	0.71
How many are venture backed? (%)	49	40	0.00

Note: For a detailed description of the construction of the insider database see table 18.3. The sample of insider sales consists of 1,436 events by 429 IPOs. We report descriptive statistics both for the sample IPOs in which insider sales occurred versus the remaining 2,317 IPOs in which sales did not occur. Note that the sum of the two subsamples does not add up to 2,974 as we discard events in which insiders' sales coincide with seasoned equity offerings. The variables, average number of insider sales, sale time as a fraction of lockup length, shares locked relative to shares outstanding, shares locked relative to post-IPO insiders' shares, and the sum of shares sold relative to shares locked are described in table 18.3. For the no-sale sample we measure the 30-day abnormal return as the abnormal return over the whole lockup period standardized to 30 days. Similarly the daily share turnover for the no-sale IPOs is measured over the whole lockup period. Underwriter rank is the Carter, Dark, and Singh (1997) underwriter reputation rank taking values from 1 (lowest rank) to 9 (highest rank). In the last row we report the frequency of venture-backed IPOs in each subsample. We report *p*-values for the test that the reported averages are unequal (assuming unknown but equal variances).

which sales did not occur. We find that insiders sell prior to lockup expiration in firms that are associated with less asymmetric information, namely large firms, firms with higher turnover, firms backed by venture capitalists, and firms with higher abnormal returns in the preceding 30-day period. The public is potentially less concerned that these firms will exploit some informational advantage by selling overvalued shares. Investors would potentially be very concerned by insider selling activity at low liquidity firms, firms not backed by venture capital, and firms with low returns because of the higher level of asymmetric information.

A final set of tests relating to insider transactions is presented in table 18.6. We estimate logit regressions to determine which firms are likely to have insiders released prior to lockup expiration. The dependent variable in table 18.6 takes the value of one if an early sale occurred prior to the lockup

Table 18.6
Logit analysis of early release

Variable	Estimate	Standard error	p-Value
Intercept	9.873	2.163	0.001
Prior abnormal return	0.224	0.023	0.000
Turnover (%)	0.065	0.077	0.402
Underpricing (%)	0.019	0.002	0.000
Venture backing	0.901	0.115	0.000
Lockup length in days	0.005	0.0004	0.000
Log of market value of equity (1992$ mil)	0.355	0.059	0.001
Percent of post-IPO insider shares locked	−0.005	0.002	0.025
High-tech industry	0.300	0.103	0.004
Annual time dummy	−0.151	0.024	0.000
Percent concordant		79.7	
Pseudo R^2		22.1	

Note: The sample is 1,436 insider sales prior to lockup expiration by 429 IPOs and 2,317 IPOs where no sales occurred. We calculate the probability that an early sale occurs prior to the expiration of the lockup agreement. The sum of the two subsamples does not add up to 2,974 as we discard events in which insiders' sales coincide with seasoned equity offerings. The explanatory variables are: The abnormal return prior to an insider sale, measured over the period beginning 30 days prior to a sale through a day beforehand. It is calculated as the difference between the firm's annualized buy-and-hold return minus the annualized Nasdaq return over the same time period. If no sale occurred, we use the annualized abnormal return calculated from the end of the IPO day through the end of the lockup period. Turnover is the average daily share turnover measured over the period beginning 30 days preceding a sale through a day before the transaction. If no sale occurred, we use the average daily turnover measured from the end of the IPO day through the end of the lockup period. Percentage of post-IPO insider shares locked is the fraction of post-IPO shares held by insiders that is subject to the lockup restriction. To eliminate the influence of outliers, when the number of shares locked exceeds the number of post-IPO shares held by insiders, we set the number of shares locked equal to 99 percent of post-IPO shares held by insiders. A high-tech industry dichotomous variable which is constructed using a subsample of 1003 IPOs from the following industries: computer manufacturing (SIC codes 3570–3579), electronic equipment (SIC codes 3660–3669, 367–3679, 3610–3659, 3680–3699), computer and data processing services (SIC codes 7370–7379), optical, medical, and scientific equipment (SIC codes 3810–3849), and communications (SIC codes 4800–4899). The remaining variables are the firm underpricing, measured as the percent return from the offering price to the first day closing price, a venture capital dichotomous variable taking the value 1 if the firm was venture backed, the length of the underwriter lockup in days, log of market value of equity in 1992 dollars, and an annual time dichotomous variable taking the values 1988 through 1996. To eliminate the possible influence of outliers, for each explanatory variable (except for the dichotomous variables) we replace observations whose values are either lower than the 1st or higher than the 99th percentiles by the sample median. We report the standard errors for each variable as well as the associated p-values. Percent concordant is the percentage times that the fitted model correctly predicts an early release.

expiration. As predicted by the commitment hypothesis, firms that have potentially lower or reduced information asymmetry problems are more likely to have early insider sales. The abnormal return over the preceding 30-day period is positively related to the probability of early sales; that is, firms with high abnormal returns are more likely to be associated with insiders being released early from their lockup restrictions. Firms with high returns are likely to have received a series of good news events and investors would be less concerned about adverse selection. Similarly high turnover, venture capital backing, and larger firm size are all related to a greater probability of early lockup release.

Large firms and firms with high turnover could have more information available about themselves. Venture capital-financed firms have the reputation of their venture capital investors to certify the firms' quality and limit potential adverse selection. Those firms with a greater fraction of their post-IPO insider shares locked are less likely to have insiders selling shares prior to the lockup expiration, consistent with the need for insiders in these firms to commit to not selling equity.

Event-Day Abnormal Return

Summary Statistics

In this section we explore the market price reaction around lockup expiration. Because the parameters of the lockup are well specified in the IPO prospectus, a simple rational expectations prediction is that the average price reaction at the time of the expiration be insignificantly different from zero. We first test this implication and then examine cross-sectional differences in abnormal returns around this event. This way we are able to provide additional evidence about the role of investment bankers and the function of the lockup provision. In particular, we are interested whether, conditional on the number of shares that might be sold by insiders, the public reacts more negatively to sales by insiders at lockup expiration in those firms that have had lower returns between the IPO and lockup expiration, those taken public by lower tier underwriters, or those firms that were not financed by venture capitalists. The commitment story predicts lower abnormal returns for firms that have had good news or are less subject to information asymmetry. The signaling hypothesis, however, has little to say on cross-sectional differences in abnormal returns. Hence later in this section we further explore differences in prices reaction to lockup expiration using tests of the commitment hypothesis.

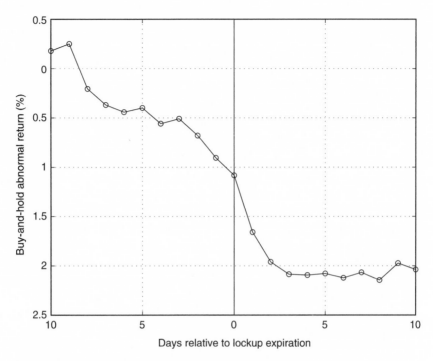

Figure 18.1
Buy-and-hold abnormal returns around lockup expirations. Beginning on day $t - 10$ and lasting through $t + 10$, we calculate the difference between the IPO firm's buy-and-hold return and the benchmark buy-and-hold return. We follow Michaely, Thaler, and Womack (1995) and use the return on a market index as a benchmark return.

We calculate abnormal returns for each IPO beginning in day $t - 10$ through $t + 10$ as the difference between the IPO firm's buy-and-hold return and the benchmark buy-and-hold return. We follow Michaely, Thaler, and Womack (1995) and use the return on a market index as a benchmark return. We employ the NYSE-AMEX value weight index throughout the analysis below.[12] In figure 18.1 we plot the average abnormal buy-and-hold return over the 21 event-days. From day -10 through day -2, abnormal returns appear to be quite small. From day -1 to day $+2$, however, abnormal returns are large and negative. Prices drop by nearly 1.5 percent around lockup expiration.

While at first glance the price decline appears to be consistent with a simple downward-sloping demand curves story, it is difficult to explain the

---

12. Our results are qualitatively similar if we use other benchmark returns such as the NYSE-AMEX equal weight index, S&P 500, or the Nasdaq buy-and-hold returns.

pattern within a rational expectations framework. The literature on additions to the S&P 500 show that a price increase occurs when a firm's addition to the S&P 500 is announced (Shleifer 1986; Harris and Gurel 1986; Beneish and Whaley 1996; Wurgler and Zhuravskaya 1999). The price rises on announcement because investors know that there will be increased demand in the future from index funds when the firm is added to the index. Similarly, in the case of underwriter lockups, investors know that a larger fraction of shares are freely tradable after a certain date. While investors may sell everything at that time, the market should get the number of shares sold at lockup expiration right on average. As such, some prices should decline at lockup expiration and some prices should rise. On average, however, abnormal return should be insignificantly different from zero (Allen and Postlewaite 1984). In order for downward-sloping demand curves to explain the average price decline that we observe, the market must hold consistently incorrect prior beliefs about how much equity will be sold at expiration and must therefore be consistently surprised by how many shares actually come to market.

Costly arbitrage (Pontiff 1996) might prevent investors from undertaking investments that would correct the temporary mispricing even if they know how many shares were coming to market. Investors may not want to try to "bet against" the stock by selling it short, since these newly public firms are very volatile. Good news may come to market that increases the price and causes a loss on the short position before the expiration of the lockup. Indeed, 40 percent of the event-day abnormal returns that we calculate are actually positive. Furthermore we find that transaction costs, calculated as the percentage bid-ask spread relative to the bid price, equal 6.3 percent on average, and are likely to eliminate the ability of investors to make money from the abnormal return that we document.[13] Finally, it may simply be hard to borrow shares in order to set up a short position given the small amount of shares that have been floated. Therefore, even if the market knows with a high degree of certainty the number of shares that will come to market, costly arbitrage may imply that the price may still decline on average at the expiration of the lockup.

Table 18.7 provides the daily abnormal returns as well as the buy-and-hold returns. The table reveals that each of the daily average abnormal returns (ARs) from day -3 to day $+2$ are negative, although only the ARs on day $+1$ is significant. Table 18.7 also tabulates the buy-and-hold abnor-

---

13. For this calculation we use bid and ask prices from CRSP on Nasdaq listed firms for the period beginning 30 days prior to the lockup expiration through one day before the event.

Table 18.7
Event time percentage abnormal returns

Days from lockup expiration	AR (%)	t-Statistic	Percent negative	BHR (%)	t-Statistic
−10	0.18	1.69	51.8	0.18	1.69
−9	0.12	1.24	52.2	0.25	1.93
−8	−0.40	3.92	55.3	−0.21	1.34
−7	−0.10	0.97	52.5	−0.37	2.20
−6	−0.02	0.22	51.4	−0.44	2.39
−5	0.12	1.17	51.4	−0.40	2.01
−4	−0.09	0.92	52.8	−0.56	2.64
−3	0.12	1.11	51.7	−0.51	2.25
−2	−0.15	1.40	54.3	−0.68	2.74
−1	−0.15	1.37	52.4	−0.91	3.59
0	−0.12	1.26	55.2	−1.08	4.10
+1	−0.52	5.00	57.0	−1.66	6.01
+2	−0.19	1.70	54.0	−1.96	6.92
+3	−0.07	0.76	52.1	−2.09	7.15
+4	0.06	0.60	51.6	−2.09	6.97
+5	0.07	0.66	51.2	−2.08	6.72
+6	0.04	0.35	52.5	−2.12	6.70
+7	0.12	1.03	52.3	−2.07	6.24
+8	0.01	0.09	53.6	−2.14	6.37
+9	0.29	2.60	50.7	−1.97	5.76
+10	−0.02	0.14	52.1	−2.04	5.58

Note: Daily abnormal returns and buy-and-hold abnormal returns around lockup expiration. The sample is 2,794 initial public offerings (IPOs) from January 1, 1988, through December 31, 1996. Since 45 firms delist before their stated lockup expiration, the sample size is reduced to 2,749 IPOs. The benchmark return is the NYSE-AMEX value weight market return. Buy-and-hold return is calculated from event day −10 through event day +10. Abnormal return is calculated as the difference between the IPO buy-and-hold return and the buy-and-hold return on the NYSE-AMEX value weight index. We report the average daily abnormal return, denoted AR, and the average buy-and-hold abnormal return, denoted BHR, in the table below. For each event day we also calculate the percentage of negative daily abnormal returns. t-statistics are calculated using the cross-sectional standard deviation of the firm abnormal returns.

mal return around lockup expiration. Buy-and-hold abnormal returns peak at -2.14 percent and t-statistics are significantly negative for all buy-and-hold returns from day -7 through day $+10$.[14]

The propensity of insiders to sell at the termination of the lockup leads us naturally to examine whether volume is abnormally high around the event. Some of this abnormal volume represents shares that are being sold on the market for the first time. A large part of the volume, however, may be due to increased information flowing to the market as investors observe insiders selling activity. We are interested in examining whether the price drops at lockup expiration are associated with greater abnormal volume. We calculate abnormal volume as in Brav and Heaton (1999). We obtain daily volume from CRSP and define normal volume as the mean daily volume in day $t - 71$ through day $t - 11$ relative to the event day. Abnormal volume is the daily volume in an event-day minus the mean daily volume, relative to the daily mean volume. To eliminate the effect of outliers on the analysis, we set observations greater than the 99th percentile in each event-day equal to the median observation.

The results are presented in figure 18.2. Nearly all event-days prior to the lockup expiration have an insignificant abnormal volume except for event-days -3 through -1, which are marginally significant. Abnormal volume from day 1 onward, however, is positive and statistically significant, peaking at 56 percent. In unreported results we find that abnormal volume does not revert back to zero when we increase the event window, indicating that the volume has permanently changed.

Cross-sectional Differences in Abnormal Returns

Now let us examine some additional information regarding the negative average abnormal return documented earlier. Our goal is to see whether

---

14. We also examined the sensitivity of our event study results to the computation of returns (Ball, Kothari, and Wasley 1995) and to potentially confounding events. First, to address the concern that the abnormal return we document is an artifact of movement of daily closing prices within the bid-ask spread, we calculated daily returns using bid to bid prices for those IPOs with available data on CRSP. Since CRSP provides daily closing bid and ask prices for Nasdaq stocks, we employed this subset in the following analysis. We found that the results from table 18.7 are not an artifact of trading and market microstructure problems. The bid-to-bid analysis reveals price declines from day -1 to day $+1$ of similar magnitude. Field and Hanka (2001) find similar evidence.

In an earlier draft we also examined whether the lockup expirations coincide with unexpectedly bad earnings announcement news. To this end, we collected from the Zacks database all earnings announcements that occurred within two days of the lockup expiration. We found, however, that the average abnormal return is of the same magnitude as for the remaining sample. As such, the negative results appear to be robust to alternative specifications.

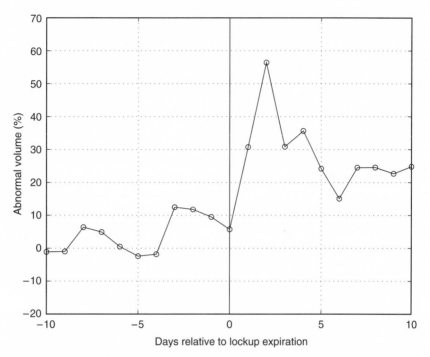

Figure 18.2
Abnormal volume around lockup expiration. We calculate abnormal volume as in Brav and Heaton (1999) and daily volume from CRSP. To eliminate the effect of outliers on the analysis, we set observations greater than the 99 percentile in each event day equal to the median observation.

cross-sectional differences in abnormal returns around this event can shed light on the competing hypotheses for the existence of lockups.

We extend this analysis in table 18.8 by considering the determinants of the price decline at lockup expiration. Our analysis is similar to Field and Hanka (2001), but while their regressions focus on downward-sloping demand curves, we focus on the potential level of asymmetric information related to firm value. The dependent variable is the buy-and-hold abnormal return from two days prior to two days after the expiration of the underwriter lockup. The independent variables are a dummy variable indicating whether the abnormal return between IPO and lockup expiration is above the median, the log of the market value of the IPO in 1992 constant dollars, the percentage of post-IPO insider shares locked, the percent of total shares offered as primary shares, the percent of the company's shares, both primary

Table 18.8
Regression results for buy-and-hold abnormal returns around lockup expirations

Dependent variable: Buy-and-hold abnormal return from two days before to two days after lockup expiration		
Constant	0.12	0.83
	[0.04]	[0.77]
Abnormal return prior to lockup expiration above median abnormal return	0.15	
	[0.33]	
Log of the market value of equity (1992$ mil)	−0.18	
	[0.60]	
Book-to-market ratio	0.65	
	[0.59]	
Venture capital backed?	−1.12	−1.12
	[2.56]	[2.89]
Underwriter rank	0.07	
	[0.58]	
Percentage of post-IPO insider shares locked	−0.02	−0.02
	[1.76]	[2.11]
Percent of offering that is primary shares	0.004	
	[0.17]	
Percent of company's shares issued in the IPO	0.02	0.03
	[1.13]	[2.10]
Cash flow margin	0.05	
	[1.06]	
Did the firm do an SEO after the IPO and before lockup expiration?	2.02	1.78
	[2.48]	[2.32]
Did IPO have any secondary shares?	0.91	
	[1.33]	
Did insiders sell any shares prior to lockup expiration?	0.46	
	[0.85]	
Firm's stock price volatility	−0.30	−0.30
	[1.85]	[2.37]
Adjusted R^2	1.3	1.4
Number of observations	1,149	1,818

Note: The dependent variable is the percentage buy-and-hold abnormal return from two days prior to two days after the expiration of the underwriter lockup. The independent variables are: The Carter, Dark, and Singh (1997) underwriter reputation rank of the lead investment bank taking values from 1 (lowest rank) to 9 (highest rank). The log of the market value of the IPO is in 1992 constant dollars. Percentage of post-IPO insider shares locked is the fraction of shares held by insiders after the IPO that are subject to the lockup restriction. To eliminate the influence of outliers, when the number of shares locked exceeds the number of post-IPO shares held by insiders, we set the number of shares locked equal to 99 percent of post-IPO shares held by insiders. The percent of total shares offered as primary shares. The percent of the company's shares, both primary and secondary, issued in the IPO relative to shares outstanding. Book-to-market ratio is the ratio of book equity to market equity in the first reporting period following the IPO (Compustat item 60) divided by the market capitalization at the IPO. A dichotomous variable takes the value 1 if the firm was financed by a venture capitalist. The cash flow margin

Table 18.8
(continued)
of the offering firm calculated as the ratio of operating cash flow to sales (Compustat items 308 and 12). The length of the underwriter lockup is in days. A dichotomous variable taking the value 1 if the buy and hold abnormal return since the offering was above the median firm's abnormal return. A dichotomous variable takes the value 1 if the firm conducted a seasoned equity offering before the lock up expiration. A dichotomous variable takes the value 1 if insider sales occurred before lockup expiration (insider transactions prior to lockup expiration are described in table 18.4). Stock price volatility measured as the daily standard deviation of the firm's abnormal return in the period beginning one day after the IPO and ending seven days prior to the lockup expiration. A dichotomous variable takes the value 1 if the firm sold secondary shares in the IPO. To eliminate the possible influence of outliers, for each variable, we replace observations whose values are either lower than the first or higher than the 99th percentiles by the sample median. [t-statistics are in brackets.]

and secondary, issued in the IPO relative to shares outstanding, the firm's market to book ratio, a dummy variable indicating whether the firm was financed by a venture capitalist, the Carter, Dark, and Singh underwriter ranking of the lead investment bank, the firm's stock price volatility, the cash flow margin of the offering firm, a dummy variable that equals one if the firm performed a seasoned equity offering between the IPO and lockup expiration, a dichotomous variable taking the value 1 if insider sales occurred before lockup expiration, and a dummy variable that equals one if any of the original IPO had any secondary shares.

The inclusion of variables indicating a firm's status as having performed a seasoned equity offering, having issued secondary shares, or having insiders sales prior to the expiration of the lockup controls for a reduced desire by insiders in this firms to sell after the lockup expiration. Similarly, in unreported results we find that doing a seasoned equity offering prior to the lockup expiration or having secondary shares in the offering are both positively related to our quality variables including venture capital backing, underwriter ranking, and cash flow margin. Hence, the information asymmetry problem is likely to be smaller for these firms and the price decline at lockup expiration reduced.[15]

---

15. In unreported results we also included in the regression a high-tech industry dichotomous variable to control for possible industry effects that may influence the nature of information and adverse selection. It was constructed using industry classifications from Brav (2000) and included a subsample of 1003 IPOs from the following industries: computer manufacturing (SIC codes 3570-3579), electronic equipment (SIC codes 3660-3669, 367-3679, 3610-3659, 3680-3699), computer and data processing services (SIC codes 7370-7379), optical, medical, and scientific equipment (SIC codes 3810-3849), and communications (SIC codes 4800-4899). We found that coefficient on this variable was insignificant, however.

The regression results are consistent with the commitment hypothesis. We find that the firm's status as a seasoned equity offering firm, having sold secondary shares, and early insider sales are related to smaller price drops, although only the seasoned equity offering dummy is statistically significant. As discussed above, insiders at these firms are less likely to sell shares at the lockup expiration; hence information asymmetry problems are reduced. Furthermore, to the extent that price volatility proxies for information asymmetry, the negative coefficient is consistent with the idea that lower transparency is associated with larger negative abnormal returns. The negative relationship, however, is also consistent with the discussion in the first part of the fifth section in which we argued that costly (risky) arbitrage limits the ability of arbitrageurs to short sell before lockup expiration. If highly volatile firms are riskier to short, then the empirical evidence indicates that these are the same firms whose abnormal return is larger in absolute value at lockup expiration.

On the other hand, the presence of venture capital investors and having a greater fraction of shares locked-up are both associated with larger price declines. Both of these variables likely proxy for a greater number of shares that are brought to market at the time of the lockup expiration. Many of these investors have automatic sell policies (see chapter 19), and hence more shares will be sold, on average, for venture capital-backed firms than similar firms not backed by venture capital, at the lockup expiration. While we would ideally be able to track all sales at the lockup expiration, including those by venture capitalists, chapter 19 notes that when venture capitalists distribute equity to their investors, they are not required to report this event to the SEC. As such, we cannot tabulate how many shares are actually sold by insiders on the lockup expiration date. What is clear, however, is that a large number of venture capital investors distribute their shares at the expiration date and many investors sell. Consequently a larger number of shares are likely to come to market at the lockup expiration for venture capital-backed companies.

Overall, the evidence from the price decline at lockup expiration is consistent with the earlier results relating to the use of IPO lockups to overcome information asymmetry. Price declines for firms which are less informationally sensitive appear to be smaller than other IPO firms.

Does the Underwriter Make Additional Compensation from Lockups?

So far we have only been able to examine the commitment hypothesis versus the signaling alternative. In this section we attempt to directly address the hypothesis that underwriters impose lockups on issuing firms to extract additional compensation. This could either be through forcing early sales to be traded by the market maker of the lead underwriter or by having the offering firm do a seasoned equity offering through the same investment bank. In the first case, the underwriter would make the bid-ask spread on the early sales by trading the insiders' shares. In the latter case, the investment bank would make additional fees underwriting the seasoned offering.

We first examine whether there are large market making profits made during the period of the lockup. We calculate a potential upper bound on the fees that the underwriter could have earned by taking all insider sales prior to lockup expiration and multiplying the number of shares sold by the bid-ask spread on the particular trading day. This way we can infer the largest gain the investment bank could have earned. First, it is important to note that only 429 of the 2,794 IPOs have any sales prior to lockup expiration. Even in those cases, the size of the transactions are relatively small, on average 5.2 percent of shares locked (median of 0.8 percent). The average market maker fee that could have been earned by the lead underwriter in this sample, conditional on an insider sale occurring, was $45,578 (median fee was $9,375). These results are in agreement with the results of Ellis, Michaely, and O'Hara (2000), who show that market making brings very little revenue to investment banks after the IPO.

A second test of the underwriter market power story entails examining firms that subsequently do seasoned equity offerings. If the underwriter is using the lockup to gain additional income, then any seasoned offering within the lockup period should be more likely to use the same investment bank as the lead underwriter, controlling for other firm and investment banker characteristics. To test this prediction, we follow Krigman, Shaw, and Womack (2001) who have recently examined in detail the determinants of underwriter changes in follow-on offerings. We first obtain information on seasoned equity offerings conducted by our sample IPOs from Securities Data Company. We include all seasoned offerings if they occur within four years of the IPO (896 events) and record those SEOs in which a firm has decided to switch its lead underwriter. The underwriter market power hypothesis predicts that if a firm does a seasoned offering, the probability of using the same lead underwriter should be higher if the offering occurs within the lockup period, controlling for the variables that Krigman and colleagues have found significant in influencing the decision of managers to switch underwriter.

Table 18.9 presents regression results for the SEOs. The dependent variable takes the value one if the firm performs a seasoned equity offering and

Table 18.9
Logit regression for the probability of switching underwriters in a seasoned equity offering

Variable	Estimate	Standard error	p-Value
Intercept	7.508	2.073	0.000
Logarithm of the expected proceeds from the IPO	−1.272	0.277	0.000
Percent revision in the IPO offering amount	−1.956	0.468	0.000
Change in the underwriter rank	0.378	0.064	0.000
Days from IPO to SEO	0.003	0.0003	0.000
Net gain/loss of lead All Star coverage	0.284	0.180	0.115
Is the SEO within the lockup period	0.060	0.268	0.822
Percent concordant		78.7	
Pseudo R^2		20.1	

Note: The sample is 896 SEOs that took place within four years of the IPO for our sample of 2,794 firms. Data on SEOs comes from SDC. The dependent variable takes the value 1 if the firm performs an SEO and uses a different lead underwriter from the lead underwriter that was used in the IPO. Independent variables include the natural logarithm of the expected IPO proceeds defined as the log of the shares offered times the midpoint of the initial filing range. The actual revision to the IPO offering amount is defined as the number of shares offered times the change in the price from the midpoint of the filing range to the final offer price, divided by the expected proceeds. The change in the rank of the underwriter from the IPO to the SEO defines underwriter rank as in Carter, Dark, and Singh (1997). The net gain/loss of lead All-Star coverage after the SEO is formed as in Krigman et al., by collecting information on analyst inclusion in the first, second or third All-America Research team. These data are collected from the October issues of the *Institutional Investor* publications for the period 1988–1999. Other variables include the number of days from the IPO to the SEO, and a dummy variable that equals one of the SEO occurs before the expiration of the lockup. To eliminate the possible influence of outliers, for each non-dichotomous variable, we replace observations whose values are either lower than the first or higher than the 99th percentiles by the sample median. Percent concordant is the percentage times that the fitted model correctly predicts an underwriter switch.

uses a different lead underwriter from the lead underwriter that was used in IPO. The independent variables are defined as in Krigman, Shaw, and Womack (2001). They are the natural logarithm of the expected IPO proceeds defined as the log of the shares offered times the midpoint of the initial filing range; the actual revision to the IPO offering amount defined as the number of shares offered times the change in the price from the midpoint of the filing range to the final offer price, divided by the expected proceeds; the change in underwriter rank from the IPO to the SEO where underwriter rank is from Carter, Dark, and Singh (1997); the number of days from the IPO to the SEO; the net gain/loss of lead All-Star coverage after the SEO, formed as in Krigman and colleagues, by collecting information on analyst inclusion in the first, second, or third All-America Research team.[16] Finally, we include a dummy variable that equals one if the SEO occurs before the expiration of the lockup. The latter variable should be negatively related to the probability of switching according to the underwriter compensation hypothesis.

Consistent with Krigman, Shaw, and Womack (2001), we find that the issuer is more likely to switch underwriter when the underwriter of seasoned offering has a higher rank (i.e., offering firms more likely to "trade up" in terms of investment banks). Similarly, an increase in All-Star coverage is positively associated with the probability of switching which, as Krigman and colleagues point out, reflects the importance of research coverage to the choice of underwriter. We also find that the probability of changing underwriters is higher the greater the time between the IPO and the SEO as documented by James (1992). Finally, the logarithm of the expected proceeds from the IPO and the percent revision in the IPO offering amount are negatively related to the probability of switching. However, the probability of retaining the same underwriter is unrelated to whether the seasoned offering is within the lockup period or not. This evidence appears to reject the underwriter market power hypothesis because the lockup variable should have increased the probability of retaining the lead underwriter.

Conclusions

The use of underwriter lockups has received considerable attention in the business press, and in this chapter we explored their use and impact on financial markets. In particular, we explored the reason that underwriter lockups exist. We found support for the notion that lockups serve as a commitment device to overcome moral hazard problems subsequent to the initial public offering. Firms that are unprofitable, that have low book-to-market ratios, that go public with lower quality underwriters, and are not venture capital backed have significantly longer lockups. In addition, while 15 percent of the firms in our sample experience insider sales prior to the expiration of the lockup agreement, early sales by insiders are more likely in firms that have less potential for managers to use private information about firm value. This includes firms that have had high post-IPO returns, firms that go public with high-quality underwriters, and firms that were financed by venture capitalists. Evidence from the price decline at the lockup expiration indicates that the negative abnormal return is smaller for firms that are more informationally transparent. We find little evidence to support the

---

16. The data are collected from the October issues of the *Institutional Investor* publications for the period 1988 to 1999.

signaling hypothesis, which predicts that firms would signal their quality to increase the offering price or perform a future seasoned equity offering. Finally, in conducting additional tests, we could refute the hypothesis that investment banks are able to extract additional compensation by imposing longer lockups.

Our work in this chapter leaves several questions unanswered. For example, what is the experience with lockups internationally? Is the trading behavior by insiders and the price reaction at expiration similar? What is the role, if any, of analysts around lockups expirations?[17] Do underwriters in other markets impose the same types of trading restrictions? How do these restrictions relate to the laws governing insider trading and information disclosure? In addition our work potentially provides some insights into policy concerning lockup provisions and insider sales. Should the SEC regulate these IPO lockup contracts?

Finally, the average abnormal return that we document at lockup expiration needs to be more fully explored. We show that the price reaction at the lockup expiration equals −2 percent on average. This abnormal return is potentially consistent with costly arbitrage and downward-sloping demand curves or investors' incorrect prior beliefs regarding the extent of insider sales. Several recent papers, including Field and Hanka (2001), have documented this price decline as well, but its existence is not fully explained. Future work would hopefully provide deeper insights into the reasons why this price decline exists and whether the price decline is temporary or permanent.

Appendix: Search for Lockup Information When Missing

In our original sample of 2,871 IPOs from SDC, 255 contained no information on a lockup provision. In order to determine whether any of these firms

---

17. Brav and Gompers (2000) provide evidence on the role of analysts around lockups expirations. We show that analysts, both affiliated and unaffiliated, tend to issue more optimistic earnings forecasts at the time of the lockup expiration. There appears to be no significant difference in the accuracy of affiliated and unaffiliated analyst earnings forecasts. Affiliated analysts, however, tend to issue more favorable recommendations at the lockup expiration. Our findings are consistent with either earnings management (Teoh, Welch, and Wong 1998) or the management of analyst expectations by insiders. It is possible that IPO firms tend to "boost" earnings around the lockup expiration and the analysts extrapolate this trend in their earnings forecasts. This could account for the increasing optimism after lockup expiration. Similarly insiders may choose to release more favorable information just prior to lockup expiration to boost analysts' recommendations. Because the insiders sell little of their holdings at IPO and are restricted from selling until after the lockup expiration, engaging in earnings management prior to the release is clearly in their self-interest (Rajan and Servaes 1995; Brav, Cornelli, and Heaton 2001; Aggarwal, Krigman, and Womack 2002).

did or did not have a lockup governing their offering, we took the 255 companies and their IPO dates. We then searched for the company prospectuses on Global Access, Microfiche, Laser Disclosure CD-Rom, and the Edgar Database on *www.sec.gov*. Of the 255 companies, we were unable to locate prospectuses for 45 of these companies (entered as N/A in our table). For the remaining 210 companies, we looked for information on their lockup agreements in the prospectuses under "Shares Eligible for Future Sale," "Underwriting," and "Additional Market Information." From the 210 companies with available prospectuses, 32 of these companies did not have any lockup agreement. The remaining 178 companies were then categorized according to the nature of their lockup agreements: 153 companies had a lockup agreement with the underwriters, 22 had lockup agreements according to SEC Rule 144, and 3 companies had some shares entered in a lockup agreement with the underwriter and other shares restricted by SEC Rule 144. The results are summarized below:

Total companies	255
Company IPO prospectuses not available (na):	45
Available prospectuses	210
Companies with no lockup agreement	32
Companies with lockup agreements	178
Companies with underwriter lockup agreements	153
Companies with shares restricted under SEC Rule 144	22

19 Why Do Venture Capitalists Distribute Shares?

An enduring issue in the corporate finance literature has been the impact of trading by informed insiders on securities prices. Two cases initiated by the U.S. Securities and Exchange Commission (SEC) in the early 1960s[1] stimulated an interest in this relationship and its implications for social welfare (e.g., Manne 1966) that continues to this day.

An extensive body of research has examined trading by corporate insiders. Notably, Seyhun (e.g., 1986, 1988) has documented the short- and long-run price impacts of trading by officers, directors, and other insiders. But as Meulbroek (1992b) notes:

Self-reported corporate transactions data [are] less appropriate for addressing [the impact of informed traders on stock prices]. The corporate transactions are by definition not based on material, nonpublic information. Because corporate insiders cannot legally trade on such information, they would most likely refrain from reporting their violative transactions to the SEC.

In this chapter we address the insider problem by examining the stock price reaction to a set of transactions by informed parties that are not affected by these legal constraints. But rather than focusing on illegal trades, as Meulbroek does, we examine a class of legal transactions that are largely exempt from SEC oversight—the distribution of shares in public companies by venture capital funds to their limited partners. Venture capitalists raise money from investors and make equity investments in young, high-risk, high-growth companies. Most successful venture capital-backed companies eventually go public in an underwritten initial public offering (IPO). Venture capitalists can liquidate their position in the company by selling shares on the open market and then paying those proceeds to investors in cash. More

---

1. In the Matter of Cady, Roberts and Co., SEC Release No. 6668, CCH Federal Securities Law Reporter par 76,803 (1961); *SEC v. Texas Gulf Sulphur Co.*, 401 F. Supp. 262 (S.D.N.Y. 1966), 401 F.2d 833 (2d Cir. 1968), 312 F. Supp. 77 (S.D.N.Y. 1970).

frequently, however, venture capitalists make distributions of shares to investors in the venture capital fund.

These distributions have several features that make them an interesting testing ground for an examination of the impact of transactions by informed insiders on securities prices. Because they are not considered to be "sales," the distributions are exempt from the antifraud and antimanipulation provisions of the securities laws. The legality of distributions provides an important advantage. Comprehensive records of these transactions are compiled by institutional investors and intermediaries who invest in venture funds, addressing concerns about sample selection bias. Like trades by corporate insiders, transactions are not revealed at the time of the transaction. Venture capitalists can immediately declare a distribution, send investors their shares, and need not register with the SEC or file a report under Rule 16(a). Rather, the occurrence of such distributions can only be discovered from corporate filings with a lag, and even then the distribution date cannot be precisely identified. To identify the time of these transactions, one needs to rely (as we do) on the records of the partners in the fund. We can also characterize in detail the features of the venture funds making the distributions, the firms whose shares are being distributed, and the changes associated with the transactions in a way that can discriminate among various alternative explanations for these patterns.

From the records of four institutions, we construct a representative set of over 700 transactions by 135 funds over a decade-long period. The results are consistent with venture capitalists possessing inside information and of the (partial) adjustment of the market to that information. After significant increases in stock prices prior to distribution, abnormal returns around the distribution are a negative and significant -2.0 percent, comparable to the market reaction to publicly announced secondary stock sales. The sign and significance of the cumulative excess returns for the twelve months following the distribution are sensitive to the benchmark used. The market's ability to discern and react to the information content of distributions is consistent with Seyhun (1986) and Meulbroek (1992b).

Significant differences appear in the returns for some subsamples. Distributions that occur in settings where information asymmetries may be greatest—especially where the firm has been taken public by a lower tier underwriter and the distribution is soon after the IPO—have larger immediate price declines. Postdistribution price performance is related to factors that predict event window returns.

At the same time we must acknowledge some important limitations to the analysis. Many of the recipients of these distributions (e.g., pension funds and endowments) will not desire to hold the distributed securities. Because distributions are not illegal, the limited partners will have no reason to disguise their sales (aside from reasons of strategic trading). In this sense the distributions resemble the legal insider transactions that have been extensively examined by Seyhun (1986) and others. Furthermore at least two other factors may cause the share price to drop at the time of distribution: the ending of the venture capitalists' value-added monitoring (since they often resign from the board at the time of the distributions) and the large increase in the public supply of shares after distribution (if demand for the company's stock is not perfectly elastic). To test these alternatives, we seek to explain the size of the short- and long-run reactions to these distributions. Variables that are consistent with these alternative hypotheses have little explanatory power.

In addition to works on insider trading, this study is related to several strands in the corporate finance literature. First, we draw upon the methodological studies on the measurement of long-run returns of securities. These works include Ball, Kothari, and Shanken (1995), Barber and Lyon (1997), Kothari and Warner (1997), and Barber, Lyon, and Tsai (1999). Second, an extensive literature (e.g., Mikkelson and Partch 1985) has shown that announcements of firms' intentions to undertake secondary issues and sales of shares by corporate insiders lead to immediate negative market reactions. Additionally Kahle (1996) has shown that firms issuing securities after insider sales experience significant negative excess returns, but other securities issuers do not. Another related strand is studies of the long-run performance of IPOs (e.g., Loughran and Ritter 1995). This analysis is closely related to chapter 20, which contrasts the post-IPO stock returns of venture-backed and nonventure firms. Although there certainly is overlap between the two analyses (most of the firms we examine had gone public, on average, one-and-a-half years prior to the distribution), our focus here is different. In particular, rather than studying the long-run returns of a particular class of securities, we seek to understand how rapidly transactions by informed insiders are incorporated into the stock price. At the same time our finding of greater efficiency in the market for venture-backed securities (when contrasted with Kahle's results) is reminiscent of that chapter's conclusions.

Venture Capitalists and Distribution Policy

As discussed in the preceding chapters, venture capitalists typically exit successful investments by taking them public. They usually do not sell shares at the time of the IPO but rather undertake a "lockup" agreement with the investment banker underwriting the offering in which they promise to refrain from selling their shares for several months.[2] Even after the lockup expires, venture capitalists will often continue to hold the shares in the company for months or even years. A more in-depth discussion of lockups is presented in chapter 18.

Once the venture capitalists decide to liquidate their positions, there are two alternatives. First, they can sell the shares they hold on the open market and distribute cash to limited partners. More often venture capitalists distribute shares to each limited partner and frequently to themselves.

A number of reasons are responsible for the preponderance of distributions in kind. First, SEC rules restrict sales by corporate insiders. Insiders, including the venture capitalist, are only allowed to sell shares each quarter up to the greater of 1 percent of the outstanding equity or the average weekly trading volume. The venture capital fund may hold a large fraction of the company's equity and selling the entire stake may take a long time. By distributing shares to limited partners, who are usually not considered insiders,[3] the venture capitalist can dispose of a large block of shares more quickly.

Second, tax motivations may also provide an incentive for the venture capitalist to distribute shares. If venture capitalists sell shares and distribute cash, taxable limited partners (e.g., individuals and corporations) and the venture capitalists themselves are subject to immediate capital gains taxes. These investors might prefer to postpone these taxes by receiving distributions in kind and selling the shares at a later date. These considerations will be unimportant to tax-exempt limited partners (e.g., pension funds and endowments). By distributing stock, venture capitalists provide limited partners with the flexibility to make their own decisions about selling the stock.

Third, if selling the shares has a large negative effect on prices, venture capitalists may want to distribute shares. The method of computing returns employed by limited partners and outside fund trackers (e.g., Venture Economics) uses the closing price of the distributed stock on the day the distribution is declared. The actual price received when the limited partners sell

---

2. Lin and Smith (1998) show that the shares sold by venture capitalists at the time of 497 venture-backed IPOs from 1979 to 1990 (representing 77 percent of the total number of venture-backed IPOs in this period) totaled less than $400 million. This represents about 1 percent of the total amount raised by venture capital funds in this period.

3. Limited partners in a venture capital fund would not be considered insiders unless they had board representation or some other affiliation with the portfolio company, or held 10 percent of the company's equity. Once the distribution is made, it is unlikely that any limited partner would hold 10 percent. A limited partner would not have board representation or it would risk losing its limited liability status.

their shares may be lower. If prices decline after the distribution, actual returns to limited partners could be substantially less than calculated returns. Venture capitalists care about stated returns on their funds because they use this information when they raise new funds.

Finally, the venture capitalist's compensation can be affected by distribution policy. If the venture capital fund has not returned committed capital to its limited partners, most funds distribute shares of portfolio companies in proportion to the partners' actual capital commitments (usually 99 percent to limited partners and 1 percent to general partners). By distributing overvalued shares prior to the return of committed capital, the venture capitalist moves closer to the point where general partners collect a larger share of the profits. Once committed capital has been returned, venture capitalists still have an incentive to distribute overvalued shares. They may be able to sell their portions at a high valuation before limited partners receive their shares and the market discerns that a distribution has occurred. This problem is exacerbated if the venture partnership agreement allows, as many do, venture capitalists to receive distributions at their discretion prior to the return of the investors' committed capital. In these instances the venture capitalist has even greater flexibility in choosing whether to be included in the distribution.

A venture capitalist's reputational concerns may not overcome the incentive to distribute overvalued shares. First, many institutional investors and advisors also care about stated return. They may be compensated based on how well the venture funds that they select do relative to a benchmark (calculated using the distribution price). This is particularly true if the shares are transferred immediately on receipt of the distribution to its public-equity managers. Any price decline may be attributed to the public-equity group. Second, certain investors may be unaware of the problem. Investors may not track stock price performance against an appropriate benchmark. Similarly record keeping of the price at which the shares were sold is often incomplete.

Few SEC regulations cover distributions by private equity investors. Rule 16(a) states that individuals who are affiliates of a firm, such as directors, officers, and holders of 10 percent of the company's shares, must disclose any transactions in the firm's stock on a monthly basis. Provision 16(a)-7, however, explicitly exempts distributions of securities that (1) were originally obtained from issuers and (2) are being distributed "in good faith, in the ordinary course of business." An interpretation widely accepted within the industry is that venture capitalists distribute investments in the normal course of business, and that they do not convey any information unless the venture capitalist makes an explicit recommendation to hold or sell the shares at the time. Venture capital lawyers have applied the same principles when considering the applicability of Rule 10(b)-5, the most general prohibition against fraudulent activity in the purchase or sale of any security.

Analysis of Distributions

Sample and Summary Statistics

We collect data on the date, size, and sources of all distributions received by two institutional investors in venture funds and three investment advisors. We eliminate distributions from funds that primarily invested in leveraged buyouts and from publicly traded Small Business Investment Companies because the nature of these funds' investments and the incentives introduced by their compensation schemes and structures were quite different. In the relatively modest number of cases where contradictory information was recorded about the same distribution, we check with the organizations to reconcile the discrepancies. These deletions and corrections leave 731 distributions of shares in 259 firms by 135 venture capital limited partnerships.

The first panel of table 19.1 summarizes the IPOs and distributions in our sample. The increasing trend in distributions reflects two factors. First, the IPO market has hot and cold periods. The early 1990s saw a prolonged "hot issue" market with many IPOs. Second, venture capital under management grew substantially during this period: the venture pool was twelve times larger (in inflation-adjusted dollars) in 1993 than in 1980. The panel also shows how the aggregate number of venture-backed IPOs and distributions by venture capitalists increased over this period.

In panel B of table 19.1 we examine the representativeness of the venture funds for which we are able to collect distribution data. We compare the venture partnerships in our sample with all the partnerships identified by Venture Economics that closed prior to 1993 (for an overview of the database and our emendations to it, see chapter 22) on several dimensions: the age of the venture organization sponsoring the fund (the span between the date when the venture organization's first fund closed and the first closing of this fund), the size of the venture organization (the sum of funds in 1997 dollars that the venture organization has raised in the decade prior to the distribution), and the ordinal rank of the fund (the count of this fund among those raised by the venture organization). While our sample is representative in terms of closing date, it is biased toward larger, older venture capital firms that have raised more previous funds.

Table 19.1
Sample summary statistics

Year	All activity (1997$ bil)		Number of IPOs in our sample	Number of distributions in our sample
	Venture stake in IPOs	Venture distributions		
Panel A: Summary of IPO and distribution activity				
1978			1	0
1979			0	0
1980	0.06	0.10	2	0
1981	0.43	0.13	3	0
1982	0.24	0.33	3	0
1983	2.42	0.58	18	1
1984	0.41	0.30	11	0
1985	0.40	0.36	8	19
1986	1.58	0.39	27	33
1987	1.42	0.68	22	55
1988	0.82	0.29	16	21
1989	0.70	0.44	15	51
1990	1.29	0.76	20	80
1991	3.48	1.63	55	134
1992	3.52	1.57	44	195
1993	3.89	1.88	14	142
Total	20.63	9.44	259	731

	Included in our sample	Not in our sample, but in venture economics database	p-Value, test of no difference
Panel B: Comparison of funds included and not included in the sample			
Number of observations	135	1139	
Date of fund's first closing	Mar 1984 (Jan 1984)	Oct 1983 (Apr 1984)	0.143 (0.908)
Size of fund (1997$ mil)	109.5 (76.5)	747.3 (31.9)	0.000 (0.000)
Size of venture firm (1997$ mil)	227.8 (130.2)	120.4 (56.1)	0.000 (0.000)
Age of venture firm at time of fund's first closing (years)	5.63 (4.17)	3.65 (1.17)	0.000 (0.000)
Ordinal rank of fund	3.20 (3)	2.65 (2)	0.000 (0.000)

Table 19.1

(continued)

	Mean	Median	Standard deviation
Panel C: Characteristics of distributions	.		
All distributions:			
Time from IPO (years)	1.78	1.02	1.90
Percent of VC's holdings distributed	67.2	68.9	33.6
First distributions only:			
Time from IPO (years)	1.69	0.90	1.87
Percent of VC's holdings distributed	81.0	100	29.4
Fifth distributions only:			
Time from IPO (years)	2.57	2.60	1.45
Percent of VC's holdings distributed	26.0	24.4	16.6
Key independent variables:			
Age of venture capital firm at time of distribution (years)	5.41	4.09	5.07
Underwriter rank	8.53	8.875	1.11
Market value of firm's equity at time of IPO (1997$ mil)	174.5	153.7	102.9

Note: In the first panel, the venture capital stake of initial public offerings (IPOs) is the value of all shares held by venture capital (VC) limited partnerships in firms that went public in that year valued at the IPO price. The distribution series is the value of shares distributed by all venture capital limited partnerships to their investors, and is based on the records of Shott Capital Management (including distributions not in our sample). The first panel also presents the number of IPOs and distributions in each year of the sample. In the second panel, in the first two columns we compare the characteristics of the funds in our sample with those within the Venture Economics funds database whose first closing was December 1992 or earlier but whose funds are not in our sample. We present both the mean and the median (in parentheses) of several measures. In the third column we present the *p*-values of *t*-tests and Wilcoxon signed-rank tests (in parentheses) of the null hypotheses that these distributions are identical. In the third panel are some key characteristics of the distributions, as well as of some important independent variables.

More information about the distributions is presented in the third panel of table 19.1. The typical distribution occurs nearly twenty months after the firm goes public. This distribution is skewed, with the median distribution occurring little more than one year after the IPO. Only 1 percent of the distributions occur in the three months immediately after going public: the lockup agreements that restrict insiders from selling shares after an IPO (typically for 40 to 180 trading days) preclude stock distributions as well.[4]

---

4. We do not present summary statistics about the time from share purchase to ultimate distribution. Because venture capitalists typically invest in successful firms in multiple rounds, it is difficult to determine how long the distributed shares have been held. Venture partnership agreements typically bar the distribution of shares covered by SEC Rule 144, which during the period under study prohibited sales for two years after the purchase of restricted stock and limited the pace of sales between the second and third year after the purchase. These restric-

In many cases there are multiple distributions for each firm. These are primarily due to the presence of several venture investors in the firm rather than multiple distributions of shares in the company by the same venture capitalist. Venture capitalists tend to distribute the entirety of their holdings at once: the third panel of table 19.1 reports that the average distribution involves 67 percent of shares that the venture capitalist holds. The table also provides summary data on two representative distributions: the first and fifth distributions of shares in a company. Not surprisingly, fifth distributions tend to occur later and involve a smaller percent of the venture capitalist's original holdings. (If there are many distributions, it is more likely that the venture capitalists are distributing their shares in several installments.) We discuss the issues posed by multiple distributions below.

Framework for the Analysis

We have already noted an important distinction between venture distributions and illegal insider trading: the limited partners may have few incentives to disguise the fact that a distribution has occurred. Additional differences stem from the fact that unlike an illegal insider trade, other events occur at the time of the distribution. First, venture capitalists hold large equity stakes and board seats even after the IPO. When the venture capitalist declares a distribution, an active, large-block shareholder is essentially dissolved. Theoretical and empirical work by Jensen and Meckling (1976), Shleifer and Vishny (1986), and others have shown that large block shareholders, who are often willing to incur the costs of monitoring management, can play an important role in increasing firm value. The unanticipated dissolution of a large block holding provides an alternative explanation for stock price declines at the time of the distribution.

The increased number of publicly tradable shares associated with distributions suggests a second explanation. While their findings are not uncontroversial, a number of studies (e.g., Harris and Gurel 1986 and Shleifer 1986) have suggested that demand curves for shares may slope downwards. If the demand for shares is not totally elastic, then increasing the supply of publicly tradable shares would decrease their price. The median lead venture capitalist controls 11.8 percent of the shares of the company subsequent to

---

tions applied not only to the venture investor but also to the limited partners in their funds. Cases involving distributions of shares held for less than two years appear to comprise at most only a few distributions in the sample, and those of less than three years under 10 percent. Conversations with practitioners similarly suggest that such distributions are very rare. For a discussion, see Denning and Painter (1994).

the IPO (Barry et al. 1990). Since a typical venture-backed IPO has only about 30 percent of the shares in the initial public float, the distribution and subsequent sale of these securities represents a substantial increase in the number of publicly traded shares and may trigger a price decline.

Liquidity may play a role in price movements even if long-run demand curves for shares are not downward sloping. Bid-ask spreads or temporary price movements may be related to abnormal volume in the market. For example, a large block of shares may trade at a lower price because the market for the company's equity is not very liquid. If liquidity is the primary reason for price movements, stock prices should decline around distributions but quickly recover thereafter.

One way to address these alternative explanations is to examine how stock price reactions to distributions are associated with the characteristics of the venture capitalist and the firm. While many of these individual items can be criticized for their imprecision, if the evidence is consistent with a considerable majority of one set of predictions, we will be more comfortable with that view. We first examine the impact of the age of the venture organization making the distribution. If the markets are reacting to insider trading by the venture capitalists, distributions by more experienced venture capitalists should produce more negative price reactions. The corporate control alternative also predicts a negative relationship, because older venture firms may be better monitors and the elimination of their oversight reduces firm value more. We determine venture firm age from the Venture Economics database.[5]

The size of the equity stake held by the venture firm may be related to the incentive to monitor and the quality of information about the company. Both our central insider trading hypothesis and the corporate control alternative predict a negative relationship between the size of the equity stake and the price reaction to the distribution. The downward-sloping demand curve suggestion predicts that only the size of the equity stake actually distributed should affect prices. The stock price reaction should be independent of total equity stake held (but not distributed) by the venture capital firm. (If the market can forecast future distributions at the time of the first distribution, stock price reaction to the first distribution may be related to the size of the equity stake held.) This information is obtained from the parties receiving the distributions.

---

5. We might anticipate that this relationship would be nonlinear: venture firms that were about to disband might behave differently from ongoing organizations. This is, however, difficult to predict in advance. Many venture firms raise series of successful funds, while others never raise a follow-on to their first fund.

Underwriters may also play a role in limiting asymmetric information. The number and quality of analysts are often correlated with the reputation of the underwriter. If the market is reacting to insider trading by the venture capitalists, then companies going public with higher quality underwriters should have less negative price reactions because there are fewer information asymmetries. The characteristics of the IPOs of the distributed companies are found in SDC's Corporate New Issues database. We denote the quality of the underwriters using their relative standing in the period from 1985 to 1991 (Carter, Dark, and Singh 1998).

The level of asymmetric information between the venture capitalists and the market may be considerably higher for companies that have been public for a short time. These firms are likely to have less analyst coverage as well as a shorter track record over which the firms' management and prospects can be assessed. If venture capitalists have access to inside information, suggesting that these firms are severely overvalued, they may quickly distribute recent IPOs. On average, the market should interpret distributions soon after IPO as a sign of relatively greater overvaluation, and the length of time from IPO to distribution should be positively related to abnormal returns. The corporate control and downward-sloping demand alternatives suggest that the price response should be independent of the length of time that the shares have been held. If the market is reacting to insider trading or the corporate control alternative holds, then most of the negative information will be conveyed in the first distribution of a company's shares. Later distributions should have much smaller price responses because the first distribution revealed that the venture capitalist considers the firm overvalued or intends to exit the investment.

The availability of information may also be related to the size of the firm. Larger firms are likely to be tracked by more and better analysts. They are also more likely to be scrutinized in the media, which also reduces asymmetric information. The ability to trade on inside information should therefore be reduced for larger firms and price declines at distribution should be smaller. The alternative views have no clear predictions about the relation between the price reaction and firm size. We employ the valuation at the close for the first trading day for this analysis.

Board representation may also be associated with greater access to inside information. Consequently, if the market is reacting to insider trades, there should be more negative price reactions to distributions by board members. The corporate control alternative would also predict that the stock price of companies declines more when venture capitalists leave the board at distribution. Not only is a large block dissipated, but also venture capitalists no longer have the same control rights or information flows once they leave the board. Board membership and share ownership at and after the IPO date are obtained from prospectuses and annual proxy statements.

Contracts governing venture partnerships can also specify whether venture capitalists must distribute or sell shares soon after the IPO. If distributions within a certain time are mandatory, the market should not infer any negative information from the distribution event. If the alternative corporate control or downward-sloping demand curves views explain price reactions, then distribution restrictions should not affect the magnitude of the price decline at distribution. Unfortunately for our empirical tests, the bulk of the distribution restrictions (which we collect from partnership agreements provided by the four institutions who contribute distribution data) are quite weak: the partnership agreements of funds with restrictions almost invariably allow distributions to be deferred with the approval of the majority (or super-majority) of the fund's advisory board. In practice, it appears that these distribution restrictions have a relatively limited effect on behavior: for the twenty venture-backed IPOs in the sample where distributions were made both by funds with and without distribution restrictions, the distribution dates were not significantly different from each other. In fact the average distribution by a fund without such a restriction occurred two weeks before that by a fund with a restriction. (This result was not driven by a single outlier among the restricted distributions. There was actually a lower variance in the time from IPO to distribution among the restricted distributions, though the difference was not significant.) Thus the extent to which this measure can help us distinguish between hypotheses seems limited.

Stock Price Reaction to Distributions during the Event Window

The stock price response to distributions is estimated using a two-factor market model employing daily Center for Research in Security Prices (CRSP) stock price data. The two-factor market model utilizes $R_{m,t}$, the return on the CRSP value-weighted Nasdaq index, and $R_{s,t}$, the return on the Nasdaq smallest decile, to determine daily abnormal returns. Equation (1) is estimated for each firm using daily data:

$$R_{j,t} = \alpha_j + \beta_{j,m} R_{m,t} + \beta_{j,s} R_{s,t} + \varepsilon_t. \tag{1}$$

The regression coefficients (factor loadings) are calculated from trading day -260 to day -61 and from trading day $+160$ to day $+360$ relative to the distribution (or for the available subsets of these periods). We designate day 0 the day that the venture capitalist declared the distribution.[6] The coefficients are then used to calculate predicted returns. The difference between the predicted and actual return is labeled an abnormal return (AR), as shown in equation (2):

$$AR_{j,t} = R_{j,t} - (\alpha_j + \beta_{j,m}R_{m,t} + \beta_{j,s}R_{s,t}).$$

(2)

Table 19.2 documents the large price appreciation before the distribution. The cumulated ARs (CARs) for the twenty days prior to distribution are +3.7 percent. The abnormal returns for the three trading days following the distribution are all negative and significant. From day 0 to day +3, the CAR is −2.0 percent. The next seventeen trading days show little price movement. Figure 19.1 plots the CARs for all distributions. After a major rise of +7.4 percent from day −60 to day −1, the three days after the distribution date have negative CARs. Over the next three weeks the stock price reacts very little. From day +20 to +100, the CAR is once again significantly negative, −5.5 percent. This overall pattern is only suggestive of long-run returns. Cumulating daily returns over long time horizons may introduce biases. The section below explores long-run returns using buy-and-hold excess returns.

The first panel of table 19.3 summarizes the short-run reactions to distributions. CARs are calculated from day 0 to day +3 (the event window). This is somewhat different from many event studies, which examine the CARs from the day before the event to the day after. Unlike many phenomena examined in event studies (e.g., takeover bids) it was unlikely that there would be any "leakage" of news prior to the event: the decision to distribute is usually made solely by the venture group without consultation with outside advisors or financial intermediaries. Thus we believe it is inappropriate to include the day prior to the distribution. (Indeed, as table 19.2 indicates, the abnormal volume in the day before the offering was little different from the other days prior to the distribution.) Because distributions are not publicly announced, we think that the market would incorporate the information into the stock price more slowly. Many distributions also occur after the market closes. Since it might take several days for investors to receive their certificates, we consequently employ a four-day window. The table also presents p-values from t-tests, comparing differences in the mean CARs for the various subsets of firms. The only significant

---

6. Of the original 731 distributions, 726 distributions have at least 60 trading days on CRSP in the estimation period. Events that have less than 60 days to calculate factor loadings are not used. The inclusion of these five observations in the sample, using the average coefficients from the other regressions, has little impact on the results. The results are also robust to one-factor market models (i.e., omitting the small firm return proxy) and to substituting other market indices for the Nasdaq indexes used in the results.

Table 19.2
Abnormal returns, cumulative abnormal returns, and trading volume around distributions

Day from distribution	AR	t-Statistic	CAR	t-Statistic	Volume (000s)	Day from distribution	AR	t-Statistic	CAR	t-Statistic	Volume (000s)
Day −20	+0.11%	(0.71)	+0.11%	(0.71)	149	Day 0	−0.18%	(−1.18)	−0.18%	(−1.18)	214
Day −19	+0.39%	(2.63)	+0.50%	(2.46)	154	Day 1	−1.03%	(−7.89)	−1.21%	(−6.72)	225
Day −18	+0.41%	(3.31)	+0.91%	(3.85)	150	Day 2	−0.33%	(−2.41)	−1.54%	(−6.76)	191
Day −17	+0.22%	(1.48)	+1.13%	(4.06)	161	Day 3	−0.43%	(−3.41)	−1.97%	(−7.79)	177
Day −16	+0.20%	(1.48)	+1.32%	(4.43)	147	Day 4	+0.18%	(1.36)	−1.79%	(−6.54)	176
Day −15	−0.03%	(−0.20)	+1.30%	(4.11)	146	Day 5	−0.37%	(−2.82)	−2.16%	(−7.18)	175
Day −14	+0.07%	(0.52)	+1.36%	(4.10)	154	Day 6	−0.03%	(−0.23)	−2.19%	(−6.83)	169
Day −13	+0.01%	(0.09)	+1.38%	(3.86)	136	Day 7	−0.05%	(−0.43)	−2.24%	(−6.87)	162
Day −12	+0.28%	(1.88)	+1.66%	(4.40)	152	Day 8	−0.03%	(−0.19)	−2.27%	(−6.69)	167
Day −11	+0.23%	(1.79)	+1.88%	(4.70)	139	Day 9	+0.01%	(0.09)	−2.25%	(−6.36)	162
Day −10	+0.32%	(2.30)	+2.21%	(5.32)	153	Day 10	+0.05%	(0.40)	−2.21%	(−5.73)	161
Day −9	+0.07%	(0.54)	+2.28%	(5.22)	160	Day 11	+0.06%	(0.41)	−2.15%	(−5.31)	168
Day −8	−0.20%	(−1.57)	+2.08%	(4.59)	172	Day 12	+0.30%	(2.26)	−1.84%	(−4.43)	171
Day −7	+0.22%	(1.60)	+2.29%	(4.80)	166	Day 13	−0.12%	(−0.85)	−1.96%	(−4.41)	176
Day −6	+0.19%	(1.43)	+2.48%	(5.10)	166	Day 14	+0.14%	(1.01)	−1.82%	(−3.94)	171
Day −5	+0.40%	(2.99)	+2.88%	(5.84)	155	Day 15	−0.07%	(−0.43)	−1.89%	(−3.73)	175
Day −4	−0.01%	(−0.04)	+2.87%	(5.75)	160	Day 16	−0.15%	(−1.10)	−2.04%	(−3.95)	180
Day −3	+0.36%	(2.49)	+3.23%	(6.25)	167	Day 17	+0.02%	(0.15)	−2.02%	(−3.75)	181
Day −2	+0.07%	(0.49)	+3.30%	(6.09)	173	Day 18	+0.06%	(0.45)	−1.96%	(−3.63)	185
Day −1	+0.42%	(2.71)	+3.72%	(6.62)	185	Day 19	−0.31%	(−2.15)	−2.27%	(−4.01)	179
						Day 20	+0.14%	(0.93)	−2.13%	(−3.74)	187

Note: The sample is 731 distributions by 135 venture capital funds between January 1983 and December 1993. The abnormal returns (ARs) are derived from a market model using both the CRSP value-weighted Nasdaq index and the Nasdaq smallest decile as factors. Cumulative abnormal returns (CARs) are calculated by summing the ARs for the period specified. (t-statistics calculated from the cross section of abnormal returns or cumulative abnormal returns are in parentheses.) Average daily trading volume is in thousands of shares.

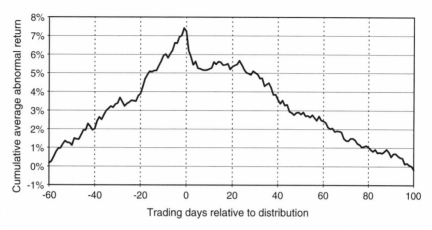

Figure 19.1
Cumulative average abnormal returns for the entire sample of distributions. The abnormal returns are derived from a market model using both the CRSP value-weighted Nasdaq index and the Nasdaq smallest decile as factors. Cumulative abnormal returns are calculated by summing the abnormal returns. The sample is 731 distributions from 135 venture capital funds between January 1983 and December 1993.

differences are among the underwriter ranking: issues brought public by less reputable underwriters experienced greater declines. As discussed above, the presence of a high-quality underwriter suggests reduced asymmetric information.[7]

The second panel of table 19.3 presents regression analyses of these patterns. The dependent variable is the CAR from day 0 to day +3. All regressions are weighted least squares, where the weight is the inverse of the

---

7. One concern about this analysis is that the use of four-day event windows increases the probability of correlation between the observations. While we are examining market- and size-adjusted returns, the clustering of distributions in particular industries may mean that the observations are not completely independent and that test-statistics are potentially overstated. We address this concern in two ways. First, we repeat the tabulations and regressions in table 19.3 using two- and three-day windows. Although the magnitude of some of the differences and coefficients are slightly smaller, the differences that are significant in the reported analyses remain so at conventional confidence levels. In these shorter windows there is less overlap across distributions and consequently less concern about inflated significance levels. Second, we calculate an upper bound for the impact of the effect, following the generalized least squares methodology of Hansen and Hodrick (1980). In particular, we create a variance-covariance matrix Ω, where each element is constrained to be zero if the two distribution windows do not overlap, 0.5 (a degree of correlation in the size- and market-adjusted abnormal returns of different distributed firms that was considerably higher than that actually observed) if the distributions occurred on the same day, and proportional to the degree of overlap otherwise. We then computed the standard errors from the matrix $(\chi'\Omega^{-1}\chi)^{-1}$. (Were there no overlap, Ω would be an identity matrix and the earlier results would be unchanged.) This way overlapping distributions are assigned less weight. Using various specifications, we find that this correction increases the standard errors on average by just under 10 percent.

Table 19.3
Returns around and after distributions

Variable	Mean CAR in distribution window			Mean ER in year after distribution		
	Above median or yes	Below median or no	p-Value from t-test	Above median or yes	Below median or no	p-Value from t-test
Venture firm age (in years)	-2.38%	-1.55%	0.104	-6.70%	-3.86%	0.544
Distributions as a percentage of equity	-1.97%	-1.97%	0.995	-6.01%	-4.77%	0.791
Underwriter ranking	-1.45%	-2.88%	0.006	1.19%	-10.82%	0.015
First distribution for firm?	-2.01%	-1.90%	0.844	-6.18%	-4.51%	0.734
Market value of IPO firm's equity at IPO (1993$ mil)	-1.57%	-2.37%	0.115	0.62%	-11.42%	0.010
Venture capitalist on board at IPO?	-2.15%	-1.74%	0.418	-5.64%	-5.09%	0.907
Venture capitalist leaves board?	-2.18%	-1.95%	0.790	-4.56%	-5.48%	0.910
Distribution restriction on venture fund?	-3.18%	-2.10%	0.235	-6.15%	-9.15%	0.712

	Dependent variable: CAR in distribution window		Dependent variable: ER in year after distribution	
			Size and book-to-market adjusted	Fama-French industry adjusted
Venture firm age (in years)	-0.0002 [0.45]	-0.0003 [0.56]	-0.0039 [0.71]	-0.0009 [0.17]
Share of IPO company's equity distributed	-0.0004 [0.64]	-0.0003 [0.55]	0.0036 [0.62]	-0.0030 [0.51]
Underwriter ranking	0.0090 [3.11]	0.0070 [2.22]	0.683 [2.38]	0.0267 [0.87]
Time from IPO to distribution [in years]	0.0042 [2.41]	0.0042 [2.42]	0.0201 [1.20]	0.0108 [0.63]
First distribution for IPO company?	-0.0001 [0.01]	0.0007 [0.12]	-0.0317 [0.53]	-0.0500 [0.84]
Share of equity held by venture firm at time of IPO	-0.0001 [0.25]	-0.0001 [0.25]	-0.0040 [0.94]	0.0037 [0.84]

	(1)	(2)	(3)	(4)
Venture capitalist on board at IPO?		−0.0003 [0.01]		−0.0476 [0.84]
Logarithm of the market value of firm's equity at IPO (1993$ mil)		0.0074 [1.57]		0.0987 [2.09]
Net-of-market returns before distribution		−0.0054 [0.30]		0.0500 [0.74]
Constant	−0.1000 [3.74]	−0.1195 [3.91]	−0.4918 [1.87]	−0.6428 [2.16]
Adjusted R^2	0.022	0.021	0.006	0.005
F-Statistic	3.34	2.52	1.56	1.35
p-Value	0.003	0.008	0.157	0.208
Number of observations	628	628	573	602

Note: The sample is 731 distributions by 135 venture capital funds between January 1983 and December 1993. The distribution window abnormal returns (ARs) are derived from a market model using both the CRSP value-weighted Nasdaq index and the Nasdaq smallest decile as factors. Cumulative abnormal returns (CARs) are calculated by summing the ARs for the period from the day of distribution to three days after the distribution. The post-distribution excess returns (ERs) are for months +1 to +12 relative to the distribution month. The ERs are the difference between the firms' returns and the buy-and-hold return on the CRSP value-weighted Nasdaq index times the mean beta for the entire sample (in the first panel), and the buy-and-hold return from a portfolio matched by size and book-to-market ratio and the matching Fama-French industry portfolio (in the second panel). In the first panel we report the sample means for observations where the variable is above the median or where the answer to the posed question is yes; the sample means for observations where the variable is below the median or where the answer to the posed question is no; and the p-values from t-tests of the difference in means. The second panel presents four regressions: the distribution window regressions are weighted least squares where the weight is the inverse of the variance of stock returns for the firm in the estimation period, while the postdistribution ones are ordinary least squares. Net-of-market returns before the distribution are the CARs from day −20 to day 0 in the second regression, and ERs from month −6 to month −1 in the fourth regression. (Absolute t-statistics are in brackets.)

variance of stock returns for the firm in the estimation period. While the regressions are very noisy and the goodness-of-fit low, the significant coefficients are consistent with the insider trading hypothesis.[8] First, companies going public with higher quality underwriters have less negative price declines at distribution. Second, as predicted by the hypothesis that the market is reacting to insider trading, distributions that occur soon after the IPO lead to more negative price reactions.

These variables are not only statistically significant, they are also economically meaningful. Consider the left-most regression in the second panel. At the mean of the independent variables, the predicted net-of-market return in the distribution window is −1.8 percent. A one-standard deviation reduction in the Carter-Manaster ranking of the book underwriter (i.e., by 1.1 rank) led to a predicted event window return of −2.8 percent. A one-standard deviation increase in the time from IPO to distribution (i.e., by 22 months) generated a predicted return of −1.0 percent. Neither the corporate control nor the liquidity alternative receives much support from the regression results.

Long-Run Excess Returns

While figure 19.1 provides some evidence of long-run price appreciation before distribution and price declines after distribution, the pattern is only suggestive. The magnitude of the price movements may be biased by cumulating abnormal returns over long horizons. To compute long-run returns, we use monthly returns from CRSP. Figure 19.2 plots the nominal buy-and-hold returns for the firms from twelve calendar months prior to twelve calendar months after distribution. For comparison, the return on the CRSP value-weighted Nasdaq index is plotted as well. The graph displays that returns increase sharply starting four months prior to the distribution. From the month after the distribution to month +8, nominal returns are quite modest. These are computed using calendar months. For a distribution occurring in January, we designate the firm's February stock return as that of month +1, whether the transfer occurred on January 2 or 31. The predis-

---

8. A natural question relates to the correlation of the independent variables. All correlation coefficients are under 0.35. We explore the impact of deleting one of these pairs of variables with correlation coefficients that are statistically significant: for instance, either the logarithm of firm market value or the market value of the stake held by the venture capitalist. These deletions have little impact on the results in this set of regressions, or those reported below. Results are little changed when we use substitutes for several independent variables such as ordinal rank of the venture fund for fund age, the market value of the company holdings by the venture capitalist for the percentage stake, and a dummy variable indicating whether the venture capitalist left the board for the board seat dummy.

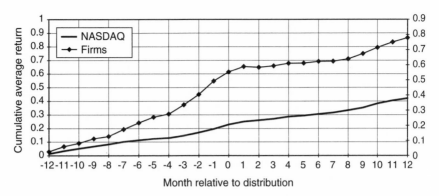

Figure 19.2
Cumulative average nominal buy-and-hold returns for the entire sample of distributions. For reference, the return on the CRSP value-weighted Nasdaq index is included. The sample is 731 distributions from 135 venture capital funds between January 1983 and December 1993.

tribution runup is not biased upwards by first-day returns of IPOs. Venture-backed firms, like other IPOs, are typically underpriced, and gain on average 8.4 percent on their first day (Barry et al. 1990). To avoid this bias, we exclude from this and subsequent analyses any firms completing an IPO in a given month: firms are included in the sample only in their second and later calendar months of trading.

We employ three approaches to calculating excess returns. First, we estimate a standard market-adjusted return. The appropriate measure of expected returns for these companies must be calculated outside the sample period. Because many of the companies went public less than one year prior to distribution, some distributions have little out-of-sample data. To overcome this problem, we estimate the beta from monthly data for all firms that have fifteen trading months of returns outside of the window from six months before to twelve months after the distribution. (We use all available monthly observations on the CRSP tapes through December 1995.) The mean beta is 1.596; the median, 1.511; and the interquartile range from 1.26 to 1.94. Excess returns (ERs) are calculated by subtracting 1.596 times the buy-and-hold return of the CRSP value-weighted Nasdaq index from the buy-and-hold return of the company,[9] as shown in equation (3):

9. One question that this procedure poses is whether we should also employ the alpha from the regression in computing our benchmark returns. The mean coefficient on the constant term, 0.0035 (or 0.35 percent per month), is positive and significant. Nonetheless, we do not include it, even though omitting it may bias our benchmark downward and make our excess returns appear more positive than they would be otherwise. Our concern is that some of the pre-distribution runup might be occurring in the estimation period (e.g., in the seventh month prior to the distribution), thereby biasing our estimate of alpha upward.

$$ER_{i,(a,b)} = \prod_{t=a}^{b} (1 + R_{i,t}) - 1.596^* \prod_{t=a}^{b} (1 + R_{Nasdaq,t}). \tag{3}$$

A second approach is to calculate returns net of benchmark portfolios comprised of firms matched by size and book-to-market equity values. Comparing performance to size and book-to-market portfolios appears reasonable given the work of Fama and French (1992), which shows that size and book-to-market are important determinants of stock returns. We form the size and book-to-market portfolios as described in Brav, Geczy, and Gompers (2000). We use all New York Stock Exchange (NYSE) stocks to create quintiles of firms based on market capitalization, with an equal number of NYSE firms in each quintile. We obtain our accounting measures from the COMPUSTAT quarterly and annual files and define book value as book common equity plus balance sheet deferred taxes and investment tax credits for the fiscal quarter ending two quarters before the sorting date, the same definition as in Fama and French (1992). Within each size quintile we form five book-to-market portfolios (with an equal number of NYSE firms in each book-to-market quintile) for a total of twenty-five (5 times 5) size and book-to-market portfolios.[10] Value-weighted returns are calculated for each portfolio for the next three months. We repeat the same procedure for April, July, and October of each year. To avoid comparing distributed firms to themselves, we eliminate firms undertaking initial or follow-on public offerings from the various portfolios for five years after their equity issue. Each issue is matched to its corresponding benchmark portfolio. Each quarter the matching is repeated, thus controlling for the time-varying firm risk characteristics of each distribution.

Finally, we calculate returns net of an industry benchmark. We match the firms to the forty-nine value-weighted industry portfolios developed by Fama and French (1997). For each distribution we compute the difference between the firm's returns and the return on the relevant industry benchmark. The sample sizes are somewhat smaller: certain firms cannot be matched to an industry portfolio due to the incompleteness of the Fama-French industry classification scheme.

If prices fully reacted to the informational content of the distribution, long-run excess returns should be zero on average in the months after the distribution. If the market underreacts or it takes time to learn that the ven-

---

10. If the book value was missing from the quarterly statements, we searched for it in the annual files. For firms that were missing altogether from the quarterly files, we used the annual files. Following the convention of Fama and French (1992) and Barber, Lyon, and Tsai (1998), we excluded all firms with negative book values from the analyses.

ture capitalist has distributed shares, then long-run drifts in prices may occur. Table 19.3 explores the long-run excess returns for the twelve months after the distribution. The results are sensitive to the benchmark used. According to market-adjusted returns, the distributed shares lose 5.4 percent of their value in the next year. The use of portfolios matched by book-to-market and size or industry groupings as a benchmark, however, leads to positive excess returns.[11] Long-run excess returns are positively correlated with underwriter rank, just as in analysis of abnormal returns in the event window. Sorting firms based on valuation at the close of the first trading day reveals that smaller firms have lower returns than their larger counterparts.

Multivariate examinations of the long-run returns are presented in the second panel. The dependent variable is the excess return from month $+1$ to month $+12$. Independent variables are the same as the ones used in the short-run analysis. Once again, the regression results are noisy. Factors that predict the short-run reaction to distributions also appear to have at least some power to explain the long-run price response. In the left regression (and several unreported ones), underwriter ranking is positively related to performance in the months after the offering. The magnitude of the effect declines when firm size (also positively associated with returns) is used as an independent variable. Overall, the market appears to quickly incorporate the information contained in the distribution into the stock price.

A major concern relates to the independence of observations. Although the magnitude of the distribution runup and rundown is similar throughout the sample period, correlations across the observations may lead to an understating of the standard errors. This problem has two dimensions. First the data set includes distributions of shares of the same firm by different venture capital funds. In addition venture capitalists may distribute shares of different firms in particular industries, such as computers and biotechnology, around the same time. Since the returns of these young firms may be quite correlated, the observations may not be truly independent.

We address the concerns about the nonindependence of the observations in two ways. First we calculate all the long-run returns using only the first distribution for each firm. Results are qualitatively similar, although significance levels fall in the regressions reflecting the smaller sample sizes. We

---

11. In unreported analyses we examined excess returns in the six months prior to distribution. Using the various market benchmarks, we found the returns to be significantly different from zero ($+15$ and $+21$ percent). Distributions of shares of smaller companies were associated with significantly greater price appreciation: excess returns for companies that are smaller than the median at the end of their first trading day varied from $+20$ to $+25$ percent, as opposed to $+10$ to $+17$ percent for large companies. Smaller companies seem to give venture capitalists more opportunity to exploit private information.

also address the correlation across different firms. Bernard (1987) discusses this problem and demonstrates that the primary source of bias in such settings is intraindustry cross-correlations as opposed to correlations across industries. One way to address this problem is to compute returns for firms net of the appropriate industry benchmark rather than a general market index. As discussed above, the results using this approach are broadly consistent with the other analysis. These anxieties are also addressed by Barber, Lyon, and Tsai (1998). These authors find that forming excess returns using size and book-to-market matched portfolios eliminates many of the biases in long horizon returns, including the skewness of the test statistics as well as much of the cross-sectional correlation induced by the clustering of observations in calendar time. At the same time it is important to acknowledge that there may still be significant cross-sectional correlations in the residuals, leading to understated standard errors and overstated t-statistics.

In a supplemental analysis, we examine trading volume, which an extensive literature (e.g., Easley and O'Hara 1987) suggests is a key mechanism through which the market discovers trades by informed insiders. Table 19.2 shows that the distribution window is associated with considerably larger trading volumes than other times.[12] We examine abnormal volume by estimating an ordinary least squares regression. Following earlier work, we use the logarithm of firm trading volume as the dependent variable and control for such variables as day of the week, news events, and Nasdaq market volume. Abnormal volume is significantly higher during the distribution window. In supplemental analyses, we show that the higher volume is associated with greater price movements, but the effect is not significantly stronger in the distribution window.

Conclusions

In this chapter we examined the distribution of venture capital investments to the investors in venture capital funds by the funds' general partners. This is a unique environment where transactions by informed insiders are exempt from antifraud provisions. The legality of these transactions allows us to build a systematic database. The evidence is consistent with the market

---

12. The average volume on the distribution day and the two subsequent days is 207,000 shares; elsewhere in the forty days around distributions, the average volume is 165,000. This comparison is limited to days without any news events. News days are defined as those on which a story about the firm (excluding routine earnings announcements) appeared in the *Wall Street Journal* (and was included in the Wall Street Journal Index), as well as the trading days immediately before and after the day the story appeared.

reacting to the inside information of the venture capitalist: the 2 percent drop around the distribution is akin to the reaction to public announcements of secondary stock sales even though venture capital distributions are not publicly disclosed.

When we disaggregated the market reactions, the patterns appeared to be consistent with the view that this is a reaction to insider trading rather than the two other explanations we offer. In particular, distributions by firms backed by high-quality underwriters also appeared to lower asymmetric information and reduce the negative cumulative abnormal returns at distribution. Distributions of less seasoned firms, which may be associated with greater asymmetric information, triggered larger immediate price declines. The long-run, postdistribution returns were more ambiguous. Although the extent and significance of the market reaction appeared to vary with the benchmark employed, at least some evidence suggested that the market does not fully incorporate information at the time of distribution.

20 How Well Do Venture-Backed Offerings Perform?

One of the central puzzles of finance—documented by Ritter (1991) and Loughran and Ritter (1995)—is the severe underperformance of initial public offerings (IPOs) over the past twenty years. These findings suggest that investors may systematically be too optimistic about the prospects of firms that are issuing equity for the first time. Recent work has shown that underperformance extends to other countries as well as to seasoned equity offerings (i.e., offering of companies whose shares are already traded).

We address three primary issues related to the underperformance of new issues. First, we examine whether the involvement of venture capitalists affects the long-run performance of newly public firms. We find that venture-backed firms do indeed outperform nonventure IPOs over a five-year period, but only when returns are weighted equally.

The second set of tests examines the effects of using different benchmarks and different methods of measuring performance to gauge the robustness of IPO underperformance. We find that underperformance in the nonventure sample is driven primarily by small issuers, that is, those with market capitalizations less than $50 million. Value weighting returns significantly reduces underperformance relative to the benchmarks we examine. In Fama-French (1993) three-factor time-series regressions, portfolios of venture-backed IPOs do not underperform. Partitioning the nonventure sample on the basis of size demonstrates that underperformance primarily resides in small nonventure issuers. Fama-French's three-factor model cannot explain the underperformance of these small, nonventure firms.

Finally we provide initial evidence on the sources of underperformance. We find that returns of IPO firms are highly correlated in calendar time, even if the firms go public in different years. Because small nonventure IPOs are more likely to be held by individuals, bouts of investor sentiment are a possible explanation for their severe underperformance. Individuals are arguably more likely to be influenced by fads or lack complete information. We also provide initial evidence that the returns of small, nonventure companies covary with the change in the discount on closed-end funds. Lee, Shleifer, and Thaler (1991) argue that this discount is a useful benchmark for investor sentiment. Alternatively, unexpected real shocks may have affected small, growth firms during this time period. We find, however, that underperformance is not exclusively an IPO effect. When issuing firms are matched to size and book-to-market portfolios that exclude all recent firms that have issued equity, IPOs do not underperform. Underperformance is a characteristic of small, low book-to-market firms regardless of whether they are IPO firms or not.

Venture Capitalists and the Creation of Public Firms

Venture capital firms specialize in collecting and evaluating information on start-up and growth companies. These types of companies are the most prone to asymmetric information and potential capital constraints (for a full discussion of these effects, see Fazzari, Hubbard, and Petersen 1988; Hoshi, Kashyap, and Scharfstein 1991). Venture capitalists, however, provide access to top-tier, national investment and commercial bankers and may partly overcome informational asymmetries that are associated with start-up companies, so we can expect the investment behavior of venture-backed firms would be less dependent upon internally generated cash flows. Venture capitalists stay on the board of directors long after the IPO and may continue to provide access to capital that nonventure firms lack. Additionally the venture capitalist may put management structures in place that help the firm perform better in the long run.

If venture-backed companies are better, on average, than nonventure companies, the market should incorporate these expectations into the price of the offering, and long-run stock price performance should be similar for the two groups. Barry et al. (1990) and Megginson and Weiss (1991) find evidence that markets react favorably to the presence of venture capital financing at the time of an IPO.

If the market underestimates the importance of a venture capitalist in the pricing of new issues, long-run stock price performance may differ. (Conversely, the market may not discount the shares of nonventure companies enough.) Such underestimation may result because those individuals most susceptible to fads and sentiment hold a larger fraction of shares after the IPO for nonventure firms (Megginson and Weiss 1991).

Venture capitalists may affect who holds the firm's shares after an IPO. Venture capitalists have contacts with top-tier, national investment banks and may be able to entice more and higher quality analysts to follow their firms, thus lowering potential asymmetric information between the firm and investors. Similarly, because institutional investors are the primary source of capital for venture funds, institutions may be more willing to hold equity in firms that have been taken public by venture capitalists with whom they have invested. The greater availability of information and the higher institutional shareholding may make venture-backed companies' prices less susceptible to investor sentiment.

Another possible explanation for better long-run performance by venture-backed IPOs is venture capitalists' reputational concerns. Chapter 16 demonstrates that reputational concerns affect the decisions venture capitalists make when they take firms public. Because venture capitalists repeatedly bring firms public, if they become associated with failures in the public market they may tarnish their reputation and ability to bring firms public in the future. Venture capitalists may consequently be less willing to hype a stock or overprice it.

Initial Public Offerings and Underperformance

Behavioral Finance

Behavioral economics demonstrates that individuals often violate rational choice theories when making decisions under uncertainty in experimental settings (Kahneman and Tversky 1982). Financial economists have also discovered long-run pricing anomalies that have been attributed to investor sentiment. Behavioral theories posit that investors weigh recent results too heavily or extrapolate recent trends too much. Eventually overoptimistic investors are disappointed and subsequent returns decline.

DeBondt and Thaler (1985, 1987) demonstrate that buying past losers and selling past winners is a profitable trading strategy. Risk, as measured by beta or the standard deviation of stock returns, does not appear to explain the results. Lakonishok, Shleifer, and Vishny (1994) show that many "value" strategies also appear to exhibit abnormally high returns. They form portfolios based on earnings-to-price ratios, sales growth, earnings growth, or cash flow-to-price and find that "value" stocks outperform "glamour" stocks without appreciably affecting risk. In addition La Porta (1996) shows that selling stocks with high forecasted earnings growth and buying low projected earnings growth stocks produces excess returns. These studies imply that investors are too optimistic about stocks that have had good performance in the recent past and too pessimistic about stocks that have performed poorly.

In addition to accounting or stock market-based trading strategies, researchers have examined financing events as sources of potential trading strategies. Ross (1977) and Myers and Majluf (1984) show that the choice of financing strategy can send a signal to the market about firm valuation. Event studies around equity or debt issues (e.g., Mikkelson and Partch 1986; Asquith and Mullins 1986) assume that all information implied by the financing choice is fully and immediately incorporated into the company's stock price. The literature on long-run abnormal performance assumes that managers have superior information about future returns and utilize that information to benefit current shareholders, and the market under-reacts to the informational content of the financing event.

Ritter (1991) and Loughran and Ritter (1995) show that nominal five year buy-and-hold returns are 50 percent lower for recent IPOs (which earned 16 percent) than they are for comparable size-matched firms (which earned 66 percent). Teoh, Welch, and Wong (1998) show that IPO underperformance is positively related to the size of discretionary accruals in the fiscal year of the IPO. Larger accruals in the IPO year are associated with more negative performance. Teoh et al. believe that the level of discretionary accruals is a proxy for earnings management and that the boosted earnings systematically fool investors.

If investor sentiment is an important factor in the underperformance of IPOs, small IPOs may be more affected. Individuals are more likely to hold the shares of small IPO firms. Many institutions like pension funds and insurance companies refrain from holding shares of very small companies. Taking a meaningful position in a small firm may make an institution a large blockholder in the company. Because the SEC restricts trading by 5 percent shareholders, institutions may want to avoid this level of ownership. Individual investors may also be more subject to fads (Lee, Shleifer, and Thaler 1991) or may be more likely to suffer from asymmetric information. These researchers use the discount on closed-end funds as a measure of investor sentiment. If investor sentiment affects returns and if closed-end fund discounts measure investor sentiment, then the returns on small IPOs would be correlated with the change in the average closed-end fund discount. Decreases in the average discount imply that investors are more optimistic and should be correlated with higher returns for small issuers.

Rational Asset Pricing Explanations

Recent work claims that multifactor asset pricing models can potentially explain many pricing anomalies in the financial economics literature. In particular, Fama and French (1996) argue that the "value" strategies in Lakonishok, Shleifer, and Vishny (1994) and the buying losers-selling winners strategy of DeBondt and Thaler (1985, 1987) are consistent with their three-factor asset pricing model.

Fama (1996) and Fama and French (1996) argue that their three-factor pricing model is consistent with Merton's (1973) intertemporal capital asset pricing model. While the choice of factor mimicking portfolios is not unique, sensitivities to Fama and French's three factors (related to the market return, size, and book-to-market ratio) have economic interpretations. Fama and French claim that anomalous performance is explained by not completely controlling for risk factors.

Tests of underperformance, however, suffer from the joint hypothesis problem discussed by Fama (1976). The assumption of a particular asset pricing model means that tests of performance are conditional on that model correctly predicting stock price behavior. If we reject the null hypothesis, then either the pricing model is incorrect or investors may be irrational. Similarly, if factors like book-to-market explain underperformance, it does not necessarily verify the model. The results may just reflect that investor sentiment is correlated with measures like book-to-market. We do not wish to argue whether factors like book-to-market reflect rational market risk measures or investor sentiment. The tests we perform are consistent with either interpretation. Another problem with long-run performance tests, however, is the nonstandard distribution of long-run run returns. Both Barber and Lyon (1997) and Kothari and Warner (1997) show that typical tests performed in the literature suffer from potential biases. Although Barber and Lyon show that size and book-to-market adjusted returns give unbiased test estimates of underperformance for random portfolios (which we report in figures 20.5 and 20.6), neither paper addresses the cross-sectional or time-series correlation in returns when tests are predicated on an event.

Analysis of Performance

Constructing the Sample

Our sample of initial public offerings is collected from various sources. The venture-backed companies are taken from three primary sources. First, firms are identified as venture-backed IPOs in the issues of the *Venture Capital Journal* from 1972 through 1992. Second, firms that are in the sample of distributions analyzed in chapter 19, but not listed in the *Venture Capital Journal*, are added to the venture-backed sample. Finally, if offering memoranda for venture capital limited partnerships used in chapters 4 and 5 list a company as being venture financed but it is not listed in either of the previous two sources, it is added to the venture-backed sample. Jay Ritter provides data on initial public offerings from 1975 to 1984. IPOs are identified in various issues of the *Investment Dealers' Digest of Corporate Financing* from 1975 to 1992. Any firm not listed in the sample of venture-backed IPOs is classified as nonventure. The data include name of the offering company, date of the offering, size of the issue, issue price, number of secondary shares, and the underwriter.[1]

For inclusion in our sample, a firm performing an initial public offering had to be followed by the Center for Research in Security Prices (CRSP) at some point after the offering date. Our final sample includes 934 venture-backed IPOs and 3,407 nonventure IPOs. Of the venture-backed sample 81.3 percent were still CRSP-listed five years after their IPO. A slightly smaller fraction of nonventure IPOs, 76.7 percent, was CRSP-listed after five years. The frequency of mergers was low. Only 11.2 percent of the venture-backed IPOs and 9.7 percent of the nonventure sample merged within the first five years. The number of liquidations, bankruptcies, and other delisting events is small for both groups as well. Only 7.5 percent of the venture-backed IPOs were delisted for these reasons in the first five years compared to 13.3 percent of nonventure IPOs.

We also examine the size and book-to-market characteristics of our sample. Each quarter we divide all New York Stock Exchange (NYSE) stocks into ten size groups. An equal number of NYSE firms are allocated to each of the ten groups and quarterly size breakpoints are recorded. Similarly we divide all NYSE stocks into five book-to-market groups each quarter with an equal number of NYSE firms in each group. The intersection of the ten size and five book-to-market groups leads to fifty possible quarterly classifications for an IPO firm.[2]

---

1. Our sample differs from Loughran and Ritter's in two respects. First, our sample period is not completely overlapping. Loughran and Ritter look at IPOs from 1970 to 1990 and measure performance using stock returns through December 31, 1992. We look at IPOs conducted over the period 1975 to 1992 using stock returns through December 31, 1994. The different sample period does not change the qualitative results because we replicate Loughran and Ritter's underperformance in our sample period as well. Second, we eliminate all unit offerings from our sample. Unit offerings, which contain a share of equity and a warrant, tend to be made by very small, risky companies. Calculating the return to an investor in the IPO is difficult because only the share trades publicly. Value-weighted results would change very little because unit offering companies are usually small.

2. We calculate the market value of equity at the first CRSP-listed closing price. For book value of equity, we use COMPUSTAT and record the first book value after the IPO as long as it is within one year of the offering date. The bias in book value should not be too great because the increment in book value due to retained earnings in the first year is likely to be very small. When we match firms on the basis of book-to-market values, we lose 778 firms because they lack COMPUSTAT data within one year of the offering. For most results this is unimportant because tests do not rely on book values. Where book-to-market ratios are used to either sort firms or match firms, the 778 firms are excluded.

Our sample of venture-backed IPOs is heavily weighted in the smallest and lowest book-to-market firms. 38.5 percent are in the lowest size decile with another 27.2 percent in the second decile, while 84.0 percent of the venture-backed IPOs are in the lowest book-to-market quintile. Most venture-backed firms are young, growth companies. These firms may have many good investment opportunities for which they need to raise cash. On the other hand, their low book-to-market ratios may just be indicators of relative overpricing. Loughran and Ritter (1995) and chapter 15 present evidence that issuers time the market for new shares when their firms are relatively overvalued. Most nonventure firms are also small and low book-to-market, but a substantial number of firms fall in larger size deciles or higher book-to-market quintiles: 58.6 percent of firms are in the lowest size decile, 20 percent more than are in the lowest decile for the venture-backed sample; 73.2 percent of the nonventure firms fall in the lowest book-to-market quintile; and 7.3 percent are in the two highest book-to-market quintiles. The differences between venture and nonventure IPOs may result from greater heterogeneity in nonventure IPOs.

Full Sample Results

Ritter (1991) and Loughran and Ritter (1995) document underperformance of IPO firms using several benchmarks. Our approach is an attempt to replicate their work and extend it along several dimensions. Several benchmarks are utilized throughout this chapter. First, as in Loughran and Ritter, the performance of IPO firms is matched to four broad market indexes: the S&P 500, Nasdaq value-weighted composite index, NYSE/AMEX (American Stock Exchange) value-weighted index, and NYSE/AMEX equal-weighted index (all of which include dividends). Performance of IPOs is also compared to Fama-French (1997) industry portfolios and size and book-to-market matched portfolios that have been purged of recent IPO and seasoned equity offering (SEO) firms.[3]

Matching firms to industry portfolios avoids the noise of selecting individual firms, and we can control for unexpected events that affect the returns of entire industries. We use the forty-nine industry portfolios created in Fama and French (1997). Industry groupings sort firms into the similar lines of business.

Comparing performance to size and book-to-market portfolios appears reasonable, given the effects documented by Fama and French (1992, 1993)

---

3. We purge SEO firms from our benchmark portfolios as well since it has been argued (Loughran and Ritter 1995) that these firms underperform after they make a seasoned offering.

that show size and book-to-market to be important determinants of the cross section of stock returns. We form twenty-five (5 times 5) value-weighted portfolios of all NYSE/AMEX and Nasdaq stocks on the basis of size and the ratio of book equity to market equity. We match each IPO on those two dimensions to the corresponding portfolio for comparison.

We form the size and book-to-market portfolios as described in Brav, Geczy, and Gompers (2000). Starting in January 1964, we use all NYSE stocks to create size quintile breakpoints with an equal number of NYSE firms in each size quintile.[4] Within each size quintile we form five book-to-market portfolios with an equal number of NYSE firms in each book-to-market quintile to form twenty-five (5 times 5) size and book-to-market portfolios. (We do not include stocks with negative book values.) Value-weighted returns are calculated for each portfolio for the next three months. We repeat this procedure for April, July, and October of each year. To avoid comparing IPO firms to themselves, we eliminate IPO and SEO firms from the various portfolios for five years after their equity issue. Each issue is matched to its corresponding benchmark portfolio. Each quarter the matching is repeated, creating a separate benchmark for each issue. We then proceed to equal (value) weight IPO firm returns and the individual bench-mark returns, which results in equal (value) weighted portfolios adjusted for book-to-market and size. We thus allow for time-varying firm risk charac-teristics of each IPO and each matching firm portfolio.

We do not, however, replicate Loughran and Ritter's size-matched firm adjustment for several reasons. Matching on the basis of size alone ignores evidence that book-to-market is related to returns. Book-to-market appears particularly important for small firms (Fama and French 1992). Matching to small nonissuers makes it likely that firms in the matching sample are dis-proportionately long-term losers, that is, high book-to-market firms. IPO firms tend to be small and low book-to-market. The delisting frequency is low for the IPO sample and their risk of financial distress in the first five years may be small. A similarly sized small firm that has not issued equity in the previous five years is probably a poorly performing firm with few growth prospects and not an appropriate risk match for the IPO firm if

---

4. Fama and French (1992) use only NYSE stocks to ensure dispersion of the number of firms across portfolios. Size is measured as the number of shares outstanding times the stock price at the end of the preceding month. We obtain our accounting measures from the COMPUSTAT quarterly and annual files, and we define book value as book common equity plus balance sheet deferred taxes and investment tax credits for the fiscal quarter ending two quarters before the sorting date. This is the same definition as in Fama and French (1992). If the book value is miss-ing from the quarterly statements, we search for it in the annual files. For firms that are missing altogether from the quarterly files, we use the annual files.

book-to-market is important. These firms may have higher returns because their risk of financial distress is higher. They are likely to be the DeBondt and Thaler (1985) underperformers that we know have high returns. This bias is especially strong prior to 1978 because Nasdaq returns only start in December 1972. Therefore all size-matched firms would come from the NYSE and AMEX, potentially biasing the matched firms even more toward long-term losers, that is, very high book-to-market firms.

Tests in this chapter calculate returns in two ways, although we only report buy-and-hold results. First, as in Ritter (1991) and Loughran and Ritter (1995), we calculate buy-and-hold returns. No portfolio rebalancing is assumed in these calculations. We also calculate full five year returns assuming monthly portfolio rebalancing. While the absolute level of returns changes, qualitative results are unchanged if returns are calculated using monthly rebalancing.

Table 20.1 presents the long-run buy-and-hold performance for our sample. We follow each offering event using both the CRSP daily and monthly tapes. Compound daily returns are calculated from the offering date until the end of the offering month. We then compound their returns using the monthly tapes for the earlier of fifty-nine months or the delisting date. Firms that drop out will have IPO returns and benchmark returns that are calculated over a shorter time period. Where available, we include the firm's delisting return. Our interval is set to match Loughran and Ritter's results (1995). In panel A we weight equally the returns for each IPO and their benchmark. As in Loughran and Ritter (1995) we calculate wealth relatives for the five-year period after IPO by taking the ratio of one plus the IPO portfolio return over one plus the return on the chosen benchmark. Wealth relatives less than one mean that the IPO portfolio has underperformed relative to its benchmark.

The results weighting returns equally show that venture-backed IPOs outperform nonventure IPOs by a wide margin. Over five years venture-backed IPOs earn 44.6 percent on average while nonventure IPOs earn 22.5 percent.[5] The five-year equal-weighted wealth relatives show large differences in performance as well. Wealth relatives for the venture capital sample are all close to 0.9. Wealth relatives for the nonventure capital

---

5. The five-year buy-and-hold returns are not true five-year returns because the average holding period is less than sixty months. Firms may take several months to be listed on the CRSP data tapes and so the first several return observations may be missing. Similarly firms are delisted and so are only traded for some shorter period of time than the sample period. Finally IPOs in the last two years have truncated returns because observations on returns only run through December 1994. The average holding period is approximately forty-seven months.

Table 20.1
Five-year post–initial public offering (IPO) returns and wealth relatives versus various benchmarks

Benchmarks	Venture-backed IPOs			Non-venture-backed IPOs		
	IPO return	Bench-mark return	Wealth relative	IPO return	Bench-mark return	Wealth relative
Panel A: Five-year equal-weighted buy-and-hold returns						
S&P 500 index	44.6	65.3	0.88	22.5	71.8	0.71
Nasdaq composite	44.6	53.7	0.94	22.5	52.4	0.80
NYSE/AMEX value-weighted	44.6	61.4	0.90	22.5	66.4	0.75
NYSE/AMEX equal-weighted	44.6	60.8	0.90	22.5	55.7	0.79
Size and book-to-market (5 × 5)	46.4	29.9	1.13	21.7	20.8	1.01
Fama-French industry portfolio	46.8	51.2	0.97	26.2	60.0	0.79
Panel B: Five-year value-weighted buy-and-hold returns						
S&P 500 index	43.4	64.5	0.87	39.3	62.4	0.86
Nasdaq composite	43.4	50.4	0.95	39.3	51.1	0.92
NYSE/AMEX value-weighted	43.4	60.0	0.90	39.3	57.6	0.88
NYSE/AMEX equal-weighted	43.4	56.4	0.92	39.3	47.7	0.94
Size and book-to-market (5 × 5)	41.9	37.6	1.03	33.0	38.7	0.96
Fama-French industry portfolio	46.0	45.0	1.01	45.2	53.2	0.95

Note: The sample is all venture-backed IPOs from 1972 through 1992 and all non-venture-backed IPOs from 1975 through 1992. Five-year equal-weighted returns on IPOs are compared with alternative benchmarks. For each IPO, the returns are calculated by compounding daily returns up to the end of the month of the IPO and from then on compounding monthly returns for 59 months. If the IPO is delisted before the 59th month, we compound the return until the delisting date. Wealth relatives are calculated as $\Sigma(1 + R_{i, T})/\Sigma(1 + R_{\text{bench}, T})$, where $R_{i, T}$ is the buy and hold return on IPO i for period T and $R_{\text{bench}, T}$ is the buy-and-hold return on the benchmark portfolio over the same period. Size and book-to-market benchmark portfolios are formed by intersecting five size quintiles and five book-to-market quintiles (5 × 5) and removing all firms which have issued equity in the previous five years in either an IPO or a seasoned equity offering. All IPO and benchmark returns are taken from the Center for Research in Security Prices files.

sample are substantially lower and range as low as 0.71 against the S&P 500 index.

Controlling for industry returns leaves performance differences as well. Using Fama-French (1997) industry portfolios, we find the venture capital sample to show little underperformance. The five-year wealth relative is 0.97. Nonventure IPOs show substantial underperformance relative to their industry benchmarks—0.79 for the five-year wealth relative.

Two interpretations of the industry results are possible. First, the benchmark industry returns for the venture-backed sample are lower than the industry returns for the nonventure sample. Thus venture-backed IPOs may be concentrated in industries that have lower risk and therefore expected returns should be lower. Second, the relatively lower industry returns may reflect the venture capitalist's ability to time industry overpricing.

Wealth relatives versus size and book-to-market portfolios demonstrate that underperformance is not an IPO effect. When IPOs and SEOs are excluded from size and book-to-market portfolios, we find that venture-backed IPOs significantly outperform their relative portfolio returns (average wealth relative of 1.13) while nonventure IPOs perform as well as the benchmark portfolios. The poor performance documented by Loughran and Ritter (1995) is not due to sample firms being initial public offering firms but rather results from the types of firms they are, that is, primarily small and low book-to-market firms.

Although the time frame of our sample is slightly different from Loughran and Ritter, our wealth relatives for NYSE/AMEX value and equal-weighted indexes, the Nasdaq value-weighted composite, and the S&P 500 are virtually identical to theirs. For example, five-year performance versus the NYSE/AMEX equal-weighted and S&P 500 indexes produces wealth relatives of 0.78 and 0.84 in Loughran and Ritter's sample, while (in unreported results) our entire sample (venture and nonventure IPOs) produces wealth relatives of 0.78 and 0.82. Nonventure IPOs perform worse than Loughran and Ritter's results.

Panel B of table 20.1 presents results in which returns of IPOs and their reference benchmarks are weighted by the issuing firm's first available market value. If we are concerned about how important IPO underperformance affects investors' wealth, then value-weighted results may be more meaningful. Five-year, value-weighted nominal returns on nonventure IPOs are higher than when returns are weighted equally. Value-weighted returns on the benchmark portfolios are similar to the equally weighted benchmark returns. This increases wealth relatives at five years for the nonventure capital sample and leaves venture capital wealth relatives relatively unchanged. Value-weighted performance looks similar for the two groups with little overall underperformance. Five-year wealth relatives are closer to one. Large nonventure IPOs perform substantially better than smaller nonventure firms do.

Yearly Cohort Results

Ritter (1991) and Loughran and Ritter (1995) document clear patterns in the underperformance of IPOs. In particular, years of greatest IPO activity are associated with the most severe underperformance. Results in panel A of table 20.2 present equal-weighted, buy-and-hold cohort results versus the

Table 20.2
Long-run performance of initial public offerings (IPOs) by cohort year versus NYSE/AMEX equal-weighted index

Year	Venture-backed IPOs				Non-venture-backed IPOs			
	Number	IPO return	NYSE/ AMEX	Wealth relative	Number	IPO return	NYSE/ AMEX	Wealth relative
Panel A: Equal-weighted five-year buy-and-hold returns								
1976	16	310.2	193.2	1.40	14	192.8	189.8	1.01
1977	13	253.1	128.9	1.54	9	103.0	119.0	0.93
1978	8	525.0	226.9	1.91	24	99.6	160.8	0.77
1979	8	71.1	164.4	0.65	44	51.0	141.8	0.62
1980	27	48.8	115.1	0.69	107	−23.4	107.0	0.37
1981	63	24.4	121.0	0.56	241	5.9	114.0	0.49
1982	25	32.8	142.8	0.55	75	110.8	128.9	0.92
1983	117	−14.7	51.1	0.56	507	3.6	50.7	0.69
1984	52	2.1	71.0	0.60	258	46.7	66.1	0.88
1985	46	12.6	40.4	0.80	253	5.3	41.5	0.74
1986	94	79.0	30.1	1.38	505	4.0	30.3	0.80
1987	78	25.3	27.1	0.99	379	12.3	26.0	0.89
1988	35	120.6	59.4	1.38	183	95.4	63.3	1.20
1989	33	141.1	58.3	1.52	129	48.9	58.2	0.94
1990	40	−14.3	67.8	0.51	116	30.7	66.5	0.79
1991	111	38.2	49.3	0.93	208	26.3	49.6	0.84
1992	147	17.7	28.3	0.92	343	15.0	27.7	0.90
Panel B: Value-weighted five-year buy-and-hold returns								
1976	16	166.8	208.0	0.87	14	228.7	183.0	1.16
1977	13	438.1	152.1	2.14	9	200.4	118.6	1.37
1978	8	529.4	218.1	1.98	24	141.8	181.7	0.86
1979	8	7.1	156.7	0.42	44	87.9	150.7	0.75
1980	27	1.3	115.6	0.47	107	−32.4	108.6	0.32
1981	63	37.6	127.1	0.61	241	22.6	122.6	0.55
1982	25	−25.7	125.3	0.33	75	81.1	108.2	0.87
1983	117	−26.0	53.3	0.48	507	21.8	54.7	0.79
1984	52	0.00	75.2	0.57	258	67.6	71.4	0.98
1985	46	26.5	43.3	0.88	253	13.9	39.4	0.82
1986	94	201.6	32.5	2.28	505	25.3	32.0	0.95
1987	77	20.1	29.8	0.93	379	39.2	25.4	1.11
1988	35	120.5	58.9	1.39	183	72.0	68.5	1.03
1989	33	130.6	59.0	1.45	129	65.4	61.5	1.02
1990	40	7.9	66.1	0.65	116	45.8	65.9	0.88
1991	111	46.9	48.3	0.99	208	49.8	50.7	0.99
1992	145	25.4	28.2	0.98	343	29.2	27.5	1.01

Table 20.2
(continued)
Note: The sample is all venture-backed IPOs and all non-venture-backed IPOs from 1976 through 1992. For each IPO the returns are calculated by compounding daily returns up to the end of the month of the IPO and from then on compounding monthly returns for 59 months. If the IPO is delisted before the 59th month, we compound the return until the delisting date. Wealth relatives are calculated as $\Sigma(1 + R_{i, T})/\Sigma(1 + R_{bench, T})$, where $R_{i, T}$ is the buy-and-hold return on the IPO i for period T and $R_{bench, T}$ is the buy-and-hold return on the benchmark portfolio over the same period. All IPO and benchmark returns are taken from the Center for Research in Security Prices files.

NYSE/AMEX equal-weighted index.[6] Nominal returns and wealth relatives are high in the late 1970s but fall sharply in the early and mid-1980s. While five-year returns increase in the late 1980s and early 1990s, they increase more in the venture-backed sample. Our five-year return patterns closely follow Loughran and Ritter's results. For the venture-backed IPOs, underperformance is concentrated in the 1979 to 1985 cohorts; while for the nonventure sample, five-year underperformance is prevalent from 1978 forward. These results are largely consistent with the results of Ritter (1991) and Loughran and Ritter (1995) who find similar time-series patterns of underperformance.

We also investigate how value weighting affects yearly cohort buy-and-hold patterns in panel B. Each IPO is given a weight proportional to its market value of equity using the first available CRSP-listed closing price. Value weighting has different effects on the venture capital and nonventure capital samples. Value-weighting the venture capital IPOs has little impact on the pattern of performance. Value-weighting returns of the nonventure capital sample improves their nominal performance and wealth relatives in most cohorts. There is still some evidence of underperformance in the early 1980s, but it is much smaller. Most five-year nonventure capital wealth relatives are closer to one.

The yearly cohort results suggest several patterns that we examine more deeply. The level and pattern of underperformance previously documented appear to be sensitive to the method of calculating returns. When returns are value weighted, underperformance of nonventure IPOs is reduced in most years.

---

6. We use the NYSE/AMEX equal-weighted index because it produces wealth relatives that are somewhere in the middle of all benchmarks utilized. Replacing the NYSE/AMEX equal-weighted index with the S&P 500, Nasdaq composite index, or industry portfolios does not affect the time-series pattern of underperformance in any significant manner. Similarly monthly portfolio rebalancing yields qualitatively similar results.

Calendar-Time Results

Event-time results that are presented above may be misleading about the pervasiveness of underperformance. Cohort returns in table 20.2 may overstate the number of years in which IPOs underperform because the returns of recent IPO firms may be correlated. If firms that have recently gone public are similar in terms of size, industry, or other characteristics, then their returns will be highly correlated in calendar time. For example, if a shock to the economy in 1983 substantially decreased the value of firms that issued equity, then it makes the cohort years from 1979 through 1983 underperform, even though all the underperformance is concentrated in one year. Similarly, as discussed in De Long et al. (1990), investor sentiment is likely to be marketwide rather than specific to a particular firm and may cause returns to be correlated in calendar time.

To address this correlation we calculate the annual return on a strategy that invests in recent IPO firms. In panel A of table 20.3 we calculate the monthly return on portfolios which buy equal amounts of all IPO firms that went public within the previous five years. We calculate the annual return by compounding monthly returns on the IPO portfolios, starting in January and ending in December of each year. These calendar-time returns are presented and compared to calendar-time returns on the NYSE/AMEX equal-weighted index and the Nasdaq composite index. The wealth relatives on the venture capital IPO portfolio are above one in nine of nineteen years and are higher than the nonventure capital portfolio wealth relative in eleven of nineteen years. Underperformance for the venture capital sample is primarily concentrated from 1983 through 1986, and it is concentrated from 1981 through 1987 for the nonventure capital portfolio.

In panel B the calendar-time portfolio is formed by investing an amount that is proportional to the market value of the IPO firm's equity in a given month. Value-weighting the calendar-time portfolio does not have a major impact on the pattern of underperformance for venture-backed IPOs but reduces underperformance in the nonventure sample.

The cross-sectional correlation between cohort years can be seen graphically in figures 20.1 and 20.2. The cumulative wealth relative is calculated for each IPO cohort year from 1979 through 1982 by taking the ratio of one plus the compound return on the portfolio that invests in each IPO that went public in a given year divided by the compound return on the Nasdaq composite index. Figure 20.1 plots the cumulative wealth relative for venture-backed IPOs, and figure 20.2 plots the cumulative wealth relative for nonventure IPOs. All cohort years move in almost identical time-series

Table 20.3
Calendar time initial public offering (IPO) performance

Year	VC-IPOs	Non-VC-IPOs	NYSE/AMEX	VC wealth relative	Non-VC wealth relative	Nasdaq	VC wealth relative	Non-VC wealth relative
Panel A: Equal-weighted IPO calendar-time portfolio returns								
1976	48.9	14.6	26.5	1.18	0.91	29.3	1.15	0.89
1977	32.3	22.2	−4.2	1.38	1.28	10.5	1.20	1.11
1978	44.7	10.5	7.8	1.34	1.03	16.1	1.25	0.95
1979	43.8	53.9	23.6	1.16	1.25	32.3	1.09	1.16
1980	78.0	89.7	32.7	1.34	1.43	37.7	1.29	1.38
1981	−7.1	−20.9	−4.3	0.97	0.83	−0.7	0.94	0.80
1982	34.6	5.8	20.2	1.12	0.88	22.4	1.10	0.87
1983	10.5	28.5	23.1	0.90	1.04	21.3	0.91	1.06
1984	−34.4	−21.1	5.1	0.62	0.75	−9.1	0.72	0.87
1985	30.1	23.5	31.2	0.99	0.94	33.8	0.97	0.92
1986	−8.9	3.4	16.9	0.78	0.88	8.0	0.84	0.96
1987	−11.4	−19.9	2.8	0.86	0.78	−4.6	0.93	0.84
1988	23.9	20.1	17.5	1.05	1.02	18.4	1.05	1.01
1989	7.9	11.4	29.4	0.83	0.86	21.1	0.89	0.92
1990	−15:0	−27.3	−4.8	0.89	0.76	−15.3	1.00	0.86
1991	97.4	50.5	30.6	1.51	1.15	60.0	1.23	0.94
1992	8.1	19.1	8.0	1.00	1.10	16.3	0.93	1.02
1993[a]	5.3	16.1	11.0	0.95	1.05	14.5	0.92	1.01
1994[a]	−3.1	−10.5	−0.3	0.97	0.90	−2.3	0.99	0.92
Panel B: Value-weighted IPO calendar-time portfolio returns								
1976	1.1	2.7	26.5	0.80	0.81	29.3	0.78	0.79
1977	13.3	−5.9	−4.2	1.18	0.98	10.5	1.03	0.85
1978	44.9	12.7	7.8	1.34	1.05	16.1	1.25	0.97
1979	27.8	49.6	23.6	1.03	1.21	32.3	0.97	1.13
1980	67.3	99.3	32.7	1.26	1.50	37.7	1.22	1.45
1981	−7.6	−21.7	−4.3	0.97	0.82	−0.7	0.93	0.79
1982	29.6	14.6	20.2	1.08	0.95	22.4	1.06	0.94
1983	2.2	16.9	23.1	0.83	0.95	21.3	0.84	0.96
1984	−30.2	−19.4	5.1	0.66	0.77	−9.1	0.77	0.89
1985	21.4	30.5	31.2	0.93	0.99	33.8	0.91	0.97
1986	−7.0	8.9	16.9	0.80	0.93	8.0	0.86	1.01
1987	5.5	−11.3	2.8	1.03	0.86	−4.6	1.11	0.93
1988	14.0	15.4	17.5	0.97	0.98	18.4	0.96	0.97
1989	32.4	20.8	29.4	1.02	0.93	21.1	1.10	1.00
1990	0.1	−12.6	−4.8	1.05	0.92	−15.3	1.18	1.03
1991	78.6	38.3	30.6	1.37	1.06	60.0	1.12	0.86

Table 20.3
(continued)

Year	VC-IPOs	Non-VC-IPOs	NYSE/AMEX	VC wealth relative	Non-VC wealth relative	Nasdaq	VC wealth relative	Non-VC wealth relative
1992	7.5	10.9	8.0	1.00	1.03	16.3	0.92	0.95
1993[a]	10.48	38.3	11.0	1.00	1.25	14.5	0.97	1.21
1994[a]	−4.7	10.9	−0.3	0.96	1.11	−2.3	0.98	1.14

Note: Annual performance of initial public offerings from 1976 through 1992 relative to the NYSE/AMEX value-weighted index and the Nasdaq value weighted composite index. The sample is all venture capital (VC) IPOs from 1972 through 1992 and all non-venture-backed (non-VC) IPOs from 1975 through 1992. Each month, the return on all IPOs that went public within the past five years is calculated. The annual return in each year is the compound return from January through December of these average monthly returns. The annual benchmark returns are the compounded monthly returns on either the NYSE/AMEX value-weighted or Nasdaq composite index. IPO and benchmark returns are taken from the Center for Research in Security Prices files.
a. Returns for 1993 and 1994 only include IPOs that went public prior to December 31, 1992.

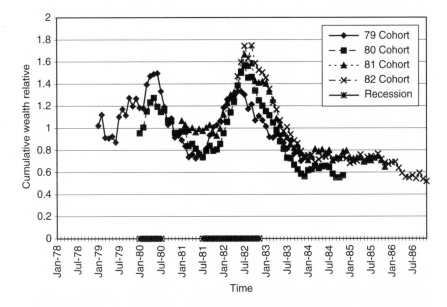

Figure 20.1
Time series of wealth relatives for selected venture-backed IPO yearly cohorts. The sample is all venture-backed IPOs from 1979 through 1982. Performance of the portfolio of IPO firms is compared to the Nasdaq composite benchmark. The cumulative wealth relative from issue date through the calendar month is plotted by taking the ratio of one plus the equal weighted buy-and-hold return for the portfolio of issuing firms in a cohort year, starting from the beginning of the cohort year up to the given month divided by one plus the compounded Nasdaq return over the same period.

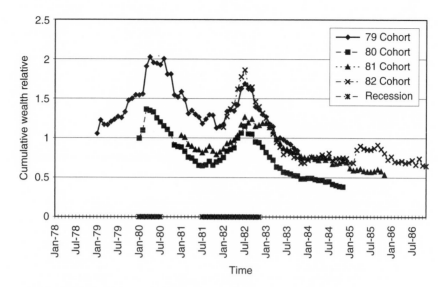

Figure 20.2
Time series of wealth relatives for selected non-venture-backed initial public offering (IPO) yearly cohorts. The sample is all non-venture-backed IPOs from 1979 through 1982. Performance of the portfolio of IPO firms is compared to the Nasdaq composite benchmark. The cumulative wealth relative from issue date through the calendar month is plotted by taking the ratio of one plus the equal weighted buy-and-hold return for the portfolio of issuing firms in a cohort year, starting from the beginning of the cohort year up to the given month divided by one plus the compounded Nasdaq return over the same period.

patterns. Relative returns decline sharply for all cohorts·in mid-1980, rise in parallel from January 1982 through the end of 1982, and then decline in 1983. The time-series correlation of the yearly cohorts illustrates the need to be concerned about interpretation of test statistics. Viewing each IPO as an independent event probably overstates the significance of estimated underperformance. Knowing that underperformance is concentrated in time may also help determine its causes.

Risk-Adjusted Performance of the IPOs

If IPOs underperform on a risk-adjusted basis, portfolios of IPOs should consistently underperform relative to an explicit asset pricing model. Recent work by Fama and French (1993) indicates that a three-factor model may explain the cross section of stock returns. Their three factors are RMRF, which is the excess return on the value-weighted market portfolio, SMB, the return on a zero investment portfolio formed by subtracting the return on a large firm portfolio from the return on a small firm portfolio,[7] and HML, the return on a zero investment portfolio calculated as the return on a portfolio of high book-to-market stocks minus the return on a portfolio of low book-to-market stocks.[8] We use the intercept from time-series regressions as an indicator of risk-adjusted performance to determine whether the results documented by Ritter (1991) and Loughran and Ritter (1995) are consistent with the Fama-French model. The intercepts in these regressions have an interpretation analogous to Jensen's alpha in the capital asset pricing model (CAPM) framework. This approach has the added benefit that we can make statistical inferences given the assumption of multivariate normality of the residuals. This was not possible in our previous analysis due to the right skewness of long horizon returns. The disadvantage of this approach is that it weights each month equally in minimizing the sum of squares. This point can be appreciated by noting that a monthly observation in mid-1976 (the average of a few IPOs) gets the same weight as a monthly observation in mid-1986 (the average of a large number of IPOs). If underperformance is correlated with the number of IPOs in our portfolios, the Fama-French results will reduce the measured underperformance.

Table 20.4 presents the three-factor time-series regression results. IPO portfolio returns are regressed on RMRF, SMB, and HML. For the equal- and value-weighted venture-backed IPO portfolios presented in panel A, results cannot reject the three-factor model. The intercepts are 0.0007 and 0.0015. Panel B presents results for nonventure IPOs. When the nonventure returns are weighted equally, the intercept is −0.0052 (52 basis points per month) with a t-statistic of −2.80 indicating severe underperformance. Value-weighting nonventure capital returns produces a smaller intercept, −0.0029 with a t-statistic of −1.84.[9]

The coefficients on HML for venture-backed IPOs (−0.6807 and −1.0659) indicate that their returns covary with low book-to-market (growth) firms. When returns are value weighed, loadings on SMB decline

7. The breakpoints for small and large firms are determined by NYSE firms alone, but the portfolios contain all firms traded on NYSE, AMEX, and Nasdaq exchanges.

8. The high book-to-market portfolio represents the top 30 percent of all firms on COMPUSTAT, while the low book-to-market portfolio contains firms in the lowest 30 percent of the COMPUSTAT universe of firms.

9. Loughran and Ritter (1995) also run Fama-French three-factor regressions and find negative intercepts for all issuer portfolios. Loughran and Ritter's regressions, however, combine IPO and SEO firms. Their regressions are therefore not directly comparable to our results. Loughran and Ritter also sort issuing firms into large and small issuers but use the median firm on NYSE/AMEX to determine the size breakpoint. This cutoff would leave very few IPO firms in the large issuing firm portfolio.

Table 20.4
Fama-French (1993) three-factor regression on initial public offering (IPO) portfolios for the whole sample and sorted on the basis of size

	Full sample equal-weighted	Full sample value-weighted	Equal-weighted size terciles		
			Small	2	Large
Panel A: Venture capital IPOs					
Intercepts	0.0007	0.0015	0.0001	−0.0004	0.0023
	[0.35]	[0.55]	[0.02]	[−0.20]	[0.93]
RMRF	1.0978	1.2127	0.9481	1.1096	1.2333
	[22.97]	[17.64]	[11.28]	[19.41]	[19.46]
SMB	1.2745	1.1131	1.6841	1.3237	1.1373
	[18.57]	[10.37]	[12.91]	[14.83]	[11.49]
HML	−0.6807	−1.0659	−0.2765	−0.6734	−1.1373
	[−8.24]	[−8.96]	[−1.90]	[−6.81]	[−9.95]
Adjusted R^2	0.889	0.821	0.687	0.846	0.849
Panel B: Non-venture capital IPOs					
Intercepts	−0.0052	−0.0029	−0.0056	−0.0056	−0.0004
	[−2.80]	[−1.84]	[−1.63]	[−2.72]	[−0.27]
RMRF	0.9422	1.0486	0.8073	0.9900	1.0312
	[19.94]	[26.12]	[9.24]	[18.74]	[26.40]
SMB	1.1450	0.6612	1.3870	1.2245	0.8322
	[15.52]	[10.55]	[10.17]	[14.85]	[13.65]
HML	−0.1069	−0.3405	0.1909	−0.1906	−0.3229
	[−1.31]	[−4.90]	[1.26]	[−2.08]	[−4.77]
Adjusted R^2	0.825	0.868	0.544	0.813	0.879

Note: The sample is all venture capital IPOs from 1972 through 1992 and all non-venture-backed IPOs from 1975 through 1992. Portfolios of IPOs are formed by including all issues that were done within the previous five years. RMRF is the value-weighted market return on all NYSE/AMEX/Nasdaq firms (RM) minus the risk-free rate (RF) which is the one-month Treasury bill rate. SMB (small minus big) is the difference each month between the return on small firms and big firms. HML (high minus low) is the difference each month between the return on a portfolio of high book-to-market stocks and the return on a portfolio of low book-to-market stocks. The first two columns present results for the entire sample. The next three columns show portfolios sorted by size. Every six months an equal number of stocks are allocated to one of three size portfolios. Size breakpoints are the same for both the venture and non-venture-backed samples. Portfolio returns are the equal-weighted returns for IPOs within that tercile. IPOs are allowed to switch allocation every six months. All regressions are for January 1977 through December 1994 for a total of 216 observations. [*t*-statistics are in brackets.]

but the loadings on HML become more negative for both IPO groups. The returns on larger IPO firms (in market value) tend to covary more with the returns of growth companies.

Every six months we divide the sample into three size portfolios based on the previous month's IPO size distribution using all IPOs to determine the breakpoints. The portfolios are rebalanced monthly and IPOs are allowed to switch portfolios every half year. We estimate equal-weighted regressions within each size group. The venture capital terciles never underperform. No intercept is below −0.0004 and none are significant. The pattern for nonventure IPOs verifies our earlier results. Underperformance is concentrated in the two smallest terciles. Intercepts for the smallest two size terciles in the nonventure sample are large, −0.0056, with t-statistics of −1.63 and −2.72. Coefficients on SMB decline monotonically from the portfolio of smallest issuers to largest issuers. Returns of the smallest IPOs covary more with returns on small stocks.

Coefficients on HML show two interesting patterns. Coefficients for venture-backed IPO portfolios decline monotonically. The larger the firm, the more it covaries with low book-to-market firms. Venture-backed firms are similar in age and amount of capital invested (book value of assets). Venture-backed firms become large by having high market values. Large firms (in market value) will have low book-to-market ratios and hence covary with growth companies.

This pattern is not as clear in the nonventure sample. First, the smallest tercile has a positive coefficient on HML and the largest two portfolios have negative coefficients. Similarly venture-backed IPOs load more negatively on HML than nonventure firms, which indicates that venture-backed returns covary more with the returns of growth companies.

The results indicate that IPO underperformance is driven by nonventure IPOs in the smallest decile of firms based on NYSE breakpoints. Over 50 percent of nonventure firms are in the smallest size decile when breakpoints are determined by NYSE-listed firms. Therefore all firms in the nonventure capital smallest portfolio of table 20.4 are from the smallest size decile.

Table 20.5 presents the results sorting firms on the basis of book-to-market ratios.[10] Panel A shows that for the equal-weighted venture-backed IPO portfolio, no book-to-market portfolio underperforms. Nonventure

---

10. Results for the whole sample are not the same as in table 20.4 because sorting by book-to-market is predicated on having book equity data from COMPUSTAT. Some firms are on CRSP but not on COMPUSTAT, so the number of firms in table 20.4 is larger than the number of firms in table 20.5 by 778 observations.

Table 20.5
Fama-French (1993) three-factor regression on initial public offering (IPO) portfolios for the whole sample and sorted on the basis of book-to-market ratio

| | Full sample | Book-to-market terciles | | |
		Low	2	High
Panel A: Venture capital IPOs—equal-weighted portfolios				
Intercepts	0.0029	−0.0009	0.0026	−0.0007
	[0.15]	[−0.36]	[0.89]	[−0.23]
RMRF	1.0893	1.1128	1.1154	1.0400
	[20.94]	[16.51]	[14.75]	[13.70]
SMB	1.3416	1.2160	1.2801	1.5242
	[16.52]	[11.56]	[10.83]	[12.86]
HML	−0.6864	−0.9806	−0.8044	−0.2760
	[−7.63]	[−8.41]	[−6.15]	[−2.10]
Adjusted R^2	0.868	0.812	0.766	0.730
Panel B: Non-venture capital IPOs—equal-weighted portfolios				
Intercepts	−0.0051	−0.0042	−0.0055	−0.0054
	[−2.90]	[−1.61]	[−2.60]	[−2.33]
RMRF	0.9762	1.0394	0.9881	0.9017
	[21.71]	[15.47]	[18.16]	[15.08]
SMB	1.1946	1.2839	1.1803	1.1264
	[17.02]	[12.24]	[13.90]	[12.07]
HML	−0.1667	−0.4977	−0.2641	0.2575
	[−2.14]	[−4.28]	[−2.81]	[2.49]
Adjusted R^2	0.852	0.770	0.805	0.703
Panel C: Venture capital IPOs—value-weighted portfolios				
Intercepts	0.0012	0.0036	0.0029	−0.0030
	[0.42]	[1.09]	[0.86]	[−1.01]
RMRF	1.1991	1.1814	1.1772	1.1664
	[16.89]	[13.82]	[13.58]	[15.38]
SMB	1.0283	0.9384	1.2043	1.3184
	[9.28]	[7.03]	[8.90]	[11.13]
HML	−1.0470	−1.2152	−0.9706	−0.5252
	[−8.52]	[−8.22]	[−6.47]	[−4.00]
Adjusted R^2	0.804	0.744	0.734	0.756
Panel D: Non-venture capital IPOs—value-weighted portfolios				
Intercepts	−0.0012	0.0021	−0.0015	−0.0039
	[−0.59]	[0.66]	[−0.71]	[−1.81]
RMRF	1.0438	1.0771	1.0631	1.0269
	[20.59]	[13.55]	[20.03]	[18.86]
SMB	0.6870	0.8899	0.7483	0.5189
	[8.68]	[7.17]	[9.03]	[6.10]
HML	−0.4282	−0.7053	−0.3632	−0.0090
	[−4.88]	[−5.12]	[−3.96]	[−0.10]
Adjusted R^2	0.813	0.698	0.802	0.732

Table 20.5
(continued)
Note: The sample is all venture capital IPOs from 1972 through 1992 and all non-venture-backed IPOs from 1975 through 1992. Portfolios of IPOs are formed by including all issues that were done within the previous five years. RMRF is the value-weighted market return on all NYSE/AMEX/Nasdaq firms (RM) minus the risk-free rate (RF) which is the one-month Treasury bill rate. SMB (small minus big) is the difference each month between the return on small firms and big firms. HML (high minus low) is the difference each month between the return on a portfolio of high book-to-market stocks and the return on a portfolio of low book-to-market stocks. The first column presents results for the entire sample. The next three columns show portfolios sorted by book-to-market ratio. Every six months an equal number of stocks are allocated to one of the three book-to-market portfolios. Book-to-market breakpoints are the same for venture and non-venture-backed samples. Portfolio returns are either equal-weighted or value-weighted returns for IPOs within that tercile. IPOs are allowed to switch allocation every six months. All regressions are for January 1977 through December 1994 for a total of 216 observations. [t-statistics are in brackets.]

firms, however, show substantial underperformance in all terciles. Underperformance ranges from −0.0042 to −0.0055.

Panels C and D show that value-weighting again reduces the influence of small firm underperformance. The lowest book-to-market portfolio for the venture-backed IPOs now has a positive intercept of 0.0036 (36 basis points per month). No other venture or nonventure IPO tercile has significant underperformance relative to the Fama-French three-factor model. The Fama-French results provide evidence that underperformance remains even after controlling for size and book-to-market in time-series regressions. Venture-backed IPOs do not underperform whether the results are run on the entire sample or sortings based on size or book-to-market. Nonventure-backed IPOs exhibit severe underperformance (primarily concentrated in the smaller issuers) even relative to the Fama-French model.

To address the source of underperformance, we rerun the Fama-French three-factor regressions including an index that measures the change in the average discount on closed-end funds. We construct the index as seen in Lee, Shleifer, and Thaler (1991). The discount on a closed-end fund is the difference between the fund's net asset value and its price divided by the net asset value. We value-weight the discount across funds in a particular month and then calculate the change in the level of the index from the previous month. Lee, Shleifer, and Thaler argue that the average discount reflects the relative level of investor sentiment. If this is the case, we expect the change in the discount to be related to returns of firms that underperform relative to the Fama-French three-factor model. When the change in discount is positive, that is, the average discount increases, individual investors may be more pessimistic and returns on firms affected by investor sentiment should fall. Conversely, when the change in average discount is negative, individual investors become more optimistic and returns should rise.

Table 20.6 confirms our predictions. The change in discount is negatively related to returns of the smallest group of firms, the smallest venture-backed companies and the smallest two terciles of nonventure firms. These firms are potentially most affected by investor sentiment. The negative relation between changes in the closed-end fund discount and returns of small IPO firms indicates that investor sentiment might be an important source of underperformance. Sophisticated investors may not enter this market because the cost of gathering information about these firms may outweigh the potential returns from correcting the mispricing. Informed investors may also not want to bet against noise traders if prices can move further out of line in the short run. Finally, short selling may be constrained because shares cannot be borrowed.

Cross-Sectional Results

Given the results from the Fama-French (1993) three-factor regressions, we explore how raw returns and wealth relatives vary with size and book-to-market. In table 20.7 we present summary statistics for size and book-to-market quintiles of the full sample and the subsets of venture-backed and nonventure IPOs. In panel A, we sort the entire sample of IPOs by their real (constant dollar) market value at the first available CRSP listed closing price. Equal numbers of IPOs are allocated to each size quintile. We impose the same cutoffs for venture-backed and nonventure IPOs. Size increases from an average of $13.0 million in the first quintile to $505.2 million in the biggest. Comparing average book-to-market ratios for the two subgroups demonstrates that venture-backed IPOs have substantially lower average book-to-market ratios within any given size quintile. The smallest two-size quintiles have disproportionately more nonventure IPOs. This reflects the larger average size of venture-backed IPO firms.[11] Differences in book-to-market ratios might reflect different industry compositions between the two groups. Venture capitalists back more firms in high-growth, low book-to-market industries.

In panel B, IPOs are sorted into book-to-market quintiles. Average book-to-market ratios increase from 0.053 in the lowest quintile to 3.142 in the

---

11. No time-series bias is imparted by sorting the entire sample by the total sample breakpoints. No trend or pattern in real size or book-to-market ratios is evident that would lead to dramatic differences in the yearly representation in size or book-to-market quintiles.

Table 20.6
Fama-French (1993) three-factor regression on initial public offering (IPO) portfolios including the change in the average closed-end fund discount

	Full sample equal-weighted	Full sample value-weighted	Equal-weighted size terciles		
			Small	2	Large
Panel A: Venture-backed IPOs					
Intercepts	0.0009	0.0018	0.0011	−0.0008	0.0024
	[0.44]	[0.59]	[0.31]	[−0.34]	[0.89]
RMRF	1.0934	1.2043	0.9145	1.1258	1.2377
	[21.10]	[15.85]	[10.08]	[18.34]	[18.06]
SMB	1.3855	1.1071	1.7154	1.2986	1.1406
	[17.28]	[9.41]	[12.22]	[13.67]	[10.75]
HML	−0.7104	−1.0881	−0.4078	−0.6400	−1.0818
	[−7.51]	[−7.85]	[−2.47]	[−5.71]	[−8.65]
ΔDiscount	−0.0002	0.0018	−0.0038	0.0001	0.0031
	[−0.22]	[1.24]	[−2.18]	[0.06]	[2.34]
Adjusted R^2	0.891	0.819	0.701	0.850	0.853
Panel B: Non-venture capital IPOs					
Intercepts	−0.0049	−0.0032	−0.0050	−0.0053	−0.0004
	[−2.38]	[−1.80]	[−1.28]	[−2.32]	[−0.52]
RMRF	0.9121	1.0271	0.7801	0.9480	1.0096
	[17.61]	[23.28]	[8.03]	[16.66]	[23.50]
SMB	1.1650	0.6853	1.3910	1.2554	0.8581
	[14.53]	[10.04]	[9.25]	[14.26]	[12.91]
HML	−0.2155	−0.4172	0.0862	−0.3313	−0.4045
	[−2.28]	[−5.18]	[0.48]	[−3.19]	[−5.16]
ΔDiscount	−0.0022	−0.0000	−0.0030	−0.0031	−0.0005
	[−2.23]	[−0.06]	[−2.62]	[−2.87]	[−0.64]
Adjusted R^2	0.8290	0.871	0.543	0.824	0.882

Note: The sample is all venture capital IPOs from 1972 through 1992 and all non-venture-backed IPOs from 1975 through 1992. Portfolios of IPOs are formed by including all issues that were done within the previous five years. RMRF is the value-weighted market return on all NYSE/AMEX/Nasdaq firms (RM) minus the risk free rate (RF) which is the one-month Treasury bill rate. SMB (small minus big) is the difference each month between the return on small firms and big firms. HML (high minus low) is the difference each month between the return on a portfolio of high book-to-market stocks and the return on a portfolio of low book-to-market stocks. ΔDiscount represents the change in the average discount on closed end-fund from the end of last month to the end of this month. The first two columns present results for the entire sample. The next three columns show portfolios sorted by size. Every six months an equal number of stocks are allocated to one of the three size portfolios. Size breakpoints are the same for both venture and non-venture-backed samples. Portfolio returns are the equal-weighted returns for IPOs within that tercile. IPOs are allowed to switch allocation every six months. All regressions are for January 1977 through May 1992 for a total of 185 observations. [*t*-statistics are in brackets.]

Table 20.7
Summary statistics for size and book-to-market quintiles

Size quintile	Average size (1992$ mil)	Venture-backed IPOs		Non-venture-backed IPOs	
		Average book-to-market	Number of firms	Average book-to-market	Number of firms
Panel A: Summary data for size quintiles					
Small	13.0	0.465 [0.323]	58	1.901 [0.295]	806
2	29.6	0.360 [0.326]	132	0.531 [0.286]	732
3	59.3	0.326 [0.286]	220	0.892 [0.305]	648
4	114.9	0.248 [0.097]	285	0.907 [0.310]	579
Large	505.2	0.187 [0.235]	237	0.709 [0.280]	622

Book-to-market quintile	Average book-to-market	Venture-backed IPOs		Non-venture-backed IPOs	
		Average size	Number of firms	Average size	Number of firms
Panel B: Summary data for book-to-market quintiles					
Low	0.053	$228.5 [142.7]	198	$131.2 [49.7]	404
2	0.167	$166.9 [117.8]	182	$170.0 [58.8]	420
3	0.277	$133.0 [92.0]	181	$115.6 [51.9]	422
4	0.400	$102.4 [77.8]	157	$117.3 [44.5]	447
High	3.142	$82.2 [55.4]	92	$227.5 [55.6]	510

Note: The sample is all venture capital initial public offerings (IPOs) from 1972 through 1992 and all non-venture-backed IPOs from 1975 through 1992. IPOs are divided into quintiles based on size (market value of equity at the first Center for Research in Security Prices (CRSP) listed closing price in constant 1997 dollars) or book-to-market at the time of IPO. The first book value of equity after the IPO is taken from COMPUSTAT as long as it is within one year of the offering date. An equal number of IPOs from the entire sample are allocated to each quintile. Breakpoints are the same for venture and non-venture-backed samples. Size is in millions of 1992 dollars. [Medians are in brackets.]

highest. Once again, significant differences are apparent across the two samples. The average size of the venture-backed IPOs is higher in the first through third quintiles but lower in the fourth and fifth quintiles. Venture-backed growth (low book-to-market) firms tend to be larger and venture capital value (high book-to-market) firms tend to be smaller than comparable nonventure IPOs. Except for the highest book-to-market quintile, the quintiles have roughly constant proportions of venture and nonventure IPOs. The highest book-to-market quintile has substantially more nonventure IPOs than venture-backed IPOs. This may indicate that venture capitalists avoid investment in industries that have high book-to-market ratios (value industries) or that the nonventure firms simply have lower growth expectations.

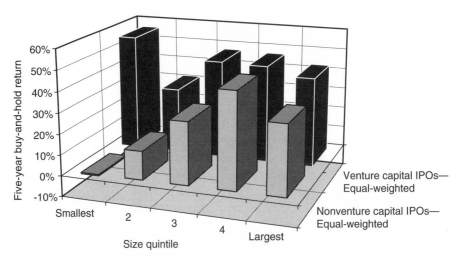

Figure 20.3
Five-year equal-weighted buy-and-hold returns for venture- and non-venture-backed IPOs by
size quintile. The sample is 3,407 non-venture-backed IPOs from 1975 through 1992 and 934
venture-backed IPOs from 1972 through 1992. Each sample of IPOs is sorted into size quintiles
based on the real (1992 dollars) size at the first closing price listed by the Center for Research in
Security Prices. Size breakpoints are the same for the venture- and non-venture-backed samples.
Quintile returns are the average buy-and-hold return for IPOs in that quintile.

Figure 20.3 plots the average equal-weighted nominal five-year, buy-and-
hold return for each size quintile classifying IPOs as venture or nonventure.
Venture-backed IPOs show no size effect. Performance of the smallest quintile of venture-backed IPOs looks very similar to performance of the largest.
A pronounced size effect is apparent in the nonventure firms, however. Average nominal returns on nonventure IPOs in size quintile 1 are negative.

Equal-weighted nominal five-year, buy-and-hold returns for book-to-
market quintiles are shown in figure 20.4. Returns show an increase from
lowest to highest quintile. The increase across book-to-market quintiles
is substantially larger for nonventure firms. On an equal-weighted basis,
all nonventure book-to-market quintiles underperform the venture-backed
quintiles.

Figures 20.5 and 20.6 show that underperformance of small, low book-to-
market IPO firms is not due to their status as equity issuers. We sort the
IPO firms into their appropriate twenty-five (5 times 5) size and book-to-
market portfolio based on the NYSE breakpoints that are discussed above.
The five-year, buy-and-hold return on the IPO firms is compared to the
five-year, buy-and-hold return on the size and book-to-market portfolio that

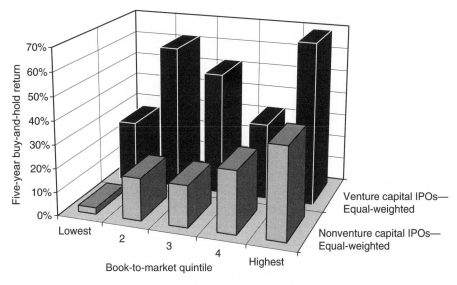

Figure 20.4
Five-year equal-weighted buy-and-hold returns for venture- and non-venture-backed IPOs by book-to-market quintile. The sample is 3,407 non-venture-backed IPOs from 1975 through 1992 and 934 venture-backed IPOs from 1972 through 1992. Each sample of IPOs is sorted into book-to-market quintiles based on the real (1992 dollars) market value at the first closing price listed by the Center for Research in Security Prices and first available book value of equity. Book-to-market breakpoints are the same for both samples. Quintile returns are the average buy-and-hold return for IPOs in that quintile.

excludes IPO and SEO firms for five years after issue. Figure 20.5 plots the average excess returns of the venture capital-backed IPO sample by portfolio. Adjusting for size and book-to-market returns, no strong pattern of performance is seen. Small, low book-to-market venture-backed IPOs (380 of 934 firms) outperform the small, low book-to-market benchmark by 42 percent.

Figure 20.6 plots size and book-to-market excess returns for nonventure capital-backed IPO firms. The small, low book-to-market nonventure IPO firms (which make up 1,465 of the 3,407 firms) outperform similar non-issuing firms by 12 percent. This positive relative performance is not the result of large returns by the IPO firms, they only earn an average of 5 percent over five years. Small, low book-to-market nonissuing firms, however, earn an average of −7 percent over the same time period. Portfolios further from the small, low book-to-market portfolio have far fewer issuing firms. Standard errors for the estimates of mean excess returns would be much larger and hence little emphasis should be placed on their significance. For

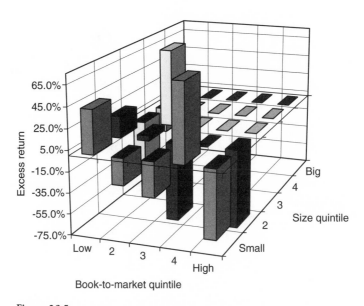

Figure 20.5
Five-year excess returns for venture-backed IPOs by size and book-to-market portfolio. The sample is 934 venture-backed IPOs from 1972 through 1992. Twenty-five (5 by 5) size and book-to-market portfolios are formed based on the NYSE breakpoints. IPO firms are assigned to their appropriate size and book-to-market portfolio at issue. The five-year excess return is calculated by subtracting the five-year buy-and-hold return on the size and book-to-market portfolio that excludes all IPO and SEO firms for five years after issue from the five-year buy-and-hold return on the IPO firm. The average excess return is plotted for each size and book-to-market portfolio.

the majority of the sample—that is, the corner of the figure near the small, low book-to-market portfolio—relative performance is close to 0.

These results indicate that IPO underperformance is not an issuing firm effect. It is a small, low book-to-market effect. Similar size and book-to-market nonissuing firms perform just as poorly as IPO firms do. This does not imply that returns are normal on a risk-adjusted basis. In fact small, low book-to-market firms appear to earn almost zero nominal returns over a five-year period that starts with IPO issuance. It may be difficult to explain this low return with a risk-based model.

In table 20.8 we present cross-sectional estimates of the determinants of five-year, buy-and-hold wealth relatives using the Nasdaq composite index as the benchmark.[12] The dependent variable is the logarithm of the five-year wealth relative. The independent variables are the logarithm of the

---

12. Because of the large cross-section that we employ, the standard 5 percent significance level should be reduced.

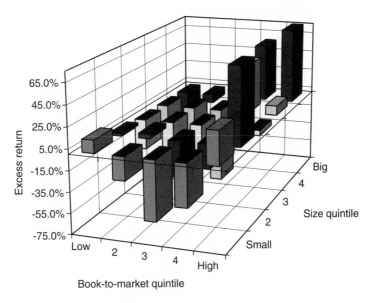

Figure 20.6
Five-year excess returns for non-venture-backed IPOs by size and book-to-market portfolio. The sample is 3,407 non-venture-backed IPOs from 1975 through 1992. Twenty-five (5 × 5) size and book-to-market portfolios are formed based on the NYSE breakpoints. IPO firms are assigned to their appropriate size and book-to-market portfolio at issue. The five-year excess return is calculated by subtracting the five-year buy-and-hold return on the size and book-to-market portfolio that excludes all IPO and SEO firms for five years after issue from the five-year buy-and-hold return on the IPO firm. The average excess return is plotted for each size and book-to-market portfolio.

firm's market value of equity (in constant dollars) at the first available CRSP listed closing price, a dummy variable indicating if the firm was venture-backed, the logarithm of the firm's book value of equity to market value, and the lagged dividend price ratio for the entire market. We include the dividend price ratio to determine whether overall market pricing affects long-run returns.

The results demonstrate that size is an important determinant of relative returns. Across all specifications the coefficient on logarithm of IPO-firm size is positive and highly significant. This result captures the essence of value-weighting returns. The presence of a venture capitalist is positively related to a firm's wealth relative, although the coefficient is only marginally significant.[13] The coefficients on lagged dividend price ratio are negative

---

13. If the regressions are run on firms below the median size, the coefficient on the venture capital dummy variable is positive and significant, indicating that returns are significantly different for small venture and nonventure companies.

Table 20.8

Cross-sectional regressions on buy-and-hold returns and wealth relatives

Independent variables	Dependent variable: Logarithm of five-year wealth relative				
Logarithm of firm size	0.2063				0.1944
	[12.68]				[10.44]
Venture-backed dummy variable		0.0953			0.0992
		[1.94]			[1.93]
Logarithm of book-to-market ratio			0.1414		0.1321
			[7.44]		[7.03]
Lagged dividend price ratio				−0.2445	−0.1386
				[−9.81]	[−5.03]
Constant	−1.6919	−0.8923	−0.7190	0.0768	−0.9904
	[−25.01]	[−39.11]	[−20.54]	[0.77]	[−6.91]
Adjusted-R^2	0.035	0.001	0.015	0.021	0.062
Number of observations	4,332	4,341	3,563	4,341	3,563

Note: The sample of initial public offerings (IPOs) is all venture-backed IPOs that went public between 1972 and 1992 and all non-venture-capital-backed IPOs that went public between 1975 and 1992. The dependent variable is the logarithm of the five-year wealth relatives using the Nasdaq composite index as the benchmark. The independent variables are the natural logarithm of the market value of the firm's equity in billions of 1992 dollars valued at the closing price on the first day for which a price from the Center for Research in Security Prices database is available, a dummy variable that equals one if the firm was venture-backed, the natural logarithm of the book-to-market ratio when the firm goes public, and the lagged dividend price ratio for the market. [t-statistics are in brackets.]

and significant. If the dividend price ratio captures the general level of market prices, IPOs that go public during periods of higher market valuation perform worse over the subsequent five years relative to the market as a whole. Finally book-to-market has an important impact on returns at five year horizons. The coefficient on the book-to-market ratio is positive and highly significant. The positive relationship between book-to-market ratio and relative performance is consistent with both Fama-French's interpretation of book-to-market as a priced risk factor and Loughran and Ritter's belief that it proxies for relative overpricing.

Conclusions

The underperformance documented in Ritter (1991) and Loughran and Ritter (1995) comes primarily from small, nonventure IPOs. We replicated Loughran and Ritter's results and showed that returns on nonventure IPOs are significantly below those of venture-backed IPOs and below relevant benchmarks when returns are weighted equally. We tested performance against several broad market indexes, Fama-French (1997) industry portfolios, and matched size and book-to-market portfolios to test the robustness of our results. Differences in performance among the groups and the level of underperformance were reduced once returns were value weighted.

We also showed that underperformance documented by Loughran and Ritter is not unique to firms issuing equity. Eliminating IPOs and SEOs from size and book-to-market portfolios demonstrates that IPOs perform no worse than similar nonissuing firms. This argues that we should look more broadly at types of firms that underperform and not treat IPO firms as a different group.

Although small, low book-to-market IPOs perform no differently from similar small, low book-to-market nonissuing firms, the pattern of relative performance in other portfolios needs to be examined in greater detail. Some of the IPO size and book-to-market portfolios appeared to exhibit either under- or overperformance. Examination of the time-series and cross-sectional properties of these patterns may be important in determining the source of performance anomalies.

The underperformance of small, low book-to-market firms may have various explanations. First, unexpected shocks may have hit small growth companies in the early and mid-1980s. The correlation of returns in calendar time may argue in favor of this explanation. Fama and French (1995) show that the earnings of small firms declined in the early 1980s but did not recover when those of large firms did. This experience was different from previous recessions. It is possible that small growth firms were constrained either in the capital or product markets after the recession. These constraints may have been unanticipated. This explanation argues that we should not view each IPO (or firm) as an event; that is, they are not all independent observations. Correcting for the cross-sectional correlation is critical.

A second explanation for the underperformance of small, low book-to-market firms is investor sentiment. The evidence from Fama-French three-factor regressions with and without the change in closed-end fund discount supports this alternative. If the IPO is small, "you can fool some of the people all of the time." If any type of firm is likely to be subject to fads and investor sentiment, it is these firms. Their equity is held primarily by individuals. Megginson and Weiss (1991) show that institutional holdings of equity after an IPO are substantially higher for venture-backed IPOs than they are for nonventure IPOs. The relatively higher institutional holdings may occur because institutions have greater information on small, venture-backed firms through their investment in venture capital funds. Furthermore, because institutions invest such large amounts of money, holding an investment in a small firm may mean that the institutional investor becomes a 5 percent shareholder, something that many institutions want to avoid for regulatory reasons. The ability to short sell small firms is extremely limited because it may be difficult to borrow their stock certificates. Field (1996) has shown that long-run IPO performance is positively related to institutional holdings. Field's effects may similarly extend to nonissuing, small growth companies.

Asymmetric information is also likely to be more prevalent for small firms because individuals spend considerably less time tracking returns than institutional investors do. Small nonventure firms go public with lower tier underwriters than similar venture-backed firms (Barry et al. 1990), and they may have fewer and lower quality analysts following the company after the offering. Michaely and Shaw (1991) provide evidence that underwriter reputation is positively related to the long-run performance of IPOs. Carter, Dark, and Singh (1998) and Nanda, Yi, and Yun (1995) have shown that the quality of the underwriter is related to long-run performance of IPOs, consistent with greater asymmetric information being associated with lower returns. It might not pay for sophisticated investors to research a small firm because they cannot recoup costs of information gathering and trading. The absolute return that investors can make is small because the dollar size of the stake they can take is limited by firm size.

Finally, individuals might derive utility from buying the shares of small, low book-to-market firms because they value them like a lottery ticket. Black (1986) argues that many finance anomalies may only be explained by this type of utility-based theory. Returns on small nonventure IPOs are more highly skewed than returns on either large IPO firms or similar sized venture-backed IPO firms.

Ritter (1991) and Loughran and Ritter (1995) have discovered an area that may allow us to test the foundations of investor sentiment and rational pricing. Future tests that identify elements of investor sentiment may show that individual investors are less than perfectly rational. Alternatively, real factors may be responsible for the measured underperformance.

What are the implications of our results? First, most institutional investors will not be significantly hurt by investing in IPOs. They usually do not buy the small issues that perform the worst. Underperformance of small growth companies, however, may be important for capital allocation. If the cost of capital for small growth companies is periodically distorted, their investment behavior may be adversely affected. If any of these small firms are future industry leaders, then we should be concerned about this mispricing. Further research is clearly warranted.

21 The Future of the Venture Capital Cycle

Over the past two decades there has been a tremendous boom in the venture capital industry. The pool of U.S. venture capital funds has grown from less than $1 billion in 1976 (Charles River Associates 1976) to over $250 billion in 2001 (Venture Economics 2002). This growth has outstripped that of almost every class of financial product.

The supply of venture capital is also likely to continue growing. Within the past two years, numerous pension funds have invested in private equity for the first time. Many experienced investors have also decided to increase their allocations to venture capital and buyout funds. These increased allocations will take a number of years to implement.

This growth naturally raises the question of sustainability. As has been highlighted throughout this volume, short-run shifts in the supply of or demand for venture capital investments have had dramatic effects. For instance, periods with a rapid increase in capital commitments have led to less restrictive partnership agreements, large investments in portfolio firms, and higher valuations for those investments. These patterns have led many practitioners to conclude that the industry is inherently cyclical. In short, this view implies that the side effects associated with periods of rapid growth generate sufficient difficulties that periods of retrenchment are sure to follow.

Neoclassical economics teaches us to examine not just the short-run supply and demand effects. It is also important to consider the nature of long-run supply and demand conditions. In the short run, intense competition between private-equity groups may lead to a willingness to pay a premium for certain types of firms (e.g., firms specializing in tools and content for the Internet). This is unlikely to be a sustainable strategy in the long run: firms that persist in such a strategy will eventually achieve low returns and be unable to raise follow-on funds.

The types of factors that will determine the long-run, steady-state supply of venture capital in the economy are likely to be more fundamental. These most likely will include the magnitude of fundamental technological innovation in the economy, the presence of liquid and competitive markets for venture capitalists to sell their investments (whether markets for stock offerings or acquisitions), and the willingness of highly skilled managers and engineers to work in entrepreneurial environments. (The last factor in turn will be a function of tax policy, legal protections, and societal preferences.) However painful the short-run adjustments, these more fundamental factors are likely to be critical in establishing the long-run level.

When one examines these more fundamental factors, there appears to have been quite substantial changes for the better over the past several decades.[1] We will briefly discuss two of these determinants of the long-run supply of venture capital in the United States, where these changes have been particularly dramatic: the extent of technological innovations and the development of regional agglomerations.

While the increase in innovative outputs can be seen through several measures, probably the clearest indication is in the extent of patenting. Patent applications by U.S. inventors, after hovering between forty and eighty thousand annually over the first eighty-five years of this century, have surged over the past decade to close to two-hundred thousand per year. This does not appear to reflect the impact of changes in domestic patent policy, shifts in the success rate of applications, or a variety of alternative explanations. (For a detailed exploration, see Kortum and Lerner 1998.) Rather, it appears to reflect a fundamental shift in the innovative fecundity in the domestic economy. The breadth of technology appears wider today than it ever has been before. The greater rate of intellectual innovation provides fertile ground for future venture capital investments.

A second change has been in the development of what economists term "agglomeration economies" in the regions with the greatest venture capital activity. The efficiency of the venture capital process itself has been greatly augmented by the emergence of other intermediaries familiar with the

---

1. Despite its growth the private-equity pool today remains relatively small. For every $1.00 of venture capital in the portfolio of U.S. institutional investors, there is about $25 of publicly traded equities. The ratios are even more uneven for overseas institutions. At the same time the size of the foreign private equity pool remains far below that of the United States. This suggests considerable possibilities for future growth. The disparity can be illustrated by comparing the ratio of the venture capital pool to the size of the economy. In 2002 this ratio was five times higher in the United States than in East and South Asia, and two times higher in the United States than in Western Europe. (These statistics are taken from the European Private Equity and Venture Capital Association 2003, *Asian Venture Capital Journal* 2003, and World Bank 2003.) At least to the casual observer, these ratios appear modest compared to the economic role of new firms, products, and processes in the developed economies.

workings of the venture process. The presence of such expertise on the part of lawyers, accountants, and real estate brokers, among others, has substantially lowered the transaction costs associated with forming and financing new firms. The increasing number of professionals and managers familiar with and accustomed to the employment arrangements offered by venture-backed firms (e.g., heavy reliance on stock options) has also been a major shift. The market for new issues by venture-backed firms appears to have become steadily more efficient, as part III of this volume makes clear. In short, the increasing familiarity with the venture capital process has itself made the long-term prospects for venture investment more attractive than they have ever been before, in this country or abroad.

A corollary to this argument is perhaps even more important. These changes appear not to have been entirely independent of the growth of venture capital, but have been at least partially triggered by the role played by these financial intermediaries. For instance, much of the growth in patenting appears to have been spurred by the growth in the number of venture capital-backed firms (Kortum and Lerner 1998). In short, it appears as if there is a somewhat of a "virtuous circle," where the growth in the activity of U.S. venture capital industry has enhanced the conditions that drive the long-run value creation of this capital, which has in turn led to more capital formation.

As the various chapters of this volume have highlighted, much is still not yet known about the venture capital industry. The extent to which the U.S. venture model will spread overseas and the degree to which the American model will—or can—be successfully adapted during this process are particularly interesting questions. Clearly, this financial intermediary will be an enduring feature on the global economic landscape in the years to come.

Information on venture capital investments is difficult to gather from public sources. Unlike mutual funds, venture capitalists are typically exempt from the Investment Company Act of 1940 and do need not reveal their investments or organizational details in public filings.

Thus the primary sources of information in previous research on venture capital have been the companies in which the funds invest. For the subset of venture-backed firms that eventually go public, information is available in IPO prospectuses and S-1 registration statements. Investments in firms that do not go public are more difficult to uncover, since these investments are usually not publicized. Similarly information on partnerships is difficult to identify.

As in this volume we seek to empirically explore the venture capital industry in considerable detail, it was necessary to devote some degree of time to the identification and development of new data sets. In this chapter we describe the data sources that are at the heart of our analyses.

Sources of Venture Capital Partnership Agreements

In the analysis of venture funds in chapters 3, 4, and 5 we include only independent private partnerships primarily engaged in venture capital investments. We define venture capital investments as investments in equity or equity-linked securities of private firms with active participation by the fund managers in the management or oversight of the firms. We eliminate funds whose stated mandate is to invest more than 50 percent of their capital in other types of assets, such as the securities of firms undergoing leveraged buyouts, "special situations," or publicly traded securities. Many venture capital organizations in the sample raised LBO funds during the 1980s. We do not include such funds, even if all the other funds associated with the organization are devoted to venture capital. Venture funds that invest more than 50 percent of their capital in other venture partnerships, known as "funds of funds," are also excluded. Similarly Small Business Investment Companies (SBICs), publicly traded venture funds, and funds with a single limited partner are eliminated. Finally we omit organizations headquartered outside the United States because their investment opportunities or regulatory environment are substantially different from domestic venture capital funds, and their negotiated partnership terms may be expected to differ.

We use the partnership agreements collected by three organizations to construct the sample. The organizations are the Harvard Management Company, Kemper Financial Services, and Venture Economics. Each of these organizations has been involved in venture investing for at least fifteen years. Nonetheless, there are substantial differences in the funds in which each invests.

The Harvard Management Company handles the private-market investments for the Harvard University endowment. The group's files on venture investments date back to the late 1970s. Harvard's venture investment strategy was shaped by the philosophy of Walter Cabot, who ran Harvard Management between 1974 and 1990. While investing in risky asset classes, such as venture capital and oil and gas, he emphasized the importance of conducting business with established and reputable financial intermediaries (Grassmuck 1990).

Kemper Financial Services is an investment manager, also known as a gatekeeper, which has invested in venture capital on a regular basis since 1978. Institutional investors, such as pension funds, frequently seek to diversify their portfolios to include privately held assets. They may not have the resources to evaluate potential investments, or may not wish to grapple with the complications posed by these investments. For instance, venture capitalists frequently liquidate investments in firms by distributing thinly traded shares to investors. Investment managers will select and manage private investments for institutions, typically for a fee of 1 percent of the funds invested (Venture Economics 1989a). Gatekeepers will usually invest in a variety of funds, but the very oldest and youngest funds are likely to be underrepresented. Very established venture capital organizations typically have close relationships with their limited partners, who have invested in several of their funds. They are unlikely to turn to gatekeepers for funding. Meanwhile gatekeepers may be reluctant to invest in new funds of unproven venture capitalists (Goodman 1990).

Venture Economics is a unit of Securities Data Company and tracks the venture capital industry. The organization was known as Capital Publishing when it was established in 1961 to prepare a newsletter on SBICs. Since its acquisition by Stanley Pratt in 1977, the company has maintained a file on venture partnerships. Venture Economics collects this information for its Fund Raiser Advisory Service, which provides consulting assistance to venture capital organizations that are drafting partnership agreements or seeking investors. The funds whose documents are in their files appear to represent a random sample of the industry.

All three organizations began collecting information on a regular basis in the late 1970s. The occasional earlier documents in their files do not appear to have been gathered systematically. We consequently restrict our analysis to funds that closed in the period from 1978 through 1992. We find two types of documents in these files. The first are private placement memoranda, the marketing documents that are circulated to potential investors. The second are limited partnership agreements. These are the contracts that govern the workings of the funds. The files at Harvard and Kemper generally contain both types of documents. The files at Venture Economics frequently only contain the former documents.

For the analysis of contractual terms in chapter 4, we use a random sample of 140 partnership agreements. For the analysis of compensation in chapter 5, we use all funds that meet our criteria. The search of these three files identifies a total of 543 venture capital funds that apparently meet our tests. We are reluctant to use some of the 142 funds with compensation information that are not included in the database of funds compiled by the Venture Economics' Investors Services Group. Our primary concern relates to those funds whose only documentation is the private placement memorandum in the Venture Economics collection. We are often unsure whether the fund ever closed. In some cases, the general partners may have been unable to raise the stipulated minimum amount of funds. Several files at Venture Economics contain a notation indicating that the fund never closed. In other cases, we know independently that the fund-raising was unsuccessful, but there is no such notation in the Venture Economics files. Since many of the offering documents in Venture Economics files are for young venture capital organizations, there is a danger of including funds that were never raised.

Consequently we do not include all 543 funds in the compensation analysis. Instead, we include funds that satisfy one of two conditions. Either the fund is included in the Venture Economics funds database and is coded as a partnership sponsored by an independent venture capital organization, or the fund itself is not included in the database, but the documentation indicates that it is a partnership sponsored by an independent venture capital organization, and independent corroboration of this fund's successful closing can be found. This corroboration can include its listing as a previous fund in a subsequent marketing document, the presence of a signed contract in one of the files, or a listing by Asset Alternatives. From our review, we find partnership agreements or private placement memoranda in the files of Harvard, Kemper, and Venture Economics for 401 funds that satisfied the first set of criteria. Eighteen funds met the second requirement.

We assess the representativeness of this sample by comparing these funds with a database of venture capital funds compiled by Venture Economics' Investors Services Group. This database includes venture capital funds, SBICs, and related organizations. The Investors Services Group database is used in preparation of directories, such as the Venture Economics annual Investment Benchmark Reports. The database is compiled from information provided by venture capitalists and institutional investors. The Venture Economics database of funds contains summary information on 1,158 funds raised between 1978 and 1992. It includes many funds whose partnership agreements or private placement memoranda were not found in the Venture Economics files.

Tables 22.1 and 22.2 examine the independent venture partnerships in the Venture Economics database that closed between 1978 and 1992. We compare the characteristics of the funds included in the sample used in chapters 4 and 5 and those not included, using t-, Wilcoxon signed-rank, and Pearson χ^2-tests. We find that larger funds by more established partnerships are significantly more likely to be included in our contract sample.[1] In addition funds based in California (the center of the U.S. venture industry) are more likely to be included. Finally the typical fund in the sample closed somewhat more recently than the other funds in the Venture Economics database.

Our sample of funds used in the compensation analysis in chapter 5 accounts for 35 percent of the 1,158 funds raised by independent venture capital organizations between 1978 and 1992 that are in the Venture Economics funds database.[2] Weighting observations by fund size, using constant 1997 dollars, our measure of sample coverage is much better: funds

---

1. We examine whether the mixture of firms may have changed over time. In each of the three periods examined—1978 to 1982, 1983 to 1987, and 1988 to 1992—the funds are significantly larger and the venture organizations are significantly more established than those not included in the sample.

2. Venture capital limited partnerships will have one or more closings, where the limited and general partners sign legal documents stating the terms of the partnership and initial cash payments are made. Having several closings enables venture funds to begin investing before fundraising is completed. Additional limited partners can be added to the partnership in the subsequent closings.

Table 22.1
Characteristics of the sample of 140 venture partnership agreements

	Included in our sample	Not included in our sample	p-Value, test of no difference
Number of observations	140	1030	
Size of fund (1997$ mil)	127.0	55.6	0.000
	[94.5]	[37.2]	[0.000]
Age of venture organization at time of first closing (years)	7.34	3.88	0.000
	[5.75]	[1.33]	[0.000]
Previous funds raised by venture organization	3.58	1.65	0.000
	[2]	[1]	[0.000]
Fund based in California?	39.4%	28.6%	{0.010}
Date of fund's first closing	Dec. 1985	Apr. 1985	0.032
	[Feb. 1986]	[Dec. 1984]	[0.027]

Note: The first two columns compare the characteristics of the independent venture partnerships in the Venture Economics funds database whose first closing was between 1978 and 1992 that were and were not included in our sample. We present both the mean and the median [in brackets] of several measures. The third column presents the p-values of t-tests, Wilcoxon signed-rank tests [in brackets], and a Pearson χ^2-test {in braces} of the null hypotheses that these distributions are identical.

in our sample account for $27.7 billion out of a total of $45.3 billion of invested capital, or 61 percent.

In the first three columns of table 22.2 we compare those entries in the Venture Economics funds database for which we do and do not have compensation data. We compare the distributions of the included and missing funds using t-tests, Wilcoxon signed-rank tests, and Pearson χ^2-tests. Larger and more recent funds, as well as funds raised by more established venture organizations, are significantly more likely to be included in our sample.[3] Funds specializing in high-technology and early-stage investments are disproportionately represented, perhaps reflecting their frequent sponsorship by established organizations. The fourth column of table 16.2 displays the characteristics of the funds in the final sample, including the ones not in the Venture Economics database and hence not included in the first column.

---

3. We also characterize the investment focus of the funds. Firms typically state in their private placement memoranda whether they intend to have an industry or stage focus. Because these are imperfectly recorded by Venture Economics, we check the original fund documents. One concern may be that funds need not make investments that are consistent with these stated objectives. The partnership agreements, which unlike the private placement memoranda are legal contracts, rarely state the funds' objectives. At the same time venture capitalists who deviate significantly from the stated goals of their partnership are likely to alienate institutional investors and the investment managers who advise them, and they may find it difficult to raise a follow-on fund (e.g., the discussion in Goodman 1990).

Table 22.2
The characteristics of the research sample of venture capital funds

	Funds in Venture Economics database			
	Included in our sample	Not included in our sample	p-Value, test of no difference	All funds included in our sample[a]
Number of observations	401	757		419
Date of fund's first closing	March 1986 [June 1986]	October 1984 [March 1984]	0.000 [0.000]	March 1986 [June 1986]
Size of fund (1997$ mil)	71.0 [45.5]	48.5 [33.4]	0.000 [0.000]	62.7 [40.1]
Size of venture organization (capital raised as % of total in past 10 years)	0.42% [0.11%]	0.40% [0.00%]	0.821 [0.000]	0.43% [0.10%]
Age of venture organization (in years)	5.35 [3.50]	4.33 [1.83]	0.006 [0.002]	4.92[a] [3.09][a]
Fund focuses on high technology?	20.4%	7.4%	{0.000}	48.0%[a]
Fund focuses on early-stage investments?	29.2%	12.8%	{0.000}	41.8%[a]

Note: The first two columns compare characteristics of funds within the Venture Economics database, both included and excluded from our sample, whose first closing was between January 1978 and December 1992. Our sample includes only those funds whose partnership agreements or private placement memoranda were found in the files of Aeneas, Kemper, and Venture Economics. We present both the mean and median [in brackets] of several measures. The third column presents the p-values of t-tests, Wilcoxon signed-rank tests [in brackets], and Pearson χ^2-tests {in braces} of the null hypotheses that these distributions are identical. The final column presents corrected summary statistics for the entire sample.
a. The data for the entire sample of 419 differ from the subsample of 401 for two reasons. In the final column, the sample size is larger and several aspects of the Venture Economics data have been corrected with information from fund documents. First, venture organization age is sometimes erroneously entered in the Venture Economics funds database. Second, the coding of investment focus is incomplete in the Venture Economics funds database. In order to allow a comparison with the 757 funds not included in our sample, for which we only have the Venture Economics data, we report the age and focus of the 401 funds as coded by Venture Economics. The summary statistics about the 419 funds incorporates our corrections based on information in the private placement memoranda.

The summary statistics in column four are also different from column one because the data reported in the fourth column were corrected using documents from the venture organizations.

While the sample is not entirely representative of the venture industry as a whole, these differences should have a limited impact on the empirical results. As a check of this claim, we repeat the analyses in chapter 5 using only the 221 observations where the partnership agreements or private placement memoranda were found in the files of Venture Economics. These observations are significantly more representative of the population of venture funds than the Harvard and Kemper samples. The results remain similar, though the significance falls, reflecting the smaller sample size.

Sources of Venture Capital Investments

The VentureOne Database

The analysis of corporate venture capital investments in chapter 6 employs the VentureOne database of financings of entrepreneurial firms. Venture-One, a unit of Reuters, established in 1987, collects data on firms that have obtained venture capital financing. The database includes firms that have received early-stage equity financing from venture capital organizations, corporate venture capital programs, and other organizations.

The companies are initially identified from a wide variety of sources, including trade publications, company Web pages, and telephone contacts with venture investors. VentureOne then collects information about the businesses through interviews with venture capitalists and entrepreneurs. Among the data collected are the names of the investors, the amount and valuation of the venture financings, and the industry, history, and current status of the firm. Data on the firms are updated and validated through monthly contacts with investors and firms.[4] VentureOne then markets the database to venture funds and corporate business development groups.

VentureOne officials suggest that two forms of selection bias may affect the completeness of their valuation data. First, in its initial years, neither the firm's data collection methodology nor its reputation in the industry were as established as today. Thus it was less likely to obtain valuation data. Second, they are sometimes able to collect information about earlier financing rounds at the time a firm seeks refinancing. Consequently the most recent data—which includes many firms that have not subsequently sought refinancing—may not be as complete as earlier years' data.

To help understand the impact of the missing data, we compared those rounds with and without valuation data. We found three patterns. First, VentureOne has had the least success in obtaining financing data about start-up transactions. This is not surprising. In these cases the number of investors is typically very small and concerns about secrecy are the greatest. VentureOne has also been less successful in obtaining valuation data about firms not in the high-technology industries traditionally funded by venture capitalists but rather in the amalgam referred to as "other industries."

---

4. Information about the financing of private firms is typically not revealed in public documents and investors and entrepreneurs may consider this to be sensitive information. Venture-One seeks to overcome this reluctance by emphasizing that its database also helps firms obtain financing. In particular, firms can alert investors whether they intend to seek further private financing or intend to go public in upcoming months.

VentureOne officials attribute this pattern to the firm's greater visibility among entrepreneurs and investors in high-technology industries. Similarly, reflecting the firm's California base, it has been more successful in obtaining information about firms based in the western United States. Finally, the observations with valuation data are disproportionately from the early to mid-1990s. Because our focus is on comparing investments by independent and corporate venture capital funds, we do not believe these patterns will bias our results.

We supplemented the VentureOne data when necessary. Some firms in the VentureOne sample were missing information, such as an assignment to one of the 103 VentureOne industry classes or information on the firm's start date. We examined a variety of reference sources to determine this information, including Corporate Technology Information Service's *Corporate Technology Directory* (1996), Dun's Marketing Services' *Million Dollar Directory* (1996), Gale Research's Ward's *Business Directory of U.S. Private and Public Companies* (1996), National Register Publishing Company's *Directory of Leading Private Companies* (1996), and a considerable number of state and industry business directories in the collections of Harvard Business School's Baker Library and the Boston Public Library. We also employed several electronic databases: the Company Intelligence and Database America compilations available through LEXIS's COMPANY/USPRIV library and the American Business Disk CD-Rom directory.

We limited the analysis reported in chapter 6 to investments in privately held firms between 1983 and 1994. While VentureOne has sought to "backfill" its database with information on earlier venture investments, its coverage of the 1970s and early 1980s is poor. Furthermore we were concerned that its methodology could have introduced selection biases. Although the database does not include all venture investments between 1983 and 1994, we believe that it provides a reasonable view of the activity in the industry during this period. We did not include investments made after 1994 because we wish to assess the outcomes of the investments: it may take several years until the fate of venture-backed firms is clear.

To identify independent and corporate venture capital organizations, we used an unpublished database of venture organizations assembled by Venture Economics' Investors Services Group discussed earlier in this chapter. We excluded from either classification a variety of other private equity investors, including individuals, SBICs, funds sponsored by banks and other financial institutions, and funds associated with financial subsidiaries of nonfinancial corporations (e.g., General Electric Capital). To determine whether a company was a nonfinancial corporation, we consulted the firm directories noted above to determine the main lines of business in the year of the investment. We also eliminated a variety of investments outside the scope of this analysis, such as purchases of shares of publicly traded firms and other financings.

The Venture Intelligence Database

The analyses described in chapters 8 through 11, 15, and 16 employ Venture Economics' Venture Intelligence Database. The relative performance of venture funds is an important issue for investors. Venture capitalists typically raise funds every few years; limited partners (wealthy individuals, endowments, and institutional investors) provide the bulk of the capital. An investment in a venture fund is almost always for at least a ten-year period, and funds may only be withdrawn under extreme circumstances. Thus potential investors scrutinize the performance of venture capitalists' past funds. While venture partnerships present historical performance data in offering documents, the methodology of these calculations is frequently idiosyncratic. Furthermore, because the IPO market is so variable, potential investors usually look for a measure of relative, rather than absolute, performance.

Venture Economics addresses the need for information on performance by confidentially gathering data from venture funds and institutional investors on venture investments. The Venture Intelligence Database includes the dates of venture financings, the investors in each round, and the amount of funds disbursed. It includes firms that did and did not go public. While the database was begun in 1977, the firm subsequently encoded its earlier records on venture financing dating back to the early 1960s.

Researchers' access to this data was very restricted prior to the firm's purchase by Securities Data Company (SDC) in 1991. Venture Economics did, however, publish the names of investors in firms that went public in their *Venture Capital Journal*. Barry et al. (1990) and Megginson and Weiss (1991) use this information (and, in the former article, cross-tabulations of these records). Much of the Venture Economics data are now publicly available as the SDC Venture Intelligence Database.

To assess the presence of potential biases in the Venture Economics database, the sample of biotechnology firms analyzed in chapters 10, 11, and 15 is examined. There is extensive data collection about biotechnology firms in other sources, which enables a detailed assessment of the Venture Intelligence Database's strengths and weaknesses. The database identifies 307 biotechnology firms that received venture capital as privately held entities between 1978 and 1989. (While the database contains earlier records, data collection was not a primary focus prior to mid-1977.) Dropped from the original sample were thirteen foreign firms that were funded by U.S. capital providers (who may face different regulatory, tax, or institutional environments), four buyouts or divisional "spin-outs" involving private capital providers, three duplicative entries of the same firm under different names (name changes are found in Commerce Clearing House's *Capital Changes Reporter*, 1992; Financial Stock Service Guide's *Directory of Obsolete Securities*, 1992; North Carolina Biotechnology Center's [NCBC] database of biotechnology companies, 1990b; Oryx Press's *BioScan: The Worldwide Biotech Industry Reporting Service*, 1992; Predicast's *F&S Index of Corporate Change*, 1992; and other sources), and sixteen firms that received venture capital only after going public.

To assess the completeness of the remaining 271 firms, U.S. biotechnology firms that received venture capital as privately held firms but are not in the Venture Economics sample are identified. Documents used include U.S. Securities and Exchange Commission (SEC) filings,[5] the records of a consulting firm specializing in the biotechnology industry, Recombinant Capital (1991, 1992), the several industry directories that list privately held firms and provide information about their financing sources cited above, press releases in Mead Data Central's (1988) NEXIS/ALLNEWS and LEXIS/PATENT/GENBIO files, and contacts with venture capitalists and biotechnology firms. These efforts lead to the identification of an additional thirty-seven U.S. biotechnology firms that received venture capital as privately held entities between 1978 and 1989.[6]

The significance of the thirty-seven omitted firms is assessed using three measures. First, a U.S. Patent and Trademark Office (1990) compilation of all biotechnology patent awards from January 1978 through June 1989 is used. Patenting is extremely important in biotechnology and is the focus of virtually every small biotechnology firm. Of the entire number of patents

---

5. A firm going public discloses its investors in its prospectus (the "certain transactions" and "financial statements" sections) and the accompanying S-1 registration statement (the "recent sales of nonregistered securities" section and exhibits). Detailed financial information is often available about private firms that have been acquired by public firms in the acquirers' proxy, 10-K, or 10-Q statements. Information on firms that file for an aborted IPO is available in the ultimately withdrawn registration statements. Firms likely to have made such filings are identified by the sources cited above.

6. Because firms are usually financed by multiple venture funds, the comprehensiveness of Venture Economics' information on venture-backed firms is considerably higher than their coverage of funds. When Venture Economics obtains information on the same company from several sources, its staff attempts to reconcile any inconsistencies. If they are unable to resolve conflicts, their tendency is to error on the side of inclusiveness. This is part of the reason for the inclusion of multiple records for a single venture round discussed below.

awarded to venture-backed biotechnology firms during this period, the Venture Economics sample accounts for over 98 percent. Second, the NCBC (1990a) compiles an "actions" database of events in the biotechnology industry (including regulatory approvals, product introductions, and ownership changes) from press releases and specialized trade journals. Firms in the Venture Economics sample account for over 95 percent of the entries about venture-backed firms between November 1978 (the inception of the database) and December 1989. Finally, altogether data from Venture Economics, Recombinant Capital, SDC's Corporate New Issues database, SEC filings, and press releases allowed the total amount of external financing received by venture-backed firms to be determined. The Venture Economics sample accounts for over 91 percent of the financing raised by these firms between 1978 and 1989. Taken together, the results suggest that the omitted firms are less significant than the ones included.

The information on these firms' financing rounds is corrected as follows:

• *Firms included in Recombinant Capital database.* The Venture Economics records are compared to those of Recombinant Capital. If they are identical, the Venture Economics records are considered as corroborated.[7] If they conflict and SEC filings are available, these are used to resolve the conflict. If they conflict and SEC filings are not available, company and venture capitalist contacts are used. If no contacts can be made, the Venture Economics data are used.

• *Firms not included in Recombinant Capital database, but with SEC filings.* The Venture Economics records are compared to the SEC filings. If they conflict, the SEC filings are used.

• *Firms not included in Recombinant Capital database without SEC filings.* Company and venture capitalist contacts are used to confirm the Venture Economics data. Frequently venture capitalists can be identified through *Pratt's Guide to Venture Capital Sources* (Venture Economics 1996). This guide is indexed by both individual and fund, so those venture capitalists associated with terminated partnerships who are still employed in the industry can often be located. Companies are identified through industry directories (Corporate Technology 1996; MegaType 1992; NCBC 1990a; Oryx 1992). Some of the firms most difficult to obtain information about are

---

7. External financing rounds are not included in some cases: instances when founders contributed a small amount of funds (typically under $20,000) in exchange for common stock, or bridge loans by venture capital providers in the six months prior to the IPO, due immediately after the offering. These entries are relatively infrequent in the Venture Economics data set.

those that failed before going public. If no contacts can be made, the Venture Economics data are used.

The Venture Economics dataset is compared to the corrected information, omitting the cases where no corroboration of the Venture Economics records could be obtained. For each firm the ratio of the reported to the actual size and number of private financings is computed. The reporting of the amount of external financing provided is unbiased, with the ratio of total funds recorded in the Venture Economics database to the actual amount being 1.04.

The number of venture rounds, however, is overstated: the database reports 28 percent more rounds than actually occurred. The data are disaggregated to determine whether the bias in the number of rounds varies in a systemic manner: rounds are divided by the age of the firm and the date at the time of the venture round. The spurious rounds are most frequent in older firms and in chronologically earlier records.

This pattern may arise for three reasons. First, a contract between a company and its venture financiers may call for the staged distribution of the funds in a single venture round. This may be recorded in the database as several distinct venture rounds. Second, staggered disbursements arise without design. Venture capital funds typically do not keep large cash balances but rather draw down funds from their limited partners as needed. Limited partners will have between two weeks and several months to provide the funds. Since several venture funds normally participate in a financing round, investments may be received over the course of several months and be recorded in the database as several rounds. Finally, Venture Economics aggregates information about venture investments from reports by pension fund managers, individual investors, and investment managers. If the date of the investment differs in these records, a single investment round may be recorded as two or more events. All these problems are likely to be more severe in later rounds, which typically have more investors. While data accuracy has increased over time, the overreporting of rounds is a significant factor in the historical Venture Economics data.

Sources of Venture-Backed IPOs and Distributions

In the analysis of IPOs and distributions in chapters 16, 17, 19, and 20, we do not rely on a single data set to identify venture-backed offerings. Rather, the sample is compiled from a variety of sources. Although the precise sources used in each analysis differed (as mentioned in the chapters), this section summarizes the three primary information sources used to identify venture-backed offerings.

The first of these is listings in Venture Economics' *Venture Capital Journal*, which regularly publishes information on such IPOs. In the analysis in chapters 3, 16, and 17, the collection of 433 venture-backed IPOs compiled by Barry et al. (1990) and Megginson and Weiss (1991) are used. Barry et al. identify their sample using the *Venture Capital Journal* but exclude any IPOs for which a venture capital investor could not be identified, reverse LBOs, and IPOs for which they could not find the offering prospectus.[8] For the longer time period covered in chapter 20, all entries in the *Venture Capital Journal* were recorded and checked against the IPO prospectuses.

The second of these are listings of all IPOs and distributions by venture funds. Venture capitalists typically unwind their successful investments by distributing the shares to their limited partners. They avoid selling the shares themselves and distributing the proceeds to their limited partners because their investors include both tax-exempt and tax-paying parties. To sell the share would generate an immediate tax liability, which some of the limited partners may wish to avoid. We obtain lists of the distributions received by US WEST Investment Trust (a pension fund which was among the largest venture investors) and by a major corporate pension fund as well as by three investment advisors (Brinson Partners, Kemper Financial Services, and RogersCasey Alternative Investments). These investment advisors allocated funds from numerous pension funds into venture capital and other asset classes. All the mentioned investors compiled, among other information, the date of the IPO, as well as the date, size, and source of each stock distribution.

Finally, many of the private placement memoranda by venture capital groups list previous investments that have gone public. While in most cases these are included in the other sources above, occasionally some additional venture-backed IPOs are identified in this manner. For the analysis in chapter 3 and 17, we examined over four hundred of these memoranda in the files of Venture Economics. We identify any investments listed as having gone public. Most of the offering documents compiled by Venture Economics are from young venture organizations. This is because its Fund Raiser Advisory Service counsels less experienced firms on strategies for raising capital.

---

8. This information was supplemented and cross-checked in a variety of ways. For the age of the venture capital firm and the offering company at IPO, the LEXIS/NEXIS's COMPNY database was searched for incorporation and partnership filings. Ritter's (1991) IPO data set was used to cross-check incorporation dates, offering size, and underpricing. For age at IPO, the earliest incorporation date is used.

We include in the IPO sample all firms if a venture investor listed in the "Management" and "Principal and Selling Shareholders" sections of the IPO prospectus is listed in the Venture Economics database. In many cases it is not immediately obvious whether a venture investor or director is an exact match with a venture organization listed in the database.[9] To address these ambiguities, we consult the edition of Venture Economics' *Pratt's Guide to Venture Capital Sources* (1996) published in the year of the IPO. We compare the addresses and key personnel of each of these ambiguous venture organizations with the information reported in the prospectus. If we are not virtually certain that the venture organizations in the prospectus and the database are the same, we do not code it as a match. For each investor we code the venture organization, the particular venture fund investing in the firm, and the size of the stake before and after the offering. This process leads to the identification of 885 IPOs in which a venture capitalist served as a director or a venture capital fund was a blockholder.

---

9. In many cases individual investors (often called angels) will describe themselves as venture capitalists. Groups of individual investors often make their investments through partnerships that are given names not unlike those of venture capital organizations.

References

AbuZayyad, T., T. J. Kosnick, J. Lerner, and P. C. Yang. 1996. GO Corporation. Harvard Business School case 9-297-021 (and teaching note 5-298-153).

Admati, A. R., and P. Pfleiderer. 1994. Robust financial contracting and the role of venture capitalists. *Journal of Finance* 49: 371–402.

Aggarwal, R., L. Krigman, and K. L. Womack. 2002. Strategic IPO underpricing, information momentum, and lockup expiration selling. *Journal of Financial Economics* 66: 105–37.

Aggarwal, R. 2000. Stabilization activities by underwriters after initial public offerings. *Journal of Finance* 55: 1075–1104.

Akerlof, G. A. 1970. The market for "lemons": Qualitative uncertainty and the market mechanism. *Quarterly Journal of Economics* 84: 488–500.

Allen, F., and A. Postlewaite. 1984. Rational expectations and the measurement of a stock's elasticity of demand. *Journal of Finance* 39: 1119–25.

Allen, F., and G. R. Faulhaber. 1989. Signaling by underpricing in the IPO market. *Journal of Financial Economics* 23: 303–24.

Armstrong, L. 1993. Nurturing an employee's brainchild. *Business Week* (October 23): 196.

Anand, B. 1996. Tax Effects on Venture Capital. Unpublished working paper. Yale University.

Asian Venture Capital Journal. 1996. *Venture Capital in Asia: 1996/97 Edition.* Hong Kong: Asian Venture Capital Journal.

Asian Venture Capital Journal. 2003. *The 2003 Guide to Venture Capital in Asia,* 14th ed. Hong Kong: Asian Venture Capital Journal.

Asquith, P., and D. W. Mullins Jr. 1986. Equity issues and offering dilution. *Journal of Financial Economics* 15: 61–89.

Asset Alternatives. 1994a. Iowa suits test LPs' authority to abolish fund. *Private Equity Analyst* 4 (May): 1, 9.

Asset Alternatives. 1994b. Warburg points the way toward a lower carry. *Private Equity Analyst* 4 (July): 7.

Asset Alternatives. 1996. Private equity managers struggle to avoid hubris in hot market. *Private Equity Analyst* 6: 28–31.

Asset Alternatives. 2003. *Private Equity Partnership Terms and Conditions*. Wellesley, MA: Asset Alternatives.

Athey, S., and S. Stern. 1998. An empirical framework for testing theories about complementarity in organizational design. National Bureau of Economic Research Working Paper 6600.

Audretsch, D. B. 1995. *Innovation and Industry Evolution*. Cambridge: MIT Press.

Bagwell, L. 1992. Dutch auction repurchases: An analysis of shareholder heterogeneity. *Journal of Finance* 47: 71–106.

Baker, M., and P. A. Gompers. 2000. Executive ownership and control in newly public firms: The role of venture capitalists. Unpublished working paper. Harvard University.

Ball, R., S. P. Kothari, and J. Shanken. 1995. Problems in measuring portfolio performance: An application to contrarian investment strategies. *Journal of Financial Economics* 38: 79–107.

Ball, R., S. P. Kothari, and C. Wasley. 1995. Can we implement research on stock trading rules? The case of short-term contrarian strategies. *Journal of Portfolio Management* 21: 54–63.

Balvers, R. J., B. McDonald, and R. E. Miller. 1988. Underpricing of new issues and the choice of auditor as a signal of investment banker reputation. *Accounting Review* 63: 605–22.

Barber, B. M., and J. D. Lyon. 1997. Detecting long-run abnormal stock returns: The empirical power and specification of test statistics. *Journal of Financial Economics* 43: 341–72.

Barber, B. M., J. D. Lyon, and C.-L. Tsai. 1999. Improved methods for tests of long-run abnormal stock returns. *Journal of Finance* 54: 165–201.

Barclay, M. J., and C. W. Smith Jr. 1995. The priority structure of corporate liabilities. *Journal of Finance* 50: 899–917.

Barry, C. B., C. J. Muscarella, J. W. Peavy III, and M. R. Vetsuypens. 1990. The role of venture capital in the creation of public companies: Evidence from the going public process. *Journal of Financial Economics* 27: 447–71.

Bartlett, J. W. 1988. *Venture Capital Law, Business, Strategies, and Investment Planning*. New York: Wiley.

Bartlett, J. W. 1994. *Venture Capital Law, Business, Strategies, and Investment Planning: 1994 Supplement*. New York: Wiley.

Bartlett, J. W. 1995. *Equity Finance: Venture Capital, Buyouts, Restructurings, and Reorganization*. New York: Wiley.

Baysinger, B. D., and H. N. Butler. 1985. Corporate governance and the board of directors: Performance effects of changes in board composition. *Journal of Law, Economics, and Organization* 1: 101–24.

Beatty, R. P. 1989. Auditor reputation and the pricing of initial public offerings. *Accounting Review* 64: 693–709.

Beatty, R. P., and J. R. Ritter. 1986. Investment banking, reputation, and the underpricing of initial public offerings. *Journal of Financial Economics* 15: 213–32.

Beatty, R. P., and E. J. Zajak. 1994. Firm risk and alternative mechanisms for internal corporate control: Evidence from initial public offerings. *Administrative Science Quarterly* 39: 313–35.

Beatty, R. P., and I. Welch. 1996. Issuer expenses and legal liability in initial public offerings. *Journal of Law and Economics* 39: 545–603.

Becker, G. S. 1983. A theory of competition among pressure groups for political influence. *Quarterly Journal of Economics* 98: 371–400.

Beneish, M. D., and R. Whaley. 1996. An anatomy of the "S&P game": The effects of changing the rules. *Journal of Finance* 51: 1909–30.

Bergemann, D., and U. Hege. 1998. Dynamic venture capital financing, learning, and moral hazard. *Journal of Banking and Finance* 22: 703–35.

Bettis, J. C., J. L. Coles, and M. L. Lemmon. 2000. Corporate policies restricting trading by insiders. *Journal of Financial Economics* 57: 191–220.

Berglöf, E. 1994. A control theory of venture capital finance. *Journal of Law, Economics, and Organization* 10: 247–67.

Bernard, V. L. 1987. Cross-sectional dependence and problems in inference in market-based accounting research. *Journal of Accounting Research* 25: 1–48.

Berndt, E. R. 1991. *The Practice of Econometrics: Classic and Contemporary*. New York: Addison-Wesley.

Berndt, E., and Z. Griliches. 1993. Price indexes for microcomputers: An exploratory study. In *Price Measurements and Their Uses. Studies in Income and Wealth*, vol. 57, edited by M. F. Foss, M. E. Manser, and A. H. Young. Chicago: University of Chicago Press NBER.

Bernstein, J., and I. M. Nadiri. 1986. Financing and Investment in Plant and Equipment and Research and Development. In *Prices, Competition and Equilibrium*, edited by M. H. Preston and R. E. Quandt. Oxford: Philip Allan.

BioVenture View. 1993 and earlier. *BioPeople*. San Francisco: BioVenture View.

Black, B. S., and R. J. Gilson. 1998. Venture capital and the structure of capital markets: Banks versus stock markets. *Journal of Financial Economics* 47: 243–77.

Black, F. 1986. Noise. *Journal of Finance* 41: 529–43.

Blanchard, O., F. Lopez de Silanes, and A. Shleifer. 1994. What do firms do with cash windfalls? *Journal of Financial Economics* 36: 337–60.

Block, Z., and O. A. Ornati. 1987. Compensating corporate venture managers. *Journal of Business Venturing* 2: 41–52.

Blume, M. E., and R. F. Stambaugh. 1983. Biases in computed returns: An application to the size effect. *Journal of Financial Economics* 12: 387–404.

Bradley, D., B. Jordan, I. Roten, and H.-C. Yi. 2001. Venture capital and IPO lockup expiration: An empirical analysis. *Journal of Financial Research* 24: 465–93.

Bradley, M., G. A. Jarrell, and E. Han Kim. 1984. On the existence of an optimal capital structure: Theory and evidence. *Journal of Finance* 39: 857–78.

Brav, A. 2000. Inference in long horizon event studies: A Bayesian approach with application to initial public offerings. *Journal of Finance* 55: 1979–2016.

Brav, A., and J. B. Heaton. 1999. Did ERISA's prudent man rule change the pricing of dividend omitting firms? Unpublished working paper. Duke University.

Brav, A., C. C. Geczy, and P. A. Gompers. 2000. Is the abnormal return following equity issuances anomalous? *Journal of Financial Economics* 56: 209–49.

Brav, A., and P. A. Gompers. 2000. Investment analyst recommendations around the expiration of IPO lockups. Unpublished working paper. Duke University.

Brav, A., F. Cornelli, and J. B. Heaton. 2001. Price manipulation in the presence of heterogeneous agents and short sales constraints. Unpublished working paper. Duke University.

Brennan, M. J., and A. Kraus. 1987. Efficient financing under asymmetric information. *Journal of Finance* 42: 1225–43.

Calomiris, C. W., and C. Ramirez. 1996. Financing the American Corporation, 1800–1990. In *The American Corporation Today*, edited by C. Kaysen. Oxford: Oxford University Press.

Campbell, J. Y., A. W. Lo, and A. C. MacKinlay. 1997. *The Econometrics of Financial Markets*. Princeton: Princeton University Press.

Carter, R., F. H. Dark, and A. K. Singh. 1998. A comparative analysis of underwriter prestige measures. *Journal of Finance* 53: 285–311.

Carter, R., and S. Manaster. 1990. Initial public offerings and underwriter reputation. *Journal of Finance* 45: 1045–67.

Carsey, T. M., B. Rundquist, and S. Fox. 1997. Defense spending and economic development in the American states, 1970–89: Untangling a complex relationship. Unpublished working paper. University of Illinois at Chicago.

Case-Western Reserve University, Center for Regional Economic Issues. 1997. Unpublished patent database. Case-Western Reserve University.

Chamberlain, G. 1980. Analysis of covariance with qualitative data. *Review of Economic Studies* 47: 225–38.

Chan, Y.-S. 1983. On the positive role of financial intermediation in allocation of venture capital in a market with imperfect information. *Journal of Finance* 38: 1543–68.

Charles River Associates, Inc. 1976. *An Analysis of Capital Market Imperfections: Prepared for the Experimental Technology Incentives Program, National Bureau of Standards, U.S. Department of Commerce*. Cambridge: Charles River Associates, Inc.

Chen, H.-C., and J. Ritter. 1999. The seven percent solution. *Journal of Finance* 55: 1105–31.

Chevalier, J. A., and G. D. Ellison. 1997. Risk taking by mutual funds as a response to incentives. *Journal of Political Economy* 105: 1167–1200.

Clay, L. 1991 and earlier. *The Venture Capital Report Guide to Venture Capital in Europe*. London: Pitman.

Cochrane, J. H. 2001. The risk and return of venture capital. National Bureau of Economic Research Working Paper 8066.

Cohen, L. R., and R. G. Noll, eds. 1991. *The Technology Pork Barrel*. Washington: Brookings Institution.

Cohen, W. M. 1995. Empirical Studies of Innovative Activity. In *Handbook of the Economics of Innovation and Technical Change*, edited by P. Stoneman. Oxford: Basil Blackwell.

Commerce Register. 1995 and earlier. *Massachusetts Directory of Manufacturers*. Hokokus, NJ: Commerce Register.

Commerce Clearing House. 1992 and earlier. *Capital Changes Reporter*. Chicago: Commerce Clearing House.

Cooter, R. D., and D. L. Rubinfeld. 1989. Analysis of Legal Disputes and their Resolution. *Journal of Economic Literature* 27: 1067–97.

Cordell, L. R., G. D. MacDonald, and M. E. Wohar. 1993. Corporate ownership and the thrift crisis. *Journal of Law and Economics* 36: 719–56.

Cornelli, F., and O. Yosha. 2003. Stage financing and the role of convertible securities. *Review of Economic Studies* 70: 1–32.

Corporate Technology Information Services. 1994 and earlier. *Corporate Technology Directory*. Woburn, MA: Corporate Technology Information Services.

Crocker, K. J., and K. J. Reynolds. 1993. The efficiency of incomplete contracts: An empirical analysis of Air Force engine procurement. *Rand Journal of Economics* 24: 126–46.

Courteau, L. 1995. Under-diversification and retention commitment in IPOs. *Journal of Financial and Quantitative Analysis* 30: 487–517.

Cumming, D. J., and J. G. MacIntosh. 2003. A cross-country comparison of full and partial venture capital exits. *Journal of Banking & Finance* 27: 511–48.

Dauchy, C. E., and M. T. Harmon. 1986. Structuring venture capital limited partnerships. *Computer Lawyer* 3 (November): 1–8.

DeBondt, W., and R. Thaler. 1985. Does the stock market overreact? *Journal of Finance* 40: 793–808.

DeBondt, W., and R. Thaler. 1987. Further evidence on investor overreaction and stock market seasonality. *Journal of Finance* 42: 557–81.

De Long, J. B., A. Shleifer, L. H. Summers, and R. Waldmann. 1990. Noise trader risk in financial markets. *Journal of Political Economy* 98: 703–38.

De Roover, R. 1963. The organization of trade. In *The Cambridge Economic History of Europe. Economic Organization and Policies in the Middle Ages*, vol. 3, edited by M. M. Postan, E. E. Rich, and E. Miller. Cambridge: Cambridge University Press, ch. 2.

Denning, P. F., and R. A. Painter. 1994. *Stock Distributions: A Guide for Venture Capitalists*. Boston: Robertson, Stephens & Co. and Testa, Hurwitz & Thibeault.

Devenow, A., and I. Welch. 1996. Rational herding in financial economics. *European Economic Review* 40: 603–15.

Dhillon, U., and H. Johnson. 1991. Changes in the Standard and Poor's 500 list. *Journal of Business* 64: 75–85.

Diamond, D. W. 1989. Reputation acquisition in debt markets. *Journal of Political Economy* 97: 828–62.

Dun's Marketing Services. 1996 and earlier. *Million Dollar Directory*. Parsippany, NJ: Dun's Marketing Services.

Easley, D., and M. O'Hara. 1987. Price, trade size, and information in securities markets. *Journal of Financial Economics* 19: 69–90.

Ely, E. S. 1987. Dr. Silver's tarnished prescription. *Venture* 9 (July): 54–58.

Eisinger, P. K. 1988. *The Rise of the Entrepreneurial State: State and Local Economic Development Policy in the United States*. Madison: University of Wisconsin Press.

Ellis, K., R. Michaely, and M. O'Hara. 2000. When the underwriter is the market maker: An examination of trading in the IPO aftermarket. *Journal of Finance* 55: 1039–74.

European Commission. 1995. *Green Paper on Innovation*. The European Union. *http://europa.eu. int/en/record/green/gp9512/ind_inn.htm*.

European Private Equity and Venture Capital Association. 2003. *Annual Survey of Pan-European Private Equity and Venture Capital Activity*. Zaventum, Belgium: European Private Equity and Venture Capital Association.

European Venture Capital Association. 1997. *1997 EVCA Yearbook*. Zaventum, Belgium: European Venture Capital Association.

Fama, E. F. 1976. *The Foundations of Finance*. New York: Basic Books.

Fama, E. F. 1996. Multifactor portfolio efficiency and multifactor asset pricing. *Journal of Financial and Quantitative Analysis* 31: 441–65.

Fama, E. F., and K. R. French. 1992. The cross-section of expected stock returns. *Journal of Finance* 47: 427–65.

Fama, E. F., and K. R. French. 1993. Common risk factors in the returns of stocks and bonds. *Journal of Financial Economics* 33: 3–55.

Fama, E. F., and K. R. French. 1995. Size and book-to-market factors in earnings and returns. *Journal of Finance* 50: 131–56.

Fama, E. F., and K. R. French. 1996. Multifactor explanations of asset pricing anomalies. *Journal of Finance* 51: 55–84.

Fama, E. F., and K. R. French. 1997. Industry costs of equity. *Journal of Financial Economics* 43: 153–93.

Fama, E. F., and M. C. Jensen. 1983. Separation of ownership and control. *Journal of Law and Economics* 26: 301–25.

Fast, N. D. 1978. *The Rise and Fall of Corporate New Venture Divisions*. Ann Arbor: UMI Research Press.

Fazzari, S. M., R. G. Hubbard, and B. C. Petersen. 1988. Financing constraints and corporate investment. *Brookings Papers on Economic Activity: Microeconomics* 1: 141–205.

Feenberg, D. R., and E. Coutts. 1993. An introduction to the TAXSIM model. *Journal of Policy Analysis and Management* 12: 189–94.

Fenn, G. W., N. Liang, and S. Prowse. 1998. The role of angel investors and venture capitalists in financing high-tech start-ups. Unpublished working paper. Milken Institute, Federal Reserve Board, and Federal Reserve Bank of Dallas.

Field, L. C. 1996. Is institutional investment in initial public offerings related to the long-run performance of these firms? Unpublished working paper. Pennsylvania State University.

Field, L. C., and G. Hanka. 2001. The expiration of IPO share lockups. *Journal of Finance* 56: 471–500.

Financial Stock Guide Service. 1992. *Directory of Obsolete Securities*. Jersey City, NJ: Financial Information, Inc.

Freear, J., and W. E. Wetzel Jr. 1990. Who bankrolls high-tech entrepreneurs? *Journal of Business Venturing* 5: 77–89.

Friend, I., and L. H. P. Lang. 1988. An empirical test of the impact of managerial self-interest on corporate capital structure. *Journal of Finance* 43: 271–81.

Friedenberg, H. L., and R. M. Beemiller. 1997. Comprehensive revision of Gross State Product by industry. 1977–94. *Survey of Current Business* 77 (June): 15–41.

Gale Research. 1996 and earlier. *Ward's Business Directory of U.S. Private and Public Companies*. Detroit: Gale Research.

Gallese, L. R. 1990. Venture capital strays far from its roots. *New York Times Magazine* 139 (April 1): S24–S39.

Galston, A. 1925. *Security Syndicate Operations: Organization, Management and Accounting*. New York: Roland Press.

G. D. Hall Co. 1995 and earlier. *George D. Hall's Directory of Massachusetts Manufacturers*. Boston: G. D. Hall Co.

Gee, R. E. 1994. Finding and commercializing new businesses. *Research/Technology Management* 37 (January/February): 49–56.

Gibbons, R. S., and K. J. Murphy. 1992. Optimal incentive contracts in the presence of career concerns: Theory and evidence. *Journal of Political Economy* 100: 468–505.

Gompers, P. A. 1993. *The theory, structure, and performance of venture capital*. Ph.D. dissertation. Harvard University.

Gompers, P. A. 1995. A clinical examination of convertible debt in venture capital investments. Unpublished working paper. Harvard University.

Gompers, P. A., and J. Lerner. 1997a. Risk and reward in private equity investments; The challenge of performance assessment. *Journal of Private Equity* 1 (Winter): 5–12.

Gompers, P. A., and J. Lerner. 1997b. Venture capital and the creation of public companies: Do venture capitalists really bring more than money?. *Journal of Private Equity* 1 (Winter): 15–32.

Gompers, P. A., and A. Metrick. 2001. Institutional investors and equity prices. *Quarterly Journal of Economics* 116: 229–59.

Gompers, P. A., J. Lerner, and D. Scharfstein. 2003. Entrepreneurial spawning: Public corporations and the genesis of new ventures, 1986–1999. *Journal of Finance*, forthcoming.

Good, M. L. 1997. Testimony before the subcommittee on oversight of government management and the District of Columbia. Governmental Affairs Committee, U.S. Senate. Washington, DC, June 3, 1997.

Goodman, E. A. 1990. Gatekeepers' "reforms" reap negative consequences. *Venture Capital Journal* 30 (December): 25–28.

Gorman, M., and W. A. Sahlman. 1989. What do venture capitalists do? *Journal of Business Venturing* 4: 231–48.

Grassmuck, K. 1990. The much-praised and often-criticized "architect" of Harvard's endowment growth steps down. *Chronicle of Higher Education* 36 (June 6): A25–A27.

Greenwald, B. C., J. E. Stiglitz, and A. Weiss. 1984. Information imperfections in the capital market and macroeconomic fluctuations. *American Economic Review Papers and Proceedings* 74: 194–99.

Griliches, Z. 1979. Issues in assessing the contribution of R&D to productivity growth. *Bell Journal of Economics* 10: 92–116.

Griliches, Z. 1986. Productivity, R&D, and basic research at the firm level in the 1970s. *American Economic Review* 76: 141–54.

Griliches, Z. 1990. Patent statistics as economic indicators: A survey. *Journal of Economic Literature* 28: 1661–1707.

Griliches, Z. 1992. The search for R&D spillovers. *Scandinavian Journal of Economics* 94 (suppl.): S29–S47.

Griliches, Z., and J. A. Hausman. 1986. Errors in variables in panel data. *Journal of Econometrics* 31: 93–118.

Grinblatt, M., and C. Y. Hwang. 1989. Signaling and the pricing of new issues. *Journal of Finance* 44: 383–420.

Grinblatt, M., S. Titman, and R. Wermers. 1995. Momentum investment strategies, portfolio performance, and herding: A study of mutual fund behavior. *American Economic Review* 85: 1088–1105.

Grossman, S., and O. D. Hart. 1986. The costs and benefits of ownership: A theory of vertical and lateral integration. *Journal of Political Economy* 94: 691–719.

Habib, M. A., and A. P. Ljungqvist. 2001. Underpricing and entrepreneurial wealth losses in IPOs: Theory and evidence. *Review of Financial Studies* 14: 433–58.

Hall, B., Z. Griliches, and J. A. Hausman. 1988. Patents and R&D: Is there a lag? *International Economic Review* 27: 265–83.

Halloran, M. J., L. F. Benton, R. V. Gunderson Jr., K. L. Kearney, and J. del Calvo. 1995. *Venture Capital and Public Offering Negotiation*. Englewood Cliffs, NJ: Aspen Law and Business.

Hansen, L. P., and R. J. Hodrick. 1980. Forward exchange rates as optimal predictors of future spot rates: An econometric analysis. *Journal of Political Economy* 88: 829–53.

Hardymon, G. F., M. J. DeNino, and M. S. Salter. 1983. When corporate venture capital doesn't work. *Harvard Business Review* 61 (May/June): 114–20.

Harris, L., and E. Gurel. 1986. Price and volume effects associated with changes on the S&P 500 list: New evidence for the existence of price pressures. *Journal of Finance* 41: 815–29.

Harris, M., and A. Raviv. 1991. The theory of capital structure. *Journal of Finance* 46: 297–356.

Hart, O. D. 1993. Theories of optimal capital structure: A managerial discretion perspective. In *The Deal Decade: What Takeovers and Leveraged Buyouts Mean for Corporate Governance*, edited by M. M. Blair. Washington: Brookings Institution.

Hart, O. D., and J. Moore. 1990. Property rights and the nature of the firm. *Journal of Political Economy* 98: 1119–58.

Hart, O. D., and J. Moore. 1998. Default and renegotiation: A dynamic model of debt. *Quarterly Journal of Economics* 113: 1–41.

Hayes, S. L. 1971. Investment banking: Power structure in flux. *Harvard Business Review* 49 (November/December): 136–52.

Hayes, S. L., A. M. Spence, and D. Van Praag Marks. 1983. *Competition in the Investment Banking Industry*. Cambridge: Harvard University Press.

Heinkel, R., and N. M. Stoughton. 1994. The dynamics of portfolio management contracts. *Review of Financial Studies* 7: 351–88.

Hellmann, T. F. 1998. The allocation of control rights in venture capital contracts. *Rand Journal of Economics* 29: 57–76.

Hellmann, T. F. 2002. IPOs, acquisitions, and the use of convertible securities in venture capital. Unpublished working paper. Stanford University.

Hellmann, T. F., and M. Puri. 2000. The interaction between product market and financing strategy: The role of venture capital. *Review of Financial Studies* 13: 959–84.

Henderson, R. 1993. Underinvestment and incompetence as responses to radical innovation: Evidence from the photolithographic alignment equipment industry. *Rand Journal of Economics* 24: 248–70.

Henderson, R., and I. Cockburn. 1996. Scale, scope and spillovers: The determinants of research productivity in drug discovery. *Rand Journal of Economics* 27: 32–59.

Hermalin, B. E., and M. S. Weisbach. 1988. The determinants of board composition. *Rand Journal of Economics* 19: 589–606.

Henry, P. 2000. Stock market liberalization, economic reform, and emerging market equity prices. *Journal of Finance* 55: 529–64.

Himmelberg, C. P., and B. C. Petersen. 1994. R&D and internal finance: A panel study of small firms in high-tech industries. *Review of Economics and Statistics* 76: 38–51.

Hochberg, Y. V. 2002. Venture capital and corporate governance in the newly public firm. Unpublished working paper. Stanford University.

Holmstrom, B., and P. Milgrom. 1987. Aggregation and linearity in the provision of intertemporal incentives. *Econometrica* 55: 303–28.

Hoshi, T., A. Kashyap, and D. Scharfstein. 1991. Corporate structure, liquidity, and investment: Evidence from Japanese industrial groups. *Quarterly Journal of Economics* 106: 33–60.

Howard and Company. 1992 and earlier. *Going Public: The IPO Reporter*. Philadelphia: Howard and Company.

Hubbard, R. G., and R. J. Weiner. 1991. Efficient contracting and market power: Evidence from the U.S. natural gas industry. *Journal of Law and Economics* 34: 25–67.

Huemer, J. 1992. Brinson Partners on a roll. *Venture Capital Journal* 32 (June): 32–36.

Hunt, B., and J. Lerner. 1995. Xerox Technology Ventures: March 1995. Harvard Business School case 9-295-127 (and teaching note 9-298-152).

Hsu, D. 2002. What do entrepreneurs pay for venture capital affiliation? Unpublished working paper. University of Pennsylvania.

Ibbotson, R. G., and J. F. Jaffe. 1975. "Hot" issue markets. *Journal of Finance* 30: 1027–42.

Ippolito, R. 1989. Efficiency with costly information: A study of mutual fund performance, 1965–1984. *Quarterly Journal of Economics* 104: 1–23.

Irwin, D. A., and P. J. Klenow. 1996. High tech R&D subsidies: Estimating the effects of Sematech. *Journal of International Economics* 40: 323–44.

Jain, B. A., and O. Kini. 1994. The post-issue operating performance of IPO firms. *Journal of Finance* 49: 1699–1726.

Jaffe, A. B. 1996. *Economic Analysis of Research Spillovers: Implications for the Advanced Technology Program*. Washington: Advanced Technology Program, National Institute of Standards and Technology, U.S. Department of Commerce.

James, C. M. 1987. Some evidence on the uniqueness of bank loans: A comparison of bank borrowing, private placements, and public offerings. *Journal of Financial Economics* 19: 217–35.

Jeffery, G. 1961. *Science and Technology Stocks: A Guide for Investors*. New York: Meridian.

Jeng, L. A., and P. C. Wells. 2000. The determinants of venture capital funding: Evidence across countries. *Journal of Corporate Finance* 6: 241–89.

Jensen, M. C. 1968. The performance of mutual funds in the period 1945–1964. *Journal of Finance* 23: 389–416.

Jensen, M. C. 1986. Agency cost of free cash flow, corporate finance and takeovers. *American Economic Review Papers and Proceedings* 76: 323–29.

Jensen, M. C. 1991. Corporate control and the politics of finance. *Journal of Applied Corporate Finance* 4 (Summer): 13–33.

Jensen, M. C. 1993. Presidential address: The modern industrial revolution, exit, and the failure of internal control systems. *Journal of Finance* 48: 831–80.

Jensen, M. C., and W. H. Meckling. 1976. Theory of the firm: Managerial behavior, agency costs, and ownership structure. *Journal of Financial Economics* 3: 305–60.

Jensen, M. C., and K. J. Murphy. 1990. Performance pay and top-management incentives. *Journal of Political Economy* 98: 225–64.

Jewkes, J., D. Sawers, and R. Stillerman. 1958. *The Sources of Invention*. New York: St. Martin's Press.

Jones, C. M., and M. Rhodes-Kropf. 2003. The price of diversifiable risk in VC and private equity. Unpublished working paper. Columbia University.

Judge, G., W. Griffiths, R. C. Hill, H. Lutkepohl, and T.-C. Lee. 1985. *The Theory and Practice of Econometrics*. New York: Wiley.

Kahle, K. M. 1996. *Insider Trading and New Security Issues*. Unpublished Ph.D. dissertation. Ohio State University.

Kahneman, D., and A. Tversky. 1982. Intuitive prediction: Biases and corrective procedures. In *Judgment under Uncertainty: Heuristics and Biases*, edited by D. Kahneman, P. Slovic, and A. Tversky. New York: Cambridge University Press.

Kaplan, S. N., and J. C. Stein. 1993. The evolution of buyout pricing and financial structure in the 1980s. *Quarterly Journal of Economics* 108: 313–57.

Kaplan, S. N., and P. Strömberg. 2002. Characteristics, contracts, and actions: Evidence from venture capital analyses. National Bureau of Economic Research Working Paper 8764.

Kaplan, S. N., and P. Strömberg. 2003. Financial contract theory meets the real world: An empirical analysis of venture capital contracts. *Review of Economic Studies* 70: 281–315.

Kaplan, S. N., and A. Schoar. 2003. Private equity performance: Returns, persistence, and capital. National Bureau of Economic Research Working Paper 9807.

Kiefer, N. M. 1988. Economic duration data and hazard functions. *Journal of Economic Literature* 26: 646–79.

Kim, E. H., and V. Singhal. 2000. Stock market openings: Experience of emerging economies. *Journal of Business* 73: 25–66.

King, R., Jr. 1990. The money corner. *Forbes* 145 (March 5): 38–40.

Klein, B., R. G. Crawford, and A. A. Alchian. 1978. Vertical integration, appropriable rents, and the competitive contracting process. *Journal of Law and Economics* 21: 297–326.

Kortum, S. 1992. *Inventions, R&D, and Industry Growth.* Unpublished Ph.D. dissertation. Yale University.

Kortum, S., and J. Lerner. 1998. Stronger protection or technological revolution: What is behind the recent surge in patenting? *Carnegie-Rochester Conference Series on Public Policy* 48: 247–304.

Kortum, S., and J. Putnam. 1997. Assigning patents to industries: Tests of the Yale Technology Concordance. *Economic Systems Research* 9: 161–75.

Kothari, S. P., and J. B. Warner. 1997. Measuring long-horizon security price performance. *Journal of Financial Economics* 43: 301–39.

Kraus, T. 2002. Underpricing of IPOs and the certification role of venture capitalists: Evidence from Germany's Neuer Markt. Unpublished working paper. University of Munich.

Kroszner, R. S., and R. G. Rajan. 1994. Is the Glass-Steagall Act justified? A study of the U.S. experience with universal banking before 1933. *American Economic Review* 84: 810–32.

Kroszner, R. S. 1996. The evolution of universal banking and its regulation in twentieth century America. In *Universal Banking: Financial System Design Reconsidered,* edited by A. Saunders and I. Walter. Chicago: Irwin, pp. 70–99.

Kroszner, R. S., and R. G. Rajan. 1997. Organization structure and credibility: Evidence from commercial bank securities activities before the Glass-Steagall Act. *Journal of Monetary Economics* 39: 475–516.

Krigman, L., W. H. Shaw, and K. L. Womack. 2001. Why do firms switch underwriters? *Journal of Financial Economics* 60: 245–84.

Krugman, P. 1991. *Geography and Trade.* Cambridge: MIT Press.

Kunze, R. J. 1990. *Nothing Ventured: The Perils and Payoffs of the Great American Venture Capital Game.* New York: Harper Collins.

Laffont, J.-J., and J. Tirole. 1993. *A Theory of Incentives in Procurement and Regulation.* Cambridge: MIT Press.

Lanjouw, J. O., and M. Schankerman. 1998. Stylized facts of patent litigation: Value, scope and ownership. Working paper EI/20. STICERD. London School of Economics Discussion Papers Series.

La Porta, R. 1996. Expectations and the cross-section of stock returns. *Journal of Finance* 51: 1715–42.

Lakonishok, J., A. Shleifer, R. Thaler, and R. W. Vishny. 1991. Window dressing by pension fund managers. *American Economic Review Papers and Proceedings* 81 (May): 227–31.

Lakonishok, J., A. Shleifer, and R. W. Vishny. 1992. The structure and performance of the money management industry. *Brookings Papers on Economic Activity: Microeconomics* 2: 339–91.

Lakonishok, J., A. Shleifer, and R. W. Vishny. 1994. Contrarian investment, extrapolation, and risk. *Journal of Finance* 49: 1541–78.

Lancaster, T. 1979. Econometric methods for the duration of unemployment. *Econometrica* 47: 939–56.

Lancaster, T. 1985. Generalized residuals and heterogeneous duration models: With applications to the Weibull model. *Journal of Econometrics* 28: 155–69.

Landier, A. 2001. Start-up financing: Banks vs. venture capital. Unpublished working paper. Massachusetts Institute of Technology.

Lawler, E., and J. Drexel. 1980. *The Corporate Entrepreneur*. Los Angeles: Center for Effective Organizations, Graduate School of Business Administration, University of Southern California.

Lee, C., A. Shleifer, and R. Thaler. 1991. Investor sentiment and the closed-end fund puzzle. *Journal of Finance* 46: 29–48.

Lee, P. M., and S. Wahal. 2002. Grandstanding, certification and the underpricing of venture capital backed IPOs. Unpublished working paper. Emory University.

Lehn, K., and A. Poulsen. 1991. Contractual resolution of bondholder-stockholder conflicts in leveraged buyouts. *Journal of Law and Economics* 34: 645–73.

Leland, H. E., and D. H. Pyle. 1977. Informational asymmetries, financial structure, and financial intermediation. *Journal of Finance* 33: 371–87.

Lerner, J. 1994. The importance of patent scope: An empirical analysis. *Rand Journal of Economics* 25: 319–33.

Lerner, J. 1992. ImmuLogic Pharmaceutical Corporation (C): April 1991. Harvard Business School case 9-293-071 (and teaching note 5-293-118).

Lerner, J. 1995. RogersCasey Alternative Investments: Innovative responses to the distribution challenge. Harvard Business School case 9-296-024.

Lerner, J. 1997. An empirical examination of a technology race. *Rand Journal of Economics* 28: 228–47.

Lerner, J., and A. Schoar. 2003. The illiquidity puzzle: Theory and evidence from private equity. *Journal of Financial Economics*, forthcoming.

Levin, J. S. 1995. *Structuring Venture Capital, Private Equity, and Entrepreneurial Transactions*. Boston: Little, Brown.

Liles, P. R. 1977. *Sustaining the Venture Capital Firm*. Cambridge: Management Analysis Center.

Levinsohn, J., and A. Petrin. 2003. Estimating production functions using intermediate inputs to control for unobservables. *Review of Economic Studies* 70: 317–41.

Levy, D. M., and N. E. Terleckyj. 1983. Effects of government R&D on private R&D investment and productivity: A macroeconomic analysis. *Bell Journal of Economics* 14: 551–61.

Lin, T. H., and R. L. Smith. 1998. Insider reputation and selling decisions: The unwinding of venture capital investments during equity IPOs. *Journal of Corporate Finance* 4: 241–63.

Lopez, R. S., and I. W. Raymond. 1955. *Medieval Trade in the Mediterranean World: Illustrative Documents Translated with Introductions and Notes*. New York: Columbia University Press.

Loughran, T., and J. R. Ritter. 1995. The new issues puzzle. *Journal of Finance* 50: 23–51.

Lutz, H. F. 1932. Babylonian partnership. *Journal of Economic and Business History* 4: 552–70.

Maddala, G. S. 1983. *Limited-Dependent and Qualitative Variables in Econometrics*. New York: Cambridge University Press.

Malitz, I. 1986. On financial contracting: The determinants of bond covenants. *Financial Management* 15 (Summer): 18–25.

Manne, H. A. 1966. *Insider Trading and the Stock Market*. New York: Free Press.

Mansfield, E., J. Rapoport, A. Romeo, S. Wagner, and G. Beardsley. 1977. Social and private rates of return from industrial innovations. *Quarterly Journal of Economics* 91: 221–40.

Manweller, R. L. 1997. *Funding High-Tech Ventures*. Grants Pass, OR: Oasis Press.

Marquis Who's Who. 1993 and earlier. *Who's Who in Finance and Industry*. Chicago: Marquis.

Martin, J. D., and J. W. Petty. 1983. An analysis of the performance of publicly traded venture capital companies. *Journal of Financial and Quantitative Analysis* 18: 401–10.

Marx, L. M. 1994. Negotiation and renegotiation of venture capital contracts. Unpublished working paper. University of Rochester.

McCallagh, P., and J. Nelder. 1989. *Generalized Linear Models*. New York: Chapman and Hall.

McNamee, R. 1991. How to fix the IPO market. *Upside* 3 (January): 24–27.

Mead Data Central. 1988. *Reference Manual for the LEXIS/NEXIS Services*. Dayton: Mead Data Central.

Mega-Type Publishing. 1992 and earlier. *Genetic Engineering and Biotechnology-Related Firms—Worldwide Directory*. Princeton Junction, NJ: Mega-Type Publishing.

Megginson, W. C., and K. A. Weiss. 1991. Venture capital certification in initial public offerings. *Journal of Finance* 46: 879–93.

Merton, R. C. 1973. An intertemporal capital asset pricing model. *Econometrica* 41: 867–87.

Merton, R. C. 1995. A functional perspective on financial intermediation. *Financial Management* 24 (Summer): 23–41.

Mervis, J. D. 1996. A $1 billion 'tax' on R&D funds. *Science* 272 (May 17): 942–44.

Meulbroek, L. K. 1992a. Comparison of forward and futures prices of an interest rate-sensitive financial asset. *Journal of Finance* 47: 381–96.

Meulbroek, L. K. 1992b. An empirical analysis of illegal insider trading. *Journal of Finance* 47: 1661–1700.

Michaely, R., and W. H. Shaw. 1991. The pricing of initial public offerings: Tests of adverse selection and signaling theories. *Review of Financial Studies* 7: 279–319.

Michaely, R., R. H. Thaler, and K. L. Womack. 1995. Price reactions to dividend omissions: Overreaction or drift? *Journal of Finance* 50: 573–608.

Mikkelson, W. H., and M. M. Partch. 1985. Stock price effects and costs of secondary distributions. *Journal of Financial Economics* 14: 165–94.

Mikkelson, W. H., and M. M. Partch. 1986. Valuation effects of security offerings and the issuance process. *Journal of Financial Economics* 15: 31–60.

Mikkelson, W. H., and M. M. Partch. 1988. Withdrawn security offerings. *Journal of Financial and Quantitative Analysis* 23: 119–33.

Mikkelson, W. H., M. M. Partch, and K. Shah. 1997. Ownership and operating performance of companies that go public. *Journal of Financial Economics* 44: 281–307.

Mundlak, Y. 1961. Empirical production functions free of management bias. *Journal of Farm Economics* 43: 45–56.

Mundlak, Y. 1978. On the pooling of time series and cross section data. *Econometrica* 46: 69–85.

Muscarella, C. J., and M. R. Vetsuypens. 1989. Initial public offerings and information asymmetry. Unpublished working paper. Pennsylvania State University and Southern Methodist University.

Muscarella, C. J., and M. R. Vetsuypens. 1990. Efficiency and organizational structure: A study of reverse LBOs. *Journal of Finance* 45: 1389–1414.

Myers, S. C. 1977. Determinants of corporate borrowing. *Journal of Financial Economics* 5: 147–75.

Myers, S. C., and N. S. Majluf. 1984. Corporate financing and investment decisions when firms have information that investors do not have. *Journal of Financial Economics* 13: 187–221.

Myers, S., R. L. Stern, and M. L. Rorke. 1983. *A Study of the Small Business Innovation Research Program*. Lake Forest, IL: Mohawk Research Corp.

Nanda, V., J.-H. Yi, and Y. Yun. 1995. IPO long-run performance and underwriter reputation. Unpublished working paper. University of Michigan.

Nash, J. F. 1950. The bargaining problem. *Econometrica* 18: 155–62.

National Register Publishing Co. 1992 and earlier. *Corporate Finance Sourcebook*. Wilmette, IL: National Register Publishing Co.

National Advisory Committee on Semiconductors. 1989. *A Strategic Industry at Risk: A Report to the President and the Congress from the National Advisory Committee on Semiconductors*. Washington: U.S. Government Printing Office.

National Register Publishing Co. 1996 and earlier. *Directory of Leading Private Companies, Including Corporate Affiliations*. Wilmette, IL: National Register Publishing Co.

Newey, W., and K. D. West. 1987. A simple, positive semi-definite, heteroskedasticity and autocorrelation consistent covariance matrix. *Econometrica* 55: 703–708.

Noone, C., and S. Rubel. 1970. *SBICs: Pioneers in Organized Venture Capital*. Chicago: Capital Publishing Co.

North Carolina Biotechnology Center, Biotechnology Information Division (NCBC). 1990a. *Documentation for Actions Database*. Research Triangle Park: North Carolina Biotechnology Center.

North Carolina Biotechnology Center, Biotechnology Information Division (NCBC). 1990b. *Documentation for Companies Database*. Research Triangle Park: North Carolina Biotechnology Center.

Olley, S., and A. Pakes. 1996. The dynamics of productivity in the telecommunications industry. *Econometrica* 64: 1263–97.

Olson, M. 1965. *The Logic of Collective Action*. Cambridge: Harvard University Press.

Organization for Economic Co-operation and Development. 1996. *Government Programs for Venture Capital*. Paris: OECD.

Oryx Press. 1992 and earlier. *BioScan: The Worldwide Biotech Industry Reporting Service*. Phoenix: Oryx Press.

Palepu, K. G. 1986. Predicting takeover targets: A methodological and empirical analysis. *Journal of Accounting and Economics* 8 (May): 3–35.

Patel, J., R. Zeckhauser, and D. Hendricks. 1991. The rationality struggle: Illustrations from financial markets. *American Economic Review Papers and Proceedings* 81: 232–36.

Peltzman, S. 1976. Towards a more general theory of regulation. *Journal of Law and Economics* 19: 211–40.

Pence, C. C. 1982. *How Venture Capitalists Make Investment Decisions*. Ann Arbor: UMI Research Press.

Perez, R. C. 1986. *Inside Venture Capital: Past, Present, and Future*. New York: Praeger.

Petersen, M. A., and R. G. Rajan. 1994. The benefits of lending relationships: Evidence from small business data. *Journal of Finance* 49: 3–37.

Petersen, M. A., and R. G. Rajan. 1995. The effect of credit market competition on lending relationships. *Quarterly Journal of Economics* 110: 407–44.

Pisano, G. P. 1989. Using equity participation to support exchange: Evidence from the biotechnology industry. *Journal of Law, Economics, and Organization* 5: 109–26.

Pittman, R. 1991. Specific investments, contracts, and opportunism: The evolution of railroad sidetrack agreements. *Journal of Law and Economics* 34: 565–89.

Pontiff, J. 1996. Costly arbitrage: Evidence from closed-end funds. *Quarterly Journal of Economics* 111: 1135–52.

Poterba, J. M. 1987. How burdensome are capital gains taxes? Evidence from the United States. *Journal of Public Economics* 33: 157–72.

Poterba, J. M. 1989. Venture capital and capital gains taxation. In *Tax Policy and the Economy*, edited by L. Summers. Cambridge: MIT Press.

Predicasts, Inc. 1992 and earlier. *Predicasts F&S Index of Corporate Change*. Cleveland: Predicasts, Inc.

Price, Waterhouse. 1985. Survey of small high-tech businesses shows federal SBIR awards spurring job growth, commercial sales. Washington: Small Business High Technology Institute.

Puri, M. 1994. The long term default performance of bank underwritten security issues. *Journal of Banking and Finance* 18: 397–418.

Puri, M. 1996. Commercial banks in investment banking: Conflict of interest or certification role? *Journal of Financial Economics* 40: 373–401.

Rajan, R. G. 1992. A theory of the costs and benefits of universal banking. Unpublished manuscript. University of Chicago.

Rajan, R. G. 1994. Why bank credit policies fluctuate: A theory and some evidence. *Quarterly Journal of Economics* 109: 399–441.

Rajan, R., and H. Servaes. 1994. The effect of market conditions on initial public offerings. Unpublished working paper. University of Chicago.

Rajan, R. G., and L. G. Zingales. 1995. What do we know about capital structure? Some evidence from international data. *Journal of Finance* 50: 1421–60.

Recombinant Capital. 1991. *Valuation Histories for Private Biotechnology Companies*. San Francisco: Recombinant Capital.

Recombinant Capital. 1992. *Valuation Histories for Public Biotechnology Companies*. San Francisco: Recombinant Capital.

Reinganum, J. R. 1989. The timing of innovation: Research, development and diffusion. In *The Handbook of Industrial Organization*, edited by R. L. Schmalensee and R. D. Willig. New York: North-Holland.

Riley, J. G. 1979. Information equilibrium. *Econometrica* 47: 331–59.

Rind, K. W. 1981. The role of venture capital in corporate development. *Strategic Management Journal* 2: 169–80.

Ritter, J. R. 1984. The "hot" issue market of 1980. *Journal of Business* 57: 214–40.

Ritter, J. R. 1987. The cost of going public. *Journal of Financial Economics* 19: 269–81.

Ritter, J. R. 1991. The long-run performance of initial public offerings. *Journal of Finance* 42: 365–94.

Ritter, J. R. 1998. Initial public offerings. In *Warren, Gorham, and Lamont Handbook of Modern Finance*, edited by D. Logue and J. Seward. Boston: WGL/RIA.

Ritter, J. R. 2002. Investment banking and security issuance. In *Handbook of the Economics of Finance*, edited by G. Constantinides, M. Harris, and R. Stulz. Amsterdam: Elsevier Science.

Ritter, J. R. 2003. Archived IPO Data. *http://bear.cba.ufl.edu/ritter/ipodata.htm*.

Roberts, K., and M. L. Weitzman. 1981. Funding criteria for research, development, and exploration projects. *Econometrica* 49: 1261–88.

Rock, K. 1986. Why new issues are underpriced. *Journal of Financial Economics* 15: 187–212.

Roe, M. 1990. Political and legal restraints on ownership and control of public companies. *Journal of Financial Economics* 27: 7–42.

Rosenbloom, R. S., and W. J. Spencer, eds. 1996. *Engines of Innovation: U.S. Industrial Research at the End of an Era*. Boston: Harvard Business School Press.

Ross, S. 1977. The determination of financial structure: The incentive signaling approach. *Bell Journal of Economics* 8: 23–40.

Sah, R. K., and J. E. Stiglitz. 1986. The architecture of economic systems: Hierarchies and poly-archies. *American Economic Review* 76: 716–27.

Sahlman, W. A. 1990. The structure and governance of venture capital organizations. *Journal of Financial Economics* 27: 473–521.

Sahlman, W. A., and H. Stevenson. 1986. Capital market myopia. *Journal of Business Venturing* 1: 7–30.

Scholes, M. S. 1972. The market for securities: Substitution versus price pressure and the effects of information on share prices. *Journal of Business* 45: 179–211.

Schmookler, J. 1966. *Invention and Economic Growth*. Cambridge: Harvard University.

Schultz, P. 1993. Unit initial public offerings: A form of staged financing. *Journal of Financial Economics* 34: 199–229.

Securities Data Company (SDC). 1992. *Corporate New Issues Database: A Tutorial*. Newark: Securities Data Company.

Seyhun, H. N. 1986. Insiders' profits, costs of trading, and market efficiency. *Journal of Financial Economics* 16: 189–212.

Seyhun, H. N. 1988. The information content of aggregate insider trading. *Journal of Business* 61: 1–24.

Shiller, R. J. 1990. Speculative prices and popular models. *Journal of Economic Perspectives* 4: 55–65.

Shiller, R. J., and J. Pound. 1989. Survey evidence of diffusions of interest and information among investors. *Journal of Economic Behavior and Organization* 12: 47–66.

Shleifer, A. 1986. Do demand curves for stocks slope down? *Journal of Finance* 41: 579–90.

Shleifer, A., and R. W. Vishny. 1986. Large shareholders and corporate control. *Journal of Political Economy* 94: 461–88.

Shleifer, A., and R. W. Vishny. 1992. Liquidation value and debt capacity: A market equilibrium approach. *Journal of Finance* 47: 1343–66.

Shleifer, A., and R. W. Vishny. 1997a. The limits of arbitrage. *Journal of Finance* 52: 35–55.

Shleifer, A., and R. W. Vishny. 1997b. A survey of corporate governance. *Journal of Finance* 52: 737–83.

Siegel, R., E. Siegel, and I. C. MacMillan. 1988. Corporate venture capitalists: Autonomy, obstacles, and performance. *Journal of Business Venturing* 3: 233–47.

Sirri, E. R., and P. Tufano. 1998. Competition in the mutual fund industry. *Journal of Finance* 53: 1589–1622.

Sloan, A. 1997. Feeding frenzy over Internet firms' IPOs likely to leave investors with heart-burn. *Washington Post* (May 27): E3.

Smith, C. W., Jr., and J. B. Warner. 1979. On financial contracting: An analysis of bond covenants. *Journal of Financial Economics* 7: 117–61.

Standard and Poor's Corporation. 1993 and earlier. *Daily Stock Price Record—Nasdaq.* New York: Standard and Poor's (also AMEX and NYSE volumes).

Standard and Poor's Corporation. 1993 and earlier. *Standard and Poor's Register of Corporations, Directors and Executives.* New York: Standard and Poor's.

Standard and Poor's Corporation. 1997. *Standard and Poor's Compustat Services.* New York: Standard and Poor's.

Stein, J. 1988. Takeover threats and managerial myopia. *Journal of Political Economy* 96: 61–80.

Stein, J. 1989. Efficient capital markets, inefficient firms: A model of myopic corporate behavior. *Quarterly Journal of Economics* 104: 655–69.

Stern, R. L., and T. Pouschine. 1992. Junk equity. *Forbes* 149 (March 2): 40–42.

Stigler, G. 1971. The economic theory of regulation. *Bell Journal of Economics* 2: 3–21.

Stiglitz, J. E. 1994. The role of the state in financial markets. In *Proceedings of the World Bank Annual Conference on Development Economics, 1993: Supplement to The World Bank Economic Review and The World Bank Research Observer,* edited by M. Bruno and B. Pleskovic. Washington: World Bank.

Stiglitz, J. E., and A. Weiss. 1981. Credit rationing in markets with incomplete information. *American Economic Review* 71: 393–409.

Stulz, R. M. 1997. International portfolio flows and security markets. In *International Capital Flows,* edited by M. Feldstein. National Bureau of Economic Research Conference Report series. Chicago: University of Chicago Press.

Sykes, H. B. 1990. Corporate venture capital: Strategies for success. *Journal of Business Venturing* 5: 37–47.

Teoh, S., I. Welch, and T. J. Wong. 1998. Earnings management and the long-run market performance of initial public offerings. *Journal of Finance* 53: 1935–74.

Tibbetts, R. 1996. 50 examples of SBIR commercialization. Unpublished working paper. U.S. National Science Foundation.

Titman, S., and R. Wessels. 1988. The determinants of capital structure choice. *Journal of Finance* 43: 1–19.

Trajtenberg, M. 1990. A penny for your quotes: Patent citations and the value of inventions. *Rand Journal of Economics* 21: 172–87.

Turner, N. 1997. Xerox inventions now raised instead of adopted by others. *Investors' Business Daily* (January 28): A6.

Tyebjee, T. T., and A. V. Bruno. 1984. A model of venture capitalist investment activity. *Management Science* 30: 1051–66.

U.S. Department of Commerce. Bureau of Economic Analysis. 1997. *Gross State Product by Industry: Original Experimental Estimates, 1963–1986.* Unpublished data file.

U.S. Department of Commerce, Bureau of the Census. 1996 and earlier. *Annual Survey of Manufacturers.* Washington: U.S. Government Printing Office.

U.S. Department of Commerce, Patent and Trademark Office [USPTO]. 1990. *Technology Profile Report: Genetic Engineering, 1/1963–6/1989.* Washington: USPTO.

U.S. Department of Commerce, Patent and Trademark Office, Office of Patent Depository Library Programs [USPTO/OPDLP]. 1989. *ASSIST Disk Notes.* Washington: USPTO/OPDLP.

U.S. Department of Commerce, Patent and Trademark Office, Office of Patent Depository Library Programs [USPTO/OPDLP]. 1990. *CASSIS/BIB User's Guide.* Washington: USPTO/OPDLP.

U.S. Department of Commerce, Patent and Trademark Office, Office of Electronic Information Products, Technology Assessment and Forecast Program. 1996. Unpublished tabulation of patenting trends in the United States.

U.S. Department of Commerce, Patent and Trademark Office, Office of Electronic Information Products, Technology Assessment and Forecast Program. 1997. All Technologies Report. *http://www.uspto.gov/web/offices/ac/ido/oeip/taf/all_tech.pdf.*

U.S. General Accounting Office (GAO). 1985. *Implementing the Small Business Innovation Development Act—The First Two Years.* Washington: GAO.

U.S. General Accounting Office (GAO). 1987a. *Federal Research: Small Business Innovation Research Participants Give Program High Marks.* Washington: GAO.

U.S. General Accounting Office (GAO). 1987b. *Federal Research: Effectiveness of Small Business Innovation Research Program Procedures.* Washington: GAO.

U.S. General Accounting Office (GAO). 1989. *Federal Research: Assessment of Small Business Innovation Research Programs.* Washington: GAO.

U.S. General Accounting Office (GAO). 1992. *Federal Research: Small Business Innovation Research Shows Success but Can Be Strengthened.* Washington: GAO.

U.S. General Accounting Office (GAO). 1995. *Federal Research: Interim Report on the Small Business Innovation Research Program.* Washington: GAO.

U.S. National Science Foundation. Division of Science Resource Studies. 1980. *Research and Development in Industry—1979.* Washington: U.S. Government Printing Office.

U.S. National Science Foundation, Division of Science Resource Studies. 1997. Survey of Research and Development in Industry. *http://www.nsf.gov/sbe/srs/sird/start.htm.*

U.S. National Science Foundation. Division of Science Resource Studies. 1998a. Survey of Research and Development Expenditures at Universities and Colleges. *http://caspar.nsf.gov.*

U.S. National Science Foundation. Division of Science Resource Studies. 1998b. Survey of Research and Development in Industry. *http://www.nsf.gov/sbe/srs/sind/start.htm.*

U.S. Small Business Administration (SBA). 1986 and earlier. *Listing of SBIR Awardees for FY 1985.* Washington: U.S. Government Printing Office.

U.S. Small Business Administration (SBA). 1996 and earlier. *Small Business Innovation Development Act: Twelfth-Year Results.* Washington: U.S. Government Printing Office.

Venture Economics. 1986. Corporate venture capital study. Unpublished manuscript.

Venture Economics. 1987. Stock distributions—Fact, opinion and comment. *Venture Capital Journal* 27 (August): 8–14.

Venture Economics. 1988a. *Exiting Venture Capital Investments*. Needham, MA: Venture Economics.

Venture Economics. 1988b. *Trends in Venture Capital*. Needham, MA: Venture Economics.

Venture Economics. 1989a. Investment managers—A force in the venture capital industry. *Venture Capital Journal* 29 (September): 10–17.

Venture Economics. 1989b. *Terms and Conditions of Venture Capital Partnerships*. Needham, MA: Venture Economics.

Venture Economics. 1992. *Terms and Conditions of Venture Capital Partnerships*. Needham, MA: Venture Economics.

Venture Economics. 1996 and earlier. *Pratt's Guide to Venture Capital Sources*. Needham, MA: Venture Economics.

Venture Economics. 1997. *Venture Intelligence Database*. Boston: Venture Economics.

Venture Economics. 1998 and earlier. *Investment Benchmark Reports—Venture Capital*. Newark, NJ: Venture Economics.

Venture Economics. 2002. *National Venture Capital Association Yearbook*. Newark, NJ: Venture Economics.

Venture Economics. 2003. *VentureXpert Database*. Boston: Venture Economics.

VentureOne. 1995. *Entrepreneurial Investment Report*. San Francisco: VentureOne.

VentureOne. 1996. *National Venture Capital Association 1995 Annual Report*. San Francisco: VentureOne.

VentureOne. 1998. *VentureOne 1997 Annual Report*. San Francisco: VentureOne.

Wallace, J., and J. Erickson. 1992. *Hard Drive: Bill Gates and the Making of the Microsoft Empire*. New York: Wiley.

Wallsten, S. J. 2000. The effects of government-industry R&D programs on private R&D: The case of the Small Business Innovation Research program. *Rand Journal of Economics* 31: 82–100.

Warther, V. A. 1995. Aggregate mutual fund flows and securities returns. *Journal of Financial Economics* 39: 209–35.

Weisbach, M. S. 1988. Outside directors and CEO turnover. *Journal of Financial Economics* 20: 431–60.

Weitzman, M. L., W. K. Newey, and M. Rabin. 1981. Sequential R&D strategy for synfuels. *Bell Journal of Economics* 12: 574–90.

Welch, I. 1989. Seasoned offerings, imitation costs, and the underpricing of initial public offerings. *Journal of Finance* 44: 421–49.

Welch, I. 1992. Sequential sales, learning, and cascades. *Journal of Finance* 47: 695–732.

Welch, I. 2000. Herding among security analysts. *Journal of Financial Economics* 58: 369–96.

Wermers, R. 1999. Mutual fund herding and the impact on stock prices. *Journal of Finance* 54: 581–622.

Wessner, C. W. 1999. *The Small Business Innovation Research Program: Challenges and Opportunities.* Washington: National Academies Press.

Williamson, O. E. 1979. Transaction-cost economics: The governance of contractual relations. *Journal of Law and Economics* 22: 233–61.

Williamson, O. E. 1983. Organization form, residual claimants, and corporate control. *Journal of Law and Economics* 26: 351–66.

Williamson, O. E. 1985. *The Economic Institutions of Capitalism: Firms, Markets, Relational Contracting.* New York: Free Press.

Williamson, O. E. 1988. Corporate finance and corporate governance. *Journal of Finance* 43: 567–91.

Wilson, R. 1968. The theory of syndicates. *Econometrica* 36: 119–32.

White, H. 1980. A heteroskedasticity-consistent covariance matrix estimator and a direct test for heteroskedasticity. *Econometrica* 48: 817–38.

White, L. J., ed. 1988. *Private Antitrust Litigation: New Evidence, New Learning.* Cambridge: MIT Press.

World Bank. 2003. *World Development Indicators.* Washington: World Bank.

Wurgler, J., and K. Zhuravskaya. 2002. Does arbitrage flatten demand curves for stocks? *Journal of Business* 75: 582–608.

Yuskavage, R. E. 1996. Improved estimates of gross product by industry, 1959–94. *Survey of Current Business* 76 (August): 133–55.

Zider, B. 1998. How venture capital works. *Harvard Business Review* 76 (November–December): 131–39.

Index